Bermuda Offshore Business Laws

International Law & Taxation Publishers
London

Bermuda Offshore Business Laws

ISBN 1-893713-34-2

International Law & Taxation Publishers
London

http://www.internationallawandtaxationpublishers.com

Contents

COMPANIES ACT 1981

(as amended, 2000)

ARRANGEMENT OF SECTIONS

PART I
INTERPRETATION AND APPLICATION

PART II
INCORPORATION OF COMPANIES AND MATTERS INCIDENTAL THERETO

PART III
PROSPECTUSES AND PUBLIC OFFERS

PART IV
SHARE CAPITAL DEBENTURES AND DIVIDENDS

PART V
THE REGISTRATION OF CHARGES

PART VI
MANAGEMENT AND ADMINISTRATION

PART VII
ARRANGEMENTS, RECONSTRUCTIONS AND AMALGAMATIONS

PART VIII
THE INVESTIGATION OF THE AFFAIRS OF A COMPANY
AND THE PROTECTION OF MINORITIES

PART IX
LOCAL COMPANIES

PART X
EXEMPTED COMPANIES

PART XA
CONTINUATION AND DISCONTINUANCE OF COMPANIES

PART XI
OVERSEAS COMPANIES

PART XII
MUTUAL COMPANIES

PART XIIA
MUTUAL FUND COMPANIES

PART XIII
WINDING UP

PART XIV
RECEIVERS AND MANAGERS

PART XIVA
TRANSFER OF SECURITIES

PART XV
GENERAL

FIRST SCHEDULE (Section 11(1))
Powers of a Company

SECOND SCHEDULE (Section 11(2))
Objects of a Company

THIRD SCHEDULE (Section 114)
Part I: Provisions to be complied with by a local company carrying on business in Bermuda.
Part II: Companies not required to comply with Part I.

FOURTH SCHEDULE (Section 66(2))
Fees for the provision of copies and entries in share registers.

FIFTH SCHEDULE (Section 121(1))
Part I (Section 121(1): Annual tax payable by local companies
Part II (section 131, 135): Fees payable by exempted companies and permit companies

SIXTH SCHEDULE (Section 286(3))
[DELETED]

SEVENTH SCHEDULE (Section 287(1))
[OMITTED]

NINTH SCHEDULE (Section 4A)
Restricted Business Activities

TENTH SCHEDULE (section 4B)
Prohibited business Activities

PART I

INTERPRETATION AND APPLICATION

Short title and commencement.

1. This Act may be cited as the Companies Act 1981 and shall come into force on such day as the Minister shall appoint by notice in the Gazette.

Interpretation.

2.(1) In this Act unless the context otherwise requires

"appointed day" means the day appointed by the Minister under section 1 for the Act to come into force;

"affiliated company" has the meaning assigned to it by section 86(3);

"appointed jurisdiction" means a jurisdiction appointed under subsection (10);

"appointed newspaper" means the Gazette or newspaper appointed by the Registrar under subsection (6);

"appointed stock exchange" means any stock exchange appointed by the Minister under subsection (9);

"arrangement" includes a reorganization of the share capital of a company by the consolidation of shares of different classes or by the division of shares into shares of different classes or by both these methods;

"attorney" means barrister and attorney;

"bearer shares" means shares that may be transferred by delivery of the warrant or certificate relating thereto;

"book and paper" includes minutes, financial statements, accounts, deeds, writings and documents;

"bye-laws" means the bye-laws of a company as originally passed or as lawfully altered from time to time;

"company" means a company to which this Act applies by virtue of section 4(1);

"company limited by shares" and "company limited by guarantee" have the meanings assigned to them by paragraphs (a) and (b) of section 5(2);

"contributory" has the meaning assigned to it by section 159;

"Court" means the Supreme Court;

"creditors' voluntary winding up" has the meaning assigned to it by section 206(4);

"debenture" includes debenture stock, bonds and any other securities of a company whether constituting a charge on the assets of the company or not;

"director" includes an alternate director and any person occupying the position of director by whatever name called;

"document" includes summons, notice, order or other legal process and registers;

"exempted company" has the meaning assigned to it by section 127;

"exempted undertaking" means an exempted company or permit company or an exempted partnership as defined in the Exempted Partnership Act 1992;

"general rules" means general rules made under section 288(2) and includes forms;

"holding company" has the meaning assigned to it by section 86(2);

"local company" means any company incorporated in Bermuda other than an exempted company;

"Member" has the meaning assigned to it by section 19;

"members' voluntary winding up" has the meaning described by section 201;

"memorandum" means the memorandum of association of a company, as originally delivered to the Registrar or as lawfully altered from time to time;

"minimum subscription" has the meaning assigned to it by section 28;

"Minister" means the Minister of Finance or such other Minister as may be appointed to administer this Act;

"mutual company" has the meaning attached to it by section 152;

"non-resident insurance undertaking" shall have the meaning assigned thereto by section I of the Non-Resident Insurance Undertakings Act 1967;

"Official Receiver" means the Official Receiver appointed under section 3 or such other person as may be performing his duties under this Act;

"officer" in relation to a body corporate, includes director and secretary;

"overseas company" means any body corporate incorporated outside Bermuda other than a non-resident insurance undertaking;

"permit" means a permit issued under section 134;

"permit company" means any company with a valid permit;

"prescribed" means prescribed by statutory instrument made under this Act;

"prospectus" means any prospectus, notice, circular, advertisement, or other invitation offering to the public for subscription or purchase of any shares or debentures in a company;

"receiver" or "manager" shall have the meaning assigned to them by section 272;

"register" means the register of companies maintained under subsection (1) of section 14;

"Registrar" means the Registrar of Companies appointed under section 3 or such other person as may be performing his duties under this Act;

"share" means share in the share capital of a company and includes stock;

"statutory meeting" means the meeting required to be held under section 70;

"subsidiary company" has the meaning assigned to it by section 86;

"unlimited liability company" has the meaning given in section 5(2)(c).

(2) Wherever in this Act an obligation or duty is placed on a company or a company is authorized to do any act then unless it is otherwise provided such obligation, duty or act may be carried out by the directors of the company.

(3) A person shall not be deemed within the meaning of any provision of this Act to be a person in accordance with whose directions or instructions the directors of a company are accustomed to act, by reason only that the directors of the company act on advice given by him in a professional capacity.

(4) The expressions "shall be liable to a fine" or "shall be liable to imprisonment" when used in this Act shall mean "shall be guilty of a summary offence and shall be liable on conviction to a fine" or "shall be guilty of a summary offence and shall be liable on conviction to imprisonment", as the case may be, and all fines and terms of imprisonment shall be deemed to be maximum fines or periods of imprisonment, as the case may be.

(5) Where it is stated that a person shall be guilty of contempt of court he shall be deemed to have committed an offence under section 5 of the Administration of Justice (Contempt of Court) Act 1979.

(6) The registrar shall from time to time publish in the Gazette a list of newspapers appointed for the purposes of this Act.

(7) Any requirement in this Act to use the word "Limited" may be met by the use of the abbreviation "Ltd".

(8) In this Act the expression "member" includes shareholder and the expression "shareholder" includes member.

(9) The Minister may appoint a stock exchange and shall cause the appointment to be published in an appointed newspaper.

(10) The Minister may appoint a jurisdiction and shall cause the appointment to be published in an appointed newspaper.

Appointment

3. There shall be appointed a Registrar of Companies and an Official Receiver both of whom shall be public officers and shall have the powers and discharge the duties conferred or imposed upon them by this Act.

Application.

4.(1) This Act shall apply to -

(a) all companies registered under it or registered before the appointed day under the Companies (Incorporation by Registration) Act 1970;

(b) all companies limited by shares incorporated by Act in Bermuda prior to or after the appointed day, except to such extent (if any) as may otherwise be expressly provided in the incorporating Act;

(c) all mutual companies incorporated prior to the appointed day to which Part XII applies; and

(d) any overseas company so far as any provision of this Act requires it to apply.

(1A) In respect of -

(a) non-resident insurance undertakings, section 2 and Parts XIII and XIV shall apply to them except those sections in Part XIII relating exclusively to members' voluntary liquidations and for the purposes of section 2 and Parts XIII and XIV "insurance business" has the meaning assigned to it in the Non-Resident Insurance Undertakings Act 1967;

(b) permit companies, section 2 and Parts III, V, XI and XIII except those sections in Part XIII relating exclusively to members' voluntary liquidations shall apply to them.

(2) Where the provisions of a private Act incorporating a company conflict with the provisions of this Act the provisions of the private Act shall prevail provided that -

(a) where reference is made in the private Act to any provision of an Act repealed by this Act then if there is a provision in this Act corresponding or nearly corresponding to the provision repealed then that provision shall apply;

(b) when reference is made in the private Act to any provision of an Act repealed by this Act and there is no provision in this Act corresponding or nearly corresponding to the provision repealed then that provision shall continue to have effect; and

(c) notwithstanding any provision in the private Act twelve months after the appointed day Parts VI (excepting section 91), VII, VIII, XIII, XIV, and XV shall apply to the company.

Restricted business activities

4A.(1) No company shall have objects that enable it to carry on any restricted business activity set out in the Ninth Schedule without the consent of the Minister.

(2) The Minister may, by order subject to the negative resolution procedure, amend the Ninth Schedule by addition, deletion or variation of any restricted business activity.

(3) An application for consent under subsection (1) shall be in such form and accompanied by such documents as the Minister may determine.

(4) Where the Minister refuses to grant his consent under subsection (1), he shall not be bound to assign any reason for his refusal and his decision shall not be subject to appeal or review in any court.

(5) The Registrar shall refuse to register a company that has objects as referred to in subsection (1) unless the consent of the Minister is first obtained.

(6) Any person aggrieved by a decision of the Registrar under subsection (5) may appeal to the Minister whose decision shall be final.

(7) Subject to subsection (8), an application for consent and any documents accompanying any such application shall be treated as confidential by the Minister and all public officers having access thereto.

(8) Subsection (7) does not preclude -

(a) the disclosure of information for the purpose of enabling or assisting the Minister to exercise or perform any functions conferred upon him by this Act;

(b) the disclosure of information or the transmitting of an application for consent and its accompanying documents to the Bermuda Monetary Authority for the purpose of enabling or assisting that Authority to exercise or perform any functions conferred upon the Authority by the Bermuda Monetary Authority Act 1969.

Prohibited business activities

4B.(1) No company shall carry on any prohibited business activity set out in the Tenth Schedule.

(2) The Minister may, by order subject to the negative resolution procedure, amend the Tenth Schedule by addition, deletion or variation of any prohibited business activity.

(3) Where a company carries on any prohibited business activity in contravention of subsection (1), the company may, on the application of the Registrar, be wound up by the Court pursuant to section 161.

PART II

INCORPORATION OF COMPANIES AND MATTERS INCIDENTAL THERETO

Mode of forming a company.

5.(1) Any one or more persons by subscribing their names to a memorandum of association and otherwise complying with the requirements of this Act in respect of registration may form a company with or without limited liability.

(2) Such a company may be -

(a) a company having the liability of its members limited by the memorandum to the amount, if any, unpaid on the shares held by them, in this Act termed "a company limited by shares";

(b) a company having the liability of its members limited by the memorandum to such an amount as the members may respectively thereby undertake to contribute to the assets of the company in the event of it being wound up, in the Act termed "a company limited by guarantee"; or

(c) a company not having any limit on the liability of its members, in this Act termed "an unlimited liability company".

(3) A company limited by guarantee shall only be formed if -

(a) its purpose is to promote art, science, religion, charity, sport, education or any other social or useful purpose and its profits, if any, and other income is to be used in promoting its purposes and no dividends are to be paid to its members; or

(b) it is a mutual company.

Registration of companies

6.(1) An application for registration of a company shall be in such form as may be prescribed by rules made under section 288 and shall be accompanied by such documents as the Minister may determine.

(2) Not more than three months prior to an application for registration of a local company the applicant shall publish in an appointed newspaper an advertisement announcing the intention to incorporate the local company specifying the name and stating its proposed objects.

(3) The Minister may, by order subject to the negative resolution procedure, prohibit the registration of companies or a class of companies the minimum share capital of which is less than an amount stated in the order.

(4) The Registrar shall refuse to register a company if he is of the opinion that -

(a) in the case of a company limited by guarantee its purpose is not one of the purposes referred to in section 5(3); or

(b) its memorandum shows that its minimum share capital will be less than the amount required by the Minister by order under subsection (3).

(5) Any person aggrieved by a decision of the Registrar under subsection (4) may appeal to the Minister whose decision shall be final.

Requirements of memorandum.

7.(1) The memorandum of every Company must state -

(a) the name of the company and, in the case of a company limited by shares or a company limited by guarantee, subject to section 9, the word "Limited" as the last word of the name;

(aa) in the case of a company limited by shares or a company limited by guarantee, that the liability of its members is limited;

(b) the objects of the Company;

(c) [deleted];

(d) the names, addresses and nationalities of the persons who subscribe their names to the memorandum and which of them, if any, has Bermudian status;

(e) whether the company is to be an exempted company;

(f) [deleted];

(g) the maximum land holding powers of the company in relation to land situate in Bermuda and, where it is proposed that the company shall acquire a particular parcel of land, a full description of that parcel; and

(h) the period, if any, fixed for the duration of the company, or the event, if any, on the occurrence of which the company is to be dissolved.

(2) In the case of a company limited by shares the memorandum must also state -

(a) the amount of share capital with which the company proposes to be registered including the minimum that must be subscribed and the division thereof into shares of fixed amount; and

(b) that the persons who subscribe their names to the memorandum agree to take such number of shares of the company as may be allotted to them respectively by the provisional directors, not exceeding the number of shares for which they respectively subscribe, and that they agree to satisfy such calls as may be made on them by the directors, provisional directors or promoters in respect of the shares allotted to them.

(3) Subject to section 154 the memorandum of a company limited by guarantee must state that each member undertakes to contribute to the assets of the company in the event of it being wound up while he is a member, or within one year after he ceases to be a member, for the payment of the debts and liabilities of the company contracted before he ceases to be a member, and of the costs charges and expenses of winding up, and for the adjustment of the rights of the contributories amongst themselves, such amount as may be required, not exceeding a specified amount.

(4) The memorandum of every company shall be signed by each subscriber in the presence of at least one witness who shall attest the signature.

(5) A company may not alter the provisions of its memorandum except in a manner provided in this Act.

Prohibition of registration of companies with undesirable names.

8.(1) No company shall be registered with a name which in the opinion of the Registrar is undesirable.

(2) Without prejudice to the generality of subsection (1), no company shall be permitted to be registered with a name which -

(a) is identical with the name by which a company is registered or incorporated under this Act or any other Act or so nearly resembles that name as to be likely to deceive unless that company signifies its consent in such manner as the Registrar may require;

(b) contains the words "Chamber of Commerce", or in the opinion of the Registrar suggests or is likely to suggest the patronage of Her Majesty or of any member of the Royal Family or connection with any government whether of Bermuda or elsewhere;

(c) contains the word "municipal" or "chartered" or in the opinion of the Registrar suggests, or is likely to suggest, connection with any public board or other local authority or with any society or body incorporated by Royal Charter;

(d) contains the word "co-operative";

(e) contains the words "building society"; or

(f) in the case of a company limited by shares or a company limited by guarantee, subject to section 9, does not contain the word "Limited"; or

(g) in the case of an unlimited liability company ends with the word "Limited".

(3) If, through inadvertence or otherwise, a company on its first registration or on its registration with a new name is registered with a name which in the opinion of the Registrar too closely resembles the name by which a company in existence is already registered, the first mentioned company may, with the sanction of the Registrar, change its name, and shall, if the Registrar so directs within six months of its being registered by that name, change its name within six weeks of the date of such direction or within such longer period as the Registrar may think fit to allow.

(4) If at any time after a company has been registered it appears to the Registrar that the name under which it is registered is undesirable, the Registrar may notify the company accordingly and may in such notification direct the company to change its name, and the company shall change its name within six weeks of such direction unless within that time it shall have lodged an appeal to the Court against such direction. The Court shall thereupon either cancel or confirm such direction and its decision shall be final and conclusive.

(5) If a company makes default in complying with a direction under subsection (3) or a confirmed direction under subsection (4) it shall be liable to a default fine:

Provided that in the case of an appeal under subsection (4) the period of default shall not commence until six weeks after the decision of the Court.

(6) Subsections (1), (3) and (4) of section 10 shall apply to a change of name under this section as they apply to a change of name under that section.

Power to dispense with "Limited" in name of charitable and other companies.

9.(1) Where it is proved to the satisfaction of the Minister that an association about to be formed as a limited company is to be formed for promoting art, science, religion, charity, sport or any other useful object, and intends to apply its profits, if any, or other income promoting its objects, and to prohibit the payment of any dividend to its members, the Minister may by licence direct that the association may be registered as a company, without the addition of the word "Limited" to its name, and the association may be registered accordingly.

(2) Where it is proved to the satisfaction of the Minister -

(a) that the objects of an existing company, are restricted to those specified in subsection (1) and to objects incidental or conducive thereto; and

(b) that by its constitution the company is required to apply its profits, if any, in promoting its objects and is prohibited from paying any dividend to its

members, the Minister may by licence, subject to such conditions as he thinks fit to impose, authorize the company to change by resolution its name by the omission of the word "Limited", and subsections (2), (3) and (4) of section 10 shall apply to a change of name under this subsection as they apply to a change of name under that section.

(3) A licence under this section may at any time be revoked by the Minister and thereupon the Registrar shall enter the word "Limited" at the end of the name of the company in the register: Provided that before a licence is revoked the Minister shall give the company an opportunity of being heard.

Change of name of a company.

10.(1) Subject to sections 8(1) and (2), a company may by resolution change its name if the Registrar has approved the proposed name.

(2) [DELETED].

(3) The Registrar shall, on receipt of a certified copy of the resolution referred to in subsection (1) together with such fee as may be prescribed -

(a) enter the new name on the register in place of the former name;

(b) enter on the register the effective date of the change of name which shall be the date of entry of the new name on the register;

(c) issue a certificate of change of name.

(4) The change of name of a company shall not affect any rights or obligations of the company, or render defective any legal proceedings by or against it, and any legal proceedings that might have been continued or commenced against it in its former name may be continued or commenced against it in its new name.

(5) Sections 8(3) and (4) shall apply mutatis mutandis to any name adopted by a company under this section.

Powers and objects of a company.

11.(1) Subject to any provision of the law a company limited by shares shall without reference in its memorandum have the powers set out in the First Schedule unless any of such powers are excluded by its memorandum.

(2) A company limited by shares, or other company having a share capital may amongst its objects by reference include in its memorandum any of the objects set out in the Second Schedule.

(3) The Minister may by notice vary the First and Second Schedules but any such variation shall not affect a company incorporated prior to the publication of the notice unless such company alters its memorandum to effect the change contained in the notice.

(4) A notice under subsection (3) shall be subject to affirmative resolution procedure.

(5) The objects set out in the different paragraphs of the objects clause in the memorandum of a company or included therein by reference shall not, unless otherwise stated, be limited or restricted in any way by reference to or inference from the terms of any other paragraph in the memorandum and such objects may be carried out in as full and ample a manner and construed in such a manner as if each paragraph defined the objects of a separate and independent company and each is construed as a primary object.

Procedure for alteration of memorandum.

12.(1) Subject to the provisions of this section, a company may, by resolution passed at a general meeting of members of which due notice has been given, alter the provisions of its memorandum.

(2) Section 6 shall apply to a company wishing to change its memorandum as if the company were applying to be registered save that the advertisement provided for in section 6(2) shall detail the proposed changes to the memorandum rather than the matters set out in section 6(3).

(3) An application may be made to the Court for an alteration to the memorandum of a company passed in accordance with subsection (1) to be annulled and where such an application is made the alteration shall not have effect except in so far as it is confirmed by the Court.

(4) An application under subsection (3) may only be made -

(a) by the holders of not less in the aggregate than twenty per centum in par value of the company's issued share capital or any class thereof; or

(b) by the holders of not less in the aggregate than twenty per centum of the company's debentures entitled to object to alterations to its memorandum; or

(c) in the case of a company limited by guarantee by not less than twenty per centum of the members;

Provided that an application shall not be made by any person who has voted in favour of the alteration or has given to the company a statement in writing duly signed that he, having had notice, consents to the alteration.

(5) An application under subsection (3) shall be made within twenty-one days after the date on which the resolution altering the company's memorandum was passed, and may be made on behalf of the persons entitled to make the application by one or more of their number as they may appoint in writing for the purpose.

(6) On an application under subsection (3) the Court may make an order annulling or confirming the alteration, either wholly or in part, and on such terms and conditions as it thinks fit, and may, if it thinks fit, adjourn the proceedings in order that an arrangement may be made to the satisfaction of the Court for the purchase of the interests of dissentient members, and may give such directions and make such orders as it may think expedient for facilitating or carrying into effect any such arrangement:

Provided that no part of the capital of the company shall be expended in the purchase of the interests of dissentient members.

(7) Where a company passes a resolution altering the provisions of its memorandum -

(a) if no application is made to the Court with respect thereto under this section, it shall within thirty days after the end of the period for making such an application deliver to the Registrar a copy of its memorandum as altered; and

(b) if such application is made it shall -

(i) forthwith give notice of that fact to the Registrar; and

(ii) within thirty days after the date of any order annulling or confirming the alteration, either wholly or in part, deliver to the Registrar an office copy of the order and, in the case of an order confirming the alteration, a copy of its memorandum as altered.

(7A) On receipt of the copy of the memorandum altered pursuant to this section, the Registrar shall, subject to section 4A, forthwith register it and the amendment shall be effective from the date of such registration.

(8) If a company makes default in giving notice or delivering any document to the Registrar as required by subsection (7), the company and every officer of the company who is in default shall be liable to a fine of one hundred dollars for every day during which the default continues.

(9) Notwithstanding anything in this section, if within twenty-one days of the passing of a resolution a company delivers to the Registrar a copy of the memorandum as altered and an affidavit sworn by at least two directors of the company stating that the company does not know of any person who could make an application to the Court under subsection (3), the Registrar shall register the memorandum and the amendment shall be effective from the date of such registration.

(10) A company shall give the same notice to the holders of debentures who are entitled to object to alterations to the company's memorandum under subsection (3) as it is required under subsection (1) to give to members of the company.

(11) This section shall not apply to any alteration of the memorandum of a company authorised by section 45 or 46.

Bye-laws.

13.(1) The administration of every company shall be regulated by bye-laws; a company limited by shares shall in its bye-laws make provision for all the matters hereafter set out in subsection (2); a company limited by guarantee shall in its bye-laws make provision for the matters set out in paragraphs (b), (c), (d) and (f) of that subsection.

(2) A company limited by shares, or other company having a share capital, shall in its bye-laws make provision for -

(a) the transfer of shares and the registration of estate representatives of decreased shareholders;

(b) a general meeting of the company once at least in every year;

(c) the keeping of its accounts and the laying of financial statements before general meetings of the company;

(d) an audit of the accounts of the company once at least in every year by an independent representative of the shareholders;

(e) the duties of the secretary to the company; and

(f) the number of members required to constitute a quorum at any general meeting of the members of the company.

(3) In addition any company may at the time of registration or from time to time make bye-laws if appropriate to regulate -

(i) and to restrict the entry into and the transfer of membership in the company;

(ii) the allotment of shares;

(iii) the making of calls on shares;

(iv) the payment for shares;

(v) the issue and registration of certificates of shares;

(vi) the forfeiture of shares for non-payment of calls;

(vii) the disposal of forfeited shares, and of the proceeds thereof;

(viii) the transfer of shares;

(ix) the declaration and payment of dividends;

(x) the duties and responsibilities of its president and vice presidents and of any other officers with special responsibilities or duties;

(xi) the appointment, functions, duties, remuneration and removal of all agents, officers, and servants of the company, and the security, if any, to be given by them to the company;

(xii) the date on which the annual meetings of the company shall be held;

(xiii) the calling of meetings of the company, and of the board of directors, the requirements as to proxies and requisite majorities in voting on any particular matter or class of matters and the procedure at such meetings;

(xiv) the quorum at meetings of directors which in no case shall be a quorum of less than two individuals;

(xv) the voting rights and restrictions relating to any class of shares in companies limited by shares, or other company having a share capital, and the voting rights and restrictions of members of companies limited by guarantee including mutual companies;

(xvi) the imposition and recovery of all penalties and forfeitures admitting of regulation by bye-laws;

(xvii) the conduct in all other particulars of the affairs of the company, as well as for the application of its funds and profits; and

(xviii) the use of its common seal and any duplicate common seal.

(4) The persons subscribing their names to the memorandum of association of a company may likewise subscribe their names to bye-laws which shall become operative if approved at the statutory meeting.

(5) The directors of a company may after its registration amend the bye-laws but any such amendment shall be submitted to a general meeting of the company, and shall become operative only to such extent as they are approved at such meeting.

Registration of companies.

14.(1) The Registrar shall maintain a register of companies in such form as he shall determine.

(2) The memorandum shall be delivered to the Registrar who, if he is satisfied -

(a) that the company will be in compliance with this Act; and

(b) that, where applicable, the Controller of Foreign Exchange has given permission under the Exchange Control Act 1972 for the issue of shares in the company, shall register the memorandum, issue a certificate of incorporation showing the date of registration and attach to the certificate a facsimile of the memorandum delivered to him.

(3) From the date of the registration of a company the subscribers of the memorandum, together with such other persons as may from time to time become members of the company, shall be a body corporate by the name contained in the memorandum, capable forthwith of exercising all the functions of an incorporated company, and having perpetual succession and power to adopt a common seal, but with such liability on the part of the members to contribute to the assets of the company in the event of its being wound up as is mentioned in this Act.

Re-registration of limited liability company as unlimited liability company.

14A.(1) Subject to the provisions of this section, a company which is registered as a company limited by shares may be re-registered as an unlimited company in accordance with the requirements of this section.

(2) No application to re-register a company limited by shares as an unlimited company shall be lodged with the Registrar unless such application has been agreed by all the members of the company.

(3) For the purposes of subsection (2) all the members of a company shall be deemed to have agreed at a general meeting if either -

(a) all the members are present in person or by proxy at the meeting and agree; or

(b) if some of the members are not present in person or by proxy at the meeting, then, if the members present in person at the meeting agree and there are produced at the meeting statements in writing from the members not present in person stating that they agree.

(4) DELETED.

(5) The application shall set out such alterations in the company's memorandum as are requisite in order to conform with the memorandum of a company to be formed as an unlimited liability company and be accompanied by the documents specified in subsection (6).

(6) The documents referred to in subsection (5) are -

(a) a certified copy, of the agreement referred to in subsection (3)(a), or certified copies of the agreement and the written statements referred to in subsection (3)(b); and

(b) a statutory declaration made by at least two directors of the company that the persons who have signified their agreement pursuant to subsection (3) constitute the whole membership of the company.

(c) DELETED

(7) Sections 6 and 12(7A) shall apply, with the necessary changes, to a re-registration under this section as they apply to the registration of a company and the registration of a company's memorandum that has been altered.

Re-registration of unlimited liability company as company limited by shares or by guarantee

14B.(1) Subject to the provisions of this section, a company which is registered as an unlimited liability company may, by resolution passed at a general meeting of members of the company, be re-registered as a company limited by shares or by guarantee in accordance with the requirements of this section.

(2) No application to re-register an unlimited liability company as a company limited by shares or by guarantee shall be lodged with the Registrar unless such application is accompanied by a certified copy of a resolution that it should be so re-registered passed at a general meeting of the company.

(3) The resolution must state whether the company is to be limited by shares or by guarantee and -

(a) if it is to be limited by shares, must state what the share capital is to be and provide for; or

(b) if it is to be limited by guarantee, must provide for, the making of such alterations to its memorandum and bye-laws as are necessary to bring them (in substance and in form) into conformity with the requirements of this Act with respect to the memorandum and bye-laws of a company so limited.

(4) The application shall be accompanied by a written copy of the memorandum of the company as altered by the resolution.

(5) Sections 6 and 12(7A) shall apply, with the necessary changes, to a re-registration under this section as they apply to the registration of a company and the registration of a company's memorandum that has been altered.

Certificate of incorporation to be conclusive evidence.

15. No defect in the formalities leading up to the incorporation of a company shall affect the validity of its incorporation and the certificate of incorporation shall be conclusive evidence of the due incorporation of the company and the date of its incorporation.

Effect of memorandum and bye-laws.

16.(1) Subject to this Act the memorandum of association when registered and the bye-laws when approved shall bind the company and the members thereof to the same extent as if they respectively had been signed and sealed by each member, and contained covenants on the part of each member to observe all the provisions of the memorandum and of the bye-laws.

(2) All money payable by any member to the company under the memorandum or bye-laws shall be a debt due from him to the company.

(3) [DELETED].

Alterations in memorandum or bye-laws increasing liability to contribute to share capital not to bind existing members without consent.

17. Notwithstanding anything in the memorandum or bye-laws of a company, no member of the company shall be bound by an alteration made in the memorandum or bye-laws after the date on which he became a member, if and so far as the alteration requires him to take or subscribe for more shares than the number held by him at the date on which the alteration is made, or in any way increases his liability as at that date to contribute to the share capital of, or otherwise to pay money to, the company:

Provided that this section shall not apply in any case where the member agrees in writing, either before or after the alteration is made, to be bound thereby.

Copies of memorandum and bye-laws to be given to members.

18.(1) A company shall, on being so required by a member send him a copy including all alterations of the memorandum of the company, the Act establishing the company or its bye-laws subject to the payment by the member of the cost thereof.

(2) If a company makes default in complying with this section, the company and every officer of the company who is in default shall be liable to a fine of fifty dollars.

Definition of member.

19.(1) The subscribers to the memorandum of a company shall be deemed to have agreed to become members of the company, and on its registration shall be entered as members in its register of members but in the case of a company limited by shares, or other company having a share capital, only if shares have been allotted to them.

(2) Every other person who agrees to become a member of a company, and whose name is entered in its register of member, shall be a member of the company.

(3) In this section "register of members" includes any branch register kept under section 65.

20. [REPEALED].

Form of contracts.

21.(1) Contracts on behalf of a company may be made as follows -

(a) a contract which if made between private persons would be by law required to be under seal may be made on behalf of the company under the common seal of the company if the seal be affixed thereto attested by a director of the company and either the secretary of the company or another director thereof or some other person expressly authorised for the purpose, or in such other manner as the bye-laws may provide;

(b) a contract which if made between private persons would be by law required to be in writing, signed by the parties to be charged therewith, may be made on behalf of the company in writing signed by any person acting under its authority, express or implied;

(c) a contract which if made between private persons would by law be valid although made by parole only, and not reduced into writing, may be made by parole on behalf of the company by any person acting under its authority, express or implied.

(2) A contract made according to this section shall be effectual in law, and shall bind the company and its successors and all other parties thereto.

(3) A contract made according to this section may be varied or discharged in the same manner in which it is authorized by this section to be made.

(4) Where a contract purports to be made by a company or by a person as agent for a company, at a time when the company has not yet been formed, then subject to any agreement to the contrary, the contract shall have effect as a contract entered into by the person purporting to act for the company or as agent for it and he shall be personally liable on the contract accordingly.

(5) Any contract purported to be made in the manner set out in subsection (4) may subsequently be unilaterally adopted by the company and the company shall thereupon become a party thereto to the same extent as if the contract had been made after the incorporation and in substitution for and discharge of the agent or person purporting to act on its behalf.

Bills of exchange and promissory notes.

22. A bill of exchange or promissory note shall be deemed to have been made, accepted or endorsed on behalf of a company if made, accepted or endorsed in the name of, or by or on behalf or on account of the company by any person acting under its authority and if so endorsed the person signing the endorsement shall not be liable thereon.

Execution of deeds abroad.

23.(1) A company may, by writing under its common seal, empower any person, either generally or in respect of any specified matters, as its agent, to execute deeds on its behalf in any place outside Bermuda.

(2) A deed signed by such an agent on behalf of the company and under his seal shall bind the company and have the same effect as if it were under its common seal.

(3) A company may in addition to its common seal for use in Bermuda, have for use in any territory or place one or more duplicate common seals and a deed or other document to which such seal is duly affixed binds the company as if it had been sealed with the company's common seal.

Authentication of documents.

24. A document or proceeding requiring authentication by a company may be signed by a director, secretary or other authorized officer of the company, and need not be under its common seal.

PART III

PROSPECTUSES AND PUBLIC OFFERS

Interpretation of expressions relating to prospectuses.

25.(1) In this Part unless the context otherwise requires -

"company" includes any association of person seeking to be registered as such a company;

"competent regulatory authority" means any authority appointed by the Minister by notice in an appointed newspaper to approve the offering of shares or debentures to the public by companies;

"expert" includes engineer, valuer, accountant and any other person whose profession gives authority to a statement made by him;

"promoter" means a promoter who was a party to the preparation of the prospectus, but does not include any person by reason of his acting in a professional capacity for persons engaged in procuring the formation of the company;

"share" includes debentures, units or sub-units of a unit trust or a warrant conferring an option to acquire shares.

(2) Any reference in this Act to offering shares to the public shall, subject to any provision to the contrary contained therein, be construed as including a reference to offering them to any section of the public, whether selected as members or debenture holders of the company concerned or as clients of the person issuing the prospectus or in any other manner, and references in this Act or in a company's bye-laws to invitations to the public to subscribe for shares shall, subject as aforesaid, be similarly construed

.

(3) For the purposes of this Part of this Act -

(a) a statement included in a prospectus shall be deemed to be untrue if it is misleading in the form and context in which it is included; and

(b) a statement shall be deemed to be included in a prospectus if it is contained therein or in any report or memorandum appearing on the face thereof or by reference incorporated therein or issued therewith.

(4) Subsection (2) shall not be taken as requiring any offer or invitation to be treated as made to the public if it is -

(a) an offer to existing holders of shares in the company of the same class as the shares comprised in the offer without any right of renunciation; or

(b) an offer without any right of renunciation to the holders of convertible

debentures or debentures having subscription rights in respect of shares into or in respect of which the rights of conversion or subscription exists; or

(c) an offer certified in writing by an officer of the company on behalf of the board of directors to be an offer which the board considers as not being calculated to result, directly or indirectly, in the shares becoming available -

(i) in the case of a local company, to more than twenty persons; and

(ii) in the case of an exempted company or a permit company, to more than thirty-five persons; or

(d) an offer having a private character whether by reason of the connection between the company issuing the shares and those to whom they are issued or otherwise; or

(e) an offer certified in writing by an officer of the company on behalf of the board of directors to be an offer which the board considers as not being calculated to result, directly or indirectly, in shares becoming available to persons other than persons whose ordinary business involves the acquisition, disposal or holding of shares, whether as principal or agent.

(5) The Minister may, on the application by or on behalf of a company, direct that the provisions of Part III or any provision of that Part and section 35 of the Act shall not apply to a proposed offer of shares.

(6) A direction of the Minister given under subsection (5) may be subject to conditions and may at any time be revoked by the Minister.

(7) It is hereby declared for the avoidance of doubt that a direction of the Minister given under subsection (5) is not a statutory instrument having legislative effect.

Company offering shares to public shall publish a prospectus.

26.(1) Subject to subsection (1A) and the provisions of any other enactment no company shall offer shares to the public unless prior to such offer it publishes in writing a prospectus signed by or on behalf of all the directors or provisional directors of the company and files a copy with the Registrar.

(1A) It is not necessary to publish and file a prospectus under subsection (1) where -

(a) the shares are listed on an appointed stock exchange and the rules of the appointed stock exchange do not require the company to publish a prospectus; or

(b) the company is subject to the rules or regulations of a competent regulatory authority and such rules or regulations do not require the company to publish a prospectus, except where exemption from publication of a prospectus is

given by reason of the offer being made only to persons who are resident outside the jurisdiction of the authority.

(2) The Registrar shall not accept for filing a copy of a prospectus unless it is accompanied by a certificate signed by an attorney certifying -

(a) that the prospectus contains the particulars required by section 27(1) and is accompanied by a written statement from the auditor of the company, dated within seven days prior to the date of such filing, which confirms -

(i) the auditor's consent to the inclusion of his name in the prospectus to be issued by the company as having accepted the appointment as auditor of the company; or

(ii) the auditor's consent to the inclusion in that prospectus of any or all reports prepared by him; or

(b) that an appointed stock exchange or a competent regulatory authority has received or otherwise accepted the prospectus as a basis for offering shares to the public.

(3) The directors, provisional directors and promoters of any company that fails to comply with this section shall each be liable to a fine of one thousand dollars.

Contents of a prospectus.

27.(1) Every prospectus shall contain or there shall be attached thereto documents showing -

(a) the names, descriptions and addresses of the promoters, officers or proposed officers;

(b) the business or proposed business of the company;

(c) the minimum subscription which, in the opinion of the promoters, directors or provisional directors must be issued as provided in section 28;

(d) any rights or restrictions on the shares that are being offered;

(e) all commissions payable on the sale of the shares referred to in the prospectus and the net amount receivable by the company in respect of the sale;

(f) the name and address of any person who owns five percent or more of the shares of the company;

Provided that this paragraph shall not apply to an exempted company or a permit company;

(g) any shareholding in the company of an officer of the company;

(h) financial statements of the company prepared in such manner and containing such information and copies of such documents as may be required by rules made under section 34;

(i) a report or statement by the auditor of the company prepared in such manner and containing such information as shall be required by rules made under section 34;

(j) the date and time of the opening and closing of subscription lists.

(2) Where an appointed stock exchange or any competent regulatory authority has received or otherwise accepted the prospectus then subsection (1) shall not apply.

Minimum amount required to be raised to be stated in prospectus.

28.(1) Every prospectus shall contain the following particulars -

(a) the minimum subscription which must be raised by the issue of shares in order to provide the sums, or, if any part thereof is to be defrayed in any other manner, the balance of the sums, required to be provided in respect of each of the following matters -

(i) the purchase price of any assets purchased or to be purchased which is to be defrayed in whole or in part out of the proceeds of the issue;

(ii) any preliminary expenses payable by the company, and any commission so payable to any person in consideration of his agreeing to subscribe for, or of his procuring or agreeing to procure subscriptions for, any shares in the company;

(iii) the repayment of any moneys borrowed by the company in respect of any of the foregoing matters;

(iv) working capital; and

(b) the amounts to be provided in respect of the matters aforesaid otherwise than out of the proceeds of the issue and the sources out of which those amounts are to be provided.

(2) Where an appointed stock exchange or any competent regulatory authority has received or otherwise accepted the prospectus, then subsection (1) shall not apply.

Companies continuously offering shares to the public.

29.(1) Where -

(a) any company continuously over a period offers shares to the public; and

(b) any of the particulars in a prospectus issued by that company ceases to be accurate in a material respect, the company as soon as reasonably practicable after becoming aware of that fact, shall -

(c) publish supplementary particulars disclosing the material changes;

(d) file a copy of the supplementary particulars with the Registrar; and

(e) give a copy of the supplementary particulars to each shareholder of the company.

(2) Each of the directors of any company that fails to comply with this section shall be liable to a fine of one thousand dollars.

Offences relating to the issue of a prospectus.

30. Any person who makes or authorizes the making of an untrue statement in a prospectus unless he proves either that the statement was immaterial or that at the time he made the statement he had reasonable grounds to believe it was true shall be liable -

(a) on conviction on indictment, to imprisonment for a period of five years or to a fine of five thousand dollars or to both such imprisonment and fine; or

(b) on summary conviction to imprisonment for a period of one year or to a fine of two thousand dollars or to both such imprisonment and fine.

Civil liability for mis-statements in prospectus.

31.(1) Where a prospectus invites persons to subscribe for shares in a company, the following persons shall be liable to pay compensation to all persons who subscribe for any shares on the faith of the prospectus for the loss or damage they may have sustained by reason of any untrue statement included therein, that is to say -

(a) every person who is an officer of the company at the time of the issue of the prospectus;

(b) every person who has authorized himself to be named and is named in the prospectus as an officer or as having agreed to become an officer either immediately or after an interval of time;

(c) every person being a promoter of the company; and

(d) every person who has authorized the issue to the public of the prospectus.

(2) No person shall be liable under subsection (1) of this section if he proves -

(a) that, having consented to become an officer of the company, he withdrew his consent before the issue of the prospectus, and that it was issued without his authority or consent; or

(b) that the prospectus was issued without his knowledge or consent, and that on becoming aware of its issue he forthwith gave reasonable public notice that it was issued without his knowledge or consent; or

(c) that, after the issue of the prospectus and before allotment thereunder, he, on becoming aware of any untrue statement therein, withdrew his consent thereto and gave reasonable public notice of the withdrawal and of the reason therefor; or

(d) that -

(i) as regards every untrue statement not purporting to be made on the authority of an expert or of a public official document or statement, he had reasonable ground to believe, and did up to the time of the allotment of the shares believe, that the statement was true; and

(ii) as regards every untrue statement purporting to be a statement by an expert or contained in what purports to be a copy of or extract from a report or valuation of an expert, it fairly represented the statement, or was a correct and fair copy of or extract from the report or valuation, and he had reasonable ground to believe and did up to the time of the issue of the prospectus believe that the person making the statement was competent to make it and had not withdrawn or altered it; and

(iii) as regards every untrue statement purporting to be a statement made by an official person or contained in what purports to be a copy of or extract from a public official document, it was a correct and fair representation of the statement or copy of or extract from the document.

(3) Where the prospectus contains -

(a) the name of a person as an officer of the company or as having agreed to become an officer of the company thereof, and he has not consented to become

an officer, or has withdrawn his consent before the issue of the prospectus, and has not authorized or consented to the issue thereof, or

(b) a statement by an expert or contains what purports to be a copy of or extract from a report or valuation of any expert, which the expert has withdrawn or altered, the officers of the company, except any without whose knowledge or consent the prospectus was issued, and any other person who authorized the issue thereof shall be liable to indemnify the person named as aforesaid or whose consent was required as aforesaid, as the case may be, against all damages, costs and expenses to which he may be made liable by reason of his name having been inserted in the prospectus or of the inclusion therein of a statement purporting to be made by him as an expert, as the case may be, or in defending himself against any action or legal proceeding brought against him in respect thereof:

Provided that a person shall not be deemed for the purposes for this subsection to have authorized the issue of a prospectus by reason only of the inclusion therein of a statement purporting to be made by him as an expert.

When experts are not liable.

32. A person referred to as an expert in a prospectus shall not be liable under section 30 or 31 if any untrue statement was not made by him or that as regards any untrue statement made by him he was competent to make the statement and had reasonable grounds to believe and did believe up to the date of the issue of the prospectus that it was true or on becoming aware that the statement was untrue before the issue of the prospectus he had given reasonable public notice of his disassociation from the prospectus and the reasons therefor.

Restriction on alteration of terms mentioned in prospectus.

33. A company limited by shares, or other company having a share capital, shall not prior to the statutory meeting vary the terms of a contract referred to in a prospectus.

Rules.

34. The Minister after consultation with the Institute of Chartered Accountants of Bermuda may make rules providing for -

(a) the information that shall be contained in, and the copies of documents that shall be attached to, any financial statement required to be attached to a prospectus by section 27(1)(h); and

(b) the information that shall be contained in any report or statement of an auditor required to be attached to a prospectus by section 27(1)(i).

PART IV

SHARE CAPITAL DEBENTURES AND DIVIDENDS

Prohibition of allotment unless minimum subscription received.

35.(1) No allotment shall be made of any share capital of a company offered to the public for subscription unless the minimum subscription provided for in paragraph (a) of section 28 has been paid to and received by the company.

For the purposes of this subsection, a sum shall be deemed to have been paid to and received by the company if a cheque or other draft for that sum has been received in good faith by the company and the officers of the company have no reason for suspecting that the cheque or other draft will not be paid.

(2) The amount so stated in the prospectus shall be reckoned exclusively of any amount payable otherwise than in cash.

(3) If the conditions aforesaid have not been complied with on the expiration of one hundred and twenty days after the first publication of the prospectus, all money received from applicants for share shall be forthwith repaid to them without interest, and, if any such money is not so repaid within one hundred and twenty eight days after the issue of the prospectus the directors, provisional directors as the case may be and promoters of the company shall be jointly and severally liable to repay that money with interest at the rate of five percent per annum from the expiration of the one hundred and twenty-eighth day:

Provided that such a person shall not be liable if he proves that the default in the repayment of the money was not due to any misconduct or negligence on his part.

(4) Any condition requiring or binding any application for shares to waive compliance with any requirement of this section shall be void.

(5) This section shall not apply to any allotment of shares subsequent to the first allotment of shares offered to the public for subscription.

Effect of irregular allotment.

36. An allotment made by a company to an applicant in contravention of section 35 shall be voidable at the instance of the applicant within one month after the holding of the statutory meeting of the company and not later, or, in any case where the company is not required to hold a statutory meeting, or where the allotment is made after the holding of the statutory meeting, within one month after the date of the allotment, and not later, and shall be so voidable notwithstanding that the company is in the course of being wound up.

Penalty for the contravention of section 36.

37. If any officer, provisional director, or promoter of a company knowingly contravenes, or permits or authorizes the contravention of, any of the provisions relating to the allotment of shares, he shall be liable to compensate the company and the allottee respectively for any loss, damages or costs which the company or the allottee may have sustained or incurred thereby:

Provided that proceedings to recover any such loss, damages, or costs shall not be commenced after the expiration of two years from the date of the allotment.

Power to pay certain commissions and prohibition of payment of other commissioners etc.

38.(1) It shall be lawful for a company to pay a reasonable commission to any person in consideration of his subscribing or agreeing to subscribe, whether absolutely or conditionally for any shares in the company, or procuring or agreeing to procure subscriptions, whether absolute or conditional for any shares in the company.

(2) Save as aforesaid, no company shall apply any of its shares or capital money either directly or indirectly in payment of any commission, discount or allowance to any person in consideration of his subscribing or agreeing to subscribe, whether absolutely or conditionally, for any shares in the company, or procuring or agreeing to procure subscriptions, whether absolute or conditional, for any shares in the company, whether the shares or money be so applied by being added to the purchase money of any property acquired by the company, or the money be paid out of the nominal purchase money or contract price, or otherwise.

(3) Nothing in this section shall affect the power of any company to pay such brokerage as it has heretofore been lawful for a company to pay.

(4) A vendor to, promoter of, or other person who receives payment in money or shares from a company shall have and shall be deemed always to have had power to apply any part of the money or shares so received in payment of any commission, the payment of which, if made directly by the company, would have been legal under this section.

Financial assistance generally prohibited.

39.(1) Subject to sections 39A to 39C (inclusive), where a person is acquiring or is proposing to acquires shares in a company, it shall not be lawful for the company or any of its subsidiaries to give financial assistance directly or indirectly for the purpose of that acquisition before or at the same time as the acquisition takes place.

(2) Subject to sections 39A to 39C (inclusive), where a person has acquired shares in a company and any liability has been incurred (by that or any other person), for the purpose of that acquisition, it shall not be lawful for the company or any of its subsidiaries to give financial assistance directly or indirectly for the purpose of reducing or discharging the liability so incurred.

(3) In this section and sections 39A to 39C (inclusive) -

(a) a reference to a person incurring a liability includes his changing his financial position by making an agreement or arrangement (whether enforceable or unenforceable, and whether made on his own account or with any other person) or by any other means, and

(b) a reference to a company giving financial assistance for the purpose of reducing or discharging a liability incurred by a person for the purpose of the acquisition of shares includes its giving such financial assistance for the purpose of wholly or partly restoring his financial position to what it was before the acquisition took place.

(4) If a company acts in contravention of this section, it shall be liable to a fine, and every officer of it who is in default shall be liable to imprisonment or fine, or both.

Exclusion from prohibition on financial assistance

39A.(1) Section 39(1) does not prohibit a company from giving financial assistance for the purpose of an acquisition of shares in it or in its holding company if -

(a) the company's principal purpose in giving that assistance is not to give it for the purpose of any such acquisition, or the giving of the assistance for that purpose is but an incidental part of some larger purpose of the company, and

(b) the assistance is given in good faith in the interests of the company.

(2) Section 39(2) does not prohibit a company from giving financial assistance if -

(a) the company's principal purpose in giving the assistance is not to reduce or discharge any liability incurred by a person for the purpose of the acquisition of shares in the company or its holding company, or the reduction or discharge of any such liability is but an incidental part of some larger purpose of the company, and

(b) the assistance is given in good faith in the interests of the company.

(2A) Section 39 shall only prohibit a company from giving financial assistance if, on the date from which the financial assistance is to be given, there are reasonable grounds for believing that the company is, or after the giving of such financial assistance would be, unable to pay its liabilities as they become due.

(3) Section 39 does not prohibit any transaction which is permitted by this Act or any other statutory provision including -

(a) a distribution of a company's assets out of funds of the company which would otherwise be available for dividend or distribution,

(*b*) a distribution made in the course of the company's winding up,

(*c*) the allotment of bonus shares,

(*d*) a reduction of capital made in accordance with the provisions of this Act,

(*e*) a redemption or purchase or shares made in accordance with the provisions of this Act.

(4) Section 39 does not prohibit -

(*a*) where the lending of money is part of the ordinary business of the company, the lending of money by the company in the ordinary course of its business;

(*b*) the provision by a company in accordance with an employees' share scheme of money for the acquisition of fully or partly paid shares in the company or any holding company; and for the purposes of this Act, an employees' share scheme is a scheme for encouraging or facilitating the holding of shares or debentures in a company by or for the benefit of the bona fide employees or former employees (including, notwithstanding section 96, any such bona fide employee or former employee who is or was also a director) of the company, the company's subsidiary or holding company or a subsidiary of the company's holding company, or the wives, husbands, widows, widowers or children or step-children under the age of twenty-one of such employees or former employees;

(*c*) the making by a company, the company's subsidiary or holding company or a subsidiary of the company's holding company of loans to persons (including, notwithstanding section 96, any such bona fide employee or former employee who is or was also a director) employed in good faith by the company with a view to enabling those persons to acquire fully or partly paid shares in the company or its holding company to be held by them by way of beneficial ownership.

(5) Where a company makes provision for the giving of financial assistance in accordance with subsection (4)(b) and (c), such company may make further provision in its bye-laws requiring or allowing the sale of such shares to the company when an employee ceases to be employed by the company and the purchase of shares by a company by virtue of this subsection shall not be taken as reducing the amount of the company's authorised share capital.

Circumstances where financial assistance is permitted

39B.(1) Section 39 does not prohibit a company from giving financial assistance in a case where the acquisition of shares in question is or was an acquisition of shares in the company or, if it is a subsidiary of another company, in that other company if the following provisions of this section and section 39C are complied with as respects the giving of that financial assistance.

(2) The financial assistance may only be given if the company has net assets which are not thereby reduced or, to the extent that they are reduced, if the financial assistance is provided out of funds of the company which would otherwise be available for dividend or distribution.

(3) Unless the company proposing to give the financial assistance is a wholly-owned subsidiary of the company whose shares are to be acquired, the giving of assistance under this section must be approved by a resolution of the company in general meeting.

(4) Where the financial assistance is to be given by the company in a case where the acquisition of shares in question is or was an acquisition of shares in its holding company, that holding company and any other company which is both the company's holding company and a subsidiary of that other holding company (except, in any case, a company which is a wholly-owned subsidiary) shall also approve by resolution in general meeting the giving of the financial assistance.

(5) The directors of the company proposing to give the financial assistance and, where the shares acquired or to be acquired are shares in its holding company, the directors of that company and of any other company which is both the company's holding company and a subsidiary of that other holding company shall before the financial assistance is given swear an affidavit in accordance with section 39C.

Conditions applicable to giving of financial assistance under s.39B

39C.(1) No company shall provide financial assistance pursuant to section 39B unless before the date as from which the financial assistance is to be given, an affidavit is sworn by at least two directors of the company declaring either that on that date after taking into account the giving of the financial assistance, the company will be solvent or that all the creditors of the company on that date have expressed in writing their concurrence in the giving of the financial assistance. The affidavit shall contain particulars of the financial assistance to be given and identify the person to whom the financial assistance is to be given.

(2) A resolution required by section 39B to be passed by a company approving the giving of financial assistance must be passed on the date on which the directors of that company swear the affidavit required by that section in connection with the giving of that financial assistance or within fifteen days immediately following that date.

(3) Where such a resolution has been passed, an application may be made to the Court within twenty-one days of the passing of that resolution for the cancellation of the resolution -

(a) by the holders of not less in the aggregate than 10 per cent in nominal value of the company's issued share capital or any class of issued share capital, or

(b) if the company is not limited by shares or does not have a share capital, by not less than 10 per cent of the company's members;

but the application shall not be made by a person who has consented to or voted in favour of the resolution. On the hearing of the application the Court may make an order cancelling or confirming the resolution and may make that order on such terms and conditions as it thinks fit, and may, if it thinks fit, adjourn the proceedings in order that an arrangement may be made to the satisfaction of the Court for the purchase of the interests of dissentient members, and may give such directions and make such orders that it thinks expedient for facilitating or carrying into effect any such arrangement.

(4) The affidavit of the directors together with a certified copy of any resolution passed by the company and by any other company as required by section 39B shall be delivered to the Registrar within twenty-one days of the swearing of the affidavit.

(5) Where a resolution is required by section 39B to be passed approving the giving of the financial assistance, the financial assistance shall not be given before the expiry of the period of thirty days beginning with -

(a) the date on which the resolution is passed; or

(b) where more than one resolution is passed, the date on which the last of them is passed;

unless, as respects that resolution (or if more than one, each of them), no person or persons when taken together are entitled to make an application to the Court in accordance with subsection (3).

(6) The financial assistance shall not be given after the expiry of the period of sixty days beginning with -

(a) the date on which the directors of the company proposing to give the financial assistance swore their affidavit as required by section 39B; or

(b) where the company is a subsidiary and both its directors and the directors of its holding companies swore such an affidavit, the date on which the earliest of the affidavits is sworn;

unless the Court, on an application under subsection (3), otherwise orders.

(7) Where a company fails to comply with subsection (4), the company and every officer who is in default shall be liable to a fine and, for continued contravention, to a daily default fine.

(8) A director of a company who swears an affidavit under section 39B without having reasonable grounds for the opinion expressed in it shall be liable to imprisonment or a fine, or both.

Application of premiums received on issue of shares.

40.(1) Where a company issues shares at a premium, whether for cash or otherwise, a sum equal to the aggregate amount or value of the premiums on those shares shall be transferred to an account, to be called "the share premium account", and the provisions of this Act relating to the reduction of the share capital of a company shall, except as provided in this section, apply as if the share premium account were paid-up share capital of the company:

Provided that in the case of an exchange of shares the excess value of the shares acquired over the nominal value of the shares being issued may be credited to a contributed surplus account of the issuing company.

(2) Subject to subsection (2A), the share premium account may, notwithstanding anything in subsection (1) be applied by the company -

(a) in paying up unissued shares of the company to be issued to members of the company as fully paid bonus shares;

(b) in writing off -

(i) the preliminary expenses of the company; or

(ii) the expenses of, or the commission paid or discount allowed on, any issue of shares or debentures of the company; or

(c) in providing for the premiums payable on redemption of any shares or of any debentures of the company.

(2A) Only premiums arising on the same class of shares can be used under subsection (2)(a) and (c).

(3) Where a company has before the appointed day issued any shares at a premium this section shall apply to the premiums received in respect of such shares as if the shares had been issued after such day:

Provided that any part of such premiums which do not on the appointed day form an identifiable part of the company's reserves shall be disregarded in determining the sum to be included in the share premium account.

The meaning of "reserve".

41. For the purpose of section 40 the expression "reserve" shall not include any amount written off or retained by way of providing for depreciation, renewals or diminution in the value of assets or retained by way of providing for any known liability of which the amount cannot be determined with substantial accuracy.

Power to issue redeemable preference shares.

42.(1) Subject to this section, a company limited by shares, or other company having a share capital, may issue preference shares which -

(i) if so authorized by its bye-laws, are, or at the option of the company are to be liable, to be redeemed;

(ii) if so authorized by its memorandum at the option of the holder are to be liable to be redeemed:

Provided that -

(a) no such shares shall be redeemed except out of the capital paid up thereon or out of the funds of the company which would otherwise be available for dividend or distribution or out of the proceeds of a fresh issue of shares made for the purposes of the redemption; and

(b) the premium, if any, payable on redemption, is provided for out of the funds of the company which would otherwise be available for dividend or distribution or out of the company's shares premium account before the shares are redeemed.

(2) Subject to this section, the redemption of preference shares thereunder may be effected on such terms and in such manner as may be provided by the bye-laws of the company; however no redemption of preference shares may be effected if, on the date on which the redemption is to be effected, there are reasonable grounds for believing that the company is, or after the redemption would be, unable to pay its liabilities as they become due.

(2A) [*repealed*]

(3) The redemption of preference shares under this section shall not be taken as reducing the amount of the company's authorized share capital.

(4) On the redemption of preference shares under this section, any amount due to a shareholder may -

(a) be paid in cash;

(b) be satisfied by the transfer of any part of the undertaking or property of the company having the same value; or

(c) be satisfied partly under paragraph (a) and partly under paragraph (b).

Purchase by a company of its own shares.

42A.(1) Subject to the following provisions of this section, a company limited by shares, or other company having a share capital, may, if authorized to do so by its memorandum or bye-laws, purchase its own shares.

(2) Section 42 shall apply in relation to the purchase by a company under this section of its own shares as it applies in relation to the redemption of redeemable preference shares by a company under that section, save that the terms and manner of purchase need not be determined by the bye-laws as provided in subsection (2) of that section.

(3) A company may not purchase any of its own shares if, as a result of the purchase of the shares in question, the issued share capital of the company would be reduced below the minimum capital specified for the company in its memorandum.

(4) A purchase by a company of its own shares may be authorized by its board of directors or otherwise by or in accordance with the provisions of its bye-laws.

(5) No purchase by a company of its own shares may be effected if, on the date on which the purchase is to be effected, there are reasonable grounds for believing that the company is, or after the purchase would be, unable to pay its liabilities as they become due.

(6) Shares purchased under this section shall be treated as cancelled and the amount of the company's issued capital shall be diminished by the nominal value of those shares accordingly; but the purchase of shares under this section shall not be taken as reducing the amount of the company's authorized share capital.

(6A) On the purchase of its own shares under this section, any amount due to a shareholder may -

(a) be paid in cash;

(b) be satisfied by the transfer of any part of the undertaking of property of the company having the same value; or

(c) be satisfied partly under paragraph (a) and partly under paragraph (b).

(7) Where a company agrees, or is obliged, to purchase any of its shares then -

(a) the company shall not be liable in damages in respect of any failure to purchase any of the shares;

(b) the court shall not grant an order for specific performance of the purchase if the company shows that to do so would render it insolvent or cause it to breach the provisions of any Act, regulations or licence;

(c) on a liquidation, other shares which carry rights whether as to capital or income which are preferred to the rights attaching to the shares agreed to be purchased, shall be paid in priority to the purchase price.

Power to convert preference shares into redeemable preference shares.

43. A company limited by shares, or other company having a share capital, may by resolution at a general meeting convert any preference shares into redeemable preference shares:

Provided that -

(a) the consent in writing has first been obtained of the holders of three-fourths of such shares that have been issued;

(b) at a date not more than thirty days and not less than fifteen days before the

date it is proposed to convert the shares the company shall cause a notice to be published in an appointed newspaper stating the intention to convert the shares and the date on which the conversion is to take place;

(c) on the date on which the conversion is to take place an affidavit shall be sworn by at least two directors of the company declaring either that on that date the company is solvent or that all the creditors of the company on that date have expressed in writing their concurrence in the conversion; and

(d) the provisions of subsection (1) of section 42 shall apply to such shares.

Power of company to arrange for different amounts being paid on shares.

44. A company limited by shares, or other company having a share capital, if so authorized by its bye-laws may do any one or more of the following things -

(a) make arrangements on the issue of shares for a difference between the members in the amounts and times of payment of calls on their shares;

(b) accept from any member the whole or a part of the amount remaining unpaid on any shares held by him, although no part of that amount has been called up;

(c) pay dividends in proportion to the amount paid up on each share where a larger amount is paid up on some shares than on others;

(d) issue its shares in fractional denominations and deal with such fractions to the same extent as its whole shares and shares in fractional denominations shall have in proportion to the respective fractions represented thereby all of the rights of whole shares including (but without limiting the generality of the foregoing) the right to vote, to receive dividends and distributions and to participate in a winding up.

Power of company limited by shares, or other company having a share capital, to alter its share capital.

45.(1) A company limited by shares, or other company having a share capital, if authorized by a general meeting and by its bye-laws, may alter the conditions of its memorandum as follows, that is to say, it may -

(a) increase its share capital by new shares of such amount as it thinks expedient;

(b) divide its shares into several classes and attach thereto respectively any preferential, deferred, qualified or special rights, privileges or conditions;

(c) consolidate and divide all or any of its share capital into shares of larger amount than its existing shares;

(d) subdivide its shares, or any of them, into shares of smaller amount than is fixed by the memorandum, so, however, that in the subdivision the proportion between the amount paid and the amount, if any, unpaid on each reduced share shall be the same as it was in the case of the share from which the reduced share is derived;

(dd) change the currency denomination of its share capital;

(e) make provision for the issue and allotment of shares which do not carry any voting rights; and

(f) cancel shares which, at the date of the passing of the resolution in that behalf, have not been taken or agreed to be taken by any person, and diminish the amount of its share capital by the amount of the shares so cancelled.

(2) A cancellation of shares in pursuance of this section shall not be deemed to be a reduction of share capital within the meaning of this Act.

(3) Whenever a company alters the conditions of its memorandum under subsection (1)(a), (dd) or (f), then within thirty days thereafter the company shall file a memorandum with the Registrar setting out the altered conditions.

(4) If any company fails to file a memorandum in accordance with subsection (3) it shall be liable to a default fine.

Reduction of share capital.

46.(1) A company having share capital if authorized in a general meeting may subject to any order made by the Minister under section 6(4) and to its memorandum and bye-laws on such terms as it may decide reduce its share capital in any way, and in particular, without prejudice to the generality of the foregoing power, by -

(a) extinguishing or reducing the liability on any of its shares in respect of capital not paid up; or

b) either with or without extinguishing or reducing liability on any of its shares cancel any paid up capital that is lost or unrepresented by available assets; or

(c) either with or without extinguishing or reducing liability of any of its shares and either with or without reducing the number of such shares pay off any paid up capital that is in excess of the requirements of the company.

(2) No company shall reduce the amount of its share capital -

(a) unless, at a date not more than thirty days and not less than fifteen days before the date on which the reduction of the share capital is to have effect, the company causes a notice to be published in an appointed newspaper stating -

(i) the amount of the share capital as last determined by the company;

(ii) the amount to which the share capital is to be reduced; and

(iii) the date on which the reduction is to have effect; and

(b) if, on the date the reduction is to be effected, there are reasonable grounds for believing that the company is, and after the reduction would be, unable to pay its liabilities as they become due.

(3) Unless the bye-laws otherwise provide where the capital of a company is reduced by the cancellation of shares and part only of a class of shares is to be cancelled, the shares to be cancelled shall be selected -

(a) by lot in such manner as the directors shall determine; or

(b) as nearly as may be in proportion to the number of shares of the class registered in the name of each shareholder; or

(c) in such other manner as the directors determine with the consent of the majority of the holders of the shares of the class to be cancelled.

(4) Where shares are to be cancelled in order to reduce the capital of a company the shares shall be acquired at the lowest price at which, in the opinion of the directors, the shares are obtainable, but not exceeding an amount, if any, stated in or determined by the bye-laws.

(5) Where a company having share capital reduces the amount of its share capital, then within thirty days after the date as from which the reduction has effect the company shall file a memorandum, with a copy of the notice referred to in paragraph (a), in the office of the Registrar stating that the provisions of this section have been duly complied with.

(6) If any company fails to comply with subsection (2), (3) or (4) every officer of the company shall be liable to a fine of five thousand dollars and if the company fails to comply with subsection (5) the company shall be liable to a default fine.

Rights of holders of special classes of shares.

47.(1) If in the case of a company the share capital of which is divided into different classes of shares, provision is made by the memorandum or bye-laws for authorizing the variation of rights attached to any class of shares in the company, subject to the consent of any specified proportions of the holders of the issued shares of that class or the sanction of a resolution passed at a separate meeting of the holders of those shares, and in pursuance of the said provision the rights attached to any such class of shares are at any time varied, the holders of not less than in the aggregate than ten percent of the issued shares of that class, may apply to the Court to have the variation cancelled, and, where any such application is made, the variation shall not have effect unless and until it is confirmed by the Court.

(2) An application under this section must be made within twenty-eight days after the date on which the consent was given or the resolution was passed, as the case may be, and may be made on behalf of the shareholders entitled to make the application by such one or more of their number as they may appoint in writing for the purpose.

(3) On any such application the Court, after hearing the applicant and any other persons who apply to the Court to be heard and appear to the Court to be interested in the application, may, if it is satisfied, having regard to all the circumstances of the case, that the variation would unfairly prejudice the shareholders of the class represented by the applicant, disallow the variation and shall, if not so satisfied, confirm the variation.

(4) The decision of the Court on any such application shall be final.

(5) The company shall within twenty-one days after the making of an order by the Court on any such application forward a copy of the order to the Registrar, and, if default is made in complying with this provision, the company and every officer of the company who is in default shall be liable to a default fine.

(6) Nothing in this section shall be deemed to modify the rights of any member of a company under section 111.

(7) If the memorandum or bye-laws of a company with share capital which is divided into different classes of shares makes no provision for varying the rights attached to any class of share and nothing in the memorandum or bye-laws precludes a variation of such rights, the rights attached to any class, unless otherwise provided by the terms of issue of the shares of that class may, whether or not the company is being wound up, be varied with the consent in writing of the holders of three-fourths of the issued shares of that class, or with the sanction of a resolution passed at a separate general meeting of the holders of the shares of the class. To every such separate general meeting the provisions of the bye-laws or other rules of the company relating to general meetings shall apply, but so that the necessary quorum shall be two persons at least holding or representing by proxy one-third of the issued shares of the class and that any holder of shares of the class present in person or by proxy may demand a poll; however, in the case of a company having only one member, one member present in person or by proxy constitutes the necessary quorum.

(8) The expression “variation” in this section includes abrogation and the expression “varied” shall be construed accordingly.

Nature and transfer of shares.

48.(1) Subject to any other enactment the shares or other interest of any member in a company shall be personal estate, transferable in manner provided by the bye-laws of the company.

(2) Notwithstanding anything in the bye-laws of a company, it shall not be lawful for the company to register a transfer of shares in or debentures of the company unless a proper instrument of transfer has been delivered to the company:

Provided that nothing in this section shall prejudice any power of the company to register as shareholder or debenture holder any person to whom the right to any shares in or debentures of the company has been transmitted by operation of law.

Transfer by estate representative.

49. A transfer of the share or other interest of a deceased member of a company made by his estate representative shall, although the estate representative is not himself a member of the company, be as valid as if he had been such a member at the time of the execution of the instrument of transfer.

Notice of refusal to register transfer.

50.(1) If a company refuses to register a transfer of any shares or debentures, the company shall, within three months after the date on which the transfer was lodged with the company, send to the transferor and transferee notice of the refusal.

(2) If default is made in complying with this section, the company and every officer of the company who is in default shall be liable to a default fine.

Duties of company with respect to the issue of certificates.

51.(1) Every company shall, so soon as practicable after the allotment of any of its shares, or debentures and in any case within two months after a demand for a certificate of such shares or debentures has been made by the person to whom they have been allotted, complete and have ready for delivery such certificates unless the conditions of issue of the shares or debentures otherwise provide.

(2) If default is made in complying with this section, the company and every officer of the company who is in default shall be liable to a default fine.

(3) If any company on whom a notice has been served requiring the company to make good any default in complying with the provisions of subsection (1) of this section fails to make good the default within ten days after the service of the notice, the Court may, on the application of the person entitled to have the certificates or the debentures delivered to him, make an order directing the company and any officer of the company to make good the default within such time as may be specified in the order, and any such order may provide that all costs of and incidental to the application shall be borne by the company or by any officer of the company responsible for the default.

Certificate to be evidence of title and evidence of grant of probate etc.

52.(1) A certificate, under the common seal of the company specifying any shares or debentures held by any member, shall be prima facie evidence of the title of the member to the shares or debentures.

(2) The production to a company of any document which is by law sufficient evidence of probate of the will, or the grant of letters of administration of the estate, or confirmation as executor of a deceased person having been granted to some person shall be accepted by the company, notwithstanding anything in its bye-laws, as sufficient evidence of the grant.

(3) "Law" in subsection (2) includes the law of Bermuda and of any country in the Commonwealth and the law in any part of the United States of America.

Bearer shares prohibited.

53. It shall not be lawful for any company to issue bearer shares.

Dividends and other distributions.

54.(1) A company shall not declare or pay a dividend, or make a distribution out of contributed surplus, if there are reasonable grounds for believing that -

(a) the company is, or would after the payment be, unable to pay its liabilities as they become due; or

(b) the realisable value of the company's assets would thereby be less than the aggregate of its liabilities and its issued share capital and share premium accounts.

(2) For the purposes of this section, "contributed surplus" includes proceeds arising from donated shares, credits resulting from the redemption or conversion of shares at less than the amount set up as nominal capital and donations of cash and other assets to the company.

Rights to claim damages

54A. A person is not debarred from obtaining damages or other compensation from a company by reason only of his holding or having held shares in the company or any right to apply or subscribe for shares or to be included in the company's register of members in respect of shares.

PART V

THE REGISTRATION OF CHARGES

Register of charges, the registration of charges and their priority.

55.(1) The Registrar shall keep with respect to each company a register of charges on the assets of the company and any person, including the company, interested in a charge on the assets of the company may apply to have that charge registered, and the Register shall register the charge in such form as may be prescribed.

(2) Any charge registered shall have priority based on the date that it is registered and not on the date of its creation and shall have such priority over any unregistered charge.

(3) Subsection (2) of this section shall not apply to charges created before the appointed day. Such charges shall continue to have the priority they had prior to that date:

Provided that any person interested in a charge on the assets of a company created before the appointed day may register that charge but the charge shall continue to have the priority it had prior to registration.

(4) Where a charge is created by a company but is a charge on assets outside Bermuda, the instrument creating or purporting to create the charge may be registered under this section notwithstanding that further proceedings may be necessary to make the charge valid or effectual according to the law of the country in which the property is situate.

(5) Notwithstanding anything in this section, a charge on -

(a) land in Bermuda shall be registered under the Mortgage Registration Act 1786 or any Act replacing it and not under this Act and the priority of such charge shall be determined in accordance with the said Mortgage Registration Act 1786 or any Act replacing it;

(b) any ship registered in Bermuda or any interest therein registerable under the Merchant Shipping Act 1894 or any Act replacing it shall be registered thereunder and not under this Act and the priority of such charge shall be determined in accordance with the said Merchant Shipping Act 1894 or any Act replacing it.

(6) [DELETED]

(7) The register of charges shall be available for inspection by members of the public during normal working hours.

(8) In this Part, "charge" includes mortgage.

Correction of register.

56.(1) The Registrar on being satisfied that an omission or misstatement of any particulars with respect to any registered charge on the assets of a company was accidental, or due to inadvertence or to some other sufficient cause, and is not of a nature to prejudice the position of creditors or shareholders of the company, may, on the application of the company or any person interested rectify the register; and any such rectification shall have effect from the date of the first entry of the charge in the register.

(2) Any creditor or member of the company aggrieved by a decision of the Registrar either to rectify or not rectify the register may within six months of the decision of the Registrar appeal to the Court which shall have the same powers as the Registrar. No appeal shall lie from a decision of the Court.

Special provision with regard to debentures.

57. Where a series of debentures containing, or giving by reference to any other instrument, any charge to the benefit which the debenture holders of that series are entitled pari passu is created by a company, it shall, for the purposes of the registration of the series under section 55, be sufficient if the following particulars are registered with the Registrar -

(a) the total amount secured by the whole series; and

(b) the dates of the resolutions authorizing the issue of the series and the date of the covering deed, if any, by which the security is created or defined; and

(c) a general description of the property charged; and

(d) the names of the trustees, if any, for the debenture holders, together with a copy of the deed containing the charge, or, if there is no such deed, a copy of one of the debentures of the series:

Provided that, where more than one issue is made of debentures in the series, there shall be sent to the Registrar for entry in the register particulars of the date and amount of each issue, but an omission to do this shall not affect the validity of the debentures issued.

Particulars required to be registered when commission paid in respect of debentures.

58. Where any commission, allowance or discount has been paid or made either directly or indirectly by a company to any person in consideration of his subscribing or agreeing to subscribe, whether absolutely or conditionally, for any debentures of the company, or procuring or agreeing to procure subscriptions, whether absolute or conditional, for any such debentures, the particulars sent for registration shall include particulars as to the amount or rate per cent of the commission, discount or allowance so paid or made, but omission to do this shall not affect the validity of the debentures issued.

Entries of satisfaction and release of property from charge.

59. The Registrar, on evidence being given to his satisfaction with respect to any registered charge

(a) that the debt for which the charge was given has been paid or satisfied in whole or in part; or

(b) that part of the property or undertaking charged has been released from the charge or has ceased to form part of the company's property or undertaking,shall enter on the register a memorandum of satisfaction in whole or in part, or of the fact that part of the property or undertaking has been released from the charge or has ceased to form part of the company's property or undertaking, as the case may be, and where he enters a memorandum of satisfaction in whole he shall, if required, furnish the company with a copy thereof.

Registration of appointment of a receiver or manager.

60.(1) If any person obtains on order for the appointment of a receiver or manager of the property of a company, or appoints such a receiver or manager under any powers contained in any instrument, he shall, within seven days from the date of the order or of the appointment under the said powers give notice of the fact to the Registrar, and the Registrar shall, on payment of such fee as may be specified by rules made by the Minister, enter the fact in the register of charges.

(2) Where any person appointed receiver or manager of the property of a company under the powers contained in any instrument ceases to act as such receiver or manager, he shall on so ceasing, give the Registrar notice to that effect, and the Registrar shall enter the notice in the register of charges.

(3) If any person makes default in complying with the requirements of this section, he shall be liable to a default fine.

(4) Rules made under this section shall be subject to affirmative resolution procedure.

Application of this Part to charges created and acquired, by company incorporated outside Bermuda.

61. The provisions of this Part shall extend to charges on property in Bermuda which are created, and to charges on property in Bermuda which are acquired, by a company incorporated outside Bermuda.

PART VI

MANAGEMENT AND ADMINISTRATION

Registered office of company.

62.(1) A company shall at all times have a registered office in Bermuda which shall not be a post office box to which all communications and notices may be addressed.

(2) On incorporation the situation of the company's registered office is that specified in a notice in the prescribed form given to the Registrar under section 69(2)(e).

(3) The company may change the situation of its registered office from time to time by giving notice in the prescribed form to the Registrar and such change takes effect upon the notice being registered by the Registrar.

(4) If default is made in complying with this section the company or every officer of the company who is in default shall be liable to a default fine.

Service of documents.

62A. A document may be served on a company by leaving it at the registered office of the company or, in the case of a non-resident insurance undertaking the principal office in Bermuda, or in the case of a permit company, the principal place of business in Bermuda from which the company engages in or carries on its trade or business in Bermuda.

Publication of name of company.

63.(1) Every company shall have its name mentioned in legible characters in all business letters of the company and in all notices and other official publications of the company, and in all bills of exchange, promissory notes, endorsements, cheques and orders for money or goods purporting to be signed by or on behalf of the company, and in all bills of parcels, invoices, receipts and letters of credit of the company.

(2) If default if made in complying with this section the company and every officer of the company who is in default shall be liable to a fine of five hundred dollars.

Restrictions on commencement of business.

64.(1) No company shall commence or carry on business or exercise any borrowing powers unless and until the minimum capital as stated in its memorandum in accordance with section 7 has been subscribed.

(2) If any company commences or continues business or exercises borrowing powers in contravention of this section every person who is responsible for the contravention shall without prejudice to any other liability, be liable to a fine of one hundred dollars for every day during which the contravention continues.

Register of members.

65.(1) Every company shall keep a register of its members and enter therein in respect of every member becoming a member after the appointed day the following particulars -

(a) the names and addresses of the members, and in the case of a company having a share capital a statement of the shares held by each member, distinguishing each share by its number so long as the share has a number, and of the amount paid or agreed to be considered as paid on the shares of each member;

(b) the date at which each person was entered in the register as a member;

(c) the date at which any person ceased to be a member for one year after he so ceased.

(2) The register of members shall be kept at the registered office of the company or after giving written notice to the Registrar of the place at such other place in Bermuda convenient for inspection by members of the company and other persons entitled to inspect it.

(3) A company the shares of which are traded on an appointed stock exchange or have been offered to the public pursuant to a prospectus filed under section 26, may keep in any place outside Bermuda, one or more branch registers after giving written notice to the Registrar of the place where each such register is to be kept.

(4) A branch register shall be kept in the same manner in which the register of members is by subsection (1) required to be kept.

(5) Every company shall, as soon as reasonably practicable, after the date on which any entry or alteration is made in a branch register, make any necessary alteration in the register of members.

(6) If the register of members or any branch register is not made easily available for inspection by members the company and every officer of the company shall be liable to a fine of five hundred dollars and the Court convicting the company or the officers, as the case may be, may order the company to make the register immediately available for inspection.

(7) A company shall not be bound to see to the execution of any trust, whether express, implied or constructive, to which any of its shares are subject and whether or not the company had notice of such trust; and the receipt of the person, firm or corporation in whose name any share stands shall be sufficient discharge to the company for any money paid by the company in respect of such shares notwithstanding any trust to which it may be subject.

Inspection of register.

66.(1) Except when the register of members is closed under the provisions of this Act, the register of the members of a company shall during business hours (subject to such reasonable restrictions as the company may impose, so that not less than two hours in each day be allowed for inspection) be open for inspection by any member without charge and by any other person on payment of five dollars, or such less sum as the company may determine, for each inspection.

(2) Any member or other person may require a copy of the register, or of any part thereof, on payment of the appropriate fee prescribed in the Fourth Schedule.

(3) If any inspection required under this section is refused or if any copy required under this section is not sent within fourteen days from the receipt of a written request, the company and every officer of the company who is in default shall be liable in respect of each offence to a default fine.

(4) In the case of any such refusal or default, the Court may by order compel an intermediate inspection of the register or direct that the copies required shall be sent to the persons requiring them.

(5) A company may on giving notice by advertisement in an appointed newspaper close the register of members for any time or times not exceeding in the whole thirty days in a year.

(6) This section applies to a branch register kept under section 65 except that in relation to a branch register subsection (5) shall have effect as if for reference to an appointed newspaper there were substituted reference to a national newspaper in the jurisdiction in which the branch register is kept.

Power of Court to rectify register.

67.(1) If -

(a) the name of any person is, without sufficient cause, entered in or omitted from the register of members of a company; or

(b) default is made or unnecessary delay takes place in entering on the register the fact of any person having ceased to be a member, the person aggrieved, or any member of the company, may apply to the Court for rectification of the register.

(2) Where an application is made under this section, the Court may either refuse the application or may order rectification of the register and payment by the company of any damages sustained by any party aggrieved.

(3) On an application under this section the Court may decide any question relating to the title of any person who is a party to the application to have his name entered in or omitted from the register, whether the question arises between members or alleged members, or between members or alleged members on the one hand and the company on the other hand, and generally may decide any question necessary or expedient to be decided for rectification of the register.

Register to be evidence.

68. The register of members shall be prima facie evidence of any matters by this Act directed or authorized to be inserted therein.

Provisional directors and their powers.

69.(1) The persons whose names are subscribed to the memorandum of association shall be the provisional directors of the company to which the memorandum of association relates and shall have power to add to their number.

(2) The provisional directors of a company shall hold office as such until the first board of directors is elected, as hereinafter provided, and subject to subsection (1) shall have the following powers only that is to say -

(a) power to cause books to be opened for the purpose of recording the subscriptions of such persons as may desire to become members of the company, and power to keep open such books for so long as the provisional directors may consider necessary;

(b) power, at any time after the minimum subscription has been subscribed to allot to any subscriber such number of shares, not exceeding the number subscribed for by him, as the provisional directors may deem expedient;

(c) power to appoint any person to be secretary of the company to hold office until the election of the first board of directors of the company;

(d) power by resolution to make such calls upon any subscriber in respect of shares allowed to him as the provisional directors may consider necessary; and in case any subscriber fails to satisfy any such call in the time limited by the provisional directors, to recover the amount of the call as a debt due by the subscriber;

(e) power to give notice of the registered office under subsection 62(2) but, if the provisional directors fail to do so, an officer of the company shall give the notice; and

(f) power to complete and execute all documentation necessary and incidental to incorporating a company.

(3) Any power vested in the provisional directors or any act authorized to be done by them may be exercised by a majority of them.

First general meeting of members to elect directors.

70.(1) As soon as convenient after the minimum share capital set out in the memorandum as provided in section 7 has been subscribed, the provisional directors shall convene the statutory meeting which shall be a general meeting of the members of the company for the purpose of electing the first board of directors.

(2) At least five days' notice in writing of the statutory meeting shall be given to each member of the company unless the members unanimously agree to waive such notice; the notice shall specify the place, date and hour at which the meeting is intended to be held, and shall state that at the meeting the members present or represented by proxy will elect the first board of directors.

(3) For the purposes of this section "member" shall not include any member who has failed to satisfy any call made upon him which came due to be satisfied before the date on which the general meeting under this section is held.

(4) The procedure at a meeting called under this section shall be the same as that for an annual general meeting called under section 71.

(5) The quorum for a meeting called under this section shall be a majority of the members of the company present in person or by proxy.

(6) A meeting called under subsection (1) shall be deemed to be the annual general meeting for the year in which it is convened.

General meetings.

71.(1) A meeting of members of a company shall be convened at least once in every calendar year; this meeting shall be referred to as the annual general meeting.

(2) The directors may, whenever they think fit, convene a general meeting; all meetings other than annual general meetings shall be called special general meetings.

(3) Notice of all general meetings shall specify the place, the day and hour of the meeting, and, in case of special general meetings, the general nature of the business to be considered.

(4) The accidental omission to give notice of a meeting to, or the non-receipt of a notice of a meeting by any persons entitled to receive notice shall not invalidate the proceedings of the meeting.

(5) Where the bye-laws so provide, a general meeting of the members of a company may be held with only one individual present if the requirement for a quorum is satisfied and, where a company has only one shareholder or only one holder of any class of shares, the shareholder present in person or by proxy constitutes a general meeting.

Failure to hold annual general meeting or to elect directors.

72.(1) If default is made in calling or holding a general meeting in accordance with section 71(1) the directors shall use their best endeavours to call or hold the meeting at the earliest practicable date.

(2) If an annual general meeting is not held within three months of the date it should have been held or the required number of directors required to be elected, if any have not been elected at such a meeting the company may apply to the Registrar to sanction the holding of a general meeting to put the affairs of the company in order. Upon receipt of such an application the Registrar may in his discretion make an order allowing the application under such conditions as he thinks fit to impose including ordering the date by which the affairs of the company shall be put in order.

(3) Subject to subsection (2) if default is made in calling an annual general meeting in accordance with section 71 or to elect the required number of directors at such meeting the Registrar, any creditors or member of the company may apply to the Court for the winding up of the company and the Court on such application may order the company to be wound up or make any order that the Registrar might have made under subsection (2).

(4) Where an application is made to the Registrar for an order under subsection (2) a fee of two hundred and fifty dollars shall be paid to the Registrar if there has been a failure to hold one annual general meeting and if there has been failure to hold more than one meeting a further fee shall be payable of one hundred dollars in respect of each such meeting.

Position when election of directors does not take place.

73. If the annual general meeting or the election of any directors, if such election is required by the bye-laws of the company does not take place at the proper time, it shall be lawful for the company to continue its business and for the existing directors to continue in office.

Convening of special general meeting on requisition.

74.(1) The directors of a company, notwithstanding anything in its bye-laws shall, on the requisition of members of the company holding at the date of the deposit of the requisition not less than one-tenth of such of the paid-up capital of the company as at the date of the deposit carries the right of voting at general meetings of the company, or, in the case of a company not having a share capital, members of the company representing not less than one-tenth of the total voting rights of all the members having at the said date a right to vote at general meetings of the company, forthwith proceed duly to convene a special general meeting of the company.

(2) The requisition must state the purposes of the meeting, and must be signed by the requisitionists and deposited at the registered office of the company, and may consist of several documents in like form each signed by one or more requisitionists.

(3) If the directors do not within twenty-one days from the date of the deposit of the requisition proceed duly to convene a meeting, the requisitionists, or any of them representing more than one half of the total voting rights of all of them, may themselves convene a meeting, but any meeting so convened shall not be held after the expiration of three months from the said date.

(4) A meeting convened under this section by the requisitionists shall be convened in the same manner, as nearly as possible, as that in which meetings are to be convened by directors.

(5) Any reasonable expenses incurred by the requisitionists by reason of the failure of the directors duly to convene a meeting shall be repaid to the requisitionists by the company, and any sum so repaid shall be retained by the company out of any sums due or to become due from the company by way of fees or other remuneration in respect of their services to such directors as were in default.

Length of notice for calling meetings.

75.(1) Notwithstanding any provision in the bye-laws of a company at least five days' notice shall be given of a meeting of a company, other than an adjourned meeting.

(2) A meeting of a company shall, notwithstanding that it is called by shorter notice than that specified in subsection (1) be deemed to have been duly called if it is so agreed -

(a) in the case of a meeting called as the annual general meeting, by all the members entitled to attend and vote thereat; and

(b) in the case of any other meeting, by a majority in number of the members having a right to attend and vote at the meeting, being a majority together holding not less than ninety-five per cent in nominal value of the shares giving a right to attend and vote at the meeting, or, in the case of a company not having a share capital, together representing not less than ninety-five per cent of the total voting rights at that meeting of all the members.

Telephonic etc. meeting.

75A. Unless the bye-laws otherwise provide, a meeting of directors or of a committee of directors or of the members or any class thereof may be held by means of such telephone, electronic or other communication facilities as permit all persons participating in the meeting to communicate with each other simultaneously and instantaneously, and participation in such a meeting shall constitute presence in person at such meeting.

Power of Court to order meeting.

76.(1) If for any reason it is impracticable to call a meeting of a company in any manner in which meetings of that company may be called, or to conduct the meeting of the company in the manner prescribed by the bye-laws or this Act, the Court may, either of its own motion or on the application of any director of the company or of any member of the company who would be entitled to vote at the meeting, order a meeting of the company to be called, held and conducted in such manner as the Court thinks fit, and where any such order is made may give such ancillary or consequential directions as it thinks expedient.

(2) Any meeting called, held and conducted in accordance with an order under the foregoing subsection shall for all purposes be deemed to be a meeting of the company duly called, held and conducted.

Voting at meetings.

77.(1) Subject to the provisions of this section, the bye-laws of the company and to any rights or restrictions lawfully attached to any class of shares, at any general meeting each member of the company shall be entitled in the case of a company limited by shares, or other company having a share capital, to one vote for each share held by him and in the case of a company limited by guarantee one vote; such votes may be given in person or by proxy.

(2) At any general meeting of a company any question proposed for consideration shall be decided on a simple majority of votes or by such majority as the bye-laws of the company may prescribe, and such majority shall be ascertained in accordance with this section.

(3) Subject to subsection (5), it shall be lawful for any question proposed for consideration at a general meeting of a company to be decided on a show of hands and in any such case, and subject to any rights or restrictions for the time being lawfully attached to any class of shares, every member present in person or by proxy at such meeting shall be entitled to one vote and shall cast such vote by raising his hand.

(4) At any general meeting of a company a declaration by the chairman that a question proposed for consideration has, on a show of hands, been carried, or carried unanimously or by a particular majority or lost and an entry to that effect in a book containing the minutes of the proceedings of the company shall, subject to subsection (5), be conclusive evidence of that fact without proof of the number or proportion of the votes recorded in favour of or against such question.

(5) Notwithstanding subsection (3), at any general meeting of a company, it shall be lawful, in respect of any question proposed for the consideration of the members, whether before or on the declaration of the result of a show of hands as provided for in subsection (3) for a poll to be demanded by any of the following persons -

(a) the Chairman of such meeting; or

(b) at least three members present in person; or represented by proxy; or

(c) any member or members present in person or represented by proxy and holding between them not less than one-tenth of the total voting rights of all the members having the right to vote at such meeting; or

(d) a member or members present in person or represented by proxy holding shares in such company conferring the right to vote at such meeting, being shares on which an aggregate sum has been paid equal to not less than one-tenth of the total sum paid up on all such shares conferring such right.

(6) Where, in accordance with subsection (5), a poll is demanded, and subject to any rights or restrictions for the time being lawfully attached to any class of shares, every member present in person or by proxy at such meeting shall have one vote for each share of which he is the holder or for which he holds a proxy or in the case of a company limited by guarantee he shall have one vote for himself and one vote for each member for whom he holds a proxy and such votes shall be counted in such manner as the bye-laws of the company may provide or, in default of such provision, as the chairman may direct and the result of such poll shall be deemed to be the resolution of the meeting at which the poll was demanded and shall replace any previous resolution upon the same matter which has been the subject of a show of hands.

(7) A poll demanded, in accordance with subsection (5), for the purpose of electing a chairman, or on a question of adjournment, shall be taken forthwith and a poll demanded on any other question shall be taken at such time at such meeting as the chairman may direct.

(8) In the case of an equality of votes, whether on a show of hands or on a poll, the chairman of the meeting at which such show of hands takes place, or at which such poll is demanded, shall unless the bye-laws of the company otherwise provide, be entitled to a second or casting vote.

(9) Nothing contained in this section shall be construed as prohibiting a member who is the holder of two or more shares from appointing more than one proxy to represent him and vote on his behalf, whether on a show of hands or on a poll, at a general meeting of the company or at a class meeting.

Resolution in writing

77A.(1) Subject to subsection (6), anything which may be done by resolution of a company in general meeting or by resolution of a meeting of any class of the members of a company, may, without a meeting and without any previous notice being required, be done by resolution in writing signed by, or, in the case of a member that is a corporation whether or not a company within the meaning of this Act, on behalf of, all the members of the company who at the date of the resolution would be entitled to attend the meeting and vote on the resolution.

(2) A resolution in writing may be signed by, or, in the case of a member that is a corporation whether or not a company within the meaning of this Act, on behalf of, all the members of a company, or any class thereof, in as many counterparts as may be necessary.

(3) For the purposes of this section, the date of the resolution is the date when the resolution is signed by, or, in the case of a member that is a corporation whether or not a company within the meaning of this Act, on behalf of, the last member to sign and any reference in any enactment to the date of passing of a resolution is, in relation to a resolution made in accordance with this section, a reference to such date.

(4) A resolution in writing made in accordance with this section is as valid as if it had been passed by the company in general meeting or by a meeting of the relevant class of members of the company, as the case may be; and any reference in any enactment to a meeting at which a resolution is passed or to members voting in favour of a resolution shall be construed accordingly.

(5) A resolution in writing made in accordance with this section shall constitute minutes for the purposes of sections 81 and 82.

(6) This section shall not apply to:

(a) a resolution passed pursuant to section 89(5); or

(b) a resolution passed for the purpose of removing a director before the expiration of his term of office under section 93.

Representation of corporations at meetings.

78.(1) A corporation, whether a company within the meaning of this Act or not, may -

(a) if it is a member of another corporation, being a company within the meaning of this Act, authorize such person or, to the extent expressly permitted by the bye-laws of that company, such persons as it thinks fit to act as its representative or representatives, as the case may be, at any meeting of the company or at any meeting of any class of members of the company, provided that, if more than one person is authorised, the authority shall specify the number and class of share held by the relevant member in respect of which each such person is authorised to act as such representative;

(b) if it is a creditor (including a holder of debentures) of another corporation, being a company within the meaning of this Act, authorize such person or persons as it thinks fit to act as its representative or representatives, as the case may be, at any meeting of any creditors of the company held in pursuance of this Act or of any rules made thereunder, or in pursuance of the provisions contained in any debenture, trust deed or warrant agreement, as the case may be.

(2) The number of persons a member or creditor of a company may be authorized to act as its representative or representatives pursuant to the authorities set out in subsection (1) shall not exceed the number of shares or securities held by that member or creditor, being shares or securities in respect of which there is an entitlement to attend and vote at the relevant meeting.

(3) Each representative authorised pursuant to subsection (1) shall be entitled to exercise the same powers on behalf of the corporation or its nominee which he represents as that corporation or its nominee could exercise as if it were an individual member, creditor or holder or debentures of that other company and, in addition, the right to vote individually on a show of hands.

Circulation of members' resolution, etc.

79.(1) Subject to the following provisions of this section it shall be the duty of a company, on the requisition in writing of such number of members as is hereinafter specified, at the expense of the requisitionists unless the company otherwise resolves -

(a) to give to members of the company entitled to receive notice of the next annual general meeting notice of any resolution which may properly be moved and is intended to be moved at that meeting;

(b) to circulate to members entitled to have notice of any general meeting sent to them any statement of not more than one thousand words with respect to the matter referred to in any proposed resolution or the business to be dealt with at that meeting.

(2) The number of members necessary for a requisition under the foregoing subsection shall be -

(a) either any number of members representing not less than one-twentieth of the total voting rights of all the members having at the date of the requisition a right to vote at the meeting to which the requisition relates; or

(b) not less than one hundred members.

(3) Notice of any such intended resolution shall be given, and any such statement shall be circulated, to members of the company entitled to have notice of the meeting sent to them by serving a copy of the resolution or statement on each such member in any manner permitted for service of notice of the meeting, and notice of any such resolution shall be given to any other member of the company by giving notice of the general effect of the resolution in any manner permitted for giving him notice of meetings of the company:

Provided that the copy shall be served, or notice of the effect of the resolution shall be given, as the case may be, in the same manner and, so far as practicable, at the same time as notice of the meeting and, where it is not practicable for it to be served or given at that time, it shall be served or given as soon as practicable thereafter.

Conditions to be met before company bound to give notice of resolution.

80. A company shall not be bound under section 79 to give notice of any resolution or to circulate any statement unless -

(a) a copy of the requisition signed by the requisitionists, or two or more copies which between them contain signatures of all the requisitionists, is deposited at the registered office of the company -

(i) in the case of a requisition requiring notice of a resolution, not less than six weeks before the meeting; and

(ii) in the case of any other requisition, not less than one week before the meeting; and

(b) there is deposited or tendered with the requisition a sum reasonably sufficient to meet the company's expenses in giving effect thereto:

Provided that if, after a copy of the requisition requiring notice of a resolution has been deposited at the registered office of the company, an annual general meeting is called for a date six weeks or less after the copy has been deposited, the copy though not deposited within the time required by this subsection shall be deemed to have been properly deposited for the purposes thereof.

Minutes of proceedings to be kept.

81.(1) Every company shall cause minutes of all proceedings of general meetings and of all proceedings of meetings of its directors to be entered in books kept for that purpose and such minutes shall be signed by the person presiding over the proceedings or over the proceedings at which the minutes are approved.

(2) Minutes prepared in accordance with subsection (1) shall be kept by the secretary at the registered office of the company and shall be evidence of the proceedings and until the contrary is proved, the proceedings shall be deemed to have been duly held and convened and the business conducted thereat shall be deemed to be valid.

(3) If a company fails to comply with subsection (1) the company and every officer of the company who is in default shall be liable to a default fine.

Inspection of minute books.

82.(1) Minutes of general meetings of a company shall be open for inspection by any member or director of the company without charge for not less than two hours during business hours each day subject to such reasonable restrictions as the company may impose.

(2) Any member or director shall be entitled to be furnished within seven days after he has made a request in that behalf to the company with a copy of any such minutes on the payment of a reasonable charge.

(3) If any inspection required under this section is refused or if any copy required under this section is not sent within the proper time, the company and every officer of the company who is in default shall be liable to a fine of ten dollars and further to a fine of ten dollars for each day there is a default.

(4) In the case of any such refusal or default, the Court may by order compel an immediate inspection of the minutes or direct that the copies required shall be sent to the persons properly requiring them.

Keeping of books of account.

83.(1) Every company shall cause to be kept proper records of account with respect to -

(a) all sums of money received and expended by the company and the matters in respect of which the receipt and expenditure takes place;

(b) all sales and purchases of goods by the company;

(c) the assets and liabilities of the company.

(2) The records of account shall be kept at the registered office of the company or at such other place as the directors think fit and shall at all times be open to inspection by the directors or a resident representative referred to in section 130(1)(d):

Provided that if the records of account are kept at some place outside Bermuda, there shall be kept at an office of the company in Bermuda such records as will enable the directors or a resident representative referred to in section 130(1)(d) to ascertain with reasonable accuracy the financial position of the company at the end of each three month period, except where the company is listed on an appointed stock exchange, there shall be kept such records as will enable the directors or a resident representative to ascertain with reasonable accuracy the financial position of the company at the end of each six month period.

(3) If a company fails to comply with subsection (1) the company and every officer of the company shall be liable to a fine of five hundred dollars.

(4) In the case of records of account not being made available for inspection by a director or a resident representative referred to in section 130(1)(d) the Court may by order compel immediate inspection of such records.

Financial statements to be laid before general meetings.

84.(1) The directors of every company shall subject to section 88 at such intervals and for such period as this Act and the bye-laws of the company provide lay before the company in general meeting -

(a) financial statements for the period, which shall include -

(i) a statement of the results of operations for the period;

(ii) a statement of retained earnings or deficit;

(iii) a balance sheet at the end of such period;

(iiiA) a statement of changes in financial position for the period;

(iv) notes to the financial statements and the notes thereto shall be in accordance with subsection (1A); and

(v) such further information as required by this Act and the company's own Act of incorporation or its memorandum, and its bye-laws; and *(b)* the report of the auditor as set out in section 90(2), in respect of the financial statements described in paragraph (1)(a).

(1A) The notes mentioned in subsection (1)(a)(iv) shall include a description of the generally accepted accounting principles used in the preparation of the financial statements which principles may be -

(a) those of Bermuda or a country or jurisdiction other than Bermuda; or

(b) such other generally accepted accounting principles as may be appointed by the Minister under subsection (5) for the purpose of this subsection, and, where the generally accepted accounting principles used are other than those of Bermuda, the notes shall identify the generally accepted accounting principles so used.

(2) Financial statements shall before being laid before a general meeting of a company be signed on the balance sheet page by two of the directors of the company.

(3) Notwithstanding the provisions of subsection (1) if at a general meeting at which financial statements should be laid the statements have not been so laid, it shall be lawful for the Chairman to adjourn the meeting for a period of up to ninety days or such longer period as the members may agree.

(4) Subject to subsection (3) if any director of a company fails to take all reasonable steps to comply with subsection (1) he shall be liable to a fine of one thousand dollars:

Provided that in any proceedings against a person in respect of an offence under this section, it shall be a defence to prove that he had reasonable ground to believe and did believe that a competent and reliable person was charged with the duty of seeing that the provisions of this section were complied with and was in a position to discharge that duty.

(5) The Minister may, after consultation with the Institute of Chartered Accountants of Bermuda, appoint generally accepted accounting principles promulgated by an accounting standard setting body and shall cause the appointment to be published in an appointed newspaper.

85. DELETED

Definition of subsidiary and holding companies.

86.(1) For the purposes of this Act, a company is a subsidiary of another company only if -

(a) it is controlled by -

(i) that other company; or

(ii) that other company and one or more companies each of which is controlled by that other company; or

(iii) two or more companies each of which is controlled by that other company; or

(b) it is a subsidiary of a subsidiary of that other company.

(2) For the purposes of this Act, a company is the holding company of another only if that other company is its subsidiary.

(3) For the purposes of this Act, one company is affiliated with another company only if one of them is the subsidiary of the other or both are subsidiaries of the same company or each of them is controlled by the same person.

(4) For the purposes of this section, a company is controlled by another company or person or by two or more companies only if -

(a) shares of the first-mentioned company carrying more than fifty percent of the votes for the election of directors are held, otherwise than by way of security only, by or for the benefit of that other company or person or by or for the benefit of those other companies; and

(b) the votes carried by such shares are sufficient, if exercised, to elect a majority of the board of directors of the first-mentioned company.

Right to receive copies of balance sheet etc.

87.(1) A copy of the financial statements of a company, including every document required by law or the bye-laws of the company shall be made available to every member of the company and if such financial statements and other documents are not sent to each member seven days before the general meeting any member may move a resolution at the general meeting that it be adjourned for seven days:

Provided that this subsection shall not require the making available of the financial statements and other documents to -

(a) any person not entitled to receive notices of general meetings;

(b) more than one of the joint holders of any shares or debentures;

(c) any person whose address is not known to the company.

(2) If default is made in complying with subsection (1) the company and every officer of the company who is in default shall be liable to a fine of one hundred dollars, and if, when any person makes a demand for any document with which he is by virtue of subsection (1) of this section entitled to be furnished, default is made in complying with the demand within seven days after the making thereof, the company and every officer of the company who is in default shall be liable to a default fine, unless it is proved that that person has already made a demand for and been furnished with a copy of the document:

Provided that it shall be a defence to any prosecution for the company or any officer to show that it was not possible to comply with subsection (1) owing to circumstances beyond the control of the company or the officer, as the case may be.

Power to waive laying of accounts and appointment of auditor.

88.(1) Notwithstanding paragraphs (c) and (d) of subsection (2) of section 13, sections 84, 87 and 89 if all members and directors of a company, either in writing or at a general meeting, agree that in respect of a particular interval no financial statements or auditor's report thereon need be laid before a general meeting or that no auditor shall be appointed to the close of the next annual general meeting then there shall be no obligation to lay financial statements for such period or to appoint an auditor until the close of the next annual general meeting, as the case may be.

(2) For the purposes of subsection (1) all the members of a company shall be deemed to have agreed at a general meeting if either -

(a) all the members are present in person at the meeting and agree; or

(b) if some of the members are not present in person at the meeting then if the members present in person at the meeting agree and there are produced at the meeting statements in writing from the members not present in person stating that they agree.

Appointment and disqualification of auditor.

89.(1) The members of a company at the statutory meeting shall subject to section 88 appoint one or more auditors to hold office until the close of the next annual general meeting, and, if the members fail to do so, the directors shall forthwith make such appointment or appointments.

(2) The members of a company at each annual general meeting shall appoint one or more auditors to hold office until the close of the next general meeting, and, if an appointment is not so made, the auditor in office shall continue in office until a successor is appointed.

(3) A person, other than an incumbent auditor, shall not be capable of being appointed auditor at an annual general meeting unless notice in writing of an intention to nominate that person to the office of auditor has been given not less than twenty-one days before the annual general meeting; and the company shall send a copy of any such notice to the incumbent auditor, and shall give notice thereof to the members either by advertisement in an appointed newspaper or in any other mode provided by the bye-laws of the company, not less than seven days before the annual general meeting:

Provided that an incumbent auditor may by notice in writing to the secretary of the company waive the requirements of this subsection which shall then not have effect.

(3A) No person shall accept appointment or consent to be appointed as auditor of a company if he is replacing an auditor who has resigned, been removed or whose term of office has expired or is about to expire, or who has vacated office, until he has requested and received from that auditor a written statement of the circumstances and the reasons why, in that auditor's opinion, he is to be replaced.

(3B) Notwithstanding subsection (3A), a person may accept appointment or consent to be appointed as auditor of a company if, within fifteen days after making the request referred to in that subsection, he does not receive a written statement as requested.

(3C) No auditor of a company is in breach of any duty to which he is subject as auditor of that company by reason of his communicating in good faith to the person making the request referred to in subsection (3A) any information or opinion in response to such request.

(4) The directors may fill any casual vacancy in the office of auditor, but while the vacancy continues the surviving or continuing auditor, if any, may act.

(5) The members, by a resolution passed by at least two-thirds of the votes cast at a general meeting of which notice specifying the intention to pass such resolution was given, may remove any auditor before the expiration of his term of office, and shall by a majority of the votes cast at that meeting appoint another auditor in his stead for the remainder of his term:

Provided that, not less than twenty-one days before the date of the meeting, notice in writing of the proposed resolution is given to the incumbent auditor and to the auditor proposed to be appointed.

(5A) An auditor of a company who has resigned, been removed, or whose term of office has expired or is about to expire, or who has vacated office, shall be entitled -

(a) to attend the general meeting of the company at which he is to be removed or his successor is to be appointed;

(b) to receive all notices of, and other communications relating to, that meeting which a member is entitled to receive; and

(c) to be heard at that meeting on any part of the business of the meeting that relates to his duties as auditor or former auditor;

(6) The remuneration of an auditor appointed by the members shall be fixed by the members or by the directors, if they are authorized to do so by the members, and the remuneration of an auditor appointed by the directors shall be fixed by the directors.

(7) Subject to section 88 where for any reason no auditor is appointed, the Registrar may, on the application of any member, appoint one or more auditors to hold office until the close of the next annual general meeting and fix the remuneration to be paid by the company for his or their services.

(8) Except as provided in subsection (9), no person shall be appointed as auditor of a company who is an officer or employee of that company or of an affiliated company or who is a partner, employer or employee of any such officer or employee.

(9) Upon the unanimous vote of the members of a company limited by guarantee, other than a mutual company present or represented at the meeting at which the auditor is appointed, an officer or employee of that company or an affiliated company, or a partner, employer or employee of an officer or employee may be appointed as auditor of that company, if he has no personal responsibility for the care of the funds of the company and is not concerned in the day to day management or recording of its finances.

(10) A person appointed as auditor under subsection (9) shall indicate in his report to the members that he is an officer or employee of the company or an affiliated company or a partner, employer or employee of an officer or employee, as the case may be.

(11) Any oral or written statement made under subsection (3A) or (5A) by an auditor or former auditor enjoys qualified privilege.

(12) An appointment as auditor of a person who has not requested a written statement from the former auditor under subsection (3A) is voidable by a resolution of the shareholders at a general meeting.

Annual audit.

90.(1) The auditor shall audit any financial statements to be laid pursuant to section 84 as will enable him to report to the members.

(2) Based on the results of his audit under subsection (1) which audit shall be made in accordance with generally accepted auditing standards, the auditor shall make a report to the members.

(3) The generally accepted auditing standards referred to in subsection (2) may be those of Bermuda or a country or jurisdiction other than Bermuda or such other generally accepted auditing standards as may be appointed by the Minister under subsection (4) for the purpose of this subsection; and where the generally accepted auditing standards used are other than those of Bermuda, the report of the auditor shall identify the generally accepted auditing standards used.

(3A) No action shall lie against an auditor in the performance of any function as an auditor contemplated by this Act except in the instance of -

(a) the company who engaged the auditor to perform such function; or

(b) any other person expressly authorized by the auditor to rely on his work.

(4) The Minister may, after consultation with the Institute of Chartered Accountants of Bermuda, appoint generally accepted auditing standards promulgated by an audit standard setting body and shall cause the appointment to be published in an appointed newspaper.

Election of directors.

91.(1) The affairs of the company shall be managed by not less than two directors who shall be individuals elected in the first place at the statutory meeting and thereafter at each annual general meeting of the company or elected or appointed by the members in such other manner and for such term as may be provided in the bye-laws.

(1A) A maximum number of directors may be determined by the members at a general meeting of the company or in such other manner as may be provided in the bye-laws.

(2) Where a maximum number of directors has been determined in accordance with subsection (1A), a general meeting of a company may authorise the directors of the company to elect or appoint on their behalf an individual or individuals to act as additional directors up to such maximum.

(2A) Any individual may be appointed an alternate director by or in accordance with a resolution of the members or by a director in such manner as may be provided in the bye-laws, and the individual so appointed shall have all the rights and powers of the director for whom he is appointed in the alternative, except that he shall not be entitled to attend and vote at any meeting of the directors otherwise than in the absence of such director.

(2B) An alternate director shall only be a director for the purposes of this Act and shall only be subject to the provisions of this Act insofar as they relate to the duties and obligations of a director when performing the functions of the director for whom he is appointed in the alternative.

(3) So long as a quorum of directors remains in office, unless the bye-laws of a company otherwise provide, any vacancy occurring in the board of directors may be filled by such directors as remain in office. If no quorum of directors remains the vacancy shall be filled by a general meeting of members.

(4) Every company shall have a president and a vice-president or a chairman and a deputy chairman who shall be directors of the company and may have such other officers who may or may not be directors and who shall be appointed in such manner and hold office for such period, as the bye-laws shall provide.

Representation of directors by another director.

91A.(1) Subject to any express provision to the contrary in the bye-laws of the company, a director of a company may appoint another director of the company to represent him and to vote on his behalf at any meeting of the directors of the company:

Provided that a director so appointed -

(a) shall not be entitled to vote at any such meeting on behalf of the director who appointed him if the director who appointed him is himself present at that meeting; and

(b) may, subject to the provisions of the foregoing paragraph, vote at any such

meeting on his own behalf as well as on behalf of the director who appointed him.

(2) Any such appointment as aforesaid -

(a) shall not have effect unless notice thereof is given in writing to the secretary of the company by the director making the appointment;

(b) may be either general or in respect of a particular meeting or meetings specified in the notice of the appointment; and

(c) may be revoked at any time by notice in writing given to the secretary of the company by the director who made the appointment.

Directors entitled to receive notice of meetings, etc.

91B.(1) The directors of a company shall upon written request deposited at the registered office of the company be entitled to receive notice of, and to attend and be heard at, any or all general meetings.

(2) Notwithstanding section 75 (length of notice for calling meetings) a notice given under subsection (1) shall be valid if in all the circumstances, such notice is reasonable.

Appointment of secretary.

92.(1) The directors of a company shall appoint a secretary to the company who shall hold office in accordance with the bye-laws.

(2) Anything required or authorized to be done by or to the secretary may, if the office is vacant or there is for any other reason no secretary capable of acting, be done by or to any assistant or deputy secretary or, if there is no assistant or deputy secretary capable of acting, by or to any officer of the company authorized generally or specially in that behalf by the directors.

Register of directors and officers

92A.(1) Subject to subsection (8), every company shall keep at its registered office a register of its directors and officers and the register shall, with respect to the particulars to be contained in it of those persons, comply with subsection (6).

(2) The company shall, within the period of fourteen days from the occurrence of -

(a) any change among its directors; or

(b) any change in the particulars contained in the register, enter on its register the particulars of the change.

(3) The register shall during business hours (subject to such reasonable restrictions as the company may impose, so that not less than two hours in each day be allowed for inspection) be open for inspection by members of the public without charge.

(4) If an inspection required under this section is refused, or if default is made in complying with subsection (1) or (2) the company which is in default shall be liable in respect of each offence to a default fine.

(5) In the case of a refusal or default, the Court may by order compel an immediate inspection of the register.

(6) The register shall contain the following particulars with respect to each director and officer -

(a) in the case of an individual, his present first name, surname and address; and

(b) in the case of a company, its name and registered office.

(6A) The register of a local company shall state whether any individual possesses Bermudian status within the meaning of the Bermuda Immigration and Protection Act 1956.

(7) For the purposes of this section "officer" means:

(a) a president, vice-president, chairman or deputy chairman provided that each such person is a director, and

(b) a secretary.

(8) Any company whose objects are wholly and exclusively charitable and which does not solicit funds from the public shall, on filing a copy of its memorandum of association and of its register of directors and officers with the Registrar and on obtaining from the Registrar a confirmation of the filing, be exempt from the provisions of this section.

(9) Notwithstanding any other statutory provision the documents filed for the purposes of subsection (8) shall be treated as confidential by the Minister and any public officer having access to them.

Removal of directors.

93.(1) Subject to its bye-laws the members of a company may at a special general meeting called for that purpose remove a director:

Provided that notice of any such meeting shall be served on the director concerned not less than fourteen days before the meeting and he shall be entitled to be heard at such meeting:

Provided further that nothing in this section shall have effect to deprive any person of any compensation or damages which may be payable to him in respect of the termination of his appointment as a director or of any other appointment with the company.

(2) A vacancy created by the removal of a director at a special general meeting may be filled at that meeting by the election of another director in his place or in the absence of any such election by the other directors.

Undischarged bankrupt not to take part in management of a company.

94.(1) If any person being an undischarged bankrupt in any country acts as director of, or directly or indirectly takes part in or is concerned in the management of, any company except with the leave of the Court, he shall be liable on conviction on indictment to imprisonment for a term of two years, or on summary conviction to imprisonment for a term of six months or to a fine of five hundred dollars or to both such imprisonment and fine:

Provided that a person shall not be guilty of an offence under this section by reason that he, being an undischarged bankrupt, has acted as director of, or taken part or been concerned in the management of, a company, if he was on the appointed day acting as a director of that company or taking part or being concerned in its management.

(2) The leave of the Court for the purposes of this section shall not be given unless notice of intention to apply therefor has been served on the Official Receiver, and it shall be the duty of the Official Receiver, if he is of opinion that it is contrary to the public interest that any such application should be granted, to attend on the hearing of and oppose the granting of the application.

A court may order that a convicted person shall not take part in the management of the affairs of a company.

95.(1) Where any court convicts any person of an offence relating to the affairs of a company which, in the opinion of such court, involves dishonestly it may order that such person shall not directly or indirectly take part in or be concerned in the management of any company without leave of the Supreme Court.

(2) Section 94(2) shall apply to any application for leave under subsection (1).

(3) The same right of appeal shall lie in respect of an order made under subsection (1) as it does from a sentence of imprisonment

(4) Any person who contravenes an order of a court made under subsection (1) shall be liable to the punishments set out in section 94(1).

Prohibition of loans to directors without consent of members.

96.(1) Without the consent of any member or members holding in the aggregate not less than nine-tenths of the total voting rights of all the members having the right to vote at any meeting of the members of the company it shall not be lawful for a company to make a loan to any person who is its director or a director of its holding company, or to enter into any guarantee or provide any security in connection with a loan made to such person as aforesaid by any other person:

Provided that nothing in this section shall apply either -

(a) subject to the next following subsection, to anything done to provide any such person as aforesaid with funds to meet expenditure incurred or to be incurred by him for the purposes of the company or for the purpose of enabling him properly to perform his duties as an officer of the company; or

(b) in the case of a company whose ordinary business includes the lending of money or the giving of guarantees in connection with loans made by other persons, to anything done by the company is the ordinary course of that business.

(2) Proviso (a) to the foregoing subsection shall not authorise the making of any loan, or the entering into any guarantee, or the provision of any security, except either -

(a) with the prior approval of the company given at a general meeting at which the purposes of the expenditure and the amount of the loan or the extent of the guarantee or security, as the case may be, are disclosed; or

(b) on condition that, if the approval of the company is not given as aforesaid at or before the next following annual general meeting, the loan shall be repaid or the liability under the guarantee or security shall be discharged, as the case may be, within six months from the conclusion of that meeting.

(3) Where the approval of the company is not given as required by any such condition, the directors authorizing the making of the loan, or the entering into the guarantee, or the provision of the security, shall be jointly and severally liable to indemnify the company against any loss arising therefrom.

(4) A loan shall be deemed to be a loan to a director if it is made to -

(a) the spouse or children of a director; or

(b) to any company (other than a company which is a holding company or a subsidiary of the company making the loan) which a director, his spouse or children own or control directly or indirectly more than twenty per cent of the capital or loan debt.

(5) For the purposes of this section a loan shall not be deemed to have been made in the ordinary course of business of a company if it has not been made on normal commercial terms in respect of interest rates, repayment terms and security.

(6) This section applies to a mutual company.

Duty of care of officers.

97.(1) Every officer of a company in exercising his powers and discharging his duties shall -

(a) act honestly and in good faith with a view to the best interests of the company; and

(b) exercise the care, diligence and skill that a reasonably prudent person would exercise in comparable circumstances.

(2) Every officer of a company shall comply with this Act, the regulations, and the bye-laws of the company.

(3) [DELETED].

(4) Without in any way limiting the generality of subsection (1) an officer of a company shall be deemed not to be acting honestly and in good faith if -

(a) he fails on request to make known to the auditors of the company full details of -

(i) any emolument, pension or other benefit that he has received or it is agreed that he should receive from the company or any of the company's subsidiaries, or

(ii) any loan he has received or is to receive from the company or any of its subsidiaries;

(b) he fails to disclose at the first opportunity at a meeting of directors or by writing to the directors -

(i) his interest in any material contract or proposed material contract with the company or any of its subsidiaries;

(ii) his material interest in any person that is a party to a material contract or proposed material contract with the company or any of its subsidiaries.

(5) For the purposes of this section -

(a) a general notice to the directors of a company by an officer of the company declaring that he is an officer of or has a material interest in a person and is to be regarded as interested in any contract with that person is a sufficient declaration of interest in relation to any such contract;

(b) the word material in relation to a contract or proposed contract shall be construed as relating to the materiality of that contract or proposed contract in relation to the business of the company to which disclosure must be made;

(c) an interest occurring by reason of the ownership or direct or indirect control of not more than ten per centum of the capital of a person shall not be deemed material.

(5A) An officer is not liable under subsection (1) if he relies in good faith upon -

(a) financial statements of the company represented to him by another officer of the company; or

(b) a report of an attorney, accountant, engineer, appraiser or other person whose profession lends credibility to a statement made by him.

(6) Any officer of a company who fails to make known a matter he is required to make known under subsection (4) shall be liable to a fine of one thousand dollars.

(7) Nothing in this section shall be taken to prejudice any rule of law or any bye-law restricting officers of a company from having any interest in contracts with the company.

Exemption, indemnification and liability of officers, etc.

98.(1) Subject to subsection (2), a company may in its bye-laws or in any contract or arrangement between the company and any officer, or any person employed by the company as auditor, exempt such officer or person from, or indemnify him in respect of, any loss arising or liability attaching to him by virtue of any rule of law in respect of any negligence, default, breach of duty or breach of trust of which the officer or person may be guilty in relation to the company or any subsidiary thereof.

(2) Any provision, whether contained in the bye-laws of a company or in any contract or arrangement between the company and any officer, or any person employed by the company as auditor, exempting such officer or person from, or indemnifying him against any liability which by virtue of any rule of law would otherwise attach to him in respect of any fraud or dishonesty of which he may be guilty in relation to the company shall be void:

Provided that -

(a) nothing in this section shall operate to deprive any person of any exemption or right to be indemnified in respect of anything done or omitted to be done by him while any such provision was in force; and

(b) notwithstanding anything in this section, a company may, in pursuance of any such provision as aforesaid indemnify any such officer or auditor against any liability incurred by him in defending any proceedings, whether civil or

criminal in which judgment is given in his favour or in which he is acquitted or when relief is granted to him by the Court under section 281.

Insurance of officers etc.

98A. A company may purchase and maintain insurance for the benefit of any officer of the company against any liability incurred by him under paragraph (b) of subsection (1) of section 97 in his capacity as an officer of the company or indemnifying such an officer in respect of any loss arising or liability attaching to him by virtue of any rule of law in respect of any negligence, default, breach of duty or breach of trust of which the officer may be guilty in relation to the company or any subsidiary thereof and nothing in this Act shall make void or voidable any such policy.

Liability of auditor or officer

98B.(1) Where an auditor or an officer is found liable to any person for damages arising out of the performance of any function as such auditor or officer as contemplated by this Act, then the following provisions of this section shall apply.

(2) An auditor or officer may be liable jointly and severally only if it is proved that he knowingly engaged in fraud or dishonesty.

(3) In any case other than that contemplated by subsection (2) hereof, the liability of the auditor or officer, as the case may be, shall be determined as follows -

(a) the Court shall determine the percentage of responsibility of the plaintiff, of each of the defendants, and of each of the other persons alleged by the parties to have caused or contributed to the loss of the plaintiff. In considering the percentages of responsibility, the Court shall consider both the nature of the conduct of each person and the nature and extent of the causal relationship between the conduct and the loss claimed by the plaintiff;

(b) the liability of the auditor or officer, as the case may be, shall be equal to the total loss suffered by the plaintiff multiplied by the auditor's or officer's, as the case may be, percentage of responsibility as determined under paragraph (a) hereof.

(4) No auditor or officer whose liability is determined under subsection (3) hereof shall have any liability in respect of any judgment entered against any other party to the action.

(5) Except where agreed in writing between the parties, where the liability of an auditor or officer has been determined in accordance with subsection (3) no other person shall have any right to recover from such auditor or officer any portion of any judgment entered against such other person in respect of the action.

PART VII

ARRANGEMENTS, RECONSTRUCTIONS AND AMALGAMATIONS

Power to compromise with creditors and members.

99.(1) Where a compromise or arrangement is proposed between a company and its creditors or any class of them or between a company and its members or any class of them, the Court may, on the application of the company or of any creditor or member of the company, or, in the case of a company being wound up, of the liquidator, order a meeting of the creditors or class of creditors, or of the members of the company or class of members, as the case may be, to be summoned in such manner as the Court directs.

(2) If a majority in number representing three-fourths in value of the creditors or class of creditors or members or class of members, as the case may be, present and voting either in person or by proxy at the meeting, agree to any compromise or arrangement, the compromise or arrangement shall if sanctioned by the Court, be binding on all the creditors or the class of creditors, or on the members or class of members, as the case may be, and also on the company or, in the case of a company in the course of being wound up, on the liquidator and contributories of the company.

(3) An order made under subsection (2) shall have no effect until a copy of the order has been delivered to the Registrar for registration, and a copy of every such order shall be annexed to every copy of the memorandum of association of the company issued after the order has been made.

(4) If a company makes default in complying with subsection (3), the company and every officer of the company who knowingly or wilfully authorizes or permits the default shall be liable to a fine of ten dollars for each copy in respect of which default is made.

Information as to compromises with creditors and members.

100.(1) Where a meeting of creditors or any class of creditors or of members or any class of members is summoned under section 99 there shall -

(a) with every notice summoning the meeting which is sent to a creditor or member, be sent also a statement explaining the effect of the compromise or arrangement and in particular stating any material interests of the directors of the company whether as directors or as members or as creditors of the company or otherwise, and the effect thereon of the compromise or arrangement, in so far as it is different from the effect on the like interests of other persons; and

(b) in every notice summoning the meeting which is given by advertisement, be included either such a statement as aforesaid or a notification of the place at which and the manner in which creditors or members entitled to attend the meeting may obtain copies of such a statement as aforesaid.

(2) Where the compromise or arrangement affects the rights of debenture holders of the company, the said statement shall give the like explanation as respects the trustees of any deed for securing the issue of the debentures as it is required to give as respects the company's directors.

(3) Where a notice given by advertisement includes a notification that copies of a statement explaining the effect of the compromise or arrangement proposed can be obtained by creditors or members entitled to attend the meeting, every such creditor or member shall, on making application in the manner indicated by the notice, be furnished by the company free of charge with a copy of the statement.

(4) Where a company makes default in complying with any requirement of this section, the company and every officer of the company who knowingly or wilfully authorizes or permits the default shall be liable to a fine of one thousand dollars, and for the purpose of this subsection any liquidator of the company, and any trustee of a deed for securing the issue of debentures of the company shall be deemed to be an officer of the company:

Provided that a person shall not be liable under this subsection if that person shows that the default was due to the refusal of any other person, being a director or trustee for debenture holders, to supply the necessary particulars as to his interests.

(5) It shall be the duty of any director of the company and of any trustee for debenture holders of the company to give notice to the company of such matters relating to himself as may be necessary for the purposes of this section, and any person who makes default in complying with this subsection shall be liable to a fine of two hundred dollars.

Provisions for facilitating reconstruction of companies.

101.(1) Where an application is made to the Court under section 99 for the sanctioning of a compromise or arrangement proposed between a company and any such persons as are mentioned in that section, and it is shown to the Court that the compromise or arrangement has been proposed for the purposes of or in connection with a scheme for the reconstruction of any company or companies and that under the scheme the whole or any part of the undertaking or the property of any company concerned in the scheme (in this section referred to as "a transferor company") is to be transferred to another company (in this section referred to as "the transferee company"), the Court may, subject to subsection (2), either by the order sanctioning the compromise or arrangement or by any subsequent order, make provision for all or any of the following matters -

(a) the transfer to the transferee company of the whole or any part of the undertaking and of the property or liabilities of any transferor company;

(b) the allocation or appropriation by the transferee company of any shares, debentures, policies or other like interests in that company which under the compromise or arrangement are to be allotted or appropriated by that company to or for any person;

(c) the continuation by or against the transferee company of any legal proceedings pending by or against any transferor company;

(d) the dissolution, without winding up, of any transferor company;

(e) the provision to be made for any persons, who within such time and in such manner as the Court directs, dissent from the compromise or arrangement;

(f) such incidental, consequential and supplemental matters as are necessary to secure that the reconstruction or amalgamation shall be fully and effectively carried out.

(2) No order shall be made under subsection (1) for the transfer to the transferee company of the whole or any part of the undertaking or of the property or liabilities of any transferor company unless notice of the application for the sanctioning of the compromise or arrangement of which the order is to form a part is given in writing to the Minister and an affidavit signifying the consent of the Minister to the making of the order has been lodged with the Court.

(3) Where an order under this section provides for the transfer of property or liabilities, that property shall, by virtue of the order, be transferred to and vest in, and those liabilities shall, by virtue of the order, be transferred to and become the liabilities of, the transferee company, and in the case of any property, if the order so directs, freed from any charge which is by virtue of the compromise or arrangement to cease to have effect.

(4) Where an order is made under this section, every company in relation to which the order is made shall cause a copy thereof to be delivered to the Registrar for registration within seven days after the making of the order, and if default is made in complying with this subsection, the company and every officer of the company who knowingly or wilfully authorizes or permits the default shall be liable to a fine of two hundred dollars.

(5) In this section the expression "property" includes all assets, rights and powers of every description, and the expression "liabilities" includes duties.

Power to acquire shares of shareholders dissenting from scheme or contract approved by majority.

102.(1) Where a scheme or contract involving the transfer of shares or any class of shares in a company (in this section referred to as "the subject company") to another company, whether a company within the meaning of this Act or not (in this section referred to as "the transferee company"), has, within four months after the making of the offer in that behalf by the transferee company been approved by the holders of not less than nine-tenths in value of the shares whose transfer is involved, other than shares already held at the date of the offer by, or by a nominee for, the transferee company or its subsidiary, the transferee company may, at any time within two months beginning with the date on which such approval is obtained, give notice to any dissenting shareholder that it desires to acquire his shares, and when such a notice is given the transferee company shall, unless on an application made by the dissenting shareholder within one month from the date on which the notice was given the Court thinks fit to order otherwise, be entitled and bound to acquire those shares on the terms on which, under the scheme or contract, the shares of the approving shareholders are to be transferred to the transferee company:

Provided that where shares in the subject company of the same class or classes as the shares whose transfer is involved are already held as aforesaid to a value greater than one-tenth of the aggregate of their value and that of the shares, other than those already held as aforesaid, whose transfer is involved, the foregoing provisions of this subsection shall not apply unless -

(a) the transferee company offers the same terms to all holders of the shares, other than those already held as aforesaid, whose transfer is involved, or, where those shares include shares of different classes, of each class of them; and

(b) the holders who approve the scheme or contract, besides holding not less than nine-tenths in value of the shares, other than those already held as aforesaid, whose transfer is involved, are not less than three-fourths in number of the holders of those shares.

(2) Where, in pursuance of any such scheme or contract as aforesaid, shares in a company are transferred to another company or its nominee, and those shares together with any other shares in the first-mentioned company held by, or by a nominee for, the transferee company or its subsidiary at the date of the transfer comprise or include nine-tenths in value of the shares in the first-mentioned company or of any class of those shares, then -

(a) the transferee company shall within one month from the date of the transfer, unless on a previous transfer in pursuance of the scheme or contract it has already complied with this requirement, give notice of that fact to the holders of the remaining shares or of the remaining shares of that class, as the case may be, who have not assented to the scheme or contract; and

(b) any such holder may within three months from the giving of the notice to him, himself give notice requiring the transferee company to acquire the shares in question, and where a shareholder gives notice under paragraph (b) of this subsection with respect to any shares, the transferee company shall be entitled and bound to acquire those shares on the terms on which under the scheme or contract the shares of the approving shareholders were transferred to it, or on such other terms as may be agreed or as the Court on the application of either the transferee company or the shareholder thinks fit to order.

(3) Where a notice has been given by the transferee company under subsection (1) of this section and the Court has not, on an application made by the dissenting shareholder, ordered to the contrary, the transferee company shall, on the expiration of one month from the date on which the notice has been given, or, if an application to the Court by the dissenting shareholder is then pending, after that application has been disposed of, transmit a copy of the notice to the subject company together with an instrument of transfer executed on behalf of the shareholder by any person appointed by the transferee company and on its own behalf by the transferee company, and pay or transfer to the subject company the amount or other consideration representing the price payable by the transferee company for the shares which by virtue of this section that company is entitled to acquire, the subject company shall thereupon register the transferee company as the holder of those shares.

(4) Any sums received by the subject company under this section shall be paid into a separate bank account, and any such sums and any other consideration so received shall be held by that company on trust for the several persons entitled to the shares in respect of which the said sums or other consideration were respectively received.

(5) In this section the expression "dissenting shareholder" includes a shareholder who has not assented to scheme or contract and any shareholder who has failed or refused to transfer his shares to the transferee company in accordance with the scheme or contract.

Holders of ninety-five percent of shares may acquire remainder.

103.(1) The holders of not less than ninety-five percent of the shares or any class of shares in a company (hereinafter in this section referred to as the "purchasers") may give notice to the remaining shareholders or class of shareholders of the intention to acquire their shares on the terms set out in the notice. When such a notice is given the purchasers shall be entitled and bound to acquire the shares of the remaining shareholders on the terms set out in the notice unless a remaining shareholder applies to the Court for an appraisal under subsection (2):

Provided that the foregoing provisions of this subsection shall not apply unless the purchasers offer the same terms to all holders of the shares whose acquisition is involved.

(2) Any shareholder to whom a notice has been given under subsection (1) may within one month of receiving the notice apply to the Court to appraise the value of the shares to be purchased from him and the purchasers shall be entitled to acquire the shares at the price so fixed by the Court.

(3) Within one month of the Court appraising the value of any shares under subsection (2) the purchasers shall be entitled either -

(a) to acquire all the shares involved at the price fixed by the Court; or

(b) cancel the notice given under subsection (1).

(4) Where the Court has appraised any shares under subsection (2) and the purchaser have prior to the appraisal acquired any shares by virtue of a notice under subsection (1) then within one month of the Court appraising the value of the shares if the price of the shares they have paid to any shareholder is less than that appraised by the Court they shall either -

(a) pay to such shareholder the difference in the price they have paid to him and the price appraised by the Court; or

(b) cancel the notice given under subsection (1) and return to the shareholder any shares they have acquired and the shareholder shall repay the purchasers the purchase price.

(5) No appeal shall lie from an appraisal by the Court under this section.

(6) The costs of any application to the Court under this section shall be in the discretion of the Court.

(7) In this section -

"price" shall include not only monetary price but also the monetary value of any shares or other securities offered by the purchasers in exchange for the shares to be acquired.

Amalgamation of companies.

104.(1) Two or more companies which are registered in Bermuda may subject to section 4A amalgamate and continue as one company:

Provided that if the amalgamated company is to be a local company it shall comply with the Third Schedule.

(2) DELETED.

Amalgamation of exempted company and foreign corporation and continuation as an exempted company

104A.(1) One or more exempted companies and one or more bodies incorporated outside Bermuda (each such body hereinafter in this section and in sections 104B and 104D referred to as a "foreign corporation") may amalgamate and continue as an exempted company registered in Bermuda to which the provisions of this Act and any other relevant laws of Bermuda shall apply.

(2) A foreign corporation shall obtain all necessary authorizations, if any, required under the laws of the jurisdiction in which it was incorporated or is presently registered in order to enable it to amalgamate and continue as an exempted company registered in Bermuda, and shall file with the Registrar documentary proof of such authorizations.

(3) DELETED

(4) The provisions of sections 105 to 109, mutatis mutandis, apply to an amalgamation under this section in the same way as they apply to an amalgamation under this section 104.

(5) DELETED

Amalgamation of exempted company and foreign corporation and continuation as a foreign corporation.

104B.(1) One or more exempted companies and one or more foreign corporations may amalgamate and continue as a foreign corporation (in this section and in sections 104C and 104D referred to as "the amalgamated corporation") to which the laws of the jurisdiction in which it is proposed that the amalgamated corporation will continue (in this section and sections 104C and 104D referred to as "the foreign jurisdiction") shall apply.

(2) An exempted company shall not amalgamate pursuant to subsection (1) unless -

(a) an officer of such company has made a statutory declaration to the effect that there are reasonable grounds for believing that -

(i) such company is, and the amalgamated corporation will be, able to pay its liabilities as they fall due;

(ii) the realizable value of the amalgamated corporation's assets will not be less than the aggregate of its liabilities and issued share capital and share premium account of all classes; and

(iii) either no creditor of such company will be prejudiced by the amalgamation or adequate notice has been given in accordance with section 104D(4) to all known creditors of such company and no creditor objects to the amalgamation otherwise than on grounds that are frivolous or vexatious;

(b) an irrevocable deed poll is executed by such company and its directors, pursuant to which -

(i) such company and each of its directors may be served with legal process in Bermuda in any proceeding arising out of actions or omissions of such company occurring prior to the amalgamation, and provision is made for the appointment of a person within Bermuda as agent for such company for the service of process for a period of not less than three years from the effective date of amalgamation and for a signed acceptance of the appointment; or

(ii) such company and each of its directors may be served with legal process at a specified address in the United Kingdom, the United States of America or any appointed jurisdiction, and whereby such company and such directors submit to the non-exclusive jurisdiction of the courts of that country or jurisdiction;

(c) each foreign corporation which is amalgamating has obtained all necessary

authorizations, if any, required under the laws of the jurisdiction in which it was incorporated or is presently registered to enable it to so amalgamate;

(d) the foreign jurisdiction is -

(i) an appointed jurisdiction; or

(ii) approved by the Minister, upon application by the company for the purpose of the amalgamation of the company with a foreign corporation and continuance as a foreign corporation.

(e) not more than three months prior to the effective date of the amalgamation -

(i) each exempted company which is amalgamating shall advertise in an appointed newspaper; and

(ii) each foreign corporation which is amalgamating shall advertise in a national newspaper in the jurisdiction in which it was incorporated or is presently registered,

its intention to amalgamate and continue as a company in the foreign jurisdiction.

Documents to be filed on amalgamation and continuation as a foreign corporation.

104C.(1) An exempted company shall not amalgamate pursuant to section 104B unless on or before the effective date of the amalgamation such company files with the Registrar a notice of the amalgamation which shall contain or have attached thereto the following information:

(a) the effective date of the amalgamation;

(b) the name of the foreign jurisdiction;

(c) the address of the registered office or the principal business address of the amalgamated corporation in the foreign jurisdiction;

(d) a copy of the statutory declaration required pursuant to section 104B(2)(a); and

(e) a copy of the irrevocable deed poll required pursuant to section 104B(2)(b).

(2) Within thirty days after the date of the issue thereof, the amalgamated corporation continuing as a result of an amalgamation pursuant to section 104B shall file with the Registrar a copy of the certificate of amalgamation issued by the appropriate authority of the foreign jurisdiction, or, if no such certificate of amalgamation is issued, such other documentary evidence of the amalgamation as shall be issued by such authority.

(3) The documents filed with the Registrar pursuant to subsections (1) and (2) shall be open to public inspection.

Provisions applicable to amalgamation and continuation as a foreign corporation

104D.(1) The provisions of sections 105 to 107 shall apply, with the necessary changes, to an amalgamation pursuant to section 104B in the same way as they apply to an amalgamation pursuant to section 104, except that the provisions of section 106 shall apply only to amalgamating exempted companies.

(2) The effect of an amalgamation pursuant to section 104B shall be the same as in the case of an amalgamation pursuant to section 104A, except insofar as the laws of the foreign jurisdiction otherwise provide.

(3) The effective date of an amalgamation pursuant to section 104B shall be the date that the amalgamation is effective pursuant to the laws of the foreign jurisdiction.

(4) For the purposes of section 104B(2)(a), adequate notice is given if -

(a) a notice in writing is sent to each known creditor having a claim against the company that exceeds $1,000; and

(b) notice is published in an appointed newspaper stating that such company intends to amalgamate with any specified exempted companies or one or more specified foreign corporations, or both, and that a creditor of such company may object to the amalgamation within thirty days from the date of the notice.

104E. DELETED

104F. DELETED

104G DELETED

Amalgamation agreement.

105.(1) Each company proposing to amalgamate shall enter into an agreement setting out the terms and means of effecting the amalgamation and, in particular, setting out -

(a) the provisions that are required to be included in the memorandum;

(b) the name and address of each proposed director of the amalgamated company;

(c) the manner in which the shares of each amalgamating company are to be converted into shares or other securities of the amalgamated company;

(d) if any shares of an amalgamating company are not to be converted into securities of the amalgamated company, the amount of money or securities that the holders of such shares are to receive in addition to or instead of securities of the amalgamated company;

(e) the manner of payment of money instead of the issue of fractional shares of the amalgamated company or of any other securities which are to be received in the amalgamation;

(f) whether the bye-laws of the amalgamated company are to be those of one of the amalgamating companies and, if not, a copy of the proposed bye-laws; and

(g) details of any arrangements necessary to perfect the amalgamation and to provide for the subsequent management and operation of the amalgamated company.

(2) If shares of one of the amalgamating companies are held by or on behalf of another of the amalgamating companies, the amalgamation agreement shall provide for the cancellation of such shares when the amalgamation becomes effective without any repayment of capital in respect thereof, and no provision shall be made in the agreement for the conversion of such into shares of the amalgamated company.

Shareholder approval.

106.(1) The directors of each amalgamating company shall submit the amalgamation agreement for approval to a meeting of the holders of shares of the amalgamating company of which they are directors and, subject to subsection (4), to the holders of each class of such shares.

(2) A notice of a meeting of shareholders complying with section 75 shall be sent in accordance with that section to each shareholder of each amalgamating company, and shall -

(a) include or be accompanied by a copy or summary of the amalgamation agreement; and

(b) subject to subsection (2A) state -

(i) the fair value of the shares as determined by each amalgamating company; and

(ii) that a dissenting shareholder is entitled to be paid the fair value of his shares.

(2A) Notwithstanding subsection 2(b)(ii), failure to state the matter referred to in that subsection does not invalidate an amalgamation.

(3) Each share of an amalgamating company carries the right to vote in respect of an amalgamation whether or not it otherwise carries the right to vote.

(4) The holders of shares of a class or series of shares of an amalgamating company are entitled to vote separately as a class in respect of an amalgamation if the amalgamation agreement contains a provision which would constitute a variation of the rights attaching to any such class of shares for the purposes of section 47.

(4A) The provisions of the bye-laws of the company relating to the holding of general meetings shall apply to general meetings and class meetings required by this section provided that, unless the bye-laws otherwise provide, the resolution of the shareholders or class must be approved by a majority vote of three-fourths of those voting at such meeting and the quorum necessary for such meeting shall be two persons at least holding or representing by proxy more than one-third of the issued shares of the company or the class, as the case may be, and that any holder of shares present in person or by proxy may demand a poll.

(5) An amalgamation agreement shall be deemed to have been adopted when it has been approved by the shareholders as provided in this section.

(6) Any shareholder who did not vote in favour of the amalgamation and who is not satisfied that he has been offered fair value for his shares may within one month of the giving of the notice referred to in subsection (2) apply to the Court to appraise the fair value of his shares.

(6A) Subject to subsection (6B), within one month of the Court appraising the fair value of any shares under subsection (6) the company shall be entitled either -

(a) to pay to the dissenting shareholder an amount equal to the value of his shares as appraised by the Court; or

(b) to terminate the amalgamation in accordance with subsection (7).

(6B) Where the Court has appraised any shares under subsection (6) and the amalgamation has proceeded prior to the appraisal then, within one month of the Court appraising the value of the shares, if the amount paid to the dissenting shareholder for his shares is less than that appraised by the Court the amalgamated company shall pay to such shareholder the difference between the amount paid to him and the value appraised by the Court.

(6C) No appeal shall lie from an appraisal by the Court under this section.

(6D) The costs of any application to the Court under this section shall be in the discretion of the Court.

(7) An amalgamation agreement may provide that at any time before the issue of a certificate of amalgamation the agreement may be terminated by the directors of an amalgamating company, notwithstanding approval of the agreement by the shareholders of all or any of the amalgamating companies.

Short form amalgamation.

107.(1) A holding company and one or more of its wholly-owned subsidiary companies may amalgamate and continue as one company without complying with sections 105 and 106 if -

(a) the amalgamation is approved by a resolution of the directors of each amalgamating company; and

(b) the resolutions provide that -

(i) the shares of each amalgamating subsidiary company shall be cancelled without any repayment of capital in respect thereof;

(ii) the memorandum shall be the same as the memorandum of the amalgamating holding company; and

(iii) no securities shall be issued by the amalgamated company in connection with the amalgamation.

(2) Two or more wholly-owned subsidiary companies of the same holding company may amalgamate and continue as one company without complying with section 105 and 106 if -

(a) the amalgamation is approved by a resolution of the directors of each amalgamating company; and

(b) the resolutions provide that -

(i) the shares of all but one of the amalgamating subsidiary companies shall be cancelled without any repayment of capital in respect thereof;

(ii) the memorandum shall be the same as the memorandum of the amalgamating subsidiary company whose shares are not cancelled.

(3) The amalgamating companies may elect to combine their respective authorised share capitals and in the resolutions approving the amalgamation they shall state whether or not they so elect.

(4) *Deleted*

(5) *Deleted*

Registration of amalgamated companies.

108.(1) Subject to subsections (2) and (3) after the amalgamation of companies has been adopted, the amalgamated company shall on application be registered by the Registrar and a certificate of amalgamation issued to the company.

(2) Any application for the registration of an amalgamated company shall be accompanied by -

(a) a certified copy of the resolution or other authority, if any, of each amalgamating company;

(b) the registered address of the amalgamated company;

(c) the memorandum of the amalgamated company; and

(d) the documents referred to in subsection (3).

(3) An application for registration of an amalgamated company shall have attached thereto a statutory declaration by an officer of each amalgamating company that establishes to the satisfaction of the Registrar that -

(a) there are reasonable grounds for believing that -

(i) each amalgamating company is and the amalgamated company will be able to pay its liabilities as they become due; and

(ii) the realizable value of the amalgamated company's assets will not be less than the aggregate of its liabilities and issued capital of all classes; and

(b) there are reasonable grounds for believing that -

(i) no creditor will be prejudiced by the amalgamation; or

(ii) adequate notice has been given to all known creditors of the amalgamating companies and no creditor objects to the amalgamation otherwise than on grounds that are frivolous or vexatious.

(4) For the purposes of subsection (3)(d), adequate notice is given if -

(a) a notice in writing is sent to each known creditor having a claim against the company that exceeds one thousand dollars; and

(b) a notice is published in an appointed newspaper stating that the company intends to amalgamate with one or more specified companies in accordance

with this Act and that a creditor of the company may object to the amalgamation within thirty days from the date of the notice.

Effect of certificate of amalgamated companies.

109. On the date shown in a certificate of amalgamation -

(a) the amalgamation of the amalgamating companies and their continuance as one company shall become effective;

(b) the property of each amalgamating company shall become the property of the amalgamated company;

(c) the amalgamated company shall continue to be liable for the obligations of each amalgamating company;

(d) an existing cause of action, claim or liability to prosecution shall be unaffected;

(e) a civil, criminal or administrative action or proceeding pending by or against an amalgamating company may be continued to be prosecuted by or against the amalgamated company;

(f) a conviction against, or ruling, order or judgment in favour of or against, an amalgamating company may be enforced by or against the amalgamated company; and

(g) the certificate of amalgamation shall be deemed to be the certificate of incorporation of the amalgamated company, however, the date of incorporation of a company is its original date of incorporation and its amalgamation with another company does not alter its original date of incorporation.

PART VIII

THE INVESTIGATION OF THE AFFAIRS OF A COMPANY AND THE PROTECTION OF MINORITIES

Investigation of the affairs of a company.

110.(1) Subject to subsection (10) the Minister may, at any time of his own volition or on the application of that proportion of the members of a company, as in his opinion warrants the application, based in respect of a company limited by shares, or other company having a share capital, on their shareholding, appoint one or more inspectors to investigate the affairs of the company and report thereon in such manner as he may direct.

(2) The application by the members of a company shall be supported by such evidence as the Minister may require for the purpose of showing that the applicants have good reason for, and are not actuated by malicious motives in requiring the investigation; and the Minister may, before appointing an inspector require the applicants to give security for payment of the costs of the inquiry.

(3) All officers and agents of the company shall produce to the inspector all books and documents in their custody or power.

(4) An inspector may examine on oath the officers and agents of the company in relation to its business, and may administer an oath accordingly.

(5) Where any officer or agent refuses to produce any book or document that under this section it is his duty to produce, or to answer any questions relating to the affairs of the company, he shall be liable to a default fine and the court convicting him may order him to produce to the inspector the books or documents in respect of which he was convicted.

(6) Any person who fails to obey an order of a court made under subsection (5) requiring the production of any books or documents shall be guilty of contempt of Court and may be punished accordingly.

(7) On the conclusion of the investigation the inspector shall report his opinion to the Minister, and a copy of the report shall be forwarded by the Minister to the company and a further copy may in his discretion, at the request of the applicants for the investigation, be delivered to them.

(8) All expenses of and incidental to the investigation shall be defrayed by the applicants, unless the Minister directs that they be paid by the company.

(9) A copy of a report made under this section shall be admissible in any legal proceeding as evidence of the opinion of the inspector in relation to any matter contained in the report.

(10) The Minister shall not have the power under this section to appoint an inspector to investigate the affairs of an exempted company or a permit company.

Alternative remedy to winding up in cases of oppressive or prejudicial conduct.

111.(1) Any member of a company who complains that the affairs of the company are being conducted or have been conducted in a manner oppressive or prejudicial to the interests of some part of the members, including himself, or where a report has been made to the Minister under section 110 the Registrar on behalf of the Minister, may make an application to the Court by petition for an order under this section.

(2) If on any such petition the Court is of opinion -

(a) that the company's affairs are being conducted or have been conducted as aforesaid; and

(b) that to wind up the company would unfairly prejudice that part of the members, but otherwise the facts would justify the making of a winding up order on the ground that it was just and equitable that the company should be wound up,

the Court may, with a view to bringing to an end the matters complained of, make such order as it thinks fit, whether for regulating the conduct of the company's affairs in future, or for the purchase of the shares of any members of the company by other members of the company or by the company and, in the case of a purchase by the company, for the reduction accordingly of the company's capital, or otherwise.

(3) Where an order under this section makes an alteration in or addition to any company's memorandum or bye-laws, then, notwithstanding anything in any other provision but subject to the provisions of the order, the company concerned shall not have power without the leave of the Court to make further alteration in or addition to the memorandum or bye-laws as so altered or added to accordingly.

(4) An office copy of any order under this section altering or adding to, or giving leave to alter or add to, a company's memorandum or bye-laws shall, within fourteen days after the making thereof, be delivered by the company to the Registrar for registration; and if a company makes default in complying with this subsection, the company and every officer of the company who is in default shall be liable to a default fine.

Preservation of the books and assets of a company.

112.(1) The Registrar in any case where the Minister has made an order under subsection (1) of section 110 or where he has made an application under subsection (1) of section 111 may apply to the Court ex parte for an order that the assets, books and papers of the company be preserved and not moved.

(2) If on any such application the Court is satisfied that there is a likelihood that the assets of the company will be transferred or that the books and papers of the company may be destroyed or removed it shall make an order that the assets of the company shall not be transferred to any other person, removed from Bermuda or otherwise dealt with and that the books or papers of the company shall not be destroyed or moved until a further order is made by the Court.

(3) Where an order under subsection (1) is served on a company the company may apply to the Court for the order to be discharged and the Court may -

(a) confirm the order;

(b) vary the order in such manner as it considers just; or

(c) discharge the order, and in any case make such orders as it thinks desirable for the preservation of the assets of the company and the custody, inspection and copying of the books and papers of the company.

(4) The company and any officer or employee of the company who acts in contravention of an order of the Court made under subsection (2) or (3) shall be guilty of contempt of Court.

PART IX

LOCAL COMPANIES

Interpretation.

113.(1) In this Part and in the Third Schedule the following shall be deemed to be "Bermudian" -

(a) The Government or any corporation of which the majority of the directors, managers, or trustees are subject to appointment by the Governor or a Minister;

(b) any person who has Bermudian status by virtue of the law relating to immigration from time to time in force;

(c) a local company in which the percentage of shares beneficially owned by Bermudians is not less than eighty percent of the total issued share capital of that company;

(cc) a local statutory corporation;

(d) an institution licensed as a bank under section 14(5)(a) of the Banks and Deposit Companies Act 1999;

(e) a wholly owned subsidiary of a local company so far, and or so long as, that local company is complying with the Third Schedule and for so long as it abides by all the obligations of its parent company and does nothing in Bermuda that its parent company is unable lawfully to do; and

(f) a trust of which the majority of the trustees are persons with Bermudian status by virtue of the law relating to immigration from time to time in force and the trust is established for the benefit of Bermuda, Bermudians or things Bermudian.

(2) For the purposes of subsection (1), a company shall be deemed to be a wholly owned subsidiary of another company if the latter company enjoys the beneficial interest in all the shares of the former company through beneficial ownership or as beneficiary under a trust, express or implied, or through a nominee shareholder, to the exclusion of any other person, and control in the former company cannot, by means of any arrangement, artifice or device, be exercised either directly or indirectly by persons who are not Bermudians.

(3) No share shall be deemed to be beneficially owned by a Bermudian if -

(a) that Bermudian is in any way under any obligation to exercise any right attaching to that share at the instance of, or for the benefit of, any person who is not Bermudian; or

(b) that share is held jointly or severally with any person who is not Bermudian; or

(c) that share is owned by a subsidiary company of the company concerned.

(4) For the purposes of this Part, the expression "local statutory corporation" means a corporation sole or a corporation aggregate, other than a company, incorporated by an Act, the principal functions of which relate to operations and affairs in Bermuda.

Circumstances in which local companies may carry on business.

114.(1) No local company shall carry on business of any sort in Bermuda unless

(a) it is a company which, at the relevant time, complies with Part I of the Third Schedule or is a wholly-owned subsidiary of such a company; or

(b) it is a company mentioned in Part II of the said Schedule; or

(c) it is licensed under section 114B and, at the relevant time is carrying on such business in accordance with the terms and conditions imposed in such licence, and not otherwise.

(2) Any local company that carries on business in contravention of subsection (1) shall be liable to a fine of one hundred dollars in respect of each day that it carries on business in contravention of the subsection.

(3) The Minister may by regulations amend Part I of the Third Schedule, and any such regulations shall be subject to affirmative resolution procedure.

(4) Section 132 shall apply mutatis mutandis to any company mentioned in Part II of the Third Schedule as if it were an exempted company.

Application for licence.

114A.(1) Any local company may apply to the Minister for a licence to carry on business in Bermuda.

(2) An application for a licence under this section shall be made to the Minister in such form and accompanied by such documents as the Minister may determine.

(3) Before an application is made, the local company shall not less than seven days prior to the date of application advertise its intention to apply for a licence under this section in an appointed newspaper.

Granting and revocation of licence.

114B.(1) Subject to the provisions of this section, the Minister may, in his discretion, grant a licence in respect of which application has been made under section 114A, but if the Minister is of opinion that it would not be in the public interest to grant a licence, he may refuse to grant one without giving any reason for so refusing.

(2) A licence issued under this section shall be for such duration and may be subject to such terms as the Minister may see fit to specify therein.

(3) The Minister shall, in deciding whether or not to grant a licence to a local company to carry on business in Bermuda, have regard to -

(a) the economic situation in Bermuda and the protection of persons already engaged in business in Bermuda;

(b) the nature and previous conduct of the company and the persons having an interest in the company whether as directors, shareholders or otherwise;

(c) any advantage or disadvantage which may result from the company carrying on business in Bermuda; and

(d) the desirability of retaining in the control of Bermudians the economic resources of Bermuda.

(4) The Minister may at any time revoke a licence -

(a) for a contravention of any condition subject to which the licence is granted;

(b) if the company concerned is carrying on business in a manner detrimental to the public interest;

(c) if the company concerned ceases to carry on business in Bermuda;

(d) if the company concerned goes into liquidation or is wound up or otherwise dissolved; or

(e) if the company concerned fails to comply with any directive or requirement issued by the Minister under this Act.

(5) Before revoking a licence under subsection (4) the Minister shall give the company concerned notice in writing of his intention to do so specifying therein the grounds on which he proposes to revoke the licence and shall afford the company concerned an opportunity of submitting to him a written statement of objections to the revocation of the licence; and thereafter the Minister shall advise the company concerned of his decision in the matter.

(6) The Minister shall lodge with the Registrar a copy of every licence granted under this section and the licence shall be available for public inspection by members of the public at the office of the Registrar during normal business hours.

Fees payable by local licensed company.

114C.(1) Every local company to which a licence is granted under this Act shall, upon the issue of such licence, pay to the Government a fee of one thousand dollars.

(2) On or before the 31st day of January of every year after the year in which a licence has been granted to a local company, that company shall, during the subsistence of such licence, pay to the Government a fee of one thousand dollars.

(3) Any licensed local company which fails to pay the fee provided by this section shall be guilty of an offence and liable on conviction by a court of summary jurisdiction to a fine not exceeding one hundred dollars for each month during which such fee remains unpaid.

(4) The Minister shall publish annually in the Gazette the name of every licensed local company that has paid the fee provided by this section.

Special provisions relating to hotel companies.

115.(1) In relation to any hotel company the Minister shall exercise his powers under section 114B after consultation with the Minister responsible for tourism.

(2) Notwithstanding any provision of a private Act restricting the transfer of shares in any hotel company, the Minister may, without prejudice to his powers under section 114B(2) impose conditions on the grant of a licence to a hotel company restricting the transfer of shares in the company without the consent of such authority as the Minister may specify.

(3) Where a hotel company is a subsidiary of a corporation incorporated outside Bermuda the Minister may without prejudice to his powers under section 114B, revoke a licence in the event of the transfer of effective control of the corporation to persons who are not Bermudians.

(3a) The provisions of subsection (5) of section 114B shall apply to the revocation of a licence under subsection (3) as they apply to the revocation of a licence under subsection (4) of that section.

(4) In this section -

> "hotel" has the meaning assigned to that expression in section I of the Hotels (Licensing and Control) Act 1969; "hotel company" means a company whose principal business in Bermuda is the ownership or the operation of a hotel in Bermuda.

Penalty for improper exercise of voting rights etc.

116.(1) Any person who, after a notice has been served upon him under sub-paragraph (2) of paragraph (2) of Part I of the Third Schedule exercises any voting rights or fails to divest himself of his shares within three years, or within such further period as the Minister may allow under the proviso to that sub-paragraph shall be liable to a fine of one thousand dollars.

(2) A court when convicting any person under subsection (1) of failing to divest himself of any shares shall, if the person convicted still holds the shares, fix a date by which he shall divest himself of the shares and if he fails so to do by such date he shall be guilty of a further offence and shall be liable to a fine of one hundred dollars for each day he has held the shares since the date the Court ordered him to divest himself of them.

(3) If any person fails to divest himself of any shares after having been found guilty of a further offence under subsection (2) he shall be guilty of contempt of court and the Court may summarily deal with him for such contempt until such time as he does divest himself of the shares.

(4) It shall be a good defence to a prosecution under subsection (2) for the owner to show that the company had at the relevant time ceased to carry on business in Bermuda or that the shares were valueless and that he was, therefore, unable to divest himself of them.

Return of shareholdings.

117.(1) Before any local company limited by shares, or other company having a share capital, first commences business the company shall forward to the Registrar a return of shareholdings in the company as at the date of making the return signed by two directors of the company.

(2) Every local company limited by shares, or other company having a share capital, shall, not later than the 31st March each year after the year in which the company first commenced business, forward to the Registrar a return of shareholdings in the company as at the 31st day of December of the immediately preceding year signed by two directors:

Provided that the Registrar may in any particular case grant an extension of time for compliance with this subsection if he is satisfied that non-compliance is not wilful or is due to circumstances beyond the control of the directors of the company.

(3) A return of shareholdings under this section -

(a) shall contain the following particulars -

(i) the number and par value of each class of shares issued by the company;

(ii) the voting and other rights attached to each class of shares;

(iii) a statement of the number and par value of each class of shares beneficially owned by Bermudians;

(iv) a statement of the number and par value of each class of shares held by other persons; and

(b) may be combined with a return made for the purpose of the payment of annual tax.

(4) Any local company which fails to comply with the provisions of this section shall be liable to a default fine.

(5) Any person who knowingly signs a return made for the purposes of this section which is false in a material particular shall be liable on conviction by a court of summary jurisdiction to a fine of one thousand dollars and on conviction on indictment to a fine of two thousand dollars.

Allotment and transfer of shares.

118.(1) No allotment of shares in a local company shall be made by the officers of the company if such allotment will, to the knowledge or belief of them, or any of them, result in the number of shares beneficially owned by persons who are not Bermudians exceeding the amount such persons are entitled to own by virtue of the Third Schedule unless the prior written consent of the Minister is obtained.

(2) The officers of a local company shall decline to register any transfer of shares in the company if such transfer will, to the knowledge or belief of the officers, or any of them, result in the number of shares beneficially owned by persons who are not Bermudian exceeding the amount such persons are entitled to own by virtue of the Third Schedule unless the prior written consent of the Minister is obtained.

(3) No allotment of shares in a local company shall be made to any person unless the application for those shares sets out whether or not the applicant is Bermudian.

(4) No transfer of shares in a local company shall be registered unless the instrument of transfer of those shares sets out with respect to both the transferor and transferee whether or not they are Bermudian.

(5) Any officer of a local company who is knowingly a party to any allotment of shares contrary to subsection (1) or subsection (3) or who is knowingly a party to authorizing or permitting any transfer, or registration of a transfer, of shares contrary to subsection (2) or subsection (4), shall be liable on conviction by a court of summary jurisdiction to a fine of one thousand dollars and on conviction on indictment to a fine of two thousand dollars.

(6) In any case where it is stated in an application for allotment, or in an instrument of transfer, of shares in a local company that an applicant, transferor or transferee is Bermudian the officers of the company may request that person to furnish such proof of the correctness of such statement as the officers consider necessary; and, in the absence of such proof, the officers may decline to allot any shares or register the transfer.

(7) The officers of a local company may at any time enquire in writing of any person who owns a share in the company -

(a) whether or not he is Bermudian;

(b) whether or not he is the beneficial owner of the shares;

(c) whether or not he is in any way under any obligation to exercise any right attaching to that share at the instance of, or for the benefit of, another person and, if so, the name of that other person and whether or not that other person is Bermudian; and

(d) whether he owns that share jointly or severally with another person and, if so, the name of the other person who has such an interest and whether or not that other person is Bermudian

and, if it is stated in any reply made to an enquiry under this subsection that any person is Bermudian, the officers may further require the person making that statement to furnish such proof of the correctness of that statement as the directors consider necessary.

(8) Any person to whom a request is made, or to whom an enquiry is addressed, under this section shall reply in writing, within fourteen days after the receipt of the request or the enquiry and shall give the information required; and no person shall be liable for breach of any contract, trust or other obligation which is binding on him in law for supplying such information.

(9) Any person who fails to reply in accordance with subsection (7) or subsection (8) or who makes a reply or furnishes information or purported proof which is false in a material particular shall be liable on conviction by a court of summary jurisdiction to a fine of one thousand dollars and on conviction on indictment to a fine of two thousand dollars.

(10) This section does not apply to a local company that is licensed under section 114B.

Minister may require information.

119.(1) The Minister may at any time by notice in writing require the officers of a local company to forward to him such information as to the officers of and shareholdings (including the classes of shares and the voting and other rights attached to each class) in the local company as the Minister may specify.

(2) A notice under subsection (1) may require that the officers set out in writing within such period as may be specified in the notice the facts in relation to the officers, shareholdings and other matters relating to the control of the company which the officers contend establishes that the local company is Bermudian controlled and such facts shall specify the extent to which the control of any corporate body holding shares in the local company is vested in Bermudians.

(3) If the officers of a local company fail to comply with the requirements specified in a notice issued under this section, or fail to comply with the requirements thereof in such a manner as to establish, prima facie, that the company is Bermudian controlled, the company shall be deemed not to be Bermudian controlled until the contrary is proved.

Acquisition of land by local companies.

120. Without prejudice to paragraph 12 of the First Schedule, a local company may acquire and hold in its corporate name with the previous sanction in each case of the Minister, but not otherwise, any land in Bermuda, bona fide required for the purpose of the company, not exceeding in the whole the limit of its landholding powers specified in its memorandum.

(1) DELETED

(2) Notwithstanding subsection (1) of this section and section 7(1)(g) but subject to subsection (3) of this section, where a local company is licensed under the Trust Companies Act 1991, the company shall have the power to acquire and hold in its corporate name any land in Bermuda provided it holds such land in its capacity as trustee of any trust or settlement established by written instrument.

(3) Nothing in subsection (2) overrides any provision in Part VIII of the Bermuda Immigration and Protection Act 1956 relating to the acquisition of land, or the holding of land, in trust.

Companies to make declarations and pay annual tax.

121.(1) Every local company shall within one month of filing its memorandum and thereafter not later than the 31st March of each year -

(a) send to the Registrar a declaration in writing by an officer of the company stating what the issued capital of the company will be when it commences business or if it is in business what the issued capital of the company was on the 1st of January of that year and, in the case of a company whose business includes the management of any unit trust scheme, stating the number of unit trust schemes managed by the company on the first day of each calendar year; and

(b) pay the appropriate fee, if applicable, and the appropriate annual tax as shown in Part I of the Fifth Schedule:

Provided that, where the filing of the memorandum is effected after the 31st August in any year, the fee payable, if applicable, and tax payable in respect of that year shall be half the fee, if applicable and half the tax shown in the Schedule.

(2) If a company fails to send a declaration to the Registrar in compliance with paragraph (a) of subsection (1) or pay the appropriate fee, if applicable, and the annual tax the company and every officer of the company shall be liable to a default fine.

(3) It shall be lawful for the Registrar, in any case where a company has not made a declaration and payment in accordance with subsection (1) and where he is satisfied that such non-payment is not due to wilful neglect or default, to accept payment of the sum due together with a penalty of one hundred and fifty dollars, and in any such case subsection (2) shall not apply.

(4) In addition to any penalty it may incur if a company fails to pay the appropriate fee, if applicable, and the annual tax within three months of it becoming due it shall cease to carry on business until the fee, if applicable, and the tax and any penalty it may have incurred have been paid.

(5) Any company that carries on business in contravention of subsection (4) shall be liable to a fine of one hundred dollars in respect of each day that it carries on business in contravention of that subsection.

(6) If any question arises as to the appropriate fee, if applicable, and the annual tax payable by a local company the decision of the Minister as to what fee, if applicable, and tax are payable shall be final.

(7) The Minister may from time to time by order vary the fees shown in Part I of the Fifth Schedule. Any such order shall be subject to affirmative resolution procedure.

Accountant General may call for auditor's certificate.

122.(1) The Accountant General may by notice in writing require a company to produce the certificate of an auditor approved by him setting out the issued capital of that company on the first day of January of such year as the Accountant General may specify in the notice.

(2) If a company without lawful excuse fails to comply with subsection (1), then that company shall be deemed to be liable for the maximum annual tax payable by a company pursuant to this Act in respect of the year to which the notice relates unless that company satisfies the Accountant General that it is liable to a lesser sum by way of annual tax.

Recovery of annual tax.

123. Annual tax and any penalty payable pursuant to this Act may be recovered by the Accountant General in a court of summary jurisdiction as a civil debt, irrespective of the amount so payable.

Companies in liquidation.

124.(1) The liability of a company to annual tax shall not be affected by reason only of the fact that it is being wound up:

Provided that, where it is shown to the satisfaction of the Accountant General that in any year the income of a company being wound up is less than twelve hundred dollars, the company shall not be liable to annual tax in respect of that year and the Accountant General shall refund to that company the annual tax, if any, paid in respect of that year.

(2) The Accountant General may require the production of such audited or other accounts and such other documents as may be reasonable to determine whether exemption provided in this section shall have effect.

(3) The Accountant General may enter into such arrangement with the liquidator or Official Receiver, as the case may be, for the suspension of the payment of annual tax during the winding up of a company pending the determination of whether the exception provided by this section shall have effect and in the event that failure by the company to pay annual tax during the period of its winding up shall not, if the company complies with the provisions of any such arrangement, attract any penalty.

Certain companies exempt from tax.

125.(1) A company shall be exempt from the payment of annual tax in any year if it satisfies the Accountant General that it is -

(a) a company limited by guarantee and is not a mutual company; or

(b) that it is operated for a charitable purpose; or

(c) that the company does not pursue any commercial enterprise for profit and that the income during each of the past years since its incorporation has not exceeded five hundred dollars.

(2) A company shall not be deemed to be operated for a charitable purpose for the purposes of subsection (1) if -

(i) it has power to engage or engages in any commercial enterprise otherwise than in furtherance of its charitable objects;

(ii) any dividend has at any time been paid on any of its share capital;

(iii) any interest has been paid on any capital employed other than capital employed in furtherance of its charitable purpose; or

(iv) any person is employed or remunerated for services otherwise than for services in furtherance of its charitable or reasonable administrative purposes.

Interpretation.

126. For the purposes of section 121 to 125 unless the context otherwise requires -

"issued capital" means in relation to -

(a) any company limited by shares, or other company having a share capital, the aggregate of the nominal value of the shares actually issued by the company whether or not the shares so issued are fully paid up; and

(b) in the case of a mutual company the nominal value of the reserve fund;

"year" means a calendar year.

PART X

EXEMPTED COMPANIES

Meaning of exempted company.

127. For the purposes of this Act, an exempted company means a company which does not comply with the requirements of this Act in respect of a local company and which -

(i) was recognized as an exempted company immediately before the appointed day;

(ii) is a company registered under this Act and stated in its memorandum to be an exempted company;

(iii) is a company incorporated by virtue of a private Act enacted after the appointed day and is declared by its incorporating Act to be an exempted company for the purposes of this Act.

Exempted company to be an exempted undertaking.

128.(1) An exempted company shall be an exempted undertaking for the purposes of the Exempted Undertakings Tax Protection Act 1966.

(2) An exempted company shall be subject to the provisions of this Act and to the provisions of law save where otherwise expressly provided in this or any other Act.

Restriction on acquisition of property etc.

129.(1) Unless otherwise authorized by its incorporating Act or any other Act or, with the consent of the Minister, by its memorandum an exempted company shall not have power -

(a) to acquire or hold land in Bermuda except -

(i) land required for its business by way of lease or tenancy agreement for a term not exceeding fifty years; or

(ii) with the consent of the Minister granted in his discretion, land by way of lease or tenancy agreement for a term not exceeding twenty-one years in order to provide accommodation or recreational facilities for its officers and employees.

(b) except as provided by section 144 to take any mortgage of land in Bermuda;

(c) to acquire any bonds, or debentures secured on any land in Bermuda except bonds or debentures issued by the Government or a public authority;

(d) DELETED*;*

(e) to carry on business of any kind or type whatsoever in Bermuda either alone or in partnership or otherwise except -

(i) carrying on business with persons outside Bermuda;

(ii) doing business in Bermuda with an exempted undertaking in furtherance only of the business of the exempted company carried on exterior to Bermuda;

(iii) buying or selling or otherwise dealing in shares, bonds, debenture stock obligations, mortgages or other securities or investments issued or created by an exempted undertaking, or a local company, or any partnership which is not an exempted undertaking;

(iv) transacting banking business in Bermuda with and through a bank licensed under the Banks Act 1969;

(v) effecting or concluding contracts in Bermuda, and exercising in Bermuda all other powers, so far as may be necessary for the carrying on of its business with persons outside Bermuda;

(vi) as manager or agent for, or consultant or adviser to, the business of an exempted undertaking whether or not such business is the sole business of the exempted company provided that the company has an object to enable it to carry on the kind or type of business as specified in this subparagraph;

(vii) carrying on the business of reinsuring risks undertaken by any company incorporated in Bermuda and permitted to engage in insurance and reinsurance business; or

(viii) in accordance with subsection (7) -

(aa) marketing of shares or dealing with the holders of shares of an exempted company where the exempted company is a mutual fund;

(bb) marketing interests in or dealing with holders of interests in a limited partnership in respect of which the exempted company is a general partner;

(cc) marketing units in or dealing with holders of units in a unit trust scheme in respect of which the exempted company is a manager.

(1A) Nothing in paragraph (e) of subsection (1) shall be taken to prohibit an exempted company from effecting or concluding contracts or arrangements with persons in Bermuda for the supply of goods and services to the company necessary for the purpose of enabling the company to carry on its business with persons outside Bermuda.

(1B) Nothing in subsection (1)(e) shall prohibit an exempted company from offering goods or services electronically from a place or business in Bermuda or through an Internet or other electronic service provider located in Bermuda.

(2) Notwithstanding anything in any Act under authority of which an exempted company is incorporated such a company shall not engage or carry on the business of conveying or arranging for the conveyance of passengers, goods or mails by ships whether such conveyance is within waters of Bermuda except -

(i) where the ship is owned, operated or chartered by or on behalf of an exempted company;

(ii) where the conveyance is of a passenger employed by the exempted company or of goods which are or are to become the property of the exempted company; or

(iii) when the business is negotiated by a local company.

(3) Notwithstanding anything in this Act as exempted company at the date of the commencement of this Act having in its memorandum among its objects an object empowering the company to reinsure all or any risks undertaken by the company shall be deemed in addition to have and always to have had the power to accept insurance and reinsurance of any risks of another exempted company similarly empowered.

(4) Notwithstanding anything in this Act, any object in the memorandum of an exempted company empowering the company to engage in retail trade in Bermuda, including retail trade with another exempted company or an exempted undertaking or any other person, shall be void to the extent that it purports so to empower that exempted company.

(5) If an exempted company does anything in contravention of the provisions of subsection (1), then the land, merchandise, stocks, shares, bonds, debentures, securities, property or other interests so acquired or disposed of, taken or held , will be liable to escheat under the Escheats Act 1871 or under any other Act relating to escheat.

(6) It is hereby declared that in any proceedings for escheat under subsection (5), the question whether any land, merchandise, stocks, shares, bonds, debentures, securities, property or other interests have been taken, acquired, disposed of or held in contravention of the provisions of subsection (1), shall be decided as a question of fact.

(7) For the purposes of subsection (1)(e)(vii), an exempted company shall be deemed to be marking, or dealing with holders of shares, interests or units if it undertakes any of the following activities in Bermuda, that is to say -

(i) the offering of such shares, interests or units for subscription or purchase by way of a prospectus or otherwise;

(ii) the acceptance of subscriptions for, or of offers to purchase, or of applications to redeem, such shares, interests or units;

(iii) the distribution of shareholder, limited partnership or unitholder information to holders of such shares, interests or units;

(iv) the making known, by way of advertisement or otherwise, that it may be contacted at a particular address in Bermuda for the purpose of communicating with the holders of such shares, interests or units or the distribution and collection of shareholder, limited partnership or unitholder information; and

(v) any other dealing with the holders of such shares, interests or units with respect to any such shares, interests or units held by them.

Circumstances in which exempted company may carry on business in Bermuda.

129A.(1) Except as provided in subsection (4), no exempted company shall carry on business in Bermuda unless the Minister, on application made by the company in such form as the Minister may determine, grants a licence to the company empowering it so to do or to carry on in Bermuda a business or an activity prohibited by subsection (1) or (2) of section 129:

Provided that such a licence shall not authorize an exempted company to engage in retail trade in Bermuda with any other person.

(1A) The company shall not less than seven days prior to an application for a licence under subsection (1) advertise its intention to apply for a licence under this section in an appointed newspaper.

(2) A licence issued under subsection (1) shall be for such duration and may be subject to such terms and conditions as the Minister may see fit to specify therein.

(3) Subsections (3), (4) and (5) of section 114B and section 114C shall apply mutatis mutandis to an exempted company licensed under this section.

(4) An exempted company shall not require a licence to carry on in Bermuda -

(a) a business or activity specified as an exception in section 129(1)(a) to (e) (inclusive); or

(b) trust business as defined in the Trust Companies Act 1991 if -

(i) the exempted company holds under the Trust Companies Act 1991 a licence which is in force; and

(ii) the settlor of the trust being managed or administered in Bermuda by the exempted company is not ordinarily resident in Bermuda at the date of creation of the settlement.

(4A) The Minister shall lodge with the Registrar a copy of every licence granted under this section and the licence shall be available for inspection by members of the public at the office of the Registrar during normal business hours.

(5) An exempted company which contravenes the provisions of subsection (1) shall be guilty of an offence and liable on summary conviction to a fine not exceeding five hundred dollars for each day the offence continues or on conviction on indictment to a fine not exceeding one thousand five hundred dollars for each day the offence continues.

Requirements for officers or representatives in Bermuda.

130.(1) Subject to subsection (2), every exempted company shall -

(a) have a minimum of two directors, other than alternate directors, ordinarily resident in Bermuda; or

(b) have a secretary who is ordinarily resident in Bermuda and a director, other than an alternate director, who is ordinarily resident in Bermuda; or

(c) have a secretary who is ordinarily resident in Bermuda and a resident representative; or

(d) in the case of a company the shares of which are listed on an appointed stock exchange, have a resident representative.

(2) The requirements of subsections (1)(b) and (1)(c) shall not be satisfied if the secretary of a company is also appointed as the director or the resident representative referred to in such subsections.

(3) For the purposes of this section, the secretary shall be an individual ordinarily resident in Bermuda but an exempted company may appoint, in addition to a secretary, assistant or deputy secretaries, whether individuals or corporations and whether or not resident in Bermuda.

(4) A resident representative of a company, other than an exempted company, the shares of which are listed on an appointed stock exchange, or any wholly-owned subsidiary of such company, shall be an individual ordinarily resident in Bermuda but any exempted company may appoint, in addition, assistant or deputy resident representatives, whether individuals or corporations and whether or not resident in Bermuda.

(5) A resident representative shall:

(a) be entitled to attend, to be heard at, and to receive minutes of all proceedings of, all meetings of the directors and members of the company or of any committee of such directors;

(b) upon giving notice to the company of an address for the purposes of receipt of notices, be entitled to receive notice of any meeting of the directors or members, or any committee of such directors; but accidental omission to give such notice shall not invalidate any action taken at any such meetings;

(c) act as agent for the service of process in Bermuda;

(d) be entitled to file all documents and make all applications required or permitted by this Act.

(6) It shall be the duty of the resident representative in any circumstances where the resident representative becomes aware that -

(a) the company has committed a breach of any provision of this Act or any regulation made hereunder which will have a material effect on the affairs of the company; or

(b) any issue or transfer of shares of the company has been effected in contravention of any other statute regulating the issue on transfer of shares, to make a written report to the Registrar within thirty days of becoming so aware and the report shall contain all relevant particulars unless before such report is made the company has remedied such breach or contravention.

(7) Where the shares of an exempted company are listed on an appointed stock exchange and that exempted company complies with the requirement specified in subsection (1)(d), the resident representative shall -

(a) within thirty days of becoming aware that the shares of the company have ceased to be listed on an appointed stock exchange, make a written report to the Registrar setting out all particulars in respect of such cessation;

(b) [*deleted*]

(c) maintain at his or its office in Bermuda originals or copies of minutes of all proceedings of meetings of directors and members of the company, all financial statements required to be prepared by the company under this Act together with the auditor's report thereon, and all records of account required by section 83 to be kept in Bermuda.

(8) So long as the shares of an exempted company are listed on an appointed stock exchange, the provisions of subsections (1)(d), (7)(b) and (7)(c) shall apply to a wholly owned subsidiary of such company which, in accordance with subsection (1)(d), has a resident representative.

(9) For the purposes of section 92A only, "officer" shall include a resident representative.

(10) The duty of the resident representative under subsections (6) and (7) shall be owed to the Registrar and no resident representative shall be liable to the company or any other person for any report made by the resident representative pursuant to subsections (6) or (7) or any failure or purported failure to make any report under those subsections.

(11) The Minister may make regulations providing for the qualifications of a secretary for the purposes of this section; and any such regulations shall be subject to the affirmative resolution procedure.

(12) Wilful failure by the resident representative to comply with any of the provisions of this section shall be an offence and shall render the resident representative or the company liable on conviction to a fine not exceeding five thousand dollars.

Annual fees.

131.(1) Subject to subsections (2A) and (2B), every exempted company shall within one month of filing its memorandum with the Registrar and thereafter during the month of January in each year -

(a) send to the Registrar a declaration in writing signed on behalf of the company -

(i) stating what or is intended to be the principal business of the company and, in the case of a company whose business is to include the management of any unit trust scheme, stating the number of unit trust schemes to be managed by the company; and

(ii) further stating -

(aa) where the company is one limited by shares, or other company having a share capital, -

1. the amount of the company's authorised share capital; and

2. the amount of the company's share premium account; and

3. the amount of the company's assessable capital, that is to say, the total of the amounts at 1 and 2 above or, in the case of a mutual fund as defined in section 156A, the amount at 1 above; and

4. the amount of the company's assessable capital expressed in Bermuda area currency, where the amount of the company's assessable capital is not already so expressed; and

5. the exchange rate used to convert into Bermuda area currency the company's assessable capital, where that capital is denominated in a currency other than Bermuda area currency; and

6. the appropriate fee payable in respect of the company according to Part II of the Fifth Schedule; and

(bb) where the company is a mutual company -

1. the amount of the company's assessable capital, that is to say, the amount of the company's reserve fund; and

2. the amount of the company's assessable capital expressed in Bermuda area currency, where that amount is not already so expressed; and

3. the exchange rate used to convert into Bermuda area currency the company's assessable capital, where that capital is denominated in a currency other than Bermuda area currency; and

4. the appropriate fee payable in respect of the company according to Part II of the Fifth Schedule.

For the purposes of this paragraph -

(iii) the information called for thereby shall -

(aa) where it is to be given upon the incorporation of a company, be given as at the date of the filing of the company's memorandum;

(bb) where it is to be given in January in any year in relation to a company which was incorporated after 31st August of the next preceding year, be given as at the date of the filing of the company's memorandum;

(cc) in any other case, be given as at 31st August of the year next preceding the year in which the information is given, except

that the date to be taken for converting a company's assessable capital into Bermuda area currency where that capital is denominated in a currency other than Bermuda area currency shall -

A. in the case of a company limited by shares, or other company having a share capital, be the later of the following dates, that is to say, the date of the filing of the company's memorandum and the date on which the company's authorised share capital was last lawfully altered; and

B. in the case of a mutual company, be the later of the following dates, that is to say, the date of the filing of the company's memorandum and the date on which the company's reserve fund was last lawfully altered;

(iv) the exchange rate for converting into Bermuda area currency on any day a currency that is not Bermuda area currency shall be the middle market rate for that currency on that day as determined, in accordance with the provisions of subsection (4) of section 15 of the Stamp Duties Act 1976 mutatis mutandis, by the Registrar, whose determination in any case shall be final and conclusive;

(v) currency of the United States of America shall be converted into Bermuda area currency at par;

(vi) where a calculation produces a fraction of a dollar, the result shall be rounded up to the next whole dollar; and

(vii) "authorised capital", in relation to a company, means the amount stated in the company's memorandum as the company's authorised capital, as lawfully altered from time to time; and

(b) pay the appropriate fee payable in respect of the company according to Part II of the Fifth Schedule:

Provided that, where the memorandum is filed after 31st August in any year, the fee payable shall be half that fee.

(2) If a company fails to comply with subsection (1), the company and every officer of the company shall be liable to a default fine.

(2A) A company liable to pay the fees provided for in sub-paragraph A(b) of paragraph 1 of Part II of the Fifth Schedule must pay those fees in addition to any other fee that the company is liable to pay under subsection (1).

(2B) A company liable to pay a fee pursuant to sub-paragraph A(c) of paragraph 1 of Part II of the Fifth Schedule is not liable to pay any other fee prescribed by subsection (1).

(3) It shall be lawful for the Registrar, in any case where a company has failed to comply with subsection (1) and he is satisfied that such non-compliance is not the result of wilful neglect or default, to accept late compliance and payment of the sum due together with a penalty of three hundred dollars; and in such a case subsection (2) shall not apply.

(4) In addition to any penalty it may incur if a company fails to pay the appropriate fee within three months of it becoming due it shall cease to carry on business until the fee and any penalty it may have incurred have been paid.

(5) Any company that carries on business in contravention of subsection (4) shall be liable to a fine of one hundred dollars in respect of each day that it carries on business in contravention of that subsection.

(6) If any question arises as to the appropriate fee payable by an exempted company the decision of the Minister as to what fee is payable shall be final.

(7) The Minister may from time to time by order vary all or any of the fees shown in Part II of the Fifth Schedule. Any such order shall be subject to affirmative resolution procedure.

Investigation of the affairs of an exempted company.

132.(1) The Minister may at any time appoint one or more inspectors to investigate the affairs of an exempted company and to report on them in such manner as he may direct.

(2) All expenses of and incidental to the investigation shall be defrayed by the exempted company unless the Minister otherwise directs.

(3) Every officer, agent or employee of the company shall produce to the inspector such books or documents as the inspector may require for the purpose of his investigation.

(3A) A foreign corporation shall within one month after the date of registration of the memorandum of continuance under this section pay the appropriate fee payable in respect of the corporation as an exempted company according to Part II of the Fifth Schedule, but where the registration is effected after 31st August in any year, the fee payable in respect of that year shall be half the appropriate fee.

(4) Any officer, agent or employee of the exempted company who, in the course of an investigation of the affairs of the company -

(a) refuses to produce any book or document required by the inspector to be produced; or

(b) refuses to answer any question relating to the affairs of the company, shall be liable to a fine of one hundred dollars.

(5) The inspector may take evidence upon oath in investigating the affairs of the exempted company, and for that purpose may administer an oath or affirmation.

(6) Any investigation under this section shall be held in private unless the company requests that it be held in public.

(7) The inspector may from time to time report to the Minister and shall on the completion of his investigation report to him and shall send copies of such reports to the company. No other person shall be informed of the nature or contents of the report save at the request of the company or on the direction of the Minister.

(8) If the Minister considers, after examining any such report that the company or any of its officers, agents or employees -

(a) have knowingly and wilfully done anything in contravention of this Act or of any licence, permit or permission granted under this Act, he may direct the Registrar to petition the Court for the winding up of the company;

(b) are carrying on its affairs in a manner detrimental to the interests of the members of the company or the creditors of the company he may require the company to take such measures as he may consider necessary in relation to its affairs.

(9) A copy of any petition referred to in subsection (8) shall be served on the company at least seven clear days before the day set by the Court for the hearing thereof.

(10) If the Court, on the hearing of any such petition, is satisfied that the company or any of its officers, agents or employees have done anything in contravention of the provisions of this Act or of any licence, permit or permission granted under the Act, the Court may;

(a) make an order for the winding up of the company; or

(b) impose a fine of two thousand dollars on the company; or

(c) impose a like fine on any officer, agent or employee of the company who has knowingly and wilfully authorized or permitted any such contravention.

(11) Where the Court makes an order for the winding up of a company under subsection (10) the company shall be wound up in the same manner and with the same procedure as if the circumstances leading to the order were circumstances referred to in section 161.

(12) Any proceedings in connection with the holding of an investigation by the inspector in pursuance of the provisions of this section shall, for the purposes of those provisions of the Criminal Code relating to perjury, be deemed to be judicial proceedings.

(13) Whenever the Minister appoints an inspector or inspectors by virtue of subsection (1) the Registrar may make an application to the Court under section 112 for an order that the assets books and papers of the company be preserved and not moved, and this section shall apply to such application mutatis mutandis.

Denomination of capital of exempted companies.

132A. Notwithstanding the provisions of the Bermuda Monetary Authority Act 1969, the share capital of an exempted company and its share certificates may be denominated in such currency as the Minister may permit.

Section 124 applies to an exempted company.

132B. Section 124 applies mutatis mutandis to an exempted company.

PART XA

CONTINUATION AND DISCONTINUATION OF COMPANIES

Continuance in Bermuda.

132C.(1) A body incorporated outside Bermuda (hereafter in this Part referred to as a "foreign corporation") may, subject to section 4A, be continued in Bermuda as an exempted company to which the provisions of this Act and any other relevant laws of Bermuda shall apply.

(2) A foreign corporation seeking to be continued in Bermuda shall -

(a) obtain all necessary authorizations, if any, required under the laws of the jurisdiction in which it was incorporated or is presently registered in order to enable it to continue as an exempted company registered in Bermuda;

(b) provide a memorandum of continuance in such form as the Minister may determine;

(c) provide financial statements of the foreign corporation prepared for a period ending within twelve months of the proposed date of continuance.

(3) A foreign corporation shall deliver to the Registrar the memorandum of continuance for registration.

(3A) A foreign corporation shall within one month after the date of registration of the memorandum of continuance under this section pay the appropriate fee payable in respect of the corporation as an exempted company according to Part II of the Fifth Schedule, but where the registration is effected after 31 August in any year, the fee payable in respect of that year shall be half the appropriate fee.

(4) If the Registrar is satisfied that the foreign corporation will be in compliance with this Act, he shall register the memorandum of continuance whereupon it will become effective and -

(a) the Registrar shall issue a certificate of deposit of the memorandum of continuance in such form as the Minister may determine

(b) the foreign corporation will become a company to which this Act and any other laws of Bermuda apply as if it had been incorporated in Bermuda on the date of the registration;

(c) the memorandum of continuance shall be deemed to be the memorandum of association of the foreign corporation in lieu of its original, re-stated or amended memorandum of association, articles of incorporation or other constituting documents;

(d) the Registrar shall issue a certificate of continuance in such form as the Minister may determine;

(e) the foreign corporation shall forward a copy of the certificate of continuance to the competent authority in the country or jurisdiction from which it has been continued.

(5) Notwithstanding the provisions of Part XI and the provisions of the Insurance Act 1978, with effect from the date of continuance -

(a) any permit issued under section 134 shall cease to apply to the continued company; and

(b) any current registration of the continued company under section 4 of the Insurance Act 1978 shall continue with suitable endorsement by the Registrar as to the date of continuance.

(6) DELETED

(7) DELETED

(8) DELETED

(9) DELETED

(10) DELETED

(11) DELETED

(12) DELETED

Provisions of Act applying to memorandum of continuance and

certificate of continuance.

132D.(1) The provisions of this Act respecting a memorandum of association shall, mutatis mutandis, apply to a memorandum of continuance.

(2) The provisions of this Act respecting a certificate of incorporation shall, mutatis mutandis, apply to a certificate of continuance.

(3) The memorandum of continuance and a copy of the certificate of continuance shall be documents open to public inspection.

Consequences of continuance of foreign corporation.

132E.(1) Upon continuance of a foreign corporation as a company under this Act -

(a) the property of the foreign corporation continues to be the property of the company;

(b) the company continues to be liable for the obligations of the foreign corporation;

(c) any existing cause of action, claim or liability to prosecution in respect of the foreign corporation is unaffected;

(d) any civil, criminal or administrative action or proceeding pending by or against the foreign corporation may be continued by or against the company; and

(e) any conviction against, or any ruling, order or judgment in favour of or against the foreign corporation may be enforced by or against the company.

(2) The registration of the continuance of a foreign corporation under this Part shall not be deemed to -

(a) create a new legal entity; or

(b) prejudice or affect the continuity of the body corporate which was formerly a foreign corporation, now a company continued in Bermuda under this Part.

(3) The courts shall apply the laws of evidence and the rules of procedure with the intent that no claimant against the continued company shall be prejudiced in pursuing in or under the laws of Bermuda a bona fide claim that existed prior to the date of continuance and which could have been pursued under the laws then governing such foreign corporation.

Continued company to adopt bye-laws.

132F. The continued company shall, as soon as practicable from the date of continuation in Bermuda, ensure that it has adopted bye-laws which conform to the requirements of this Act and any other law of Bermuda.

Exempted company may discontinue out of Bermuda

132G.(1) An exempted company may be discontinued under this Act and be continued in a jurisdiction outside Bermuda as if it had been incorporated under the laws of that other jurisdiction.

(2) An exempted company shall not be discontinued pursuant to subsection (1) unless -

(a) **(i)** a resolution of the members or each class of members is passed in

general meeting approving the discontinuance, provided that at any such meeting each share of the company shall carry the right to vote in respect of such discontinuance whether or not it otherwise carries the right to vote; or

(iii) the discontinuance is approved in such manner as may be authorised by the bye-laws of the company;

(b) a statutory declaration has been signed by the directors of the company stating that the company is solvent and can meet all of its liabilities and obligations and that the discontinuance will not adversely affect the interests or rights of bona fide creditors and members;

(c) an irrevocable deed poll is executed by such company and its directors pursuant to which -

(i) such company and each of its directors may be served with legal process in Bermuda in any proceeding arising out of actions or omissions of such company prior to the discontinuance and provision is made for the appointment of a person within Bermuda as agent for such company for the service of process for a period of not less than three years from the date of discontinuance and for a signed acceptance of the appointment; or

(ii) such company and each of its directors may be served with legal process at a specified address in the United Kingdom, the United States of America or any appointed jurisdiction, and whereby such company and such directors submit to the non-exclusive jurisdiction of the courts of that country or jurisdiction;

(d) at least fourteen days prior to the discontinuance such company advertises in an appointed newspaper and in a national newspaper in each jurisdiction within which it carried on a substantial part of its trade or business activities its intention to discontinue under this Act and continue in the named jurisdiction; and

(e) the jurisdiction in which such company is to be continued is -

(i) an appointed jurisdiction; or

(ii) approved by the Minister, upon application by the company for the purpose of the discontinuance of the company out of Bermuda.

Documents to be filed on discontinuance.

132H.(1) An exempted company shall not be discontinued pursuant to section 132G unless on or before the effective date of the discontinuance, such company files with the Registrar a notice of the discontinuance which shall contain or have attached thereto the following information:

(a) the effective date of the discontinuance;

(b) the name of the jurisdiction in which the company will continue;

(c) the address of the registered office or the principal business address of the company in the jurisdiction in which the company will continue;

(d) a copy of the statutory declaration required pursuant to section 132G(2)(b); and

(e) a copy of the irrevocable deed poll required pursuant to section 132G(2)(c).

(2) Within thirty days after the date of the issue thereof a company which has been discontinued pursuant to section 132G shall file with the Registrar a copy of the instrument of continuance issued to the company by the appropriate authority of the jurisdiction into which the company has been continued, or, if no such instrument of continuance is issued, such other documentary evidence of such continuance as shall be issued by such authority.

(3) On receipt of the copy of the instrument of continuance or other documentary evidence of continuance, the Registrar shall file that instrument or document and issue a certificate of discontinuance which shall be in such form as the Minister may determine and thereupon the company shall cease to be registered as a company in Bermuda.

(4) The documents filed with the Registrar pursuant to subsections (1), (2) and (3) shall be open to public inspection.

Effect of discontinuance

132I.(1) The effective date of the discontinuance of a company pursuant to section 132H shall be the date that such company's continuance in the appointed jurisdiction is effective pursuant to the laws of such other jurisdiction, and such discontinuance and continuance shall not be deemed to operate to -

(a) create a new legal entity; or

(b) prejudice or affect the continuity of the body corporate which was formerly the company that was subject to this Act.

(2) On the effective date of the discontinuance of a company pursuant to section 132H this Act shall cease to apply to such company except as is required by the provisions hereof.

132J. DELETED

132K. DELETED

Public inspection of documents

132L. The instrument of continuance, the certificate of discontinuance and the declaration of discontinuance shall be documents open to public inspection.

Regulations

132M. The Minister may make Regulations for carrying out the purposes and provisions of this Part into effect.

PART XI

OVERSEAS COMPANIES

Overseas company not to carry on business without a permit.

133.(1) An overseas company shall not engage in or carry on any trade or business in Bermuda without a permit from the Minister issued under section 134.

(2) Any permit issued to an overseas company enabling it lawfully to engage in or carry on any trade or business in Bermuda under the authority of any Act other than this Act or the Non-Resident Insurance Undertakings Act 1967 shall be deemed to be a permit issued under section 134 if valid on the appointed day and for so long as it remains valid.

(3) For the purposes of this section and this Part, the expression "engage in or carry on any trade or business in Bermuda" includes the engaging in or carrying on any trade or business outside Bermuda from a place of business in Bermuda.

(4) A company shall be deemed to engage in or carry on any trade or business in Bermuda if it occupies premises in Bermuda or if it makes known by way of advertisement, or by an insertion in a directory or by means of letter heads that it may be contacted at a particular address in Bermuda or is otherwise seen to be engaging in or carrying on any trade or business in or from within Bermuda on a continuing basis:

Provided that a company shall not be deemed to engage in or carry on any trade or business in Bermuda by reason only that -

(a) a travelling salesman representing the company who has been permitted to land in Bermuda as such establishes a temporary place of business in Bermuda; or

(b) meetings of its officers or members are held in Bermuda; or

(c) the company is buying or selling or otherwise dealing in shares, bonds, debenture stock obligations, mortgages or other securities issued or created by an exempted undertaking, or a local company, or any partnership which is not an exempted undertaking.

(5) A company shall be deemed to engage in or carry on any trade or business in Bermuda if it makes known by way of advertisement or by any statement on a web site or by an electronic record as defined in the Electronic Transactions Act 1999 that it may be contacted at a particular address in Bermuda or if it uses a Bermudian domain name.

Grant of permit to overseas company.

134.(1) An overseas company without a permit may apply to the Minister for a permit to engage in or carry on any trade or business in Bermuda.

(2) Every application for a permit shall be accompanied by such documents and particulars as the Minister may from time to time require and shall be accompanied by the application fee prescribed under the Government Fees Act 1965.

(3) Within three months prior to an application for a permit under subsection (1) the company shall publish in an appointed newspaper an advertisement announcing the intention to apply for a permit specifying its name and stating the trade or business it proposes to engage in or carry on in Bermuda.

(4) Where the Minister refuses to grant a permit he shall not be bound to assign any reason therefor.

(5) Without prejudice to the discretion conferred on the Minister by this section, he shall, in deciding whether or not to grant a permit, have regard to -

(a) the economic situation in Bermuda and the due protection of persons already engaged in or carrying on any trade or business in Bermuda;

(b) the nature and previous conduct of the company and the persons having an interest in the company whether as directors, shareholders or otherwise;

(c) any advantage or disadvantage which may result from the company engaging in or carrying on a trade or business in Bermuda.

Annual fees.

135.(1) Subject to subsection (1A), every permit company shall before engaging in or carrying on any trade or business in Bermuda, and thereafter during the month of March each year, pay the appropriate fee payable in respect of the company according to Part II of the Fifth Schedule, but where a permit is issued after 31 October in any year, the fee payable in respect of that year shall be half the appropriate fee; and sub-paragraph (i) of paragraph (a) of subsection (1) of section 131 shall apply mutatis mutandis to every such company.

(1A) A company liable to pay the fees provided for in sub-paragraph B(c) of paragraph 1 of Part II of the Fifth Schedule must pay those fees in addition to any other fee that the company is liable to pay under subsection (1).

(2) If a company fails to pay the appropriate fee as provided in subsection (1) it shall be liable to a default fine.

(3) Subsections (2), (3), (4), (5) and (6) of section 131 shall apply mutatis mutandis to permit companies.

Conditions subject to which permits may be granted.

136.(1) Permits shall be subject to such conditions as the Minister may think fit to impose which shall be specified in the permit and, without derogation from the generality of this provision a permit may require that the company shall have one or more directors ordinarily resident in Bermuda and shall inform the Minister of any change in its beneficial ownership.

(2) Subject to any conditions which may be specified in a permit pursuant to subsection (1), an overseas company which has been granted a permit shall have power in Bermuda -

(a) if it is a mutual fund as defined in subsection (5), to market its shares or deal with holders of its shares in Bermuda;

(b) if it is a general partner in a limited partnership, as so defined, to market interests in, or deal with the holders of interests in, such limited partnership; or

(c) if it is the manager of a unit trust scheme, as so defined, to market units in or deal with holders of units in, such unit trust scheme, in accordance with subsection (3).

(3) For the purpose of subsection (2), an overseas company shall be deemed to be marketing or dealing with the holders of the shares of that overseas company, interests in a limited partnership, or units in a unit trust scheme, if it undertakes in Bermuda any of the activities specified in subsection (4).

(4) The activities referred to in subsection (3) are -

(i) the offering of such shares, interests or units for subscription or purchase by way of a prospectus or otherwise;

(ii) the acceptance of subscriptions for, or of offers to purchase, or of applications to redeem, such shares, interests or units;

(iii) the distribution of shareholder, limited partnership or unitholder information to holders of such shares, interests or units;

(iv) the making known, by way of advertisement, or otherwise, that it may be contacted at a particular address in Bermuda for the purpose of communication with the holders of such shares, interests or units or the distribution and collection of shareholder, limited partnership or unitholder information; and

(v) any other dealing with the holders of such shares, interests or units with respect to any such shares, interests or units held by them.

(5) In this section -

(a) "mutual fund" means a company incorporated outside Bermuda but having the characteristics set out in section 156A of this Act;

(b) "limited partnership" means a limited partnership formed under the laws of a country outside Bermuda, but having the characteristics set out in section 2(1) of the Limited Partnership Act 1883;

(c) "unit trust scheme" means a unit trust scheme formed under the laws of a country outside Bermuda, but having the characteristics set out in section 1 of the Exempted Undertakings Tax Protection Act 1966.

Principal representative.

136A.(1) Every permit company shall appoint and maintain a principal representative in Bermuda and shall give notice in writing to the Registrar of such particulars of its principal representative as the Minister may determine.

(2) If any particulars of a principal representative required by subsection (1) to be notified to the Registrar are altered the company shall give in writing to the Registrar particulars of the alteration within twenty-one days after the alteration is made.

(3) If a company fails to comply with the provisions of this section it shall be liable to a default fine.

Form and proof of a permit.

137.(1) A permit shall be in such form as the Minister shall determine.

(2) A copy of every permit shall be lodged by the Minister with the Registrar.

(3) A certificate purporting to be signed by the Registrar -

(a) certifying that a permit was or was not in force in respect of an overseas company at the time specified in the certificate; and

(b) specifying the conditions of the permit,

shall be admissible in evidence in proceedings under this Act without further proof and shall be prima facie evidence of the facts certified or specified therein.

Alteration of conditions of a permit.

138.(1) The Minister may on the application of a permit company vary the terms of its permit.

(2) Where under subsection (1) the Minister varies the terms of a permit he shall notify the Registrar who shall amend his copy of the permit accordingly.

Revocation of a permit.

139. The Minister may at any time revoke the permit of an overseas company if -

(a) the company or any of its servants or agents contravenes a condition of its permit;

(b) in the opinion of the Minister the company is carrying on business in a manner detrimental to the public interest;

(c) the company ceases to engage in or carry on any trade or business in Bermuda;

(d) a court or other competent authority in any country makes an order for the winding up, dissolution or judicial management of the company or of any person who directly or indirectly controls the company;

(e) the company is otherwise wound up or if any person who directly or indirectly controls the company is wound up or ceases to carry on business;

(f) there is a substantial change in the effective control of the company;

(g) there is a substantial change in the nature of the business carried on by the company; or

(h) the company contravenes or fails to comply with any provision of this Part of this Act.

Revocation procedure.

140.(1) The Minister shall give a company reasonable notice in writing of his intention to revoke its permit under section 139 and shall afford the company an opportunity of making representations to him.

(2) A notice under subsection (1) shall specify the ground on which the Minister intends to revoke the permit.

(3) Upon the revocation of its permit a company shall forthwith cease to engage in or carry on any trade or business in Bermuda unless the Minister in his discretion authorizes the company so to do -

(a) pending the determination of an appeal against the revocation;

(b) for such period as the Minister may specify for the purpose of closing its business in Bermuda.

(4) When the Minister revokes the permit of an overseas company the Registrar may, if he is satisfied that it would be in the interests of any creditor of the company or of any other person to whom the company has an obligation that the affairs of the company in Bermuda shall be wound up in the same manner as a company incorporated in Bermuda, petition the Court to wind up such affairs and the court may make such orders for the winding up of such affairs as is practicable.

Appeals to the Court.

141.(1) A company aggrieved by the revocation by the Minister of its permit may appeal to the Court within twenty-one days or such longer period as the Court may allow after receipt of notification of such revocation.

(2) If an appeal is allowed by the Court, the company shall be entitled to engage in or carry on any trade or business in Bermuda in the same manner as it did before its permit was revoked.

(3) If an appeal is dismissed by the Court, the company shall, forthwith or in such time as the Minister may allow, cease to engage in or carry on any trade or business in Bermuda.

(4) The provisions of section 62 of the Supreme Court Act 1905 shall be deemed to extend to the making of rules under that section to regulate the practice and procedure on an appeal under this section.

Register of permit companies.

142.(1) The Registrar shall keep a register of permit companies in such form as he shall determine but which shall show -

(a) the name of the company;

(b) the principal place in Bermuda from which the company engages in or carries on any trade or business in Bermuda and the address of its registered office outside Bermuda;

(c) the date and place of its incorporation; and

(d) the date of its permit.

(2) The register shall be open to inspection by members of the public during ordinary office hours on payment of such fee not exceeding five dollars as the Minister may determine.

(3) Every permit company lawfully engaging in or carrying on any trade or business in Bermuda on the appointed day shall within one month of that day deliver to the Registrar -

(i) a copy of its memorandum or in the event of it not having a memorandum, a document setting out the objects of the company, the names of the directors and their nationalities, the trade or business it is permitted to engage in or carry on in Bermuda and the amount of its authorized and paid up share capital;

(ii) a copy of its permit;

(iii) particulars of its place or places of business in Bermuda and the address of its registered office outside Bermuda;

(iv) a list of persons resident in Bermuda authorized to accept on its behalf service of process and any notices required to be served on it.

(4) Every overseas company in receipt of a permit after the appointed day shall deliver to the Registrar such of the particulars set out in subsection (3) as it has not delivered to the Minister on its application for a permit.

(5) An alteration of any of the matters details of which are required to be delivered to the Registrar under subsection (3) shall be notified to the Registrar by every permit company within thirty days of the alteration becoming effective.

Restrictions on activities of a permit company.

143. Unless authorized this Act or by any other Act or its permit a permit company shall not -

(a) acquire or hold land in Bermuda except -

(i) land required for its business by way of lease or tenancy agreement for a term not exceeding fifty years; or

(ii) with the consent of the Minister granted in his discretion, land by way of lease or tenancy agreement for a term not exceeding twenty-one years in order to provide accommodation or recreational facilities for its officers and employees;

(b) subject to section 144 take any mortgage of land in Bermuda;

(c) acquire any bonds or debentures secured on any land in Bermuda other than bonds or debentures issued by the Government or a public authority;

(d) *Deleted*;

(e) carry on business of any kind or type whatsoever in Bermuda either alone or in partnership or otherwise except -

(i) carrying on business with persons outside Bermuda;

(ii) doing business in Bermuda with an exempted undertaking in furtherance only of the business of the permit company carried on exterior to Bermuda;

(iii) buying or selling or otherwise dealing in shares, bonds, debenture stock obligations, mortgages or other securities issued or created by an exempted undertaking, or a local company, or any partnership which is not an exempted undertaking;

(iv) transacting banking business in Bermuda with and through a bank licensed under the Banks Act 1969;

(v) effecting or concluding contracts in Bermuda, and exercising in Bermuda all other powers, so far as may be necessary for the carrying on of its business with persons outside Bermuda;

(vi) as manager or agent for, or consultant or adviser to, the business of an exempted undertaking whether or not such business is the sole business of the permit company provided that the permit company is authorised by law to carry on the kind or type of business in Bermuda;

(vii) notwithstanding the Non-Resident Insurance Undertakings Act 1967, carrying on the business of re-insuring risks undertaken by any company incorporated in Bermuda and permitted to engage in insurance and reinsurance business.

Permit company and reinsuring.

143A. Where a permit company carries on the kind or type of business specified in section 143(e)(vii) that company shall be deemed not to be a non-resident insurance undertaking.

Power of overseas and exempted companies to hold mortgages.

144.(1) Subject to subsection (2) an overseas company may hold in its corporate name a mortgage on real and personal property of every description in Bermuda in the same manner and in the same respects as a local company and shall as mortgagee have all the rights of a local company.

(2) No overseas company without the prior consent of the Minister shall take any mortgage on land in Bermuda to secure any principal sum exceeding $50,000; or whereby any such mortgage shall together with any other principal sum or sums received by any other mortgage or mortgages held by such company from the same mortgagor or mortgagors exceed the sum of $50,000:

Provided that:

(a) the Minister may withhold such consent without assigning any reason;

(b) if any overseas company enters into possession of any land in Bermuda as mortgagee it shall cause the land to be sold within five years of so entering into possession thereof, or within such further period as the Minister may from time to time sanction in any such case, and any such land which is not sold within the time hereby limited shall be liable to escheat.

(3) For the purposes of this section an exempted company shall be deemed to be an overseas company.

(4) The Minister may by rule vary the principal sum exceeding which his consent is necessary prior to the taking out of a mortgage under this section.

Records to be kept by permit company.

145. Every permit company shall keep at the principal place in Bermuda from which the company engages in or carries on any trade or business in Bermuda such records of its acts and financial affairs as will show adequately the trade or business it is engaging in or carrying on or has engaged in or carried on in Bermuda except that if the records of its acts and financial affairs are kept at some place outside Bermuda, there shall be kept at an office of the company in Bermuda such records as will enable the directors to ascertain with reasonable accuracy the financial position of the company at the end of each three month period.

Provisions relating to the enforcement of restrictions on permit companies.

146. The Minister shall have the same power to appoint an inspector to investigate the affairs of a permit company as he has under section 132 to appoint an inspector to investigate the affairs of an exempted company and subsections (2) to (12) of that section shall apply mutatis mutandis to such an investigation.

Letter heads and service of notice.

147.(1) Every permit company shall have the following particulars on all letters sent from a place of business in Bermuda in connection with its business -

(a) its name;

(b) its place of incorporation; and

(c) the principal place in Bermuda from which the company engages in or carries on any trade or business in Bermuda.

(2) Any process or notice required to be served on an overseas company shall be sufficiently served if served on any person named in the list of persons delivered to the Registrar or the Minister pursuant to paragraph (iv) of subsection (3) of section 142 or if left at a place of business notified to the Registrar or the Minister pursuant to paragraph (iii) of such subsection.

Offences.

148. Where any overseas company, whether a permit company or not, fails to comply with any provision of this Part where no other penalty is provided the company, its officers and the person who appears to the court trying the case to be in charge of its affairs in Bermuda shall be liable to a fine of one thousand dollars.

Contractors to the United States Government.

149. Nothing in this Part of this Act shall apply to a company incorporated in the United States in respect of any business carried on by that company in or in connection with the Bases as defined in the United States Bases (Agreement) Act 1952.

Effect of repeals or amendments of other enactments and savings.

150.(1) Notwithstanding the repeal or amendment of any enactment by this Act, any licence or permit granted under the Acts so repealed or amended enabling any overseas company to carry on business in or from within Bermuda shall continue to have effect according to the tenor thereof until such licence or permit is either revoked under section 139 or the company is granted a permit under this Act.

(2) This part shall be read in addition to and not in derogation of the External Companies (Jurisdiction in Actions) Act 1885.

Application of certain sections of Act to non-resident insurance undertakings.

150A. The provisions of sections 136A, 137(2) and (3), 138, 142, 144, 145, 146, 147 and 151 shall apply to non-resident insurance undertakings as if they were permit companies.

Application of No 41 of 1966 to permit companies.

151. The Exempted Undertakings Tax Protection Act 1966 shall apply to permit companies as if there were exempted companies.

PART XII

MUTUAL COMPANIES

Interpretation.

152.(1) In this Part unless the context otherwise requires -

> "mutual company" means any company, other than a company limited by shares, or other company having a share capital, whether incorporated before or after the appointed day, which is authorized to engage in or carry on as a principal object insurance or reinsurance business of all kinds on the mutual principle.

(2) For the purposes of this Part, a mutual company shall be deemed to engage in or carry on insurance or reinsurance business on the mutual principle where the members thereof who are exposed to some contingency associate themselves together by contributing by way of premiums on the basis that if the contemplated contingency befalls any member he shall receive a compensatory payment.

Mutual companies to create and maintain a reserve fund.

153.(1) A mutual company shall create and maintain a reserve fund of not less than an amount approved by the Minister in respect of such company.

(2) The memorandum of a mutual company shall in addition to the requirements of section 7 state the amount of its reserve fund.

(3) The reserve fund of a mutual company shall be treated in all respects as if it were share capital.

Liability of members on a winding up.

154.(1) Subsection (3) of section 7 shall not apply to mutual companies and the liability of a member of such a company in the event of it being wound up shall be limited to the premiums or any unpaid premiums or undischarged portion thereof due to the company on the date of the commencement of the winding up from such member.

(2) For the purposes of this section "premiums" means the premiums, including retrospective premium adjustments or calls payable for insurance issued or effected by a mutual company to, for or on behalf of each member of the company and any capital contribution or other such assessment that is due under the bye-laws or any other contractual obligation with a member of the company.

Apportionment of assets of mutual companies.

155. When a mutual company is wound up, after its liabilities have been satisfied the person carrying out the winding up shall either apportion the remaining assets in accordance with the bye-laws of the company or if there is no provision in the bye-laws for such apportionment then in such a fair and equitable manner amongst the members of the company as such person may decide.

Criteria for determining membership.

155A.(1) Subject to subsection (2), a mutual company shall in its bye-laws make provision to establish the criteria by reference to which membership in the company and eligibility therefor shall be determined.

(2) Without prejudice to the generality of subsection (1) and notwithstanding subsection (2) of section 152, the following persons shall, unless the bye-laws of the company otherwise provide, be members of a mutual company:

(a) any person who is for the time being a provisional director thereof;

(b) any person whose risks are insured, whether directly or indirectly, by the company and who has been accepted by the company as a member; or

(c) any person who provides some part of the funds necessary to establish or maintain the reserve fund of the company.

(3) For the purposes of subsection (2), the reference to a risk of a person being indirectly insured by the company is a reference to that risk being covered by the company by reinsurance through one or more intermediaries.

Provisions of Act to apply to mutual companies.

156.(1) Subject to section 4 the provisions of this Act relating to companies limited by guarantee shall apply to all mutual companies:

Provided that the Minister from time to time may by regulations declare that any provision of this Act shall not apply to mutual companies or that in its application it shall be varied in such manner as shall be set out in the regulations.

(2) Any regulations made by the Minister under subsection (1) shall be subject to affirmative resolution procedure.

(3) For the avoidance of doubt it is declared that -

(a) sections 104 to 109 apply, with the necessary changes, to mutual companies;

(b) in sections 105 to 108 references to "shares" and to "capital" shall be read as if they were references to "membership interests" and to "a reserve fund" respectively.

PART XIIA

MUTUAL FUND COMPANIES

Interpretation.

156A. In this Part, unless the context otherwise requires "mutual fund" means a company limited by shares, or other company having a share capital and incorporated for the purpose of investing the moneys of its members for their mutual benefit and having the power to redeem or purchase for cancellation its shares without reducing its authorized share capital and stating in its memorandum that it is a mutual fund.

Redemption and purchase of shares by mutual fund.

156B.(1) No shares of a mutual fund shall be redeemed or purchased by another mutual fund unless such shares are fully paid.

(2) No shares of a mutual fund shall be redeemed or purchased as aforesaid unless the respective par values of the fully paid shares which will remain outstanding after such redemption or purchase exceed in the aggregate the minimum capital prescribed by the Minister under subsection (4) of section 6.

Redemption and purchase by mutual company of its own shares.

156C.(1) A mutual fund shall, if authorized by its memorandum or bye-laws, have power to redeem or purchase for cancellation its issued shares at the option of the company or at the option, or on the request, of a member.

(2) A mutual fund, on the redemption or purchase of its own shares, may -

(a) repay the capital paid up on such shares out of paid in capital, share premium or other reserves of the company;

(b) pay the premium, if any, out of realised or unrealised profits, share premium or other reserves of the company, on such terms and in such manner and at such price as may be determined having regard to the asset value of such shares as ascertained in accordance with the bye-laws of the mutual fund.

(3) The redemption or purchase of its own shares by a mutual fund shall not be taken as reducing its authorized share capital and a mutual fund shall have power to issue shares equal in aggregate par value to the aggregate par value of the shares so redeemed or purchased as if those shares had never been issued and the issuance of such shares under the power herein contained shall not be taken as increasing the amount of its issued share capital.

(4) The power of a mutual fund referred to in subsection (3) shall be exerciseable by the directors of the mutual fund.

156D. [DELETED]

Private Act companies incorporated with certain powers deemed to be mutual funds.

156E. Every company incorporated by private Act and having the power to redeem or purchase for cancellation its issued shares at the option of, or on the request of, a member shall be deemed for the purpose of this Act to be a mutual fund.

Certain sections do not to apply to mutual fund.

156F. Sections 40, 42, 42A, 54(1)(b), 65(6) and 66 shall not apply to a mutual fund.

Provisions applicable to certain companies incorporated after appointed day.

156G. Every company incorporated after the appointed day and before the commencement of the Companies Amendment Act 1984 having the power to redeem or purchase for cancellation its issued shares or any class of shares at the option of, or on the request of, a member and which is an open-ended company (as defined in Part 11 of the Fifth Schedule) shall be deemed for the purposes of this Act to be a mutual fund and to have and always to have had the powers set out in section 156C.

Certification by the Minister of fund as United Kingdom class scheme.

156H. Subject to section 156I, upon application by a mutual fund, the Minister may, in such form as he may determine, certify that the mutual fund is, in his opinion, a United Kingdom class scheme.

Conditions to be satisfied for certification.

156I.(1) The Minister shall not certify a mutual fund in accordance with the provisions of section 156H unless he is satisfied that -

(a) the applicant is a mutual fund within the meaning of this Part;

(b) the applicant is in compliance with the provisions of this Act;

(c) the custodian of the mutual fund is a bank incorporated in Bermuda;

(d) the manager of the mutual fund is a company incorporated in Bermuda which is separate and apart from the custodian and is in compliance with the provisions of this Act;

(e) the mutual fund is fit and proper to be approved as a United Kingdom Class scheme;

(f) the bye-laws of the mutual fund comply with such requirements as are described;

(g) the members of the mutual fund are entitled to have their shares redeemed or purchased by the fund in accordance with the bye-laws of the fund;

(h) the officers, directors, manager and custodian of the mutual fund are of good standing and repute, financially sound, and have sufficient qualifications and experience to fulfill properly their respective roles; and

(i) the custodian and manager of the mutual fund are or will, upon certification, be participants in a compensation arrangement.

(2) For the purposes of this section and section 156O(2) -

"compensation arrangement" means an arrangement, approved by the Minister, in which the custodian and manager of a mutual fund are participants, providing for compensation to any member or former member of the mutual fund who has suffered loss as a result of any material breach by the custodian or manager of the fund -

(i) of the bye-laws of the fund; or

(ii) of any provision of this Act;

and where the custodian or manager, as the case may be, is or is likely to be unable otherwise to satisfy any judgment against it for such breach.

Right of member to bring action against custodian or manager for loss suffered as a result of breach of bye-laws.

156J. A member or a former member of a mutual fund certified under section 156H shall have a right of action against the custodian or manager of the fund, as the case may be, for any loss incurred by him as a result of any material breach of the bye-laws of the fund by the custodian or manager respectively; or as a result of any material breach by the custodian or manager respectively of any provision of this Act, subject to the defences applying to action for breach of statutory duty.

Power of Minister to require reclarification where fund no longer complies with statutory conditions.

156K. Where the Minister is of the opinion that any of the conditions set forth in section 156I are no longer fulfilled by a mutual fund, he shall immediately notify the mutual fund thereof and may, after affording the mutual fund an opportunity of making representation to him, require rectification thereof within such reasonable time as shall be set out in the said notice, failing which rectification as aforesaid, the Minister may revoke the certification made under section 156H, and so notify the mutual fund and the Secretary of State of the United Kingdom or his designate.

Custodian and manager required to be independent of one another.

156L. The custodian and manager of a mutual fund certified under section 156H shall in fulfilling their respective duties act independently of one another.

Manager of fund deemed to be an officer of fund.

156M. For the purposes of this Act the manager of a mutual fund certified under section 156H shall be deemed to be an officer of such fund whether or not such manager would otherwise be treated as an officer of the fund for the purposes of this Act.

Power of directors to amend bye-laws to ensure compliance with prescribed requirements.

156N.(1) Notwithstanding section 13(5), the directors of a mutual fund certified under section 156H shall have the right to amend the bye-laws of the mutual fund to the extent required to ensure continued compliance of such bye-laws with the requirements prescribed from time to time and no such amendment shall require the approval of the company in general meeting.

(2) Notwithstanding anything in this Act contained, no amendment may be made to the bye-laws of a mutual fund certified under section 156H if the effect thereof would be that the bye-laws of the mutual fund would no longer comply with such requirements as are prescribed from time to time.

Power of the Minister to direct custodian or manager of fund to furnish information.

156O.(1) For the purposes of obtaining any information which the Minister needs to ensure that the provisions of this Part are fulfilled, the Minister may direct the custodian or the manager of a mutual fund certified under section 156H to furnish him with such information in such form and manner and within such time as he may specify.

(2) The custodian and manager of a mutual fund certified under section 156H shall furnish the trustee or administrator of any compensation arrangement with such information as he may require for the proper performance of his duties as such.

Regulations.

156P.(1) The Minister may make regulations prescribing anything required or authorised to be prescribed under this Part and generally for the better carrying out of the provisions of this Part.

(2) Subject to subsection (3), the Minister shall -

(a) cause a copy of all regulations made under this Part to be available at the office of the Registrar of Companies for inspection by any interested person free of charge at any time when the office of the Registrar of Companies is open to the public;

(b) cause to be published in the Gazette a notice briefly describing the nature of any regulations made under this Part, stating the date on which such regulations may be inspected at the office of the Registrar of Companies.

(3) Section 6 of the Statutory Instruments Act 1977 shall not apply to any regulations made under this Part. The provisions of subsection (2) shall be deemed to be deposit for public inspection for the purposes of subsection (1) of section 5 of that Act.

PART XIII

WINDING UP

Modes of winding up.

157. The winding up of a company may be either by the Court or voluntary and this Act, subject to any other Act, shall be applied to the winding up of a company by either of these modes.

Liability as contributories of present and past members.

158. Subject to section 158A, in the event of a company being wound up, every present and past member shall be liable to contribute to the assets of the company to an amount sufficient for payment of its debts and liabilities, and the costs, charges and expenses of the winding up, and for the adjustment of the rights of the contributories among themselves, subject to the following qualifications -

(a) a past member shall not be liable to contribute if he has ceased to be a member for one year or upwards before the commencement of the winding up;

(b) a past member shall not be liable to contribute in respect of any debt or liability of the company contracted after he ceased to be a member;

(c) a past member shall not be liable to contribute unless it appears to the Court that the existing members are unable to satisfy the contributions required to be made by them in pursuance of this Act;

(d) in the case of a company limited by shares, subject to the special provisions relating to banks under the Banks Act 1969, no contribution shall be required from any member exceeding the amount, if any, unpaid on the shares in respect of which he is liable as a present or past member;

(e) in the case of company limited by guarantee, no contribution shall, subject to the special provisions relating to mutual companies, be required from any member exceeding the amount undertaken to be contributed by him to the assets of the company in the event of its being wound up;

(ee) in the case of an unlimited liability company there shall be no limitation on the liability of any member;

(f) nothing in this Act shall invalidate any provision contained in any policy of insurance or other contract whereby the liability of individual members on the policy or contract is restricted, or whereby the funds of the company are alone made liable in respect of the policy or contract;

(*g*) a sum due to any member of a company, in his character as a member, by way of dividends, profits or otherwise shall not be deemed to be a debt of the company payable to that member in a case of competition between himself and any other creditor not a member of the company, but any such sum may be taken into account for the purpose of the final adjustment of the rights of the contributories among themselves.

Winding up of limited company that was formerly unlimited

158A.(1) This section applies in the case of a company being wound up which was at some former time registered as unlimited but has re-registered as a company limited by shares or by guarantee under section 14B.

(2) Notwithstanding section 158(a), a past member of the company who was a member of it at the time of re-registration, if the winding up commences within the period of three years beginning on the day on which the company was re-registered, is liable to contribute to the assets of the company in respect of debts and liabilities contracted before that time.

(3) If no persons who were members of the company at that time are existing members of it, a person who at that time was a present or past member is liable to contribute as provided in subsection (2) notwithstanding that the existing members have satisfied the contributions required to be made by them under this Act.

(4) Subsection (3) applies subject to section 158(a) and to subsection (2), but notwithstanding section 158(c).

(5) Notwithstanding section 158(d) and (e), there is no limit on the amount which a person who, at that time, was a past or present member of the company is liable to contribute.

Definition and nature of liability of a contributory.

159.(1) The term "contributory" means every person liable to contribute to the assets of a company in the event of its being wound up, and for the purposes of all proceedings prior to the final determining of the persons who are to be deemed contributories, includes any person alleged to be a contributory.

(2) The liability of a contributory shall create a debt of the nature of a specialty accruing due from him at the time when his liability commenced but payable at the times when calls are made for enforcing the liability.

Contributories in a case of death or bankruptcy of a member.

160.(1) If a contributory dies either before or after he has been placed on the list of contributories, his estate representatives shall be liable in the due course of the administration to contribute to the assets of the company in discharge of his liability and shall be contributories accordingly.

(2) If the estate representatives make default in paying any money ordered to be paid by them, proceedings may be taken for administering the estate of the deceased contributory and for compelling payment thereout of the money due.

(3) If a contributory becomes bankrupt, either before or after he has been placed on the list of contributories -

(a) his trustee in bankruptcy shall represent him for all the purposes of the winding up, and shall be a contributory accordingly, and may be called on to admit to proof against the estate of the bankrupt, or otherwise allow to be paid out of his assets in due course of law, any money due from the bankrupt in respect of his liability to contribute to the estate of the company; and

(b) there may be proved against the estate of the bankrupt the estimated value of his liability to future calls as well as calls already made.

Circumstances in which a company may be wound up by the Court.

161. In addition to any other provision in this or any other Act prescribing for the winding up of a company a company may be wound up by the Court if -

(a) the company has by resolution resolved that the company be wound up by the Court;

(b) subject to section 88 default is made in holding the statutory meeting or failing to comply with section 84 or section 89;

(c) the company does not commence its business within a year of its incorporation or suspends its business for a whole year;

(d) the company engages in a prohibited business activity in contravention of section 4B;

(e) the company is unable to pay its debts;

(f) the consent by the Minister for the registration of the company, where such consent was required, was obtained as a result of a material mis-statement in the application for consent; or

(g) the Court is of the opinion that it is just and equitable that the company should be wound up.

Definition of inability to pay debts.

162. A company shall be deemed to be unable to pay its debts -

(a) if a creditor, by assignment or otherwise, to whom the company is indebted in a sum exceeding five hundred dollars then due has served on the company, by leaving it at the registered office of the company, a demand under his hand requiring the company to pay the sum so due and the company has for three weeks thereafter neglected to pay the sum or to secure or compound for it to the reasonable satisfaction of the creditor; or

(b) if the execution or other process issued on a judgment, decree or order of any court in favour of a creditor of the company is returned unsatisfied in whole or in part; or

(c) if it is proved to the satisfaction of the Court that the company is unable to pay its debts; in determining whether a company is unable to pay its debts, the Court shall take into account the contingent and prospective liabilities of the company.

Provisions as to applications for winding up.

163.(1) An application to the Court for the winding up of a company shall be by petition, presented either by the company or by any creditor or creditors, including any contingent or prospective creditor or creditors, contributory or contributories, or by all of those parties, together or separately:

Provided that -

(a) a contributory shall not be entitled to present a winding up petition unless the shares in respect of which he is a contributory, or some of them, either were allotted to him or have been held by him and registered in his name, for at least six months during the eighteen months before the commencement of the winding up, or have devolved on him through the death of a former holder; and

(b) a winding up petition shall not, if the ground of the petition is default in holding the statutory meeting, be presented by any person except a member, nor before the expiration of fourteen days after the last day on which the meeting ought to have been held; and

(c) the Court shall not give a hearing to a winding up petition presented by a contingent or prospective creditor until such security for costs has been given as the Court thinks reasonable and until a prima facie case for winding up has been established to the satisfaction of the Court; and

(d) in a case falling within paragraph (g) of section 161 the winding up petition may be presented by the Registrar.

(2) When a company is being wound up voluntarily a winding up petition may be presented by the Official Receiver as well as by any other person authorized in that behalf under this section, but the Court shall not make a winding up order on the petition unless is it satisfied that the voluntary winding up cannot be continued with due regard to the interest of the creditors or contributories.

(3) Where the petition is presented on the ground that a material mis-statement was made in the application for the consent of the registration of the company the Court shall not make a winding up order unless it is satisfied -

(a) that but for the mis-statement the consent of the Minister would not have been given; and

(b) that an order winding up the company will not cause hardship to any person who was not responsible for the mis-statement.

(4) Where the petition is presented on the ground that a material mis-statement was made in the application for the consent for the registration of the company the Court, if it finds that a material mis-statement was made, whether it makes an order winding up the company or not, may -

(a) impose on the company a fine of two thousand dollars; and

(b) require the company to pay the costs of the proceedings.

Powers of Court on hearing petition.

164.(1) On hearing a winding up petition the Court may dismiss it, or adjourn the hearing conditionally or unconditionally, or make any interim order, or any other order that it thinks fit, but the Court shall not refuse to make a winding up order on the ground only that the assets of the company have been mortgaged to an amount equal to or in excess of those assets or that the company has no assets.

(2) Where the petition is presented by members of the company as contributories on the ground that it is just and equitable that the company should be wound up, the Court, if it is of the opinion, -

(a) that the petitioners are entitled to relief either by winding up the company or by some other means; and

(b) that in the absence of any other remedy it would be just and equitable that the company should be wound up, shall make a winding up order, unless it is also of the opinion both that some other remedy is available to the petitioners and that they are acting unreasonably in seeking to have the company wound up instead of pursuing that other remedy.

(3) Where the petition is presented on the ground of default in holding the statutory meeting the Court may -

(a) instead of making a winding up order, direct that a meeting shall be held; and

(b) order the costs to be paid by any person who, in the opinion of the Court, is responsible for the default.

Powers to stay or restrain proceedings against a company.

165.(1) At any time after the presentation of a winding up petition, and before a winding up order has been made, the company or any creditor or contributory may, where an action or proceeding against the company is pending, apply to the Court for a stay of those proceedings.

(2) On an application being made under subsection (1) the Court may stay the proceedings accordingly on such terms as it thinks fit.

Avoidance of dispositions of property etc. after commencement of winding up.

166.(1) In a winding up by the Court, any disposition of the property of the company, including things in action, and any transfer of shares, or alteration in the status of the members of the company, made after the commencement of the winding up, shall, unless the Court otherwise orders, be void.

(2) Where any company is being wound up by the Court, any attachment, sequestration, distress or execution put in force against the estate or effects of the company after the commencement of the winding up shall be void to all intents.

Commencement of winding up by the Court.

167.(1) Where, before the presentation of a petition for the winding up of a company by the Court, a resolution has been passed by the company for voluntary winding up, the winding up of the company shall be deemed to have commenced at the time of the passing of the resolution, and unless the Court, on proof of fraud or mistake, thinks fit otherwise to direct, all proceedings taken in the voluntary winding up shall be deemed to have been validly taken.

(2) In any other case, the winding up of a company by the Court shall be deemed to commence at the time of the presentation of the petition for the winding up.

(3) On the making of a winding up order, a copy of the order must forthwith be forwarded by the company to the Registrar, who shall make a minute thereof in his books relating to the company.

(4) When a winding up order has been made or a provisional liquidator has been appointed, no action or proceeding shall be proceeded with or commenced against the company except by leave of the Court and subject to such terms as the Court may impose.

(5) An order for winding up a company shall operate in favour of all the creditors and of all the contributories of the company as if made on the joint petition of a of a creditor and of a contributory.

Statement of company affairs to be submitted to Official Receiver.

168.(1) Where the Court has made a winding up order or appointed a provisional liquidator, there shall, unless the Court thinks fit to order otherwise and so orders, be made out and submitted to the Official Receiver a statement as to the affairs of the company in the prescribed form, verified by affidavit, and showing the particulars of its assets, debts and liabilities, the names, residences and occupations of its creditors, the securities held by them respectively, the dates when the securities were respectively given, and such further or other information as may be prescribed or as the Official Receiver may require.

(2) The statement shall be submitted and verified by one or more of the persons who are at the relevant date the directors and by the person who is at that date the secretary of the company, or by such of the persons hereinafter in this subsection mentioned as the Official Receiver, subject to the direction of the Court, may require to submit and verify the statement, that is to say, persons -

(a) who are or have been officers of the company;

(b) who have taken part in the formation of the company at any time within one year before the relevant date;

(c) who are in the employment of the company, or have been in the employment of the company within the said year, and are in the opinion of the Official Receiver capable of giving the information required;

(d) who are or have been within the said year officers of or in the employment of a company which is, or within the said year was, an officer of the company to which the statement relates.

(3) The statement shall be submitted within thirty days from the relevant date or within such extended time as the Official Receiver or the Court may for special reasons appoint.

(4) Any person making or concurring in making the statement and affidavit required by this section shall be allowed, and shall be paid by the Official Receiver or provisional liquidator, as the case may be, out of the assets of the company such costs and expenses, incurred in and about the preparation and making of the statement and affidavit, as the Official Receiver may consider reasonable, subject to an appeal to the Court.

(5) If any person, without reasonable excuse, makes default in complying with the requirements of this section, he shall be liable to a default fine.

(6) Any person stating himself in writing to be a creditor or contributory of the company shall be entitled by himself or by his agent at all reasonable times, on payment of the prescribed fee, to inspect the statement submitted in pursuance of this section and a copy thereof or extract therefrom.

(7) Any person falsely stating himself to be a creditor or contributory shall be liable to a fine of one thousand dollars or imprisonment for a period of six months or both such fine and imprisonment.

(8) In this section the expression "the relevant date" means, in a case where a provisional liquidator is appointed, the date of his appointment and, in a case where no such appointment is made, the date of the winding up order.

Report by Official Receiver.

169.(1) In a case where a winding-up order is made, the Official Receiver shall, as soon as practicable after receipt of the statement to be submitted under the last foregoing section, or, in a case where the Court orders that no statement shall be submitted, as soon as practicable after the date of the order, submit a preliminary report to the Court -

(a) as to the amount of capital issued, subscribed and paid up, and the estimated amount of assets and liabilities; and

(b) if the company has failed, as to the causes of the failure; and

(c) whether in his opinion further inquiry is desirable as to any matter relating to the promotion, formation or failure of the company or the conduct of the business thereof.

(2) The Official Receiver may also, if he thinks fit, make a further report, or further reports, stating the manner in which the company was formed and whether in his opinion any fraud has been committed by any person in its promotion or formation or by any officer of the company in relation to the company since the formation thereof, and any other matters which in his opinion it is desirable to bring to the notice of the Court.

(3) If the Official Receiver states in any such further report as aforesaid that in his opinion a fraud has been committed as aforesaid, the Court shall have the further powers provided in section 196.

Power of Court to appoint liquidators.

170.(1) For the purpose of conducting proceedings in winding up a company and performing such duties in reference thereto as the Court may impose, the Court may appoint a liquidator or liquidators.

(2) The Court may on the presentation of a winding up petition or at any time thereafter and before the first appointment of a liquidator appoint a provisional liquidator who may be the Official Receiver or any other fit person.

(3) When the Court appoints a provisional liquidator, the Court may limit his powers by the order appointing him.

Provisions relating to the appointment of liquidators.

171. The following provisions with respect to liquidators shall have effect on a winding-up order being made -

(*a*) if the Court has appointed no other provisional liquidator prior to the winding up order being made the Official Receiver shall become the provisional liquidator and he or the provisional liquidator appointed by the Court shall continue to act as provisional liquidator until another person becomes liquidator and is capable of acting as such;

(*b*) the provisional liquidator shall summon separate meetings of the creditors and contributories of the company for the purpose of determining whether or not an application is to be made to the Court for appointing a liquidator in the place of the provisional liquidator;

(*c*) the Court may make any appointment and order required to give effect to any such determination and, if there is a difference between the determinations of the meetings of the creditors and contributories in respect of the matter aforesaid, the Court shall decide the difference and make such order thereon as it thinks fit;

(*d*) in a case where a liquidator is not appointed by the Court, the Official Receiver shall be the liquidator of the company;

(*e*) the Official Receiver shall be the liquidator during any vacancy;

(*f*) a liquidator shall be described when a person other than the Official Receiver is liquidator, by the style of "the liquidator", and, where the Official Receiver is liquidator, by the style of "the Official Receiver and liquidator", of the particular company in respect of which he is appointed and not by his individual name.

Provisions where person other than Official Receiver is appointed liquidator.

172. Where, in the winding up of a company by the Court, a person other than the Official Receiver is appointed liquidator, that person -

(*a*) shall not be capable of acting as liquidator until he has notified his appointment to the Registrar and given security in the prescribed manner to the satisfaction of the Registrar; and

(*b*) shall give the Official Receiver such information and such access to and facilities for inspecting the books and documents of the company and generally such aid as may be requisite for enabling that officer to perform his duties under this Act.

General provisions as to liquidators.

173.(1) A liquidator appointed by the Court may resign or, on cause shown, be removed by the Court.

(2) Where a person other than the Official Receiver is appointed liquidator, he shall receive such salary or remuneration by way of percentage or otherwise as the Court may direct, and, if more persons than one are appointed liquidators, their remuneration shall be distributed among them in such proportion as the Court directs.

(3) A vacancy in the office of a liquidator appointed by the Court shall be filled by the Court.

(4) If more than one liquidator is appointed by the Court, the Court shall declare whether any act by this Act required or authorized to be done by the liquidator is to be done by all or any one or more of the persons appointed.

(5) Subject to section 249, the acts of a liquidator shall be valid notwithstanding any defects that may afterwards be discovered in his appointment or qualifications.

Custody and vesting of company's property.

174.(1) Where a winding up order has been made or where a provisional liquidator has been appointed, the liquidator or the provisional liquidator, as the case may be, shall take into his custody or under his control all the property and things in action to which the company is or appears to be entitled.

(2) Where a company is being wound up by the Court, the Court may on the application of the liquidator by order direct that all or any part of the property of whatsoever description belonging to the company or held by trustees on its behalf shall vest in the liquidator by his official name, and thereupon the property to which the order relates shall vest accordingly, and the liquidator may, after giving such indemnity, if any, as the Court may direct, bring or defend in his official name any action or other legal proceeding which relates to that property or which it is necessary to bring or defend for the purpose of effectually winding up the company and recovering its property.

Powers of liquidator.

175.(1) The liquidator in a winding-up by the Court shall have power, with the sanction either of the Court or of the committee of inspection -

(a) to bring or defend any action or other legal proceeding in the name and on behalf of the company;

(b) to carry on the business of the company so far as may be necessary for the beneficial winding up thereof;

(c) to appoint an attorney to assist him in the performance of his duties;

(d) to pay any classes of creditors in full;

(e) to make any compromise or arrangement with creditors or persons claiming to be creditors or having or alleging themselves to have any claim, present or future, certain or contingent ascertained or sounding only in damages against the company, or whereby the company may be rendered liable;

(f) to compromise all calls and liabilities to calls, debts and liabilities capable of resulting in debts, and all claims, present or future, certain or contingent, ascertained or sounding only in damages, subsisting or supposed to subsist between the company and a contributory or alleged contributory or other debtor or person apprehending liability to the company, and all questions in any way relating to or affecting the assets of the winding up of the company, on such terms as may be agreed, and take any security for the discharge of any such call, debt, liability or claim and give a complete discharge in respect thereof.

(2) The liquidator in a winding up by the Court shall have power -

(a) to sell the real and personal property and things in action of the company by public auction or private contract, with power to transfer the whole thereof to any person or to sell the same in parcels;

(b) to do all acts and to execute, in the name and on behalf of the company, all deeds, receipts and other documents, and for that purpose to use, when necessary, the company's seal;

(c) to prove, rank and claim in the bankruptcy, insolvency or sequestration of any contributory for any balance against his estate, and to receive dividends in the bankruptcy, insolvency or sequestration in respect of that balance, as a separate debt due from the bankrupt or insolvent, and rateably with the other separate creditors;

(d) to draw, accept, make and endorse any bill of exchange or promissory note in the name and on behalf of the company, with the same effect with respect to the liability of the company as if the bill or note had been drawn, accepted, made or endorsed by or on behalf of the company in the course of its business;

(e) to raise on the security of the assets of the company any money required;

(f) to take out in his official name letters of administration to any deceased

contributory and to do in his official name any other act necessary for obtaining payment of any money due from a contributory or his estate which cannot be conveniently done in the name of the company, and in all such cases the money due shall, for the purpose of enabling the liquidator to take out the letters of administration or recover the money, he deemed to be due to the liquidator himself;

(g) to appoint an agent to do any business which the liquidator is unable to do himself;

(h) to do all such other things as may be necessary for winding up the affairs of the company and distributing its assets.

(3) The exercise by the liquidator in a winding up by the Court of the powers conferred by this section shall be subject to the control of the Court, and any creditor or contributory may apply to the Court with respect to any exercise or proposed exercise of any of those powers.

Exercise and control of liquidator's powers.

176.(1) Subject to this Act, the liquidator of a company which is being wound up by the Court shall, in the administration of the assets of the company and in the distribution thereof among its creditors, have regard to any directions that may be given by resolution of the creditors or contributories at any general meeting or by the committee of inspection, and any directions given by the creditors or contributories at any general meeting shall in case of conflict be deemed to override any directions given by the committee of inspection.

(2) The liquidator may summon general meetings of the creditors or contributories for the purpose of ascertaining their wishes, and it shall be his duty to summon meetings at such times as the creditors or contributories, by resolution, either at the meeting appointing the liquidator or otherwise, may direct, or whenever requested in writing to do so by one-tenth in value of the creditors or contributories as the case may be.

(3) The liquidator may apply to the Court in manner prescribed for directions in relation to any particular matter arising under the winding up.

(4) Subject to this Act, the liquidator shall use his own discretion in the management of the estate and its distribution among the creditors.

(5) If any person is dissatisfied by any act, omission or decision of the liquidator, that person may apply to the Court, and the Court may confirm, reverse or modify the act or decision complained of, and may give such directions or make such order in the premises as it thinks just.

Books to be kept by liquidator.

177. Every liquidator of a company which is being wound up by the Court shall keep, in the manner prescribed, proper books in which he shall cause to be made entries or minutes of proceedings at meetings, and of such other matters as may be prescribed, and any creditor or contributory may, subject to the control of the Court, personally or by his agent inspect any such books.

Release of liquidators.

178.(1) When the liquidator of a company which is being wound up by the Court has realized all the property of the company or as much thereof as can, in his opinion, be realized without needlessly protracting the liquidation and has distributed a final dividend, if any, to the creditors and has adjusted the rights of the contributories among themselves, and made a final return, if any, to the contributories, or has resigned, or has been removed from his office, the Court shall on his application and on his complying with all its requirements after hearing any objection that may be urged by any creditor, contributory or person interested against the release of the liquidator either release or withhold his release.

(2) An appeal shall lie to the Court of Appeal against a decision withholding the release of a liquidator under subsection (1).

Receipts by liquidators.

179.(1) Every liquidator of a company which is being wound up by the Court shall deal with the money received by him in such manner as the Court shall direct.

(2) If any liquidator at any time retains for more than thirty days a sum exceeding five thousand dollars after he has received directions of the Court as to how he is to deal with the money, he shall pay interest on the sum so retained at the statutory rate of interest fixed under the Interest and Credit Charges (Regulation) Act 1975 unless the Court otherwise orders.

(3) A liquidator of a company which is being wound up by the Court shall not pay any sums received by him as liquidator into his private banking account.

Audit of liquidators' accounts.

180. Every liquidator of a company which is being wound up by the Court shall at such times as the Court shall direct send to the Court audited accounts of his receipts and payments as liquidator.

Meetings of creditors and contributories to determine whether committee of inspection shall be appointed.

181.(1) When a winding-up order has been made by the Court, it shall be the business of the separate meetings of the creditors and contributories summoned for the purpose of determining whether or not an application should be made to the Court for appointing a liquidator in place of the Official Receiver to determine further whether or not an application is to be made to the Court for the appointment of a committee of inspection to act with the liquidator and who are to be members of the committee if appointed.

(2) The Court may make any appointment and order required to give effect to any such determination, and if there is a difference between the determinations of the meetings of the creditors and contributories in respect of the matters aforesaid the Court shall decide the difference and make such order thereon as the Court may think fit.

Constitution and proceedings of committee of inspection.

182.(1) A committee of inspection appointed in pursuance of this Act shall consist of creditors and contributories to the company or persons holding general powers of attorney from creditors or contributories in such proportions as may be agreed upon by the meetings of creditors and contributories or as, in case of difference, may be determined by the Court.

(2) The Committee shall meet at such times as it shall from time to time determine and the liquidator and any member of the committee may also call a meeting of the committee as and when either of them consider it necessary.

(3) The committee may act by a majority of their members present at a meeting but shall not act unless a majority of the committee are present.

(4) A member of the committee may resign by notice in writing signed by him and delivered to the liquidator.

(5) If a member of the committee becomes bankrupt or compounds or arranges with his creditors or is absent from five consecutive meetings of the committee without the leave of those members who together with himself represent the creditors or contributories, as the case may be, his office shall thereupon become vacant.

(6) A member of the committee may be removed by an ordinary resolution at a meeting of creditors, if he represents creditors, or of contributories, if he represents contributories of which seven days notice has been given stating the object of the meeting.

(7) On a vacancy occurring in the committee the liquidator shall forthwith summon a meeting of creditors or of contributories, as the case may require, to fill the vacancy, and the meeting may, by resolution, reappoint the same or appoint another creditor or contributory to fill the vacancy:

Provided that if the liquidator, having regard to the position in the winding up, is of the opinion that it is unnecessary for the vacancy to be filled he may apply to the Court and the Court may make an order that the vacancy shall not be filled, or shall not be filled except in such circumstances as may be specified in the order.

(8) The continuing members of the committee, if not less than two, may act notwithstanding any vacancy in the committee.

Powers of Registrar where no committee of inspection.

183. Where in the case of a winding up there is no committee of inspection, the Registrar may, on the application of the liquidator, do any act or thing or give any direction or permission which is by this Act authorized or required to be done or given by a committee.

Power to stay winding up.

184.(1) The Court may at any time after an order for winding up on the application either of the liquidator or the Official Receiver or any creditor or contributory and on proof to the satisfaction of the Court that all proceedings in relation to the winding up ought to be stayed, make an order staying the proceedings, either altogether or for a limited time, on such terms and conditions as the Court thinks fit.

(2) Where the Court makes an order staying the proceedings altogether it may on hearing the liquidator, the Official Receiver, if he desires to be heard, and the interested creditors or contributories make such orders it considers desirable to enable the company to be as near as practicable as it was before the winding-up order was made.

(3) On any application under this section the Court may, before making an order, require the Official Receiver to furnish to the Court a report with respect to any facts or matters which are in his opinion relevant to the application.

(4) A copy of every order made under this section shall forthwith be forwarded by the company, or otherwise as may be prescribed, to the Registrar, who shall make a minute of the order in his books relating to the company.

Settlement of list of contributories and application of assets.

185.(1) As soon as may be after making a winding-up order, the Court shall settle a list of contributories with power to rectify the register of members in all cases where rectification is required in pursuance of this Act, and shall cause the assets of the company to be collected and applied in discharge of its liabilities:

Provided that, where it appears to the Court that it will not be necessary to make calls on or adjust the rights of the contributories, the Court may dispense with the settlement of a list of contributories.

(2) In settling the list of contributories the Court shall distinguish between persons who are contributories in their own right and persons who are contributories as being representatives or liable for the debts of others.

Delivery of property to liquidator.

186. The Court may, at any time after making a winding-up order, require any contributory for the time being on list of contributories and any trustee, receiver, banker, agent or officer of the company to pay, deliver, convey, surrender or transfer forthwith, or within such time as the Court directs, to the liquidator any money, property or books and papers in his hands to which the company is prima facie entitled.

Payment of debts due by contributory to company and extent to which set-off allowed.

187.(1) The Court may, at any time after making a winding-up order make an order on any contributory for the time being on the list of contributories to pay, in manner directed by the order, any money due from him or from the estate of the person whom he represents to the company, exclusive of any money payable by him or the estate by virtue of any call in pursuance of this Act.

(2) In the case of any company when all the creditors are paid in full, any money due on any account whatever to a contributory from the company may be allowed to him by way of set-off against any subsequent call.

Power of Court to make calls.

188.(1) The Court may, at any time after making a winding-up order, and either before or after it has ascertained the sufficiency of the assets of the company to make calls on all or any of the contributories for the time being settled on the list of the contributories to the extent of their liability, for the payment of any money which the Court considers necessary to satisfy the debts and liabilities of the company, and the costs, charges and expenses of winding up, and for the adjustment of the rights of the contributories among themselves, and make an order for payment of any calls so made.

(2) In making a call the Court may take into consideration the probability that some of the contributories may partly or wholly fail to pay the call.

Order on contributory conclusive evidence.

189.(1) An order made by the Court on a contributory shall, subject to any right of appeal, be conclusive evidence that the money, if any, thereby appearing to be due or ordered to be paid is due.

(2) All other pertinent matters stated in the order shall be taken to be truly stated as against all persons and in all proceedings.

Appointment of special manager.

190.(1) Where in proceedings the Official Receiver becomes the liquidator of a company, whether provisionally or otherwise, he may, if satisfied that the nature of the estate of business of the company, or the interests of the creditors or contributories generally, require the appointment of a special manager of the estate or business of the company other than himself, apply to the Court, and the Court may on such application appoint a special manager of the said estate or business to act during such time as the Court may direct, with such powers, including any of the powers of a receiver or manager, as may be entrusted to him by the Court.

(2) The special manager shall give such security and account in such manner as the Court shall direct.

(3) The special manager shall receive such remuneration as may be fixed by the Court.

Power to exclude creditors not proving in time.

191. The Court may fix a time or times within which creditors are to prove their debts or claims or be excluded from the benefit of any distribution made before those debts are proved.

Adjustment of rights of contributories.

192. The Court shall adjust the rights of the contributories among themselves and distribute any surplus among the persons entitled thereto.

Inspection of books by creditors and contributories.

193.(1) The Court may, at any time after making a winding up order, make such order for inspection of the books and papers of the company by creditors and contributories as the Court thinks just, and any books and papers in the possession of the company may be inspected by creditors or contributories accordingly, but not further or otherwise.

(2) Nothing in this section shall be taken as excluding or restricting any statutory rights of a government department or person acting under the authority of a government department.

Power to order costs of winding up to be made out of assets.

194. The Court may, in the event of the assets being insufficient to satisfy the liabilities, make an order as to the payment out of the assets of the costs, charges and expenses incurred in the winding up in such order of priority as the Court thinks just.

Power to summon persons suspected of having property of company etc.

195.(1) The Court may, at any time after the appointment of a provisional liquidator or the making of a winding up order, summon before it any officer of the company or persons known or suspected to have in his possession any property of the company or supposed to be indebted to the company, or any person whom the Court deems capable of giving information concerning the promotion, formation, trade, dealings, affairs or property of the company.

(2) The Court may examine such person on oath, concerning the matters aforesaid, either by word of mouth or on written interrogatories, and may reduce his answers to writing and require him to sign them.

(3) The Court may require such person to produce any books and papers in his custody or power relating to the company, but, where he claims any lien on books or papers produced by him, the production shall be without prejudice to that lien, and the Court shall have jurisdiction in the winding up to determine all questions relating to that lien.

(4) If any person so summoned, after being tendered a reasonable sum for his expenses, refuses to come before the Court at the time appointed, not having a lawful excuse, made known to the Court at the time of its sitting and allowed by it, the Court may cause him to be apprehended and brought before the Court for examination.

Power to order public examination of promoter and officer.

196.(1) Where an order has been made for winding up a company by the Court the Official Receiver may make a report under this Act stating that in his opinion any person in the promotion or formation of the company or any officer of the company since its formation has been guilty of fraud or dishonesty or has been in default in complying with the provisions of the law relating to companies or has shown himself to have acted in an improper, reckless or incompetent manner in relation to the company's affairs.

(2) Where a report is made to the Court under subsection (1) the Court may, after consideration of the Official Receiver's report, direct that the person or officer referred to in the report shall attend before the Court on a day appointed for that purpose and be publicly examined as to his conduct in relation to the company.

(3) The Official Receiver shall take part in the examination either in person or by attorney.

(4) The liquidator, where the Official Receiver is not the liquidator, and any creditor or contributory may also take part in the examination either personally or by attorney.

(5) The Court may put such questions to the person examined as the Court thinks fit.

(6) The person examined shall be examined on oath and shall answer all such questions as the Court may put or allow to be put to him.

(7) A person ordered to be examined under this section shall at his own cost, before his examination, be furnished with a copy of the Official Receiver's report, and may at his own cost employ an attorney who shall be at liberty to put to him such questions as the Court may deem just for the purpose of enabling him to explain or qualify any answers given by him:

Provided that, if any such person applies to the Court to be exculpated from any charges made or suggested against him, it shall be the duty of the Official Receiver to appear on the hearing of the application and call the attention of the Court to any matters which appear to the Official Receiver to be relevant, and if the Court, after hearing any evidence given or witnesses called by the Official Receiver, grants the application, the Court may allow the applicant such costs as in its discretion it may think fit.

(8) Notes of the examination shall be taken down in writing, and shall be read over to or by, and signed by, the person examined, and may thereafter be used in evidence against him, and shall be open to the inspection of any creditor or contributory at all reasonable times.

(9) An examination under this section, may if the Court so directs, be held by any person appointed by the Court for that purpose. Such person shall have all the powers of the Court in conducting such examination.

Power to arrest absconding contributory.

197. The Court, at any time either before or after making a winding-up order, on proof of probable cause for believing that a contributory is about to quit Bermuda or otherwise to abscond or to remove or conceal any of his property for the purpose of evading payment of calls or of avoiding examination respecting the affairs of the company, may cause the contributory to be arrested and his books and papers and movable personal property to be seized and him and them to be safely kept until such time as the Court may order.

Powers of Court cumulative.

198. Any powers by this Act conferred on the Court shall be in addition to and not in restriction of any existing powers of instituting proceedings against any contributory or debtor of the company or the estate of any contributory or debtor, for the recovery of any call or other sums.

Delegation to liquidator of certain powers of the Court.

199.(1) The Chief Justice may make rules enabling all or any of the powers and duties conferred or imposed on the Court by this Act in respect of the following matters -

(a) the holding and conducting of meetings to ascertain the wishes of creditors and contributories;

(b) the settling of lists of contributories and the rectifying of the register of members where required, and the collecting and applying of the assets;

(c) the paying, delivery, conveyance, surrender or transfer of money, property, books or papers to the liquidator;

(d) the making of calls;

(e) the fixing of a time within which debts and claims must be proved, to be exercised or performed by the liquidator as an officer of the Court, and subject to the control of the Court:

Provided that the liquidator shall not, without the special leave of the Court, rectify the register of members, and shall not make any call without either the special leave of the Court or the sanction of the committee of inspection.

(2) Rules made under subsection (1) shall not be subject to Parliamentary scrutiny by virtue of section 6 of the Statutory Instruments Act 1977.

Early dissolution.

199A.(1) This section applies where an order for the winding up of a company has been made by the Court.

(2) The Official Receiver, if -

(a) he is the liquidator of the company, and

(b) it appears to him -

(i) that the realisable assets of the company are insufficient to cover the expenses of the winding up; and

(ii) that the affairs of the company do not require any further investigation, may at any time apply to the Registrar for the early dissolution of the company.

(3) Before making that application, the Official Receiver shall give not less than twenty-eight days' notice of his intention to do so to the company's creditors and contributories and, if there is a receiver of the company, to that receiver.

(4) With the giving of that notice the Official Receiver ceases (subject to any directions under section 199B) to be required to perform any duties imposed on him in relation to the company, its creditors or contributories by virtue of any provision of this Act, apart from a duty to make an application under subsection (2).

(5) On the receipt of the Official Receiver's application under subsection (2) the Registrar shall forthwith register it and, at the end of the period of three months beginning with the day of the registration of the application, the company shall be dissolved; however, the Minister may, on the application of the Official Receiver or any other person who appears to the Minister to be interested, give directions under section 199B at any time before the end of that period.

Consequences of notice under section 199A.

199B.(1) Where a notice has been given under section 199A(3), the Official Receiver or any creditor of or contributory to the company or the receiver of the company (if there is one) may apply to the Minister for directions under this section.

(2) The grounds on which that application may be made are -

(a) that the realisable assets of the company are sufficient to cover the expenses of the winding up;

(b) that the affairs of the company do require further investigation; or

(c) that for any other reason the early dissolution of the company is inappropriate.

(3) Directions under this section -

(a) are directions making such provision as the Minister thinks fit for enabling the winding up of the company to proceed as if no notice had been given under section 199A(3), and

(b) may, in the case of an application under section 199A(5), include a direction deferring the date at which the dissolution of the company is to take effect for such period as the Minister thinks fit.

(4) An appeal to the Court lies from any decision of the Minister on an application for directions under this section.

(5) It is the duty of the person on whose application any directions are given under this section, or in whose favour an appeal with respect to an application for such directions is determined, within seven days after the giving of the directions or the determination of the appeal, to deliver to the Registrar for registration such a copy of the directions or determination as is prescribed.

(6) If a person without reasonable excuse fails to deliver a copy as required by subsection (5), he is liable to a fine of two hundred and fifty dollars and, for continued contravention, to a daily default fine.

Dissolution of company.

200.(1) When the affairs of a company have been completely wound up, the Court, if the liquidator makes an application in that behalf, shall make an order that the company be dissolved from the date of the order, and the company shall be dissolved accordingly.

(2) A copy of the order shall within fourteen days from the date thereof be forwarded by the liquidator to the Registrar who shall make in his books a minute of the dissolution of the company.

(3) If the liquidator makes default in complying with the requirements of this section, he shall be liable to a default fine.

Circumstances in which a company may be wound up voluntarily.

201. A company may be wound up voluntarily -

(a) when the company resolves in general meeting that the company be wound up voluntarily; or

(b) pursuant to section 201A.

Appointment of liquidator and dissolution of company of limited duration.

201A.(1) A company shall be wound up voluntarily upon the expiration of the period fixed for the duration of the company by its incorporating Act or its memorandum or upon the occurrence of the event on the occurrence of which its incorporating Act or its memorandum provides that the company is to be dissolved and thereafter the company shall be dissolved in accordance with this Part.

(2) Where a company is being wound up pursuant to subsection (1) -

(a) references in this Part to the resolution for voluntary winding up shall be deemed to be references to the expiration of the period, or the occurrence of the event, referred to in subsection (1);

(b) section 216(1) shall be read as requiring the meeting of the creditors of the company to be summoned within thirty days of the expiration of the period, or the occurrence of the event, referred to in subsection (1);

(c) sections 208(1), 216(5) and 230 shall not apply to the company.

(3) Subject to section 227, where a company is being wound up pursuant to subsection (1) by way of members' voluntary winding up, within ninety days after the expiration of the period, or the occurrence of the event, referred to in that subsection the members of the company shall appoint one or more liquidators for the purpose of winding up the affairs, and distributing the assets, of the company, and may fix their remuneration, and in the absence of such an appointment within that time period, the Official Receiver shall be the liquidator.

(4) Where a company is being wound up pursuant to subsection (1) by way of a creditor's voluntary winding up and no liquidator has been appointed within ninety days after the expiration of the period, or the occurrence of the event, referred to in subsection (1), the Official Receiver shall be the liquidator.

Notice of resolution to wind up voluntarily.

202.(1) Where a company is being wound up voluntarily, then within twenty-one days after -

(a) the expiration of the period fixed for the duration of the company by its incorporating Act or memorandum;

(b) the occurrence of the event, on the occurrence of which the incorporating Act or memorandum provides that the company is to be dissolved; or

(c) the passing of the resolution that the company be wound up voluntarily, the company shall give notice thereof by advertisement in an appointed newspaper.

(2) If default is made in complying with this section, the company and every officer of the company shall be liable to a default fine. For the purpose of this section the liquidator of the company shall be deemed to be an officer of the company.

Commencement of voluntary winding up.

203. A voluntary winding up shall be deemed to commence -

(a) on the expiration of the period, if any, fixed in the incorporating Act or the memorandum for the duration of a company;

(b) on the occurrence of the event, if any, on the occurrence of which it is provided in the incorporating Act or the memorandum that a company is to be dissolved; or

(c) at the time of the passing of the resolution for voluntary winding up.

Effect of voluntary winding up on business and status of company.

204. In case of a voluntary winding up, the company shall, from the commencement of the winding up, cease to carry on its business, except so far as may be required for the beneficial winding up thereof.

Provided that the corporate state and corporate powers of the company shall, notwithstanding any thing to the contrary in its memorandum or bye-laws, continue until it is dissolved.

Avoidance of transfers etc. after commencement of voluntary winding up.

205. Any transfer of shares, not being a transfer made to or with the sanction of the liquidator, and any alteration in the status of the members of the company, made after the commencement of a voluntary winding up shall be void.

Statutory declaration of solvency in case of proposal to wind up voluntarily.

206.(1) Where it is proposed to wind up a company voluntarily, the majority of the directors, shall each make a statutory declaration to the effect that they have formed the opinion that the company will be able to pay its debts in full within such period not exceeding twelve months from the commencement of the winding up as may be specified in the declaration.

(2) A declaration made as aforesaid shall have no effect for the purposes of this Act unless -

(a) it is made within five weeks immediately preceding -

(i) the expiration of the period, if any, fixed in the incorporating Act or the memorandum for the duration of the company;

(ii) the occurrence of the event, if any, on the occurrence of which it is provided in the incorporating Act or the memorandum that the company is to be dissolved; or

and is delivered to the Registrar for registration before that date.

(b) it embodies either -

(i) a statement of the company's assets and liabilities as at the latest practicable date before the making of the declaration; or

(ii) statement to the effect that the opinion of the directors was based on an indemnity, undertaking or pledge made in favour of the company in respect of its liabilities.

(3) Any director of a company making a declaration under this section without having any reasonable grounds for the opinion that the company will be able to pay its debts in full within the period specified in the declaration, shall be liable to imprisonment for a period of six months or to a fine of two thousand five hundred dollars or to both; and if the company is wound up in pursuance of a resolution passed within the period of five weeks after the making of the declaration, but its debts are not paid or provided for in full within the period stated in the declaration it shall be presumed until the contrary is shown that the director did not have reasonable grounds for his opinion.

(4) A winding up in the case of which a declaration has been made and delivered in accordance with this section is in this Act referred to as "a member's voluntary winding up", and a winding up in the case of which a declaration has not been made and delivered as aforesaid is in this Act referred to as "a creditors' voluntary winding up".

Provisions applicable to members' winding up.

207. The provisions contained in the seven sections next following shall, subject to the provisions of the last of them, apply in relation to a members' voluntary winding up.

Power of company to appoint and fix remuneration of liquidators.

208.(1) The company in general meeting shall appoint one or more liquidators for the purpose of winding up the affairs and distributing the assets of the company, and may fix their remuneration.

(2) On the appointment of a liquidator all the powers of the officers shall cease, except so far as the company in general meeting or the liquidator sanctions the continuance thereof.

Power to fill vacancy in office of liquidator.

209.(1) If a vacancy occurs by death, resignation or otherwise in the office of liquidator appointed by the company, the company in general meeting may, subject to any arrangement with its creditors, fill the vacancy.

(2) For that purpose a general meeting may be convened by any contributory or, if there were more liquidators than one, by the continuing liquidators.

(3) The meeting shall be held in manner provided by this Act or by the bye-laws, or in such manner as may, on application by any contributory or by the continuing liquidators, be determined by the Court.

Power of liquidator to accept shares etc as consideration for sale of property of company.

210.(1) Where a company is proposed to be, or is in the course of being, wound up voluntarily, and the whole or part of its business or property is proposed to be transferred or sold to another company whether a company within the meaning of this Act or not, in this section called "the transferee company", the liquidator of the first-mentioned company, in this section called "the transferor company", may, with the sanction of a resolution of the company, conferring either a general authority on the liquidator or an authority in respect of any particular arrangement, receive, in compensation or part compensation for the transfer or sale, shares, policies or other like interests in the transferee company for distribution among the members of the transferor company, or may enter into any other arrangement whereby the members of the transferor company may, in lieu of receiving cash, shares, policies or other like interests or in addition thereto, participate in the profits or receive any other benefits from the transferee company.

(2) Any sale or arrangement in pursuance of this section shall be binding on the members of the transferor company.

(3) If any member of the transferor company who did not vote in favour of the resolution expresses his dissent therefrom in writing addressed to the liquidator, and left at the registered office of the company within seven days after the passing of the resolution, he may require the liquidator either to abstain from carrying the resolution into effect or to purchase his interest at a price to be determined by agreement or by arbitration

.

(4) If the liquidator elects to purchase the member's interest, the purchase money must be paid before the company is dissolved and be raised by the liquidator in such manner as may be determined by resolution.

(5) A resolution shall not be invalid for the purposes of this section by reason that it is passed before or concurrently with a resolution for voluntary winding up or for appointing liquidators, but if an order is made within a year for winding up the company by the Court, the resolution shall not be valid unless sanctioned by the Court.

Duty of liquidator to call creditors' meeting in case of insolvency.

211.(1) If the liquidator is at any time of the opinion that the company will not be able to pay its debts in full within the period stated in the declaration under section 206 he shall forthwith summon a meeting of the creditors, and shall lay before the meeting a statement of the assets and liabilities of the company.

(2) If the liquidator fails to comply with this section, he shall be liable to a fine not exceeding two hundred and fifty dollars.

Duty of liquidator to call general meeting at end of each year.

212.(1) Subject to section 214, in the event of the winding up continuing for more than one year, the liquidator shall summon a general meeting of the company at the end of the first year from the commencement of the winding up, and of each succeeding year, or at the first convenient date within three months from the end of the year or such longer period as the Registrar may allow, and shall lay before the meeting an account of his acts and dealings and of the conduct of the winding up during the preceding year.

(2) If the liquidator fails to comply with this section, he shall be liable to a fine not exceeding fifty dollars.

Final meeting and dissolution: members voluntary winding-up.

213.(1) Subject to section 214, as soon as the affairs of the company are fully wound up, the liquidator shall make up an account of the winding-up, showing how the winding-up has been conducted and the property has been disposed of, and thereupon shall call a general meeting of the company for the purpose of laying before it the account, and giving any explanation thereof.

(2) The meeting shall be called by advertisement in an appointed newspaper, specifying the time, place and object thereof, and published one month at least before the meeting.

(3) Within one week after the meeting the liquidator shall notify the Registrar that the company has been dissolved and the Registrar shall record that fact and the date of the dissolution in the appropriate register:

Provided that, if a quorum is not present at the meeting the liquidator, in lieu of notifying the Registrar as herebefore mentioned, shall notify him that the meeting was duly summoned and that no quorum was present thereat and on such notification the requirements of this subsection shall be deemed to have been complied with.

(4) If the liquidator fails to call a general meeting of the company as required by this section or fails to comply with the requirements of subsection (3), he shall be liable to a default fine.

Alternative provisions as to annual and final meetings in case of insolvency.

214. Where section 211 has effect, sections 222 and 223 shall apply to the winding up, as if the winding up were a creditor's voluntary winding up:

Provided that the liquidator shall not be required to summon a meeting of creditors under section 222 at the end of the first year from the commencement of the winding up, unless the meeting held under section 211, is held more than three months before the end of the year.

Provisions applicable to creditors' winding up.

215. The provisions contained in the eight sections next following shall apply in relation to a creditor's voluntary winding up.

Meeting of creditors.

216.(1) The company shall cause a meeting of the creditors of the company to be summoned for the day, or the next day following the day, on which there is to be held the meeting which the resolution for voluntary winding up is to be proposed, and shall cause the notices of the meeting of creditors to be sent by post to the creditors simultaneously with the sending of the notices of the meeting of the company.

(2) The company shall cause notice of the meeting of creditors to be advertised in an appointed newspaper on at least two occasions.

(3) The directors of the company shall -

(a) cause a full statement of the position of the company's affairs together with a list of the creditors of the company and the estimated amount of their claims to be laid before the meeting of the creditors to be held as aforesaid; and

(b) appoint one of their number to preside at such meeting.

(4) It shall be the duty of the director appointed to preside at the meeting of creditors to attend the meeting and preside thereat.

(5) If the meeting of the company at which the resolution for voluntary winding up is to be proposed is adjourned and the resolution is passed at an adjourned meeting, any resolution passed at the meeting of the creditors held in pursuance of subsection (1) of this section shall have effect as if it has been passed immediately after the passing of the resolution for winding up the company.

(6) If default is made -

(a) by the company in complying with subsection (1) and (2) of this section;

(b) by the directors of the company in complying with subsection (3) of this section;

(c) by any director of the company in complying with subsection (4) of this section, the company, directors or director, as the case may be, shall be liable to a fine of five hundred dollars, and in the case of default by the company, every officer of the company who is in default shall be liable to like penalty.

Appointment of liquidator.

217. The creditors and the company at their respective meetings mentioned in the last foregoing section may nominate a person to be liquidator for the purpose of winding up the affairs and distributing the assets of the company, and if the creditors and the company nominate different persons, the person nominated by the creditors shall be liquidator, and if no person is nominated by the creditors the person, if any, nominated by the company shall be liquidator:

Provided that in the case of different persons being nominated, any director, member or creditor of the company may within seven days after the date on which the nomination was made by the creditors, apply to the Court for an order either directing that the person nominated as liquidator by the company shall be liquidator instead of or jointly with the person nominated by the creditors or appointing some other person to be liquidator instead of the person appointed by the creditors.

Appointment of committee of inspection.

218.(1) The creditors at the meeting to be held in pursuance of section 216 or at any subsequent meeting may, if they think fit, appoint a committee of inspection consisting of not more than five persons, and if such a committee is appointed the company may, either at the meeting at which the resolution for voluntary winding up is passed or at any time subsequently in general meeting, appoint such number of persons as they think fit to act as members of the committee not exceeding five in number:

Provided that the creditors may, if they think fit, resolve that all or any of the persons so appointed by the company ought not to be members of the committee of inspection, and, if the creditors so resolve, the persons mentioned in the resolution shall not, unless the Court otherwise directs, be qualified to act as members of the committee, and on any application to the Court under this provision the Court may, if it thinks fit, appoint other persons to act as such members in place of the persons mentioned in the resolution.

(2) Subject to this section and to general rules, section 182 except subsection (1), shall apply with respect to a committee of inspection appointed under this section as it applies with respect to a committee of inspection appointed in a winding up by the Court.

Fixing of liquidator's remuneration and cessor of officers' powers.

219.(1) The committee of inspection, or if there is no such committee, the creditors, may fix the remuneration to be paid to the liquidator or liquidators.

(2) On the appointment of a liquidator, all the powers of the officers shall cease, except so far as the committee of inspection, or if there is no such committee, the creditors, sanction the continuance thereof.

Power to fill vacancy in office of liquidator.

220. If a vacancy occurs, by death, resignation or otherwise, in the office of a liquidator, other than a liquidator appointed by, or by the direction of, the Court, the creditors may fill the vacancy.

Application of s.210 to a creditors' voluntary winding up.

221. Section 210 shall apply in the case of a creditors' voluntary winding up as in the case of a members' voluntary winding up, with the modification that the powers of the liquidator under the said section shall not be exercised except with the sanction either of the Court or of the committee of inspection.

Duty of liquidator to call meetings of company and creditors at end of each year.

222.(1) In the event of the winding up continuing for more than one year, the liquidator shall summon a general meeting of the company and a meeting of the creditors at the end of the first year from the commencement of the winding up, and of each succeeding year, or at the first convenient date within three months from the end of the year or such longer period as the Registrar may allow, and shall lay before the meetings an account of his acts and dealings and of the conduct of the winding up during the preceding year.

(2) If the liquidator fails to comply with this section, he shall be liable to a fine not exceeding fifty dollars.

Final meeting and dissolution.

223.(1) As soon as the affairs of the company are fully wound up, the liquidator shall make an account of the winding up showing how the winding up has been conducted and the property of the company has been disposed of, and thereupon shall call a general meeting of the company and a meeting of the creditors for the purpose of laying the account before the meetings and giving any explanation thereof.

(2) Each such meeting shall be called by advertisement in an appointed newspaper specifying the time, place and object thereof, and published one month at least before the meeting.

(3) Within one week after the date of the meetings, or, if the meetings are not held on the same date, after the date of the later meeting, the liquidator shall send to the Registrar a copy of the account, and shall make a return to him of the holding of the meetings and of their dates, and if the copy is not sent or the return is not made in accordance with this subsection the liquidator shall be liable to a default fine:

Provided that, if a quorum is not present at either such meeting, the liquidator shall, in lieu of the return hereinbefore mentioned, make a return that the meeting was duly summoned and that no quorum was present thereat and upon such a return being made the provisions of this subsection as to the making of the return shall, in respect of that meeting, be deemed to have been complied with.

(4) The Registrar on receiving the account and, in respect of each such meeting, either of the returns herein before mentioned, shall forthwith register them, and on the expiration of three months from the registration thereof the company shall be deemed to be dissolved:

Provided that the Court may, on the application of the liquidator or of any other person who appears to the Court to be interested, make an order deferring the date at which the dissolution of the company is to take effect for such time as the Court thinks fit.

(5) It shall be the duty of the person on whose application an order of the Court under this section is made, within seven days after the making of the order, to deliver to the Registrar an office copy of the order for registration, and if the person fails to do so he shall be liable to a default fine.

(6) If the liquidator fails to call a general meeting of the company or a meeting of the creditors as required by this section, he shall be liable to a fine of two hundred and fifty dollars.

Provisions applicable to every winding up.

224. The provisions contained in the nine sections of this Act next following shall apply to every winding up whether a member's or creditor's winding up.

Distribution of property of company.

225. Subject to this Act as to preferential payment the property of a company shall, on its winding up, be applied in satisfaction of its liabilities pari passu, and, subject to such application, shall, unless the bye-laws otherwise provide, be distributed among the members according to their rights and interests in the company.

Powers and duties of liquidator in voluntary winding up.

226.(1) The liquidator may -

(a) in the case of a members' voluntary winding up, with the sanction of a resolution of the company, and, in the case of a creditor's voluntary winding up, with the sanction of the Court or the committee of inspection or if there is no such committee a meeting of the creditors, exercise any of the powers given by paragraphs (d), (e) and (f) of subsection (1) of section 175 to a liquidator in a winding up by the Court;

(b) without sanction, exercise any of the other powers by this Act given to the liquidator in a winding up by the Court;

(c) exercise the power of the Court under this Act of settling a list of contributories, and the list of contributories shall be prima facie evidence of the liability of the persons named therein to be contributories;

(d) exercise the power of the Court to make calls;

(e) summon general meetings of the company for the purpose of obtaining the sanction of the company by resolution or for any other purpose he may think fit.

(2) The liquidator shall pay the debts of the company and shall adjust the rights of the contributories among themselves.

(3) When several liquidators are appointed, any power given by this Act may be exercised by such one or more of them as may be determined at the time of their appointment, or, in default of such determination, by any number not less than two.

Power of Court to appoint and remove liquidator in voluntary winding up.

227.(1) If for any cause whatever there is no liquidator acting, the Court may appoint a liquidator.

(2) The Court may, on cause shown, remove a liquidator and appoint another liquidator.

Notice by liquidator of his appointment.

228.(1) The liquidator shall, within twenty-one days after his appointment, publish in an appointed newspaper and deliver to the Registrar for registration a notice of his appointment.

(2) If the liquidator fails to comply with the requirements of this section he shall be liable to a default fine.

Arrangement when binding on creditors.

229.(1) Any arrangement entered into between a company about to be, or in the course of being, wound up and its creditors shall, subject to the right of appeal under this section, be binding on the company if sanctioned by a resolution and on the creditors if acceded to by three-fourths in number and value of the creditors.

(2) Any creditor or contributory may, within three weeks from the completion of the arrangement, appeal to the Court against it, and the Court may thereupon, as it thinks just, amend, vary or confirm the arrangement.

Liquidators power to stay voluntary winding up.

230.(1) The liquidator of a company may at any time after he has been appointed stay the winding up either altogether or for a limited time if he is satisfied that such a stay is in the best interests of the contributories or the creditors.

(2) The liquidator shall three weeks prior to staying the winding up of a company under subsection (1) publish in an appointed newspaper his intentions and his reasons for so doing and shall give notice of such intention to the Registrar.

(3) The Official Receiver or any contributory or creditor may within three weeks of the publication of a notice under subsection (2) apply to the Court under section 231 for an order requiring the liquidator to continue the winding up proceedings.

(4) When a liquidator stays the winding up of a company altogether he shall, after the period allowed for an application under subsection (3) has expired, take such steps as he considers desirable to enable the company to be as near as practicable as it was before the resolution to wind up the company was made.

Power to apply to Court to have questions determined or powers exercised.

231.(1) The liquidator or any contributory or creditor may apply to the Court to determine any question arising in the winding up of a company, or to exercise, as respects the enforcing of calls or any other matter, all or any of the powers which the Court might exercise if the company were being wound up by the Court.

(2) The Court, if satisfied that the determination of the question or the required exercise of power will be just and beneficial, may accede wholly or partially to the application on such terms and conditions as it thinks fit or may make such other order on the application as it thinks just.

(3) A copy of an order made by virtue of this section staying the proceedings in the winding up shall forthwith be forwarded by the company, or otherwise as may be prescribed to the Registrar who shall make a minute of the order in his books relating to the company.

Costs of voluntary winding up.

232. All costs, charges and expenses properly incurred in the winding up, including the remuneration of the liquidator, shall be payable out of the assets of the company in priority to all other claims.

Saving for rights of creditors and contributories.

233. The winding up of a company shall not bar the right of any creditor or contributory to have it wound up by the Court, but in the case of an application by a contributory the Court must be satisfied that the rights of the contributories will be prejudiced by a voluntary winding up.

Debts of all description may be proved.

234. In every winding up, subject in the case of insolvent companies to the rules of bankruptcy as applied by this Act all debts payable on a contingency, and all claims against the company, present or future, certain or contingent, ascertained or sounding only in damages, shall be admissible to proof against the company, a just estimate being made so far as possible, of the value of such debts or claims as may be subject to any contingency or sound only in damages, or for some other reason do not bear a certain value.

Application of bankruptcy rules in winding up of insolvent companies.

235. In the winding up of an insolvent company the same rules shall prevail and be observed with regard to the respective rights of secured and unsecured creditors and to debts provable and to the valuation of annuities and future and contingent liabilities as are in force for the time being under the law of bankruptcy with respect to the estates of persons adjudged bankrupt, and all persons who in any such case would be entitled to prove for and receive dividends out of the assets of the company may come in under the winding up and make such claims against the company as they respectively are entitled to by virtue of this section.

Preferential payments.

236.(1) In a winding up there shall be paid in priority to all other debts -

(a) all taxes owing to the Government and rates owing to a municipality at the relevant date;

(b) all wages or salary, whether or not earned wholly or in part by way of commission or whether payable for time or piece work of any employee of the company in respect of services rendered to the company during four months next before the relevant date;

(c) all accrued holiday remuneration becoming payable to any employee, or in the case of his death to any other person in his right, on the termination of his employment before or by the effect of the winding-up order or resolution;

(d) unless the company is being wound up voluntarily merely for the purposes of reconstruction or of amalgamation with another company, all amounts due in respect of contributions payable during the twelve months next before the relevant date by the company as the employer of any persons under the Contributory Pensions Act 1970 or any contract of insurance;

(e) unless the company is being wound up voluntarily merely for the purposes of reconstruction or of amalgamation with another company, or unless the company has, at the commencement of the winding up, under a contract with insurers capable of being transferred to and vested in the workman, all amounts due in respect of any compensation or liability for compensation under the Workmen's Compensation Act 1965, being amounts which have accrued before the relevant date.

(2) Notwithstanding anything in paragraph (b) of the foregoing subsection, the sum to which priority is to be given under that paragraph shall not, in the case of any one claimant, exceed two thousand five hundred dollars:

Provided that where a claimant under the said paragraph (b) has entered into a contract for the payment of a portion of his wages in a lump sum or for the payment of a gratuity at the end of his hiring, he shall have priority in respect of the whole of each sum, or a part thereof, as the Court may decide to be due under the contract, proportionate to the time of service up to the relevant date.

(3) Where any compensation under the Workmen's Compensation Act 1965, is a weekly payment, the amount due in respect thereof shall, for the purposes of paragraph (e) of subsection (1) of this section, be taken to be the amount of the lump sum for which the weekly payment could, if redeemable, be redeemed if the employer made an application for that purpose under the said Act.

(4) Where any payment has been made -

(a) to any employee of a company, on account of wages or salary; or

(b) to any such employee or, in the case of his death, to any other person in his right, on account of accrued holiday remuneration, out of money advanced by some person for that purpose, the person by whom the money was advanced shall in a winding up have a right of priority in respect of the money so advanced and paid up to the amount by which the sum in respect of which the employee or other person in his right, would have been entitled to priority in the winding up has been diminished by reason of the payment having been made.

(5) The foregoing debts shall -

(a) rank equally among themselves and be paid in full, unless the assets are insufficient to meet them, in which case they shall abate in equal proportions; and

(b) so far as the assets of the company available for payment of general creditors are insufficient to meet them, have priority over the claims of holders of debentures under any floating charge created by the company, and be paid accordingly out of any property comprised in or subject to that charge.

(6) Subject to the retention of such sums as may be necessary for the costs and expenses of the winding up, the foregoing debts shall be discharged forthwith so far as the assets are sufficient to meet them, and in the case of the debts to which priority is given by paragraph (d) of subsection (1) of this section formal proof thereof shall not be required.

(7) In the event of a landlord or other person distraining or having distrained on any goods or effects of the company within three months next before the date of a winding-up order, the debts to which priority is given by this section shall be a first charge on the goods or effects so distrained on, or the proceeds of the sale thereof:

Provided that, in respect of any money paid under any such charge, the landlord or other person shall have the same rights of priority as the person to whom the payment is made.

(8) For the purpose of this section -

(a) any remuneration in respect of a period of holiday or absence from work through sickness or other good cause shall be deemed to be wages in respect of services rendered to the company during that period;

(b) the expression "accrued holiday remuneration" includes in relation to any person, all sums which, by virtue either of his contract of employment or of any enactment, including any order made or direction given under an Act, are payable on account of the remuneration which would, in the ordinary

course, have become payable to him in respect of a period of holiday had his employment with the company continued until he became entitled to be allowed the holiday;

(c) the expression "the relevant date" means -

(i) in the case of a company ordered to be wound up compulsorily, the date of the appointment, or first appointment, of a provisional liquidator, or, if no such appointment was made, the date of the winding up order, unless in either case the company had commenced to be wound up voluntarily before that date; and

(ii) in any case where the foregoing sub-paragraph does not apply, means the date of the passing of the resolution for the winding up of the company.

Fraudulent preference.

237.(1) Any conveyance, mortgage, delivery of goods, payment, execution or other act relating to property made or done by or against a company within six months before the commencement of its winding up which, had it been made or done by or against an individual within six months before the presentation of a bankruptcy petition on which he is adjudged bankrupt, would be deemed in his bankruptcy a fraudulent preference, shall in the event of the company being wound up be deemed a fraudulent preference of its creditors and be invalid accordingly.

(2) Any conveyance or assignment by a company of all its property to trustees for the benefit of all its creditors shall be void to all intents.

Liability and rights of certain fraudulently preferred persons.

238.(1) Where anything made or done is void under the last foregoing section as a fraudulent preference of a person interested in property mortgaged or charged to secure the company's debt, when, without prejudice to any rights or liabilities arising apart from this provision, the person preferred shall be subject to the same liabilities, and shall have the same rights, as if he had undertaken to be personally liable as surety for the debts to the extent of the charge on the property or the value of his interest, whichever is the less.

(2) The value of the said person's interest shall be determined as at the date of the transaction constituting the fraudulent preference, and shall be determined as if the interest were free of all incumbrances other than those to which the charge for the company's debts was then subject.

(3) On any application made to the Court with respect to any payment on the ground that the payment was a fraudulent preference of a surety or guarantor, the Court shall have jurisdiction to determine any questions with respect to the payment arising between the person to whom the payment was made and the surety or guarantor and to grant relief in respect thereof, notwithstanding that it is not necessary so to do for the purposes of the winding up and for that purpose may give leave to bring in the surety or guarantor as a third party as in the case of an action for the recovery of the sum paid.

This subsection shall apply, with the necessary modifications, in relation to transactions other than the payment of money as it applies in relation to payments.

Effect of floating charge.

239.(1) Where a company is being wound up, a floating charge on the undertaking or property of the company created within twelve months of the commencement of the winding up shall, unless it is proved that the company immediately after the creation of the charge was solvent, be invalid, except to the amount of any cash paid to the company at the time of or subsequently to the creation of, and in consideration for, the charge, together with interest on that amount at the statutory rate fixed under the Interest and Credit Charges (Regulation) Act 1975.

Disclaimer of onerous property.

240.(1) The liquidator of a company may with the leave of the Court disclaim any property belonging to the company whether real or personal including any right of action or right under a contract which in his opinion is onerous for the company to hold or is unprofitable or unsalable.

(2) The disclaimer shall operate to determine, as from the date of disclaimer, the rights, interest and liabilities of the company, and the property of the company in or in respect of the property disclaimed, but shall not, except so far as is necessary for the purpose of releasing the company and the property of the company from liability, affect the rights or liabilities of any other person.

(3) The Court, before or on granting leave to disclaim, may require such notices to be given to persons interested, and impose such terms as a condition of granting leave, and make such other order in the matter as the Court thinks just.

(4) The Court may, on an application by any person who either claims any interest in any disclaimed property or is under any liability not discharged by this Act in respect of any disclaimed property and on hearing any such persons as it thinks fit, make an order for the vesting of the property in or the delivery of the property to any persons entitled thereto, or to whom it may seem just that the property should be delivered by way of compensation for such liability as aforesaid, or a trustee for him, and on such terms as the Court thinks just, and on any such vesting order being made, the property comprised therein shall vest accordingly in the person therein named in that behalf without any conveyance or assignment for the purpose.

(5) Any person injured by the operation of a disclaimer under this section shall be deemed to be a creditor of the company to the amount of the injury, and may accordingly prove the amount as a debt in the winding up.

Restriction of rights of creditor as to execution or attachment in case of company being wound up.

241.(1) Where a creditor has issued execution against the goods or lands of a company or has attached any debt due to the company, and the company is subsequently wound up, he shall not be entitled to retain the benefit of the execution or attachment against the liquidator in the winding up of the company unless he has completed the execution or attachment before the commencement of the winding up:

Provided that -

(a) where any creditor has had notice of a meeting having been called at which a resolution for voluntary winding up is to be proposed, the date on which the creditor so had notice shall for the purpose of the foregoing provision, be substituted for the date of the commencement of the winding up;

(b) a person who purchases in good faith under a sale by the Provost Marshal any goods of a company on which an execution has been levied shall in all cases acquire a good title to them against the liquidator; and

(c) the rights conferred by this subsection on the liquidator may be set aside by the Court in favour of the creditor to such extent and subject to such terms as the Court may think fit.

(2) For the purposes of this section, an execution against goods shall be taken to be completed by seizure and sale, and an attachment of a debt shall be deemed to be completed by receipt of the debt, and an execution against land shall be deemed to be completed by seizure or by the appointment of a receiver.

(3) In this and the next section the expression "goods" includes all chattels personal, and the expression Provost Marshal includes any officer charged with the execution of a writ or other process.

Duties of Provost Marshal as to goods taken in execution.

242.(1) Subject to the provisions of subsection (3) of this section, where any goods of a company are taken in execution, and, before the sale thereof or the completion of the execution by the receipt or recovery of the full amount of the levy, notice is served on the Provost Marshal that a provisional liquidator has been appointed or that a winding-up order has been made or that a resolution for voluntary winding up has been passed, the Provost Marshal shall, on being so required, deliver the goods and any money seized or received in part satisfaction of the execution to the liquidator, but the costs of the execution shall be a first charge on the goods or money so delivered, and the liquidator may sell the goods, or a sufficient part thereof for the purpose of satisfying that charge.

(2) Subject to the provisions of subsection (3) of this section, where under an execution in respect of a judgment for a sum exceeding five hundred dollars the goods of a company are sold or money is paid in order to avoid sale, the Provost Marshal shall deduct the costs of the execution from the proceeds of the sale or the money paid and retaining the balance for fourteen days, and if within that time notice is served on him of a petition for the winding up of the company having been presented or of a meeting having been called at which there is to be proposed a resolution for the voluntary winding up of the company and an order is made or a resolution is passed, as the case may be, for the winding up of the company, the Provost Marshal shall pay the balance to the liquidator, who shall be entitled to retain it as against the execution creditor.

(3) The rights conferred by this section on the liquidator may be set aside by the Court in favour of the creditor to such extent and subject to such terms as the Court thinks fit.

Offences by officers of companies in liquidation.

243.(1) If any person, being a past or present officer of a company which at the time of the commission of the alleged offence is being wound up, whether by the Court or voluntarily, or is subsequently ordered to be wound up by the Court or subsequently passes a resolution for voluntary winding up -

(a) does not to the best of his knowledge and belief fully and truly discover to the liquidator all the property, real and personal, of the company, and how and to whom and for what consideration and when the company disposed of any part thereof, except such part as has been disposed of in the ordinary way of the business of the company; or

(b) does not deliver up to the liquidator, or as he directs, all such part of the real and personal property of the company as is in his custody or under his control, and which he is required by law to deliver up; or

(c) does not deliver up to the liquidator, or as he directs, all books and papers in his custody or under his control belonging to the company and which he is required by law to deliver up;

(d) within twelve months next before the commencement of the winding up or at any time thereafter conceals any part of the property of the company to the value of three hundred dollars or upwards, or conceals any debt due to or from the company; or

(e) within twelve months next before the commencement of the winding up or at any time thereafter fraudulently removes any part of the property of the company to the value of fifty dollars or upwards; or

(f) makes any material omission in any statement relating to the affairs of the company; or

(*g*) knowing or believing that a false debt has been proved by any person under winding up, fails for the period of a month to inform the liquidator thereof; or

(*h*) after the commencement of the winding up prevent the production of any book or paper affecting or relating to the property or affairs of the company; or

(*i*) within twelve months next before the commencement of the winding up or at any time thereafter, conceals, destroys, mutilates or falsifies, or is privy to the concealment, destruction, mutilation or falsification of, any book or paper affecting or relating to the property or affairs of the company; or

(*j*) within twelve months next before the commencement of the winding up or at any time thereafter makes or is privy to the making of any false entry in any book or paper affecting or relating to the property or affairs of the company; or

(*k*) within twelve months next before the commencement of the winding up or at any time thereafter fraudulently parts with, alters or makes any omission in, or is privy to the fraudulent parting with, altering or making any omission in, any document affecting or relating to the property or affairs of the company; or

(*l*) after the commencement of the winding up or at any meeting of the creditors of the company within twelve months next before the commencement of the winding up attempts to account for any part of the property of the company by fictitious losses or expenses; or

(*m*) has within twelve months next before the commencement of the winding up or at any time thereafter, by any false representation or other fraud, obtained any property for or on behalf of the company on credit for which the company does not subsequently pay for; or

(*n*) within twelve months next before the winding up or any time thereafter, under false pretence that the company is carrying on its business, obtains in credit, for or on behalf of the company, any property which the company does not subsequently pay for; or

(*o*) within twelve months next before the commencement of the winding up or at any time thereafter pawns, pledges or disposes of any property of the company which has been obtained on credit and has not been paid for, unless such pawning, pledging, or disposing is in the ordinary way of the business of the company; or

(*p*) is guilty of any false representation or other fraud for the purpose of obtaining the consent of the creditors of the company or any of them to an agreement with reference to the affairs of the company or to the winding up, he shall, in the case of the offences mentioned respectively in paragraphs (m), (n), and (o) of this subsection, be liable on indictment to imprisonment for a term of five years, or on summary conviction to imprisonment for a term of twelve months, and in the case of any other offence he shall be liable on conviction on indictment to imprisonment for a term of two years, or on summary conviction of imprisonment for a period of twelve months:

Provided that it shall be a good defence to a charge under any of paragraphs (a), (b), (c), (d), (f), (m), (n), and (o), if the accused proves that he had not intent to defraud, and to a charge under any of paragraphs (h), (i) and (j), if he proves that he had no intent to conceal the state of affairs of the company or to defeat the law.

(2) Where any person pawns, pledges or disposes of any property in circumstances which amount to an offence under paragraph (o) of subsection (1) of this section, every person who takes in pawn or pledge or otherwise receives the property knowing it to be pawned, pledged or disposed of in such circumstances as aforesaid shall be liable to be punished in the same way as if he had committed an offence under such paragraph.

(3) For the purpose of this section the expression "officer" shall include any person in accordance with whose directions or instructions the directors of a company have been accustomed to act.

Penalty for falsification of books.

244. If any officer or contributory of any company being wound up destroys, mutilates, alters or falsifies any books, papers or securities, or makes or is privy to the making of any false or fraudulent entry in any register, book of account or document belonging to the company with intent to defraud or deceive any person, he shall be liable on conviction on indictment to imprisonment for a period of five years.

Frauds by officers of companies which have gone into liquidation.

245. If any person, being at the time of the commission of the alleged offence an officer of a company which is subsequently ordered to be wound up by the Court or subsequently passes a resolution for voluntary winding up, -

(a) has by false pretence or by means of any other fraud induced any person to give credit to the company;

(b) with intent to defraud creditors of the company, has made or caused to be made any transfer of or charge on, or has caused or connived at the levying of any execution against, the property of the company; or

(c) with intent to defraud creditors of the company, has concealed or removed

any part of the property of the company since, or within two months before, the date of any unsatisfied judgment or order for payment of money obtained against the company, shall be liable on conviction on indictment to imprisonment for a term of two years, or on summary conviction to imprisonment for a term of twelve months.

Persons concerned responsible for fraudulent trading.

246.(1) If in the course of the winding up of a company it appears that any business of the company has been carried on with intent to defraud creditors of the company or creditors of any other person or for any fraudulent purpose, the Court, on the application of the Official Receiver, or the liquidator or any creditor or contributory of the company, may, if it thinks proper so to do, declare that any persons who were knowingly parties to the carrying on of the business in manner as aforesaid shall be personally responsible, without any limitation of liability, for all or any of the debts or other liability of the company as the Court may direct.

On the hearing of an application under this subsection the Official Receiver or the liquidator, as the case may be, may himself give evidence or call witnesses.

(2) Where the Court makes any such declaration, it may give such further directions as it thinks proper for the purpose of giving effect to that declaration, and in particular may make provision for making the liability of any such person under the declaration a charge on any debt or obligation due from the company to him, or on any mortgage or charge or any interest in any mortgage or charge on any assets of the company held by or vested in him, or any company or person on his behalf, or any person claiming as assignee from or through the person liable or any company or person acting on his behalf, and may from time to time make such further order as may be necessary for the purpose of enforcing any charge imposed under this subsection.

For the purpose of this subsection, the expression “assignee” includes any person to whom or in whose favour, by the directions of the person liable, the debt, obligation, mortgage or charge was created, issued or transferred or the interest created, but does not include an assignee for valuable consideration, not including consideration by way of marriage, given in good faith and without notice of any of the matters on the ground of which the declaration is made.

(3) Where any business of a company is carried on with such intent or for such purpose as is mentioned in subsection (1) of this section, every person who was knowingly a party to the carrying on of the business in manner aforesaid, shall be liable on conviction on indictment to imprisonment for a term of two years or to a fine of two thousand five hundred dollars, or to both.

(4) This section shall have effect notwithstanding that the person concerned may be criminally liable in respect of the matters on the ground of which the declaration is to be made, and where the declaration under subsection (1) of this section is made unless the person concerned pays the debts and liabilities which the Court in the declaration has directed that he should pay within a space of three weeks of the declaration he shall be deemed to have been guilty of an act of bankruptcy under section (3) of the Bankruptcy Act 1989.

Power of Court to assess damages against delinquent officers.

247.(1) If in the course of winding up a company it appears that any person who has taken part in the formation or promotion of the company, or any past or present director, manager or liquidator, or any officer of the company, has misapplied or retained or become liable or accountable for any money or property of the company, or been guilty of any misfeasance or breach of trust in relation to the company, the Court may, on the application of the Official Receiver, or of the liquidator, or of any creditor or contributory, examine the conduct of the promoter, director, manager, liquidator or officer, and compel him to repay or restore the money or property or any part thereof respectively with interest at such rate as the Court thinks just, or to contribute such sum to the assets of the company by way of compensation in respect of the misapplication, retainer, misfeasance or breach of trust as the Court thinks just.

(2) The provisions of this section shall have effect notwithstanding that the offence is one for which the offender may be criminally liable.

(3) When an order is made under this section, if the person concerned fails to comply with the order within the space of three weeks of it being served upon him or within such time, or such further time that the Court may allow, unless he satisfies the Court that he has a counter-claim, set-off or cross demand which equals or exceeds the amount he has been ordered to pay he shall be guilty of an act of bankruptcy for the purposes of section 3 of the Bankruptcy Act 1989.

Prosecution of delinquent officers and members of company.

248.(1) If it appears to the Court in the course of a winding up by the Court that any past or present officer, or any member, of the company has been guilty of any offence in relation to the company for which he is criminally liable, the Court may, either on the application of any person interested in the winding up or of its owns motion, direct the liquidator to refer the matter to the Attorney-General.

(2) If it appears to the liquidator in the course of a voluntary winding up that any past or present officer, or any member, of the company has been guilty of any offence in relation to the company for which he is criminally liable, he shall forthwith report the matter to the Attorney-General and shall furnish him with such information as he shall require and give him such access to and facilities for inspecting and taking copies of any documents in his possession or control relating to the matter in question.

Body corporate disqualified for appointment as liquidator.

249. A body corporate, unless empowered so to do by an incorporating Act, shall not be qualified for appointment as liquidator of a company whether in a winding up by the Court or in a voluntary winding up and -

(a) any appointment made in contravention of this provision shall be void; and

(b) any body corporate which acts in contravention of this section shall be liable to a fine not exceeding five hundred dollars.

Corrupt inducement affecting appointment as liquidator.

250. Any person who gives or agrees or offers to give to any member or creditor of a company any valuable consideration with a view to securing his own appointment or nomination, or to securing or preventing the appointment or nomination of some person other than himself, as the company's liquidator shall be liable to a fine of five hundred dollars.

Enforcement of duty of liquidator to make returns etc.

251.(1) If any liquidator who has made any default in filing, delivering or making any return, account or other document, or in giving any notice which he is by law required to file, deliver, make or give, fails to make good the default within fourteen days after the service on him of a notice requiring him to do so, the Court may, on an application made to the Court by any contributory or creditor of the company or by the Registrar, make an order directing the liquidator to make good the default within such time as may be specified in the order.

(2) Any such order may provide that all costs of and incidental to the application shall be done by the liquidator.

(3) Nothing in this section shall be taken to prejudice the operation of any provision imposing penalties on a liquidator in respect of any such default as aforesaid.

Notification that a company is in liquidation.

252.(1) Where a company is being wound up, whether by the Court or voluntarily, every invoice, order for goods or business letter issued by or on behalf of the company or a liquidator of the company, or a receiver or manager of the property of the company, being a document on or in which the name of the company appears, shall contain a statement that the company is being wound up.

(2) If default is made in complying with this section, the company and any of the following persons who knowingly and wilfully authorizes or permits the default, namely, any officer of the company, any liquidator of the company and any receiver or manager, shall be liable to a fine of one hundred dollars.

Exemption of certain documents from stamp duty.

253.(1) When a company is being wound up by the Court or when a company is the subject of a creditors' voluntary winding up -

(a) every assurance relating solely to freehold property, or to any estate, right or interest in, any real or personal property, which forms part of the assets of the company and which, after the execution of the assurance, either at law or in equity, is or remains part of the assets of the company; and

(b) every power of attorney, proxy paper, writ, order, certificate, bond or other instrument or writing relating solely to the property of any company which is being wound up, or to any proceeding under any such winding up, shall be exempt from duties chargeable under the enactments relating to stamp duties.

(2) In this section the expression "assurance" includes deed, conveyance, assignment and surrender.

Books of company to be evidence.

254. Where a company is being wound up, all books and papers of the company and of the liquidators shall, as between the contributories of the company, be prima facie evidence of the truth of all matters purporting to be therein recorded.

Disposal of books and papers of company.

255.(1) When a company has been wound up and is about to be dissolved, the books and papers of the company and of the liquidators may be disposed of as follows, that is say -

(a) in the case of a winding up by the Court, in such way as the Court directs;

(b) in the case of a members' voluntary winding up, in such way as the company by resolution directs, and, in the case of a creditors' voluntary winding up, in such a way as the committee of inspection or, if there is no such committee, as the creditors of the company may direct.

(2) No responsibility shall rest on the company, the liquidator or any person to whom the custody of the books and papers has been committed, by reason of any book or paper not being forthcoming to any person claiming to be interested therein that the company, liquidator or person, as the case may be, retains custody of such books and papers -

(i) in the case of a company dissolved pursuant to Section 213, for a period of at least ten years;

(ii) in the case of a company dissolved pursuant to Section 261, for a period of at least twenty years; and

(iii) in any other case, for a period of at least two years, commencing on the date of the dissolution of the company.

(3) The Minister may make rules for enabling the Registrar to prevent, for such period from the dissolution of the company, as the Registrar thinks proper, the destruction of the books and papers of a company which has been wound up, and for enabling any creditor or contributory of the company to make representations to the Registrar and to appeal to the Court from any direction which may be given by the Registrar in the matter, provided that such period shall not exceed -

(a) in the case of a company dissolved pursuant to Section 213, ten years;

(b) in the case of a company dissolved pursuant to Section 261, twenty years; and

(c) in any other case, two years, commencing on the date of the dissolution of the company.

(4) If any person acts in contravention of any rules made for the purposes of this section or of any direction of the Registrar thereunder, he shall be liable to a fine of five hundred dollars.

(5) Any rules made under subsection (3) shall be subject to negative resolution procedure.

Information as to pending liquidations.

256.(1) If where a company is being wound up the winding up is not concluded within one year after its commencement, the liquidator shall, at such intervals as may be prescribed, until the winding up is concluded, send to the Registrar such particulars as the Registrar may require with respect to the proceedings in and position of the liquidation.

(2) If a liquidator fails to comply with this section, he shall be liable to a default fine.

(3) This section shall not apply in the case of a members' voluntary winding up of a company.

Unclaimed assets to be paid into consolidated fund.

257.(1) If, where a company is being wound up, it appears either from any statement sent to the Registrar under the last foregoing section or otherwise that a liquidator has in his hands or under his control any money representing unclaimed or undistributed assets of the company which have remained unclaimed or undistributed for six months after the date of their receipt or any money held by the company in trust in respect of dividends or other sums due to any person as a member of the company, the liquidator shall forthwith pay the said money to the Accountant General who shall pay it into the Consolidated Fund and the liquidator shall be entitled to a receipt for the money so paid which shall be an effectual discharge to him in respect thereof.

(2) Any person claiming to be entitled to any money paid into the Consolidated Fund in pursuance of this section may apply to the Accountant General for payment thereof, and the Accountant General, on receipt of a certificate by the liquidator that the person claiming is entitled, may make an order for the payment to that person of the sum due.

(3) Any person dissatisfied with the decision of the liquidator or the Accountant General in respect of a claim made under this section may appeal to the Court.

Appointment of commissioner to take evidence.

258.(1) The Court may appoint a commissioner for the purpose of taking evidence under this Act and may refer the whole or any part of the examination of any witnesses under this Act to any person it has appointed as commissioner.

(2) Every commissioner shall have in relation to any matter referred to him all the powers of the Court to summon and to examine witnesses, to require the delivery of documents, to punish defaults by witnesses, and to allow their costs and expenses to witnesses.

(3) Any examination so taken shall be returned or reported to the Court.

The swearing of affidavits etc.

259.(1) Any affidavit or declaration required to be sworn under or for the purposes of this Part may be sworn in Bermuda or elsewhere before any Court or person lawfully authorized to take and receive affidavits or before any of Her Majesty's consuls, vice consuls or high commissioners.

(2) All courts, judges, justices, commissioners and persons acting judicially shall for the purposes of subsection (1) take judicial notice of the seal or stamp or signature of any court, judge or person in Bermuda and of any court, consul, vice consul or high commissioner elsewhere but may in its discretion require the seal or stamp of any other person to be authenticated by a court, consul, vice consul or high commissioner or require evidence that the person is lawfully authorized to seal and receive affidavits.

Power of Court to declare dissolution of company void.

260.(1) Where a company has been dissolved, the Court may -

(a) in the case of a dissolution pursuant to section 213, at any time not later than ten years from the date of such dissolution; and

(b) in any other case, at any time not later than two years from such date, on an application being made for the purpose by the liquidator of the company or by any other person who appears to the Court to be interested, make an order declaring the dissolution to have been void.

(2) It shall be the duty of the person on whose application the order was made, within seven days after the making of the order, or such further time as the Court may allow, to deliver to the Registrar for registration a copy of the order, and if that person fails so to do he shall be liable to a default fine.

(3) Where the Court makes an order under subsection (1), the Court may make such consequential orders, or impose such terms and conditions, as to the Court may seem appropriate in the circumstances.

(4) Where an order is made and registered pursuant to this section, the company shall be deemed to have continued in existence as if it had not been dissolved.

Registrar may strike defunct company off register.

261.(1) Where the Registrar has reasonable cause to believe that a company is not carrying on business or is not in operation, he may send to the company by post a letter inquiring whether the company is carrying on business or is in operation.

(2) If the Registrar does not within one month of sending the letter receive any answer thereto, he shall within fourteen days after the expiration of the month send to the company a registered letter referring to the first letter, and stating that no answer thereto has been received, and that if an answer is not received to the second letter within one month from the date thereof, a notice will be published in an appointed newspaper with a view to striking the name of the company off the register.

(3) If the Registrar either receives an answer to the effect that the company is not carrying on business or is not in operation, or does not within one month after sending the second letter receive any answer, he may publish in an appointed newspaper, and send to the company by post, a notice that at the expiration of three months from the date of that notice the name of the company mentioned therein will, unless cause is shown to the contrary, be struck off the register and the company will be dissolved.

(4) If, in any case where a company is being wound up, the Registrar has reasonable cause to believe either that no liquidator is acting, or that the affairs of the company are fully wound up, and the returns required to be made by the liquidator have not been made for a period of six consecutive months, the Registrar shall publish in an appointed newspaper and send to the company or the liquidator if any, a like notice as is provided in the last foregoing subsection.

(5) At the expiration of the time mentioned in subsection (3) the Registrar may, unless cause to the contrary is previously shown by the company, strike its name off the register, and shall publish notice thereof in an appointed newspaper, and on such publication the company shall be dissolved:

Provided that -

(a) the liability, if any, of every officer, manager and member of the company shall continue and may be enforced as if the company had not been dissolved; and

(b) nothing in this subsection shall affect the power of the Court to wind up a company the name of which has been struck off the register.

(6) If a company or any member or creditor thereof feels aggrieved by the company having been struck off the register, the Court on an application made by the company or member or creditor before the expiration of twenty years from the publication of the notice aforesaid may, if satisfied that the company was at the time of the striking off carrying on business or in operation, or otherwise that it is just that the company be restored to the register, order the name of the company to be restored to the register, and upon a copy of the order being delivered to the Registrar for registration the company shall be deemed to have continued in existence as if its name had not been struck off; and the Court may by the order give such directions and make such provisions as seems just for placing the company and all other persons in the same position as nearly as may be as if the name of the company had not been struck off.

(7) A notice to be sent under this section to a liquidator may be addressed to the liquidator at his last known place of business, and a letter or notice to be sent under this section to a company may be addressed to the company at its registered office, or, if no office has been registered to the care of some officer of the company, or, if there is no officer of the company whose name and address are known to the Registrar, may be sent to each of the persons who subscribed the memorandum, addressed to him at the address mentioned in the memorandum.

Property of dissolved company to be bona vacantia.

262. Where a company is dissolved, all property and rights whatsoever vested in or held on trust for the company immediately before its dissolution, including leasehold property but not including property held by the company on trust for any other person, shall, subject and without prejudice to any order which may at any time be made by the Court under the two last foregoing sections, be deemed to be bona vacantia and shall accordingly belong to the Crown.

Power of Crown to disclaim title to property vesting under foregoing section.

263.(1) Where any property vests in the Crown under the last preceding section, the Crown's title thereto under that section may be disclaimed by a notice signed by the Attorney General.

(2) When a notice of disclaimer is executed under this section as respects any property, that property shall be deemed not to have been vested in the Crown under the last preceding section and section 240 shall apply to the property as if it had been disclaimed under subsection (1) of that section.

Investment of surplus funds.

264.(1) When the cash balance standing to the credit of the account of any company in liquidation is in excess of the amount which, in the opinion of the liquidator is required for the time being to answer demands in respect of the company's debts, the liquidator may invest the amount not so required in investments that the committee of inspection authorises, or in the absence of a committee of inspection that the Court authorises.

(2) In the case of a winding up by the Court the liquidator shall not make any investment under subsection (1) without the sanction of the Court; in the case of a members' or creditors' voluntary winding up the liquidator shall not act without the sanction of the committee of inspection or when there is no committee of inspection without the sanction of a general meeting of members or a meeting of creditors, as the case may be.

PART XIV

RECEIVERS AND MANAGERS

Disqualification of undischarged bankrupt from acting as receiver or manager.

265.(1) If any person being an undischarged bankrupt under the laws of any country acts as receiver or manager of the property of a company on behalf of debenture holders, he shall, subject to the following subsection, be liable on conviction on indictment to imprisonment for a term of not exceeding two years, or on summary conviction to imprisonment for a term not exceeding six months or to a fine not exceeding one thousand dollars or both.

(2) The foregoing subsection shall not apply to a receiver or manager where -

(a) the appointment under which he acts and the bankruptcy were both before the commencement of this Act; or

(b) he acts under an appointment made by order of a court.

Receivers and managers appointed out of Court.

266.(1) A receiver or manager of the property of a company appointed under the powers contained in any instrument may apply to the Court for directions in relation to any particular matter arising in connection with the performance of his functions and on any such application the Court may give such directions, or may make such order declaring the rights of persons before the Court or otherwise, as the Court thinks just.

(2) A receiver or manager of the property of a company appointed under the powers contained in any instrument shall, to the same extent as if he had been appointed by order of a Court, be personally liable on any contract entered into by him in the performance of his functions, except in so far as the contract otherwise provides, and entitled in respect of that liability to indemnity out of the assets; but nothing in this subsection shall be taken as limiting any right to indemnity which he would have apart from this subsection, or as limiting his liability on contracts entered into without authority or as conferring any right to indemnity in respect of that liability.

(3) This section shall apply whether the receiver or manager was appointed before or after the commencement of this Act but subsection (2) thereof shall not apply to contracts entered into before the appointed day.

Notification that receiver or manager appointed.

267.(1) Where a receiver or manager of the property of a company has been appointed, every invoice, order for goods or business letter issued by or on behalf of the company the receiver or manager or the liquidator of the company, being a document on or in which the name of the company appears, shall contain a statement that a receiver or manager has been appointed.

(2) If default is made in complying with the requirements of this section, the company and any of the following persons who knowingly and wilfully authorizes or permits the default namely, any officer of the company, any liquidator of the company and any receiver or manager, shall be liable to a fine of one hundred dollars.

Power of Court to fix remuneration on application of liquidator.

268. The Court may, on an application made to the Court by the liquidator of a company, by order fix the amount to be paid by way of remuneration to any person who, under the powers contained in any instrument, has been appointed as receiver or manager of the property of the company and may from time to time, on an application made either by the liquidator or by the receiver or manager, vary or amend any order so made.

Provisions as to information where receiver or manager appointed.

269.(1) Where a receiver or manager of the whole or substantially the whole of the property of the company (hereafter in this section and in the next following section referred to as "the receiver") is appointed on behalf of the holders of any debentures of the company secured by a floating charge, then subject to the provisions of this and the next following section -

(a) the receiver shall forthwith send to the company notice of his appointment; and

(b) the company shall, within fourteen days after receipt of the notice, or such longer time as may be allowed by the Court or the receiver, submit to the receiver a statement showing as at the date of the receiver's appointment particulars of the company's assets, debts and liabilities, the names, addresses and occupations of its creditors, the securities held by them respectively and such further information as the receiver shall require and the company is able to give.

(2) The receiver may require any statement or part of a statement submitted under subsection 1(b) to be verified by an affidavit from an officer of the company.

(3) If any person without reasonable excuse makes default in complying with the requirements of this section, he shall be liable to a default fine.

Delivery to Registrar of accounts of receivers and managers.

270.(1) Every receiver of the property of a company who has been appointed under the powers contained in any instrument shall, within one month, or such longer period as the Registrar may allow, after the expiration of the period of six months from the date of his appointment and of every subsequent period of six months and within one month after he ceases to act as receiver or manager, deliver to the Registrar for registration an abstract showing his receipts and his payments during that period of six months, or, where he ceases to act as aforesaid, during the period from the end of the period to which the last preceding abstract related up to the date of his so ceasing, and the aggregate amount of his receipts and of his payments during all preceding periods since his appointment.

(2) Any receiver or manager who makes default in complying with the provisions of this section shall be liable to a default fine.

Enforcement of duty of receiver to make returns.

271.(1) If -

(a) any receiver of the property of a company, who has made default in filing, delivering or making any return, account or other document or in giving any notice, which a receiver is by law required to file, deliver, make or give, fails to make good the default within 14 days after the service on him of a notice requiring him to do so; or

(b) any receiver of the property of a company who has been appointed under the powers contained in any instrument, has, after being required at any time by the liquidator of the company so to do, failed to render proper accounts of his receipts and payments and to pay over to the liquidator the amount properly payable to him, the Court may, on an application made for the purpose, make an order directing the receiver or manager, as the case may be, to make good the default within such time as may be specified in the order.

(2) An application for the purposes of this section may be made by any member or creditor of the company or by the Registrar or in the case of a default under subsection 1(b) by the liquidator and the order may provide that all costs of and incidental to the application shall be borne by the receiver.

Construction of references to receivers and managers.

272. It is hereby declared that, except where the context otherwise requires -

(a) any reference in this Act to a receiver or manager of the property of a company, or to a receiver thereof, includes a reference to a receiver or manager, or, as the case may be, to a receiver, of part only of that property and to a receiver only of the income arising from that property or from part thereof; and

(b) any reference in this Act to the appointment of a receiver or manager under powers contained in any instrument includes a reference to an appointment made under powers which, by virtue of any enactment are implied in and have effect as if contained in an instrument.

PART XIVA

TRANSFER OF SECURITIES

Transfer of securities.

272A.(1) Notwithstanding any statutory provision or any rule of law to the contrary, title to securities of companies whose securities are traded or listed on an appointed stock exchange may be evidenced and transferred without a written instrument by an appointed agent or in accordance with Regulations made under this section.

(2) Subsection (1) shall not relieve companies registered in Bermuda from complying with section 65.

(3) The Minister may make Regulations enabling title to securities to be evidenced and transferred without a written instrument.

(4) In this section -

(a) "appointed agent" means a person appointed by the Minister for the purposes of this section;

(b) "securities" means shares, stock, debentures, debenture stock, loan stock, bonds and other securities of any description;

(c) references to title to securities include any legal or equitable interest in securities; and

(d) references to a transfer of title include a transfer by way of security.

(5) The Regulations may make provision -

(a) for procedures for recording and transferring title to securities; and

(b) for the regulation of those procedures and the persons responsible for or involved in their operation.

(6) The Regulations shall contain such safeguards as appear to be appropriate for the protection of investors and for ensuring that competition is not restricted, distorted or prevented.

(7) The Regulations may for the purpose of enabling or facilitating the operation of the new procedures make provision with respect to the rights and obligations of persons in relation to securities dealt with under the procedures, but the Regulations shall be framed so as to secure that the rights and obligations in relation to securities dealt with under the new procedures correspond, so far as practicable, with those which would arise apart from any Regulations under this section.

(8) The Regulations may include such supplementary, incidental and transitional provisions as appear to the Minister to be necessary or expedient and in particular, provision may be made for the purpose of giving effect to -

(a) the transmission of title to securities by operation of law;

(b) any restriction on the transfer of title to securities arising by virtue of the provisions of any statutory provision or instrument, court order or agreement;

(c) any power conferred by any such provision on a person to deal with securities on behalf of the person entitled.

(9) The Regulations may make provision with respect to the persons responsible for the operation of the new procedures -

(a) as to the consequences of their insolvency or incapacity; or

(b) as to the transfer from them to other persons of their functions in relation to the new procedures.

(10) The Regulations may make different provision for different cases.

(11) The Minister shall cause the appointment of an appointed agent to be published in an appointed newspaper.

PART XV

GENERAL

Form of Registers etc.

273.(1) Any book or paper required by this or any other Act, whether public or private, to be kept by the Registrar or a company may be kept by recording the matters in question in bound books or in any other permanent manner including a form otherwise than legible.

(2) Where any such book or paper is not kept in a bound book adequate precautions shall be taken for guarding against falsification and facilitating its discovery and where the book or paper is kept in a form otherwise than legible it shall be capable of being reproduced in a legible form

.

(3) Where in this or any other Act, whether public or private, provision is made for the inspection or reproduction of any book or paper then it shall be treated as a provision to allow inspection or reproduction in a legible form.

(4) Copies of minutes referred to in section 81 and financial statements referred to in section 84 shall be preserved in the registered office of the company for a period of six years from the date when they were first required.

(5) Where any company fails to comply with any provision of this section the company and any officer responsible for the default shall be liable to a fine of one thousand dollars.

Certain officers to be exempt from company fees and charges.

274. The Accountant General, the Registrar, the Official Receiver and any person acting on their behalf shall be exempt from the payment of any fee or charges for inspecting or copying the register or any books or papers of a company when lawfully entitled so to do.

Penalty for improper use of word "Limited".

275. If any person or persons trade or carry on business under any name or title of which "Limited" or any contraction or imitation of such word is the last word, that person or those persons shall, unless duly incorporated with limited liability, be liable to a default fine.

Protection and inspection of books when offence suspected.

276.(1) Without prejudice to any other provision of law, where, on an application to the Minister by or on behalf of the Attorney-General, it appears to the Minister that an offence under this Act may have been committed, and that evidence relating to the commission of such offence may be found in any books or papers of or under the control of the company, a direction in writing may be made by the Minister requiring the secretary to the company or such other officer or person as may be named in the direction to produce the said books or papers or any of them to a person named in the direction at a place and time so named.

(2) When a direction has been made under subsection (1), the person named in the direction to whom the said books or papers are to be produced, shall inspect and may take copies thereof for the purpose of investigating and obtaining evidence of any offence under this Act.

(3) A person to whom books and papers are produced pursuant to subsection (1) shall on completion of his investigation forward a report of the results thereof to the Attorney-General together with all copies of documents made by him pursuant to subsection (2).

(4) Any person who fails to comply with a direction of the Minister made under subsection (1) is guilty of a summary offence and is liable to a fine not exceeding one thousand dollars or to imprisonment for a term not exceeding six months or to both such fine and imprisonment.

(5) A certificate purporting to be signed by the Minister certifying that a person has failed to comply with a direction made by him under subsection (1) shall, in any prosecution for an offence under subsection (3) be prima facie proof of such failure to comply.

(6) For the purpose of this section "company" shall include an overseas company.

Appeals to the Court.

276A.(1) An appeal shall lie to the Court against an order of the Minister revoking a licence under section 114B or section 129A.

(2) An appeal under this section shall lie at the instance of the company affected thereby and shall be commenced by notice in writing served upon the Attorney-General within twenty-one days after the day on which the revocation made under section 114B or section 129A takes effect.

(3) Subject to subsection (2), the Chief Justice may make rules of court under section 62 of the Supreme Court Act 1905 for the purpose of regulating the practice and procedure on appeals under this section.

(4) On an appeal under this section, the Court may confirm, reverse, or modify the decision of the Minister or remit the matter to him with the opinion of the Court thereon.

(5) Unless the Court otherwise orders, an appeal under this section shall not have the effect of suspending the execution of the decision appealed against, pending the determination of the appeal.

Onus of proof.

276B. In any proceedings under this Act in which the right of any company to carry on business in Bermuda is in issue, the onus of proving that the company had, at the relevant time, the right to carry on business in Bermuda, shall be on that company unless, at the relevant time, that company was licensed under this Act.

Proof of certificate.

276C. A certificate purporting to be under the hand of the Minister specifying that any particular company was or was not licensed under this Act during any period specified in the certificate shall be receivable in evidence in any proceedings under this Act without further proof and shall be prima facie evidence of the facts specified therein.

Publication of orders.

276D. Every revocation of the licence of a company made under section 114B or section 129A shall be published in the Gazette and shall take effect from the date of such publication or such later date as may be specified therein.

Penalty for false statements or failure to make a statement.

277.(1) If any person in any return, report, certificate, book or paper or other document, required by or for the purposes of any provision of this Act wilfully makes a statement false in any material particular, knowing it to be false, he shall be guilty of an offence and liable on conviction on indictment to imprisonment for a term of two years, or on summary conviction to imprisonment for a term of twelve months or to a fine of two thousand dollars or to both such fine and imprisonment.

(2) Any person in any return, report, certificate, book or paper or other document, required by or for the purposes of any provision of this Act fails to make a statement he is required to make in such return, report, certificate, book or paper or other document and any person who wilfully fails to make a return, report or document which he is required to make shall be liable to a fine of one thousand dollars.

Section 452 of Criminal Code not to apply.

278. Section 452 of the Criminal Code shall not apply to offences against the provisions of this Act:

Provided that no prosecution for a summary offence shall be begun more than three years after the offence was committed.

Application of fines.

279. A court imposing any fine under this Act may direct that the fines whole or any part thereof shall be applied in or towards payment of the costs of the proceedings.

Default fines.

280.(1) Where in this Act it is provided that any person who is in default shall be liable to a default fine, such person shall, for every day during which the default, refusal or contravention continues, be liable to a fine of twenty dollars.

(2) Notwithstanding subsection (1) an individual who is in default shall only be liable to a fine if he knowingly is guilty of the default or knowingly and wilfully authorizes or permits the default.

(3) It shall be lawful for the Registrar, in any case where a person fails to comply with a provision of this Act which is subject to a default fine and the failure is not due to wilful neglect or default, to accept payment of a penalty of two hundred and fifty dollars, and in such case subsection (1) shall not apply.

(4) Any penalty payable under this Act may be recovered by the Accountant General in the Supreme Court or in a court of summary jurisdiction as a civil debt.

Power of Court to grant relief in certain cases.

281.(1) If in any proceedings for negligence, default, breach of duty or breach of trust against an officer of a company or a person employed by a company as auditor, whether he is or is not an officer of the company, it appears to the Court hearing the case that that officer or person is or may be liable in respect of the negligence, default, breach of duty or breach of trust, but that he has acted honestly and reasonably, and that, having regard to all the circumstances of the case, including those connected with his appointment, he ought fairly to be excused for the negligence, default, breach of duty or breach of trust, that Court may relieve him, either wholly or partly, from his liability on such terms as the Court may think fit.

(2) Where any such officer or person aforesaid has reason to apprehend that any claim will or might be made against him in respect of any negligence, default, breach of duty or breach of trust, he may apply to the Court for relief, and the Court on any such application shall have the same power to relieve him as under this section it would have had if it had been a Court before which proceedings against that person for negligence, default, breach of duty or breach of trust had been brought.

(3) Where any case to which subsection (1) of this section applies is being tried by a judge with a jury, the judge, after hearing the evidence, may, if he is satisfied that the defendant ought in pursuance of that subsection to be relieved either in whole or in part from the liability sought to be enforced against him, withdraw the case in whole or in part from the jury and forthwith direct judgment to be entered for the defendant on such terms as to costs or otherwise as the judge may think proper.

Suits and actions against Registrar and Official Receiver.

282.(1) No suit or action shall lie against the Registrar or the Official Receiver or any person acting on their behalf in respect of anything done or omitted to be done in their official capacity in good faith without negligence.

(2) Nothing in subsection (1) shall be deemed to interfere with applications or references to the Court under Part XIII.

Registrar and Official Receiver to be indemnified in respect of foreign suits.

283. Neither the Registrar nor the Official Receiver shall be required to prosecute, defend or take part in any proceedings outside the jurisdiction of the Court unless he is indemnified by or on behalf of the person who wishes him to act against any judgment, order or costs that may be awarded against him by deed guarantee or deposit, as he may require.

Mode of making applications to Court.

284.(1) Subject to any other provision of the law including the Rules of the Supreme Court 1952 any application under this Act shall be made by originating summons.

(2) An originating summons may in the first place be heard ex parte when the Court may direct that the summons shall be served on such persons, if any, as it shall think fit and that the summons shall be supported by such evidence as it shall require.

Power to enforce orders.

285. Orders made by any Court under this Act may be enforced as orders made in an action pending therein.

Amendment of private Acts.

286.(1) Subject to subsections (3), (4) and the other provisions of this Act which enable private Acts incorporating companies to be amended a company to which this Act applies may amend any provision of its incorporating Act by resolution passed at a general meeting of members of which due notice has been given:

Provided that before notice of the meeting is given to the members the Minister has consented to the amendment.

(2) Subject to subsections (3) and (4) the provisions of section 12, other than subsection (1) thereof, shall apply to a company wishing to amend a provision of its incorporating Act as if it were altering its memorandum and in the application of such provisions the words "private Act" shall be substituted for the word "memorandum".

(3) No amendment shall be made to any private Act which amends the provisions of any public Act including this Act or amends any provision of law referred to in paragraphs (a) to (e) of the proviso to subsection (2) of section 35 of the Constitution.

(4) The change of name of a company incorporated by private Act shall be made in accordance with section 10.

Repeal of, and amendments to, other Acts, and savings, Seventh Schedule.

287.(1) The enactments specified in Part I of the Seventh Schedule are repealed, and the enactments specified in Part 11 of that Schedule are amended in the respects specified in that Part of that Schedule.

(2) Nothing in this Act shall affect any appointment, conveyance, mortgage, deed or agreement made, resolution passed, direction given, proceeding taken, instrument issued or thing done under any enactment repealed or amended by subsection (1) (in this Act referred to as a "former enactment relating to companies"), but any such appointment, conveyance, mortgage, deed, agreement, resolution, direction, proceeding, instrument or thing shall, if in force immediately before the appointed day, continue in force and, so far as it could have been made, passed, given, taken, issued or done under this Act, shall have effect as if made, passed, given, taken, issued or done under this Act.

(2A) Where immediately before the appointed day -

(a) a permit under section 9 of the Companies (Incorporation by Registration) Act 1970 had not either been granted or refused by the Minister in response to an application made to him under the Act before that day for the incorporation of a company; or

(b) such a permit had in fact been granted by the Minister but a certificate of incorporation had not been issued in respect of the company under that Act,

the repeals and amendments effected by subsection (1) of this section shall be deemed not to have had effect in relation to such an application but the enactments repealed or, as the case may be, amended by that subsection shall be deemed to continue in full force and effect on and after that day to such extent as to enable the Minister, if he thinks fit, to grant the permit, and the Registrar to issue the certificate of incorporation, under the Companies (Incorporation by Registration) Act 1970; and where a certificate of incorporation is issued in respect of a company on or after the appointed day by virtue of this subsection, the company shall be deemed to be a company registered before the appointed day for the purposes of paragraph (a) of subsection (1) of section 4.

(2B) Where before the appointed day a company has made proposals to the Minister under section 19 of the Companies (Incorporation by Registration) Act 1970 for the alteration of its memorandum of association and immediately before that day the Minister had not either approved or rejected the proposals, the repeals and amendments effected by subsection (1) of this section shall be deemed not to have had effect in relation to those proposals, but the enactments repealed or, as the case may be, amended by the said subsection (1) shall be deemed to continue in full force and effect on and after that day to such extent as to enable the Minister, if he thinks fit, to approve the proposals, and the Registrar to register the altered memorandum, under the Companies (Incorporation by Registration) Act 1970; and where an altered memorandum is so registered on or after the appointed day by virtue of this subsection, the alteration to the memorandum shall be deemed for the purposes of this Act to have been effected before the appointed day.

(3) Any legal proceedings, winding up or inspection taking place on the appointed day shall continue as if this Act had not been enacted unless the Court orders that this Act shall apply to the proceeding, winding up or inspection.

(4) Any document referring to any former enactment relating to companies shall be construed as referring to the corresponding enactment of this Act.

(5) Any person appointed to any office under or by virtue of any former enactment relating to companies shall be deemed to have been appointed to that office under or by virtue of this Act.

(5A) Any person holding the office of Registrar of Companies immediately before the appointed day shall be deemed as from the appointed day to have been duly appointed Registrar of Companies and Official Receiver under section 3.

(5B) Any person holding the office of Registrar of Companies on or after the commencement of the Companies (Winding Up) Act 1977 and before the appointed day shall be deemed to have been the Official Receiver in relation to any function performed by him in that name in purported pursuance of any power conferred by that Act upon the Registrar of Companies in Bermuda to perform the functions of the Official Receiver in England, anything to the contrary notwithstanding.

(6) Any register kept under any former enactment relating to companies shall be deemed part of the register to be kept under the corresponding provisions of this Act.

(7) All funds and accounts constituted under this Act shall be deemed to be in continuation of the corresponding funds and accounts constituted under the former enactments relating to companies.

(7A) Where immediately before the appointed day an exempted company incorporated by registration under any former enactment relating to companies specified its objects or powers by reference to all or any paragraphs of the First Schedule to the Companies (Incorporation by Registration) Act 1970 (now repealed) such company shall after the appointed day continue to have the objects or powers so specified by reference and shall be capable of exercising such objects or powers whether or not stated as such, anything to the contrary notwithstanding.

(7B) Where immediately before the appointed day a company in its incorporating Act specified its objects or powers by reference to all or any paragraphs of the Schedule to the Exempted Companies Act 1950 (now repealed) or the First Schedule to the Companies (Incorporation by Registration) Act 1970 (now repealed), such company shall after the appointed day continue to have and shall be deemed always to have had the objects or powers, as the case may be, so specified by reference and further shall be deemed to be and always to have been capable of exercising such objects or powers, whether or not stated as such, anything to the contrary notwithstanding.

(7C) Notwithstanding the repeal of any enactment by this Act, any licence granted under any enactment so repealed to an exempted company enabling such company to carry on business in or from within Bermuda shall, if valid immediately before the appointed day, continue in full force and effect according to its tenor as if it were a licence granted under section 129A.

(7D) Notwithstanding the repeal of any enactment by this Act, any licence granted under any enactment so repealed to a local company or an hotel company enabling such company to carry on business in Bermuda shall, if valid immediately before the appointed day, continue in full force and effect according to its tenor as if it were a licence granted under section 114B.

(8) Where any offence, being an offence for the continuance of which a penalty was proved, has

been committed under any former enactment relating to companies, proceedings may be taken under this Act in respect of the continuance of the offence after the appointed day, in the same manner as if the offence had been committed under the corresponding provisions of this Act.
(9) Save where otherwise provided in this Act nothing in this section shall affect the provisions of the Interpretation Act 1951 relating to the repeal, re-enactment or amendment of Acts.

Rules.

288.(1) The power of the Chief Justice to make rules of Court under section 62 of the Supreme Court Act 1905, shall include a like power in relation to all Court proceedings under this Act including any matters to be prescribed in relation to the winding up of a company by the Court and the fees to be paid in respect of Court proceedings.

(2) The Minister may by rule prescribe any matter to be prescribed under this Act in respect of which the Chief Justice is not entitled to make rules and may make rules prescribing the manner and form in which any application or declaration under this Act may be made and may by regulations under the Government Fees Act 1965 or the Stamp Duties Act 1976 whichever is appropriate fix fees for any function performed under this Act unless otherwise prescribed.

(3) All rules made by the Chief Justice, other than rules prescribing fees shall not be subject to section 6 of the Statutory Instruments Act 1977.

(4) All rules by whomsoever made under this Act prescribing fees shall be subject to affirmative resolution procedure.

(5) All rules unless otherwise expressly provided and those referred to in subsections (3) and (4) shall be subject to negative resolution procedure.

Saving.

289. Nothing in this Act shall affect the provisions of section 61 of the Bermuda Housing Act 1980.

FIRST SCHEDULE

(Section 11(I))

A company limited by shares, or other company having a share capital, may exercise all or any of the following powers subject to any provision of the law or its memorandum -

1. [*Deleted*]

2. to acquire or undertake the whole or any part of the business, property and liabilities of any person carrying on any business that the company is authorized to carry on;

3. to apply for register, purchase, lease, acquire, hold, use, control, licence, sell, assign or dispose of patents, patent rights, copyrights, trade marks, formulae, licences, inventions, processes, distinctive marks and similar rights;

4. to enter into partnership or into any arrangement for sharing of profits, union of interests, co-operation, joint venture, reciprocal concession or otherwise with any person carrying on or engaged in or about to carry on or engage in any business or transaction that the company is authorized to carry on or engage in or any business or transaction capable of being conducted so as to benefit the company;

5. to take or otherwise acquire and hold securities in any other body corporate having objects altogether or in part similar to those of the company or carrying on any business capable of being conducted so as to benefit the company;

6. subject to section 96 to lend money to any employee or to any person having dealings with the company or with whom the company proposes to have dealings or to any other body corporate any of whose shares are held by the company;

7. to apply for, secure or acquire by grant, legislative enactment, assignment, transfer, purchase or otherwise and to exercise, carry out and enjoy any charter, licence, power, authority, franchise, concession, right or privilege, that any government or authority or any body corporate or other public body may be empowered to grant, and to pay for, aid in and contribute toward carrying it into effect and to assume any liabilities or obligations incidental thereto;

8. to establish and support or aid in the establishment and support of associations, institutions, funds or trusts for the benefit of employees or former employers of the company or its predecessors, or the dependants or connections of such employees or former employees, and grant pensions and allowances, and make payments towards insurance or for any object similar to those set forth in this paragraph, and to subscribe or guarantee money for charitable, benevolent, educational or religious objects or for any exhibition of for any public, general or useful objects;

9. to promote any company for the purpose of acquiring or taking over any of the property and liabilities of the company or for any other purpose that may benefit the company;

10. to purchase, lease, take in exchange, hire or otherwise acquire any personal property and any rights or privileges that the company considers necessary or convenient for the purpose of its business;

11. to construct, maintain, alter, renovate and demolish any buildings or works necessary or convenient for its objects;

12. to take land in Bermuda by way of lease or leasing agreement for a term not exceeding fifty years, being land "bona fide" required for the purposes of the business of the company and with the consent of the Minister granted in his discretion to take land in Bermuda by way of lease or leasing agreement for a term not exceeding twenty-one years in order to provide accommodation or recreational facilities for its officers and employees and when no longer necessary for any of the above purposes to terminate or transfer the lease or leasing agreement;

13. except to the extent, if any, as may be otherwise expressly provided in its incorporating Act or memorandum and subject to the provisions of this Act every company shall have power to invest the moneys of the Company by way of mortgage of real or personal property of every description in Bermuda or elsewhere and to sell, exchange, vary, or dispose of such mortgage as the company shall from time to time determine;

14. to construct, improve, maintain, work, manage, carry out or control any roads, ways, tramways, branches or sidings, bridges, reservoirs, watercourses, wharves, factories, warehouses, electric works, shops, stores and other works and conveniences that may advance the interests of the company and contribute to, subsidize or otherwise assist or take part in the construction, improvement, maintenance, working, management, carrying out of control thereof;

15. to raise and assist in raising money for, and aid by way of bonus, loan, promise, endorsement, guarantee or otherwise, any person and guarantee the performance or fulfilment of any contracts or obligations of any person, and in particular guarantee the payment of the principal of and interest on the debt obligations of any such person;

16. to borrow or raise or secure the payment of money in such manner as the company may think fit;

17. to draw, make, accept, endorse, discount, execute and issue bills of exchange, promissory notes, bills of lading, warrants and other negotiable or transferable instruments;

18. when properly authorized to do so, to sell, lease, exchange or otherwise dispose of the undertaking of the company or any part thereof as an entirety or substantially as an entirety for such consideration as the company thinks fit;

19. to sell, improve, manage, develop, exchange, lease, dispose of, turn to account or otherwise deal with the property of the company in the ordinary course of its business;

20. to adopt such means of making known the products of the company as may seem expedient, and in particular by advertising, by purchase and exhibition of works of art or interest, by publication of books and periodicals and by granting prizes and rewards and making donations;

21. to cause the company to be registered and recognized in any foreign jurisdiction, and designate persons therein according to the laws of that foreign jurisdiction or to represent the company and to accept service for and on behalf of the company of any process or suit;

22. to allot and issue fully-paid shares of the company in payment or part payment of any property purchased or otherwise acquired by the company or for any past services performed for the company;

23. to distribute among the members of the company in cash, kind, specie or otherwise as may be resolved, by way of dividend, bonus or in any other manner considered advisable, any property of the company, but not so as to decrease the capital of the company unless the distribution is made for the purpose of enabling the company to be dissolved or the distribution, apart from this paragraph, would be otherwise lawful;

24. to establish agencies and branches;

25. to take or hold mortgages, hypothecates, liens and charges to secure payment of the purchase price, or of any unpaid balance of the purchase price, of any part of the property of the company of whatsoever kind sold by the company, or for any money due to the company from purchasers and others and to sell or otherwise dispose of any such mortgage, hypothec, lien or charge;

26. to pay all costs and expenses of or incidental to the incorporation and organization of the company;

27. to invest and deal with the moneys of the company not immediately required for the objects of the company in such manner as may be determined;

28. to do any of the things authorized by this subsection and all things authorized by its memorandum as principals, agents, contractors, trustees or otherwise, and either alone or in conjunction with others;

29. to do all such other things as are incidental or conducive to the attainment of the objects and the exercise of the powers of the company.

Every company may exercise its powers beyond the boundaries of Bermuda to the extent to which the laws in force where the powers are sought to be exercised permit.

SECOND SCHEDULE

(Section 11(2))

Subject to section 4A, a company may by reference include in its memorandum any of the following objects that is to say the business of -

(a) insurance and reinsurance of all kinds;

(b) packaging of goods of all kinds;

(c) buying, selling dealing in goods of all kinds;

(d) designing and manufacturing of goods of all kinds;

(e) mining and quarrying and exploration for metals, minerals, fossil fuel and precious stones of all kinds and their preparation for sale or use;

(f) exploring for, the drilling for, the moving, transporting and refining petroleum and hydro carbon products including oil and oil products;

(g) scientific research including the improvement discovery and development of processes, inventions, patents and designs and the construction, maintenance and operation of laboratories and research centres;

(h) land, sea and air undertakings including the land, ship and air carriage of passengers, mails and goods of all kinds;

(i) ships and aircraft owners, managers, operators, agents, builders and repairers;

(j) acquiring, owning, selling, chartering, repairing or dealing in ships and aircraft;

(k) travel agents, freight contractors and forwarding agents;

(l) dock owners, wharfingers, warehousemen;

(m) ship chandlers and dealing in rope, canvas oil and ship stores of all kinds;

(n) all forms of engineering;

(o) developing, operating, advising or acting as technical consultants to any other enterprise or business;

(p) farmers, livestock breeders and keepers, graziers, butchers, tanners and processors of and dealers in all kinds of live and dead stock, wool, hides, tallow, grain, vegetables and other produce;

(q) acquiring by purchase or otherwise and holding as an investment inventions, patents, trade marks, trade names, trade secrets, designs and the like;

(r) buying, selling, hiring, letting and dealing in conveyances of any sort;

(s) employing, providing, hiring out and acting as agent for artists, actors, entertainers of all sorts, authors, composers, producers, directors, engineers and experts or specialists of any kind; and

(t) to acquire by purchase or otherwise and hold, sell, dispose of and deal in real property situated outside Bermuda and in personal property of all kinds wheresoever situated;

(u) to enter into any guarantee, contract of indemnity or suretyship and to assure, support or secure with or without consideration or benefit the performance of any obligations of any person or persons and to guarantee the fidelity of individuals filling or about to fill situations of trust or confidence

(v) to be and carry on the business of a mutual fund within the meaning of section 156A.

Provided that none of these objects shall enable the company to carry on restricted business activity as set out in the Ninth Schedule except with the consent of the Minister.

THIRD SCHEDULE

(Section 114)

PART I

PROVISIONS TO BE COMPLIED WITH BY A LOCAL COMPANY CARRYING ON BUSINESS IN BERMUDA

1.(1) The company shall be controlled by Bermudians.

(2) Without prejudice to the generality of sub-paragraph (1), at least sixty per centum of the total voting rights in the company shall be exerciseable by Bermudians.

2.(1) The percentage of Bermudian directors, and the percentage of shares beneficially owned by Bermudians, in the company shall not be less than sixty per centum in each case:

Provided that the company shall not be deemed to be in breach of this paragraph in so far as, and so long as, it is acting in accordance with sub-paragraph (2).

(2) The company shall act in accordance with this subparagraph if the percentage of shares beneficially owned by Bermudians in it falls below sixty per centum by virtue of factors which are beyond its control and it gives notice in writing to the person who is not Bermudian and whose ownership of shares results in the percentage so falling, as soon as the directors become aware of that fact, that -

(a) he must divest himself of his interest in those shares as soon as may be and, in any event, not later than three years from the date upon which he receives the notice; and

(b) he must not exercise any voting rights attaching to such shares from the date upon which he receives the notice, and the three years calculated in accordance with paragraph (a) have not elapsed:

Provided that the Minister may in any particular case, for good cause, extend the period of three years for a further period not exceeding one year.

(3) For the purposes of sub-paragraph (2), the directors of a company shall be deemed to become aware that the percentage of shares beneficially owned by Bermudians in their company is less than the percentage specified in sub-paragraph (1) three days after the day upon which any director of a company would, if acting with due diligence, have become aware of that fact.

PART II

COMPANIES NOT REQUIRED TO COMPLY WITH PART I

The Shell Company of Bermuda Limited within the scope of any enactment authorizing the carrying on of its business operation in Bermuda.

FOURTH SCHEDULE

(SECTION 66(2))

Fees for Provision of Copies and Entries in Share Registers

The fee prescribed for the purposes of section 66(2) of the Act is as follows:

(a) for the first one hundred entries or part thereof copied	$ 5.00
(b) the next one thousand entries or part thereof copied	$20.00
(c) for every subsequent one thousand entries or part thereof copied	$20.00

FIFTH SCHEDULE

PART I

(Section 121)

1. The appropriate fee in the case of a company whose business includes the management of any unit trust scheme, shall be two thousand four hundred and seventy dollars in respect of each unit trust scheme managed by that company at the date of the declaration made under section 121;

2. Issued capital

When the issued capital of company if a company limited by shares, or other company having a share capital, is -	Tax payable
(i) less than $50,000	$ 550
(ii) $50,000 or more but less than $250,000	$ 825
(iii) $250,000 or more but less than $500,000	$ 1,375
(iv) $500,000 or more but less than $1,000,000	$ 2,745
(v) $1,000,000 or more but less than $5,000,000	$ 5,485
(vi) $5,000,000 or more but less than $10,000,000	$10,450
(vii) $10,000,000 or more	$15,675

In the case of a local company which is a mutual company, the tax payable by such company shall be on the same scale as a company limited by shares, but the basis shall be the reserve fund of such a company in place of the issued capital.

In the case of a local company which is a company limited by guarantee, other than a mutual company no fee shall be payable.

In the case of a local company engaging in or carrying on wholesale trading business in respect of petroleum and other oils or liquefied petroleum gas the tax payable by such company shall be $15,675.

PART II

(Section 131, 135)

1. A EXEMPTED COMPANIES (Section 131)

Conditions	Fee
(a) Where the assessable capital of the exempted company -	
(i) is $0 - £12,000	$ 1,695
(ii) is $12,001 - $120,000	$ 3,460
(iii) is $120,001 - $1,200,000	$ 5,340
(iv) is $1,200,001 - $12,000,000	$ 7,120
(v) is $12,000,001 - $100,000,000	$ 8,900
(vi) is £100,000,001 - $500,000,000	$15,900
(vii) is $500,000,001 or more	$25,500
(b) Where the exempted company's business includes the management of any unit trust scheme: in respect of each unit trust scheme managed by the company at the date the declaration under section 131(1) was made	$ 2,470
(bb) (i) Where the exempted company is a small foreign sales corporation which does not lease aircraft	$500
(ii) Where the exempted company is a regular foreign sales corporation which does not lease aircraft	$1,000
(iii) Where the exempted company is a foreign sales corporation, whether small or regular, which leases aircraft	$1,680

(c)	(i) Where the exempted company is one whose capital is denominated in a currency other than Bermuda area currency or currency of the United States of America, and the Bermuda area currency equivalent is $15,000 or less	$ 1,695
	(ii) Where the exempted company is one limited by guarantee (but is not a mutual company)	$ 1,695
	(iii) Where the exempted company is one whose memorandum provides that the company's principal object is that of holding beneficially all the shares in another exempted company which has, as an object specified in its own memorandum, the object of carrying on insurance business as defined in the Insurance Act 1978	$ 1,695
	(iv) Where the exempted company is one whose capital is denominated in a currency other than Bermuda area currency or currency of the United States of America, and the Bermuda area currency equivalent is $150,000 or less	$ 3,510
	(v) Where the exempted company is one which is engaging in or carrying on, in Bermuda, wholesale trading business in respect of petroleum and other oils or liquified petroleum gas	$16,460

2. B <u>PERMIT COMPANIES</u> (Section 135)

Conditions	Fee
(a) Where the permit company is one which is engaging in or carrying on, in Bermuda, wholesale trading business in respect of petroleum and other oils or liquified petroleum gas	$16,460
(b) Where the principal business of the permit company is finance business or insurance business or, in the case of a permit company which is open-ended, mutual fund business	$ 3,510

(c) Where the permit company's business includes the management of any unit trust scheme: in respect of each unit trust scheme managed by the company at the date the declaration under section 135 (as read with section 131) was made $ 2,470

(d) in any other case $ 1,695

For the above purposes, the following expressions have the following meanings -

"finance business" means the business of raising money from the public by the issue of bonds or other securities;

"foreign sales corporation" means a company which -

(a) has been registered under this Act as an exempted company; and

(b) has been designated as a foreign sales corporation under the Internal Revenue Code, of the United States of America, and has submitted to the Registrar a certified copy of the document which -

(i) evidences such designation; and

(ii) specifies whether the company is a small or regular foreign sales corporation;

"insurance business" means the business of effecting or carrying out contracts of insurance or reinsurance as a principal, but excluding insurance management or insurance brokerage business;

"mutual fund business" means the business of raising money from the public for investment in real property, shares, stocks or personal property;

"small foreign sales corporation" means a foreign sales corporation which, under the Internal Revenue Code of the United States of America, has been so designated;

"regular foreign sales corporation" means a foreign sales corporation which, under the Internal Revenue Code of the United States of America, has been so designated.

3. "Open-ended company" means a company which has power under the terms of its incorporation to redeem or purchase for cancellation its issued shares at the option of, or on the request of, a shareholder;

"unit trust scheme" means any arrangements made for the purpose, or having the effect, of providing, for persons having funds available for investment, facilities for the participation by them as beneficiaries under a trust, in profits or income arising from the acquisition, holding, management or disposal of any property whatsoever.

4. Where a company liable to pay the higher fee in any year does not carry on the business attracting the higher fee, it shall only pay the lower. Where a company liable to pay the higher fee at any time during a year carries on the business attracting the higher fee, it shall pay that fee for that year.

C SEGREGATED ACCOUNTS COMPANIES

In addition to the annual fee or tax otherwise payable under this Schedule a segregated accounts company registered under section 6 of the Segregated Accounts Companies Act 2000 shall pay an annual fee of $250 in respect of each segregated account operated by the company, subject to a maximum annual fee of $1000 in the aggregate.

SIXTH SCHEDULE

DELETED

SEVENTH SCHEDULE

(S.227(1)

OMITTED

NINTH SCHEDULE

(section 4A)

RESTRICTED BUSINESS ACTIVITIES

B.R. 10/99 effective 29th March, 1999

Restricted business activities are any business activity which is not specified in paragraphs (b) to (n) and (p) to (v) of the Second Schedule.

TENTH SCHEDULE

(section 4B)

PROHIBITED BUSINESS ACTIVITIES

The following are prohibited business activities -

(a) trafficking in armaments as defined in the Armaments (Control) Act 1964;

(b) except as authorized by law, operating lotteries as defined in the Lotteries Act 1944 or gambling facilities, including the operation thereof through the Internet;

(c) except as authorized by law, importation, exportation trading in, manufacture, production or supply of controlled drugs as defined by the Misuse of Drugs Act 1972.

THE SEGREGATED ACCOUNTS COMPANIES ACT 2000

ARRANGEMENT OF SECTIONS

WHEREAS it is expedient to provide for the registration and regulation of companies that operate segregated accounts:

Be it enacted by The Queen's Most Excellent Majesty, by and with the advice and consent of the Senate and the House of Assembly of Bermuda, and by the authority of the same, as follows:—

PART I - INTERPRETATION AND APPLICATION

Citation

1. This Act may be cited as the Segregated Accounts Companies Act 2000.

Interpretation and application

2.(1) In this Act—

"beneficial owner" means any person who is—

(a) identified in or by reference to a governing instrument as having a legal or beneficial interest in a segregated account;

(b) the registered holder of any security linked to a segregated account; or

(c) designated as having a beneficial interest in a segregated account in the records of a segregated accounts company;

and includes that person's successors in title or assigns;

"counterparty" means any party (other than the segregated accounts company itself), or any person deriving any interest or title from a party, to a transaction to which the company is a party, which transaction does not by its terms go to the beneficial ownership of a segregated account;

"court" means the Supreme Court;

"general account" means an account maintained under section 16(1)(c) which records all of the assets and liabilities of a segregated accounts company which are not linked to a segregated account of that company;

"general shareholder" means any member of a segregated accounts company not being the holder of a share linked to a segregated account;

"governing instrument" in relation to a segregated account, means a written instrument evidencing a transaction and conforming to the provisions of section 11;

"insurance business" means insurance business as defined in section 1(1) of the Insurance Act 1978;

"linked" means linked by means of an entry made in the records of a segregated accounts company used in the preparation of the financial statements of the company in accordance with generally accepted accounting principles and made in respect of a transaction which—

(a) records movement in value or changes in characteristics necessarily consequent on that transaction; and

(b) identifies assets, rights, liabilities, obligations or contributions as belonging to or pertaining to a segregated account;

"manager" means any person who, by virtue of the terms of a governing instrument or otherwise with the consent of a segregated accounts company and the beneficial owners of any segregated account, has control of a segregated account;

"operative date" means the date on which this Act comes into force;

"the Minister" means the Minister of Finance;

"register" means the register of segregated accounts companies maintained under section 6;

"registered" means registered under section 6;

"Registrar" means the Registrar of Companies appointed under section 3 of the Companies Act 1981;

"security" in relation to a segregated accounts company, means any share, note, bond, debenture, evidence of indebtedness, certificate, unit, warrant, or right conferring an option to acquire shares or any other right issued by or pertaining to the company, but does not include a contract of insurance unless the terms of the contract so provide;

"segregated account" means a separate and distinct account (comprising entries recording data, assets, liabilities, rights and obligations linked to such account) of a segregated accounts company maintained in respect of a beneficial owner or a counterparty in accordance with this Act;

"segregated accounts company" means a company which is registered under section 6;

"transaction" means any dealing of whatever nature, including the issue of any security, by which the assets or liabilities linked to a segregated account are affected, or, in the case of assets intended by the parties to be applied to a risk of any nature, any dealing which exposes such assets to liability or loss.

(2) For the purposes of this Act—

(a) a segregated accounts company shall be deemed to be solvent if the general account is able to pay its liabilities as they become due;

(b) a segregated account shall be deemed to be solvent if it is able to pay its liabilities as they become due.

(3) Nothing in this Act shall be construed as requiring a company which operates segregated accounts under the authority of a Private Act or otherwise to be registered.

(4) For the avoidance of doubt it is declared that, notwithstanding section 18, a segregated accounts company is not by reason only of the operation of segregated accounts carrying on trust business in or from within Bermuda for the purposes of the Trust Companies Act 1991.

PART II - REGISTRATION

Application for registration to operate segregated accounts

3.(1) Any company to which the Companies Act 1981 applies—

(a) if it is engaged in insurance business; or

(b) if it is not so engaged, with the approval of the Minister, may, by filing a notice under section 4, apply to be registered under section 6.

(2) From the date of registration of a segregated accounts company the provisions of this Act shall apply thereto and the company may enter into transactions.

(3) The establishment of a segregated account does not create a legal person distinct from the segregated accounts company.

Companies to notify Registrar

4.(1) Where a company intends to operate segregated accounts, the company shall file with the Registrar a notice thereof in writing not less than 28 days before establishing the segregated accounts.

(2) Notice given pursuant to subsection (1) shall not of itself confer any power under this Act, and the company shall not be entitled to avail itself of the provisions of this Act until it has been registered under section 6.

Documents to be filed

5.(1) The notice under section 4 shall be in such form as the Registrar may determine but shall contain the following information—

(a) the name of the company, which, subject to a direction from the Minister pursuant to section 26, shall include the expression "(SAC)";

(b) a statement that the company intends to operate segregated accounts;

(c) the address of the registered office of the company;

(d) the name and address of the segregated account representative of the company;

(e) the nature of the business of the company;

(f) the date of incorporation of the company; and

(g) a statement that the company has made provision to account for segregated accounts in the manner set out in section 16.

(2) Where the company has conducted business prior to its registration, the company, in filing a notice under section 4, shall—

(a) file with the Registrar a statutory declaration as at the date of the notice setting out a true and accurate statement of—

(i) the assets and liabilities of the company as at a date within three months prior to the date of the notice;

(ii) a description of any transaction or event which, as of the date of the notice, has occurred, or is expected to occur, between the date of the statement of assets and liabilities prepared pursuant to subparagraph (i) and the date of registration of the company as a segregated accounts company which, if it had occurred before the date of that statement, would have caused significant changes to the assets and liabilities disclosed therein; and

(iii) the segregated accounts the company intends to operate and the assets and liabilities which the company proposes to assign to each of those segregated accounts;

and declaring that—

(iv) on registration, the company will be solvent in respect of each segregated account and the general account as if each segregated account and the general account were a separate legal entity;

(v) no creditor of the company will be prejudiced; or

(vi) the creditors of the company have consented in writing to the company proceeding to register; and

(b) attach evidence of the consent in writing to registration of 75% in number of those persons who would, on the registration of the company, be the beneficial owners of the segregated accounts of the company and 75% in number of those persons who would, on the registration of the company, be counterparties to any undischarged or open transactions linked to a segregated account.

(3) Any person who, on the registration of the company, would be a beneficial owner or counterparty to an open or undischarged transaction and who does not consent to the registration of the company as a segregated accounts company under this Act may, within one month of the date of the notice under section 4, apply to the court for an order that such notice shall not have effect and that the company shall remain unregistered for the purposes of this Act.

(4) Without prejudice to the provisions of subsection (2)(b) and subsection (3), a beneficial owner or counterparty to an open or undischarged transaction linked to a segregated account who is aggrieved by a notice under section 4 may, within 21 days of receipt of the notice, apply to the Registrar to refuse to register the company.

(5) Where a company—

(a) has conducted business prior to filing a notice under section 4; and

(b) has filed such notice, it shall cause a copy of the notice to be contemporaneously given to all beneficial owners and to all counterparties to any open or undischarged transactions linked to a segregated account.

(6) If there is any material alteration of the particulars set out in subsection (2) between the date of the notice filed pursuant to section 4 and the date of registration, then the company shall give further notice to the Registrar of such alteration of particulars.

(7) The notice filed pursuant to section 4 and any documents accompanying that notice shall be treated as confidential by the Registrar and all public officers having access thereto, but this subsection does not preclude the disclosure of information for the purpose of enabling the Minister to exercise any functions conferred upon him by this Act.

Register of segregated accounts companies

6.(1) The Registrar shall maintain a register of segregated accounts companies.

(2) Upon application and upon payment of such fee as may be prescribed under the Government Fees Act 1965, the Registrar, if satisfied—

(a) that the company will be in compliance with this Act; and

(b) in the case of a financial institution as defined in section 1(1) of the Bermuda Monetary Authority Act 1969, that the Bermuda Monetary Authority has no objection to the registration, shall register the company as a segregated accounts company.

(3) The Registrar may—

(a) impose such conditions on the registration of a company as he may consider necessary to ensure the reputation of Bermuda and in particular, to vet the beneficial owners of segregated accounts and to ensure compliance with this Act;

(b) require the company to take certain steps or to refrain from adopting or pursuing a particular course of action or to restrict the scope of its segregated accounts business in a particular way.

(4) The Registrar may revoke or vary any condition or requirement imposed under subsection (3) by giving notice thereof to the company.

(5) After registering a company pursuant to subsection (2), the Registrar shall issue a certificate showing the date of registration.

(6) The Registrar shall place a copy of the certificate referred to in subsection (5) on the public file maintained by him in respect of the company.

(7) The register shall be available for inspection by members of the public.

(8) Where the Registrar refuses to register a company pursuant to subsection (2), he shall not be bound to assign any reason for his refusal and his decision shall not be subject to appeal or review in any court.

Removal from the register

7.(1) Subject to this section, the Registrar, on receipt of a request in writing by a segregated accounts company attaching thereto evidence of the consent in writing of 75% in number of the beneficial owners of the segregated accounts of the company and of 75% in number of any counterparties to any undischarged or open transactions linked to segregated accounts, shall remove the company from the register and the provisions of this Act shall cease to apply to the company.

(2) A request under subsection (1) shall be in such form as the Registrar may determine, but shall include a statutory declaration averring that no creditor of the segregated accounts company will be prejudiced by, or that the creditors have consented in writing to, the removal of the company from the register and shall have attached to the declaration a true and accurate statement of—

(a) the assets and liabilities of the company as at a date within the three months prior to the date of the request;

(b) a description of any transaction or event which, as of the date of the request, is expected to occur between the date of the statement of assets and liabilities prepared pursuant to paragraph (a) and the date of the removal of the company as a segregated accounts company which, if it had occurred before the date of the statement of assets and liabilities, would have caused significant changes to the assets and liabilities disclosed therein; and

(c) the segregated accounts which the company has operated and the assets and liabilities which were linked to each of those segregated accounts.

(3) If there is any material alteration of the particulars set out in subsection (2) between the date of the request given pursuant to subsection (1) and the removal of the company from the register, the company shall give notice to the Registrar of such alteration in particulars.

(4) A segregated accounts company shall circulate contemporaneously with the request to the Registrar under subsection (1) notice of that request to all beneficial owners of the segregated accounts company and to all counterparties to any undischarged or open transactions linked to a segregated account.

(5) A beneficial owner of a segregated account or any counterparty to any undischarged or open transaction linked to a segregated account who is aggrieved by a request made pursuant to subsection (1) may, within 21 days of receipt of notice of the request, apply to the Registrar to refuse to remove the segregated accounts company from the register or, if the removal has already occurred, to reinstate the company on the register.

(6) Where an application has been made under subsection (5) and the Registrar has made a decision on the application, any person who is aggrieved by that decision may, within 21 days of the decision, appeal to the court and the court shall hear the matter and make such order as it thinks fit.

(7) The making of a request pursuant to subsection (1) shall not of itself effect the removal of a segregated accounts company from the register and the Registrar in his absolute discretion shall determine whether to give effect to the removal of the company from the register and, in this regard, may require such information from the company as he considers necessary to render such decision.

(8) Without prejudice to the provisions of Part VIII of the Companies Act 1981 (which relates to the powers of the Minister to investigate the affairs of a company), the Registrar may, whether on his own initiative or on application by a beneficial owner or a counterparty, remove a segregated accounts company from the register where the company has materially breached—

(a) the provisions of this Act or a condition or requirement imposed under section 6(3); or

(b) the terms of any direction given pursuant to section 26 or regulation made under section 27, but the rights and obligations of any beneficial owner and of any counterparty to an open or undischarged transaction linked to a segregated account shall be unaffected by the removal, and the powers of the company shall continue in respect of such accrued rights and obligations but solely for the discharge thereof.

(9) Where the Registrar intends to remove a segregated accounts company from the register pursuant to subsection (8), he shall give the company notice of that intention and, before giving effect to the removal of the company from the register, he shall take into account any representations made by the company within such period as may be specified in the notice.

Provisions relating to operation of segregated accounts pursuant to Private Act

8.(1) Where a company has operated segregated accounts by virtue of authority conferred by a Private Act and the company has registered—

(a) the provisions of this Act shall apply to that company and, to the extent of any inconsistency between this Act and the provisions of that Private Act, the provisions of this Act shall prevail;

(b) any contracts to which the company was a party on the date of registration shall be construed in accordance with the Private Act but contracts renewed or entered into after the date of registration shall be construed in accordance with this Act.

(2) A company which has by virtue of authority conferred by a Private Act the right to operate segregated accounts shall, within six months from the operative date or, in the case of a Private Act that comes into force after the operative date, within six months of the coming into force of the Private Act, give notice of that fact in writing to the Registrar, attaching thereto a copy of the Private Act together with a copy of its most recent financial statements.

(3) For the avoidance of doubt it is declared that any provision of a Private Act that confers authority on a company to operate segregated accounts which does not go to the operation of such accounts shall not be affected by the registration of the company.

PART III - MANAGEMENT AND ADMINISTRATION

Company to inform persons they are dealing with segregated accounts company

9. A segregated accounts company shall—

(a) inform any person with whom it enters into a transaction that it is a segregated accounts company; and

(b) where the transaction relates to a segregated account, for the purposes of that transaction identify or specify that segregated account.

Segregated account representative

10.(1) A segregated accounts company shall appoint and maintain a segregated account representative in Bermuda.

(2) The particulars of the segregated account representative of a segregated accounts company shall be included in the register of directors and officers of the company maintained pursuant to section 92A of the Companies Act 1981.

(3) It is the duty of the segregated account representative within 30 days of—

(a) his reaching the view that there is a likelihood of a segregated account or the general account of a segregated accounts company for which he acts becoming insolvent; or

(b) it coming to his knowledge or his having reason to believe that the segregated accounts company for which he acts—

(i) has failed to comply with—

(A) any requirement or condition imposed under section 6(3),

(B) any requirement imposed by section 11 or 15,

(C) any direction given under section 26, or

(D) any regulation made under section 27; or

(ii) has become involved in any criminal proceedings in Bermuda or elsewhere, to make a written report to the Registrar setting out all the particulars of the case that are available to him relating to the insolvency, failure or involvement.

Governing instrument

11.(1) A transaction which is effected in connection with a segregated account shall be evidenced in a governing instrument which may consist of one or more agreements, instruments or other writings and may include or incorporate by reference bye-laws or other documents containing provisions setting out—

(a) the beneficial ownership of the segregated account linked to that transaction;

(b) the governance of the business of the segregated account;

(c) the conduct of its affairs and the rights, powers and duties of the company, any manager and the beneficial owner and their respective servants, agents, employees, successors or assigns;

(d) the identity of the segregated account to which the transaction and any assets or liabilities (and the respective proportions thereof as provided in section 12) are linked; and

(e) the extent of the interest of the parties therein and subordination thereof (if any).

(2) The governing instrument of a transaction which goes to the beneficial ownership of a segregated account shall provide that—

(a) the transaction is governed by Bermuda law;

(b) a person shall become a beneficial owner and shall become bound by the governing instrument if such person complies with the conditions for becoming a beneficial owner as set out in the governing instrument;

(c) a beneficial owner shall take such interest in a segregated account as is stipulated in respect of him and that, absent such stipulation, the extent of the interest of such beneficial owner shall be nil;

(d) if no other provision for management is specified in the governing instrument, the segregated accounts company shall manage the segregated account and may—

(i) appoint and supervise the officers, managers, employees and other persons who have management of the segregated account; and

(ii) enter into financial arrangements for payment for services including the charging of fees, disbursements and other charges which the manager shall be authorized to withdraw from the segregated account;

(e) unless otherwise provided in the governing instrument, the segregated accounts company may take any action, including—

(i) the amendment of the governing instrument subject, in relation to contracts of insurance and other contracts with third parties, to the consent of those parties;

(ii) the accomplishment of an amalgamation or consolidation pursuant to section 13;

(iii) the appointment of one or more managers;

(iv) for the benefit of the segregated account only, the sale, lease, exchange, transfer, pledge or other disposition of all or any part of the assets of the segregated account, or the dissolution of the segregated account;

or may provide for the taking of any action to create under the provisions of the governing instrument a class, group or series of beneficial interests that was not previously outstanding, without the vote or approval of any particular manager or beneficial owner, or class, group or series of managers or beneficial owners;

(f) the segregated accounts company may grant to, or withhold from, all or certain managers or beneficial owners, or a specified class, group or series of managers or beneficial owners, the right to vote, separately or with any or all other classes, groups or series of managers or beneficial owners, on any matter, such voting being on a per capita, number, financial interests, class, group, series or any other basis;

(g) the segregated accounts company may, if and to the extent that voting rights are granted under the governing instrument, set forth provisions relating to—

(i) notice of the time, place or purpose of any meeting at which any matter is to be voted on;

(ii) waiver of any such notice;

(iii) action by consent without a meeting;

(iv) the establishment of record dates;

(v) quorum requirements;

(vi) voting in person, by proxy or in any other manner; or

(vii) any other matter with respect to the exercise of any voting rights;

(h) the segregated accounts company may create further segregated accounts to which all or any part of the assets, liabilities, profits or losses linked to any existing segregated account may be transferred, and for the conversion of beneficial interests in an existing segregated account into beneficial interests in the separate segregated account; and

(i) any property linked to a segregated account which, on dissolution of the segregated accounts company, is found not to be linked to a beneficial owner, shall become *bona vacantia* and escheat to the Crown.

(3) The governing instrument of a transaction which does not go to the beneficial ownership of a segregated account shall provide—

(a) the name and the extent of the interest of the counterparty and that the company is a segregated accounts company and that the transaction is to be linked to a segregated account and whether or not the transaction is subject to abatement pursuant to paragraph (d);

(b) unless otherwise provided in the governing instrument, that the transaction is governed by the laws of Bermuda, and that the parties shall submit to the jurisdiction of the Bermuda courts;

(c) that the counterparty to the transaction shall only have recourse to the assets which are linked to the segregated account to which the transaction relates;

(d) subject to subsection (4), that the liabilities linked to a segregated account shall abate proportionately (either equally or otherwise in accordance with the terms of the transaction) if the assets linked to that segregated account prove insufficient to meet those liabilities.

(4) Where it is intended by the segregated accounts company and counterparty that there shall be no abatement as provided in subsection (3)(d), the governing instrument evidencing the transaction shall, and, if it does not do so, shall be deemed to contain a statement that in the event of the exhaustion of the assets linked to a segregated account the counterparty shall not have recourse to the assets which are linked to any other segregated account or to the general account.

(5) The provisions of this section shall operate to the exclusion of any law relating to trusts treating with the same subject matter, and no rule of law relating to trusts may be pleaded by any person to augment or modify the operation of this Act, but nothing in this section shall be construed to deny the remedy of tracing in law and in equity the assets or the proceeds of the assets of any segregated account where such assets or proceeds have been commingled.

(6) Where a transaction was entered into and the governing instrument does not comply with subsection (1), (2) or (3), the court may, either on the winding up of the segregated accounts company or on the application of any party to the transaction, declare that the provisions of subsection (1), (2) or (3) were implied terms of the transaction and, upon such declaration, they shall be deemed to be implied terms.

(7) In any proceedings before the court for a declaration pursuant to subsection (6), the onus of proof shall be on the party moving the court.

Apportionment of assets among segregated accounts

12.(1) A segregated accounts company may apportion an asset or liability among two or more segregated accounts.

(2) Where a segregated accounts company has apportioned an asset or liability pursuant to subsection (1), the proportion in which the value of the asset or the extent of the liability is linked to each segregated account shall be clearly shown, by way of a percentage, in the governing instrument of the transaction linked to each segregated account.

Amalgamations and consolidations

13.(1) A segregated accounts company may by agreement in writing amalgamate or consolidate a segregated account with or into one or more segregated accounts formed, organized or existing under the laws of any jurisdiction, or with such other segregated accounts company as the agreement shall provide.

(2) In relation to the amalgamation or consolidation of a segregated account pursuant to subsection (1), section 105 of the Companies Act 1981 shall have effect with the following modifications:—

(a) references to "memorandum" or "bye-laws" shall be construed as including references to "governing instrument";

(b) references to "director" shall be construed as including references to "manager";

(c) references to "shares" shall be construed as including references to "securities".

(3) Unless otherwise provided in the governing instrument, an amalgamation or consolidation shall be approved by the managers of each segregated account which is to be amalgamated or consolidated and by all of the beneficial owners of that segregated account.

(4) In connection with an amalgamation or consolidation, rights or securities or interests linked to a segregated account which is a party to the amalgamation or consolidation may be exchanged or converted into cash, property, rights or securities of, or interests in, the resulting segregated account or, in addition to or in lieu thereof, may be exchanged for or converted into cash, property, rights or securities of, or interests in, a segregated account in the amalgamation or consolidation.

(5) Notwithstanding prior approval, an agreement of amalgamation or consolidation may be terminated or amended pursuant to a provision for such termination or amendment contained in the agreement.

(6) An amalgamation or consolidation of a segregated account with some other segregated account shall be effected in the same manner as a long-form amalgamation under Part VII of the Companies Act 1981 (which relates to arrangements, reconstructions and amalgamations), except that where Part VII refers to any member or creditor of the company it shall be construed as a reference to the beneficial owners or counterparties to an open or undischarged transaction, as the case may be, linked to the relevant segregated account.

Issue of securities linked to a segregated account

14.(1) A segregated accounts company may create and issue securities in one or more classes linked to the same segregated account, the proceeds of issue of which shall be included in the assets linked to that segregated account.

(2) Where a segregated accounts company has effected a transaction by issuing a security linked to a segregated account, the issue of the security shall be identified as being linked to the segregated account in the accounts, books and records required to be kept by the company pursuant to this Act.

(3) The proceeds of the issue of shares or other securities, other than securities linked to a segregated account, shall be included in the general assets of the segregated accounts company only and the general shareholders shall have no rights to the assets of any segregated account by reason only of being a general shareholder.

Dividends, distributions, redemptions and repurchases

15.(1) A segregated accounts company may pay a dividend or make a distribution in respect of securities of any class linked to a segregated account whether or not a dividend or distribution is declared on any other class of securities linked to the same or any other segregated account or any other securities issued by the company.

(2) Notwithstanding any other provision of this Act, a dividend shall not be declared or paid, or a distribution declared or made, in respect of securities linked to a segregated account if there are reasonable grounds for believing that—

(a) the segregated account is, or would after the payment be, unable to pay its liabilities as they become due; or

(b) the realisable value of the assets of the segregated account would thereby be

less than the aggregate of its liabilities and its issued shared capital and share premium accounts.

(3) Dividends or distributions in respect of securities linked to a segregated account shall be paid or made on or in respect of those securities by reference only to the assets and liabilities of the segregated account linked to those securities, and not by reference to the general account or any other segregated account, and otherwise in accordance with the rights of such securities.

(4) Section 54 of the Companies Act 1981 does not apply to a segregated accounts company in relation to a dividend or distribution in respect of a segregated account, declared, paid or made under this section.

(5) Subject to subsections 42(2) and 42A(5) of the Companies Act 1981, a segregated accounts company may redeem or repurchase a security using the assets linked to the relevant segregated account provided that—

(a) on the date of redemption or repurchase, after taking into account the redemption or repurchase, the relevant segregated account is solvent; or

(b) any counterparties to open or undischarged transactions linked to that segregated account on that date have expressed in writing their concurrence to the redemption or repurchase.

Accounts, records and registers

16.(1) A segregated accounts company shall—

(a) maintain records in accordance with generally accepted accounting principles used in the preparation of the financial statements of the company prepared in accordance with section 84 of the Companies Act 1981, and the records shall clearly show the share capital, proceeds of securities, reserves, assets, liabilities, income and expenses, dividends and distributions that are linked to each segregated account;

(b) maintain a record of each transaction linked to a segregated account maintained by the company; and

(c) maintain a general account which records in accordance with this Act all of the assets and liabilities of the company which are not linked to a segregated account and which discloses any assets intended by the parties to be applied to a risk of any nature, and which therefore exposes such assets to liability or loss.

(2) For the purposes of subsection (1)(a), "reserves" includes retained earnings, contributed surplus and share premium.

(3) The records referred to in subsection (1) shall be kept in accordance with section 83 of the Companies Act 1981, provided that in the case of a segregated accounts company to which the Insurance Act 1978 applies, the records may be kept at the principal office.

(4) The records maintained with respect to a segregated account may be inspected by any beneficial owner of that segregated account, but a beneficial owner shall not have a right to inspect the records relating to any other segregated account.

(5) A segregated accounts company shall prepare or cause to be prepared financial statements in respect of each segregated account. and the provisions of sections 84, 88 and 90 of the Companies Act 1981 shall apply, with the necessary modifications, to the preparation of financial statements under this section and any reference in those provisions to "member" shall be construed as a reference to the beneficial owner of the segregated account.

(6) Subject to subsection (5), a copy of the financial statements of a segregated account shall be made available to the beneficial owner of a segregated account at such intervals and for such periods as are agreed between the segregated accounts company and the beneficial owner of the segregated account, but in any event shall be made available not less frequently than once in each financial year.

(7) If—

(a) the records maintained with respect to a segregated account; or

(b) the financial statements of a segregated account, are not made available for inspection by any beneficial owner of that segregated account, the court may by order compel immediate production of the records or financial statements.

(8) A segregated accounts company shall maintain a register of beneficial owners setting out their respective interests in any segregated account together with the particulars required in respect of members of the company as set out in section 65(1) of the Companies Act 1981.

(9) The register of beneficial owners shall not be open to public inspection.

Nature of segregated accounts; application of assets and liabilities

17.(1) Notwithstanding any enactment or rule of law to the contrary, any asset which is linked by a segregated accounts company to a segregated account—

(a) shall be held by the company as a separate fund which is not part of the general account exclusively for the benefit of the beneficial owner of the segregated account and any counterparty to a transaction linked to that segregated account and in such proportions as may be specified in the governing instrument and shall only be available to meet liabilities to the creditors of that segregated account; and

(b) shall not be available or used to meet liabilities to, and shall be absolutely and for all purposes protected from, the general shareholders and from the creditors of the company who are not creditors in respect of the particular segregated account identified in the governing instrument.

(2) For the purposes of this Act, the Companies Act 1981 and otherwise at law, the assets recorded in the general account shall be the only assets of a segregated accounts company available to meet liabilities of the company that are not linked to a segregated account.

(3) No assets may be transferred from the general account to a segregated account unless, on the date from which the transfer is to be effective, and taking into account that transfer, the general account of the segregated accounts company is solvent or all the general shareholders and creditors entitled to the assets thereof on that date have expressed in writing their concurrence to the transfer.

(4) Where a liability of a segregated accounts company to a person arises from a matter relating to, or is otherwise imposed in respect of or attributable to, a particular segregated account, that liability—

(a) shall extend only to, and that person shall, in respect of that liability, be entitled to have recourse only to, the assets attributable to that segregated account;

(b) shall not extend to, and that person shall not, in respect of that liability, be entitled to have recourse to, the segregated account assets linked to any other segregated account; and

(c) unless the parties otherwise provide, shall not extend to, and that person shall not in respect of that liability, be entitled to have recourse to, the general account.

(5) Where a liability of a segregated accounts company to a person—

(a) arises otherwise than from a matter in respect of a particular segregated account; or

(b) is imposed otherwise than in respect of a particular segregated account, that liability shall extend only to, and that person shall, in respect of that liability, be entitled to have recourse only to, the general account.

(6) Where—

(a) the governing instrument of a segregated account so provides; and

(b) the aggregate entitlements of the beneficial owners or counterparties, as the case may be, exceed at any given time the value of the assets linked to that

account, the entitlement of each beneficial owner or counterparty shall, to the extent of the excess, be reduced pro rata.

(7) The order and priority of the paying out of funds from a segregated account shall be determined by the terms of the governing instrument of that segregated account taken together, and failing a sufficient statement of particulars governing the priority of those payments, they shall be made in order of the dates of the respective transactions, so that the first in time shall be first to be paid.

(8) A segregated accounts company may, with the consent in writing of any relevant beneficial owner or counterparty, transfer to the general account an asset from the segregated account to which it is linked, if—

(a) the terms of the governing instrument so allow; and

(b) the segregated account to which such asset is linked, taking into account the proposed transfer, remains solvent.

(9) Any asset transferred in accordance with subsection (8) shall cease to be linked to the segregated account from which it was transferred on the date of the transfer.

(10) Any asset linked to a segregated account which, on a dissolution of the segregated accounts company is found not to be linked to a beneficial owner, shall become *bona vacantia* and escheat to the Crown.

Rights and obligations with respect to segregated accounts

18.(1) Notwithstanding any enactment or rule of law to the contrary, any asset of a segregated accounts company which is linked to a particular segregated account is deemed to be owned by the company as a separate fund which is not part of the general account and which is not part of the company's own assets, in respect of which the company has the powers and the duties as managers pursuant to section 11(2)(d) and for which the company is accountable pursuant to the terms of the governing instrument.

(2) The governing instrument may provide that no creditor of a beneficial owner of a segregated account shall have any right or interest in any asset linked to that segregated account, and such provision shall have like effect for all purposes except that the provisions of section 36A to section 36G of the Conveyancing Act 1983 (which relate to fraudulent conveyances) continue to apply.

(3) To the extent provided in the governing instrument any person (including a beneficial owner) may give directions to the segregated accounts company or other persons in the management of the segregated account and the managers shall have regard to such directions.

(4) Except to the extent otherwise provided in the governing instrument but subject to subsection (7)(b), neither the power to give directions to the segregated accounts company or other persons nor the exercise thereof by any person (including a beneficial owner) shall cause the person giving directions to be a trustee or officer of the company.

(5) Except to the extent otherwise provided in the governing instrument, the beneficial owners are entitled to the same limitation of personal liability as is enjoyed by members of companies limited by shares under section 158(d) of the Companies Act 1981.

(6) Except to the extent otherwise provided in the governing instrument but subject to subsection (7)(b), neither the segregated accounts company nor any of its officers, agents or employees is liable to any person other than the beneficial owners of the segregated account and any counterparty to a transaction to which that segregated account is linked for any contractual obligation of the segregated account or any act or omission of such officers, agents or employees.

(7) A segregated accounts company may—

(a) sue and be sued in respect of a particular segregated account, and service of process upon the company in accordance with subsection (9) shall be sufficient;

(b) be sued for debts and other obligations or liabilities contracted or incurred by the company in respect of a particular segregated account under the governing instrument, and for any damages to persons or property resulting from the negligence of the company acting in the performance of duties with respect to that account.

(8) The property of a segregated account is subject to orders of the court as if it were a separate body corporate.

(9) A segregated accounts company may be served with process in the manner prescribed in section 62A of the Companies Act 1981 in all civil actions or proceedings involving or relating to the activities of a segregated account or a breach by the company of a duty to the segregated account, or to any beneficial owner thereof or to a counterparty to a transaction linked thereto.

(10) Except to the extent otherwise provided in the governing instrument, a beneficial owner has an undivided beneficial interest in the assets linked to a segregated account by the relevant transaction and shall share in the profits and losses of the segregated account in the proportion (expressed as a percentage) of the entire undivided beneficial interest in the segregated account owned by that beneficial owner.

(11) A beneficial owner's beneficial interest in a segregated account is personal property notwithstanding the nature of the property of the segregated account.

(12) Except to the extent otherwise provided in the governing instrument, a beneficial owner has no interest in specific segregated account property.

(13) Except to the extent otherwise provided in the governing instrument, a beneficial owner's beneficial interest in the segregated account is freely transferable.

(14) Except to the extent otherwise provided in the governing instrument, at the time a beneficial owner becomes entitled to receive a payment, distribution, allocation or dividend pursuant to any governing instrument, he has the status of, and is entitled to all remedies available to, a creditor of the segregated account with respect to the payment, distribution, allocation or dividend, and the governing instrument may provide for the establishment of record dates with respect to such payment, distribution, allocation or dividend.

(15) To the extent that, at law or in equity, a segregated accounts company or manager has duties (including fiduciary duties) and liabilities relating to a segregated account or to a beneficial owner or to a counterparty—

(a) that company or manager acting under a governing instrument is not liable to the segregated account or to any beneficial owner or counterparty for the company's good faith reliance on the provisions of that governing instrument; and

(b) the company's or manager's duties and liabilities may be expanded or restricted by provisions in a governing instrument.

(16) The provisions of this section and section 11 operate to the exclusion of any law relating to trusts treating with the same subject matter, and no rule of law relating to trusts may be pleaded by any person to augment or modify the operation of this Act, but nothing in this section shall be construed to deny the remedy of tracing in law and in equity the assets or the proceeds of the assets of any segregated account where such assets or proceeds have been commingled.

PART IV - RECEIVERSHIP AND WINDING UP

Receivership orders

19.(1) Subject to the provisions of this section, if, in relation to a segregated accounts company, the court is satisfied that-

(a) without regard to any abatement provisions contained in the governing instrument, the assets linked to a particular segregated account are or are likely to be insufficient to discharge the claims of creditors in respect of that segregated account; and

(b) the making of a receivership order under this section would achieve the purposes set out in subsection (3), the court may make a receivership order in respect of that segregated account.

(2) A receivership order may be made in respect of one or more segregated accounts.

(3) A receivership order shall direct that the business and assets linked to a segregated account shall be managed by a receiver specified in the order for the purposes of—

(a) the orderly termination of the business of, or attributable to, the segregated account; and

(b) the distribution of the assets linked to the segregated account to those entitled thereto.

(4) No resolution for the voluntary winding up of a segregated accounts company of which any segregated account is subject to a receivership order shall be effective without leave of the court.

Application for receivership orders

20.(1) An application for a receivership order in respect of a segregated account may be made by—

(a) the segregated accounts company;

(b) the directors of the segregated accounts company;

(c) any creditor of the segregated accounts company in respect of that segregated account;

(d) any beneficial owner of that segregated account;

(e) any counterparty to any open or undischarged transactions linked to that segregated account; or

(f) the Registrar.

(2) The court, on hearing an application—

(a) for a receivership order; or

(b) for leave, pursuant to section 19(4), for a resolution for voluntary winding up, may make an interim order or adjourn the hearing conditionally or unconditionally.

(3) Notice of an application to the court for a receivership order in respect of a segregated account shall be served upon—

(a) the segregated accounts company;

(b) the Registrar; and

(c) such other persons (if any) as the court may direct, each of whom shall be given an opportunity to make representations to the court before the order is made.

Functions and powers of receiver

21.(1) The receiver of a segregated account—

(a) may do all such things as may be necessary for the purposes set out in section 19(3); and

(b) shall have all the functions and powers of the directors and managers of the segregated accounts company in respect of the business and assets linked to the segregated account.

(2) The receiver may at any time apply to the court for—

(a) directions as to the extent or exercise of any function or power; or

(b) the receivership order to be discharged or varied.

(3) In exercising his functions or powers the receiver is deemed to act as the agent of the segregated accounts company in respect of the segregated account, and does not incur personal liability except to the extent that his conduct amounts to fraud or dishonesty.

(4) Any person dealing with the receiver in good faith is not concerned to enquire whether the receiver is acting within his powers.

(5) During the period of operation of a receivership order the functions and powers of the directors and managers of the segregated accounts company cease in respect of the business and assets linked to the segregated account in respect of which the order was made.

Discharge and variation of receivership orders

22.(1) The court shall not discharge a receivership order unless it appears to the court that the purpose for which the order was made has been achieved or substantially achieved or is incapable of achievement.

(2) The court, on hearing an application for the discharge or variation of a receivership order, may make any interim order it thinks fit or adjourn the hearing, conditionally or unconditionally.

Remuneration of receiver

23. The remuneration of a receiver and any expenses properly incurred by him shall be payable in priority to all other claims from the assets linked to the segregated account in respect of which the receiver was appointed but not from any other assets of the segregated accounts company.

Winding up of segregated accounts companies

24.(1) Subject to this section, a segregated accounts company shall be wound up in accordance with the provisions of this Act, the Companies Act 1981 and any other Act which applies to the winding up of a company, save that in the event of any conflict, the provisions of this Act shall prevail.

(2) Where—

(a) a petition for the winding up of a segregated accounts company is presented pursuant to Part XIII of the Companies Act 1981 (which relates to winding up); and

(b) the general account is otherwise solvent for the purposes of section 162 of that Act, the court shall not proceed on the petition on any ground provided for in paragraph (a), (b), (c) or (d) of section 161 of that Act and shall not proceed unless the court is satisfied that to proceed would be just and equitable in all the circumstances.

Application of assets

25.(1) Notwithstanding any statutory provision or rule of law to the contrary, in the winding up of a segregated accounts company the liquidator shall deal with the assets and liabilities which are linked to each segregated account only in accordance with this Act and accordingly the liquidator shall ensure that the assets linked to one segregated account are not applied to the liabilities linked to any other segregated account or to the general account, unless an asset or liability is linked to more than one segregated account, in which case the liquidator shall deal with the asset or liability in accordance with the terms of any relevant governing instrument.

(2) The remuneration to be paid to the liquidator shall be apportioned by the liquidator to each segregated account and the general account in such amounts as would best reflect the duties performed by the liquidator and the court must first approve that apportionment.

(3) The liquidator, or any person affected by a decision of the liquidator, may apply to the court for directions in relation to the remuneration of the liquidator.

PART V - GENERAL

Directions of Minister to modify the provisions of this Act

26.(1) The Minister may, on the application, or with the consent in writing, of any segregated accounts company or any company intending to file a notice pursuant to section 4, direct that—

(a) any or all of the provisions of sections 5, 7, 11 and 16, shall not apply to such company; or

(b) those provisions or any of them shall apply to it subject to such modifications as may be specified in the direction.

(2) A direction under this section may be made subject to conditions.

(3) A direction under this section may be revoked by the Minister at any time provided that the company shall be given an opportunity to make representations to the Minister before the revocation takes effect.

(4) An application for a direction under this section shall be supported by a statutory declaration to the effect that no creditor of the company or of any segregated account thereof shall be prejudiced by the effect of the direction, if given, or that each creditor has consented in writing to the giving of such direction.

(5) A direction under this section is a public document available for inspection on the records maintained by the Registrar in respect of the company.

(6) A direction under this section is not a statutory instrument having legislative effect

.

(7) Where a direction is given under subsection (1), the relevant provision shall have effect subject to the direction.

Minister may make regulations

27.(1) The Minister may make regulations for the better carrying out of the provisions of this Act.

(2) The negative resolution procedure applies to regulations made under subsection (1).

Suits and actions against Registrar and Official Receiver

28.(1) No suit or action shall lie against the Registrar or Official Receiver or any person acting on their behalf in respect of anything done or omitted to be done in their official capacity in good faith without negligence.

(2) Nothing in subsection (1) shall be deemed to interfere with applications or references to the court under Part XIII of the Companies Act 1981 (which relates to winding up).

Registrar and Official Receiver to be indemnified in respect of foreign suits

29. Neither the Registrar nor the Official Receiver shall be required to prosecute, defend or take part in any proceedings outside the jurisdiction of the court unless he is indemnified by or on behalf of the person who wishes him to act against any judgment, order or costs that may be awarded against that person by deed, guarantee or deposit, as he may require.

Offences

30. Any person who—

(a) for any purpose under this Act makes a statement or declaration that he knows or has reasonable grounds to believe to be false, deceptive or misleading in a material particular;

(b) fails to comply with a condition or requirement under section 6(3); or

(c) being a segregated account representative, fails to perform his duty under section 10(3), is guilty of an offence and is liable on summary conviction to a fine of $5000 or imprisonment for 12 months, or both.

Fees

31. The Fifth Schedule to the Companies Act 1981 is amended by the addition of the following—

"C SEGREGATED ACCOUNTS COMPANIES

In addition to the annual fee or tax otherwise payable under this Schedule a segregated accounts company registered under section 6 of the Segregated Accounts Companies Act 2000 shall pay an annual fee of $250 in respect of each segregated account operated by the company, subject to a maximum annual fee of $1000 in the aggregate.".

Commencement

32. This Act comes into operation on such day as the Minister may appoint by notice published in the Gazette.

THE PARTNERSHIP ACT, 1902 (as amended)

ARRANGEMENT OF SECTIONS

NATURE OF PARTNERSHIP

RELATIONS OF PARTNERS TO PERSONS DEALING WITH THEM

RELATIONS OF PARTNERS TO ONE ANOTHER

MISCELLANEOUS PROVISIONS

NATURE OF PARTNERSHIP

Definition of partnership.

1.(1) Partnership is the relation which subsists between persons carrying on a business in common with a view of profit.

(2) Notwithstanding anything in the foregoing subsection, it is hereby declared that the relation between members of any company or association -

(a) which is registered under any Act of the Legislature of these Islands which is hereafter passed for the incorporation and regulation of joint stock companies, or any other Act of the Legislature of these Islands, or any Act of the Parliament of the United Kingdom for the time being in force in these Islands relating to the registration of joint stock companies; or

(b) which is formed or incorporated by or in pursuance of any other Act of the Legislature of these Islands, or of the Parliament of the United Kingdom or letters patent, or Royal Charter, is not a partnership within the meaning of this Act.

Rules for determining existence of partnership.

2. In determining whether a partnership does or does not exist, regard should be had to the following rules, that is to say, -

(a) joint tenancy, tenancy in common, joint property, common property, or part ownership does not of itself create a partnership as to anything so held or owned, whether the tenants or owners do or do not share any profits made by the use thereof;

(b) the sharing of gross returns does not of itself create a partnership, whether the persons sharing such returns have or have not a joint or common right or interest in any property from which or from the use of which the returns are derived;

(c) the receipt by a person of a share of the profits of a business is prima facie evidence that he is partner in the business, but the receipt of such a share, or of a payment contingent on or varying with the profits of a business, does not of itself make him a partner in the business; and in particular -

(i) the receipt by a person of a debt or other liquidated amount by instalments or otherwise out of the accruing profits of a business does not of itself make him a partner in the business or liable as such;

(ii) a contract for the remuneration of a servant or agent of a person engaged in a business by a share of the profits of the business does not of itself make the servant or agent a partner in the business or liable as such;

(iii) a person being the widow or child of a deceased partner, and receiving by way of annuity a portion of the profits made in the business in which the deceased person was a partner, is not by reason only of such receipt a partner in the business or liable as such;

(iv) the advance of money by way of loan to a person engaged or about to engage in any business on a contract with that person that the lender shall receive a rate of interest varying with the profits, or shall receive a share of the profits arising from carrying on the business, does not of itself make the lender a partner with the person or persons carrying on the business or liable as such:

Provided that the contract is in writing, and signed by or on behalf of all the parties thereto;

(v) a person receiving by way of annuity or otherwise a portion of the profits of a business in consideration of the sale by him of the goodwill of the business is not by reason only of such receipt a partner in the business or liable as such.

Postponement of rights of person lending or selling in consideration of share of profits in case of insolvency.

3. In the event of any person to whom money has been advanced by way of loan upon such a contract as is mentioned in the last forgoing section, or of any buyer of a goodwill in consideration of a share of the profits of the business, being adjudged a bankrupt, entering into an agreement to pay his creditors less than one hundred cents in the dollar, or dying in insolvent circumstances, then the lender of the loan shall not be entitled to recover anything in respect of his loan, and the seller of the goodwill shall not be entitled to recover anything in respect of the share of profits contracted for, until the claims of the other creditors of the borrower or buyer for valuable consideration in money or money's worth have been satisfied.

Meaning of firm and firm-name.

4. Persons who have entered into partnership with one another are for the purposes of this Act called collectively a firm, and the name under which their business is carried on is called the firm-name.

RELATIONS OF PARTNERS TO PERSONS DEALING WITH THEM

Power of partner to bind firm.

5. Every partner is an agent of the firm and of his other partners for the purpose of the business of the partnership; and the acts of every partner who does any act for carrying on in the usual way business of the kind carried on by the firm for which he is a member bind the firm and his partners, unless the partner so acting has in fact no authority to act for the firm in the particular matter, and the person with whom he is dealing either knows that he has no authority, or does not know or believe him to be a partner.

Partners bound by acts on behalf of firm.

6. An act or instrument relating to the business of the firm and done or executed in the firm-name or in any other manner showing an intention to bind the firm, by any person thereto authorized, whether a partner or not, is binding on the firm and all the partners:

Provided that this section shall not affect any general rule of law relating to the execution of deeds or negotiable instruments.

Partner using credit of firm for private purposes.

7. Where one partner pledges the credit of the firm for a purpose apparently not connected with the firm's ordinary course of business, the firm is not bound unless he is in fact specially authorized by the other partners:

Provided that this section shall not affect any personal liability incurred by an individual partner.

Effect of notice that firm will not be bound by acts of partners.

8. If it has been agreed between the partners that any restriction shall be placed on the power of any one or more of them to bind the firm, no act done in contravention of the agreement is binding on the firm with respect to persons having notice of the agreement.

Liability of partners.

9. Every partner in a firm is liable jointly with the other partners for all debts and obligations of the firm incurred while he is a partner; and after his death his estate is also severally liable in a due course of administration for such debts and obligations, so far as they remain unsatisfied, but subject to the prior payment of his separate debts.

Liability of firm for wrongful act, etc., of partner, etc.

10. Where, by any wrongful act or omission of any partner acting in the ordinary course of the business of the firm, or with the authority of his co-partners, loss or injury is caused to any person not being a partner is the firm, or any penalty is incurred, the firm is liable therefor to the same extent as the partner so acting or omitting to act.

Misapplication of money or property received for or in custody of firm.

11. In the following cases, that it so say -

(a) where one partner acting within the scope of his apparent authority receives the money or property of a third person and misapplies it; and

(b) where a firm in the course of its business receives money or property of a third person, and the money or property so received is misapplied by one or more of the partners while it is in the custody of the firm;

the firm is liable to make good the loss.

Liability for wrongs joint and several.

12. Every partner is liable jointly with his co-partners and also severally for everything for which the firm while he is a partner therein becomes liable under either of the last two foregoing sections.

Improper employment of trust-property for partnership purposes.

13. If a partner, being a trustee, improperly employs trust-property in the business or on the account of the partnership, no other partner is liable for the trust-property to the persons beneficially interested therein:

Provided that -

(a) this section shall not affect any liability incurred by any partner by reason of his having notice of a breach of trust; and

(b) nothing in this section shall prevent trust-money from being followed and recovered from the firm if still in its possession or under its control.

Persons liable by holding out as partners.

14. Every one who by words spoken or written or by conduct represents himself, or who knowingly suffers himself to be represented, as a partner in a particular firm, is liable as a partner to any one who has on the faith of any such representation given credit to the firm, whether the representation has or has not been made or communicated to the person so giving credit by or with the knowledge of the apparent partner making the representation or suffering it to be made:

Provided that where after a partner's death the partnership business is continued in the old firm-name, the continued use of that name or of the deceased partner's name as part thereof shall not of itself make his executor's or administrator's estate or effects liable for partnership debts contracted after his death.

Admissions and representations of partners.

15. An admission or representation made by any partner concerning the partnership affairs, and in the ordinary course of its business, is evidence against the firm.

Notice to acting partners to be notice to the firm.

16. Notice to any partner who habitually acts in the partnership business of any matter relating to partnership affairs operates as notice to the firm, except in the case of a fraud on the firm committed by or with the consent of that partner.

Liabilities of incoming and outgoing partners.

17.(1) A person who is admitted as a partner into an existing firm does not thereby become liable to the creditors of the firm for anything done before he became a partner.

(2) A partner who retires from a firm does not thereby cease to be liable for partnership debts or obligations incurred before his retirement.

(3) A retiring partner may be discharged from any existing liabilities by an agreement to that effect between himself and the members of the firm as newly constituted and the creditors, and this agreement may be either express or inferred as a fact from the course of dealing between the creditors and the firm as newly constituted.

Revocation of continuing guaranty by change in firm.

18. A continuing guaranty or cautionary obligation given either to a firm or to a third person in respect of the transactions of a firm is, in the absence of agreement to the contrary, revoked as to future transactions by any change in the constitution of the firm to which, or of the firm in respect of the transactions of which, the guaranty or obligation was given.

RELATIONS OF PARTNERS TO ONE ANOTHER

Variation by consent of terms of partnership.

19. The mutual rights and duties of partners, whether ascertained by agreement or defined by this Act, may be varied by the consent of all the partners, and such consent may be either express or inferred from a course of dealing.

Partnership property.

20.(1) All property and rights and interests in property originally brought into the partnership stock or acquired, whether by purchase or otherwise, on account of the firm, or for the purposes and in the course of the partnership business, are called in this Act partnership property, and must be held and applied by the partners exclusively for the purposes of the partnership and in accordance with the partnership agreement:

Provided that the legal estate or interest in any land which belongs to the partnership shall devolve according to the nature and tenure thereof, and the general rules of law thereto applicable, but in trust, so far as necessary, for the persons beneficially interested in the land under this section.

(2) Where co-owners of an estate or interest in any land, not being itself partnership property, are partners as to profits made by the use of that land or estate, and purchase other land or estate out of the profits to be used in like manner, the land or estate so purchased belongs to them, in the absence of an agreement to the contrary, not as partners but as co-owners for the same respective estates and interests as are held by them in the land or estate first mentioned at the date of the purchase.

Property bought with partnership money.

21. Unless the contrary intention appears, property bought with money belonging to the firm is deemed to have been brought on account of the firm.

Conversion into personal estate of land held as partnership property.

22. Where land has become partnership property, it shall, unless the contrary intention appears, be treated as between the partners (including the representatives of a deceased partner), and also as between the heirs of a deceased partner and his executors or administrators, as personal and not real estate.

Procedure against partnership property for a partner's separate judgment debts.

23.(1) A writ of execution shall not issue against any partnership property except on a judgment against the firm.

(2) The Supreme Court may, on the application by petition of any judgment creditor of a partner, make an order charging that partner's interest in the partnership property and profits with payment of the amount of the judgment debt and interest thereon, and may by the same or a subsequent order appoint a receiver of that partner's share of profits (whether already declared or accruing), and of any other money which may be coming to him in respect of the partnership, and direct all accounts and inquiries, and give all other orders and directions which might have been directed or given if the charge had been made in favour of the judgment creditor by the partner, or which the circumstances of the case may require.

(3) The other partner or partners shall be at liberty at any time to redeem the interest charged, or, in case of a sale being directed, to purchase the same.

Rules as to interests and duties of partners subject to special agreement.

24. The interest of partners in the partnership property and their rights and duties in relation to the partnership shall be determined, subject to any agreement express or implied between the partners, by the following rules, that is to say -

(a) all the partners are entitled to share equally in the capital and profits of the business, and must contribute equally towards the losses whether of capital or otherwise sustained by the firm;

(b) the firm must indemnify every partner in respect of payments made and personal liabilities incurred by him -

(i) in the ordinary and proper conduct of the business of the firm; or

(ii) in or about anything necessarily done for the preservation of the business or property of the firm;

(c) a partner making, for the purposes of the partnership, any actual payment or advance beyond the amount of capital which he has agreed to subscribe, is entitled to interest at the rate of five per cent. per annum from the date of the payment or advance;

(d) a partner is not entitled, before the ascertainment of profits, to interest on the capital subscribed by him;

(e) every partner may take part in the management of the partnership business;

(f) no partner shall be entitled to remuneration for acting in the partnership business;

(g) no person may be introduced as a partner without the consent of all existing partners;

(h) any difference arising as to ordinary matters connected with the partnership business may be decided by a majority of the partners, but no change may be made in the nature of the partnership business without the consent of all existing partners;

(i) the partnership books shall be kept at the place of business of the partnership (or the principal place, if there is more than one), and every partner may, when he thinks fit, have access to and inspect and copy any of them.

Power to expel partner.

25. No majority of the partners can expel any partner unless a power to do so has been conferred by express agreement between the partners.

Retirement from partnership at will.

26.(1) Where no fixed term has been agreed upon for the duration of the partnership, any partner may determine the partnership at any time on giving notice of his intention so to do all the other partners.

(2) Where the partnership has originally been constituted by deed, a notice in writing, signed by the partner giving it, shall be sufficient for this purpose.

Where partnership for term is continued over, continuance on old terms presumed.

27.(1) Where a partnership entered into for a fixed term is continued after the term has expired, and without any express new agreement, the rights and duties of the partners remain the same as they were at the expiration of the term, so far as is consistent with the incidents of a partnership at will.

(2) A continuance of the business by the partners or such of them as habitually acted therein during the term, without any settlement or liquidation of the partnership affairs, is presumed to be a continuance of the partnership.

Duty of partners to render accounts, etc.

28. Partners are bound to render true accounts and full information of all things affecting the partnership to any partner or his legal representatives.

Duty of partners to account for private profits.

29.(1) Every partner must account to the firm for any benefit derived by him without the consent of the other partners, from any transaction concerning the partnership, or from any use by him of the partnership property, name or business connection.

(2) The foregoing provisions of this section apply in relation to transactions undertaken after a partnership has been dissolved by the death of a partner, and before the affairs thereof have been completely wound up, either by any surviving partner or by the representatives of the deceased partner.

Duty of partner not to compete with firm.

30. If a partner, without the consent of the other partners, carries on any business of the same nature as and competing with that of the firm, he must account for and pay over to the firm all profits made by him in that business.

Rights of assignee of share in partnership.

31.(1) An assignment by any partner of his share in the partnership, either absolute or by way of mortgage or redeemable charge, does not, as against the other partners, entitled the assignee, during the continuance of the partnership, to interfere in the management or administration of the partnership business of affairs, or to require any accounts of the partnership transactions, or to inspect the partnership books, but entitles the assignee only to receive the share of profits to which the assigning partner would otherwise be entitled, and the assignee must accept the account of profits agreed to by the partners.

(2) In case of a dissolution of the partnership, whether as respects all the partners or as respects the assigning partner, the assignee is entitled to receive the share of the partnership assets to which the assigning partner is entitled as between himself and the other partners, and, for the purpose of ascertaining that share, to an account as from the date of the dissolution.

Dissolution of expiration of notice.

32. Subject to an agreement between the partners, a partnership is dissolved -

(a) if entered into for a fixed term, by the expiration of that term;

(b) if entered into for a single adventure or undertaking, by the termination of that adventure or undertaking;

(c) if entered into for an undefined time, by any partner giving notice to the other or others of his intention to dissolve the partnership.

In the last-mentioned case the partnership is dissolved as from the date mentioned in the notice as the date of dissolution or, if no date is so mentioned, as from the date of the communication of the notice.

Dissolution by bankruptcy, death or charge.

33.(1) Subject to any agreement between the partners, every partnership is dissolved as regards all the partners by the death or bankruptcy of any partner.

(2) A partnership may, at the option of the other partners, be dissolved if any partner suffers his share of the partnership property to be charged under this Act for his separate debt.

Dissolution by illegality of partnership.

34. A partnership is in every case dissolved by the happening of any event which makes it unlawful for the business of the firm to be carried on or for the members of the firm to carry it on in partnership.

Dissolution by Supreme Court.

35. On application by a partner the Supreme Court may decree a dissolution of the partnership in any of the following cases, that is to say -

(a) when a partner is found by the Supreme Court to be an insane person, or is shown to the satisfaction of the Supreme Court to be permanently of unsound mind, in either of which cases the application may be made as well on behalf of that partner by his committee or next friend or person having title to intervene as by any other partner;

(b) when a partner, other than the partner suing, becomes in any other way permanently incapable of performing his part of the partnership contract;

(*c*) when a partner, other than the partner suing, has been guilty of such conduct as, in the opinion of the Supreme Court, regard being had to the nature of the business, is calculated prejudicially to affect the carrying on of the business;

(*d*) when a partner, other than the partner suing, wilfully or persistently commits a breach of the partnership agreement, or otherwise so conducts himself in matters relating to the partnership business that it is not reasonably practicable for the other partner or partners to carry on the business in partnership with him;

(*e*) when the business of the partnership can only be carried on at a loss;

(*f*) whenever in any case circumstances have arisen which, in the opinion of the Supreme Court, render it just and equitable that the partnership should be dissolved.

Rights of persons dealing with firm against apparent members of firm.

36.(1) Where a person deals with a firm after a change in its constitution he is entitled to treat all apparent members of the old firm as still being members of the firm until he has notice of the change.

(2) An advertisement in the Gazette shall be notice as to persons who had not dealings with the firm before the date of the dissolution or change so advertised.

(3) The estate of a partner who dies, or who becomes bankrupt, or of a partner who, not having been known to the person dealing with the firm to be a partner, retires from the firm, is not liable for partnership debts contracted after the date of the death, bankruptcy, or retirement respectively.

Rights of partners to notify dissolution.

37. On the dissolution of a partnership or retirement of a partner any partner may publicly notify the same, and may require the other partner or partners to concur for that purpose in all necessary or proper acts, if any, which cannot be done without his or their concurrence.

Continuing authority of partners for purposes of winding up.

38. After the dissolution of a partnership the authority of each partner to bind the firm, and the other rights and obligations of the partners, continue notwithstanding the dissolution so far as may be necessary to wind up the affairs of the partnership, and to complete transactions begun but unfinished at the time of the dissolution, but not otherwise:

Provided that the firm is in no case bound by the acts of a partner who has become bankrupt, but this proviso does not affect the liability of any person who has after the bankruptcy represented himself or knowingly suffered himself to be represented as a partner of the bankrupt.

Rights of partners as to application of partnership property on dissolution.

39. On the dissolution of a partnership every partner is entitled, as against the other partners in the firm, and all persons claiming through them in respect of their interests as partners, to have the property of the partnership applied in payment of the debts and liabilities of the firm, and to have the surplus assets after such payment applied in payment of what may be due to the partners respectively after deducting what may be due from them as partners to the firm; and for that purpose any partner or his representatives may on the termination of the partnership apply to the Supreme Court to wind up the business and affairs of the firm.

Appropriation of premium dissolution where partnership prematurely dissolved.

40. Where one partner has paid a premium to another on entering into a partnership for a fixed term, and the partnership is dissolved before the expiration of that term otherwise than by the death of a partner, the Supreme Court may order the repayment of the premium, or of such part thereof as it thinks just, having regard to the terms of the partnership contract and to the length of time during which the partnership has continued, unless -

(a) the dissolution is, in the judgment of the Supreme Court, wholly or chiefly due to the misconduct of the partner who paid the premium; or

(b) the partnership has been dissolved by an agreement containing no provision for a return of any part of the premium.

Rights where partnership dissolved for fraud or misrepresentation.

41. Where a partnership contract is rescinded on the ground of the fraud, or misrepresentation of one of the parties thereto, the party entitled to rescind is, without prejudice to any other right, -

(a) entitled to a lien on, or right of retention of, the surplus of the partnership assets, after satisfying the partnership liabilities, for any sum of money paid by him for the purchase of a share in the partnership and for any capital contributed by him; and

(b) entitled to stand in the place of the creditors of the firm for any payments made by him in respect of the partnership liabilities; and

(c) entitled to be indemnified by the person guilty of the fraud or making the representation against all the debts and liabilities of the firm.

Right of outgoing partner in certain cases to share profits made after dissolution.

42. Where any member of a firm has died or otherwise ceased to be a partner, and the surviving or continuing partners carry on the business of the firm with its capital or assets without any final settlement of accounts as between the firm and the outgoing partner or his estate, then, in the absence of any agreement to the contrary, the outgoing partner or his estate is entitled at the option of himself or his representative to such share of the profits made since the dissolution as the Supreme Court may find to be attributable to the use of his share of the partnership assets, or to interest at the rate of five per cent. per annum on the amount of his share of the partnership assets:

Provided that where by the partnership contract an option is given to surviving or continuing partners to purchase the interest of a deceased or outgoing partner, and that option is duly exercised, the estate of the deceased partner, or the outgoing partner or his estate, as the case may be, is not entitled to any future or other share of profits; but if any partner assuming to act in exercise of the option does not in all material respects comply with the terms thereof, he is liable to account under the foregoing provisions of this section.

Retiring or deceased partner's share to be a debt.

43. Subject to any agreement between the partners, the amount due from surviving or continuing partners to an outgoing partner or the representatives of a deceased partner in respect of the outgoing or deceased partner's share is a debt accruing at the date of the dissolution or death.

Rules for distribution of assets on final settlement of accounts.

44. In settling accounts between the partners after a dissolution of partnership, the following rules shall, subject to any agreement, be observed, that is to say, -

(a) losses, including losses and deficiencies of capital, shall be paid first out of profits, next out of capital, and lastly, if necessary, by the partners individually in the proportion in which they were entitled to share profits;

(b) the assets of the firm, including the sums, if any, contributed by the partners to make up losses or deficiencies of capital, shall be applied in the following manner and order, that is to say, -

(i) in paying the debts and liabilities of the firm to persons who are not partners therein;

(ii) in paying to each partner rateably what is due from the firm to him for advances as distinguished from capital;

(iii) in paying to each partner rateably what is due from the firm to him in respect of capital; and

(iv) the ultimate residue, if any, shall be divided among the partners in the proportion in which profits are divisible.

MISCELLANEOUS PROVISIONS

Definition of "business".

45. In this Act, unless the contrary intention appears, the expression "business" includes every trade, occupation, or profession.

Saving for rules of equity and common law.

46. The rules of equity and of common law applicable to partnership shall continue in force except so far as they are inconsistent with the express provisions of this Act.

Power of Supreme Court to make rules or orders for carrying Act into effect.

47.(1) The Supreme Court shall have power to make such rules or orders as it may deem necessary for carrying into effect the provisions of this Act so far as they relate to the jurisdiction of the Supreme Court.

(2) Section 6 of the Statutory Instruments Act 1977 shall not apply to rules made under subsection (1).

The Limited Partnership Act 1883

(as amended, 1998)

Arrangement of Sections

Be it enacted by the Governor, Council and Assembly of the Bermudas or Sommers Islands as follows:

General Powers to Form Limited Partnerships

1. Limited partnerships for the transaction of all mercantile, mechanical, manufacturing or other business, except banking or insurance, may be formed by two or more persons.

Interpretation

1A. In this Act, unless a contrary intention appears:

"Court" means the Supreme Court;

"the limited partners' capital" means the sum referred to in section 3(d) [Section 3(d) was deleted by the Limited Partnership Amendment Act 1995];

"the minimum limited partners' capital" means the amount specified by the Minister as such in an order under section 5(3);

"the Minister" means the Minister of Finance;

"the register" means the register referred to in section 4(1)(b);

"the Registrar" means the Registrar of Companies;

"statutory value" means the statutory value referred to in section 2(2)(a).".

Constitution of, and Contribution to, Limited Partnership

2.(1) Limited partnerships may consist of -

(a) one or more general partners who shall be jointly and severally responsible as partners now are by law; and

(b) any other persons who contribute, or undertake to contribute, to the limited partnership cash or other property (but not services) as capital, who shall be called limited partners and who, except as provided by this Act, shall not be liable for any debts of the limited partnership.

(2) Where the capital contribution of a limited partner, or a part of that contribution, is made or is undertaken to be made otherwise than in cash -

(a) there shall forthwith be assigned to that contribution or part or intended contribution or part, in accordance with the partnership agreement, a value to be known as the statutory value; and

(b) the statutory value shall, for the purposes of this Act, be accepted as the value of that contribution or part or intended contribution or part, as the case may be.

(3) Within thirty days after a limited partner makes, or undertakes to make, a capital contribution to a limited partnership, a general partner shall -

(a) deliver a notice thereof, containing the particulars specified in subsection (4), to the Registrar for registration by him in the register; and

(b) delivery a copy of such notice to the Bermuda Monetary Authority.

(4) The notice referred to in subsection (3) shall contain the following particulars, that is to say,

(a) the name of the limited partnership;

(b) the name and address of the limited partner that made, or undertook to make, the capital contribution; and

(c) the amount of the capital contribution made or undertaken to be made and the date of such making or undertaking.

(5) The Minister may on application in writing made by a general partner exempt -

(a) a limited partnership the interests in which are traded on an appointed stock exchange or on a market which is supervised by a competent regulatory authority; or

(b) such other limited partnership as the Minister considers appropriate,from complying with the requirements of subsection (3).

Particulars of Limited Partnership

3. The persons forming a limited partnership shall make and severally sign a certificate which shall contain the following particulars, that is to say -

(a) the name of the limited partnership;

(b) the names and respective places of residence of the general partners;

(c) the general nature of the business to be transacted by the limited partnership;

(d) the address of the registered office, in Bermuda, of the limited partnership; and

(e) the date when the limited partnership is to commence and the term, if any, for which it is entered into.

Formation of Limited Partnership

4.(1) A limited partnership shall be deemed to have been formed when -

(a) the consent of the Minister has been obtained thereto under section 5; and

(b) the certificate specified in section 3 has been registered in the office of the Registrar in a register to be kept by him for that purpose open to public inspection.

(2) An application for the Minister's consent under section 5 shall be in such form, and be accompanied by such documents, as the Minister may require.

(3) The persons forming a limited partnership shall, not earlier than three months before making an application under subsection (2), publish in the Gazette an advertisement announcing the intention to form the limited partnership and specifying -

(a) the name of the limited partnership;

(b) the names and respective places of residence of the general partners; and

(c) the general nature of the business to be transacted by the limited partnership.

Consent of Minister

5.(1) The Minister may grant or refuse his consent to an application made to him under section 4(2).

(2) The Minister shall not be bound to give any reason for a decision under subsection (1) and that decision shall not be subject to appeal or review in any court.

(3) The Minister may from time to time by order subject to the negative resolution procedure prohibit the formation of limited partnerships, or any class of limited partnerships, the limited partners' capital of which is less than an amount specified in the order as the minimum limited partners' capital.

Name and Registered Office of Limited Partnership

6.(1) The Registrar may refuse to register a limited partnership if, in the opinion of the Registrar, the name of the limited partnership is undesirable.

(2) The Registrar may, if in his opinion the name is not undesirable, on application by any person intending to form a limited partnership, reserve a name for the exclusive use of the applicant for a period not exceeding three months next after the date of the receipt of such application.

(3) [Repealed]

(4) Every limited partnership shall have and use the words "Limited Partnership" or the abbreviation "L.P." at the end of its name; and those words and that abbreviation may be used interchangeably.

(5) A limited partnership shall, at all times, maintain a registered office, which shall not be a post office box, in Bermuda, to which all communications may be sent.

(6) [Repealed]

Register of Limited Partners

7.(1) The general partners shall establish and maintain up to date in the registered office of the limited partnership in Bermuda a register of limited partners which shall contain the particulars specified in subsection (2).

(2) The particulars referred to in subsection (1) are -

(a) the name and address of each limited partner;

(b) the date a person becomes, and the date, if applicable, he ceases to be, a limited partner;

(c) the amount of cash contributed or undertaken to be contributed by each limited partner as capital; and

(d) where a capital contribution or a part of a capital contribution has been made or undertaken to be made otherwise than in cash, a statement of the statutory value of that contribution or part or intended contribution or part.

(3) Where a person ceases to be a limited partner, the particulars specified in subsection (2) in respect of that limited partner shall be maintained on the register of limited partners for a period of not less than six years commencing with the date of such cessation.

(4) A limited partnership the interests in which are traded on an appointed stock exchange or on a market which is supervised by a competent regulatory authority may keep, in any place outside Bermuda, one or more branch registers of limited partners after giving written notice to the Registrar of the place where each such branch register is to be kept.

(5) A branch register shall be kept in the same manner in which the register of limited partners is by subsections (1) and (3) required to be kept.

(6) A limited partnership shall, as soon as reasonably practicable after the date on which an entry or alteration is made in a branch register of limited partners, make any necessary alteration in the register of limited partners.

(7) In this section and in section 11 -

(*a*) "appointed stock exchange" means any stock exchange; and

(*b*) "competent regulatory authority" means any authority, appointed by the Minister by notice in the Gazette to approve the offering of shares or debentures to the public by companies.

Inspection of Register of Limited Partners

8.(1) The register of limited partners shall, during business hours and subject only to such reasonable restrictions as the general partners may impose, be open for inspection -

(*a*) by any limited partner, without charge; and

(*b*) by any other person on payment of five dollars, or such less sum as the general partners may determine, for each inspection.

(2) A limited partner or other person may require a copy the register of limited partners, or any part thereof, on payment of five dollars or such less sum as the general partners may determine, for every hundred words or fractional part thereof required to be copied.

(3) If an inspection or a copy required by this section is refused, every general partner who is in default shall be liable in respect of each offence to a default fine not exceeding twenty dollars for every day during which the default continues.

(4) In this section and in section 8A the expression "register of limited partners" includes a branch register.

Power of Court to Rectify Register

8A.(1) If default is made or unnecessary delay occurs in entering on the register of limited partners a particular required by section 7, a limited partner may apply to the Court for rectification of the register.

(2) Where an application is made under this section, the Court may either refuse the application or order rectification of the register of limited partners and payment by any partner in default of any damages sustained by the limited partner.

(3) On an application under this section the Court may decide any question necessary or expedient to be decided for rectification or otherwise of the register of limited partners.

(4) The register of limited partners shall be prima facie evidence of any matter by this Act required to be inserted therein.

Change of Particulars of Limited Partnership

8B.(1) Subject to the provisions of this section, the partners in a limited partnership may, from time to time, change any of the particulars specified in the certificate referred to in section 3.

(2) The general partners shall, not earlier than three months before such change other than a change referred to in section 3(d) or (e), publish an advertisement in the Gazette announcing the particular that it intends to change and specifying the proposed change.

(3) Where a change referred to in subsection (1) is in relation to -

(a) a change of the name of the limited partnership;

(b) a change of general partners; or

(c) a change in the general nature of the business transacted by the limited partnership, the Minister's consent thereto shall be obtained by application by the general partners.

(4) The general partners shall, not later than thirty days after a change referred to in subsection (1) is made -

(a) make and severally sign a supplementary certificate supplementing, as the circumstances may require, the certificate referred to in that subsection; and

(b) deliver the supplementary certificate to the Registrar for registration by him in the register.

(5) Subject to the provisions of this section, a change referred to in subsection (1) is effective on the date of registration of the supplementary certificate by the Registrar under subsection (4)(b).

(6) The provisions of section 5(1) and (2) shall, mutatis mutandis, apply to an application under subsection (3) of this section as they apply to an application under section 4(2).

(7) Where a change referred to in subsection (3) is made otherwise than in accordance with the provisions of this section, the Minister may petition the Court for the dissolution of the limited partnership.

(8) If the Court, on hearing of a petition under subsection (7) is satisfied that a general partner or a person duly authorised by the general partners has contravened or caused or permitted the contravention of subsection (3), the Court may:

(a) make an order for the dissolution of the limited partnership; or

(b) impose a fine not exceeding five thousand dollars on any general partner or duly authorised person, as the case may be, who knowingly and wilfully contravened, or otherwise caused or permitted the contravention of, that subsection; or

(c) make such order and impose such fine.

Management of Limited Partnership

8C.(1) A general partner in a limited partnership shall have all the rights and powers and be subject to all the restrictions and liabilities of a partner in a partnership that is not a limited partnership, except that, without the express prior consent, or the express ratification, in writing, of every other partner, a general partner shall not have authority -

(a) to admit a person as a general or a limited partner to the limited partnership; or

(b) to do any act which makes it impossible to carry on the ordinary business of the limited partnership.

(2) A limited partner in a limited partnership shall be liable as a general partner if he takes part in the management of the limited partnership.

(3) For the purposes of subsection (2), a limited partner does not take part in the management of a limited partnership by reason only of the inclusion of the limited partner's name, or any part of it, in the name of the limited partnership, or of his:-

(a) being a contractor for, or an agent or employee of, the limited partnership or a general partner;

(b) consulting or advising a general partner with respect to the business of the limited partnership;

(bb) taking any actions, or making any decisions, in respect of any investment made by the limited partnership;

(c) acting as surety for the limited partnership;

(d) approving or disapproving an amendment to the partnership agreement;

(e) voting on any of the matters specified in subsection (4).

(4) The matters referred to in subsection (3)(e) are -

(a) the dissolution or winding up of the limited partnership;

(b) the sale, exchange, lease, mortgage, pledge or other transfer of all or substantially all of the assets of the limited partnership otherwise than in the ordinary course of business of the limited partnership;

(c) the incurring of indebtedness by the limited partnership otherwise than in the ordinary course of business of the limited partnership;

(d) a change in the general nature of the business transacted by the limited partnership; or

(e) the removal of a general partner.

(5) The doing of any other act or thing or the voting on any other matter by a limited partner in relation to a limited partnership shall not, by reason only that such act or thing or such matter is not specified in subsection (3) or (4), be construed as taking part in the management of the limited partnership.

Limited Partner's Liability to Partnership

8D.(1) A limited partner is liable to a limited partnership for the difference, if any, between -

(a) the value of money and the value of other property actually contributed; and

(b) the value of money and the statutory value of other property undertaken to be contributed, to the limited partnership.

(2) A limited partner holds as trustee for the limited partnership -

(a) specified property stated in the partnership agreement as contributed by him, but which has not in fact been contributed or which has been returned contrary to this Act; and

(b) money or other property paid or conveyed to him on account of his contribution to the limited partnership contrary to this Act.

(3) Where, in accordance with section 11, a limited partner -

(a) has received the return of the whole or part of his capital contribution to a limited partnership;

(b) has been released from the whole or part of the capital contribution that he has undertaken to make to a limited partnership; or

(c) has received such return and been so released in whole or in part, he is nevertheless, for the period of one year following the date of any such return or release, liable to the limited partnership or, where the limited partnership is dissolved, to its creditors for any amount, not exceeding the amount returned with interest or the value of money or other contribution from which he has been released or the value of both such return and release, necessary to discharge the liabilities of the limited partnership to all creditors who extended credit to the limited partnership or whose claim otherwise arose before the return of the contribution or release or the return and release, as the case may be.

(4) Where, in violation of section 11, a limited partner -

(a) has received the return of the whole or part of his capital contribution to the limited partnership;

(b) has been released from the whole or part of the capital contribution that he has undertaken to make to the limited partnership; or

(c) has received such return and been so released in whole or in part, he is, for the period of six years following the date of any such return or release, liable to the limited partnership or, where the limited partnership is dissolved, to its creditors for the amount of the contribution wrongfully returned with interest, or the value of the contribution wrongfully released, or the value of both (as the case may be).

Liability for False Statements in Certificates, Etc.

8E.(1) If a certificate of limited partnership, a supplementary certificate or a certificate of cancellation, contains a false statement and a person who relied on that statement suffers loss, that person may recover damages for that loss from -

(a) any person who signed the certificate, or caused another to sign it on his behalf, and knew, and any general partner who knew or should have known, the statement to be false at the time the certificate was signed; and

(b) any general partner who thereafter knows or should have known that any statement specified in the certificate has changed, making the statement false in any respect within a sufficient time before the statement was relied upon reasonably to have enabled that general partner to cancel or change the certificate, or to file a petition for its change or cancellation under section 8G.

Cancellation of Limited Partnership

8F.(1) A certificate of limited partnership shall be cancelled -

(a) upon the commencement of the winding up of the affairs of a limited partnership consequent on the dissolution of that limited partnership; and

(b) at any other time, if there are no limited partners.

(2) A certificate of cancellation shall, in respect of a limited partnership, specify -

(a) the name and the date of registration of the limited partnership;

(b) that the limited partnership is dissolved or that there are no limited partners, as the case may be; and

(c) the effective date of the cancellation (which shall be a date certain) if cancellation is not to be effective upon registration of the certificate by the Registrar under subsection (4).

(3) A certificate of cancellation shall be signed by at least one general partner.

(4) The general partners shall, within thirty days after the happening of an event referred to in subsection (1), deliver the certificate of cancellation to the Registrar for registration by him in the register.

Amendment or Cancellation by the Court

8G.(1) If a person required -

(a) by section 8B(4)(a) to sign a supplementary certificate in respect of a change of particular; or

(b) by section 8F(3) to sign a certificate of cancellation, fails or refuses so to do, any other partner, and any assignee of a partnership interest, who is adversely affected by the failure or refusal, may petition the Court to direct the change or cancellation, as the case may be.

(2) If the Court finds that it is appropriate that a certificate referred to in subsection (1) should be signed and that a person referred to in that subsection has failed or refused to sign the certificate, the Court shall order the Registrar to enter in the register an appropriate change or cancellation, as the case may be.

Offences in Relation to Certificates

8H. A person who fails, without reasonable excuse -

(a) to publish an advertisement announcing the intention to change a particular under section 8B(2);

(b) to sign a certificate of cancellation under section 8F(3); or

(c) to deliver a certificate of cancellation to the Registrar under section 8F(4), is guilty of an offence and liable, on summary conviction, to a fine not exceeding five thousand dollars.

General Partners' Liability to Account

9. The general partners shall be liable to account to each other, and to the limited partners, for their management of the concern, both at law and in equity, as other partners are now liable.

Civil and Criminal Liability of Partners

10. Every partner who is guilty of any fraud in the affairs of the partnership shall be liable civilly to the party injured to the extent of his damage, and shall also be guilty of an offence against this Act, and shall be liable on conviction on indictment to imprisonment for a term not exceeding four years, to a fine not exceeding ten thousand dollars, or to both such imprisonment and fine.

Restriction on Reduction of Capital

11.(1) Subject to the provisions of this section, no part of the limited partners' capital shall be withdrawn, nor shall any payment of a share of the profits or other compensation by way of income be made to a limited partner from the assets of the limited partnership if the withdrawal or payment, as the case may be, would result in the limited partnership becoming insolvent.

(2) For the purposes of determining whether a withdrawal or a payment under subsection (1) would result in a limited partnership becoming insolvent, all the partners may agree that any liabilities of the limited partnership in respect of the partners shall not be taken into account.

(3) Subsection (1) shall not apply on the winding up of a limited partnership consequent on the dissolution of that limited partnership.

(4) Subject to agreement between all the partners, a contribution reduction may be made in a limited partnership if -

(a) the conditions specified in subsection (5) are satisfied; and

(b) the requirements specified in subsection (6) are fulfilled.

(5) The conditions referred to in subsection (4)(a) are -

(a) a contribution reduction under subsection (8)(a)(i) shall not be made otherwise than in the form of a payment of cash unless all the partners otherwise agree;

(b) where there is in force under section 5(3) an order specifying the minimum limited partners' capital in respect of limited partnerships of a description to which the limited partnership belongs, a contribution reduction shall not be made so as to cause the amount of the limited partners' capital in that limited partnership to fall below the minimum, whether or not that limited partnership was formed after the making of that order; and

(c) on the effective contribution reduction date:

(i) all the liabilities of the limited partnership (not counting liabilities to general partners and limited partners on account of their capital contributions to the limited partnership) have been discharged; or

(ii) the limited partnership will be solvent immediately after the contribution reduction.

(6) Subject to subsection (6A), the requirements referred to in subsection (4)(b) are -

(a) on the effective contribution reduction date an affidavit shall be sworn by at least one general partner declaring either that on that date, after taking into account the contribution reduction, the limited partnership is solvent or that all the creditors of the limited partnership on that date have expressed in writing their concurrence in the contribution reduction;

(b) within thirty days after the effective contribution reduction date a general partner shall -

(i) deliver the affidavit referred to in paragraph (a) and a notice of the contribution reduction containing the particulars specified in paragraph (c) to the Registrar for registration by him in the register; and

(ii) deliver a copy of the affidavit and the notice to the Bermuda Monetary Authority; and

(c) the notice referred to in paragraph (b) shall contain the following particulars, that is to say -

(i) the name of the limited partnership in respect of which the contribution reduction was made;

(ii) the name and address of the limited partner in favour of whom the contribution reduction was made; and

(iii) the amount and the effective date of the contribution reduction.

(6A) The Minister may on application in writing made by a general partner exempt -

(a) a limited partnership the interests in which are traded on an appointed stock exchange or on a market which is supervised by a competent regulatory authority; or

(b) such other limited partnership as the Minister considers appropriate, from complying with the requirements of subsection (6).

(7) Subject to subsection (6A), if a provision of this section is contravened in relation to a limited partnership, every general partner shall be guilty of an offence and shall be liable, upon the contravention being proved in a court of summary jurisdiction, to a fine not exceeding five thousand dollars.

(8) In this section "the Bermuda Monetary Authority" means the Bermuda Monetary Authority established under section 2 of the Bermuda Monetary Authority Act 1969.

(8) In this section -

a) "contribution reduction", in relation to a limited partner in a limited partnership, means -

(i) in the case of a limited partner who has actually made a contribution or part contribution to the capital of the limited partnership, the return to him of such capital contribution or part thereof;

(ii) in the case of a limited partner who has undertaken to contribute to the capital of the limited partnership, a release, in whole or in part, from that undertaking; or

(iii) both such return and release, in whole or in part; and

(b) "the effective contribution reduction date" means the date on which a contribution reduction is to take, or took, effect, as the case may be.

Assignment of Limited Partner's Interest

12. Subject to the provisions of the partnership agreement, a limited partner may -

(a) with the consent of the general partners; and

(b) by instrument in writing signed by the assignor and the assignee, assign his share or a part thereof, in a limited partnership.

Restriction on Assignment of Partnership Assets

13. No general assignment by a limited partnership in case of insolvency or insufficiency of assets for the payment of the partnership debts shall be valid without the consent in writing of two-thirds in value of the creditors of the partnership, nor unless it provides for a distribution of the partnership property among all the creditors in proportion to the amount of their several claims, of which notice shall be given in the Gazette; but debts due to the Crown shall first be paid or secured.

Avoidance of Assignments and Securities in Fraud of Creditors

14. Every sale, assignment or transfer, of the property or effects of any limited partnership made by such partnership when actually insolvent or bankrupt, or in contemplation of insolvency or bankruptcy, or after or in contemplation of insolvency or bankruptcy of any partner, with intent to give a preference to any creditor or creditors of such partnership over any other creditor or creditors thereof, and every judgment confessed, lien created, or security given, by such partnership, or any partner thereof, under the like circumstances, and with the like intent, shall be void as against the creditors of such partnership.

Postponement of Claims of Limited Partners in case of Bankruptcy to other Creditors

15. In case of the insolvency or bankruptcy of the partnership no limited partner shall under any circumstances be allowed to claim as a creditor until the claims of all the other creditors of the partnership are satisfied.

Provisions Relating to Suits Respecting Business of Limited Partnership

16. All suits respecting the business of a limited partnership shall be prosecuted by and against the general partners only, except in those cases where limited partners are held severally responsible.

17. [Repealed]

18. [Repealed]

19. [Repealed]

Rights and Liabilities of Members of Limited Partnerships

20. In all cases not otherwise herein provided for, the members of limited partnerships shall be subject to all the liabilities, and entitled to all rights, of general partners.

21. [Repealed]

Registration, etc., of Certificates, etc.; Evidence

22.(1) The Registrar shall establish and maintain a register in which shall be registered or recorded all certificates, notices and affidavits required by this Act.

(2) The register shall be open, during office hours, to the inspection of all persons desiring to view the register on payment to the Registrar of the fee of five dollars.

(3) A sum of one hundred and fifty dollars shall be paid to the Registrar for registering or recording every certificate, notice or affidavit required by this Act.

(4) A certificate of the Registrar certifying that a certificate, notice or affidavit required by this Act to be registered or recorded by him has been so registered or recorded shall be received in all courts and in all proceedings whatsoever as evidence of the matter to which the certificate relates.

Meaning of the Gazette

23. For the purposes of this Act the Gazette shall mean an appointed newspaper as defined in the Companies Act 1981.

THE LIMITED PARTNERSHIP AMENDMENT ACT 1990

Savings, Transitional etc.

9.(1) Subject to subsections (3) and (4), a limited partnership formed and in existence prior to the coming into operation of this Act, shall continue under this Act, and everything lawfully done by such limited partnership shall be of full force and effect.

(2) Subject to subsections (3) and (4), where, immediately prior to the coming into operation of this Act, a certificate in respect of a limited partnership has been registered in the office of the Registrar-General pursuant to section 4 of the principal Act, the provisions of section 5 of that Act shall, notwithstanding the provisions of this Act, apply to and in relation to that limited partnership as if this Act had not been enacted.

(3) The general partners shall, in respect of a limited partnership referred to in subsection (1) and (2), within six months of the coming into operation of this Act:

(a) make and severally sign a supplementary certificate which shall:

(i) specify the name of the limited partnership in accordance with the provisions of section 6(4); and

(ii) specify the address of the registered office of the limited partnership in Bermuda in accordance with section 6(5).

(b) deliver the supplementary certificate to the Registrar for registration by him in the register; and

(c) if applicable, establish a registered office in Bermuda, in accordance with section 6(5); and

(d) establish a register of limited partners in accordance with section 7.

(4) The expression "limited partner" used in relation to a limited partnership shall apply, and shall be deemed to have always applied, in relation to a limited partnership in existence prior to the coming into operation of this Act.

(5) The Registrar-General shall, upon the coming into operation of this Act, forthwith deliver to the Registrar the book referred to in section 22 of the principal Act and the information contained in that book modified in such manner as the Registrar considers appropriate, having regard to the provisions of this Act, shall form a part of, and be included in, the register required to be kept by the Registrar under this Act.

(6) Failure to comply with any of the provisions of subsection (3) shall render every general partner liable to a default fine not exceeding one hundred dollars for every day during which the default continues.

OVERSEAS PARTNERSHIPS ACT 1995

(as amended, 1999)

WHEREAS it is expedient to make provisions for the purpose of enabling overseas partnerships to be granted permits to engage in or carry on a trade or business in Bermuda and for matters incidental to such propose:

Be it enacted by The Queen's Most Excellent Majesty, by and with the advice and consent of the Senate and the House of Assembly of Bermuda, and by the authority of the same, as follows:-

PART I

PRELIMINARY

Citation

1. This Act may be cited as the Overseas Partnerships Act 1995 and shall come into operation on a day to be appointed by the Minister by notice published in the Gazette.

Interpretation

2.(1) In this Act, unless the context otherwise requires -

"appointed newspaper" means the Gazette, or newspaper appointed by the Registrar under section 2(2) of the Exempted Partnerships Act 1992;

"certificate of overseas partnership" means the certificate referred to in section 4(3);

"Court" means the Supreme Court;

"default fine" has the meaning given in section 24;

"exempted undertaking" has the meaning assigned to it by section 2(1) of The Companies Act 1981;

"Minister" means the Minister of Finance;

"overseas partnership" means a partnership formed under a law other than the law of Bermuda;

"permit" means a permit issued under section 7;

"registered office" means the registered office referred to in section 12;

"Registrar" means the Registrar of Companies;

"resident representative" means the person appointed under section 13;

(2) For the purposes of this Act the expression "engage in or carry on any trade or business in Bermuda" has the meaning assigned to that expression by section 133 of the Companies Act 1981.

PART II

OVERSEAS PARTNERSHIPS

Overseas partnership not to carry on business with a permit

3. An overseas partnership shall not engage in or carry on any trade or business in Bermuda without a permit from the Minister issued under section 7.

Application for permit by overseas partnership

4.(1) Subject to the provisions of this Act, an overseas partnership may apply to the Minister for a permit to engage in or carry on any trade or business in Bermuda.

(2) An application for the Minister's consent to the issue of a permit shall be in such form, and be accompanied by such documents, as the Minister may require.

(3) The persons seeking to obtain a permit shall make and severally sign a certificate which shall contain the following particulars, that is to say -

(a) the name of the partnership;

(b) the names of all the general partners and their respective addresses;

(c) the name of the resident representative and his address if his address is different from the address of the registered office;

(d) the address of the registered office in Bermuda of the overseas partnership;

(e) the general nature of the business to be transacted by the overseas partnership;

(f) the law governing the overseas partnership;

(g) the address outside Bermuda of the principal place of business, if any, of the partnership; and

(h) the term, if any, for the duration of the partnership.

(4) Within three months prior to an application for a permit under subsection (1), the partnership shall publish in an appointed newspaper an advertisement announcing the intention to apply for a permit and specifying -

(a) the name of the partnership;

(b) the names of all the general partners;

(c) the law governing the partnership; and

(d) the general nature of the business to be transacted by the partnership.

Consent of Minister

5.(1) The Minister may grant or refuse consent to an application made to him under section 4(1).

(2) Where the Minister refuses consent to an application he shall not be bound to give any reason for such refusal and that refusal shall not be subject to appeal or review in any court.

Matters to be taken into consideration by Minister

6. Without prejudice to the discretion conferred on the Minister by section 5, the Minister shall, in deciding whether or not to grant a permit, have regard to -

(a) the economic situation in Bermuda and the due protection of persons already engaged in or carrying on any trade or business in Bermuda;

(b) the nature and previous conduct of the overseas partnership; and

(c) any advantages or disadvantages which may result from the overseas partnership engaging in or carrying on a trade on business in Bermuda.

Form and proof of permit

7.(1) A permit shall be in such form as the Minister may determine and shall -

(a) state that the Minister approves the names of all the general partners and the general nature of the business to be transacted by the overseas partnership;

(b) specify any conditions or restrictions subject to which the permit is granted; and

(c) be signed by the Minister.

(2) A copy of every permit shall be lodged by the Minister with the Registrar.

(3) A certificate purporting to be signed by the Registrar -

(a) certifying that a permit was or was not in force in respect of an overseas partnership at the time specified in the permit; and

(b) specifying the conditions or restrictions, if any, subject to which the permit was granted, shall be admissible in evidence in proceedings under this Act without further proof and shall be prima facie evidence of the facts certified or specified therein.

Permit may be subject to conditions, etc.

8.(1) Where the Minister grants a permit pursuant to an application under section 4, that permit may be subject to such conditions or restrictions, if any, as the Minister may think fit to impose.

(2) Without prejudice to the generality of subsection (1), a permit may require that an overseas partnership shall have one or more partners ordinarily resident in Bermuda.

(3) The Minister may, on the application of the general partners, vary any condition or restriction subject to which a permit is granted.

(4) Where under subsection (3) the Minister varies the conditions or restrictions of a permit he shall cause the variation to be delivered to the Registrar for registration by him in the register.

Registration of permit, etc.

9.(1) Subject to the provisions of this section, a permit issued by the Minister may be delivered to the Registrar for registration and shall be effective on the date that it is so registered by the Registrar.

(2) The persons seeking to register a permit shall deliver to the Registrar the certificate of overseas partnership and the permit.

(3) If the Registrar does not consider the name of the overseas partnership undesirable, the Registrar shall register the permit and shall issue a certificate of registration which shall specify the date of registration of the permit and to which shall be attached a facsimile of the certificate of overseas partnership and a copy of the permit.

(4) The Registrar may -

(a) refuse to register a permit if, in the opinion of the Registrar, the name of the overseas partnership is undesirable; and

(b) if in his opinion a name is not undesirable, on application by any person intending to register a permit, reserve that name for the exclusive use of the applicant for a period not exceeding three months next after the date of receipt of such application.

Register of overseas partnerships

10.(1) The Registrar shall establish and maintain in such form as he shall determine a register of overseas partnerships in which shall be registered -

(a) the certificate of overseas partnership; and

(b) the permit issued by the Minister.

(2) The register shall be open to inspection by members of the public during ordinary business hours on payment of such fee, not exceeding five dollars, as the Minister may determine.

Restrictions on activities of overseas partnership

11.(1) An overseas partnership shall not -

(a) acquire or hold land in Bermuda other than by way of lease or tenancy agreement for a term not exceeding twenty-one years, being land required for the business of the overseas partnership;

(b) take any mortgage of land in Bermuda without the prior written consent of the Minister;

(c) acquire any bonds, or debentures secured on any land in Bermuda other than bonds or debentures issued by the Government or a public authority;

(d) except as provided in paragraph (e)(iii), acquire any shares issued by any company incorporated in Bermuda, or acquire any interest in any business or undertaking in Bermuda:

(e) carry on business of any kind or type whatsoever in Bermuda either alone or in partnership or otherwise except -

(i) carrying on business with persons outside Bermuda;

(ii) doing business in Bermuda with an exempted undertaking in furtherance only of the business of the overseas partnership carried on outside Bermuda;

(iii) buying or selling or otherwise dealing in shares, loans, debenture stock, obligations, mortgages or other securities issued or created by an exempted undertaking;

(iv) transacting banking business in Bermuda with and through a bank licensed under the Banks Act 1969;

(v) effecting or concluding contracts in Bermuda, and exercising in Bermuda all other powers, so far as may be necessary for the carrying on of its business with persons outside Bermuda;

(vi) if the articles of partnership expressly so provide, acting as manager or agent for, or consultant or adviser to the business of any exempted undertaking whether or not such business is the sole business of the overseas partnership.

(2) Nothing in subsection (1)(e) shall be taken to prohibit an overseas partnership from effecting or concluding contracts or arrangements with persons in Bermuda for the supply of goods and services to the overseas partnership necessary for the purpose of enabling the overseas partnership to carry on its business with persons outside Bermuda.

(2A) Nothing in subsection (1)(e) shall prohibit an overseas partnership from offering goods or services electronically from a place of business in Bermuda or through an internet or other electronic service provider located in Bermuda.

(2B) An overseas partnership shall be deemed to engage in or carry on any trade or business in Bermuda if it makes known by way of advertisement or by any statement on a web site or by an electronic record as defined in the Electronic Transactions Act 1999 that it may be contacted at a particular address in Bermuda or if it uses a Bermudian domain name.

(3) An overseas partnership shall not engage in, or carry on the business of, conveying or arranging for the conveyance of passengers, goods or mail by ship within the waters of Bermuda except -

(i) where the ship is owned, operated or chartered by or on behalf of the overseas partnership;

(ii) where the conveyance is of a passenger employed by the overseas partnership or of goods which are or are to become the property of the overseas partnership; or

(iii) when the business is negotiated by a local company as defined by the Companies Act 1981.

(4) An overseas partnership shall not engage in retain trade in Bermuda, including retail trade with an exempted undertaking or any other person.

(5) An overseas partnership shall transact all banking business conducted in Bermuda with and through a bank incorporated in Bermuda.

(6) If an overseas partnership does anything in contravention of the provisions of subsection (1), then the land, merchandise, stocks, shares, bonds, debentures, securities, property or other interests so acquired or disposed of, taken or held, will be liable to escheat under the Escheats Act 1871 or under any other Act relating to escheat.

(7) It is hereby declared that in any proceedings for escheat under subsection (6), the question whether any land, merchandise, stocks, shares, bonds, debentures, securities, property or other interests have been taken, acquired, disposed of or held in contravention of the provisions of subsection (1), shall be decided as a question of fact.

Registered office

12. An overseas partnership shall, at all times, maintain in Bermuda a registered office, which shall not be a post office box, to which all communications may be sent.

Resident representative

13. An overseas partnership shall -

(a) appoint, and at all times maintain in Bermuda, a resident representative; and

(b) within thirty days after the appointment of a resident representative notify the Registrar of his name and address.

Duties of resident representative

14.(1) Where a resident representative knows or has reasonable cause to believe -

(a) that an overseas partnership has changed a matter referred to in section 22, and in a case where -

(i) the Minister's consent is required under subsection (1)(a) of that section, no consent has been obtained; or

(ii) the Minister is required to be notified under subsection (4) of that section, the Minister has not been so notified:

(b) that there is a breach of any condition or restriction subject to which the Minister consented to the registration of a permit under section 8(1) or to a change of a matter under section 22(1)(a);

(c) that the overseas partnership has failed to deliver to the Registrar for registration by him a supplementary certificate referred to in section 22(5);

(d) that the overseas partnership has failed to pay any fee required by any provision of this Act; or

(e) that the overseas partnership is not keeping records of its acts and financial affairs in accordance with section 15, the resident representative shall within thirty days of any of the matters specified in paragraph (a) to (e) coming to his knowledge or belief, as the case may be, make a written report to the Minister and such report shall contain all the information that is available to the resident representative.

(2) Where a resident representative knows or has reasonable cause to believe that an overseas partnership has commenced winding up its affairs consequent on the dissolution of the overseas partnership, the resident representative shall forthwith give written notice of that fact or that belief, as the case may be, to the Minister.

(3) A resident representative who fails to comply with subsection (1) or (2) is guilty of an offence and liable on conviction by a court of summary jurisdiction to a fine not exceeding five thousand dollars.

Records to be kept by overseas partnership

15. Every overseas partnership shall keep at its registered office in Bermuda such records of its acts and financial affairs as will show adequately the trade or business it is engaging in or carrying on or has engaged in or carried on in Bermuda except that if the records of its acts and financial affairs are kept at some place outside Bermuda there shall be kept at the registered office of the overseas partnership in Bermuda such records as will enable all the partners to ascertain with reasonable accuracy the financial position of the partnership at the end of every three months.

Appointment and duties of inspector

16.(1) The Minister may at any time appoint one or more inspectors to investigate the affairs of an overseas partnership and to report thereon in such manner as the Minister may direct.

(2) The expenses of and incidental to such investigation shall be defrayed by the overseas partnership unless the Minister otherwise directs.

(3) A general partner or a resident representative of an overseas partnership shall take such steps as are reasonable to produce to an inspector such books or documents as the inspector may require for the purposes of an investigation.

(4) A general partner or a resident representative of an overseas partnership who, in the course of an investigation of the affairs of the overseas partnership -

(a) refuses to produce any book or document which is in his possession and which is required by the inspector to be produced; or

(b) refuses to answer any question relating to the affairs of the overseas partnership which he might reasonably be expected to know, is guilty of an offence and liable on conviction by a court of summary jurisdiction to a fine not exceeding five thousand dollars.

(5) An inspector may take evidence upon oath in investigating the affairs of an overseas partnership and for that purpose may administer an oath.

(6) An investigation under this section shall be held in private unless the overseas partnership requests that it be held in public.

(7) An inspector investigating the affairs of an overseas partnership may from time to time report to the Minister and shall, on completion of the investigation -

(a) submit a written report to the Minister; and

(b) submit a copy of such report to all the partners.

(8) Except at the request of an overseas partnership or on the direction of the Minister, no other person shall be informed of the nature or contents of a report referred to in subsection (7).

(9) If the Minister, after examining a report referred to in subsection (7), considers that an overseas partnership, a partner, the resident representative or any officer, agent or employee of the overseas partnership -

(a) has knowingly and wilfully done anything in contravention of this Act, the Minister may revoke the permit granted under section 7;

(b) is carrying on the affairs of the overseas partnership in a manner that is detrimental to the interests of the creditors of the overseas partnership,the Minister may require the overseas partnership to take such measures as he considers necessary in relation to its affairs.

(10) Any proceedings in connection with the holding of an investigation by an inspector in pursuance of the provisions of this section shall for the purposes of those provisions of the Criminal Code relating to perjury, be deemed to be judicial proceedings.

Letterheads and service of process

17.(1) Every overseas partnership shall have the following particulars on all letters set from a place of business in Bermuda in connection with that business, that is to say, -

(a) the name of the overseas partnership;

(b) the law governing the partnership; and

(c) the address of its registered office.

(2) Any notice, instrument or other document, and any legal process to be delivered to, or served on, an overseas partnership for the purposes of this Act may be delivered or served by leaving it at the registered office of the overseas partnership or by delivering it to a general partner or to the resident representative.

(3) If the registered office cannot reasonably be found, any such notice, instrument, document or legal process may be delivered or served by leaving it at the office of the Registrar and publishing a notice of the fact in an appointed newspaper.

(4) Delivery or service pursuant to subsection (3) shall be deemed to be delivery to, or service on, an overseas partnership.

Revocation of a permit

18. The Minister may at any time revoke the permit of an overseas partnership if -

(a) the partnership or any of its servants or agents contravenes a condition of its permit;

(b) in the opinion of the Minister the partnership is carrying on business in a manner detrimental to the public interest;

(c) the partnership ceases to engage in or carry on any trade or business in Bermuda;

(d) a court or other competent authority in any country makes an order for the dissolution of the partnership; or

(e) there is a substantial change in the nature of the business carried on by the partnership and the Minister had not, pursuant to section 22(1)(a), consented to such change.

Revocation procedure

19.(1) The Minister shall give an overseas partnership reasonable notice in writing of his intention to revoke its permit under section 18 and shall afford the partnership an opportunity of making representations to him.

(2) A notice under subsection (1) shall specify the grounds on which the Minister intends to revoke the permit.

(3) Upon the revocation of its permit an overseas partnership shall forthwith cease to engage in or carry on any trade or business in Bermuda unless the Minister in his discretion authorises the partnership so to do -

(a) pending the determination of an appeal against the revocation; and

(b) for such period as the Minister may specify for the purpose of ceasing its business in Bermuda.

(4) When the Minister revokes the permit of an overseas partnership the Registrar may, if he is satisfied that it would be in the interests of any creditor of the partnership or of any other person to whom the partnership has an obligation that the affairs of the partnership in Bermuda should be wound up, petition the Court to wind up its affairs and the Court may make such orders for the winding up of the affairs of the overseas partnership as is practicable.

Appeals to Supreme Court

20.(1) A partnership aggrieved by the revocation by the Minister of a permit may appeal to the Court within twenty-one days or such longer period as the Court may allow after receipt of notification of such revocation.

(2) If an appeal is allowed by the Court, the partnership shall be entitled to engage in or carry on any trade or business in Bermuda in the same manner as it did before its permit was revoked.

(3) If an appeal is dismissed by the Court, the partnership shall, forthwith or in such time as the Minister may allow, cease to engage in or carry on any trade or business in Bermuda.

(4) Section 62 of the Supreme Court Act 1905 shall be deemed to extend to the making of rules under that section to regulate the practice and procedure on an appeal under this section.

Surrender of permit

21.(1) Where an overseas partnership ceases to carry on any trade or business in Bermuda, a general partner or the resident representative may deliver to the Registrar for registration by him in the register a certificate of surrender of the permit issued by the Minister under section 7.

(2) A certificate of surrender shall specify -

(a) the name of the overseas partnership and the date of registration of the permit granted by the Minister; and

(b) that the overseas partnership has ceased to engage in or carry on any trade or business in Bermuda.

(3) A certificate of surrender shall be signed by at least one general partner or by a person duly authorised to sign on behalf of the overseas partnership.

(4) Subject to subsection (5), upon delivery to the Registrar of a certificate of surrender, the provisions of this Act shall cease to have effect in respect of the overseas partnership.

(5) Subsection (4) is without prejudice to any proceedings by, or against, the overseas partnership.

Change in respect of overseas partnership

22.(1) Subject to the provisions of this section, the general partners of an overseas partnership may, from time to time -

(a) subject to subsection (2), with the prior written consent of the Minister obtained by application of the general partners -

(i) change the general partners;

(ii) change the name of the overseas partnership; or

(iii) change the general nature of the business transacted by the overseas partnership;

(b) subject to subsection (4), change the resident representative; or

(c) change any of the following matters, that is to say, -

(i) the registered office;

(ii) the term, if any, for the duration of the partnership; or

(iii) the principal place of business, if any, outside Bermuda, of the partnership.

(2) The general partners shall, not earlier than three months before making a change referred to in subsection (1)(a), publish an advertisement in an appointed newspaper specifying the proposed change.

(3) The provisions of section 5(1) and (2) and section 8 shall, mutatis mutandis, apply to an application made under subsection (1)(a) of this section as they apply to an application made under section 4.

(4) The general partners shall, not later than thirty days before making a change referred to in subsection (1)(b), in writing, notify the Minister of the proposed change.

(5) The general partners shall, not later than thirty days after a change referred to in this section is made -

(a) make and severally sign a supplementary certificate supplementing, as the circumstances require, the certificate of overseas partnership; and

(b) deliver the supplementary certificate to the Registrar for registration by him in the register.

(6) Where an overseas partnership fails to comply with subsections (1), (2), (4) or (5) the overseas partnership shall be liable to a default fine.

Fees

23.(1) The fee specified in Part I of the Schedule to this Act shall accompany an application for the Minister's consent under section 4.

(2) The persons seeking to register a permit shall -

(a) at the time of registration of that permit; and

(b) thereafter, on or before 31 January in each year, pay to the Registrar the fee specified in Part II of the Schedule.

(3) Where a permit is registered after 31 August in any year, the fee payable at the time of such registration shall be one half of the amount referred to in subsection (2)(a).

(4) If an overseas partnership fails to comply with subsection (2)(b) the overseas partnership shall be liable to a default fine.

(5) The fees specified in Part III of the Schedule shall, in addition to the fees specified in Part I and II, be payable in respect of the matters specified in the said Part III.

(6) The Minister may, from time to time, by order, amend the Schedule to this Act and such order shall be subject to the affirmative resolution procedure.

(7) In this section "annual fee" means the fee referred to in subsection (2)(b).+

Default fine

24.(1) Where in this Act it is provided that an overseas partnership, or any person who is in default shall be liable to a default fine, such overseas partnership or such person shall, for every day during which the default, refusal or contravention continues, be liable to a fine of twenty dollars.

(2) Notwithstanding subsection (1), an individual who is in default shall only be liable to a fine if he knowingly is guilty of the default or knowingly and wilfully authorizes or permits the default.

(3) It shall be lawful for the Registrar, in any case where a person fails to comply with a provision of this Act which is subject to a default fine and the failure is not due to wilful neglect or default, to accept payment of a penalty of three hundred dollars, and in such case subsection (1) shall not apply.

(4) Any penalty payable under this Act may be recovered by the Accountant General in the Supreme Court or in a court of summary jurisdiction as a civil debt.

Construction of "partner"

25. For the avoidance of a doubt it is hereby declared that where a permit is registered under this Act, then, for the purposes of the overseas partnership to which the permit was granted, unless the context otherwise requires -

(a) references to "partner" shall be construed as references to "general partner"; and

(b) anything required to be done or suffered by a partner shall be construed as being required to be done or suffered, as the case may be, by a general partner.

Application of Act No. 41 of 1966 to overseas partnerships

26. The Exempted Undertakings Tax Protection Act 1966 shall apply to overseas partnerships as if they were exempted partnerships.

Amendment of Act No. 15 of 1990

27. The Stamp Duties (International Business) Relief Act 1990 is amended -

(a) in section 2(3) -

(i) in the definition of the expression "international business" by inserting immediately before the words "or exempted partnership" the words ", overseas partnership"; and

(ii) by deleting the full stop at the end of the definition of the expression "international business" and substituting therefore a semi-colon; and by inserting next after the definition of that expression the following:

"overseas partnership" has the meaning assigned to it by section 2(1) of the Overseas Partnerships Act 1995.".

Amendment of Act No. 57 of 1969

28. The Bermuda Monetary Authority Act 1969 is amended in section 21(1)(d) by inserting next after the words "Companies Act 1981" the words "or pursuant to section 4 of the Overseas Partnerships Act 1995".

SCHEDULE (section 23)

PART I

Activity

Fee to accompany application for Minister's consent under section 4	$185.00

PART II

Fee payable on registration of overseas partnership under section 23(2)(a)	$250.00
Annual fee payable by overseas partnership under section 23(2)(b)	$2000.00

PART III
(Additional Fees)

On delivery of documents to Registrar for registration of permit under section 9(2)	$50.00
On an application for Minister's consent to change a matter under section 22(1)(a)	$50.00
For preparation of a copy of any document by a public officer: -	
(a) for the first 3 pages or part thereof	$3.00
(b) for each additional 3 pages or part thereof	$3.00
For a search by a public officer of the records maintained by the Registrar for the purpose of obtaining a certificate that the Overseas Partnership Act 1995 has been complied with	$50.00
For certifying and sealing a copy of any document or set of documents	$50.00
For registering or recording every certificate required by this Act	$150.00
For each inspection of the register under section 10(2)	$5.00

THE EXEMPTED PARTNERSHIPS ACT 1992

(as amended, 1999)

ARRANGEMENT OF SECTIONS

WHEREAS it is expedient to replace the Exempted Partnerships Act, 1958, by new provisions in respect of the registration, regulation and control of exempted partnerships and for purposes connected with those matters:

Be It enacted by the Queen's Most Excellent Majesty, by and with the advice and consent of the Senate and the House of Assembly of Bermuda, and by the authority of the same, as follows:-

Short title.

1. This Act may be cited as the Exempted Partnerships Act 1992.

Interpretation.

2.(1) In this Act, unless the context otherwise requires -

"appointed newspaper" means the Gazette, or newspaper appointed by the Registrar under subsection (2);

"certificate of exempted partnership" means the certificate referred to in section 5;

"Court" means the Supreme Court;

"exempted partnership" means a partnership which satisfies the requirements of section 7(1);

"limited partnership" means a limited partnership within the meaning of section 2(1) of the Limited Partnership Act 1883 and references to "general partner" and "limited partner" shall be construed accordingly;

"Minister" means the Minister of Finance;

"register" means the register referred to in section 22;

"registered office" means the registered office referred to in section 10(10);

"Registrar" means the Registrar of Companies;

"resident representative" means the person appointed under section 17.

(2) The Registrar shall from time to time publish in the Gazette a list of newspapers appointed for the purposes of this Act.

Application.

3. This Act applies to every exempted partnership whether such exempted partnership was registered under the Exempted Partnerships Act 1958 or is registered after the coming into operation of this Act.

Commencement.

4. This Act shall come into operation on a day to be appointed by the Minister by notice published in the Gazette.

Certificate of exempted partnership.

5.(1) The persons seeking to register a partnership as an exempted partnership shall make and severally sign a certificate which shall contain the following particulars, that is to say -

(a) the name of the exempted partnership;

(b) subject to subsection (2), the names of all the partners;

(c) the date when the exempted partnership is to commence and the term, if any, for which it is entered into;

(d) the name of the resident representative and his address if his address is different from the address of the registered office;

(e) the address of the registered office in Bermuda of the exempted partnership; and

(f) the general nature of the business to be transacted by the exempted partnership.

(2) Notwithstanding subsection (1)(b), in the case of a partnership which is registered, or which the persons are seeking to register, as a limited partnership, the certificate shall contain the names and respective principal places of residence of the general partners only.

Articles of partnership.

6. The articles of partnership of an exempted partnership registered after the coming into operation of this Act shall -

(a) expressly provide that the law applicable to be exempted partnership is the law of Bermuda: and

(b) specify the general nature of the business to be transacted by the exempted partnership.

Requirements for registration of exempted partnership.

7.(1) Subject to the provisions of this Act, a partnership may be registered as an exempted partnership under section 9 if -

(a) one or more of the partners -

(i) is an individual who does not possess Bermudian status under the provisions of the Bermuda Immigration and Protection Act 1956;

(ii) is a company which is not a local company for the purposes of part IX of the Companies Act 1981; or

(iii) is not otherwise Bermudian for the purposes of any other law; and

(b) the Minister has granted consent thereto under section 8.

(2) An application for the Minister's consent to the registration of an exempted partnership shall be in such form, and be accompanied by such documents, as the Minister may require.

(3) The persons seeking to register a partnership as an exempted partnership shall, not earlier than three months before making an application under subsection (2), publish in an appointed newspaper an advertisement announcing the intention and specifying -

(a) the name of the exempted partnership;

(b) subject to subsection (4), the names of all the partners; and

(c) the general nature of the business to be transacted by the exempted partnership.

(4) Notwithstanding subsection (3)(b), in the case of a partnership which is registered, or which the persons are seeking to register, as a limited partnership, the advertisement shall contain the names and respective principal places of residence of the general partners only.

(5) Notwithstanding section 4(3) of the Limited Partnership Act 1883 (which makes provision in respect of the advertisement of an intention to form a limited partnership), where the persons seeking to register an exempted partnership under this Act are also seeking to register, at the same time, that partnership as a limited partnership under that Act, an advertisement under this section shall be deemed to include an advertisement under section 4(3) of that Act, so, however, that that advertisement shall comply with the requirements specified in subsection (3) of this section and those specified in section 4(3) of that Act.

Consent of Minister.

8.(1) The Minister may grant or refuse consent to an application made to him under section 7(2).

(2) Where the Minister refuses consent to an application he shall not be bound to give any reason for such refusal and that refusal shall not be subject to appeal or review in any court.

(3) Where the Minister consents to an application that consent may be subject to such conditions and restrictions as the Minister may specify.

(4) Conditions or restrictions subject to which the Minister consents to an application shall be included in a certificate of exempted partnership and shall be registered in the register.

(5) The Minister may from time to time by order subject to the negative resolution procedure prohibit the registration of exempted partnerships, or any class of exempted partnerships, the capital of which is less than an amount specified in the order.

(6) Where an exempted partnership contravenes any condition or restriction specified by the Minister under subsection (3) every partner shall be guilty of an offence and shall be liable -

(a) on conviction by a court of summary jurisdiction to a fine not exceeding five hundred dollars; or

(b) on conviction on indictment to a fine not exceeding five thousand dollars, for each day the offence continues.

Registration of exempted partnership, etc.

9.(1) Not later than six months later the Minister has consented to an application under section 8, the partners shall deliver to the Registrar -

(a) the certificate of exempted partnership;

(b) the consent of the Minister referred to in that section; and

(c) a copy of the articles of partnership.

(2) The articles of partnership referred to in subsection (1)(c) shall not be registered in the register.

(3) If the Registrar

(a) is presented with a certificate which -

(i) states that the Minister has approved the names of all the partners and the nature of the business to be transacted by the exempted partnership; and

(ii) is signed by the Minister; and

(b) does not consider the name of the exempted partnership undesirable, the Registrar shall register the certificate of exempted partnership and shall issue a certificate of registration which shall specify the date of registration of the exempted partnership and to which shall be attached a facsimile of the certificate of exempted partnership.

(4) Where the persons seeking to register a partnership as an exempted partnership under this section are also seeking, at the same time, to register that partnership as a limited partnership under the Limited Partnership Act 1883 and the Registrar thinks it appropriate so to do the Registrar may issue one certificate of registration and that certificate of registration shall -

(a) specify the date of registration; and

(b) have attached to it a facsimile of the certificate of exempted partnership specified in section 5 of this Act and a facsimile of the certificate specified In section 3 of the Limited Partnership Act 1883.

Name and registered office of exempted partnership.

10.(1) The Registrar may refuse to register an exempted partnership if, in the opinion of the Registrar, the name of the exempted partnership is undesirable.

(2) The Registrar may, if in his opinion the name is not undesirable, on application by any person seeking to register an exempted partnership, reserve a name for the exclusive use of the applicant for a period not exceeding three months from the date of receipt of the application.

(3) Without prejudice to the generality of subsection (1), no exempted partnership shall be permitted to be registered with a name which is identical with the name by which another exempted partnership is registered under this Act or so nearly resembles that name as to be likely to deceive unless that other exempted partnership signifies its consent in such manner as the Registrar may require.

(4) I f, through inadvertence or otherwise, an exempted partnership on its first registration or on its registration with a new name is registered with a name which in the opinion of the Registrar too closely resembles the name by which an exempted partnership in existence is already registered, the first mentioned exempted partnership may, with the sanction of the Registrar, change its name. and shall, if the Registrar so directs within six months of its being registered by that name, change its name within six weeks of the date of such direction or within such longer period as the Registrar may think fit to allow.

(5) If at any time after an exempted partnership has been registered it appears to the Registrar that the name under which it is registered is undesirable, the Registrar may notify the exempted partnership accordingly and may in such notification direct the exempted partnership to change its name, and the exempted partnership shall change its name within six weeks of such direction unless within that time it shall have lodged an appeal to the Court against such direction.

(6) Where an exempted partnership lodges an appeal under subsection (5), the Court may either confirm or cancel the direction of the Registrar and the decision of the Court shall be final.

(7) If an exempted partnership makes default in complying -

(a) with a direction under subsection (4); or

(b) subject to subsection (8), with a confirmed direction under subsection (6).

it shall be liable to a default fine of one hundred dollars for every day during which the default continues,

(8) Notwithstanding subsection (7)(b), where an exempted partnership lodges an appeal under subsection (5), the period of default shall not commence until six weeks after the decision of the Court.

(9) Section 13, other than subsection (4), shall not apply to a change of name under this section.

(10) An exempted partnership shall, at all times, maintain a registered office, which shall not be a post office box, in Bermuda, to which all communications may be sent.

(11) Notice of the address of the registered office of an exempted partnership and every change thereof shall, within fourteen days of the establishment of the office or of the making of the change, as the case may be, be given to the Registrar.

(12) If default is made in complying with subsection (11) the exempted partnership shall be liable to a default fine of one hundred dollars for every day during which the default continues.

Fees. Schedule.

11.(1) Subject to subsection (2), the fee specified in Part I of the First Schedule to this Act shall accompany an application for the Minister's consent under section 7(2).

(2) Where the persons applying for the Minister's consent to register a partnership as an exempted partnership under section 7(2) are also applying, at the same time, for the Minister's consent to register that partnership as a limited partnership under section 4(2) of the Limited Partnership Act 1883, then, notwithstanding any provision with respect to the payment of fee in relation to an application for consent under that Act, the fee specified in Part II of the First Schedule to this Act shall be the fee payable in respect of, and shall accompany, such application.

(3) Subject to subsections (4), (5) and (6) and section 25(3), the persons seeking -

(a) to register a partnership as an exempted partnership; or

(b) to register a partnership as an exempted partnership and as a limited partnership pursuant to section 9(4), shall -

(c) at the time of registration of that partnership; and

(d) thereafter, on or before January 31 in each year, pay to the Registrar the fee specified in Part Ill of the First Schedule to this Act.

(4) Where a partnership referred to in subsection (3)(a) or (b) is registered after August 31 in any year, the fee payable at the time of such registration shall be one half the amount specified in Part III of the First Schedule to this Act.

(5) Subject to subsection (6), where in any year a partnership referred to in subsection (3)(a) or (b) fails to pay the annual fee, every partner shall be guilty of an offence and shall be liable on conviction by a court of summary jurisdiction to a fine not exceeding one hundred dollars for every day during which the default continues.

(6) Notwithstanding subsection (5), but subject to subsection (7), where -

(a) in any year a partnership referred to in subsection (3)(a) or (b) fails to pay the annual fee; and

(b) the Registrar is satisfied that that failure is not due to the wilful neglect of the partners, the Registrar may accept payment of the sum due together with a penalty of three hundred dollars and upon such acceptance the provisions of subsection (5) shall not apply.

(7) Notwithstanding the provisions of subsections (5) and (6), where -

(a) in any year a partnership referred to in subsection (3)(a) or (b) fails to pay the annual fee; and

(b) thereafter fails for a period of three months commencing on the first day of February in that year to pay that fee, the partnership may, by order of the Court on petition to that court by the Registrar, be dissolved.

(8) For the avoidance of doubt it is hereby declared that subsection (7) does not affect the application of subsection (5).

(9) The fees specified in Part IV of the First Schedule shall, in addition to the fees specified in Parts I to III of that Schedule, be payable in respect of the matters specified in Part IV.

(10) The Minister may, from time to time, by order, amend the First Schedule to this Act and such order shall be subject to the affirmative resolution procedure.

(11) In this section and in section 12, "annual fee" means the fee referred to in subsection (3)(d).

Submission of declaration.

12.(1) An exempted partnership shall, on or before January 31 in each year, send to the Registrar, together with the annual fee, a declaration in writing signed by a partner or by a person duly authorized to sign on behalf of the partnership stating the general nature of the business transacted by the exempted partnership.

(2) If an exempted partnership fails to send a declaration to the Registrar in compliance with subsection (1), every partner shall be liable to a penalty of two hundred and fifty dollars, payable to the Registrar.

Change in respect of exempted partnership.

13.(1) Subject to the provisions of this section, the partners of an exempted partnership may, from time to time -

(a) with the prior consent of the Minister, obtained by application by the partners, change any of the matters specified in subsection (2); and

(b) change the resident representative.

(2) The matters referred to in subsection (1)(a) are -

(a) the name of the exempted partnership;

(b) the general partners; and

(c) the general nature of the business transacted by the exempted partnership.

(3) Where an exempted partnership proposes to change the resident representative, the partners shall, not later than thirty days before such change, in writing, notify the Minister of the proposed change.

(4) The partners shall, not earlier than three months before making a change referred to in subsection (2), publish an advertisement in an appointed newspaper, announcing the matter that it is intended to change and specifying the proposed change.

(5) The partners shall, not later than thirty days after a change referred to in this section is made -

(a) make and severally sign a supplementary certificate supplementing, as the circumstances require, the certificate of exempted partnership; and

(b) deliver the supplementary certificate to the Registrar for registration by him in the register.

(6) The provisions of section 8(1), (2), (3) and (4) shall, mutatis mutandis, apply to an application made under subsection 1(a) of this section as they apply to an application made under section 7(2).

(7) Where a change referred to in subsection 1(a) is made otherwise than in accordance with the provisions of this section, the Minister may petition the Court for the dissolution of the exempted partnership.

(8) If the Court, on the hearing of a petition under subsection (7), is satisfied that a partner or a person duly authorised by the partners has contravened or caused or permitted the contravention of a provision of subsection 1(a), the Court may -

(a) make an order for the dissolution of the exempted partnership;

(b) impose a fine not exceeding five thousand dollars on any partner or duly authorized person, as the case may be, who knowingly and wilfully contravened, or otherwise caused or permitted the contravention; or

(c) make such order and impose such fine.

(9) Where a change referred to in subsection (3) is made otherwise than in accordance with that subsection every partner is guilty of an offence and liable on conviction by a court of summary jurisdiction to a fine not exceeding two thousand dollars.

Records of accounts.

14.(1) An exempted partnership shall keep proper records of account with respect to its business including, without limiting the generality of the foregoing, records of account with respect to its assets, liabilities and capital, cash receipts and disbursements, purchases and sales and income costs and expenses.

(2) Subject to subsection (3), the records of account shall be kept at the registered office or at such other place as the partners think fit, and shall at all times be open to inspection by the partners, including limited partners, if any, and the resident representative.

(3) If the records of account are kept at a place outside Bermuda, there shall be kept at the registered office such records of account as will enable the financial position of the exempted partnership, at the end of each three month period, to be ascertained with reasonable accuracy.

(4) If an exempted partnership fails to comply with the provisions of subsection (1), (2) or (3), every partner shall be guilty of an offence and liable on conviction by a court of summary jurisdiction to a fine not exceeding five hundred dollars.

(5) If any partner refuses to make available the records of account for inspection by another partner or by the resident representative, the Court may, on application by the second mentioned partner or the resident representative, order the partner so refusing to make the records of account available.

Financial statements.

15.(1) The partners of an exempted partnership shall, subject to section 16, at such intervals and for such periods as the articles of partnership provide, cause to be prepared -

(a) in accordance with generally accepted accounting principles, financial statements which shall include -

(i) a statement of the results of operations for the period;

(ii) a statement of retained earnings or deficit;

(iii) a balance sheet at the end of such period; and

(iv) such further information as may be required by the articles of partnership; and

(b) the report of an auditor in respect of the financial statements specified in paragraph (a).

(2) Subject to section 16, if an exempted partnership fails to comply with subsection (1), every partner shall be guilty of an offence and liable on conviction by a court of summary jurisdiction to a fine not exceeding one thousand dollars.

Power to waive preparation of financial statements.

16. Notwithstanding section 15, if in respect of a particular interval all the partners, including limited partners, if any, agree in writing that no financial statement or auditor's report thereon needs to be prepared, there shall be no obligation to cause a financial statement or auditor's report to be prepared for that interval.

Resident representative.

17.(1) An exempted partnership shall -

(a) appoint, and at all times maintain in Bermuda, a resident representative; and

(b) within one month of the appointment of a resident representative notify the Registrar of his name and address.

(2) Where a resident representative knows or has reasonable cause to believe -

(a) that an exempted partnership has changed a matter referred to in section 13, and in a case where -

(i) the Minister's consent is required under subsection(1)(a) of that section, no consent has been obtained; or

(ii) the Minister is required to be notified under subsection (3) of that section, the Minister has not been so notified;

(b) that there is a breach of any condition or restriction subject to which the Minister consented to the registration of the exempted partnership under section 8(3) or to a change of a matter under section 13(1)(a);

(c) that the exempted partnership has failed to deliver to the Registrar for registration by him a supplementary certificate referred to in section 13(5)(b);

(d) that the exempted partnership has failed to pay any fee required by any provision of this Act; or

(e) that the exempted partnership is not keeping records of account in accordance with section 14, or is in contravention of any requirement in respect of the preparation of financial statements or audit under section 15, the resident representative shall, within thirty days of any of the matters specified in paragraphs (a) to (e) coming to his knowledge or belief, as the case may be, make a written report to the Minister and such report shall contain all the information that is available to the resident representative.

(3) Where a resident representative knows or has reasonable cause to believe that an exempted partnership has commenced winding up its affairs consequent on the dissolution of the exempted partnership, the resident representative shall forthwith give written notice of that fact or that belief, as the case may be, to the Minister.

(4) A resident representative who fails to comply with sub-section (2) or (3) is guilty of an offence and liable on conviction by a court of summary jurisdiction to a fine not exceeding five thousand dollars.

Appointment of duties of inspector.

18.(1) The Minister may at any time appoint one or more inspectors to investigate the affairs of an exempted partnership and to report thereon in such manner as the Minister may direct.

(2) The expenses of and incidental to such investigation shall be defrayed by the exempted partnership unless the Minister otherwise directs.

(3) A partner or a resident representative of an exempted partnership shall produce to an inspector such books or documents as the inspector may require for the purposes of his investigation.

(4) A partner or a resident representative of an exempted partnership who, in the course of an investigation of the affairs or the exempted partnership -

(a) refuses to produce any book or document required by the inspector to be produced; or

(b) refuses to answer any question relating to the affairs of the exempted partnership, shall be guilty of an offence and shall be liable on conviction by a court of summary jurisdiction to a fine not exceeding five thousand dollars.

(5) An inspector may take evidence upon oath in investigating the affairs of an exempted partnership and for that purpose may administer an oath.

(6) An investigation under this section shall be held in private unless an exempted partnership requests that it be held in public.

(7) An inspector investigating the affairs of an exempted partnership may from time to time report to the Minister and shall, on completion of the investigation

(a) submit a written report to the Minister; and

(b) submit a copy of such report to all the partners, including limited partners, if any.

(8) Except at the request of an exempted partnership or on the direction of the Minister, no other person shall be informed of the nature or contents of a report referred to in subsection (7).

(9) If the Minister, after examining a report referred to in subsection (7)(a), considers that an exempted partnership, a partner, the resident representative or any officer, agent or employee of the exempted partnership -

(a) has knowingly and wilfully done anything in contravention of this Act, the Minister may direct the Registrar to petition the Court for the dissolution of the exempted partnership; or

(b) is carrying on the affairs of the exempted partnership in a manner that is detrimental to the interests of the creditors of the exempted partnership, the Minister may require the exempted partnership to take such measures as he considers necessary in relation to its affairs.

(10) A copy of a petition referred to in subsection (9)(a) shall be served on the exempted partnership at least seven clear days before the day set by the Court for the hearing thereof.

(11) If the Court, on the hearing of a petition referred to in subsection (9)(a), is satisfied that the exempted partnership or a partner, or the resident representative or any officer, agent or employee of the exempted partnership, has done anything in contravention of the provisions of this Act, the Court may -

(a) make an order for the dissolution of the exempted partnership;

(b) impose a fine not exceeding two thousand dollars on the exempted partnership;

(c) impose a like fine on any partner or resident representative or any officer, agent or employee of the exempted partnership who knowingly and wilfully authorized or permitted such contravention; or

(d) make an order under paragraph (a) and impose a fine under paragraph (b) and (c).

(12) Any proceedings in connection with the holding of an investigation by an inspector in pursuance of the provisions of this section shall, for the purposes of those provisions of the Criminal Code relating to perjury, be deemed to be judicial proceedings.

Restrictions on carrying on business, etc.

19.(1) An exempted partnership shall not -

(a) acquire or hold land in Bermuda except land required for its business held by way of lease or tenancy agreement for a term not exceeding twenty-one years;

(b) take any mortgage of land in Bermuda without the prior written consent of the Minister;

(c) acquire any bonds, or debentures secured on any land in Bermuda except bonds or debentures issued by the Government or a public authority;

(d) except as provided in paragraph (e)(iii), acquire any shares issued by any company incorporated in Bermuda or acquire any interest in any business or undertaking in Bermuda;

(e) carry on business of any kind or type whatsoever in Bermuda either alone or in partnership or otherwise except -

(i) carrying on business with persons outside Bermuda;

(ii) doing business in Bermuda with an exempted undertaking in furtherance only of the business of the exempted partnership carried on outside Bermuda;

(iii) buying or selling or otherwise dealing in shares, loans, debenture stock obligations, mortgages or other securities issued or created by an exempted undertaking;

(iv) transacting banking business in Bermuda with and through a bank licensed under the Banks Act 1969;

(v) effecting or concluding contracts in Bermuda, and exercising in Bermuda all other powers, so far as may be necessary for the carrying on of its business with persons outside Bermuda;

(vi) if the articles of partnership expressly so provide, acting as manager or agent for, or consultant or adviser to, the business of an exempted undertaking whether or not such business is the sole business of the exempted partnership.

(2) Nothing in subsection (1)(e) shall be taken to prohibit an exempted partnership from effecting or concluding contracts or arrangements with persons in Bermuda for the supply of goods and services to the exempted partnership necessary for the purpose of enabling the exempted partnership to carry on its business with persons outside Bermuda.

(2A) Nothing in subsection (1)(e) shall prohibit an exempted partnership from offering goods or services electronically from a place of business in Bermuda or through an internet or other electronic service provider located in Bermuda.

(3) An exempted partnership shall not engage in, or carry on the business of, conveying or arranging for the conveyance of passengers, goods or mail by ship whether such conveyance is within or outside the waters of Bermuda or partly within and partly outside those waters except -

(i) where the ship is owned, operated or chartered by or on behalf of the exempted partnership;

s

(ii) where the conveyance is of a passenger employed by the exempted partnership or of goods which are or are to become the property of the exempted partnership; or

(iii) when the business is negotiated by a local company as defined by the Companies Act 1981.

(4) Notwithstanding anything in this Act any provision in the articles of partnership empowering an exempted partnership to engage in retail trade in Bermuda, including retail trade with another exempted undertaking or any other person, shall be void to the extent that it purports so to empower that exempted partnership.

(5) An exempted partnership shall transact all banking business conducted in Bermuda with and through a bank incorporated in Bermuda.

(6) If an exempted partnership does anything in contravention of the provisions of subsection (1), then the land, merchandise, stocks, shares, bonds, debentures, securities, property or other interests so acquired or disposed of, taken or held, will be liable to escheat under the Escheats Act 1871 or under any other Act relating to escheat.

(7) It is hereby declared that in any proceedings for escheat under subsection (6), the question whether any land, merchandise, stocks, shares, bonds, debentures, securities, property or other interests have been taken, acquired, disposed of or held in contravention of the provisions of subsection (1), shall be decided as a question of fact.

(8) In this section the expression "exempted undertaking" has the meaning assigned to it by section 2 of the Companies Act 1981.

Cancellation of exempted partnership.

20.(1) Within thirty days after the commencement of the winding up of the affairs of an exempted partnership consequent on the dissolution of the exempted partnership a partner or a person duly authorized by the exempted partnership shall deliver a certificate of cancellation of the exempted partnership to the Registrar for registration by him in the register.

(2) A certificate of cancellation shall, in respect of an exempted partnership, specify -

(a) the name and date of registration of the exempted partnership;

(b) that the exempted partnership is dissolved; and

(c) the effective date of the cancellation (which shall be a date certain) if cancellation is not to be effective upon registration of the certificate by the Registrar under subsection (1).

(3) A certificate of cancellation shall be signed by at least one partner or by a person duly authorised to sign on behalf of the exempted partnership.

Offences in relation to certificate, etc.

21. A person who fails, without reasonable excuse -

(a) to publish an advertisement announcing an intention to change a matter under section 13(4);

(b) to deliver a certificate of cancellation to the Registrar under section 20(1); or

(c) to sign a certificate of cancellation under section 20(3), is guilty of an offence and liable, on conviction by a court of summary jurisdiction to a fine not exceeding five thousand dollars.

Establishment of register evidence.

22.(1) The Registrar shall establish and maintain in such form as he shall determine, a register of exempted partnerships in which shall be registered all certificates and advertisements required by this Act.

(2) The register shall be open, during office hours, to the inspection of all persons desiring to view the register.

(3) A certificate of the Registrar certifying that a certificate required by this Act to be registered by him has been so registered shall be received in all courts and in all proceedings whatsoever as evidence of the matter to which the certificate relates.

Service on exempted partnership.

23.(1) Any notice, instrument or other document, and any legal process to be delivered to, or served on, an exempted partnership for the purposes of this Act may be delivered or served by leaving it at the registered office of the exempted partnership or by delivering it to a partner or to the resident representative.

(2) If the registered office cannot reasonably be found, any such notice, instrument, document or legal process may be delivered or served by leaving it at the office of the Registrar and publishing a notice of the fact in an appointed newspaper.

(3) Delivery or service pursuant to subsection (2) shall be deemed to be delivery to, or service on, an exempted partnership.

General provision in respsect of exempted partnership registered as limited partnership.

24. Except as expressly provided, nothing contained in this Act shall affect any provision of law relating to a limited partnership registered under the Limited Partnership Act 1883 and, accordingly, where a partnership is registered as an exempted partnership under this Act and as a limited partnership under the Limited Partnership Act 1883, unless the context otherwise requires -

(a) references to "partner" shall be construed as references to "general partner"; and

(b) anything required to be done or suffered by a partner shall be construed as being required to be done or suffered, as the case may be, by a general partner.

Savings, transitional, etc.

25.(1) Subject to subsections (2), (3) and (4), an exempted partnership registered under the repealed Act and in existence prior to the coming into operation of this Act, shall continue under this Act, and everything lawfully done by such exempted partnership shall be of full force and effect.

(2) The partners or a person duly authorized by the exempted partnership shall, in respect of an exempted partnership referred to in subsection (1), within six months of the coming into operation of this Act -

(a) make and severally sign a certificate which shall contain the particulars specified in section 5;

(b) deliver the certificate to the Registrar for registration by him in the register; and

(c) if applicable, establish a registered office in Bermuda in accordance with section 10.

(3) The fee referred to in section 11(3)(a) does not apply to the registration of a certificate under subsection (2)(b) of this section.

(4) A person who was a resident manager of an exempted partnership under section 6 of the repealed Act shall be deemed to be the resident representative of that partnership for the purposes of section 17 of this Act.

(5) Where immediately prior to the coming Into operation of this Act an application has been made for the Minister's consent to the registration of an exempted partnership that application shall be deemed to have been made under this Act and the provisions of this Act shall apply accordingly.

(6) All information contained in books, registers and other records maintained by the Registrar in respect of exempted partnerships under the repealed Act, modified in such manner as the Registrar considers appropriate, having regard to the provisions of this Act, shall form part of, and be included in, the register required to be kept by the Registrar under this Act.

(7) Failure to comply with any of the provisions of subsection (2) shall render every partner liable to a default fine of one hundred dollars for every day during which the default continues.

(8) In this section "the repealed Act", means the Exempted Partnerships Act 1958.

Consequential amendments.

26. The provisions of the enactments specified in the first column of the Second Schedule to this Act are amended In the manner specified in the second column of that Schedule.

Repeal.

27. The Exempted Partnerships Act 1958 is repealed.

FIRST SCHEDULE (Section 11)

PART I

Fee Payable

Fee to accompany application for Minister's consent under section 7(2)	$185.00

PART II

Fee on application for consent to limited partnership and exempted partnership under section 11(2)	$250.00

PART III

Fee payable on registration of a partnership as an exempted partnership and on registration of a partnership as an exempted partnership and limited partnership under section 11(3)	$2000.00
Annual fee payable by exempted partnership and by exempted partnership registered as limited partnership under section 1 I(3)(d)	$2000.00

PART IV

Additional Fees

Fee Payable

On delivery of documents to Registrar for registration of exempted partnership under section 9(1)	$50.00
On an application for Minister's consent to change a matter under section 13(1)(a)	$50.00
For preparation of a copy of any document by a public officer:-	
*a)*or the first 3 pages or part thereof	$3.00
*b)*for each additional 3 pages or part thereof	$3.00

For a search by a public officer of the records maintained by the Registrar for the purpose of obtaining a certificate that

The Exempted Partnership Act 1992 has been complied with	$50.00
For certifying and sealing a copy of any document or set of documents	$50.00
For registering or recording every certificate or advertisement required by this Act	$150.00
For each inspection of the register under section 22(2)	$5.00

SECOND SCHEDULE (Section 25)

Exempted Undertakings Tax Protection Act 1966	
Section 1(b)	Delete the words "section 1" and the figure "1958" and substitute therefor respectively the words "section 2" and the figure "1992".
Interest and Credit Charges (Regulation) Act 1975	
Section 6(2)(b)	Delete the words "Exempted Partnerships Act 1958" and substitute the words "Exempted Partnerships Act 1992".
Companies Act	
Section 2(1)	In the definition of the expression "exempted undertaking", delete the figure "1958" and substitute the figure "1992".
Municipalities Act 1923 First Schedule Paragraph 4(l)(d)(iii)	Delete the words "Exempted Partnerships Act 1958" and substitute the words "Exempted Partnerships Act 1992

BR 18/93

STATUTORY INSTRUMENT

made by the Minister of Finance under the Exempted Partnership Act 1992

The Exempted partnerships (Prohibition of Registration) Order 1993

In exercise of the power conferred upon the Minister of Finance by section 8(5) of the Exempted Partnership Act 1992 the following Order is hereby made:-

1. This Order may be cited as the Exempted Partnerships (Prohibition of Registration) Order 1993.

2. The registration of an exempted partnership the capital of which is less than U.S.$12,000 or, where the capital is specified in a currency, other than United States currency, less than the equivalent in that currency of U.S.$12,000, is hereby prohibited.

THE TRUSTEE ACT 1975

(as amended, 1999)

ARRANGEMENT OF SECTIONS

PART I - PRELIMINARY

PART II - GENERAL POWERS OF TRUSTEES AND ESTATE REPRESENTATIVES

General Powers

Indemnities

PART I - PRELIMINARY

Interpretation.

1. In this Act, unless the context otherwise requires -

"authorised investments" means investments authorised by the instrument, if any, creating the trust for the investment of money subject to the trust, or by any provision of law;

"contingent right" as applied to land includes a contingent or executory interest, a possibility coupled with an interest, whether the object of the gift or limitation of the interest, or possibility is or is not ascertained, also a right of entry, whether immediate or future, and whether vested or contingent;

"convey" and "conveyance" as applied to any person include the execution by that person of every necessary or suitable assurance for conveying, assigning, appointing, surrendering, or otherwise transferring or disposing of land whereof he is seized or possessed, or wherein he is entitled to a contingent right, either for his whole estate or for any less estate, together with the performance of all formalities required by law for the validity of the conveyance;

"court" means the Supreme Court;

"estate representative" means the executor, original or by representation, or administrator for the time being of a deceased person;

"income" includes rents and profits;

"instrument" includes a statutory provision;

"mortgage" and "mortgagee" relate to every estate and interest regarded in equity as merely a security for money, and every person deriving title under the original mortgagee;

"pay" as applied in relation to stocks and securities in connection with the expression "into court" includes a deposit or transfer of the same in or into court;

"possession" includes receipt of rents and profits or the right to receive the same, if any; and "possessed" applies to receipt of income of and to any vested estate less than a life estate or interest in possession or in expectancy in any land;

"property" includes real and personal property, and any estate, share and interest in any property, real or personal, and any debt, and any thing in action, and any other right or interest, whether in possession or not;

"rights" include estates and interests;

"sale" includes an exchange;

"securities" include stocks, funds and shares and "securities payable to bearer" include securities transferable by delivery or by delivery and endorsement;

"stock" includes fully paid up shares, and so far as relates to vesting orders made by the court under this Act, includes any fund, annuity, or security transferable in books kept by any company or society, or by instrument of transfer either alone or accompanied by other formalities, and any share or interest therein;

"transfer" in relation to stock or securities, includes the performance and execution of every deed, power of attorney, act, and thing on the part of the transferor to effect and complete the title in the transferee;

"trust" does not include the duties incident to an estate or interest conveyed by way of mortgage, but with this exception the expressions "trust" and "trustee" extend to implied and constructive trusts, and to cases where the trustee has a beneficial interest in the trust property, and to the duties incident to the office of an estate representative, and "trustee" includes an estate representative, and "new trustee" includes an additional trustee;

"trust corporation" means -

(a) a corporation either appointed by the court in any particular case to be a trustee or licensed as a trust company under the Trust Companies Act 1991; and

(b) the person for the time being holding office as public trustee in his capacity as corporation sole under the Public Trustee Act 1906 of the Parliament of the United Kingdom;

"trust for sale" in relation to land means an immediate trust for sale, whether or not exercisable at the request or with the consent of any person, and with or without power at discretion to postpone the sale;

"trust funds" include any funds in the hands of a trustee, whether at the time in a state of investment or not.

Application of Act.

2.(1) This Act, except where otherwise expressly provided, applies to trusts including, so far as this Act applies thereto, executorships and administratorships constituted or created either before or after the 1st March, 1975.

(2) The powers conferred by this Act on trustees are in addition to the powers conferred by the instrument, if any, creating the trust, but those powers, unless otherwise stated, apply if and so far only as a contrary intention is not expressed in the instrument, if any, creating the trust, and have effect subject to the terms of that instrument.

(3) This Act does not affect the legality or validity of anything done before the 1st March, 1975, except as otherwise herein expressly provided.

PART II - GENERAL POWERS OF TRUSTEES AND ESTATE REPRESENTATIVES

General Powers

Power of trustees to sell by auction etc.

3.(1) Where a trust for sale or a power of sale of property is vested in a trustee, he may sell or concur with any other person in selling all or any part of the property, either subject to prior charges or not, and either together or in lots, by public auction or by private contract, subject to any such conditions respecting title or evidence of title or other matter as the trustee thinks fit, with power to vary any contract for sale, and to buy in at any auction, or to rescind any contract for sale and to re-sell, without being answerable for any loss.

(2) Where a trust for sale or a power of sale of land held on lease is vested in a trustee, he may make, on such terms and conditions as he may think proper, a sub-lease of the land or any part thereof with a nominal reversion, where such sub-lease amounts in substance to a sale and the trustees have satisfied themselves that it is the most appropriate method of disposing of the land.

(3) Where trustees lease any land pursuant to any power conferred on them by subsection (2) they may sell any rent reserved on any reversion expectant upon the determination of such lease.

(4) Where any sub-lease purports to have been made in exercise of a power conferred by this section, that power shall, until the contrary is proved, be assumed to have been properly exercised and -

(a) the sub-lessee shall not, either before or on the execution of the sub-lease, be concerned to see or enquire whether a case has arisen to authorise the execution of that sub-lease; and

(b) neither the sub-lessee nor any of his successors in title shall be concerned to see to the application of any moneys paid in consideration of the lease.

(5) A trust or power to sell or dispose of land includes a trust or power to sell or dispose of part thereof whether the division is horizontal, vertical, or made in any other way.

(6) *(a)* A trust or power to sell or dispose of land includes a power, either with or without consideration, to grant by writing an option to purchase or take a lease of the land, or any part thereof, or any easement, right, or privilege over or in relation to the same, at a price or rent fixed at the time of granting the option;

(b) every such option shall be made exercisable within an agreed number of years not exceeding ten.

Power to sell subject to depreciatory conditions.

4.(1) No sale made by a trustee shall be impeached by any beneficiary upon the ground that any of the conditions subject to which the sale was made may have been unnecessarily depreciatory, unless it also appears that the consideration for the sale was thereby rendered inadequate.

(2) No sale made by a trustee shall, after the execution of the conveyance, be impeached as against the purchaser upon the ground that any of the conditions subject to which the sale was made may have been unnecessarily depreciatory, unless it appears that the purchaser was acting in collusion with the trustee at the time when the contract for sale was made.

(3) No purchaser, upon any sale made by a trustee, shall be at liberty to make any objection against the title upon any of the grounds aforesaid.

(4) This section applies to sales and purchases made before or after the 1st March, 1975.

Power of trustee to give receipts.

5. The receipt in writing of any trustee for any money, securities, or other personal property or effects payable, transferable, or deliverable to him under any trust or power shall be a sufficient discharge for the same, and shall effectually exonerate the person paying, transferring, or delivering the same from seeing to the application or being answerable for any loss or misapplication thereof.

Power to compound liabilities.

6.(1) Any one of several estate representatives, or a sole estate representative, or two or more trustees acting together, or a sole acting trustee where by the instrument, if any, creating the trust, or by any statutory provision, a sole trustee is authorised to execute the trusts and powers reposed in him, may, if and as he or they think fit -

(a) accept any property, real or personal, before the time at which it is made transferable or payable; or

(b) sever and apportion any blended trust funds or property; or

(c) pay or allow any debt or claim on any evidence that he or they may think sufficient; or

(d) accept any composition or any security, real or personal, for any debt or for any property, real or personal, claimed; or

(e) allow any time for payment of any debt; or

(f) compromise, compound, abandon, submit to arbitration, or otherwise settle any debt, account, claim, or thing whatever relating to the trust, and for any of those purposes may enter into, give, execute, and do such agreements, instruments of composition or arrangement, releases, and other things as to him or them seem expedient, without being responsible for any loss occasioned by any act or thing so done by him or them in good faith.

Power to raise money by sale, mortgage, etc.

7.(1) Where trustees are authorised by the instrument, if any, creating the trust or by any provision of law to pay or apply capital money subject to the trust for any purpose or in any manner, they shall have and shall be deemed always to have had power to raise the money required by sale, conversion, calling in, or mortgage of all or any part of the trust property for the time being in possession.

(2) This section applies notwithstanding anything to the contrary contained in the instrument, if any, creating the trust.

Protection to purchasers and mortgagees dealing with trustees.

8. No purchaser or mortgagee, paying or advancing money on a sale or mortgage purporting to be made under any trust or power vested in the trustees, shall be concerned to see that such money is wanted, or that no more than is wanted is raised, or otherwise as to the application thereof.

Devolution of powers or trusts.

9.(1) Where a power or trust is given to or imposed on two or more trustees jointly, the same may be exercised or performed by the survivors or survivor of them for the time being.

(2) Until the appointment of new trustees, the estate representatives or representative for the time being of a sole trustee, or, where there were two or more trustees, of the last surviving or continuing trustee, shall be capable of exercising or performing any power or trust which was given to, or capable of being exercised by, the sole or last surviving or continuing trustee, or other the trustees or trustee for the time being of the trust.

(3) In this section "estate representative" does not include an executor who has renounced or has not proved.

Power to insure.

10. A trustee may insure against loss or damage from any cause any building or other insurable property to any amount, including the amount of any insurance already in force, not exceeding the full value of the building or property, and pay the premiums for such insurance out of the income thereof or out of the income of any other property subject to the same trusts without obtaining the consent of any person who may be entitled wholly or partly to such income.

Application of insurance money where policy kept up under any trust, power or obligation.

11.(1) Money receivable by trustees or any beneficiary under a policy of insurance against the loss or damage of any property subject to a trust or settlement, from whatever cause, shall, where the policy has been kept up under any trust in that behalf or under any power statutory or otherwise, or in performance of any covenant or of any obligation statutory or otherwise, be capital money for the purposes of the trust or settlement, as the case may be.

(2) If any such money is receivable by any person, other than the trustees of the trust or settlement, that person shall use his best endeavours to recover and receive the money, and shall pay the net residue thereof, after discharging any costs of recovering and receiving it, to the trustees of the trust or settlement, or, if there are no trustees capable of giving a discharge therefor, into court.

(3) Any such money -

(a) if it was receivable in respect of property held upon trust for sale, shall be held upon the trusts and subject to the powers and provisions applicable to money arising by a sale under such trust;

(b) in any other case, it shall be held upon trusts corresponding as nearly as may be with the trusts affecting the property in respect of which it was payable.

(4) Such money, or any part thereof, may also be applied by the trustees, or, if in court, under the direction of the court, in rebuilding, reinstating, replacing, or repairing the property lost or damaged, but any such application by the trustees shall be subject to the consent of any person whose consent is required by the instrument, if any, creating the trust to the investment of money subject to the trust.

(5) Nothing contained in this section prejudices or affects the right of any person to require any such money or any part thereof to be applied in rebuilding, reinstating, or repairing the property lost or damaged, or the rights of any mortgagee, lessor, or lessee, whether under any statutory provision or otherwise.

(6) This section applies to policies effected either before or after the 1st March, 1975, but only to money received after such date.

Power of trustees of renewable leaseholds to renew and raise money for the purpose.

12.(1) Subject to subsection (2), a trustee of any leaseholds for lives or years which are renewable from time to time either under any covenant or contract may, if he thinks fit, use his best endeavours to obtain from time to time a renewed lease of the same hereditaments on reasonable terms, and for that purpose may from time to time make or concur in making a surrender of the lease for the time being subsisting and do all such other acts as are requisite.

(2) Where by the terms of the instrument, if any, creating the trust the person in possession for his life or other limited interest is entitled to enjoy the same without any obligation to renew or to contribute to the expense of renewal, this section shall not apply unless the consent in writing of that person is obtained to the renewal on the part of the trustee.

Deposit of documents for safe custody.

13. Trustees may deposit any documents held by them relating to the trust, or to the trust property, with any bank or trust company, and any sum payable in respect of such deposit shall be paid out of the income of the trust property.

Reversionary interests, valuations, and audit.

14.(1) Where trust property includes any share, estate or interest in property not vested in the trustees, or the proceeds of the sale of any such property, or any other thing in action, the trustees on the same falling into possession, or becoming payable or transferable may -

(a) agree or ascertain the amount or value thereof or any part thereof in such manner as they may think fit;

(b) accept in or towards satisfaction thereof, at the market or current value, or upon any valuation or estimate of value which they may think fit, any authorised investments;

(c) allow any deductions for duties, costs, charges and expenses which they may think proper or reasonable;

(d) execute any release in respect of the premises so as effectually to discharge all accountable parties from all liability in respect of any matters coming within the scope of such release, without being responsible in any such case for any loss occasioned by any act or thing so done by them in good faith.

(2) The trustees shall not be under any obligation and shall not be chargeable with any breach of trust by reason of any omission -

(a) to apply for a writ of distringas or any stop or other like order upon any securities or other property out of or on which such share, estate or interest or other thing in action as aforesaid is derived, payable or charged; or

(b) to take any proceedings on account of any act, default, or neglect on the part of the persons in whom such securities or other property or any of them or any part thereof are for the time being, or had at any time been, vested;

unless and until required in writing so to do by some person, or the guardian of some person, beneficially interested under the trust, and unless also due provision is made to their satisfaction for payment of the costs of any proceedings required to be taken so, however, that nothing in this subsection shall relieve the trustees of the obligation to get in and obtain payment or transfer of such share, estate or interest or other thing in action on the same falling into possession.

(3) Trustees may, for the purpose of giving effect to the trust, or any of the provisions of the instrument, if any, creating the trust or of any Act, from time to time (by suitably qualified agents) ascertain and fix the value of any trust property in such manner as they think proper, and any valuation so made in good faith shall be binding upon all persons interested under the trust.

(4) Trustees may, in their absolute discretion, from time to time, but not more than once in every three years unless the nature of the trust or any special dealings with the trust property make a more frequent exercise of the right reasonable, cause the accounts of the trust property to be examined or audited by an independent accountant, and shall, for that purpose, produce such vouchers and give such information to him as he may require; and the costs of such examination or audit, including the fee of the auditor, shall be paid out of the capital or income of the trust property, or partly in one way and partly in the other, as the trustees, in their absolute discretion, think fit, but, in default of any direction by the trustees to the contrary in any special case, costs attributable to capital shall be borne by capital and those attributable to income by income.

Power to delegate certain functions by estate representatives.

15.(1) This section is subject to the terms of the will, if any.

(2) Estate representatives may delegate all or any of their functions as estate representative to -

(a) a delegate; or

(b) one of the estate representatives (a "co-estate representative"), and may pay such delegate or co-estate representative out of the property of the estate, whether income or capital or partly each as they may think fit.

(3) Subsections 15A(3) and (4) apply, with the necessary changes, to the exercise of the power of delegation under subsection (2).

Power to delegate certain functions by trustees

15A.(1) This section and section 15B are subject to the terms of the trust, and without prejudice to any of the powers conferred by sections 17 and 24.

(2) Trustees of a trust may delegate any or all of their delegable functions to -

(a) a delegate; or

(b) one of the trustees (a "co-trustee"), and may pay such delegate or co-trustee out of the trust property, whether income or capital or partly each as they may see fit.

(3) In exercising any power to delegate, and in supervising the delegate, the trustees shall exercise reasonable care, skill and caution.

(4) Delegation under this section to a delegate, but not to a co-trustee, may be made on terms which

(a) limit the liability of the delegate;

(b) do not prohibit actual or potential conflicts of interest dealing with the trust property; or

(c) permit sub-delegation, including on such terms as are mentioned in paragraphs (a) and (b);

and the trustees shall not, by reason of delegating on such terms, be responsible for the act or default of any delegate or sub-delegate, provided that the trustees honestly believed delegation to that delegate on those terms to be in the best interests of the trust as a whole.

(5) In this section "trustee" does not include an estate representative.

Meaning of "delegable functions"

15B.(1) For the purposes of section 15A, "delegable functions" shall be interpreted in accordance with this section.

(2) Functions of an administrative or managerial nature (including discretonary investment powers) are delegable functions.

(3) The following functions are not delegable -

(a) the formulation of policy criteria governing the investment or other application of trust property, and any decision as to the amount of money that may be raised on the security of trust property;

(b) the exercise of any discretionary duties or powers concerning distribution of income or capital to, or use of the trust property by, persons beneficially interested under the trust, or the appropriation of trust property in satisfaction of a beneficiary's entitlement to any capital;

(c) the exercise of any power to determine or to alter any interest of a person beneficially interested under the trust, including a power to deal with income or capital expenditure or receipts as if they were not of such income or capital nature and a power to bring forward or postpone the closing date for the total or partial termination of the trust;

(d) the exercise of any power to add a person or class of persons to, or exclude a person or class of person from, those who are beneficially interested under the trust;

(e) the exercise of any power to add to, revoke or vary the administrative powers under the trust or to release or restrict any powers under the trust;

(f) the exercise of any power to appoint or remove trustees;

(g) the exercise of any power to change the proper law governing the validity, administration or any other severable aspect of the trust.

Power to concur with others.

16. Where an undivided share in the proceeds of sale of land directed to be sold, or in any other property, is subject to a trust, or forms part of the estate of a testator or intestate, the trustees or estate representatives may (without prejudice to any trust for sale affecting the entirety of the land and the powers of the trustees for sale in reference thereto) execute or exercise any trust or power vested in them in relation to such share in conjunction with the persons entitled to or having power in that behalf over the other share or shares, and notwithstanding that any one or more of the trustees or estate representatives may be entitled to or interested in any such other share, either in his or their own right or in a fiduciary capacity.

Power to delegate trusts during absence abroad.

17.(1) A trustee intending to remain out of Bermuda may, notwithstanding any rule of law or equity to the contrary, by power of attorney, delegate to any person (including a trust corporation) the execution or exercise during his absence from Bermuda of all or any trusts, powers and discretions vested in him as such trustee, either alone or jointly with any other person or persons so, however, that a person being the only other co-trustee and not being a trust corporation shall not be appointed to be an attorney under this subsection.

(2) The donor of a power of attorney given under this section shall be liable for the acts or defaults of the donee in the same manner as if they were the acts or defaults of the donor.

(3) The power of attorney shall not come into operation unless and until the donor is out of Bermuda, and shall be revoked by his return.

(4) In favour of any person dealing with the donee, any act done or instrument executed by the donee shall, notwithstanding that the power has never come into operation or has been revoked by the act of the donor or by his death or return to Bermuda or otherwise, be as valid and effectual as if the donor were alive and of full capacity, and had himself done such act or executed such instrument, unless such person had actual notice that the power had never come into operation or of the revocation of the power before such act was done or instrument executed.

(5) For the purpose of executing or exercising the trusts or powers delegated to him, the donee may exercise any of the powers conferred on the donor as trustee by any Act or by the instrument creating the trust, including power, for the purpose of the transfer of any securities, himself to delegate to an attorney power to transfer such securities but not including the power of delegation conferred by this section.

(6) The fact that it appears from any power of attorney given under this section, or from any evidence required for the purposes of any such power of attorney or otherwise, that in dealing with any securities the donee of the power is acting in the execution of a trust shall not be deemed for any purpose to affect any person in whose books the securities are registered with any notice of the trust.

Indemnities

Protection against liability in respect of rents and covenants.

18.(1) Where an estate representative or trustee liable for -

(a) any rent, covenant, or agreement reserved by or contained in any lease; or

(b) any rent, covenant or agreement payable under or contained in any grant made in consideration of a rent charge; or

(c) any indemnity given in respect of any rent, covenant or agreement referred to in either of the foregoing paragraphs,

satisfies all liabilities under the lease or grant which may have accrued, and been claimed, up to the date of the conveyance hereinafter mentioned, and, where necessary, sets apart a sufficient fund to answer any future claim that may be made in respect of any fixed and ascertained sum which the lessee or grantee agreed to lay out on the property demised or granted, although the period for laying out the same may not have arrived, then and in any such case the estate representative or trustee may convey the property demised or granted to a purchaser, legatee, devisee, or other person entitled to call for a conveyance thereof and thereafter -

(i) he may distribute the residuary real and personal estate of the deceased testator or intestate, or, as the case may be, the trust estate (other than the fund, if any, set apart as aforesaid) to or amongst the persons entitled thereto, without appropriating any part, or any further part, as the case may be, of the estate of the deceased or of the trust estate to meet any future liability under the said lease or grant;

(ii) notwithstanding such distribution, he shall not be personally liable in respect of any subsequent claim under the said lease or grant.

(2) This section operates without prejudice to the right of the lessor or grantor, or the persons deriving title under the lessor or grantor, to follow the assets of the deceased or the trust property into the hands of the persons amongst whom the same may have been respectively distributed, and applies notwithstanding anything to the contrary in the will or other instrument, if any, creating the trust.

(3)

In this section "lease" includes an underlease and an agreement for a lease or underlease and any instrument giving any such indemnity as aforesaid or varying the liabilities under the lease; "grant" applies to a grant whether the rent is created by limitation, grant, reservation, or otherwise, and includes an agreement for a grant and any instrument giving any such indemnity as aforesaid or varying the liabilities under the grant; "lessee" and "grantee" include persons respectively deriving title under them.

Protection by means of advertisements.

19.(1) With a view to the conveyance to, or distribution among, the persons entitled to any real or personal property, the trustees of a settlement or of a disposition on trust for sale may give notice by advertisement published three times at intervals of not less than one week in a newspaper for the time being approved as the Gazette, of their intention to make such conveyance or distribution as aforesaid, and requiring any person interested to send to the trustees within the time, not being less than one month from the publication of the last of the notices, fixed in the notice, particulars of his claim in respect of the property or any part thereof to which the notice relates.

(2) At the expiration of the time fixed by the notice the trustees may convey or distribute the property or any part thereof to which the notice relates, to or among the persons entitled thereto, having regard only to the claims, whether formal or not, of which the trustees then had notice and shall not, as respects the property so conveyed or distributed, be liable to any person whose claim the trustees have not had notice at the time of conveyance or distribution; but nothing in this section -

(a) prejudices the right of any person to follow the property, or any property representing the same, into the hands of any person, other than a purchaser, who may have received it; or

(b) frees the trustees from any obligation to make inquiries and searches or obtain official certificates of search similar to those which an intending purchaser would be advised to make or obtain.

(3) This section applies notwithstanding anything to the contrary in the will or other instrument, if any, creating the trust.

(4) This section does not apply to the protection of estate representatives by means of advertisements under section 53 of the Administration of Estates Act 1974 [*title 26 item 12*].

Protection in regard to notice.

20. A trustee or estate representative acting for the purposes of more than one trust or estate shall not, in the absence of fraud, be affected by notice of any instrument, matter, fact or thing in relation to any particular trust or estate if he has obtained notice thereof merely by reason of his acting or having acted for the purposes of another trust or estate.

Power of trustees to pay to attorney appointed by beneficiary.

21. A trustee acting or paying money in good faith under or in pursuance of any power of attorney shall not be liable for any such act or payment by reason of the fact that at the time of the act or payment the person who gave the power of attorney was subject to any disability or bankrupt or dead, or had done or suffered some act or thing to avoid the power, if this fact was not known to the trustee at the time of his so acting or paying so, however, that -

(a) nothing in this section shall affect the right of any person entitled to the money against the person to whom the payment is made;

(b) the person so entitled shall have the same remedy against the person to whom the payment is made as he would have had against the trustee.

Implied indemnity of trustees.

22.(1) A trustee shall be chargeable only for money and securities actually received by him notwithstanding his signing any receipt for the sake of conformity, and shall be answerable and accountable only for his own acts, receipts, neglects, or defaults, and not for those of any other trustee, nor for those of any bank, broker, or other person with whom any trust money or securities may be deposited, nor for the insufficiency or deficiency of any securities, nor for any other loss, unless the same happens through his own deliberate, reckless or negligent breach of an equitable duty.

(2) A trustee may reimburse himself or pay or discharge out of the trust premises all expenses incurred in or about the execution of the trusts or power

Remuneration of trust corporations.

22A. Subject to -

(a) any contrary intention in the terms of the trust; or

(b) any order of a court, a trust corporation shall be entitled to reasonable remuneration for its services as trustee, in addition to reimbursement of its expenses under section 22(2).

Maintenance, Advancement and Protective Trusts

Power to apply income for maintenance and to accumulate surplus income during a minority.

23.(1) Where any property is held by trustees in trust for any person for any estate or interest whatsoever, whether vested or contingent, then, subject to any prior estates or interests or charges affecting that property -

(a) during the infancy of any such person, if his estate or interest so long continues, the trustees may, at their sole discretion, pay to his parent or guardian, if any, or otherwise apply for or towards his maintenance or education, or otherwise

for his benefit, the whole or such part, if any, of the income of that property as may, in all the circumstances, be reasonable, whether or not there is -

(i) any other fund applicable to the same purpose; or

(ii) any person bound by law to provide for his maintenance or education; and

(b) if such person on attaining the age of twenty-one years has not a vested estate or interest in such income, the trustees shall thenceforth pay the income of that property and of any accretion thereto under subsection (3) to him, until he either attains a vested estate or interest therein or dies, or until failure of his estate or interest.

(2) In deciding whether the whole or any part of the income of the property is during a minority to be paid or applied for the purposes aforesaid, the trustees shall have regard to the age of the infant and his requirements and generally to the circumstances of the case, and in particular to what other income, if any, is applicable for the same purposes; and where trustees have notice that the income of more than one fund is applicable for those purposes, then, so far as practicable, unless the entire income of the funds is paid or applied as aforesaid or the court otherwise directs, a proportionate part only of the income of each fund shall be so paid or applied.

(3) During the infancy of any such person, if his estate or interest so long continues, the trustees shall accumulate all the residue of that income in the way of compound interest by investing the same and the resulting income thereof from time to time in authorised investments, and shall hold those accumulations as follows:-

(a) if any such person -

(i) attains the age of twenty-one years, or marries under that age, and his estate or interest in such income during his infancy or until his marriage is a vested estate or interest; or

(ii) on attaining the age of twenty-one years or on marriage under that age becomes entitled to the property from which such income arose in fee simple, or absolutely, or for an entailed estate or interest,

the trustees shall hold the accumulation in trust for such person absolutely, but without prejudice to any provision with respect thereto contained in any settlement by him made under any statutory powers during his infancy, and so that the receipt of such person after marriage, and though still an infant, shall be a good discharge; and

(b) in any other case the trustees shall, notwithstanding that such person had a vested estate or interest in such income, hold the accumulations as an accretion

to the capital of the property from which such accumulations arose, and as one fund with such capital for all purposes, and so that, if such property is settled land, such accumulations shall be held upon the same trusts as if the same were capital money arising therefrom,

but the trustees may, at any time during the infancy of such person if his estate or interest so long continues, apply those accumulations, or any part thereof, as if they were income arising in the then current year.

(4) This section applies in the case of a contingent estate or interest only if the limitation or trust carries the intermediate income of the property, but it applies to a future or contingent legacy by the parent of, or a person standing in loco parentis to, the legatee, if and for such period as, under any provision of law, the legacy carries interest for the maintenance of the legatee, and in any such case at last aforesaid the rate of interest shall (if the income available is sufficient, and subject to any rules of court to the contrary) be five per centum per annum.

(5) This section applies to a vested annuity in like manner as if the annuity were the income of property held by trustees in trust to pay the income thereof to the annuitant for the same period for which the annuity is payable, save that in any case accumulations made during the infancy of the annuitant shall be held in trust for the annuitant or his estate representatives absolutely.

(6) This section does not apply where the instrument, if any, under which the interest arises came into operation before the 1st March, 1975.

Power of advancement.

24.(1) Trustees may at any time or times pay or apply any capital money subject to a trust, for the advancement or benefit, in such manner as they may, in their absolute discretion, think fit, of any person entitled to the capital of the trust property or of any share thereof, whether absolutely or contingently on his attaining any specified age or on the occurrence of any other event, or subject to a gift over on his death under any specified age or on the occurrence of any other event, and whether in possession or in remainder or reversion, and such payment or application may be made notwithstanding that the estate or interest of such person is liable to be defeated by the exercise of a power of appointment or revocation, or to be diminished by the increase of the class to which he belongs so, however, that -

(a) the money so paid or applied for the advancement or benefit of any person shall not exceed altogether the amount of the presumptive or vested share, estate or interest of that person in the trust property; and

(b) if that person is or becomes absolutely and indefeasibly entitled to a share in the trust property the money so paid or applied shall be brought into account as part of such share; and

(c) no such payment or application shall be made so as to prejudice any person

entitled to any prior life or other estate or interest, whether vested or contingent, in the money paid or applied unless such person is in existence and of full age and consents in writing to such payment or application.

(2) This section applies only where the trust property consists of -

(a) money or securities which are not by any provision of law or in equity considered as land; or

(b) property held upon trust for sale, calling in and conversion and the proceeds of such sale, calling in and conversion are not in equity considered as land.

(3) This section does not apply to trusts constituted or created before the 1st March, 1975.

(4) For the avoidance of doubt, when exercising the power of advancement the trustees may -

(a) create any provisions, including -

(i) discretionary trusts and dispositive, administrative or managerial powers exercisable by any person; and

(ii) the delegation of discretions and duties to any person; and

(b) provide that the capital money may become subject to the terms of any other trust, provided that the requirements of subsection (1) are satisfied.

Protective trusts.

25.(1) Where any income, including an annuity or other periodical Income payment, is directed to be held on protective trusts for the benefit of any person (in this section referred to as "the principal beneficiary") for the period of his life or any less period, then, during that period (in this section referred to as "the trust period") the said income shall, without prejudice to any prior estate or interest be held -

(a) upon trust for the principal beneficiary until whichever of the following events shall first occur -

(i) the trust period expires; or

(ii) the principal beneficiary (whether before or after the termination of any prior estate or interests) does or attempts to do or suffers any act or thing, or until any other event (not being an advance under any statutory or express power) happens whereby, if during the trust period the said income were payable to the principal beneficiary absolutely, he would be deprived of the right to receive the same or any part thereof; and

(b) upon trust, where any of the events referred to in sub-paragraph (ii) of paragraph (a) happens during the subsistence of the trust period, to apply the said income (as the trustees in their absolute discretion, without being liable to account for the exercise of their discretion, think fit) for the maintenance or support, or otherwise for the benefit, of all or any one or more exclusively of the other or others of the following persons -

(i) the principal beneficiary and his or her wife or husband, if any, and his or her children or more remote issue, if any; and

(ii) if as often as and while there is no living issue of the principal beneficiary, the principal beneficiary and his or her wife or husband, if any, and the persons who, if the principal beneficiary were actually dead without having married would for the time being be his next of kin, so that the trustees in the exercise of their discretion may apply any income accrued but unapplied in any previous year for the purposes of the trusts implied as aforesaid in any subsequent year.

(2) This section does not apply to trusts coming into operation before the 1st March, 1968, and has effect subject to any variation of the trusts implied as aforesaid contained in the instrument creating the trust.

(3) Nothing in this section operates to validate any trust which would, if contained in the instrument creating the trust, be liable to be set aside.

PART III - APPOINTMENT AND DISCHARGE OF TRUSTEES

Power of appointing new or additional trustees.

26.(1) Where a trustee, whether original, substituted or additional, and whether appointed by a court or otherwise, is dead, or remains out of Bermuda for more than twelve months, or desires to be discharged from all or any of the trusts or powers reposed in or conferred on him, or refuses or is unfit to act therein, or is incapable of acting therein, then -

(a) the person or persons nominated for the purpose of appointing new trustees by the instrument, if any, creating the trust; or

(b) if there is no such person, or no such person able and willing to act, then the surviving or continuing trustees or trustee for the time being, or the estate representatives of the last surviving or continuing trustee, may, by writing, appoint one or more other persons (whether or not being the persons exercising the power) to be a trustee or trustees in the place of the trustee so deceased, remaining out of Bermuda, desiring to be discharged, refusing, or being unfit or being incapable, as aforesaid.

(2) Where a trustee has been removed under a power contained in the instrument creating the trust, a new trustee or new trustees may be appointed in the place of the trustee who is removed, as if he were dead, or, in the case of a corporation, as if the corporation desired to be discharged from the trust, and the provisions of this section shall apply accordingly.

(3) Where a corporation being a trustee is or has been dissolved, either before or after the 1st March, 1975, then, for the purposes of this section and of any statutory provision replaced thereby, the corporation shall be deemed to be and to have been from the date of the dissolution incapable of acting in the trusts or powers reposed in or conferred on the corporation.

(4) The power of appointment given by subsection (1) or any similar previous statutory provision to the estate representatives of a last surviving or continuing trustee shall be and shall be deemed always to have been exercisable by the executors for the time being (whether original or by representation) of such surviving or continuing trustee who have proved the will of their testator or by the administrators for the time being of such trustee without the concurrence of any executor who has renounced or has not proved.

(5) But a sole or last surviving executor intending to renounce, or all the executors where they all intend to renounce, shall have and shall be deemed always to have had power, at any time before renouncing probate, to exercise the power of appointment given by this section, or by any similar previous enactment, if willing to act for that purpose and without thereby accepting the office of executor.

(6) Where a sole trustee, other than a trust corporation, is or has been originally appointed to act in a trust, or where, in the case of any trust, there are not more than three trustees (none of them being a trust corporation) whether original, substituted or additional and whether appointed by the court or otherwise, then and in any such case -

(a) the person or persons nominated for the purpose of appointing new trustees by the instrument, if any, creating the trust; or

(b) if there is no such person, or no such person able and willing to act, then the trustee or trustees for the time being, may, by writing, appoint one or more other persons (whether or not being the persons exercising the power) to be an additional trustee or additional trustees, but it shall not be obligatory to appoint any additional trustee unless the instrument, if any, creating the trust, or any statutory provision provides to the contrary.

(7) Every new trustee appointed under this section as well before as after all the trust property becomes by law, or by assurance, or otherwise, vested in him, shall have the same powers, authorities, and discretions, and may in all respects act as if he had been originally appointed a trustee by the instrument, if any, creating the trust.

(8) The provisions of this section relating to a trustee who is dead include the case of a person nominated trustee in a will but dying before the testator, and those relative to a continuing trustee include a refusing or retiring trustee, if willing to act in the execution of the provisions of this section.

(9) Where a trustee is incapable, by reason of mental disorder within the meaning of the Mental Health Act 1968 [*title 11 item 36*], of exercising his functions as trustee and is also entitled in possession to some beneficial interest in the trust property, no appointment of a new trustee in his place shall be made by virtue of subsection (1)(b) unless leave to make the appointment has been given by the judicial authority appointed to act for the purposes of Part IV of the Mental Health Act 1968.

Supplemental provisions as to appointment of trustees.

27. On the appointment of a trustee for the whole or any part of trust property -

(a) the number of trustees may be increased; and

(b) a separate set of trustees may be appointed for any part of the trust property held on trusts distinct from those relating to any other part or parts of the trust property, notwithstanding that no new trustees or trustee are or is to be appointed for other parts of the trust property, and any existing trustee may be appointed or remain one of such separate set of trustees, or, if only one trustee was originally appointed, then, save as hereinafter provided, one separate trustee may be so appointed; and

(c) it shall not be obligatory, save as hereinafter provided, to appoint more than

one new trustee where only one trustee was originally appointed, or to fill up the original number of trustees where more than two trustees were originally appointed but, except where only one trustee was originally appointed, a trustee shall not be discharged from his trust unless there will be a trust corporation, any other body corporate, wherever incorporated, with power to act as a trustee or at least two individuals to act as trustees to perform the trust; and

(d) any assurance or thing requisite for vesting the trust property, or any part thereof, in a sole trustee, or jointly in the persons who are the trustees, shall be executed or done.

Evidence as to a vacancy in a trust.

28.(1) A statement, contained in any instrument coming into operation after the 1st March, 1975 by which a new trustee is appointed for any purpose connected with land, to the effect that a trustee has remained out of Bermuda for more than twelve months or refuses or is unfit to act, or is incapable of acting, or that he is not entitled to a beneficial Interest in the trust property in possession, shall, in favour of a bona fide purchaser, be conclusive evidence of the matter stated.

(2) In favour of such purchaser any appointment of a new trustee depending on that statement, and any vesting declaration, express or implied, consequent on the appointment, shall be valid.

Retirement of trustee without a new appointment.

29.(1) Where a trustee is desirous of being discharged from the trust or a severable part of the trust, and after his discharge there will be a trust corporation, any other body corporate, wherever incorporated, with power to act as a trustee or at least two individuals to act as trustees to perform the trust, then, if such trustee as aforesaid by deed declares that he is desirous of being discharged from the trust or the severable part thereof, and if his co-trustees and such other person, if any, as is empowered to appoint trustees, by deed consent to the discharge of the trustee, and to the vesting in the co-trustees alone of the trust property, the trustee desirous of being discharged shall be deemed to have retired from the trust or a severable part thereof, and shall, by the deed, be discharged therefrom under this Act, without any new trustee being appointed in his place.

(2) Any assurance or thing requisite for vesting the trust property in the continuing trustees alone shall be executed or done.

Vesting of trust property in new or continuing trustees.

30.(1) Where by a deed a new trustee is appointed to perform any trust, then -

(a) if the deed contains a declaration by the appointor to the effect that any estate or interest in any land subject to the trust, or in any chattel so subject, or the right to recover or receive any debt or other thing in action so subject, shall vest in the persons who by virtue of the deed become or are the trustees for

performing the trust, the deed shall operate, without any conveyance or assignment, to vest in those persons as joint tenants and for the purposes of the trust the estate, interest or right to which the declaration relates; and

(b) if the deed is made after the 1st March, 1975 and does not contain such a declaration, the deed shall, subject to any express provision to the contrary therein contained, operate as if it had contained such a declaration by the appointor extending to all the estates, interests and rights with respect to which a declaration could have been made.

(2) Where by a deed a retiring trustee is discharged under the statutory power without a new trustee being appointed, then -

(a) if the deed contains such a declaration as aforesaid by the retiring and continuing trustees, and by the other person, if any, empowered to appoint trustees, the deed shall, without any conveyance or assignment, operate to vest in the continuing trustees alone, as joint tenants, and for the purposes of the trust, the estate, interest, or right to which the declaration relates; and

(b) if the deed is made after the 1st March, 1975 and does not contain such a declaration, the deed shall, subject to any express provision to the contrary therein contained, operate as if it had contained such a declaration by such persons as aforesaid extending to all the estates, interests and rights with respect to which a declaration could have been made.

(3) An express vesting declaration, whether made before or after the 1st March, 1975, shall, notwithstanding that the estate, interest or right to be vested is not expressly referred to, and provided that the other statutory requirements were or are complied with, operate and be deemed always to have operated (but without prejudice to any express provision to the contrary contained in the deed of appointment or discharge) to vest in the persons respectively referred to in subsections (1) and (2), as the case may require, such estates, interests and rights as are capable of being and ought to be vested in those persons.

(4) This section does not extend -

(a) to land conveyed by way of mortgage for securing money subject to the trust, except land conveyed on trust for securing debentures or debenture stock;

(b) to land held under a lease which contains any covenant, condition or agreement against assignment or disposing of the land without licence or consent, unless, prior to the execution of the deed containing expressly or impliedly the vesting declaration, the requisite licence or consent has been obtained, or unless, by

virtue of any rule of law, the vesting declaration, express or implied, would not operate as a breach of covenant or give rise to a forfeiture;

(c) to any share, stock, annuity or property which is only transferable in books kept by a company or other body, or in manner directed by or under any statutory provision.

In this subsection "lease" includes an underlease and an agreement for a lease or underlease.

PART IIIA - MANAGING TRUSTEES

Managing trustees

30A. A trust instrument may contain provisions by virtue of which the exercise of any of the trustees' powers may be reserved to a managing trustee, and no other trustee is liable for any of the decisions, acts or transactions of the managing trustee in so far as they amount to exercise of powers reserved by the trust instrument to the managing trustee.

PART IV - POWERS OF THE COURT

Appointment of New Trustees

Power of court to appoint new trustees.

31.(1) The court may, whenever it is expedient to appoint a new trustee or new trustees, and it is found inexpedient, difficult or impracticable so to do without the assistance of the court, make an order appointing a new trustee or new trustees either in substitution for or in addition to any existing trustee or trustees, or although there is no existing trustee.

(2) In particular and without prejudice to the generality of subsection (1), the court may make an order appointing a new trustee in substitution for a trustee who is incapable, by reason of mental disorder within the meaning of the Mental Health Act 1968 [*title 11 item 36*], of exercising his functions as trustee, or is a bankrupt, or is a corporation which is in liquidation or has been dissolved, or who for any other reason whatsoever appears to the court to be undesirable as a trustee.

(3) An order under this section, and any consequential vesting order or conveyance, shall not operate further or otherwise as a discharge to any former or continuing trustee than an appointment of new trustees under any power for that purpose contained in any instrument would have operated.

(4) Nothing in this section gives power to appoint an executor or administrator.

Power of court to authorise remuneration.

32. The court may, in any case in which the circumstances appear to it so to justify, authorise any person to charge such remuneration for his services as trustee as the court may think fit.

Powers of new trustee appointed by the court.

33. Every trustee appointed by a court of competent jurisdiction shall, as well before as after the trust property becomes by law, or by assurance, or otherwise, vested in him, have the same powers, authorities, and discretions, and may in all respects act as if he had been originally appointed a trustee by the instrument, if any, creating the trust.

Vesting Orders

Vesting orders of land.

34.(1) Subject to subsection (2), where -

(a) the court appoints or has appointed a trustee, or where a trustee has been appointed out of court under any statutory or express power; or

(b) a trustee entitled to or possessed of any land or estate or interest therein, whether by way of mortgage or otherwise, or entitled to a contingent right therein, either solely or jointly with any other person -

(i) is an infant; or

(ii) is out of the jurisdiction of the court; or

(iii) cannot be found, or, being a corporation, has been dissolved; or

(c) it is uncertain who was the survivor of two or more trustees jointly entitled to or possessed of any estate or interest in land; or

(d) it is uncertain whether the last trustee known to have been entitled to or possessed of any estate or interest in land is living or dead; or

(e) there is no estate representative of a deceased trustee who was entitled to or possessed of any estate or interest in land, or where it is uncertain who is the estate representative of a deceased trustee who was entitled to or possessed of any estate or interest in land; or

(f) a trustee jointly or solely entitled to or possessed of any estate or interest in land, or entitled to a contingent right therein, has been required, by or on behalf of a person entitled to require a conveyance of the land or estate or interest or a release of the right, to convey the land or estate or interest or to release the right, and has wilfully refused or neglected to convey the land or estate or interest or release the right for twenty-eight days after the date of the requirement; or

(g) land or any estate or interest therein is vested in a trustee whether by way of mortgage or otherwise, and it appears to the court to be expedient;

the court may make an order (in this Act referred to as a "vesting order") vesting the land or estate or interest therein in any such person in any such manner and for any such estate or interest as the court may direct, or releasing or disposing of the contingent right to such person as the court may direct.

(2) Where an order made under subsection (1) -

(a) is consequential on the appointment of a trustee the land or estate or interest therein shall be vested for such estate or interest as the court may direct in the persons who on the appointment are the trustees; and

(b) relates to a trustee entitled or formerly entitled jointly with another person, and such trustee is an infant or out of the jurisdiction of the court or cannot be found, or being a corporation has been dissolved, the land estate interest or right shall be vested in such other person who remains entitled, either alone or with any other person the court may appoint.

Orders as to contingent rights of unborn persons.

35. Where any estate or interest in land is subject to a contingent right in an unborn person or class of unborn persons who, on coming into existence would, in respect thereof, become entitled to or possessed of that estate or interest on any trust, the court may make an order -

(a) releasing the land or estate or interest therein from the contingent right; or

(b) vesting in any person the estate or interest to or of which the unborn person or class of unborn persons would, on coming into existence, be entitled or possessed in the land.

Vesting order in place of conveyance by infant mortgagee.

36. Where any person entitled to or possessed of any estate or interest in land, or entitled to a contingent right in land, by way of security for money, is an infant, the court may make an order vesting or releasing or disposing of the estate or interest in the land or the right in like manner as in the case of an infant trustee.

Vesting order in place of conveyance by estate representative of mortgagee.

37. Where -

(a) a mortgagee of land has died without having entered into possession or into the receipt of the rents and profits thereof; and

(b) the money due in respect of the mortgage has been paid to a person entitled to receive the same, or that person consents to an order for the reconveyance of the land, the court may make an order vesting the land in such person in such manner and for such estate or interest as the court may direct, where -

(i) an estate representative or devisee of the mortgagee is out of the jurisdiction of the court or cannot be found, or, being a corporation, has been dissolved; or

(ii) an estate representative or devisee of the mortgagee on demand made by or on behalf of a person entitled to require a conveyance of the land has stated in writing that he will not convey the same or does not convey the same for the space of twenty-eight days after a proper instrument for conveying the land has been tendered to him by or on behalf of the person so entitled; or

(iii) it is uncertain which of several devisees of the mortgagee was the survivor; or

(iv) it is uncertain whether the estate representative of the mortgagee or the survivor of several devisees of the mortgagee is living or dead; or

(v) there is no estate representative to a mortgagee who has died intestate as to the land, or where the mortgagee has died, and it is uncertain who is his estate representative or devisee.

Vesting order consequential on order for sale or mortgage of land.

38. Where the court gives a judgment or makes an order directing the sale or mortgage of any land, every person who is entitled to or possessed of any estate or interest in the land, or entitled to a contingent right therein, and is a party to the action or proceeding in which the judgment or order is given or made or is otherwise bound by the judgment or order, shall be deemed to be so entitled or possessed, as the case may be, as a trustee for the purposes of this Act, and the court may, if it thinks expedient, make an order vesting the land or any part thereof for such estate or interest as the court thinks fit in the purchaser or mortgagee or in any other person.

Vesting order consequential on judgment for specific performance, etc.

39. Where a judgment is given for the specific performance of a contract concerning any estate or interest in land, or for the partition, or for sale or exchange of any estate or interest in land, or generally where any judgment is given for the conveyance of any estate or interest in land either in cases arising out of the doctrine of election or otherwise, the court may declare -

(a) that any of the parties to the action are trustees of any estate or interest in the land or any part thereof within the meaning of this Act; or

(b) that the estates or interests of unborn persons who might claim under any party to the action, or under the will or voluntary settlement of any deceased person who was during his lifetime a party to the contract or transaction concerning which the judgment is given, are the estates or interests of persons who, on coming into existence, would be trustees within the meaning of this Act;

and thereupon the court may make a vesting order relating to the rights of those persons, born and unborn, as if they had been trustees.

Effect of vesting order.

40. A vesting order under any of the foregoing provisions shall in the case of a vesting order consequential on the appointment of a trustee, have the same effect -

(a) as if the persons who before the appointment were the trustees, if any, had duly executed all proper conveyances of the land for such estate or interest as the court directs: or

(b) if there is no such person, or no such person of full capacity, as if such person had existed and been of full capacity and had duly executed all proper conveyances of the land for such estate or interest as the court directs,

and shall in every other case have the same effect as if the trustee or other person or description or class of persons to whose rights or supposed rights the said provisions respectively relate had been an ascertained and existing person of full capacity, and had executed a conveyance or release to the effect intended by the order.

Power to appoint person to convey.

41. Where a vesting order can be made under any of the foregoing provisions, the court may, if it is more convenient, appoint a person to convey the land or any interest therein or release the contingent right, and a conveyance or release by that person in conformity with the order shall have the same effect as an order under the appropriate provision.

Vesting orders as to stock and things in action.

42.(1) Subject to subsection (2), where -

(a) the court appoints or has appointed a trustee, or where a trustee has been appointed out of court under any statutory or express power; or

(b) a trustee entitled, whether by way of mortgage or otherwise, alone or jointly with another person to stock or to a thing in action -

(i) is an infant; or

(ii) is out of the jurisdiction of the court; or

(iii) cannot be found, or, being a corporation, has been dissolved; or

(iv) neglects or refuses to transfer stock or receive the dividends or income thereof, or to sue for or recover a thing in action, according to the direction of the person absolutely entitled thereto for twenty-eight days next after a request in writing has been made to him by the person so entitled; or

(v) neglects or refuses to transfer stock or receive the dividends or income thereof, or to sue for or recover a thing in action for twenty-eight days next after an order of the court for that purpose has been served on him; or

(c) it is uncertain whether a trustee entitled alone or jointly with another person to stock or to a thing in action is alive or dead; or

(d) stock is standing in the name of a deceased person whose estate representative is under disability; or

(e) stock or a thing in action is vested in a trustee whether by way of mortgage or otherwise and it appears to the court to be expedient, the court may make an order vesting the right to transfer or call for a transfer of stock, or to receive the dividends or income thereof, or to sue for or recover the thing in action, in any such person as the court may appoint.

(2) Where -

(a) an order made under subsection (1) is consequential on the appointment of a trustee, the right shall be vested in the persons who, on the appointment, are the trustees; and

(b) the person whose right is dealt with by an order made under subsection (1) was entitled jointly with another person, the right shall be vested in that last-mentioned person either alone or jointly with any other person whom the court may appoint.

(3) Where a vesting order can be made under this section, the court may, if it is more convenient, appoint some proper person to make or join in making the transfer so, however, that the person appointed to make or join in making a transfer of stock shall be some proper officer of the bank, or the company or society whose stock is to be transferred.

(4) The person in whom the right to transfer or call for the transfer of any stock is vested by an order of the court under this Act, may transfer the stock to himself or any other person, according to the order, and the bank and all other companies shall obey every order under this section according to its tenor.

(5) After notice in writing of an order under this section it shall not be lawful for the bank or any other company to transfer any stock to which the order relates or to pay any dividends thereon except in accordance with the order.

(6) The court may make declarations and give directions concerning the manner in which the right to transfer any stock or thing in action vested under the provisions of this Act is to be exercised.

(7) The provisions of this Act as to vesting orders shall apply to shares in British ships registered in Bermuda as if they were stock.

Vesting orders of charity property.

43. The powers conferred by this Act as to vesting orders may be exercised for vesting any estate or interest in land, stock, or thing in action in any trustee of a charity or society over which the court would have jurisdiction upon action duly instituted, whether the appointment of the trustee was made by instrument under a power or by the court under its general or statutory jurisdiction.

Vesting orders in relation to infant's beneficial interests.

44. Where an infant is beneficially entitled to any property the court may, with a view to the application of the capital or income thereof for the maintenance, or education, or otherwise for the benefit of the infant, make an order -

(a) appointing a person to convey such property; or

(b) in the case of stock, or a thing in action, vesting in any person the right to transfer or call for a transfer of such stock, or to receive the dividends or income thereof, or to sue for and recover such thing in action, upon such terms as the court may think fit.

Orders made upon certain allegations to be conclusive evidence.

45. Where a vesting order is made as to any land under this Act or under any Act relating to persons of unsound mind founded on an allegation -

(a) of the personal incapacity of a trustee or mortgagee; or

(b) that a trustee or mortgagee or the estate representative of or other person deriving title under a trustee or mortgagee is out of the jurisdiction of the court or cannot be found, or being a corporation has been dissolved; or

(c) that it is uncertain which of two or more trustees, or which of two or more persons interested in a mortgage, was the survivor; or

(d) that it is uncertain whether the last trustee or the estate representative of or other person deriving title under a trustee or mortgagee, or the last surviving person interested in a mortgage is living or dead; or

(e) that any trustee or mortgagee has died intestate without leaving a person beneficially interested under the intestacy or has died and it is not known who is his estate representative or the person interested, the fact that the order has been so made shall be conclusive evidence of the matter so alleged in any court upon any question as to the validity of the order; but this section does not prevent the court from directing a reconveyance or surrender or the payment of costs occasioned by any such order if improperly obtained.

Application of vesting order to property out of Bermuda.

46. The powers of the court to make vesting orders under this Act shall extend to all property wherever situated.

Jurisdiction to make other Orders

Power of court to authorise transactions relating to trust property.

47.(1) Where any transaction affecting or concerning any property vested in trustees, is in the opinion of the court expedient, but the same cannot be effected by reason of the absence of any power for that purpose vested in the trustees by the instrument, if any, creating the trust, or by any provision of law, the court may by order confer upon the trustees, either generally or in any particular instance, the necessary power for the purpose, on such terms and subject to such provisions and conditions, if any, as the court may think fit and may direct in what manner any money authorised to be expended, and the costs of any transaction, are to be paid or borne as between capital and income.

(2) The court may, from time to time, rescind or vary any order made under this section or may make any new or further order.

(3) An application to the court under this section maybe made by the trustees, or by any of them, or by any person beneficially interested under the trust.

(4) In this section, "transaction" includes any sale, exchange, assurance, grant, lease, partition, surrender, reconveyance, release, reservation, or other disposition, and any purchase or other acquisition, and any covenant, contract, or option, and any investment or application of capital, and any compromise or other dealing, or arrangement.

Jurisdiction of court to vary trusts.

48.(1) Subject to subsection (2), where property is held on any trusts or settlements arising under any will, settlement or other disposition, the court may if it thinks fit by order approve on behalf of -

(a) any person having, directly or indirectly, an estate or interest, whether vested or contingent, under the trusts or settlements who by reason of infancy or other incapacity is incapable of assenting; or

(b) any person (whether ascertained or not) who may become entitled, directly or indirectly, to an estate or interest under the trusts or settlements as being at a future date or on the happening of a future event a person of any specified description or a member of any specified class of persons so, however, that this paragraph shall not include any person who would be of that description, or a member of that class, as the case may be, if the said date had fallen or the said event had happened at the date of the application to the court; or

(c) any person unborn; or

(d) any person in respect of any discretionary interest of his under protective trusts where the interest of the principal beneficiary has not failed or determined,

any arrangement (by whomsoever proposed, and whether or not there is any other person beneficially interested who is capable of assenting thereto) varying or revoking all or any of the trusts or settlements, or enlarging the powers of the trustees of managing or administering any of the property subject to the trusts or settlements.

(2) Except by virtue of subsection (1)(d) the court shall not approve an arrangement on behalf of any person unless the carrying out of the arrangement would be for the benefit of that person.

(3) In subsection (1), "protective trusts" means the trusts specified in section 25(1)(a) or any like trusts, "the principal beneficiary" has the same meaning as in section 25(1) and "discretionary interest" means an interest arising under the trust specified in section 25(1)(b) or any like trust.

(4) Nothing in this section shall be taken to limit the powers conferred by section 47.

Persons entitled to apply for orders.

49.(1) An order under this Act for the appointment of a new trustee or concerning any estate or interest in land, stock, or thing in action subject to a trust, may be made on the application of any person beneficially interested in the land, stock, or thing in action, whether under disability or not, or on the application of any person duly appointed trustee thereof.

(2) An order under this Act concerning any estate or interest in land, stock, or thing in action subject to a mortgage may be made on the application of any person beneficially interested in the equity of redemption, whether under disability or not, or of any person interested in the money secured by the mortgage.

Power to give judgment in absence of a trustee.

50. Where in any action the court is satisfied that diligent search has been made for any person who, in the character of trustee, is made a defendant in any action, to serve him with a process of the court, and that he cannot be found, the court may hear and determine the action and give judgment therein against that person in his character of a trustee as if he had been duly served, or had entered an appearance in the action, and had also appeared by his counsel at the hearing, but without prejudice to any interest he may have in the matters in question in the action in any other character.

Power to charge costs on trust estate.

51. The court may order the costs and expenses of and incidental to any application for an order under this Act or for any order or declaration in respect of any property subject to a trust, or of and incidental to any such order or declaration, or any document executed or act performed in pursuance thereof, to be raised and paid out of the property in respect whereof the same is made or performed, or out of the income thereof, or to be borne and paid in such manner and by such persons as to the court may seem just.

Power to relieve trustee from personal liability.

52.(1) If it appears to the court that a trustee, whether appointed by the court or otherwise, is or may be personally liable for any breach of trust, whether the transaction alleged to be a breach of trust occurred before or after the 1st March, 1975, but has acted honestly and reasonably, and ought fairly to be excused for the breach of trust and for omitting to obtain the directions of the court in the matter in which he committed such breach, then the court may relieve him either wholly or partly from personal liability for the same.

(2) In this section "trustee" includes a person who has ceased to be a trustee and the estate representative of a deceased trustee.

Power to make beneficiary indemnify for breach of trust.

53.(1) Where a trustee commits a breach of trust at the instigation or request or with the consent in writing of a beneficiary, the court may, if it thinks fit, make such order as to the court seems just, for impounding all or any part of the estate or interest of the beneficiary in the trust estate by way of indemnity to the trustee or persons claiming through him.

(2) This section applies to breaches of trust committed as well before as after the 1st March, 1975.

Payment into court

Payment into court by trustees.

54.(1) Trustees, or the majority of trustees, having in their hands or under their control money or securities belonging to a trust, may pay the same into court; and the same shall, subject to rules of court, be dealt with according to the orders of the court.

(2) The receipt or certificate of the proper officer shall be a sufficient discharge to trustees for the money or securities so paid into court.

(3) Where money or securities are vested in any persons as trustees, and the majority are desirous of paying the same into court, but the concurrence of the other or others cannot be obtained, the court may order the payment into court to be made by the majority without the concurrence of the other or others.

(4) Where any such money or securities are deposited with any bank, broker, or other depositary, the court may order payment or delivery of the money or securities to the majority of the trustees for the purpose of payment into court.

(5) Every transfer payment and delivery made in pursuance of any such order shall be valid and take effect as if the same had been made on the authority or by the act of all the persons entitled to the money and securities so transferred, paid, or delivered.

PART VA - INVESTMENTS

Investment powers

55A.(1) A trustee's power of investment under this section shall be subject to any enlargement or restriction of his powers of investment set out in the instrument creating the trust.

(2) Nothing in this section shall restrict the powers of the court under section 47.

(3) A trustee may invest or otherwise apply trust property in the purchase or acquisition of property of any kind, whether or not situated in Bermuda, whether or not income-producing, with or without security, and whether for the purpose of -

(a) receiving an appropriate total return from income and capital appreciation;

(b) controlling or limiting risk; or

(c) benefiting persons interested in any way whatsoever in the income produced by trust property;

or for a mixture of such purposes.

(4) In so investing or otherwise applying trust property, a trustee shall act as a prudent investor would, by considering the purposes, terms, distribution requirements and other circumstances of the trust and by exercising reasonable care, skill and caution.

(5) In determining whether a trustee has acted in accordance with this section, any decision to invest or otherwise apply trust property shall be evaluated in the context of the trust property as a whole and as part of an overall investment strategy having risk and return objectives reasonably suited to the trust.
56-63. *Repealed.*

PART VI - GENERAL PROVISIONS

Indemnify to banks and others.

64. This Act, and every order purporting to be made under this Act, shall be a complete indemnity to banks and to all persons for any acts done pursuant thereto, and it shall not be necessary for a bank or for any person to inquire concerning the propriety of the order, or whether the court by which the order was made had jurisdiction to make it.

Enactments repealed.

65. [*Omitted.*]

Commencement.

66. [*Omitted.*]

FIRST SCHEDULE

(Section 55)

Repealed.

SECOND SCHEDULE (Section 65)

ENACTMENTS REPEALED

[*omitted*]

BERMUDA

1989: No. 62

THE TRUSTS (SPECIAL PROVISIONS) ACT 1989

(as amended, 1998)

WHEREAS it is expedient to make provision on the law respecting trusts, to make provision respecting a trust for a purpose or purposes, to make provision for administrative powers in trust and for matters connected therewith and incidental thereto:

Be it enacted by The Queen's Most Excellent Majesty, by and with the advice and consent of the Senate and the House of Assembly of Bermuda, and by the authority of the same as follows:-

Short title and commencement

1. This Act may be cited as the Trusts (Special Provisions) Act 1989 and shall come into operation on such date as the Premier may appoint by notice published in the Gazette.

PART I

TRUSTS

Trust described.

2.(1) For the purposes of this Part, the term "trust" refers to the legal relationship created, either inter vivos or on death, by a person, the settlor, when assets have been placed under the control of a trustee for the benefit of a beneficiary or for a specified purpose.

(2) A trust has the following characteristics:

(a) the assets constitute a separate fund and are not a part of the trustee's own estate;

(b) title to the trust assets stands in the name of the trustee or in the name of another person on behalf of the trustee;

(c) the trustee has the power and the duty in respect of which he is accountable, to manage, employ or dispose of the assets in accordance with the terms of the trust and the special duties imposed upon him by law.

(3) The reservation by the settlor of certain rights and powers, and the fact that the trustee may himself have rights as a beneficiary, are not necessarily inconsistent with the existence of a trust.

Application.

3. This Part applies to trusts created voluntarily and evidenced in writing and also to any other trusts of property arising under the law of Bermuda or by virtue of a judicial decision whether in Bermuda or elsewhere.

Non-application.

4. This Part does not apply to the extent that the law specified by section 5 or 6 does not provide for trusts or the category of trusts involved.

Governing law.

5.(1) A trust shall be governed by the law chosen by the settlor whose choice shall be express or be implied in the terms of the instrument creating or the writing evidencing the trust, interpreted, if necessary, in the light of circumstances of the case.

(2) Where the law chosen under subsection (1) does not provide for trusts or the category of trusts involved, the choice shall not be effective and the law specified in section 6 applies.

No applicable law chosen.

6.(1) Where no applicable law has been chosen, a trust shall be governed by the law with which it is most closely connected and in ascertaining the law with which a trust is most closely connected references shall be made in particular to-

(a) the place of administration of the trust designated by the settlor;

(b) the situs of the assets of the trust;

(c) the place of residence or business of the trustee;

(d) the objects of the trust and the places where they are to be fulfilled.

(2) A trust that is governed by the law of Bermuda may provide terms to change the law governing the trust from the law of Bermuda to a new governing law but such change is valid and effective only if the new governing law recognises the validity of the trust and the respective interests of the beneficiaries.

(3) A change in the law governing a trust shall not affect the legality or validity of or render any person liable for anything done before the change.

Law governing validity and construction of trust.

7. The law specified by section 5 or 6 shall govern the validity of the trust, its construction, its effects and the administration of the trust and in particular the law shall govern -

(a) the appointment, resignation and removal of trustees, the capacity to act as a trustee, and the devolution of the office of trustee;

(b) the rights and duties of trustees among themselves;

(c) the right of trustees to delegate in whole or in part the discharge of their duties or the exercise of their powers;

(d) the power of trustees to administer or to dispose of trust assets, to create security interests in the trust assets, or to acquire new assets;

(e) the powers of investment of trustees;

(f) restrictions upon the duration of the trust, and upon the power to accumulate the income of the trust;

(g) the relationships between the trustees and the beneficiaries including the personal liability of the trustees to the beneficiaries;

(h) the variation or termination of the trust;

(i) the distribution of the trust assets;

(j) the duty of trustees to account for their administration.

Choosing different laws.

8. In applying this Part a severable aspect of the trust, particularly matters of administration, may be governed by a different law.

Jurisdiction of Supreme Court.

9. The Supreme Court has jurisdiction -

(a) where a trustee is resident in Bermuda;

(b) where any trust property is situated in Bermuda but only in respect of property so situated;

(c) where the administration of any trust is carried on in Bermuda, or

(d) where the Court thinks it appropriate.

Capacity to create trust.

10.(1) Subject to subsection (2), a person has capacity to create a trust in the following cases:

(a) where the trust property is movable -

(i) in the case of an inter vivos trust, if he has the capacity to create a trust of movable property by the law of Bermuda;

(ii) in the case of a testamentary trust, if he has the capacity to create a trust of movable property by the law of his domicile;

(b) where the trust property is immovable, if he has the capacity to create a trust by the lex situs of the immovable.

(2) All questions as to the capacity of any settlor arising in regard to a trust which is for the time being governed by the law of Bermuda or in regard to any disposition of property upon the trusts thereof are to be determined according to the law of Bermuda without reference to the law of any other jurisdiction with which the trust or disposition may be connected except that this subsection -

(a) does not validate any disposition of property which is neither owned by the settlor nor the subject of a power in that behalf vested in the settlor, nor does this subsection affect the recognition of foreign laws in determining whether the settlor is the owner of such property or the holder of such power;

(b) does take effect subject to any express contrary term of the trust or disposition;

(c) does not, as regards the capacity of a corporation, affect the recognition of the laws of its place of incorporation;

(d) does not affect the recognition of foreign laws prescribing generally (without reference to the existence or terms of the trust) the formalities for the disposition of property;

(e) does not validate any trust or disposition of immovable property situate in a jurisdiction other than Bermuda which is invalid according to the laws of such jurisdiction;

(f) does not validate any testamentary trust or disposition which is invalid according to the laws of testator's domicile.

Varying or setting aside trust.

11. Where a trust is validly created under the law of Bermuda the Court shall not vary it or set it aside pursuant to the law of another jurisdiction in respect of -

(a) the personal and proprietary effects of marriage;

(b) succession rights, testate and intestate, especially the indefeasible shares of spouses and relatives;

(c) the protection of creditors in matters of insolvency, unless the law of Bermuda has corresponding laws or public policy rules.

PART II

PURPOSE TRUSTS

Purpose trusts

12A.(1) A trust may be created for a non-charitable purpose or purposes provided that the conditions set out in subsection (2) are satisfied; and in this Part such a trust is referred to as a "purpose trust".

(2) The conditions are that the purpose or purposes are -

(a) sufficiently certain to allow the trust to be carried out,

(b) lawful, and

(c) not contrary to public policy.

(3) A purpose trust may only be created in writing.

(4) The rule of law (known as the rule against excessive duration or the rule against perpetual trusts) which limits the time during which the capital of a trust may remain unexpendable to the perpetuity period under the rule against perpetuities shall not apply to a purpose trust.

(5) The rule against perpetuities (also known as the rule against remoteness of vesting) as modified by the Perpetuities and Accumulations Act 1989 shall apply to a purpose trust.

Enforcement and variation of purpose trust by the court

12B.(1) The Supreme Court may make such order as it considers expedient for the enforcement of a purpose trust on the application of any of the following persons -

(a) any person appointed by or under the trust for the purposes of this subsection;

(b) the settlor, unless the trust instrument provides otherwise;

(c) a trustee of the trust;

(d) any other person whom the court considers has sufficient interest in the enforcement of the trust;

and where the Attorney-General satisfies the court that there is no such person who is able and willing to make an application under this subsection, the Attorney-General may make an application for enforcement of the trust.

(2) On an application in relation to a purpose trust by any of the following persons -

(a) any person appointed by or under the trust for the purposes of this subsection;

(b) the settlor, unless the trust instrument provides otherwise;

(c) a trustee of the trust, the court may if it thinks fit approve a scheme to vary any of the purposes of the trust, or to enlarge or otherwise vary any of the powers of the trustees of the trust.

(3) Where any costs are incurred in connection with any application under this section, the Supreme Court may make such order as it considers just as to payment of those costs (including payment out of the property of the trust).

Effect of non-compliance

12C. Nothing in this Part affects the creation, termination or validity of any trust created under any other law, but, save as aforesaid, purpose trusts which do not comply with section 12A are invalid.

Land in Bermuda

12D. No interest in land in Bermuda shall be held, directly or indirectly, in a purpose trust.

PART III

INCORPORATION OF ADMINISTRATIVE POWERS BY REFERENCE

Incorporation by reference. Schedule

17. Any instrument creating any trust may incorporate by reference any of the provisions set out in the Schedule, in which case the following expressions appearing in the provisions have, unless a contrary intention appears, the meanings respectively assigned to them:

"the Settlor" includes a person who provides trust property or makes a testamentary disposition on trust or to a trust;

"the Trustees" means the trustees for the time being of the trust;

"the Trust Fund" means -

(a) the property in respect of which trusts are declared;

(b) all property paid or transferred to or otherwise vested in and accepted by the Trustees and in respect of which a memorandum signed by the Trustees is conclusive evidence;

(c) all income which, in accordance with the provisions of the trust, is accumulated by the Trustees and added to the capital thereof;

(d) all money, investments and other property from time to time representing all property and income mentioned in paragraphs (a), (b) and (c) and any part of the said property or income.

SCHEDULE SECTION 17

Trust for Sale.

1.(1) The Trustees shall stand possessed of any real property from time to time comprised in the Trust Fund Upon Trust to sell the same with power to postpone the sale thereof or of any part thereof for such period as they shall in their absolute discretion think fit and shall stand possessed of all other investments comprised in the Trust Fund Upon Trust at such discretion either to retain the same in the existing state thereof for such period as they shall think fit or at any time or times to sell the same or any part thereof.

(2) The Trustees shall hold the net proceeds of any sale of investments comprised in the Trust Fund and all other monies held or received by them as capital monies Upon Trust to invest the same at their discretion in or upon any of the investments by this instrument authorised with power to vary or transpose such investments for or into any others of a like nature.

Powers of Investment.

2. TRUST moneys to be invested under the trusts of this instrument may be applied or invested in any currency and in any part of the world in the purchase of or upon the security of such common or preferred stocks shares mutual fund shares unit trust units or other securities or commodities (including precious metals) bonds notes debentures certificates of deposit or time deposits land or other investments or property of whatever nature (and whether or not income-producing or paying dividends or interest) and whether involving liabilities or not or upon such personal credit with or without security as the Trustees in their absolute discretion think fit without being restricted to trustee investments prescribed under the proper law governing this instrument and to the intent that the Trustees shall have the same powers in all respects as if they were absolute owners beneficially entitled And in addition (but without prejudice to the generality of the foregoing) the Trustees may invest the Trust Fund in the shares or debentures of any company whatsoever and wheresoever incorporated without the need for diversification and without being liable for any loss occasioned thereby.

Power with regard to mode of application of capital and income.

3. ANY power by this instrument or by law conferred on the Trustees to pay transfer appropriate or apply the Trust Fund or any income thereof for the benefit of any beneficiary may at the discretion of the Trustees be validly exercised (without prejudice to the generality of such power or to any other mode of application) -

(a) by paying or transferring the same to the trustees of any settlement (whether or not such trustees are resident in Bermuda and whether or not the proper law of such settlement is the law of Bermuda) the provisions of which are in the opinion of the Trustees for the benefit of such beneficiary notwithstanding that such settlement may also contain trusts powers or provisions (discretionary or otherwise) in favour of other persons or objects Provided however that no such payment or transfer shall be made so as to infringe the

rule against perpetuities as applicable to the trusts created by this instrument; or

(b) (in the case of any such person who is a minor) by paying or transferring the same to such minor's parent or guardian or some other person for the time being having the care or custody of such minor upon the recipient undertaking to apply the same for the benefit of the minor;

And the Trustees shall not thereafter be under any obligation to see to the further application of the capital or income so paid or transferred and the receipt of such trustees parent guardian or other person shall be a full sufficient and complete discharge to the Trustees.

Additional Powers.

4.THE Trustees shall have the following powers in addition to those conferred by law:

(1) Power to receive any property from any person as an addition to the Trust Fund either by gift inter vivos or by will or under the provisions of any other settlement or trust or otherwise;

(2) Power to borrow on the security of the Trust Fund and for such purpose to make any outlay out of the Trust Fund or the income thereof and to enter into such contracts mortgages charges or undertakings relating thereto as the Trustees may in their absolute discretion think fit;

(3) Power to lend any part of the Trust Fund to any person (whether or not a beneficiary) upon such terms (if any) as to security repayment rate of interest and otherwise as the Trustees in their absolute discretion may determine;

(4) With respect to any property comprised in the Trust Fund power to exercise all powers relating thereto as if beneficially entitled thereto and without being restricted in any way by the office of trustee including (without prejudice to the generality of the foregoing power) -

(a) Power to vote upon or in respect of any shares securities bonds notes or other evidence of interest in or obligations of any corporation trust association or concern whether or not the exercise of such power affects the security or the apparent security of the Trust Fund or the purchase or sale or lease of the assets of any such corporation trust association or concern;

(b) Power to deposit any such shares securities or property in any voting trust or with any depository designated thereby;

(c) Power to give proxies or powers of attorney with or without power of substitution for voting or acting on behalf of the Trustees as the owners of any such property; and

(d) Power to omit to register bonds or securities;

(5) Power (at the expense of the Trust Fund) to incorporate or register or to procure the incorporation or registration of any company (with limited or unlimited liability) in any part of the world for any purpose including the acquisition of the Trust Fund or any part thereof and so that (if thought fit) the consideration on the sale of the Trust Fund to any such company may consist wholly or partly of fully paid shares debentures debenture stock or other securities of the company credited as fully paid which shall be allotted to or otherwise vested in the Trustees and be capital moneys in the Trustees' hands;

(6) Power at any time to apply any part of the Trust Fund of the income thereof in effecting or joining in effecting or otherwise acquiring any policy of assurance on the life of any beneficiary or of any other person or any endowment or other policy and to maintain surrender exchange exercise any option thereunder or otherwise deal with such policies as if the Trustees were absolutely entitled thereto;

(7) Power to pay out at any time any part of the Trust Fund in purchasing or acquiring or making improvements in or repairs to or on any land or building (whether freehold leasehold or of any other tenure or interest and of whatsoever description and situate in any part of the world) in the occupation of or intended for occupation by any beneficiary And power to permit any beneficiary to occupy until sale any land or building purchased or acquired as aforesaid or otherwise comprised in the Trust Fund upon such terms (as to payment or non-payment of rent outgoings repairs or otherwise) as the Trustees may think fit;

(8) Power at any time or times to lay out any part of the Trust Fund in the purchase or other acquisition of any yachts boats motor vehicles works of art household furniture plate linen china cutlery other articles of household use ornament or equipment and other chattels for the use of any beneficiary whether occupying a building purchased or acquired as aforesaid or otherwise And power to hand over to any such beneficiary for his use any property so purchased or acquired by the Trustees as aforesaid or otherwise forming part of the Trust Fund upon and subject to such terms and conditions (if any) as to insurance preservation maintaining inventories and otherwise as the Trustees think fit;

(9) Power to grant options for such consideration and exercisable at such time or times or within such period as the Trustees think fit for the purchase of any property subject to the trusts of this instrument or the acquisition of any interest therein;

(10) Power to keep the Trust Fund either in or out of Bermuda and if the Trustees think fit to hold in any part of the world all or any securities or other property in bearer form or registered in the name of the Trustees or nominees without disclosing the fiduciary relationship;

(11) In the event of any duties fees or taxes whatsoever becoming payable in any part of the world in respect of the Trust Fund or any part thereof in any circumstances whatsoever power to pay all such duties fees or taxes out of the Trust Fund or the income thereof with discretion as to the time and manner in which the said duties fees or taxes shall be paid and the Trustees may pay such duties fees or taxes notwithstanding that the same shall not be recoverable from the Trustees or from any persons interested under the trusts of this instrument or that the payment shall not be to the advantage of such persons;

(12) Power to make such reserves out of the Trust Fund or the income thereof as the Trustees deem proper for expenses taxes and other liabilities and to pay from capital or income or to apportion between capital and income any expenses of making or changing investments and selling exchanging or leasing (including brokers commissions and charges) and generally to determine what part of the expenses of administering the trusts of this instrument shall be charged to capital and what part to income;

(13) Power to make execute and deliver deeds assignments transfers leases mortgages instruments of pledge creating liens contracts and other instruments sealed and unsealed;

(14) Power to institute prosecute and defend any suits or actions or other proceedings affecting the Trustees or the Trust Fund and to compromise any matter of difference or to submit such matter to arbitration and to compromise or compound any debt owing to the Trustees or any other claims and to adjust any disputes in relation to debts or claims against them as trustees upon evidence that the Trustees shall deem sufficient and to make partition upon such terms (including if thought fit the payment or receipt of equality money) as the Trustees shall deem desirable with co-owners or joint tenants besides the Trustees having any interest in any property in which the Trustees are interested and to make partition either by sale or by set-off or by agreement or otherwise;

(15) Power to make any distribution of the Trust Fund pursuant to the trusts of this instrument in cash or in kind or partly in cash and partly in kind and in the case of a distribution to more than one person not strictly rateably but on the basis of equal or other proportionate value (as the case may require) according to the judgment of the Trustees which shall be binding on all persons interested under this instrument;

(16) Power to take at the expense of the Trust Fund or the income thereof the opinion of legal counsel concerning any question arising under this instrument or on any matter in any way relating to the Trust Fund or the duties of the Trustees in connection with this instrument And the Trustees shall not be liable for any action taken in good faith pursuant to or otherwise in accordance with the opinion or advice of such counsel;

(17) Power -

(a) to engage the services of such investment counsel adviser or manager ("the Investment Adviser") as the Trustees may from time to time think fit (including the Settlor or any trustee of this instrument or any corporate trustee or any parent subsidiary or affiliate of such corporate trustee) in order to obtain advice on the investment and reinvestment of the Trust Fund AND to delegate to the Investment Adviser without being liable for any consequential loss discretion to manage the portfolio or any part thereof within the limits and for the period stipulated by the Trustees and the Trustees

(i) shall settle the terms and conditions for the remuneration of the Investment Adviser and the reimbursement of the Investment Adviser's expenses as in their uncontrolled discretion they deem proper and such remuneration and expenses may be paid by the Trustees from and out of the Trust Fund; and

(ii) shall not be liable for any action taken in good faith pursuant to or otherwise in accordance with the advice of the Investment Adviser;

(b) to employ and pay at the expense of the capital or income of the Trust Fund any agent or agents in any part of the world whether solicitors bankers accountants stockbrokers managers or other persons (including the Settlor or any trustee of this instrument or any corporate trustee or any parent subsidiary or affiliate of such corporate trustee) to transact any business or to do any act requiring to be transacted or done in execution of the trusts of this instrument including the receipt and payment of money and the execution of documents and in any such event the trustee, the corporate trustee or the parent subsidiary or the affiliate of such corporate trustee is entitled to charge and be paid and to retain for his or its own account all usual professional and other fees and commissions normally paid for such services including fees and commissions shared with other agents;

Trustee may exercise powers despite personal interest.

(18) Power for all or any of the Trustees

(a) to exercise or join or concur in exercising all or any of the powers and discretions by this instrument or by law given to the Trustees notwithstanding that such trustee may have a personal interest in the mode or result of exercising any such power or discretion or may be interested therein in some other fiduciary capacity but any trustee may abstain from acting except as a merely formal party in any matter in which he may be so interested as aforesaid and may allow his co-trustees to act alone in the exercise of such powers and discretions in relation to such matter; and

To effect transactions.

(b) to purchase or sell any property notwithstanding that the vendor or purchaser is the same as or includes the Trustees or any of them PROVIDED that the price payable on any such purchase or sale is certified as fair and reasonable by an independent valuer employed for the purpose by the Trustees;

Residuary power.

(19) Power to effect any transaction concerning or affecting the Trust Fund or any other property whatsoever and to do all other acts and things which the Trustees may in their absolute discretion think expedient in the interests of the Trust Fund or any beneficiary And for the purpose of this sub-paragraph "transaction" includes any sale exchange assurance conveyance grant lease surrender reconveyance release reservation or other disposition and any purchase or other acquisition and any covenant contract licence option right of pre-emption and any compromise or partition and any company reconstruction or amalgamation and any other dealing or arrangement And "effect" has the meaning appropriate to the particular transaction And references to property include references to restrictions and burdens affecting the property;

Powers of Sale, etc.

(20) All the powers of sale (by public auction or private contract) exchange mortgaging leasing or other disposition management repair building and improvement and all other powers of an absolute beneficial owner in respect of any property for the time being comprised in the Trust Fund including (without prejudice to the generality of the foregoing) the power of borrowing on the security of the Trust Fund and for such purpose to make any outlay out of the income or capital of the Trust Fund and to make such contracts and to enter into such undertakings relating thereto as the Trustees in their absolute discretion shall think fit;

Power to give guarantees.

(21) Power at any time in the Trustees' discretion and on such terms as they deem fit to appropriate or to apply the capital or income of the Trust Fund or any part thereof in order to secure the payment of money owed by any beneficiary or the performance of any obligations of any beneficiary and to give any guarantee or to become surety for any beneficiary and for such purposes to mortgage or charge any investments or property for the time being forming part of the Trust Fund or to deposit or transfer any such investments or property with or to any person by way of security.

To release fiduciary powers.

(22) Power from time to time by deed revocable or irrevocable wholly or partially to release extinguish or restrict any power by this instrument or by law conferred on the Trustees notwithstanding the fiduciary nature of any such power (but not so as to invalidate any prior exercise thereof).

Exclusion of apportionments.

5. UNLESS the Trustees in their absolute discretion shall otherwise determine all dividends and other income received shall be treated for all purposes as income accruing at the due date of payment whether or not such dividends or income may have been earned and accrued wholly or partially in respect of a period prior to such date.

Protection of third parties in dealings with trustees.

6.(1) NO person or corporation dealing with the Trustees and no purchaser on any sale made by the Trustees shall be concerned to enquire into the propriety or validity of any act of the Trustees or to see to the application of any money paid or property transferred to or upon the order of the Trustees.

(2) NO firm association or corporation any of whose securities are comprised in the Trust Fund and no purchaser or person dealing with any trustee purporting to act under any delegation of authority from any other trustee shall be required to ascertain or enquire whether a case exists in which such delegation is permitted or whether such delegated authority is still subsisting.

(3) WHEN anything is dependent upon the value of any property or the existence of any fact a certificate of the Trustees as to such value or fact shall be conclusive in favour of anyone acting thereon in good faith.

Power in relation to underlying company/ies.

7. ANY trustee of this instrument and any director officer or employee of a corporate trustee or of a parent subsidiary or affiliate of such corporate trustee may act as a director officer manager or employee of any company whose shares or debentures may be comprised in the Trust Fund or as a director officer manager or employee of any subsidiary or holding company of any such company and may retain for himself or itself any remuneration which he or it may receive as such director officer manager or employee notwithstanding that any votes or other rights attaching to such shares or debentures may have been instrumental either alone or in conjunction with other matters or by reason of their non-exercise in procuring or continuing for him or it his or its position as such director officer manager or employee or that his or its qualifications for any such position may be constituted in part or in whole by any such shares or debentures.

Trustee not bound to interfere with company management

8. THE Trustees shall not be bound or required to interfere in the management or conduct of the affairs or business of any company in which the Trust Fund may be invested (and whether or not the Trustees have the control of such company) And so long as no trustee of this instrument has notice of any wilful negligence wilful default or fraud or dishonesty on the part of the directors having the management of such company they may leave the same (including the payment or non-payment of dividends) wholly to such directors And no beneficiary is entitled as such beneficiary in any way to compel control or forbid the exercise (including in any particular manner) of any voting or other rights at any time vested in the Trustees with regard to such company including without prejudice to the generality of the foregoing any powers the Trustees may have (even if also directors of such company) of compelling such company to distribute any dividend.

[illegible] assessment upon the value of any Property of the [illegible] to any such [illegible]

THE TRUST COMPANIES ACT 1991

ARRANGEMENT OF SECTIONS

THE TRUST COMPANIES ACT 1991

WHEREAS it is expedient to regulate more effectively the doing of trust work by corporations, and to provide for connected and incidental matters:

Be it enacted by The Queen's Most Excellent Majesty, by and with the advice and consent of the Senate and the House of Assembly of Bermuda, and by the authority of the same, as follows:-

Short title.

1. This Act may be cited as the Trust Companies Act 1991.

Interpretation.

2. In this Act, unless the context requires otherwise -

"accountant" means a person entitled to practise as a public accountant under the Institute of Chartered Accountants of Bermuda Act 1973;

"application" means an application under section 5, and "applicant" has a corresponding meaning:

"approved auditor" has the meaning given to it by subsection (2) of section 14;

"the Authority" means the Bermuda Monetary Authority established by the Bermuda Monetary Authority Act 1969;

"commencement day" means the day appointed pursuant to subsection (1) of section 30;

"the Companies Act" means the Companies Act 1981;

"company" has the meaning given to it by subsection (1) of section 2 of the Companies Act;

"existing company" means a company which was carrying on trust business immediately before commencement day;

"financial statements" means the statements referred to in section 13;

"financial year", in relation to a company, means the period not exceeding fifty-three weeks at the end of which the balance of the company's accounts is struck or, if no such balance is struck or a period of more than fifty-three weeks is employed for that purpose, then calendar year;

"licence" means a licence provided for in sections 5 to 7; and "license" has a corresponding meaning;

"the Minister" means the Minister of Finance;

"officer", in relation to a body (whether corporate or unincorporate), includes director, manager or secretary of the body;

"trust" has the meaning given to it by section 2 of the Trusts (Special Provisions) Act 1989;

"trust business" means the undertaking, executing and administering of trusts, as a business, trade, profession or vocation carried on or practised in the service of the public generally;

"trust company" has the meaning given to it by subsection (1) of section 3.

Restriction on carrying on trust business without a licence.

3.(1) Subject to subsection (2), a person shall not carry on trust business in or from within Bermuda unless that person is a company which at the time holds a licence which is in force for the purpose (in this Act called a "trust company").

(2) The prohibition in subsection (1) does not extend to an individual or a partnership.

Restriction on use of certain words in names.

4. None of the words "Trust", "trust", "Trustee" and "trustee", and no grammatical variation of any of those words, shall be used in a name designating a business unless the business is that of a licensed company; and if any person, being an officer, employee or agent business, uses any of those words in a name designating the business when he knows that the business is not that of a licensed trust company, commits an offence against this Act.

Applications for licences.

5.(1) A person with an interest to do so may make an application to the Minister for a licence for a company to carry on trust business or from within Bermuda.

(2) An application -

(a) shall be accompanied by -

(i) a statement setting out the nature and scale of the trust business which is to be carried on by the company, and particulars of the arrangements proposed for the operation of that business; and

(ii) such other information and documents as the Minister may require for the purpose of considering the application; and

(iii) an application fee of $170 or such higher amount as may be prescribed under the Government Fees Act 1965; and

(b) shall otherwise be made in such manner as the Minister may direct.

(3) At any time after receiving an application and before determining it the Minister may in writing require the applicant to provide additional information or documents.

(4) Requirements or directions made or given under subsection (2) or (3) may differ as between different applications.

(5) Any statement or information to be provided to the Minister under this section shall be in such form as the Minister may specify; and the Minister may in writing require the applicant to provide a report by an accountant or other person approved by the Minister on such aspects of any such statement or information as the Minister may specify.

(6) An application may be withdrawn by notice in writing to the Minister at any time before he has determined the application.

Power to grant licences.

6.(1) The Minister may grant or reject an application.

(2) The Minister shall not grant an application unless he is satisfied that the criteria set forth in the First Schedule are or will be fulfilled with respect to the company to which the application relates.

(3) Notwithstanding subsection (2), the Minister shall reject an application if he determines that it is not in the public interest that the application should be granted.

(4) In deciding whether to grant or reject an application, the Minister shall take into account, among other things -

(a) the economic situation in Bermuda;

(b) any advantage or disadvantage that may result for Bermuda from the application being granted; and

(c) where the proposed trust company is a company already in being, the nature and previous conduct of the company and the character and previous conduct of any individual or body having an interest (whether as an officer, shareholder or otherwise) in the company.

(5) The Minister need not give any reason for granting or rejecting an application.

Conditions to licences.

7.(1) A licence may be granted subject to such conditions as the Minister sees fit to specify in the licence.

(2) The power given by subsection (1) to impose conditions includes, subject to the limitations specified in subsections (4) and (5), power to impose conditions whereby -

(a) the transfer of a voting share in a company; or

(b) the appointment of a top executive in a company,may be prevented by the Minister or an authority chosen by him.

(3) The expression "top executive" in this section means, in relation to a company, a person who is to perform functions of any of the following offices in the company, namely -

(a) a director;

(b) the chief executive officer;

(c) the chief financial officer;

(d) the company secretary, by whatever name called.

(4) The limitation referred to in subsection (2), in relation to a proposed transfer of a voting share, is that the Minister (or, as the case may be, the chosen authority) is entitled to consider the following, and no other, question, namely, whether, in light of -

(a) the character and previous conduct of the person to whom the share is to be transferred; and also

(b) the likely impact, in the opinion of the Minister (or, as the case may be, the chosen authority), of the transfer on the future conduct of the company's affairs,the public interest will be prejudiced by the transfer being made.

(5) The limitation referred to in subsection (2), in relation to a proposed appointment of a top executive, is that the Minister (or, as the case may be, the chosen authority) is entitled to consider the following, and no other, question, namely, whether, in light of -

(a) the character and previous conduct of the proposed appointee; and also

(b) the proposed appointee's knowledge of, and skill and experience in, trust business,the public interest will be prejudiced by the appointment being made.

Other provisions concerning licences.

8.(1) A licence shall be in such form as the Minister thinks fit, and different licences may be in different forms.

(2) A company which holds a licence shall at all times keep the licence on display at the company's registered office in Bermuda in a place where the public can see the licence.

(3) A licence remains in force until it is cancelled.

Annual licence fee.

9.(1) Subject to this section, every trust company shall, on or before the 31st day of March in every year following the year in which the company was licensed, pay a licence fee of $1,000 or such higher amount as may be prescribed under the Government Fees Act 1965.

(2) A licence fee is not payable by a company whose winding up is in progress in winding up proceedings in Bermuda, except where -

(a) the fee, being due for payment, was not paid; and

(b) the time allowed by subsection (1) for the payment of the fee had expired, before those proceedings had commenced.

(3) If a licence fee that a company is excused by subsection (2) from paying has in fact been paid, the liquidator may recover the fee from the government.

(4) An unpaid licence fee may be sued for by the Government by action as a civil debt and -

(a) the Government may (whether in such an action or not) require; and

(b) where judgment is given for the Government in such an action, the Court may order, for late payment of the fee payment of a penalty in an amount equal to the amount of the fee.

Functions of the Bermuda Monetary Authority under this Act.

10.(1) The Authority has, in addition to its other functions -

(a) the duty to supervise trust companies in accordance with this Act; and

(b) in and for the discharge of that duty, the functions conferred on the Authority by this Act.

(2) The Authority shall, to such extent as is necessary for giving effect to any arrangements made between the Minister and the Authority for the purpose, make to the Minister periodic or other reports about matters coming to the Authority's knowledge pursuant to section 12 or 16; and for that purpose or for the purpose of consultation with the Minister under subsection (2) of section 22, the Authority may disclose to the Minister any information in the Authority's possession, being information relevant to the making of such a report or the conduct of such consultation, notwithstanding that the information is information which, but for this subsection, the Authority would be forbidden by some provision of law so to disclose.

(3) Neither the Authority nor any officer or employee of the Authority is liable in damages for anything done or omitted in the discharge or purported discharge of the Authority's functions under this Act unless the act or omission was in bad faith.

Segregation of trust accounts.

11. In the records of account that a trust company is required by section 83 of the Companies Act to cause to be kept, the transactions and balances of the company shall be kept segregated from the transactions and balances of the trusts which the company administers.

Duty to file financial and other information.

12.(1) Every trust company shall, within the statutory period after the last day of each financial year, deliver to the Authority a copy of-

(a) the company's financial statements;

(b) the company's certificate of management; and

(c) the two reports of the approved auditor called for by section 14, relating to that financial year.

(2) The following provisions have effect in relation to a company's certificate of management -

(a) the certificate shall be in the form, and (subject to paragraph (b)) contain the information, and be executed in the manner, prescribed in the specimen certificate set forth in the Second Schedule;

(b) where a statement or opinion that is required to be made or expressed in the certificate cannot be so made or expressed, then -

(i) the wording of the statement or opinion shall be modified appropriately; and

(ii) a statement of the reason for, and, where appropriate, of the action that will be taken to correct, any deficiency shall be made either in the certificate itself or in an attachment to it.

(3) The expression "statutory period" in subsection (1) means one hundred and twenty days or, where the Authority thinks fit in circumstances explained to the Authority affecting a particular financial year, any longer period approved by the Authority.

Duty to prepare financial statements.

13.(1) In the case of a trust company, the financial statements described in paragraph (a) of subsection (1) of section 84 of the Companies Act shall, notwithstanding anything to the contrary in that section, be prepared in respect of each financial year.

(2) In relation to a trust company, to the extent that section 88 of the Companies Act conflicts with a requirement of this section or of section 14 or of any other provision of this Act, that requirement prevails.

Audit.

14.(1) A trust company's financial statements shall be audited annually by the company's approved auditor.

(2) In this Act the expression "approved auditor", in relation to a trust company, means an accountant who has been approved by the Minister as that company's approved auditor.

(3) The approved auditor shall conduct the above audit, and prepare his report on that audit, in accordance with generally accepted auditing standards.

(4) In addition to the above report, the approved auditor shall prepare annually a report in the form, and containing the information, prescribed in the specimen report set forth in the Third Schedule.

(5) The requirements of this section are in addition to, and do not derogate from, the requirements of section 90 of the Companies Act.

Investigation of affairs of a trust company.

15.(1) The Minister may appoint a person appearing to him to be a suitable person as an inspector to investigate and make to him a report on the affairs, or any part of the affairs, of a trust company if the Minister is satisfied that such an investigation is required in the public interest.

(2) Subject to section 17, it is the duty of any trust company in relation to whose affairs an inspector has been appointed under subsection (1) (hereinafter called a "company under investigation"), and of any past or present officer, employee or agent of such a company, to produce to the inspector on request all books, records and documents relating to the company under investigation which are in its or his possession, custody or power, and otherwise to give to the inspector all information and assistance in connection with the investigation which it or he is reasonably able to give.

(3) Subject to section 17, an inspector may -

(a) examine on oath any past or present officer, employee or agent of the company under investigation in relation to its business, and may administer an oath accordingly;

(b) if he thinks it necessary for the purposes of his investigation that a person whom he has no power to examine on oath should be so examined, make application to the Supreme Court, and that Court may, if it thinks fit, order that person to attend and be examined on oath before the Court on any matter relevant to the investigation.

(4) The expenses of an investigation of a company under this section shall be borne by the company unless the Minister directs otherwise.

(5) If any person -

(a) discloses to any person other than the Minister; or

(b) uses or applies for his own benefit,

any information that he obtained by reason of being appointed an inspector under subsection (1), he commits an offence against this Act.

Power of Authority to obtain information.

16.(1) Subject to section 17, the Authority may in writing direct any person to whom this section applies to produce to the Authority any document or information relating to any matter or thing connected with trust business which is in that person's possession, custody or power and which the Authority reasonably requires for the purpose of verifying or supplementing information otherwise provided to the Authority or the Minister under this Act; and any such person shall comply with any lawful direction so given.

(2) The expression "person to whom this section applies" in subsection (1) means any person who has at any time been an officer, employee or agent of a trust company.

Provisions supplementary to sections 15 and 16.

17.(1) Where it is desired that material relating to the affairs of a particular trust (as distinct from material relating to the affairs of a trust company or those of the trusts generally that such a company administers) shall be examined or produced pursuant to the provisions of section 15 or 16, those provisions have effect subject to subsections (2) to (6).

(2) In a case described in subsection (1), an inspector or, as the case may be, an officer of the Authority duly authorised for the purpose may apply ex parte to the Supreme Court for an order under subsection (4) in relation to material or material of a particular description; but such an application may not be made unless the material in question is material that is, or contains, or is likely to be, or to contain, evidence implicating some person in -

(a) drug trafficking or money laundering; or

(b) stealing, or other dishonesty affecting, trust property; or

(c) a contravention of a prohibition or restriction imposed by law in pursuance of a resolution or other decision of an international body, being a resolution or decision binding on Bermuda.

(3) In subsection (2) -

"drug trafficking" has the meaning given to it by section 1 of the Drug Trafficking Suppression

Act 1988;

"money laundering" means arrangements whereby -

(a) the retention or control by or on behalf of some person of that person's benefits from one or more criminal offences is facilitated; or

(b) some person's benefits from one or more criminal offences are or may be used to secure that funds are placed at that person's disposal, or are or may be used to acquire property by way of investment for him.

(4) If on such an application the Court is satisfied -

(a) that access to the material in question is necessary for the purposes stated by the inspector or the officer of the Authority making the application; and also

(b) that it is in the public interest that that access should be given, then the Court may make an order that the person who appears to the Court to be in possession of the material shall -

(aa) produce it to the inspector or an officer of the Authority for him to take away; or

(bb) otherwise give him access to it, within such period as is specified in the order.

(5) The period to be specified in an order under subsection (4) is seven days unless it appears to the Court that a longer or shorter period would be appropriate in the circumstances.

(6) Where the Court makes an order under paragraph (bb) of subsection (4) in relation to material on any premises, it may, on the application of an inspector or an officer of the Authority, order any person who appears to the Court to be entitled to grant entry to the premises to allow the inspector or an officer of the Authority to enter the premises to obtain access to the material.

(7) Where material which is sought under section 15 or 16 or this section is contained in a computer -

(a) an obligation under any of those sections to give access to the material has effect as an obligation to give access to it in a form in which it is visible and legible; and

(b) an obligation under any of those sections to produce the material has effect as an obligation to produce it in a form in which it is visible and legible and can be taken away.

(8) Any right that an inspector or the Authority or an officer of the Authority has, or may be given, under section 15 or 16 or this section -

(a) does not include any right to access to, or production of, items subject to legal privilege;

(b) has effect notwithstanding, and overrides, any obligation as to secrecy or other restriction upon the disclosure of information, being an obligation or restriction imposed by statute or otherwise.

(9) In subsection (8), "items subject to legal privilege" means -

(a) communications between a professional legal adviser and his client made in connection with the giving of legal advice to the client; and

(b) communications between a professional legal adviser and his client or between such an adviser and any other person made in connection with or in contemplation of legal proceedings and for the purpose of such proceedings,

when they are in possession of a person who is entitled to possession of them.

(10) Items held with the intention of furthering a criminal purpose are not items subject to legal privilege.

Company may be wound up in certain cases.

18.(1) After receipt of a report from the Authority under subsection (2) of section 10 or from an inspector under subsection (1) of section 15, the Minister may, if he considers that a trust company or any of its officers, employees or agents has or have knowingly or wilfully done anything in contravention of this Act or of a requirement of, or a condition attached to, the company's licence, direct the Authority to petition the Supreme Court for the winding up of the company.

(2) A copy of any petition made under subsection (1) shall be served on the company not less than seven clear days before the day set by the Court for the hearing of the petition.

(3) If the Court, on the hearing of any such petition, is satisfied that any of the allegations in the petition are well founded, then the Court may do all or any of the following -

(a) make an order for the winding up of the company;

(b) impose a fine not exceeding $2,000 on the company;

(c) impose a fine not exceeding $2,000 on any officer, employee or agent of the company whom the Court determines to be culpable, as the circumstances in the Court's opinion warrant.

(4) The Court may, after hearing representations from the Authority or the liquidator or any other person appearing to the Court to be affected, include in a winding-up order made under paragraph (a) of subsection (3) provision that all or any of the trusts which the company was administering before the making of the winding-up order shall, notwithstanding anything to the contrary in any such trust, be transferred to a new trustee for administration by him; and, where such provision is made, the Court may make or give such supplemental or incidental orders or directions as the Court deems necessary or expedient to be made or given for giving effect to any such transfer.

(5) Where the Court makes an order for the winding up of a company under paragraph (a) or subsection (3), the company shall be wound up in the same manner and by the same procedure as if the circumstances leading to the making of the order were the same as those leading to the making of a winding-up order under section 161 of the Companies Act.

Other measures against a company.

19.(1) After receipt of a report from the Authority under subsection (2) of section 10 or from an inspector under subsection (1) of section 15, the Minister may, if he considers that a trust company or any of its officers, employees or agents has or have been or is or are carrying on the company's affairs in a manner detrimental to one or more of the company's creditors or members or to the public interest, subject to subsection (2) of this section by notice in writing require the company to take such measures as the Minister considers necessary to be taken in relation to those affairs.

(2) Where any requirement made by the Minister under subsection (1) will, in the opinion of the company of which the requirement has been made, involve modifying any disposition or arrangement made or called for by a trust that the company is administering, then the company need not comply with that requirement unless the Supreme Court has sanctioned the modification; and that Court has jurisdiction to give such sanction, and in the exercise of that jurisdiction to make or give such supplemental or incidental orders or directions as the Court may deem necessary or expedient upon application being made to the Court for the purpose either by the Authority or by the company in question.

(3) Any cost or expense consequential on, or incidental to, a modification by the Court under subsection (2), and the costs of proceedings taken on an application made by the Authority or the company under that subsection, shall be borne by the company unless the Court orders otherwise.

Cancellation of licences.

20. The Minister may, subject to the provisions of this section and sections 22 and 23, in writing cancel the licence of a trust company -

(a) at the request of the company: or

(b) upon any one or more of the following grounds, namely -

(i) that the company has ceased to carry on trust business;

(ii) that the company has contravened a requirement of, or a condition attached to, its licence, or a requirement made of it by or under this Act:

(iii) that the company is insolvent;

(iv) that the company is carrying on business in a manner detrimental to one or more of the company's creditors or members or to the public interest.

Variation of licences.

21. The Minister may, subject to the provisions of this section and sections 22 and 23, in writing vary the licence of a trust company -

(a) at the request of the company; or

(b) upon any one or more of the following grounds, namely -

(i) that the company has contravened a requirement of, or a condition attached to, its licence, or a requirement made of the company by or under this Act:

(ii) that the company is insolvent;

(iii) that the company is carrying on business in a manner detrimental to one or more of the company's creditors or members or to the public interest.

Preconditions to cancelling or varying a licence.

22.(1) The Minister shall, before he cancels a licence under paragraph (b) of section 20 or varies a licence under paragraph (b) of section 21 -

(a) give the company notice in writing of the ground or grounds on which he intends to do so:

(b) afford the company an opportunity to make objection in writing within the period of thirty days after receipt of the notice; and

(c) take any such objection into consideration;

and, if the Minister decides to cancel or vary a licence, he shall cause the instrument cancelling or varying the licence to be served on the company.

(2) The Minister shall not cancel or vary a licence without first consulting the Authority about the cancellation or variation.

(3) Before the Minister cancels a licence under paragraph (a) or (b) of section 20, he shall also consider whether there is a case in the public interest for all or any of the trusts that the company has been administering to be transferred, notwithstanding anything to the contrary in any such trust, to a new trustee for administration by him, and, if the Minister so determines, he shall direct the Authority to petition the Supreme Court for that purpose; and in such a case the Court, after hearing representations from the Authority or any other person appearing to the Court to be affected, has the same power to order a transfer of any such trust, and in that connection to make or give supplemental or incidental orders or directions, as the Court has under subsection (4) of section 18 in the case of a winding-up under section 18.

(4) Subject to section 23, the cancellation or variation of a company's licence takes effect on the expiration of the period of twenty-one days beginning on the date of service on the company of the instrument cancelling or varying the licence.

Appeals.

23.(1) An existing company may appeal to the Supreme Court if the Minister -

(a) in the exercise of his powers under sections 5 and 6 refuses to grant the company a licence; or

(b) in the exercise of his powers under section 7 grants the company a licence subject to conditions.

(2) A trust company may appeal to the Supreme Court against the cancellation of its licence under paragraph (b) of section 20 or against the variation of its licence under paragraph (b) of section 21.

(3) The bringing of an appeal under subsection (2) of this section suspends the cancellation or variation appealed against pending the determination or abandonment of the appeal.

(4) An appeal under this section must be brought -

(a) where it is brought under subsection (1), within twenty-one days of the day provided for in subsection (2) of section 30;

(b) where it is brought under subsection (2), within twenty-one days of the date on which the instrument cancelling or varying the company's licence was served on the company.

(5) On an appeal under this section, the Supreme Court may confirm, vary or reverse the decision of the Minister and exercise any power that he could have exercised under this Act in the matter under appeal.

Grant, cancellation and variation of licences to be gazetted.

24. The Minister shall publish in the Gazette in such form as he thinks fit notice of every grant, cancellation or variation of a licence under this Act.

False documents or information.

25.(1) Any person who, for any purposes of this Act -

(a) issues a document, or supplies information, which is false or misleading in a material respect; or

(b) signs a document which is false or misleading in a material respect; or

(c) takes part in the preparation or issue of a document, or the supplying of information, which is false in a material respect, commits an offence against this Act unless he proves -

(aa) if an individual, that he had no knowledge of the falsity or misleading character of the document or information, and took every reasonable precaution to ensure its accuracy; and

(bb) if not an individual, that every person acting on his behalf had no such knowledge, and took every such reasonable precaution, as aforesaid.

Offences.

26.(1) A person who fails to comply with a duty or prohibition imposed upon him by or under a provision to which this section applies commits an offence against this Act.

(2) The provisions to which this section applies are those of: section 3; subsection (1) of section 12; subsection (2) of section 15: subsection (1) of section 16; and section 19.

Punishment of offences.

27. A person who commits an offence against this Act is liable -

(a) on summary conviction, to a fine not exceeding $5,000 or to imprisonment for a period not exceeding twelve months, or to both such fine and imprisonment;

(b) on conviction on indictment, to a fine not exceeding $15,000 or to imprisonment for a term not exceeding three years or to both such fine and imprisonment.

Offences by corporations.

28. Where a body corporate is guilty of an offence against this Act and the offence is proved to have been committed with the consent or connivance of, or to be attributable to neglect on the part of, a director, manager, secretary or other similar functionary of the body corporate, or a person who was purporting to act in any such capacity, he, as well as the body corporate, shall be guilty of that offence and liable to be proceeded against and punished accordingly.

Amendment of other laws.

29.(1) The Third Schedule to the Bermuda Monetary Authority Act 1969 is amended by adding the words "Trust Company (as defined in the Trust Companies Act 1991)" to the entities listed there.

(2) The definition of "trust corporation" in section 1 of the Administration of Estates Act 1974 is amended by deleting the words "entitled under the rules to act as trustee" and substituting the words "licensed as a trust company under the Trust Companies Act 1991".

(3) The Non-Contentious Probate (Designation of Trust Corporations) Rules 1974, made under section 57 of the Administration of Estates Act 1974, are revoked.

Commencement, transitional and saving.

30.(1) Subject to this section, this Act commences on such day as the Minister may appoint by notice published in the Gazette.

(2) Subject to subsection (3), in relation to existing companies this Act commences on the expiration of one year beginning on commencement day.

(3) Section 4 does not apply to, or in relation to -

(a) a business that was using the word "Trust" or "trust" or "Trustee" or "trustee", or any grammatical variation of any of those words, in its name immediately before the day on which this Act was passed; or

(b) a business that is a unit trust scheme, whether that scheme was established before, or is established on or after, commencement day; and for this purpose "unit trust scheme" has the meaning given to it by section 1 of the Stamp Duties Act 1976

FIRST SCHEDULE

(Section 6(2))

MINIMUM CRITERIA FOR A LICENCE

1. The company's objects and powers encompass the carrying on of -

(a) trust business; and

(b) all activities necessary for, or necessarily incidental to, the carrying on of trust business.

2. The company has a paid-up share capital of $250,000.

3. The company has adequate insurance.

4. The company has premises adequate for the company's business.

5. The company has available to it (whether directly employed or available through other arrangements) sufficient personnel with adequate knowledge, skill and experience necessary for the conduct of the company's business.

6. The company has an approved auditor.

SECOND SCHEDULE

(Section 12(2)(a))

TRUST COMPANY CERTIFICATE OF MANAGEMENT

THE TRUST COMPANIES ACT 1991

To: The General Manager

The Bermuda Monetary Authority

As Chief Executive Officer and Director of [name of trust company] ("the Company"), we certify, in respect of the financial year ended [date], as follows -

1. This Certificate is given pursuant to section 12 of the Trust Companies Act 1991.
2. The Company complied with every condition and requirement of its licence.
3. The Company at all times kept property and records relating to the trusts of which it was trustee duly separate from property and records not so relating.
4. The company at all times had in place procedures for ensuring that all persons involved in the carrying on of its trust business had adequate training and experience. and were adequately supervised.
5. The Company caused proper records to be kept for each trust of which it was trustee.
6. The affairs of each trust of which the Company was trustee were conducted lawfully.

Chief Executive ________________________

Officer (signature)

________________________ ____________

(typed name) (date)

____

Director (signature)

________________________ ____________

(typed name) (date)

THIRD SCHEDULE

(Section 14(4))

APPROVED AUDITOR'S REPORT

THE TRUST COMPANIES ACT 1991

To: The General Manager

The Bermuda Monetary Authority

1. This Report is made pursuant to section 14(4) of the Trust Companies Act 1991 ("the Act") in respect of [name of trust company] ("the Company").

2. In the course of the audit of the financial statements of the Company for the financial year ended [date] that I conducted pursuant to section 14(1) of the Act, nothing came to my attention that caused me to conclude that any statement in the certificate of management given on behalf of the Company in respect of that year is inaccurate or unreasonable in any material respect.*

____

(signature)

______________________ ____________

(typed name) (date)

Approved Auditor

*This statement should be modified, and particulars given in a schedule to this Report, as may be necessary.

THE PERPETUITIES AND ACCUMULATIONS ACT 1989

(as amended, 1998)

ARRANGEMENT OF SECTIONS

PRELIMINARY

PERPETUITIES

ACCUMULATIONS

Short title and commencement.

1. This Act may be cited as the Perpetuities and Accumulations Act 1989 and shall come into operation on such date as the Premier may appoint by notice published in the Gazette.

PRELIMINARY

Interpretation.

2.(1) In this Act, unless the context otherwise requires -

"disposition" includes the conferring of a power of appointment and any other disposition of an interest in or right over property, and references to the interest disposed of shall be construed accordingly;

"in being" means living or en ventre sa mere;

"power of appointment" includes any discretionary power to transfer a beneficial interest in property without the furnishing of valuable consideration;

"will" includes a codicil.

(2) For the purposes of this Act a disposition contained in a will shall be deemed to be made at the death of the testator.

(3) For the purposes of this Act a person shall be treated as a member of the class if in his case all the conditions identifying a member of the class are satisfied, and shall be treated as a potential member if in his case some only of those conditions are satisfied but there is a possibility that the remainder will in time be satisfied.

PERPETUITIES

Power to specify perpetuity period.

3.(1) Subject to section 11(3) and subsection (2) of this section, where the instrument by which any disposition is made so provides, the perpetuity period applicable to the disposition under the rule against perpetuities, instead of being of any other duration, shall be of a duration equal to such number of years not exceeding one hundred as is specified in that behalf in the instrument.

(2) Subsection (1) shall not have effect where the disposition is made in exercise of a special power of appointment, but where a period is specified under that subsection in the instrument creating such a power the period shall apply in relation to any disposition under the power as it applies in relation to the power itself.

Presumptions and evidence as to future parenthood.

4.(1) Where in any proceedings there arises on the rule against perpetuities a question which turns on the ability of a person to have a child at some future time, then -

(a) subject to paragraph (b), it shall be presumed that a male can have a child at the age of fourteen years or over, but not under that age, and that a female can have a child at the age of twelve years or over, but not under that age or over the age of fifty-five years; but

(b) in the case of a living person evidence may be given to show that he or she will or will not be able to have a child at the time in question.

(2) Where any such question referred to in subsection (1) is decided by treating a person as unable to have a child at a particular time, and he or she does so, the Supreme Court may make such order as it thinks fit for placing the persons interested in the property comprised in the disposition, so far as may be just, in the position they would have held if the question had not been so decided.

(3) Subject to subsection (2), where any such question referred to in subsection (1) is decided in relation to a disposition by treating a person as able or unable to have a child at a particular time, then he or she shall be so treated for the purpose of any question which may arise on the rule against perpetuities in relation to the same disposition in any subsequent proceedings.

(4) In the provisions of this section references to having a child are references to be getting or giving birth to a child, but those provisions (except subsection (1)(b)) shall apply in relation to the possibility that a person will at any time have a child by adoption, legitimation or other means as they apply to his or her ability at that time to beget or give birth to a child.

Uncertainty as to remoteness.

5.(1) Where, apart from the provisions of this section and section 6 and 7, a disposition would be void on the ground that the interest disposed of might not become vested until too remote a time, the disposition shall be treated, until such time (if any) as it becomes established that the vesting must occur, if at all, after the end of the perpetuity period, as if the disposition were not subject to the rule against perpetuities; and its becoming so established shall not affect the validity of anything previously done in relation to the interest disposed of by way of advancement, application of intermediate income or otherwise.

(2) Where, apart from the provisions of subsection (1), a disposition consisting of the conferring of a general power of appointment would be void on the ground that the power might not become exercisable until too remote a time, the disposition shall be treated, until such time (if any) as it becomes established that the power will not be exercisable within the perpetuity period, as if the disposition were not subject to the rule against perpetuities.

(3) Where, apart from the provisions of subsection (1), a disposition consisting of the conferring of any power, option or other right would be void on the ground that the right might be exercised at too remote a time, the disposition shall be treated as regards any exercise of the right within the perpetuity period as if it were not subject to the rule against perpetuities and, subject to the said provisions, shall be treated as void for remoteness only if, and so far as, the right is not fully exercised within that period.

(4) Where this section applies to a disposition and the duration of the perpetuity period is not determined by virtue of section 3 or 11(3), it shall be determined as follows:

(a) where any persons falling within subsection (5) are individuals in being and ascertainable at the commencement of the perpetuity period the duration of the period shall be determined by reference to their lives and no others, but so that the lives of any description of persons falling within paragraph (b) or (c) of that subsection shall be disregarded if the number of persons of that description is such as to render it impracticable to ascertain the date of death of the survivor;

(b) where there are no lives under paragraph (a) the period shall be twenty-one years.

(5) The said persons are as follows:

(a) the person by whom the disposition was made;

(b) a person to whom or in whose favour the disposition was made, that is to say -

(i) in the case of a disposition to a class of persons, any member or potential member of the class;

(ii) in the case of an individual disposition to a person taking only on certain conditions being satisfied, any person as to whom some of the conditions are satisfied and the remainder may in time be satisfied;

(iii) in the case of a special power of appointment exercisable in favour of members of a class, any member or potential member of the class;

(iv) in the case of a special power of appointment exercisable in favour of one person only, that person or, where the object of the power is ascertainable only on certain conditions being satisfied, any person as to whom some of the conditions are satisfied and the remainder may in time be satisfied;

(v) in the case of any power, option or other right, the person on whom the right is conferred;

(c) a person having a child or grandchild within subparagraphs (i) to (iv) of paragraph (b), or any of whose children or grandchildren, if subsequently born, would by virtue of his or her descent fall within those subparagraphs;

(d) any person on the failure or determination of whose prior interest the disposition is limited to take effect.

Reduction of age and exclusion of class members to avoid remoteness.

6.(1) Where a disposition is limited by reference to the attainment by any person or persons of a specified age exceeding twenty-one years, and it is apparent at the time the disposition is made or becomes apparent at a subsequent time -

(a) that the disposition would, apart from this section, be void for remoteness, but

(b) that it would not be so void if the specified age had been twenty-one years,

the disposition shall be treated for all purposes as if, instead of being limited by reference to the age in fact specified, it had been limited by reference to the age nearest to that age which would, if specified instead, have prevented the disposition from being so void.

(2) Where in the case of any disposition ages exceeding twenty-one years are specified in relation to different persons -

(a) the reference in paragraph (b) of subsection (1)(b) to the specified age shall be construed as a reference to all the specified ages, and

(b) that subsection shall operate to reduce each such age so far as is necessary to save the disposition from being void for remoteness.

(3) Where the inclusion of any persons, being potential members of a class or unborn persons who at birth would become members or potential members of the class, prevents the foregoing provisions of this section from operating to save disposition from being void for remoteness, those persons shall thenceforth be deemed for all purposes of the disposition to be excluded from the class, and the said provisions shall thereupon have effect accordingly.

(4) Where, in the case of a disposition to which subsection (3) does not apply, it is apparent at the time the disposition is made or becomes apparent at a subsequent time that, apart from this subsection, the inclusion of any persons, being potential members of a class or unborn persons who at birth would become members or potential members of the class, would cause the disposition to be treated as void for remoteness, those persons shall, unless their exclusion would exhaust the class, thenceforth be deemed for all the purposes of the disposition to be excluded from the class.

(5) Where this section has effect in relation to a disposition to which section 5 applies, the operation of this section shall not affect the validity of anything previously done in relation to the interest disposed of by way of advancement, application of intermediate income or otherwise.

Condition relating to death of surviving spouse.

7. Where a disposition is limited by reference to the time of death of the survivor of a person in being at the commencement of the perpetuity period and any spouse of that person, and that time has not arrived at the end of the perpetuity period, the disposition shall be treated for all purposes, where to do so would save it from being void for remoteness, as if it had instead been limited by reference to the time immediately before the end of that period.

Saving and acceleration of expectant interest.

8. A disposition shall not be treated as void for remoteness by reason only that the interest disposed of is ulterior to and dependent upon an interest under a disposition which is so void, and the vesting of an interest shall not be prevented from being accelerated on the failure of a prior interest by reason only that the failure arises because of remoteness.

Powers of appointment.

9. For the purposes of the rule against perpetuities, a power of appointment shall be treated as a special power unless -

(a) in the instrument creating the power it is expressed to be exercisable by one person only, and

(b) it could, at all times during its currency when that person is of full age and capacity, be exercised by him so as immediately to transfer to himself the whole of the interest governed by the power without the consent of any other person or compliance with any other condition, not being a formal condition relating only to the mode of exercise of the power.

Provided that for the purpose of determining whether a disposition made under a power of appointment exercisable by will only is void for remoteness, the power shall be treated as a general power where it would have fallen to be so treated if exercisable by deed.

Administrative powers of trustees.

10.(1) The rule against perpetuities shall not operate to invalidate a power conferred on trustees or other persons to sell, lease, exchange or otherwise dispose of any property for full consideration, or to do any other act in the administration (as opposed to the distribution) of any property, and shall not prevent the payment to trustees of other persons of reasonable remuneration for their services.

(2) Subsection (1) shall apply for the purpose of enabling a power to be exercised at any time the commencement of this Act notwithstanding that the power is conferred by an instrument which took effect before the commencement.

Options relating to land.

11.(1) The rule against perpetuities shall not apply to a disposition consisting of the conferring of an option for valuable consideration an interest reversionary (whether directly or indirectly) on the term of a lease if -

(a) the option is exercisable only by the lessee or his successors in title, and

(b) it ceases to be exercisable at or before the expiration of one year following the determination of the lease.

(2) This subsection applies in relation to an agreement for a lease as it applies in relation to a lease, and "lessee" shall be construed accordingly.

(3) In the case of a disposition consisting of the conferring of an option to acquire for valuable consideration any interest in land, the perpetuity period under the rule against perpetuities shall be twenty-one years, and section 3 does not apply; however, this subsection does not apply to a right of pre-emption conferred on a government or municipal authority or statutory corporation in respect of land used or to be used for religious purposes where the right becomes exercisable only if the land ceases to be used for such purposes.

Avoidance of contractual and other rights in cases of remoteness.

12. Where a disposition inter vivos would fall to be treated as void for remoteness if the rights and duties thereunder were capable of transmission to persons other than the original parties and had been so transmitted, it shall be treated as void as between the person by whom it was made and the person to whom or in whose favour it was made or any successor of his, and no remedy shall lie in contract or otherwise for giving effect to it or making restitution for its lack of effect.

Possibilities of resulting trust conditions subsequent, exceptions and reservations.

13.(1) In the case of a possibility of a resulting trust on the determination of any determinable interest in property the rule against perpetuities shall apply in relation to the provision causing the interest to be determinable as it would apply if that provision were expressed in the form of a condition subsequent giving rise, on breach thereof, to a right of re-entry or an equivalent right in the case of property other than land, and where the provision falls to be treated as void for remoteness the determinable interest shall become an absolute interest.

(2) Where a disposition is subject to any such provision, or to any such condition subsequent, or to any exception or reservation, the disposition shall be treated for the purposes of this Act as including a separate disposition of any rights arising by virtue of the provision, condition subsequent, exception or reservation.

Restrictions on perpetuity rule.

14. The rule of law relating to perpetuities does not apply and shall be deemed never to have applied -

(a) to any power to take possession of land or the income thereof given by way of indemnity against a rent, whether charged upon or payable in respect of any part of that land or not; or

(b) to any grant, exception, or reservation of any right of entry on, or user of, the surface of land or of any easements, rights, or privileges over or under land for the purpose of -

(i) executing repairs, alterations, or additions to any adjoining land, or the buildings and erections thereon;

(ii) constructing, laying down, altering, repairing, renewing, cleansing and maintaining any works.

ACCUMULATIONS

Accumulations of income.

15.(1) Where property is settled or disposed of in such manner that the income thereof may or must be accumulated wholly or in part, the power or discretion to accumulate that income is valid if the disposition of the accumulated income is or may be valid, but not otherwise.

(2) Nothing in this section affects the rights of any person or persons to terminate an accumulation that is for his or their benefit, or any jurisdiction or power of the court to direct payments from accumulations pursuant to any statute.

Right to stop accumulations.

16. Section 4 applies to any question as to the right of beneficiaries to put an end to accumulations of income under any disposition as it applies to questions arising on the rule against perpetuities.

Application.

17.(1) Subject to section 12A of the Trusts (Special Provisions) Act 1989 nothing in this Act shall affect the operation of the rule of law rendering void for remoteness certain dispositions under which property is limited to be applied for purposes other than the benefit of any person or class of persons in cases where the property may be so applied after the end of the perpetuity period.

(2) This Act shall apply (except as provided in section 10(2)) only in relation to instruments taking effect after the commencement of this Act, and in the case of an instrument made in the exercise of a special power of appointment shall apply only where the instrument creating the power takes effect after that commencement, however, section 9 shall apply in all cases for construing the foregoing reference to a special power of appointment.

(3) This Act shall apply in relation to a disposition made otherwise than by an instrument as if the disposition had been contained in an instrument taking effect when the disposition was made.

(4) This Act binds the Crown.

Amendment of Pension Trust Funds Act 1966, Title 17 Item 39.

18. Section 7 of the Pension Trust Funds Act, 1966 is amended by inserting immediately after the word “registered” the word “unregistered”.

THE INSURANCE ACT, 1978

(as amended)

ARRANGEMENT OF SECTIONS

Part X - Miscellaneous

WHEREAS it is expedient to regulate the carrying on of insurance business in or from Bermuda; to provide for the registration of insurers and other persons engaged in that business; and to provide for matters connected with, or incidental to, the matters aforesaid:

Be it enacted by The Queen's Most Excellent Majesty, by and with the advice and consent of the Legislative Council and the House of Assembly of Bermuda, and by the authority of the same, as follows:-

PART I - Preliminary

Interpretation.

1.(1) In this Act, unless the context otherwise requires -

"actuary" means a person qualified as an actuary by examination of the Institute of Actuaries in England or the Faculty of Actuaries in Scotland or the Society of Actuaries in the United States of America or Canada, or a person recognized by the Minister as an actuary;

"association of underwriters" means an association of individual underwriters, organized according to the system known as Lloyd's whereby each underwriting member of the association becomes liable for a separate and proportionate part of the sum secured by each policy subscribed to by that association; and, in relation to such an association as aforesaid, "recognized" means recognized by the Minister;

"auditor" means either -

(a) a person entitled to practise as a public accountant in Bermuda; or

(b) a person who has qualified as an accountant by examination of one of the Institutes of Chartered Accountants of England and Wales, Ireland and Scotland or the Canadian Institute of Chartered Accountants or the American Institute of Certified Public Accountants; or

(c) a person recognized by the Minister as an auditor;

"bank" means a bank licensed under the Banks Act 1969;

"the Court" means the Supreme Court;

"domestic business" means insurance business where, whether the contract of insurance is made in Bermuda or elsewhere, the subject-matter of the contract is either -

(a) property that at the time of the making of the contract is in, or in transit to or from Bermuda; or

(b) the life, safety, fidelity or insurable interest of an individual who at the time of the making of the contract is ordinarily resident in Bermuda; or

(c) a risk of a company formed in Bermuda that is not an exempted company within the definition of that expression in section 1 of the Exempted Companies Act 1950;

"excepted long-term business" means either -

(a) credit life business, that is to say, the business of effecting and carrying out contracts of insurance against risks of loss to persons arising from the non-payment of debts due to such persons by reason of the death of debtors of theirs, being contracts that are -

(i) not contracts of domestic business; and

(ii) expressed to be in effect for a period of five years or less; and

(iii) not either automatically renewable or convertible into contracts of insurance of any other kind or for any different period; and

(iv) of a kind which the Minister, upon application made to him by the insurer for the purpose, has given his prior approval in writing for the insurer to effect and carry out; or

(b) employee group business, that is to say, the business of effecting and carrying out contracts of insurance on the lives of employees of the insurer or of an affiliate (within the definition of "affiliate" in regulation 2 of the Insurance Accounts Regulations 1980) of the insurer, being contracts that are -

(i) not contracts of domestic business; and

(ii) expressed to be in effect for a period of five years or less; and

(iii) not either automatically renewable or convertible into contracts of insurance of any other kind or for any different period; and

(iv) made on a group insurance basis; and

(v) of a kind which the Minister, upon application made to him by the insurer for the purpose, has given his prior approval in writing for the insurer to effect and carry out.

"financial year", in relation to an insurer, means the period not exceeding fifty-three weeks at the end of which the balance of the insurer's accounts is struck or, if no such balance is struck or if a period in excess of fifty-three weeks is employed, then calendar year;

"functions" includes powers and duties;

"general business" means, subject to subsection (4), insurance business that is not long-term business;

"insolvent" means, in relation to an insurer at any relevant date, that if proceedings had been taken for the winding up of the insurer the Court could, in accordance with the provisions of sections 222 and 223 of the Winding Up Act, hold or have held that the insurer was at that date unable to pay its debts;

"inspector" means a person appointed as an inspector under section 30;

"Insurance Advisory Committee" means the Insurance Advisory Committee established by section 2;

"insurance agent" means a person who with the authority of an insurer acts on its behalf in relation to any or all of the following matters, that is to say, the initiation and receipt of proposals, the issue of policies and the collection of premiums, being proposals, policies and premiums relating to insurance business;

"insurance broker" means a person who arranges or places insurance business with insurers on behalf of prospective or existing policy-holders;

"insurance business" means the business of effecting and carrying out contracts -

(a) protecting persons against loss or liability to loss in respect of risks to which such persons may be exposed; or

(b) to pay a sum of money or render money's worth upon the happening of an event,

and includes re-insurance business;

"insurance manager" means a person who, not being an employee of any insurer, holds himself out as a manager in relation to one or more insurers, whether or not the functions performed by him as such go beyond the keeping of insurance business accounts and records;

"insurance salesman" means a person who otherwise than as an employee solicits applications for, or negotiates, insurance business on behalf of an insurer or an insurance broker or agent;

"insurer" means a person carrying on insurance business;

"long-term business" means, subject to subsection (4), insurance business of any of the following kinds, namely, -

(a) effecting and carrying out contracts of insurance on human life or contracts to pay annuities on human life;

(b) effecting and carrying out contracts of insurance against risks of the persons insured sustaining injury as the result of an accident or of an accident of a specified class or dying as the result of an accident or of an accident of a specified class or becoming incapacitated or dying in consequence of disease or disease of a specified class, being contracts that are expressed to be in effect for a period of not less than five years or without limit of time and either not expressed to be terminable by the insurer before the expiration of five years from the taking effect thereof or are expressed to be so terminable before the expiration of that period only in special circumstances therein mentioned;

(c) effecting and carrying out contracts of insurance, whether effected by the issue of policies, bonds or endowment certificates or otherwise, whereby in return for one or more premiums paid to the insurer a sum or a series of sums is to become payable to the persons insured in the future, not being contracts such as fall within either paragraph (a) or (b), but does not include excepted long-term business;

"Minister" means the Minister of Finance;

"non-resident insurance undertaking" means an insurer carrying on domestic business under a permit granted under section 3 of the Non-Resident Insurance Undertakings Act 1967;

"prescribed" means prescribed by regulations;

"to register" means to register under this Act;

"Register" means the Register for which provision is made in subsection (1) of section 13;

"Registrar" means the Registrar of Companies;

"regulations" means regulations made under section 53;

"statutory financial return" means the return provided for in section 18;

"statutory financial statements" means the accounts provided for in section 15.

(2) References in this Act to "the Winding Up Act" are references to the Companies (Winding Up) Act 1977, and references to a section of the Winding Up Act are references to the similarly numbered section of the Companies Act 1948 of the United Kingdom as adopted (subject, where modified, to modification) in Bermuda by the Winding Up Act.

(3) It is hereby declared for the avoidance of doubt that in this Act -

(a) any reference to carrying on business from within Bermuda includes reference to carrying on business outside Bermuda from a principal place of business within Bermuda;

(b) unless the context otherwise requires, any reference to carrying on the business of effecting and carrying out contracts of any kind includes reference to carrying on one aspect, or some aspects, only of that business;

(c) every company or body, being a company or body formed in Bermuda with power to carry on insurance business, shall, if carrying on insurance business anywhere, be deemed to be carrying on insurance business in or from within Bermuda for the purposes of subsection (1) of section 3.

(4) The limitations upon the meaning of "general business" and "long-term business" as defined in subsection (1) of this section shall, in relation to any insurer, not operate to disentitle that insurer

(a) if authorized to carry on general business, from carrying on long-term business; or

(b) if authorized to carry on long-term business, from carrying on general business, being -

(aa) in the case set forth in paragraph (a), long-term business as to which the Minister has given a direction under section 56 on the ground that he is satisfied that that long-term business either is or will be only incidental to the insurer's general business, or is or will be of such a limited extent that the insurer ought not to be treated in all respects as a composite within the definition of "composite" in regulation 2 of the Insurance Accounts Regulations 1930, or

(bb) in the case set forth in paragraph (b), general business as to which the Minister has given a corresponding direction *mutatis mutandis*.

Insurance Advisory Committee.

2.(1) There shall be a committee, to be known as "the Insurance Advisory Committee" for the purpose of advising the Minister on matters connected with the discharge of his functions under this Act.

(2) The Insurance Advisory Committee shall consist of such persons (not fewer than five in number) to be appointed by the Minister, as the Minister may think fit, but so that not fewer than three members of the Committee shall be persons appearing to the Minister to be knowledgeable about insurance business in Bermuda.

(3) The Minister shall appoint a person to be chairman of the Insurance Advisory Committee.

(4) It shall be the duty of the Insurance Advisory Committee to advise the Minister on any matter which he is required or permitted by or under this Act to refer to them, or which, being a matter such as is mentioned in subsection (1), he may otherwise refer to them, and they may also of their own motion make representations to the Minister as respects any such matter as is mentioned in that subsection; and the Minister shall take into account any such advice or representations that the Committee may tender or make to him.

PART II - Registration

Insurers

Insurers to be registered.

3.(1) Subject to the provisions of this Act, and notwithstanding anything in any other Act, no person shall carry on insurance business in or from within Bermuda unless he is registered by the Minister as an insurer under section 4.

(2) Any person who contravenes subsection (1) shall be guilty of an offence.

Minister may register insurers.

4.(1) Subject to sections 5 to 7 and 12, the Minister may, on application being made to him for that purpose by a body corporate, and upon payment of the relevant fee provided for by section 14, register that body as an insurer subject to it complying with such conditions as the Minister may see fit to impose.

(2) Every application under subsection (1) for registration shall be made to the Registrar in the prescribed form.

Factors to be considered in relation to such registration.

5.(1) In considering whether to register a body as an insurer, the Minister shall (but without prejudice to his discretion under section 12 to refuse registration on any grounds) have regard to whether the body appears to him to be a fit and proper body to be engaged in insurance business, and to the following additional considerations -

(a) whether the body has, or has available, adequate knowledge and expertise;

(b) whether any person to be concerned in the management of the business is a fit and proper person to be so concerned;

(c) whether the premises intended to be used in the business are adequate for the conduct of the business.

Margin of solvency

6.(1) The Minister shall not register a body under section 4 unless he is satisfied that the value of its assets exceeds the amount of its liabilities by the prescribed amount.

(2) For the purposes of this section the value of any assets and the amount of any liabilities shall, subject to subsection (3), be determined in accordance with any applicable regulations.

(3) The amount of the liabilities of the long-term business of a body at any time shall, for the purposes of this section, be taken to be -

(a) an amount equal to the total amount at that time standing to the credit of the fund or funds maintained by the body in respect of its long-term business; or

(b) the amount of those liabilities at that time as determined in accordance with any applicable regulations, whichever is the greater.

Paid up share capital.

7. The Minister shall not register a body which has a share capital unless the amount paid up on the share capital -

(a) in a case where the body proposes to carry on general business but not long-term business, is $120,000 or more;

(b) in a case where the body proposes to carry on long-term business but not general business, is $250,000 or more;

(c) in a case where the body proposes to carry on both long-term business and general business, is $370,000 or more.

Principal office and principal representative.

8.(1) Every insurer shall maintain a principal office in Bermuda.

(1A) Every insurer shall appoint and maintain a principal representative in Bermuda who satisfies the requirements of subsection (1B).

(1B) A principal representative of an insurer shall be either -

(a) a registered insurance manager; or

(b) a person approved by the Minister as that insurer's principal representative.

(2) An insurer at the time of registration shall give notice in writing to the Registrar -

(a) of the location of its principal office; and

(b) of the prescribed particulars of its principal representative, its insurance manager (if it has one), its approved auditor and any other prescribed person to be engaged or employed in, or in connection with, its business.

(3) If any information required by subsection (2) to be notified to the Registrar is altered, the insurer shall give in writing to the Registrar particulars of the alteration within twenty-one days after the alteration is made.

(3A) Without a reason acceptable to the Minister -

(a) an insurer shall not terminate the appointment of its principal representative; and

(b) a principal representative shall not cease to act as such, unless it or he gives thirty days notice in writing to the Minister of the intention to do so.

(4) An insurer shall maintain in its principal office an accurate list of all its insurance agents in Bermuda and, if required in writing at any time by the Registrar so to do, shall provide him with a copy of that list.

(5) If an insurer fails to comply with any of subsections (1) to (3A), or with a requirement made of it under subsection (4), it shall be guilty of an offence.

(6) If a principal representative wilfully fails to give to the Minister notice which he is required by subsection (3A) to give, he shall be guilty of an offence.

Principal representative to report certain events.

8A.(1) It shall be the duty of the principal representative within thirty days of -

(a) his reaching the view that there is a likelihood of the insurer for which he acts becoming insolvent; or

(b) its coming to his knowledge, or his having reason to believe, that an event to which this section applies has occurred, to make a report in writing to the Minister setting out all the particulars of the case that are available to him.

(2) As respects any principal representative, this section applies to the following events, being events in which the insurer for which he acts as principal representative is involved, that is to say -

(a) failure by the insurer -

(i) to comply substantially with a condition imposed upon the insurer by the Minister relating to a solvency margin or a liquidity or other ratio;

(ii) to comply in any respect with any other such condition not so relating;

(b) an offence by the insurer against subsection (8) of section 20 or subsection (5) of section 21 or subsection (5) of section 22;

(c) failure by the insurer to comply with a modified provision, or with a condition, being a provision or condition specified in a direction given to the insurer by the Minister in the exercise of his powers under section 56;

(d) involvement of the insurer in any criminal proceedings whether in Bermuda or abroad;

(e) the insurer's ceasing to carry on insurance business in or from within Bermuda.

(3) A principal representative who fails to perform his duty under subsection (1) shall be guilty of an offence.

Insurance Managers and Intermediaries

Insurance managers and intermediaries to be registered.

9.(1) Subject to the provisions of this Act, and notwithstanding anything in any other Act, no person shall in or from within Bermuda act as an insurance manager, broker, agent or salesman unless he is registered for the purpose by the Minister under section 10.

(2) Any person who contravenes subsection (1) shall be guilty of an offence.

Minister may register insurance managers and intermediaries.

10.(1) Subject to sections 11 and 12, the Minister may, on application being made to him for that purpose by any person, and on payment of the relevant fee provided for by section 14, register that person as an insurance manager, broker, agent or salesman, as the case may be, subject to that person complying with such conditions as the Minister may see fit to impose.

(2) Every application under subsection (1) for registration shall be made to the Registrar in the prescribed form.

Factors to be considered in relation to such registration.

11. In considering whether to register a person under section 10, the Minister shall (but without prejudice to his discretion under section 12 to refuse registration on any grounds) have regard to whether the person appears to him to be a fit and proper person to be so registered and, in particular, to whether the person has knowledge of the insurance business adequate to enable him to act in the capacity in which he has applied for registration.

General

Power of Minister in relation to registration.

12. In deciding whether to register a person under section 4 or 10 the Minister shall act as he thinks fit in the public interest, and, if of opinion that it is not in the public interest that registration should be granted, he shall refuse to grant it.

Registration.

13.(1) Where the Minister determines to register any person under section 4 or 10, he shall direct the Registrar accordingly, and the Registrar shall cause the prescribed particulars relating to that person to be entered in a register to be maintained for the purpose by the Registrar (in this Act referred to as "the Register").

(2) A person's registration shall remain in force until it is cancelled.

(3) Where a person is registered as aforesaid, the Registrar shall issue to him a certificate of registration, in which shall be specified -

(a) the name and business address of the person registered;

(b) the date of registration; and

(c) any conditions imposed under section 4 or 10.

(4) A certificate issued under this section shall be accepted in all courts as *prima facie* evidence of the fact that the person named therein is registered, and of the particulars set forth in the certificate.

(5) A copy of every certificate of registration shall be kept by the Registrar in his Office and shall be open to inspection by the public.

Fees.

14.(1) Fees shall be prescribed under the Government Fees Act 1965 in respect of -

(a) the making of any application for registration;

(b) the registration of any person:

(c) the issue of any certificate;

(d) the inspection of the Register; and

(e) the furnishing by the Registrar of any document or copy.

(2) In addition to the fees for which subsection (1) provides, there shall, subject to subsection (3), be payable by a registered insurer or insurance manager, broker, agent or salesman before the 31st day of March in every year following the year in which it or he was registered a business fee of such amount as shall be prescribed under the said Government Fees Act 1965:

Provided that

(a) a business fee shall not be payable by a company whose winding up is in progress in winding up proceedings in Bermuda, except where -

(i) the fee, being due for payment, was not paid; and

(ii) the time allowed by this subsection for its payment had expired,

before those proceedings were commenced; and

(b) if a business fee that a company is excused by paragraph (a) of this proviso from paying has in fact been paid, the liquidator may recover it from the Government.

(3) An unpaid business fee may be sued for by the Government by action as a civil debt and -

(a) the Government may (whether in such an action or not) require; and

(b) where judgment is given for the Government in any action, the court may order, for late payment of the fee payment of a penalty in an amount equal to the amount of the fee.

PART III - Regulation Of Insurers Generally

Accounts and Audit

Statutory financial statements.

15.(1) An insurer shall prepare accounts (in this Act referred to as "statutory financial statements") in respect of its insurance business for each financial year.

(2) Statutory financial statements shall be in such form (being a form calculated to enable comparison to be made between the insurer's business for the financial year in respect of which the statements are prepared and the insurer's business for the financial year immediately preceding that year), and shall contain such information, as may be prescribed.

(3) The information required to be included in statutory financial statements pursuant to subsection (2) shall be information calculated to fulfil (in addition to any other purposes for which regulations may be made) the following purposes, that is to say -

(a) to give as early warning as possible to any person examining the said statements (whether by way of notice of the observance or non-observance by the insurer of any margin of solvency, or in any other way) of any financial or operational difficulties into which the insurer's business has fallen or might appear likely to fall;

(b) to provide the basis on which the Minister or any other authority may in good time take action under this Act or any other statutory provision to exercise any statutory power available to him or it for the safeguarding of any element of the public interest involved in or affected by the insurer's business.

Audit of statutory financial statements.

16.(1) The statutory financial statements of an insurer shall be audited annually by the insurer's approved auditor.

(2) In this Act the expression "approved auditor", in relation to an insurer, means that the auditor has been approved by the Minister as the independent auditor of that insurer.

(3) In subsection (2) the expression "independent", in relation to an insurer's auditor, means that the auditor has satisfied the Minister that the auditor is not, and will not at any relevant time be, financially interested in any way in any business of the insurer apart from the audit.

Duty to keep statutory financial statements at principal office.

17.(1) Every insurer shall have a copy of its statutory financial statements (together with the auditor's report thereon) available at its principal office for production to the Registrar, if directed by him to produce it, not later than six months (or such longer period, not exceeding nine months, as the

Registrar may allow) after the end of the insurer's financial year to which the statements relate and, subject to subsection (3), at all times thereafter.

(2) Every insurer shall not later than twenty-one days after the date on which financial statements become available as required by subsection (1) inform the Registrar by notice in writing of that date.

(3) The insurer shall keep the said statements and report at the insurer's principal office for the period of five years commencing on the date referred to in subsection (1).

Insurer to make financial returns.

18.(1) Every insurer shall send to the Registrar a financial return (in this Act referred to as "the statutory financial return") at the same time as he sends to the Registrar the notice called for by subsection (2) of section 17.

(2) A statutory financial return shall be in the prescribed form, but different forms of return may be prescribed for different classes of insurers.

Segregation of insurance accounts and business.

19. An insurer which carries on any business other than insurance business shall keep separate accounts in respect of its insurance business, and shall segregate the assets and liabilities of its insurance business from those of its other business.

Investment in Bermuda by Non-Resident Insurance Undertakings

Minister may require Bermuda investment.

20.(1) The Minister may by order made under this section require that every insurer, or every insurer of a class specified in the order, being a non-resident insurance undertaking, must maintain invested in Bermuda during the currency of the order approved assets of a value fixed in the order (in this section referred to as "investment asset value").

(2) An order under this section may fix -

(a) an investment asset value of not more than 60% of the value of the domestic liabilities of insurers, being liabilities outstanding on account of long-term business;

(b) an investment asset value of not more than 40% of the premium income of insurers, being premium income arising on account of general business that is domestic business, and such an order may either fix an investment asset value under paragraph (a) alone or paragraph (b) alone, or may fix investment asset values so as to be in force concurrently under both those paragraphs.

(3) Such an order as aforesaid may contain such transitional provision (including provision reducing temporarily a percentage otherwise fixed by the order) as the Minister may deem necessary to enable insurers affected by the order, or any class of such insurers, to reorganize investments held by them immediately before the coming into force of the order with a view to meeting the requirements of the order.

(4) Where an approved asset is a security on which a value was placed by the approved auditor in the course of the latest audit of the statutory financial statements of the insurer, that value shall, in any dispute as to the value of the security, be deemed conclusively to be the true value of the security.

(5) The Minister may include provision in such an order as aforesaid that for the purposes of the order domestic liabilities shall not include any part of such liabilities which is re-insured.

(6) For the purposes of this section -

(a) **(i)** an "approved asset" is an asset approved by the Minister;

(ii) "premium income" in relation to an insurer, means the net amount, after deduction of any premiums paid by the insurer for re-insurance, of the premiums received by the insurer;

(iii) a "domestic liability" is a liability arising in respect of domestic business; and

(b) references to "premium income" and "domestic liabilities", in relation to an insurer affected by an order, are respectively references to premium income and domestic liabilities as shown in the statutory financial statements of the insurer in respect of the financial year next preceding the date of the making of the order;

(c) subject to any applicable regulations, in computing the amount of any liabilities, all contingent and prospective liabilities shall be taken into account but not liabilities in respect of share capital.

(7) Any order made under this section shall be subject to the affirmative resolution procedure.

(8) An insurer which at any time fails to comply with the provisions of an order that is in force under this section and applies to it shall be guilty of an offence.

Maintenance of assets in Bermuda.

21.(1) The Minister may by order made under this section require that every insurer, or every insurer of a class specified in the order, being a non-resident insurance undertaking, must maintain in Bermuda approved assets of the insurer of a value which at any time is equal to the whole or a specified proportion of the amount of its domestic liabilities.

(2) Such an order as aforesaid may contain provision that assets of a specified class or description shall or shall not be treated as assets maintained in Bermuda.

(3) Subsections (4), (5) and (as respects the interpretation or treatment of approved assets, liabilities and domestic liabilities) (6) of section 20 shall apply *mutatis mutandis* in relation to an order made under this section as those subsections apply in relation to an order made under section 20.

(4) Any order made under this section shall be subject to the affirmative resolution procedure.

(5) An insurer which fails at any time to comply with the provisions of an order that is in force under this section and applies to the insurer shall be guilty of an offence.

Custody of assets.

22.(1) The Minister may impose a requirement on any insurer affected by an order under section 21 that the whole or a specified proportion of the insurer's assets affected by such an order shall be held by a person approved by the Minister for the purposes of the requirement as trustee of the insurer.

(2) Assets of an insurer held by a person as trustee for an insurer shall be taken to be held by him in compliance with a requirement imposed under this section if, and only if, they are assets in whose case the insurer has given him written notice that they are to be held by him in compliance with such a requirement, or they are assets into which assets in whose case the insurer has given him a written notice as aforesaid have, by any transaction or series of transactions, been transposed by him on the instructions of the insurer.

(3) No asset held by a person as trustee of an insurer in compliance with a requirement imposed under this section shall, so long as the requirement is in force, be released except with the consent of the Minister.

(4) If a mortgage or charge is created by an insurer at a time when there is in force a requirement imposed on the insurer by virtue of this section, being a mortgage or charge conferring a security on any assets which are held by a person as trustee of the insurer in compliance with the requirement, the mortgage or charge shall, to the extent that it confers such a security, be void against the liquidator and any creditor of the insurer.

(5) An insurer which fails to comply with a requirement properly imposed upon it under this sectin shall be guilty of an offence.

PART IV - Special Provisions For Insurers Carrying On Long-Term Business

Insurers to which this Part applies.

23. This Part shall apply to insurers carrying on long-term business.

Insurer carrying on long-term business to maintain separate accounts.

24.(1) An insurer to which this Part applies shall keep its accounts in respect of its long-term business separate from any accounts kept in respect of any other business.

(2) All receipts of such an insurer's long-term business shall be carried to, and form part of, a special fund with an appropriate name, in this Act referred to as a "long-term business fund".

(3) Such an insurer shall maintain books of account and other records such that -

(a) the assets in its long-term business fund; and

(b) the liabilities of its long-term business, can be readily identified at any time.

(4) No payment from such an insurer's long-term business fund shall be made directly or indirectly for any purpose other than a purpose of the insurer's long-term business, notwithstanding any arrangement for its subsequent repayment out of receipts of business other than the long-term business, except in so far as such payment can be made out of any surplus certified by the insurer's approved actuary to be available for distribution otherwise than to policy-holders.

(5) No insurer to which this Part applies shall declare or pay a dividend to any person other than a policy-holder unless the value of the assets of its long-term business fund as certified by the insurer's approved actuary, exceeds the extent (as so certified) of the liabilities of the insurer's long-term business; and the amount of any such dividend shall not exceed the aggregate of -

(a) that excess; and

(b) any other funds properly available for the payment of dividend, being funds arising out of business of the insurer other than long-term business.

(6) This section shall not apply in relation to an insurer which, immediately before the commencement of this Act -

(a) either -

(i) was an exempted company within the definition of that expression in section 1 of the Exempted Companies Act 1950; or

(ii) had a permit under section 66 of the Bermuda Immigration and Protection Act 1956 or under section 3 or the Non-Resident Insurance Undertakings Act 1967; and *(b)* was carrying on both long-term and general business in or from within Bermuda.

Transfer of long-term business.

25.(1) Any scheme under which the whole or any part of the long-term business of any insurer to which this Part applies (in this section referred to as the "transferor") is to be transferred to another insurer (in this section referred to as the "transferee") shall be void unless it is made in accordance with the provisions of this section and the Court has sanctioned the scheme thereunder.

(2) Either the transferor or the transferee may apply to the Court, by petition, for an order sanctioning the scheme, and the Court shall have power to make such an order subject to the provisions of this section.

(3) The Court shall not entertain such a petition unless the petition is accompanied by a report on the scheme prepared by an approved actuary and the Court is satisfied that sufficient notice of the scheme has been served on each policy-holder affected and been published in the Gazette, and also that copies of the petition and the report have been served on the Minister.

(4) On any petition under this section -

(a) any person who alleges that he would be adversely affected by the carrying out of the scheme: and

(b) the Minister

shall be entitled to be heard.

(5) (deleted by Act no. 14 of 1983)

(6) (repealed by Act no. 1 of 1985)

(7) Subsections (1) to (4) shall not have effect in relation to the transfer of long-term business that is re-insurance business.

Appointment of actuary by insurer carrying on long-term business.

26.(1) An insurer shall not carry on long-term business at any time if it does not have an approved actuary (in this Act referred to as the "insurer's approved actuary") at that time.

(2) In subsection (1) "approved actuary", in relation to an insurer, means an actuary approved by the Minister as that insurer's approved actuary.

Actuarial certificates of long-term business liabilities.

27.(1) An insurer to which this Part applies shall include in the insurer's statutory financial return called for by section 18 a certificate prepared by the insurer's approved actuary in the prescribed form as to the amount of the insurer's liabilities outstanding on account of its long-term business.

(2) Notwithstanding subsection (1) the Minister may in writing at any time direct an insurer to which this Part applies to cause to be produced to him a valuation of the insurer's liabilities outstanding at the date specified in the direction on account of its long-term business, together with a certificate prepared by the insurer's approved actuary in the prescribed form relating thereto; and the insurer shall comply with any such direction.

PART V - Special Provisions Relating To Insurance Managers, Brokers, Agents And Salesmen

Insurance managers to maintain lists of insurers for which they act.

28. An insurance manager shall maintain an accurate list of all insurers for which he acts as insurance manager, and shall, if required in writing at any time by the Registrar so to do, provide the Registrar with a copy of that list.

Insurance broker, agent or salesman deemed agent of insurer in certain cases.

29. In relation to any contract of insurance to which an insurer is a party and in respect of which an insurance broker, agent or salesman having apparent authority to act for the insurer in that respect in fact receives a premium under the contract -

(a) the broker, agent or salesman shall be deemed to be the agent of the insurer; and

(b) the insurer shall be deemed to have received the premium, notwithstanding anything to the contrary in the contract.

PART VI - Powers

Investigation of affairs of an insurer.

30.(1) The Minister may appoint any person appearing to him to be a suitable person as an inspector to investigate the affairs, or any part of the affairs, of an insurer if he is satisfied that such an investigation is required in the interest of the policy-holders or of persons who may become policy-holders.

(2) It shall be the duty of any insurer in relation to whose affairs an inspector has been appointed under subsection (1) (hereinafter called an "insurer under investigation"), and of any past or present officer, employee or insurance manager of such an insurer, to produce to the inspector on request all books, records and documents relating to the insurer under investigation which are in its or his custody or control and otherwise to give to the inspector all assistance in connection with the investigation which it or he is reasonably able to give.

(3) An inspector may -

(a) examine on oath any past or present officer, employee, or insurance manager of the insurer under investigation in relation to its business, and may administer an oath accordingly;

(b) if he thinks it necessary for the purpose of his investigation that a person whom he has no power to examine on oath should be so examined, make application to the Court, and the Court may, if it thinks fit, order that person to attend and be examined on oath before the Court on any matter relevant to the investigation.

Minister may require information.

31.(1) The Minister may in writing direct any person to whom this section applies to produce to him any document or information relating to any matter or thing connected with insurance business which is in that person's custody or control and which the Minister reasonably requires for the purpose of verifying or supplementing information otherwise provided under this Act.

(2) The expression "person to whom this section applies" in subsection (1) means any person who at the time a direction under that subsection is given is, or at any time within the period of five years immediately preceding that time was, an insurer or an insurance manager, broker, agent or salesman.

(3) Any person to whom a direction is given under subsection (1) shall be guilty of an offence if he fails to comply with the direction.

Powers of Minister where insolvency of insurer is feared.

32.(1) If it appears to the Minister that the business of an insurer is being so conducted that there is a risk of the insurer becoming insolvent, he may, subject to subsection (4), in writing direct the insurer to do, or cause to be done, any or all of the following things, that is to say -

(a) not to effect any further contract of insurance, or any further contract of insurance of a specified description;

(b) not to vary any contract of insurance in force when the direction was given, if the effect of the variation would be to increase the liabilities of the insurer;

(c) not to make any investment of a specified class;

(d) before the expiration of a specified period (or such longer period as the Minister may allow) to realize any existing investment of a specified class;

(e) to maintain in Bermuda, or transfer to and keep in the custody of a specified bank, assets of the insurer of such value and description as are specified;

(f) to limit the aggregate of the premiums to be received by it during a specified period beginning not earlier than twenty-eight days after the direction was given.

(2) No assets kept in the custody of a bank pursuant to a direction given under paragraph (e) of subsection (1) shall, so long as the direction is in force, be removed from the bank except with the prior consent of the Minister in writing.

(3) In subsection (1) "specified" means specified in the direction.

(4) Before the Minister gives a direction under subsection (1), he shall give notice to the insurer of his intention to give the direction, and take any representations made by the insurer into account.

(5) Any registered insurer which fails to comply with a direction given under subsection (1), and any other person who causes such a direction to be contravened, shall be guilty of an offence.

PART VII - Insolvency And Winding Up

Margin of solvency for general business.

33.(1) An insurer, being a company that may be wound up under the Winding Up Act, carrying on general business shall be deemed for the purposes of section 222 of the Winding Up Act (winding up of company by the court) to be unable to pay its debts if at any time the value of its assets does not exceed the amount of its liabilities by the prescribed amount, and the provisions of this Act as to winding up shall have effect accordingly.

(2) For the purposes of this section in computing the amount of liabilities of an insurer, all contingent and prospective liabilities shall be taken into account but not liabilities in respect of share capital.

(3) For the purposes of this section the value of any assets and the amount of any liabilities shall, subject to subsections (4) and (5), be determined in accordance with any applicable regulations making provision as to the taking into, or leaving out of, account of assets or liabilities for any purpose.

(4) In the case of an insurer which carries on long-term business as well as general business, the amount of the liabilities of its long-term business at any time shall, for the purposes of this section, be taken to be -

(a) an amount equal to the total amount at that time standing to the credit of the insurer's long-term business fund; or

(b) the amount of those liabilities at any time as determined in accordance with any applicable regulations, whichever is the greater.

(5) Regulations may require that, in every statutory financial return prepared by an insurer carrying on general business, there shall be included a certificate as to solvency (to be called a "solvency certificate") -

(a) in such form and signed by such persons as may be prescribed by the regulations: and

(b) containing such a statement with respect to the assets and liabilities of the insurer as may be so prescribed, and if any such insurer fails to comply with the regulations so made the value of its assets shall, in any proceedings under this section for the winding up or the insurer, be deemed, until the contrary is proved, not to exceed the amount of its liabilities by the amount required by subsection (1).

(6) Nothing in this section shall be taken as affecting the manner in which, on a winding up, any assets or liabilities are required to be dealt with whether by virtue of section 36 or otherwise.

Winding up of insurers under Companies (Winding Up) Act 1977.

34. The Court may order the winding up, in accordance with the Winding Up Act, of an insurer, being a company which may be wound up under that Act, and the provisions of that Act shall apply accordingly subject to the modification that the insurer may be ordered to be wound up on the petition of ten or more policy-holders owning policies of an aggregate value of not less than $50.000:

Provided that such a petition shall not be presented except by leave of the Court, and leave shall not be granted until a *prima facie* case has been established to the satisfaction of the Court and until security for costs for such amount as the Court may think reasonable has been given.

Winding up on petition of Registrar.

35.(1) The Registrar may present a petition for the winding up, in accordance with the Winding Up Act, of an insurer, being a company which may be wound up under that Act, on the ground -

(a) that the insurer is unable to pay its debts within the meaning of sections 222 and 223 of the Winding Up Act; or

(b) that the insurer has failed to satisfy an obligation to which it is or was subject by virtue of this Act; or

(c) that the insurer has failed to satisfy the obligation imposed upon it by section 15 as to the preparation of accounts or to produce statutory financial statements pursuant to a direction given by the Registrar under subsection (1) of section 17, and that the Minister is unable to ascertain its financial position.

(2) In any proceedings on a petition to wind up an insurer presented by the Registrar under subsection (1), evidence that the insurer was insolvent -

(a) at the close of the period to which the statutory financial statements last prepared under section 15 relate; or

(b) at any date specified in a direction under subsection (2) of section 27, shall be evidence that the insurer continues to be unable to pay its debts, unless the contrary is proved.

(3) If, in the case of an insurer, being a company which may be wound up under the Winding Up Act, it appears to the Minister that it is expedient in the public interest that the insurer should be wound up, he may, unless the insurer is already being wound up by the Court, direct the Registrar to present a petition for it to be so wound up if the Court thinks it just and equitable for it to be so wound up.

(4) Where a petition for the winding up of an insurer is presented by a person other than the Registrar, a copy of the petition shall be served on the Registrar, and he shall be entitled to be heard on the petition.

Winding up of insurers carrying on long-term business.

36.(1) An insurer which carries on long-term business shall not be wound up voluntarily.

(2) Subject to subsection (3) and to rules made by virtue of section 40, in any winding up of an insurer which immediately before the winding up was carrying on or entitled to carry on long-term business -

(a) the assets in the insurer's long-term business fund shall be available only for meeting the liabilities of the insurer attributable to its long-term business;

(b) other assets of the insurer shall be available only for meeting the liabilities of the insurer attributable to its other business.

(3) Where the value of the assets mentioned in either paragraph of subsection (2) exceeds the amount of the liabilities mentioned in that paragraph the restriction imposed by that sub- section shall not apply to so much of those assets as represents the excess.

(4) In relation to the assets falling within either paragraph of subsection (2) the creditors mentioned in subsections (1) and (2) of section 246 of the Winding Up Act shall be only those who are creditors in respect of liabilities failing within that paragraph; and any general meeting of creditors summoned for the purposes of that section shall accordingly be separate general meetings of the creditors in respect of the liabilities falling within each paragraph.

(5) Where under subsection (1) of section 333 of the Winding Up Act (defalcations of directors, etc. disclosed in course of winding up) the Court orders any money or property to be repaid or restored to an insurer or any sum to be contributed to its assets then, if and so far as the wrongful act which is the reason for the making of the order related to assets belonging to an insurer's long-term business fund, the Court shall include in the order a direction that the money, property or contribution shall be treated for the purposes of this Act as assets of that fund, and this Act shall have effect accordingly.

Continuation of long-term business of insurer in liquidation.

37.(1) This section shall have effect in relation to the winding up of an insurer, being an insurer carrying on long-term business.

(2) The liquidator shall, unless the Court otherwise orders, carry on the long-term business of the insurer with a view to its being transferred as a going concern to another insurer, whether an existing insurer or an insurer formed for that purpose; and, in carrying on that business as aforesaid, the liquidator may agree to the variation of any contracts of insurance in existence when the winding up order is made, but shall not effect any new contracts of insurance.

(3) If the liquidator is satisfied that the interests of the creditors in respect of liabilities of the insurer attributable to its long-term business require the appointment of a special manager of the insurer's long-term business, he may apply to the Court, and the Court may on such application appoint a special manager of that business to act during such time as the Court may direct, with such powers, including any of the powers of a receiver or manager, as may be entrusted to him by the Court.

(4) Subsections (2) and (3) of section 263 of the Winding Up Act (special manager to give security and receive remuneration) shall apply to a special manager appointed under subsection (3) of this section as they apply to a special manager appointed under that section.

(5) The Court may, if it thinks fit and subject to such provisions (if any) as it may determine, reduce the amounts of the contracts made by the insurer in the course of carrying on its long-term business.

(6) The Court may, on the application of a liquidator, a special manager appointed under subsection (3) or the Registrar, appoint an independent actuary to investigate the long-term business of the insurer and to report to the liquidator, the special manager or the Registrar, as the case may be, on the desirability or otherwise of that business being conducted and on any reduction in the contracts made in the course of carrying on that business that may be necessary for its successful continuation.

(7) Notwithstanding subsection (1) of section 245 of the Winding Up Act (which requires the liquidator to obtain the sanction of the Court or committee of inspection for the bringing of legal proceedings in the name of and on behalf of the company) the liquidator may without any such sanction make an application in the name of and on behalf of the insurer under section 25.

Subsidiary insurers.

38.(1) Where the insurance business or any part of the insurance business of an insurer has been transferred to an insurer under an arrangement in pursuance of which the first mentioned insurer (in this section called the subsidiary insurer) or the creditors thereof has or have claims against the insurer to which the transfer was made (in this section called the principal insurer), then, if the principal insurer is being wound up by or under the supervision of the Court, the Court shall, subject to the provisions of this section, order the subsidiary insurer to be wound up in conjunction with the principal insurer, and may by the same or any subsequent order appoint the same person to be liquidator for the two insurers, and make provision for such other matters as may seem to the Court necessary, with a view to the insurers being wound up as if they were one insurer.

(2) The commencement of the winding up of the principal insurer shall, save as otherwise ordered by the Court, be the commencement of the winding up of the subsidiary insurer.

(3) In adjusting the rights and liabilities of the members of the several insurers between themselves, the Court shall have regard to the constitution of the insurers, and to the arrangements entered into between the insurers, in the same manner as the Court would have regard to the rights and liabilities of different classes of contributories in the case of the winding up of a single insurer, or as near thereto as circumstances admit.

(4) Where any insurer alleged to be subsidiary is not in process of being wound up at the same time as the principal insurer to which it is subsidiary, the Court shall not direct the subsidiary insurer to be wound up unless, after hearing all objections (if any) that may be urged by or on behalf of the insurer against it being wound up, the Court is of the opinion that the insurer is subsidiary to the principal insurer, and that the winding up of the insurer in conjunction with the principal insurer is just and equitable.

(5) An application may be made in relation to the winding up of any subsidiary insurer in conjunction with a principal insurer by any creditor of, or person interested in, the principal insurer or the subsidiary insurer.

(6) Where an insurer stands in the relation of a principal insurer to one insurer, and the relation of a subsidiary insurer to some other insurer, or where there are several insurers standing in the relation of subsidiary insurers to one principal insurer, the Court may deal with any number of such insurers together or in separate groups, as it thinks most expedient, upon the principles laid down in this section.

Reduction of contracts as alternative to winding up.

39. In the case of an insurer which has been proved to be unable to pay its debts, the Court may, if it thinks fit, reduce the amount of the contracts of the insurer on such terms and subject to such conditions as the Court thinks just instead of making a winding up order.

Winding up rules.

40.(1) The Minister may make rules under this section for determining the amount of the liabilities of an insurer to policy-holders of any class or description for the purpose of proof in a winding up and generally for carrying into effect the provisions of this Act in respect to the winding up of insurers.

(2) Without prejudice to the generality of subsection (1), rules made under this section may make provision for all or any of the following matters -

(a) the identification of the assets and liabilities falling within either paragraph of subsection (2) of section 36;

(b) the apportionment between the assets falling within paragraphs (a) and (b) of that subsection of the costs, charges or expenses of the winding up or any debts of the insurer having priority under section 319 of the Winding Up Act;

(c) the determination of the amount of liabilities of any description falling within either paragraph of that subsection for the purpose of establishing whether or not there is any such excess in respect of that paragraph as is mentioned in subsection (3) of section 36;

(d) the application of assets within paragraph (a) of the said subsection (2) for meeting the liabilities within that paragraph;

(e) the application of assets representing any such excess as is mentioned in the said subsection (3).

(3) Rules made under this section shall be subject to the negative resolution procedure.

PART VIII - Cancellation Of Registration

Cancellation of registration of insurers.

41.(1) The Minister may, subject to the provisions of this Part, by order cancel the registration of an insurer -

(a) at the request of the insurer; or

(b) upon any one or more of the following grounds, that is to say -

(i) that false, misleading or inaccurate information has been supplied by the insurer or on its behalf for the purpose of any provision of this Act or the regulations;

(ii) that two years have elapsed since the registration of the insurer, and the insurer has not commenced to carry on business;

(iii) that the insurer has ceased to carry on business;

(iv) that the insurer has persistently failed to pay fees due under section 14;

(v) that the insurer has not complied with a condition attached to its registration or with a requirement made of it under this Act or the regulations;

(vi) that the insurer has been convicted of an offence against a provision of this Act or the regulations;

(vii) that, in the opinion of the Minister, arrived at after consultation with the Insurance Advisory Committee, the insurer has not been carrying on business in accordance with sound insurance principles.

(2) Before he cancels the registration of an insurer under paragraph (b) of subsection (1), the Minister shall give the insurer notice in writing of the ground on which he proposes to cancel the registration, and shall afford the insurer an opportunity to make objection in writing within the period of thirty days after receipt of the notice; and the Minister shall take into consideration any such objection and, if he decides to cancel the registration, cause the order of cancellation to be served on the insurer.

(3) The cancellation of the registration of an insurer shall take effect on the expiration of the period of twenty-one days beginning on the date of service of the order upon the insurer, or on such later date as may be specified in the order, but subject to the right of the insurer to appeal to the Court under section 43.

(4) In this section "to carry on business" means to carry on insurance business in or from within Bermuda.

Cancellation of registration of insurance managers, etc.

42.(1) The Minister may, subject to the provisions of this Part, by order cancel the registration of an insurance manager, broker, agent or salesman -

(a) at the request of the manager, broker, agent or salesman in question; or

(b) upon any one or more of the following grounds, that is to say

(i) that false, misleading or inaccurate information has been supplied by him or on his behalf for the purposes of any provision of this Act or the regulations;

(ii) that two years have elapsed since his registration, and he has not commenced to carry on business;

(iii) that he has ceased to carry on business;

(iv) that he has persistently failed to pay fees due under section 14;

(v) that he has not complied with a condition attached to his registration or with a requirement made of him under this Act or the regulations;

(vi) that he has been convicted of an offence against a provision of this Act or the regulations;

(vii) that he has been convicted by a court (whether in Bermuda or elsewhere) of an offence involving fraud or dishonesty;

(viii) that, in the opinion of the Minister, arrived at after consultation with the Insurance Advisory Committee, he has not been carrying on business in accordance with sound insurance principles.

(2) The provisions of subsections (2) and (3) of section 41 shall apply in relation to the cancellation under this section of a registration as those provisions apply in relation to a cancellation under that section.

(3) In this section "to carry on business" means in or from within Bermuda to act as an insurance manager, broker, agent or salesman, as the case may be.

Appeals to Supreme Court.

43.(1) An appeal at the instance of an insurer or other person affected by an order made under section 41 or 42 shall lie to the Court against the order.

(2) Such an appeal shall be commenced by notice of motion, and shall -

(a) be filed in the Registry of the Supreme Court; and

(b) be served on the Attorney General,within twenty-one days after the date on which the order was served on the insurer or other person affected by the order.

(3) Rules of court may be made under section 62 of the Supreme Court Act 1905 for the purpose of regulating the practice and procedure on appeals under this section.

(4) On an appeal under this section the Court may confirm, reverse or modify the order of the Minister, or may remit the matter to him with the opinion of the Court thereon.

(5) The bringing of an appeal under this section shall operate to suspend the order of cancellation appealed against, pending the determination or abandonment of the appeal:

Provided that the insurer or other person affected by the order shall not during the period of the suspension be entitled to effect any business or perform any function other than business or a function arising out of business commenced or transacted by him before the order was served upon him.

Cancellation of registration to be gazetted.

44. The Registrar shall publish in the Gazette notice of any cancellation of a registration under this Act.

PART IX - Supplementary

Prohibition of loans to directors, etc.

45.(1) Subject to subsection (2), an insurer which carries on domestic business shall not, directly or indirectly, without the previous consent of the Minister in writing -

(a) make any loan to any director or officer of the insurer, or to the wife or child of any such director or officer; or

(b) guarantee, or provide any security in connection with, a loan by any other person to a person referred to in paragraph (a).

(2) Nothing in subsection (1) shall operate to prohibit the making of a loan -

(a) to a person referred to in paragraph (a) of that sub-section, where the amount of the loan is within the surrender value of a life policy issued to him by the insurer; or

(b) secured by a first mortgage, where the amount of the loan does not exceed three quarters of the market value of the property mortgaged.

(3) An insurer which contravenes this section shall be guilty of an offence.

Effect on business transactions of infringement of Act.

46. For the avoidance of doubt it is hereby declared that no business transaction shall be void or voidable by reason only that at the relevant time any party to the transaction is in breach of any provision of this Act.

Acting on behalf of unregistered insurer.

47.(1) Subject to subsection (2), any person who solicits another person, or causes him to enter into, or make application to enter into, a contract of domestic business with a person who is not a registered insurer shall be guilty of an offence.

(2) Subsection (1) shall not apply in relation to -

(a) any contract arranged by any person authorized in that behalf by the Minister in accordance with any conditions imposed by the Minister; or

(b) any contract of re-insurance.

Personal liability of intermediaries in certain cases.

48.(1) Any insurance broker or agent who arranges a policy of domestic business with a person who is not a registered insurer shall be personally liable on the policy as if he were the insurer.

(2) For the purposes of subsection (1) a member of a recognized association of underwriters shall be deemed to be a registered insurer.

Control of advertisements.

49. An insurer or an insurance broker or agent shall not publish any advertisement which misleads, or directly or by implication is likely to mislead or deceive, any prospective policy-holder with respect to an insurer's assets or financial standing, or in any other material respect.

Issue of false documents etc.

50.(1) Any person who, for any purposes of this Act, issues any document which is false or misleading in a material respect, and any person who takes part in the preparation or issue of such a document, or who signs such a document, shall be guilty of an offence unless he proves -

(a) if an individual, that he had no knowledge of the falsity or misleading character of the document and took every reasonable precaution to ensure its accuracy; and

(b) in any other case, that every person acting on his behalf had no such knowledge, and took every such reasonable precaution, as aforesaid.

PART X - Miscellaneous

Service on insurers.

51.(1) Any notice, instrument or other document, and any legal process, to be delivered to, or served on, an insurer for the purposes of this Act may be delivered or served by leaving it at the principal office of the insurer.

(2) If the said office cannot reasonably be found, any such notice, instrument, document or process may be delivered or served by leaving it at the office of the Registrar and publishing notice of the fact in the Gazette.

(3) Delivery or service pursuant to subsection (2) shall be deemed to be delivery to, or service on, an insurer.

Confidentiality.

52.(1) Information received by any public officer or an inspector in the course of the performance by him of any function under this Act shall not be disclosed by him except -

(a) to the Minister or a public officer or, but so far only as may be necessary or expedient for the proper discharge of any function to be performed under this Act, to other persons; or

(b) for the purposes of any criminal or civil proceedings: or

(c) in the form of a summary or other general statement which does not identify the person from whom the information was received or to whom it relates.

(2) Any person who discloses information in contravention of this section shall be guilty of an offence.

Regulations.

58.(1) The Minister may make regulations -

(a) dividing insurance business into classes for the purposes of any provision of this Act:

(b) exempting any class of insurance business from any provision of this Act;

(c) exempting any person or class of persons from any provision of this Act;

(d) determining the value of assets or the amount of liabilities for the purposes of any provision of this Act;

(e) without prejudice to paragraph (d); providing that, for any specified purpose, assets or liabilities of any specified class or description shall be left out of account or shall be taken into account only to a specified extent;

(f) prescribing the information to be contained in any statement or report required by any provision of this Act to be provided, and the manner of presentation of such information;

(g) prescribing the information to be contained in any register under this Act which is to be made available for inspection by members of the public;

(h) prescribing the number of copies and the manner of certification of any document required to be furnished under any provision of this Act;

(i) prescribing anything permitted or required by this Act to be prescribed;

(j) creating offences and prescribing penalties (including imprisonment) for such offences.

(2) Regulations prescribing the information to be contained in any statutory financial statement or any statutory financial return may provide for enabling the information to be given in a note on, or a statement or report annexed to, the statement or return; or may require there to be given in such a note, statement or report as aforesaid such information in addition to that given in the statement or return as may be prescribed.

(3) Regulations may, as respects such matters stated in any statutory financial statement or any statutory financial return or in statements or reports annexed thereto as may be prescribed, require there to be given by such persons as may be prescribed and to be annexed to the statutory financial statement or statutory financial return certificates of such matters as may be prescribed.

(4) If a form is prescribed for any statutory financial statement or as that in which information authorized or required to be given in a statement or report annexed to any statutory financial statement is to be given, or for a certificate to be so annexed, the statutory financial statement shall be prepared, the information shall be given or, as the case may be, the certificate shall be framed, in that form.

(5) In this section "Act" includes any regulations.

(6) Regulations made under this section shall be subject to the affirmative resolution procedure.

Specific offences.

54.(1) Any person who fails to comply with any duty or prohibition imposed upon him by any provision to which this section applies shall be guilty of an offence.

(2) The provisions to which this section applies are sub sections (1), (2), and (3) of section 17;

subsection (4) of section 24; subsection (2) of section 27; section 28; subsection (2) of section 30; the proviso to subsection (5) of section 43; and section 49.

General provisions relating to offences.

55.(1) Any person committing an offence against this Act or any regulation for which no penalty is specifically provided may be proceeded against either summarily or on indictment, and shall be liable on conviction -

(a) in the former case, to a fine not exceeding $5,000 or to imprisonment for a period not exceeding twelve months, or to both such fine and imprisonment; and

(b) in the latter case, to a fine not exceeding $15,000 or to imprisonment for a term not exceeding three years or to both such fine and imprisonment.

(2) Where an offence committed against this Act or any regulation by a body corporate is proved to have been committed with the consent or connivance of, or to be attributable to any neglect on the part of, any director, manager, secretary or other similar officer of the body corporate, or any person who was purporting to act in any such capacity, he, as well as the body corporate, shall be guilty of that offence and liable to be proceeded against and punished accordingly.

Power to modify accounting provisions in certain cases.

56.(1) The Minister may, on the application, or with the consent, of any insurer, direct that all or any of the provisions to which this section applies shall not apply to that insurer or shall apply to it subject to such modifications as may be specified in the direction.

(2) A direction under this section may be subject to conditions.

(3) A direction under this section may be made with retroactive effect.

(4) A direction under this section may be revoked at any time by the Minister; and the Minister may also vary any such direction at any time, provided the variation has been applied for, or is consented to, by the insurer affected by the variation.

(5) The provisions to which this section applies are -

(a) the limitations upon the carrying on of general business or, as the case may be, long-term business specified in subsection (4) of section 1;

(b) the provisions of section 6, 15 to 18 and 33; and

(c) the provisions of any regulations -

(i) relating to the limitations referred to in paragraph (a); or

(ii) made for the purposes of any of the provisions specified in paragraph (b).

(6) It is hereby declared for the avoidance of doubt that a direction given under this section is not a statutory instrument having legislative effect.

Application.

57.(1) Insurance business of any of the following kinds, that is to say -

(a) insurance business carried on by a friendly society registered under the Friendly Societies Act 1868 or by a trade union registered under the Trade Union Act 1965, being business in which risks of members of the friendly society or trade union, as the case may be, are insured;

(b) insurance business carried on by the Hospital Insurance Commission pursuant to the Hospital Insurance Act 1970;

(c) the health insurance scheme conducted pursuant to the Government Employees (Health Insurance) Act 1971;

(d) housing loan insurance carried on by the Bermuda Housing Corporation under the Bermuda Loan Insurance Act 1984.

shall be deemed not to be insurance business within the meaning of this Act.

(2) Apart from -

(a) section 43; and

(b) any provision dealt with in subsection (3) of this section, nothing in this Act or any regulation shall apply in relation to any member of a recognized association of underwriters.

(3) The provisions of this Act or the regulations specified in the table below shall apply, or, as the case may be, shall not apply, in relation to a member of a recognized association of underwriters to the extent there specified -

(a) section 3: shall not apply in relation to any member of a recognized association of underwriters, who is registered in accordance with paragraph (b) below and carries on his business in accordance with the requirements of that paragraph and with any conditions attached to his registration;

(b) sections 9 to 14, and any regulations made for the purposes of those sections shall apply in relation to a member of a recognized association of underwriters as respects the carrying on of insurance business by him in or from within

Bermuda as those provisions apply in relation to an insurance manager, broker, agent or salesman acting as such;

(c) sections 42 to 44 shall apply in relation to a member of a recognized association of underwriters in the same manner as those sections apply in relation to an insurance manager, broker, agent or salesman;

(d) section 54 shall apply as respects the proviso to subsection (5) of section 43;

(e) section 55 shall apply;

(f) section 1 shall apply to the extent necessary for the interpretation of any other section that applies.

Transitional.

58.(1) [Omitted]

(2) As respects any time after the expiration of the aforesaid period of twelve months (in this subsection referred to as "the twelve-month period"), the Minister, on application being made to him for the purpose, may by instrument in writing exempt any such person as aforesaid from the provisions of this Act or the regulations specified in the instrument for such period as the Minister may specify in the instrument as being a further period that he is satisfied that that person requires to enable him to -

(a) transfer his business or wind up his affairs (being business or affairs regulated wholly or partly by this Act); or

(b) otherwise comply with this Act or the regulations, but, save as permitted by any such instrument, any such person shall on and after the expiration of the twelve-month period be bound by the provisions of this Act.

Amendment of Act no.43 of 1971.

59. [Omitted]

Commencement.

60. [Omitted]

THE NON-RESIDENT INSURANCE UNDERTAKINGS ACT 1967

(as amended)

Arrangement Of Sections

Interpretation.

1. In this Act -

"non-resident insurance undertaking" means any undertaking conducting insurance business of any kind other than -

(a) a company incorporated in these Islands under any Act; or

(b) any other person or body of persons, ordinarily resident in these Islands, conducting insurance business from a place of business in these Islands as principals to the insurance business undertaken in these Islands and authorised by law so to do;

"insurance business" includes making out or executing policies of insurance or insurance contracts receiving any premium or giving credit therefor or receiving any other consideration therefor, paying out any sums under a policy of insurance or insurance contracts and entering into or inducing or attempting to induce any person to enter into or take out any policy of insurance or insurance contract by advertisement or otherwise;

"the Minister" means the Minister of Finance or such other Minister as may be appointed to administer this Act.

Non-resident insurance undertakings to have permits to carry on business.

2.(1) Any person who conducts insurance business in these Islands as manager of or agent for or otherwise on behalf of a non-resident insurance undertaking except under the authority and in accordance with the conditions of a permit issued to that non-resident insurance undertaking, or to some person in these Islands on its behalf, shall be guilty of an offence against this Act.

(2) The Act shall not apply to any non-resident insurance undertaking the whole of whose insurance business is conducted with persons normally resident outside these Islands and relates solely to persons, property and risks outside these Islands.

(3) For the avoidance of doubt it is hereby declared that, collectively, all members of the Society of Lloyd's of London and any insurance undertaking operating on the same basis shall, for the purposes of the Act, be deemed to be a single non-resident insurance undertaking irrespective of the combination in which such members underwrite any particular insurance risk.

Grant of permits.

3.(1) The Minister may grant a permit under this Act upon application in writing made by, or on behalf of, the non-resident insurance undertaking and such a permit shall not be issued to the non-resident insurance undertaking or person acting on its behalf until there is produced to the Minister a receipt of the Accountant General that $10,000 has been paid to him by, or on behalf of, the non-resident insurance undertaking.

(2) A permit granted by the Minister under this section -

(a) shall contain a condition that on or before the 31st day of March in each year subsequent to the year of issue thereof the non-resident insurance undertaking or any person acting on its behalf, shall pay to the Accountant General the sum of ten thousand dollars and such a condition shall be specified in the permit; and

(b) may be limited in duration to a time specified in the permit; and

(c) may be granted subject to such other conditions or limitations as the Minister may think fit to impose and as are specified in the permit, and any person conducting insurance business on behalf of any non-resident insurance undertaking who fails to comply with any condition or limitation specified in the permit relating to that non-resident insurance undertaking shall be guilty of an offence against this Act.

Power of Accountant General to grant relief.

4. Notwithstanding the provisions of subsection (2) of section 3 it shall be lawful for the Accountant General, in any case where a non-resident insurance undertaking has not made payment or where payment has not been made on its behalf in accordance with the condition specified in paragraph (a) of subsection (2) of section 3 and the Accountant General is satisfied that such non-payment is not due to wilful neglect or default, to accept payment of the sum due together with a penalty of one thousand dollars as constituting compliance with that condition and on receipt thereof the non-resident insurance undertaking shall for all purposes be deemed to have complied therewith.

Revocation of permits.

5.(1) Where it appears to the Minister that the manager or agent or other person acting on behalf of a non-resident insurance undertaking is conducting the business on behalf of that non-resident insurance undertaking in contravention of any of the conditions contained in the permit relating to that non-resident insurance undertaking, the Minister may revoke that permit:

Provided that, before so revoking any such permit, the Minister shall cause a notice to be served on such persons conducting business on behalf of that non-resident insurance undertaking as appears to the Minister equitable and shall take into account any representations made by or on behalf of those persons.

(2) Notice of any revocation pursuant to this section shall be published in the Gazette and in at least one other newspaper circulating in these Islands.

Application of other Acts.

6.(1) The provisions of Part XI of the Companies Act 1981, other than those provisions specified in section 150A of the said Act, shall not apply to a non-resident insurance undertaking to which this Act applies.

(2) Nothing in this Act shall be construed so as to derogate from or abridge any power expressly conferred upon a non-resident insurance undertaking by or under any private Act.

Offences.

7. Offences against this Act shall be prosecuted before a court of summary jurisdiction and upon conviction a person shall be liable to a fine not exceeding five thousand dollars or to imprisonment for one month or to both such fine and imprisonment, or, in respect of a second or subsequent offence, to a fine not exceeding ten thousand dollars or to imprisonment for a term not exceeding six months or to both such fine and imprisonment.

Saving with regard to existing policies.

8. Nothing in this Act shall affect any policy of insurance or insurance contract made out or executed before the date of the coming into force of this Act, or the conducting of any insurance business in relation to any such policy of insurance or insurance contract after that date.

Effect of incorporating Act.

9. For the avoidance of doubt it is hereby declared that capacity to conduct insurance business conferred on any company under its incorporating Act or permission to engage in gainful occupation granted to any person under the Bermuda Immigration and Protection Act 1956 shall not constitute permission to conduct such business in contravention of the provisions of this Act.

Commencement.

10. [*Omitted.*]

CONVEYANCING AMENDMENT ACT 1994

WHEREAS it is expedient to amend the Conveyancing Act 1983 to make new provisions in respect of certain voidable dispositions:

Be it enacted by The Queen's Most Excellent Majesty, by and with the advice and consent of the Senate and the House of Assembly of Bermuda, and by the authority of the same, as follows:-

Short title

1. This Act which amends the Conveyancing Act 1983 may be cited as the Conveyancing Amendment Act 1994.

Inserts new Part IV A

2. The Conveyancing Act 1983 is amended by inserting at the end of Part IV, immediately after section 36, the following new Part IV A -

"PART IV A - PROVISIONS AGAINST DISPOSITIONS WITH REQUISITE INTENTION

Interpretation

36A.(1) In this Part -

"appointed day" means the date on which this Part comes into operation;

"disposition" means any disposition or series of dispositions of property of any nature whatsoever and however effected, and, without limiting the generality of the foregoing, includes any exercise of a power of appointment, any trust, gift, transfer, sale, exchange, demise, assignment, assurance, grant, lease, surrender, conveyance, reconveyance, release, reservation, any purchase or other acquisition, any covenant, contract or option and any compromise or other dealing or arrangement;

"eligible creditor" means a person to whom -

(a) on, or within two years after, the material date the transferor owed an obligation and on the date of the action or proceeding to set aside the relevant disposition that obligation remains unsatisfied;

(b) on the material date the transferor owed a contingent liability and since that date the contingency giving rise to the obligation has occurred and on the date of the action or proceeding to set aside the relevant disposition that obligation remains unsatisfied; or

(c) on the date of the action or proceeding to set aside the relevant disposition, the transferor owes an obligation in consequence of a claim, made by that person against the transferor, arising from a cause of action which accrued prior to, or within two years after, the material date.

"material date" means the date on which a relevant disposition is made;

"obligation" means any obligation or liability, other than a contingent liability, to pay a sum of money or to transfer property;

"property" includes money, goods, things in action, land and every description of property wherever situated and every description of interest, whether present or future or vested or contingent, arising out of, or incidental to, property;

"relevant disposition" means a disposition to which section 36C applies;

"requisite intention" means an intention of a transferor to make a disposition the dominant purpose of which is to put the property which is the subject of that disposition beyond the reach of a person or a class of persons who is making, or may at some time make, a claim against him;

"transferor" means a person who directly or indirectly makes a relevant disposition or causes it to be made;

"transferee" means the person to whom a relevant disposition is made and includes a successor in title of such person;

"trust" includes a settlement;

"undervalue", in relation to a disposition of property, means a disposition in respect of which -

(a) no consideration is given; or

(b) the value of the consideration given is, in money or money's worth, significantly less than the value, in money or money's worth, of the property.

Application

36B.(1) Subject to subsections (2) and (3), with effect from the appointed day the provisions of this Part shall apply to every disposition of property made by any person whether that disposition was made before or after the appointed day and whether or not the property, the subject of the disposition, is situated in Bermuda or elsewhere.

(2) Notwithstanding subsection (1), where -

(a) prior to, or within six months after, the appointed day; and

(b) pursuant to a conveyance of property to which section 37 of the Conveyancing Act 1983 applies,

any action or proceeding has been commenced, this Part shall have no application, and the provisions of the said section 37 shall have effect as if this Part had not been enacted.

(3) This Part shall not affect the operation of a disentailing assurance or the law of bankruptcy for the time being in force.

Avoidance of dispositions made with the requisite intention, etc.

36C.(1) Subject to subsection (2) and the provisions of this Part, every disposition of property made with the requisite intention and at an undervalue shall be voidable at the instance of an eligible creditor thereby prejudiced.

(2) Where a person seeking to set aside a relevant disposition was not, on the material date, a person to whom an obligation was owed by the transferor, the Court shall not set aside that disposition unless the Court is satisfied that that person was, on the material date, reasonably foreseeable by the transferor as a person to whom an obligation might become owed by him.

(3) Subject to subsection (4), no action or proceeding to set aside a disposition shall be commenced pursuant to this Part unless such action or proceeding is commenced -

(a) in the case of an eligible creditor referred to in paragraph (a) of the definition of that expression, within six years after the material date or within six years after the date when the obligation became owed, whichever is the later date;

(b) in the case of an eligible creditor referred to in paragraph (b) of that definition, within six years after the material date;

(c) in the case of an eligible creditor referred to in paragraph (c) of that definition, within six years after the material date, or within six years after the date when the cause of action accrued, whichever is the later date.

(4) Except as provided in subsection (3), nothing contained in this section shall be construed as in any way affecting the operation of the Limitation Act 1984.

(5) For the avoidance of doubt it is hereby declared -

(a) that a disposition to which this Part applies shall not, by reason only that it was made at an undervalue, be set aside by the Court; and

(*b*) the Court shall, for the purpose of setting aside such a disposition determine, on a balance of probability, whether it was made with the requisite intention.

Savings of certain rights

36D.(1) Where, pursuant to this Part, a relevant disposition is set aside and the Court is satisfied that the transferee has acted in good faith, then, -

(*a*) the transferee shall have a first and paramount charge over the property, the subject of the relevant disposition, for an amount equal to all costs (and not only such costs as the Court might otherwise allow) properly incurred by the transferee in the defence of the action or proceeding to set aside that disposition;

(*b*) the relevant disposition shall be set aside subject to all fees and costs properly incurred and subject also to any pre-existing rights, claims and interests of the transferee and of any person through whom the transferee claims and who has acted in good faith; and

(*c*) in the case of a trust, the relevant disposition shall only be set aside subject to the right of a beneficiary to retain any distribution made consequent upon the prior exercise of a trust, power or a discretion vested in the trustee of such trust or any other person, and otherwise properly exercised.

(2) The burden of proving that a transferee or any person through whom the transferee claims has not acted in good faith shall be upon the person making the allegation.

Extent of avoidance of relevant disposition

36E. Subject to section 36D, a relevant disposition shall be set aside pursuant to this Part only to the extent necessary to satisfy the obligation owed to the eligible creditor at whose instance the disposition has been set aside.

Part not to validate certain dispositions

36F. Nothing contained in this Part shall be construed as -

(*a*) validating any disposition of property which is neither owned by, nor is the subject of a power of disposal with respect thereto vested in, the transferor; or

(*b*) affecting the recognition of a foreign law in determining whether the transferor is the owner of such property or the holder of such power.

Relationship with Trusts (Special Provisions) Act 1989

36G. Nothing in this Part shall be construed as creating or enabling any right, claim or interest on behalf of a creditor or person which right, claim or interest would be avoided or defeated by section 11 of the Trusts (Special Provisions) Act 1989, (which prohibits the variation or setting aside of trusts validly created under the Law of Bermuda).".

Amends Real Estates Assets Act 1787

3. The Real Estates Assets Act 1787 is amended by repealing section 3.

Repeals section 37

4. Section 37 of the Conveyancing Act 1983 is repealed.

THE ELECTRONIC TRANSACTIONS ACT 1999

ARRANGEMENT OF SECTIONS

PART VI - DATA PROTECTION

PART VII - INTERMEDIARIES AND E-COMMERCE SERVICE PROVIDERS

PART VIII - E-COMMERCE ADVISORY BOARD

PART IX - GENERAL

PART I - PRELIMINARY

Citation

1. This Act may be cited as the Electronic Transactions Act 1999.

Definitions

2. In this Act -

"accredited certificate" means an electronic record that -

(i) associates a signature verification device to a person;

(ii) confirms the identity of that person;

(iii) is issued by an authorised certification service provider; and

(iv) meets the relevant criteria;

"addressee" in relation to an electronic record, means a person who is intended by the originator to receive the electronic record, but does not include a person acting as an intermediary with respect to that electronic record;

"authorised certification service provider" means a certification service provider authorised under section 20(2) to provide accredited certificates;

"certification service provider" means a person who issues identity certificates for the purposes of electronic signatures or provides other services to the public related to electronic signatures;

"data controller" means a person who, either alone or jointly or in common with other persons, determines the purposes for which and the manner in which any personal data is, or is to be, processed;

"data processor" means a person who processes personal data on behalf of a data controller;

"e-commerce service provider" means a person who uses electronic means in providing goods, services or information;

"electronic" means relating to technology having electrical, digital, magnetic, wireless, optical, electromagnetic or similar capabilities;

"electronic agent device" means a program, or other electronic or automated means configured and enabled by a person that is used to initiate or respond to electronic records or performance in whole or in part without review by an individual;

"electronic record" means a record created, stored, generated, received or communicated by electronic means;

"electronic signature" means a signature in electronic form in, attached to, or logically associated with, information that is used by a signatory to indicate his adoption of the content of that information and meets the following requirements -

(i) it is uniquely linked to the signatory;

(ii) it is capable of identifying the signatory;

(iii) it is created using means that the signatory can maintain under his sole control; and

(iv) it is linked to the information to which it relates in such a manner that any subsequent alteration of the information is revealed;

"electronic signature product" means hardware or software, or components thereof, that are intended to be used by a certification service provider for the provision of electronic signature services;

"identifiable natural person" means an individual who can be identified, directly or indirectly, in particular by reference to an identification number or to one or more factors specific to his physiological, mental, economic, cultural or social identity;

"information" includes data, text, images, sounds, codes, computer programs, software and databases;

"information processing system" means an electronic system for creating, generating, sending, receiving, storing, displaying, or otherwise processing information;

"intermediary" with respect to an electronic record, means a person who, on behalf of another person, sends, receives or stores that electronic record or provides other services with respect to that electronic record;

"Minister" means the Minister responsible for telecommunications and electronic commerce;

"originator" in relation to an electronic record, means a person by whom, or on whose behalf, the electronic record purports to have been sent or generated prior to storage, if any, but does not include an intermediary with respect to that electronic record;

"personal data" means any information relating to an identified or identifiable natural person;

"prescribed" means prescribed by regulations under section 32;

"record" means information that is inscribed on a tangible medium or that is stored in an electronic, paper-based or any other medium and is retrievable in perceivable form;

"security procedure" means a procedure, established by law or agreement or knowingly adopted by each party, that is employed for the purpose of verifying that an electronic signature, record or performance is that of a particular person or for detecting changes or errors in the content of an electronic record;

"signature creation device" means unique data, including codes or private cryptographic keys, or a uniquely configured physical device which is used by the signatory in creating an electronic signature;

"signature verification device" means unique data, including codes or public cryptographic keys, or a uniquely configured physical device which is used in verifying an electronic signature;

Crown to be bound

3.(1) This Act binds the Crown.

(2) Notwithstanding subsection (1), nothing in this Act obliges any Government Department to generate, send, receive, store or otherwise process any record by electronic means, but the Minister may, by notice published in the Gazette, indicate that a Government Department will receive and process electronic records relating to such matters as may be specified in the notice.

Objects

4. The objects of this Act are -

(a) to enhance the reputation of Bermuda as an international business centre;

(b) to facilitate electronic transactions on a technology neutral basis by means of reliable electronic records;

(c) to remove uncertainties in relation to conducting transactions electronically with respect to the requirements for documents and for signatures to be in writing;

(d) to promote public confidence in the validity, integrity and reliability of conducting transactions electronically; and

(e) to promote the development of the legal and business infrastructure necessary to implement electronic transactions securely.

Regulatory policy

5. Transactions carried out by electronic means shall be regulated in a manner that -

(a) permits and encourages the growth of business by electronic means through

the operation of free market forces;

(b) promotes the greatest possible use of industry self-regulation;

(c) is flexible; and

(d) is technologically neutral.

Exclusions

6.(1) Part II (legal requirements respecting electronic records) and Part III (communication of electronic records) do not apply to any rule of law requiring writing or signatures for the following matters -

(a) the creation, execution or revocation of a will or testamentary instrument;

(b) the conveyance of real property or the transfer of any interest in real property.

(2) The Minister may by regulations provide that this Act, or such provisions thereof as may be specified in the regulations, does not apply to any class of transactions, persons, matters or things specified in the regulations.

Variation by agreement

7. As between parties involved in generating, sending, receiving, storing or otherwise processing records, any provision of Part II (legal requirements respecting electronic records) or Part III (communication of electronic records) may be varied by agreement.

PART II - LEGAL REQUIREMENTS RESPECTING ELECTRONIC RECORDS

Legal recognition of electronic records

8. Information shall not be denied legal effect, validity, admissibility or enforceability solely on the ground that it is -

(a) in the form of an electronic record; or

(b) not contained in the electronic record purporting to give rise to such legal effect, but is referred to in that electronic record.

Writing

9.(1) Where information is required by law to be in writing or is described in any statutory provision as being written, that requirement or description is met by an electronic record if the information contained in the electronic record is accessible and is capable of retention for subsequent reference.

(2) Subsection (1) applies whether the requirement for the information to be in writing is in the form of an obligation or the law provides consequences if it is not in writing.

Delivery

10.(1) Where information is required by law to be delivered, dispatched, given or sent to, or to be served on, a person, that requirement is met by doing so in the form of an electronic record provided that the originator of the electronic record states that the receipt of the electronic record is to be acknowledged and the addressee has acknowledged its receipt.

(2) Subsection (1) applies whether the requirement for delivery, dispatch, giving, sending or serving is in the form of an obligation or the law provides consequences for the information not being delivered, dispatched, given, sent or served.

Signature

11.(1) Where the signature of a person is required by law, that requirement is met by an electronic record if -

(a) a method is used to identify that person and to indicate that the person intended to sign or otherwise adopt the information in the electronic record; and

(b) where it is required that information be presented, that information is capable of being accurately represented to the person to whom it is to be presented.

(2) Subsection (1) applies whether the requirement for the information to be presented or retained in its original form is in the form of an obligation or the law provides consequences if it is not presented or retained in its original form.

(3) For the purposes of subsection (1)(a) -

(a) the criterion for assessing integrity is whether the information has remained complete and unaltered, apart from the addition of any endorsement and any change which arises in the normal course of communication, storage and display; and

(b) the standard of reliability required is to be assessed in the light of the purpose for which the information was generated and all the relevant circumstances.

Retention of electronic records

13.(1) Where certain documents, records or information are required by law to be retained, that requirement is met by retaining electronic records if the following conditions are satisfied -

(a) the information contained in the electronic record is accessible and is capable of retention for subsequent reference;

(b) the electronic record is retained in the format in which it was generated, sent or received, or in a format which can be demonstrated to represent accurately the information generated, sent or received; and

(c) any information that enables the identification of the origin and destination of an electronic record and the date and time when it was sent or received is retained.

(2) An obligation to retain documents, records or information in accordance with subsection (1) does not extend to any information the sole purpose of which is to enable the message to be sent or received.

(3) A person may satisfy the requirement referred to in subsection (1) by using the services of any other person, if the conditions set out in subsection (1)(a), (b) and (c) are met.

Admissibility and evidential weight of electronic records

14.(1) In any legal proceedings, nothing in the rules of evidence shall apply so as to deny the admissibility of an electronic record in evidence -

(a) solely on the ground that it is an electronic record; or

(b) if it is the best evidence that the person adducing it could reasonably be expected to obtain, on the ground that it is not in its original form.

(2) Information in the form of an electronic record will be given due evidential weight and in assessing the evidential weight of an electronic record, regard shall be had to—

(a) the reliability of the manner in which the electronic record was generated, stored or communicated;

(b) the reliability of the manner in which the integrity of the information was maintained;

(c) the manner in which the originator was identified; and

(d) any other relevant factor.

(3) This section does not affect the application of sections 27E, 27F, 43A and 43B of the Evidence Act 1905 (which relate to the admissibility of documents produced by computers).

PART III - COMMUNICATION OF ELECTRONIC RECORDS

Formation and validity of contracts

15.(1) In the context of formation of contracts, unless otherwise agreed by the parties, an offer and the acceptance of an offer may be expressed by means of electronic records.

(2) As between the originator and the addressee of an electronic record, a declaration of intention or other statement or delivery of a deed shall not be denied legal effect, validity or enforceability solely on the ground that it is in the form of an electronic record.

Attribution of electronic records

16.(1) An electronic record is attributable to a person if the electronic record resulted from the action of the person, acting in person, by his agent, or by his electronic agent device.

(2) Attribution may be proven in any manner, including by showing the efficacy of any security procedure applied to determine the person to whom the electronic record was attributable.

(3) Attribution of an electronic record by a person under this section has the effect provided for by the law, regulation, or agreement regarding the security procedure.

Acknowledgement of receipt of electronic records

17.(1) Subsections (2), (3) and (4) apply where, on or before sending an electronic record, or by means of that electronic record, the originator has requested or has agreed with the addressee that receipt of the electronic record be acknowledged.

(2) Where the originator has not agreed with the addressee that the acknowledgement be given in a particular form or by a particular method, an acknowledgement may be given by -

(a) any communication by the addressee, automated or otherwise; or

(b) any conduct of the addressee,that is reasonably sufficient to indicate to the originator that the electronic record has been received.

(3) Where the originator has stated that the electronic record is conditional on receipt of the acknowledgement, the electronic record is to be treated as though it had never been sent until the acknowledgement is received.

(4) Where the originator has not stated that the electronic record is conditional on receipt of the acknowledgement, and the acknowledgement has not been received by the originator within the time specified or agreed or, if no time has been specified or agreed, within a reasonable time, the originator -

(a) may give notice to the addressee stating that no acknowledgement has been received and specifying a reasonable time by which the acknowledgement must be received; and

(b) if the acknowledgement is not received within the time specified in paragraph (a), may, upon notice to the addressee, treat the electronic record as though it had never been sent or exercise any other rights the originator may have.

(5) Where the originator receives the addressee's acknowledgement of receipt, it is presumed that the related electronic record was received by the addressee, but that presumption does not imply that the electronic record corresponds to the record received.

(6) Where the received acknowledgement states that the related electronic record met technical requirements, either agreed upon or set forth in applicable standards, it is presumed that those requirements have been met.

(7) Except in so far as it relates to the sending or receipt of the electronic record, this section is not intended to deal with the legal consequences that may flow either from that electronic record or from the acknowledgement of its receipt.

Time and place of dispatch and receipt of electronic records

18.(1) Unless otherwise agreed between the originator and the addressee, the dispatch of an electronic record occurs when it enters an information processing system outside the control of the originator.

(2) Unless otherwise agreed between the originator and the addressee, the time of receipt of an electronic record is determined as follows -

(a) where the addressee has designated an information processing system for the purpose of receiving electronic records, receipt occurs—

(i) at the time when the electronic record enters the designated information processing system; or

(ii) if the electronic record is sent to an information processing system of the addressee that is not the designated information processing system, at the time when the electronic record comes to the attention of the addressee;

(b) where the addressee has not designated an information processing system, receipt occurs when the electronic record enters an information processing system of the addressee or otherwise comes to the attention of the addressee.

(3) Subsection (2) applies notwithstanding that the place where the information processing system is located may be different from the place where the electronic record is deemed to be received under subsection (4).

(4) Unless otherwise agreed between the originator and the addressee, an electronic record is deemed to be dispatched at the place where the originator has his place of business, and is deemed to be received at the place where the addressee has his place of business.

(5) For the purposes of subsection (4) -

(a) if the originator or the addressee has more than one place of business, the place of business is that which has the closest relationship to the transaction to which the electronic record relates or, where there is no such transaction, the place of business is presumed to be the principal place of business; or

(b) if the originator or the addressee does not have a place of business, it is presumed to be where the originator or the addressee ordinarily resides.

PART IV - ELECTRONIC SIGNATURES

Electronic signature associated with an accredited certificate

19. An electronic signature that is associated with an accredited certificate issued by an authorised certification service provider under section 20 is deemed to satisfy the requirements of subsection 11(1)(a) and (b).

Certification and revocation of certification

20.(1) The provision of certification services for electronic signatures is not subject to prior authorisation.

(2) The Minister, on application by a certification service provider and on payment of such fee as may be prescribed under the Government Fees Act 1965, may, if satisfied that the applicant meets the relevant criteria (which may include criteria in respect to electronic signature products), by notice published in the Gazette, authorise the applicant to provide accredited certificates.

(3) Subject to subsection (4), the Minister, if satisfied that an authorised certification service provider no longer meets the relevant criteria, may by notice published in the Gazette revoke an authorisation given under subsection (2).

(4) Before revoking an authorisation under subsection (3), the Minister shall give notice in writing to the authorised certification service provider of his intention to do so and indicating his reasons for the proposed revocation and shall invite the authorised certification service provider, within 14 days of the notice, to submit representations in writing as to why the authorisation should not be revoked, and the Minister shall consider those representations.

(5) In this section the "relevant criteria" means such policy criteria as the Minister may specify by notice published in the Gazette.

Recognition of external certification service providers

21.(1) The Minister may by notice published in the Gazette, recognise certificates or classes of certificates issued in, or certification service providers or classes of certification service providers established in any other jurisdiction and, upon such recognition and on payment of such fee as may be prescribed under the Government Fees Act 1965 -

(a) those certificates or classes of certificates shall be deemed to be accredited certificates; and

(b) those certification service providers or classes of certification service providers shall be deemed to be authorised under subsection 20(2).

(2) In determining to accord recognition under subsection (1) the Minister shall have regard to whether -

(a) the certificates or classes of certificates are required to, and do in fact, meet obligations equivalent to those required for an accredited certificate; and

(b) the certification service providers or classes of certification service providers are required to, and do in fact, meet criteria equivalent to those required for an authorised certification service provider.

(3) The Minister may, by notice published in the Gazette, revoke any recognition accorded under subsection (1), but, before doing so, the Minister shall advise the person affected of his intention to do so and indicating his reasons for the proposed revocation and shall invite that person, within 14 days of the notice, to submit representations in writing as to why the recognition should not be revoked, and the Minister shall consider those representations.

Pseudonyms

22.(1) Certification service providers may, at the request of a particular signatory, indicate in the relevant certificate a pseudonym instead of the signatory's name.

(2) Where a pseudonym is indicated pursuant to subsection (1), the certification service provider shall, where necessary for the investigation of an offence involving the use of electronic signatures or where otherwise required by law to do so, transfer personal data relating to the signatory.

(3) Where personal data is transferred pursuant to subsection (2), the certification service provider shall make a record of the transfer and as soon as possible thereafter give notice to the signatory of the transfer.

Liability of authorised certification service provider

23.(1) By issuing an accredited certificate, an authorised certification service provider is liable to any person who reasonably relied on the certificate for -

(a) the accuracy of all information in the accredited certificate as from the date on which it was issued, unless the authorised certification service provider has stated otherwise in the accredited certificate;

(b) assurance that the person identified in the accredited certificate held, at the time the accredited certificate was issued, the signature creation device corresponding to the signature verification device given or identified in the accredited certificate;

(c) if the authorised certification service provider generates both the signature creation device and the signature verification device, assurance that the two devices function together in a complementary manner, unless the person who relied on the accredited certificate knows or ought reasonably to have known that the authorisation of the certification service provider has been revoked.

(2) An authorised certification service provider is not liable for errors in the information in an accredited certificate where -

(a) the information was provided by or on behalf of the person identified in the accredited certificate; and

(b) the certification service provider can demonstrate that he has taken all reasonably practical measures to verify that information.

(3) An authorised certification service provider that -

(a) indicates in the accredited certificate limits on the uses of that certificate; and

(b) makes those limits known to third parties, is not liable for damages arising from the use of the accredited certificate contrary to those limits.

(4) The limits in subsection (3) may include a limit on the value of transactions for which the accredited certificate is valid.

PART V - ENCRYPTION

Regulations

24.(1) The Minister may make regulations -

(a) respecting the use, import and export of encryption programs or other encryption products;

(b) prohibiting the export of encryption programs or other encryption products from Bermuda generally or subject to such restrictions as may be prescribed.

(2) For the avoidance of doubt it is declared that, subject to any regulations made under subsection (1), it is lawful in Bermuda for a person to use any encryption program or other encryption product of any bit size or other measure of the strength of the encryption provided that it has lawfully come into the possession of that person.

Amendments to the Criminal Code

25. Section 464 of the Criminal Code Act 1907 is amended -

(a) in subsection (1), by inserting after the words "any such thing" the words ", together with any device, computer program or information necessary to secure access to, or to comprehend the meaning of, such thing or its contents";

(b) by inserting the following after subsection (1) -

"(1A) If it appears to a magistrate or to a Justice of the Peace, on complaint made on oath, that there are reasonable grounds for suspecting that a person is in possession of information or of a computer, computer program on any similar device which is relevant to the interpretation of any thing seized under subsection (1), then the magistrate or Justice of the Peace may direct that person to assist a police officer in the manner provided in subsection (7).

(c) by the addition of the following:

"(6) If the thing seized under a warrant issued under subsection (1) is a computer, computer program, or any other similar device, the magistrate may direct that a police officer be permitted to make copies of any information, software or data required for the investigation or prosecution of an offence and may direct any person arrested in connection with the warrant pursuant to which the computer, computer program or other similar device was seized to disclose or execute any procedure necessary to render the contents of the computer intelligible.

(7) If any other person is in possession of the devices, procedures or information necessary to render intelligible the contents of a computer, computer program, or any other similar device, for the purposes of subsection (6), then the magistrate may by direction pursuant to subsection (1A), require such person to surrender or provide copies of such devices or information or to execute such procedures.

(8) Any person who fails to comply with a direction under subsection (1A), (6) or (7) is guilty of an offence and is liable on summary conviction to imprisonment for 6 months or to a fine of $50,000, or to both.".

PART VI - DATA PROTECTION

Data protection

26.(1) The Minister may make regulations prescribing standards for the processing of personal data whether or not the personal data originates inside Bermuda.

(2) The regulations may provide for -

(a) the voluntary registration and de-registration to the standards by data controllers and data processors;

(b) the establishment of a register that is available for public inspection showing particulars of data controllers and data processors who have registered or de-registered to the standards and the dates thereof and the countries in respect of which the registration applies;

(c) the application of the standards to those countries specified in the regulations;

(d) different standards to be applied in respect of personal data originating from different countries.

(3) A data controller or data processor who voluntarily registers to a standard in subsection (1) must comply with the standard, as it may be amended from time to time, in respect to any personal data originating from a country to which the standard applies that is collected by the data controller during the period of registration, including any time after de-registration, and, if he fails to do so, is guilty of an offence and is liable on summary conviction to imprisonment for 6 months or to a fine of $50,000, or to both.

PART VII - INTERMEDIARIES AND E-COMMERCE SERVICE PROVIDERS

Liability of intermediaries

27.(1) An intermediary is not subject to any civil or criminal liability in respect of any information contained in an electronic record in respect of which the intermediary provides services, if the intermediary was not the originator of that electronic record and -

(a) has no actual knowledge that the information gives rise to civil or criminal liability;

(b) is not aware of any facts or circumstances from which the likelihood of civil or criminal liability in respect of the information ought reasonably to have been known; or

(c) follows the procedure set out in section 28 if the intermediary -

(i) acquires knowledge that the information gives rise to civil or criminal liability; or

(ii) becomes aware of facts or circumstances from which the likelihood of civil or criminal liability in respect of the information ought reasonably to have been known.

(2) An intermediary is not required to monitor any information contained in an electronic record in respect of which the intermediary provides services in order to establish knowledge of, or to become aware of, facts or circumstances to determine whether or not the information gives rise to civil or criminal liability.

(3) Nothing in this section relieves an intermediary from complying with any court order, injunction, writ, Ministerial direction, regulatory requirement, or contractual obligation in respect of an electronic record.

Procedure for dealing with unlawful, defamatory etc. information

28.(1) If an intermediary has actual knowledge that the information in an electronic record gives rise to civil or criminal liability, as soon as practicable the intermediary shall -

(a) remove the information from any information processing system within the intermediary's control and cease to provide or offer to provide services in respect of that information; and

(b) notify the Minister or appropriate law enforcement agency of the relevant facts and of the identity of the person for whom the intermediary was supplying services in respect of the information, if the identity of that person is known to the intermediary.

(2) If an intermediary is aware of facts or circumstances from which the likelihood of civil or criminal liability in respect of the information in an electronic record ought reasonably to have been known as soon as practicable the intermediary shall -

(a) follow the relevant procedure set out in a code of conduct approved or standard appointed under section 29 if such code or standard applies to the intermediary; or

(b) notify the Minister.

(3) If the Minister is notified in respect of any information under subsection (2), the Minister may direct the intermediary to -

(a) remove the electronic record from any information processing system within the control of the intermediary;

(b) cease to provide services to the person to whom the intermediary was supplying services in respect of that electronic record; and

(c) cease to provide services in respect of that electronic record.

(4) An intermediary is not liable, whether in contract, tort, under statute or pursuant to any other right, to any person, including any person on whose behalf the intermediary provides services in respect of information in an electronic record, for any action the intermediary takes in good faith in exercise of the powers conferred by, or as directed by the Minister under, this section.

Codes of conduct and standards for intermediaries and e-commerce service providers

29.(1) If a code of conduct is approved or a standard is appointed by the Minister under this section to apply to intermediaries or e-commerce service providers, those intermediaries or e-commerce service providers must comply with the code of conduct or standard.

(2) An intermediary or e-commerce service provider who fails to comply with an approved code of conduct or appointed standard, shall in the first instance be given a written warning by the Minister and the Minister may direct that person to cease and desist or otherwise to correct his practices, and, if that person fails to do so within such period as may be specified in the direction, he shall be guilty of an offence and be liable on summary conviction to a fine of $5,000 for each day on which the contravention continues.

(3) If the Minister is satisfied that a body or organization represents intermediaries or e-commerce service providers, the Minister may, by notice given to the body or organization, request that body or organization to -

(a) develop a code of conduct that applies to intermediaries or e-commerce service providers and that deals with one or more specified matters relating to the provision of services by those intermediaries or e-commerce service providers; and

(b) provide a copy of that code of conduct to the Minister within such time as may be specified in the request.

(4) If the Minister is satisfied with the code of conduct provided under subsection (3), the Minister shall approve the code of conduct by notice published in the Gazette and thereupon the code of conduct applies to intermediaries or e-commerce service providers as may be specified in the notice.

(5) If the Minister is satisfied that -

(a) no body or organization represents intermediaries or e-commerce service providers; or

(b) a body or organization to which notice is given under subsection (3) has not complied with the request of the Minister under that subsection, the Minister may, by notice published in the Gazette, appoint a standard that applies to intermediaries or e-commerce service providers.

(6) If the Minister has approved a code of conduct or appointed a standard that applies to intermediaries or e-commerce service providers and -

(a) the Minister receives notice from a body or organization representing intermediaries or e-commerce service providers of proposals to amend the code of conduct or standard; or

(b) the Minister no longer considers that the code of conduct or standard is appropriate,the Minister may, by notice published in the Gazette, revoke or amend any existing code of conduct or standard.

(7) A code of conduct approved or standard appointed under this section may relate to one or more of the following matters -

(a) the types of services and of customers that are permitted to be provided services by intermediaries;

(b) the types of information permitted to be contained in electronic records for which services are provided by intermediaries;

(c) the contractual application of relevant codes of conduct or standards to customers of intermediaries and e-commerce service providers;

(d) information to be disclosed by intermediaries and e-commerce service providers including name, address, e-mail address and contact and registration details;

(e) the use of a quality accreditation mark associated with Bermuda;

(f) the actions to be taken in the event of customers of intermediaries or e-commerce service providers sending bulk, unsolicited electronic records;

(g) business activities prohibited by the Tenth Schedule to the Companies Act 1981;

(h) publication of material that contravenes the Obscene Publications Act 1973 or the Criminal Code Act 1907;

(i) procedures for dealing with complaints;

(j) procedures for dispute resolution, including dispute resolution by electronic means;

(k) such other matters as the Minister may require.

(8) References in this section to intermediaries and e-commerce service providers include reference to a particular class of intermediary and a particular class of e-commerce service provider respectively.

PART VIII - E-COMMERCE ADVISORY BOARD

E-Commerce Advisory Board

30.(1) There shall be a board to be known as the "E-Commerce Advisory Board" for the purpose of providing advice to the Minister on matters connected with the discharge of his functions under this Act.

(2) The Minister shall appoint the members of the Board by notice published in the Gazette.

(3) The Board shall consist of not fewer than 5 nor more than 11 persons appearing to the Minister to be knowledgeable about electronic commerce or international business.

(4) The Minister shall designate one of the persons appointed a member under subsection (2) to be the chairman of the Board.

(5) The Board shall determine its own procedure.

(6) The function of the Board is to advise the Minister on any matter referred to it by the Minister, or which, of its own initiative, the Board considers appropriate.

PART IX - GENERAL

Offences, liability of corporate officers

31. Where a corporation is guilty of an offence under this Act or regulations made under this Act, every person who at the time of the commission of the offence was a director or officer of the corporation is guilty of the like offence unless he proves that the contravention took place without his consent or that he exercised all due diligence to prevent the commission of the offence.

Regulations

32.(1) The Minister may make regulations generally for any matter the Minister considers necessary to give effect to this Act and, in particular, -

(a) prescribing the relevant criteria for the issue of an accredited certificate;

(b) respecting any matter for which provision may be made by regulations under this Act.

(2) The regulations may provide that any contravention of a provision thereof constitutes an offence and may prescribe a penalty for that offence.

(3) Regulations made under subsection (1) are subject to the negative resolution procedure.

Consequential amendments

33. The Acts set out in column 1 of the Schedule are amended in the manner set out in column 2 of that Schedule.

Commencement

34. This Act or any provision thereof comes into operation on such day as the Minister may appoint by notice published in the Gazette.

SCHEDULE (section 32)

Arbitration Act 1986

section 20 Insert after subsection (1) the following -

"(1A) For the purposes of subsection (1) the examination of witnesses on oath or affirmation and the administering of oaths or the taking of affirmations of witnesses in the arbitration may be conducted by appropriate electronic means.".

Bermuda International Conciliation and Arbitration Act 1993

section 7 Insert next after subsection (3) the following -

"(4) For the purposes of subsection (2) -

(a) discussions with one or more parties;

(b) the hearing of witnesses, experts or parties;

(c) the inspection of documents, goods or other property; and

(d) consultation with the conciliator,

may, as far as is practicable, be conducted by electronic means and the conciliator and one or more of the parties are not required to be physically present in the same place at any time.".

section 21 Insert next after subsection (4) the following -

"(5) Conciliation proceedings need not be conducted by way of oral hearing or oral argument, or conducted on the basis of documents or other materials, and may, at the option of the parties, be conducted by electronic means, including electronic exchange of documents or by video conference.".

section 37 Insert next after subsection (4) the following -

"(5) For the purposes of subsections (1) and (2), proceedings conducted by way of oral hearings for the presentation of evidence or for oral argument, or conducted on the basis of documents or other materials, may be conducted by appropriate electronic means.".

Companies Act 1981

section 129 Insert next after subsection (1A) the following -

"(1B) Nothing in subsection (1)(e) shall prohibit an exempted company from offering goods or services electronically from a place of business in Bermuda or through an internet or other electronic service provider located in Bermuda.".

section 133 Insert next after subsection (4) the following -

"(5) A company shall be deemed to engage in or carry on any trade or business in Bermuda if it makes known by way of advertisement or by any statement on a web site or by an electronic record as defined in the Electronic Transactions Act 1999 that it may be contacted at a particular address in Bermuda or if it uses a Bermudian domain name.".

Computer Misuse Act 1996

section 6 Insert next after section 6 the following -

"Causing computer to cease to function

6A(1) A person is guilty of an offence if -

(a) he causes a computer to cease to function permanently or temporarily; and

(b) at the time he engages in conduct that causes a computer to cease to function permanently or temporarily he has -

(i) knowledge that the conduct is unauthorised;

(ii) the requisite know-ledge; and

(iii) the requisite intent.

(2) For the purposes of subsection (1)(b) -

(a) "requisite knowledge" is knowledge that the conduct would or would be likely to cause a computer to cease to function permanently or temporarily; and

(b) "requisite intent" is intent to cause a computer to cease to function and by so doing -

(i) prevent or hinder access to the computer; or

(ii) impair the operation of the computer,

but the intent need not be directed at a particular computer.

(3) A person guilty of an offence under this section is liable -

(a) on summary conviction to imprisonment for 6 months or to a fine of $6,000 or to both;

(b) on conviction or indictment to imprisonment for 5 years or to a fine of $20,000 or to both.".

section 7 In subsection (1), delete "or 5" and substitute ", 5 or 6A".

Insert next after subsection (3) the following:

"(3A) "Significant link", in relation to an offence under section 6A, means -

(a) that the accused was in Bermuda when he engaged in conduct which caused the computer to cease to function permanently or temporarily; or

(b) that the computer was in Bermuda.".

Exempted Partnerships Act 1992

section 19 Insert next after subsection (2) the following -

"(2A) Nothing in subsection (1)(e) shall prohibit an exempted partnership from offering goods or services electronically from a place of business in Bermuda or through an internet or other electronic service provider located in Bermuda.".

Government Authorities (Fees) Act 1971

First Schedule Insert after the entry relating to the Development Applications Board the following -

"E-Commerce Advisory Board established under section 30 of the Electronic Transactions Act 1999".

Interpretation Act 1951

section 7(1) Insert after the definition of "public place" the following -

""record" includes a record created, stored, generated, received or communicated by electronic, magnetic, optical or other similar means;".

Overseas Partnerships Act 1995

section 11 Insert next after subsection (2) the following -

"(2A) Nothing in subsection (1)(e) shall prohibit an overseas partnership from offering goods or services electronically from a place of business in Bermuda or through an internet or other electronic service provider located in Bermuda.

(2B) An overseas partnership shall be deemed to engage in or carry on any trade or business in Bermuda if it makes known by way of advertisement or by any statement on a web site or by an electronic record as defined in the Electronic Transactions Act 1999 that it may be contacted at a particular address in Bermuda or if it uses a Bermudian domain name.".

THE EXEMPTED UNDERTAKINGS TAX PROTECTION ACT 1966

(as amended)

ARRANGEMENT OF SECTIONS

Interpretation.

1. In this Act -

"exempted undertakings" means -

(*a*) an exempted company within the section 127 of the Companies Act 1981; or

(*b*) an exempted partnership within section 2 of the Exempted Partnerships Act 1992; or

(*c*) an exempted unit trust scheme;

"exempted unit trust scheme" means an arrangement made for the purpose, or having the effect, of providing, for persons having funds available for investment, facilities whereby those persons may participate as beneficiaries under a non-resident trust in profits or income arising from the acquisition, holding, management or disposal of any property whatsoever;

"the Minister" means the Minister of Finance;

"non-resident trust" means a trust of which the trustee has been designated under the Exchange Control Regulations 1973 as not resident in Bermuda.

Authorization to give assurance.

2.(1) The Minister is hereby authorized to enter into an arrangement with any exempted undertaking that shall make application to the Accountant-General therefor, whereby such undertakings may be given an assurance that, in the event of there being enacted in these Islands any legislation imposing tax computed on profits or income or computed on any capital asset, gain or appreciation, then the imposition of any such tax shall not be applicable to such undertakings or to any of its operations.

(2) Any such arrangement as is referred to in subsection (1) may include an assurance that the aforesaid taxes, and any tax in the nature of estate duty or inheritance tax, shall not be applicable to the shares, debentures or other obligations of such undertaking.

(3) Any such assurance as aforesaid may be for any period not exceeding fifty years from the date of the commencement of this Act and may be in such form as the Minister shall determine.

Application to persons normally resident in these Islands.

3. In the event of the enactment of any legislation in these Islands imposing any tax referred to in this Act, then nothing contained herein shall be construed so as to prevent the application of any such tax to such persons ordinarily resident in these Islands to whom it is appropriate that such tax should be applied.

Repeal and saving.

4. The Exempted Companies Tax Protection Act 1956 shall be repealed:

Provided that any undertaking given to any exempted company under the provisions of that Act shall be deemed to be an assurance given under this Act and shall continue to have full force and effect as if so given for the period therein specified.

JUDGMENTS (RECIPROCAL ENFORCEMENT) ACT 1958

(1989 Revision)

ARRANGEMENT OF SECTIONS

Interpretation

1.(1) In this Act unless the context otherwise requires -

"appeal" includes any proceeding by way of discharging or setting aside a judgment or an application for a new trial or a stay of execution;

"judgment" means a judgment or order given or made by a court in any civil proceedings, or a judgment or order given or made by a court in any criminal proceedings for the payment of a sum of money in respect of compensation or damages to an injured party; and it also includes an award in proceedings on an arbitration if the award has, in pursuance of the law in force in the place where it was made, become enforceable in the same manner as a judgment given by a court in that place;

"judgment creditor" means the person who has obtained the judgment, and includes his successors and assigns;

"judgment debtor" means the person against whom judgment has been given, and includes every person against whom the judgment is enforceable in the place where it was given;

"registration" and its cognate expressions means registration of a judgment under this Act;

"the superior courts of the United Kingdom" means the High Court in England, the Court of Sessions in Scotland, the High Court in Northern Ireland, the Court of Chancery of the County Palantine of Lancaster or the Court of Chancery of the County Palantine of Durham, and includes judgments given in any courts on appeals against any judgments so given.

(2) For the purposes of this Act, "action in personam" shall be deemed not to include any matrimonial cause or any proceedings in connection with any of the following matters, that is to say, matrimonial matters, administration of estates of deceased persons, bankruptcy, winding-up of companies, lunacy or guardianship of infants.

Judgments to which Act applies

2.(1) Any judgment given in the superior courts of the United Kingdom, other than a judgment of such a court given on appeal from a court which is not a superior court, shall be a judgment to which this Act applies, if -

(a) it is final and conclusive as between the parties thereto; and

(b) there is payable thereunder a sum of money, not being a sum payable in respect of taxes or other charges of a like nature or in respect of a fine or other penalty.

(2) For the purposes of this section, a judgment shall be deemed to be final and conclusive notwithstanding that an appeal may be pending against it, or that it may still be subject to appeal in the United Kingdom.

Application by judgment creditor to register judgment in Supreme Court

3.(1) A person, being a judgment creditor under a judgment to which this Act applies, being a judgment given after 14 December 1958, may apply to the Supreme Court at any time within six years after the date of such judgment, or, where there have been proceedings by way of appeal against the judgment, after the date of the last judgment given in those proceedings, to have the judgment registered in the Supreme Court, and on any such application the Supreme Court shall, subject to the proof of the matters required by Rules of Court and to the other provisions of this Act order the judgment to be registered:

Provided that a judgment shall not be registered if at the date of the application -

(a) it has been wholly satisfied; or

(b) it could not be enforced by execution in the United Kingdom.

(2) In the case of a judgment to which this Act applies given before the 15 December 1958, subsection (1) shall apply save that the time limited for registration shall be twelve months from the date of the judgment or such longer period as may be allowed by the Supreme Court.

(3) Subject to the provisions of this Act with respect to the setting aside of registration -

(a) a registered judgment shall, for the purposes of execution, be of the same force and effect; and

(b) proceedings may be taken on a registered judgment; and

(c) the sum for which a judgment is registered shall carry interest; and

(d) the Supreme Court shall have the same control over the execution of a registered judgment;

as if the judgment had been a judgment originally given in the Supreme Court and entered therein on the date of registration:

Provided that execution shall not issue on such judgment so long as, under this Act and rules made under section 10, it is competent for any party to make an application to have registration set aside, or, where such application is made, until after such application has been finally determined.

(4) Where the sum payable under a judgment to which this Act applies is expressed in a currency not legal tender in Bermuda, such judgment shall be registered as if it were a judgment for such sum in the currency of Bermuda, on the basis of the rate of exchange prevailing at the date of such judgment, as is equivalent to the sum so payable.

(5) If at the date of an application for registration, a judgment to which this Act applies has been partly satisfied, such judgment shall not be registered in respect of the whole sum payable thereunder but only in respect of the balance remaining payable at that date.

(6) If, on an application for registration, it appears to the Supreme Court that a judgment to which this Act applies is in respect of different matters and that some, but not all, of the provisions of such judgment are such that if those provisions had been contained in separate judgments those judgments could properly have been registered, such judgment may be registered in respect of the provisions aforesaid but not in respect of any other provisions contained therein.

(7) In addition to the sum payable under a judgment to which this Act applies, including any interest which by the law of the United Kingdom becomes due under the judgment up to the time of registration, such judgment shall be registered for the reasonable costs of and incidental to registration, including the costs of obtaining a certified copy of such judgment.

Setting aside registration

4.(1) On an application in that behalf duly made by any party against whom a registered judgment may be enforced, the registration -

(a) shall be set aside if the Supreme Court is satisfied -

(i) that the judgment is not a judgment to which this Act applies or was registered in contravention of this Act; or

(ii) that the courts of the United Kingdom had no jurisdiction in the circumstances of the case; or

(iii) that the judgment debtor, being the defendant in the proceedings giving rise to the registered judgment, did not (notwithstanding that process may have been duly served on him in accordance with the law of the United Kingdom) receive notice of those proceedings in sufficient time to enable him to defend the proceedings and did not appear; or

(iv) that the judgment was obtained by fraud; or

(v) that the rights under the judgment are not vested in the person by whom the application for registration was made:

(b) may be set aside if the Supreme Court is satisfied that the matter in dispute in the proceedings giving rise to the registered judgment had, previously to the date of such judgment, been the subject of a final and conclusive judgment by a court having jurisdiction in the matter.

(2) For the purposes of this section, the superior courts of the United Kingdom shall, subject to sub-section (3), be deemed to have had jurisdiction -

(a) in the case of a judgment given in an action in personam -

(i) if the judgment debtor, being a defendant ion the proceedings giving rise to such judgment, submitted to the jurisdiction of that court by voluntarily appearing in such proceedings otherwise than for the purpose of protecting, or obtaining the release of property seized, or threatened with seizure in such proceedings or of contesting the jurisdiction of the court; or

(ii) if the judgment debtor was a plaintiff in, or counterclaimed in, the proceedings giving rise to such judgment; or

(iii) if the judgment debtor, being a defendant in the proceedings giving rise to such judgment, had, before the commencement of such proceedings, agreed, in respect of the subject matter thereof, to submit to the jurisdiction of the court giving such judgment or of the courts of the United Kingdom; or

(iv) if the judgment debtor, being a defendant in the proceedings giving rise to such judgment, was at the time when such proceedings were instituted resident in, or being a body corporate had its principal place of business in, the United Kingdom; or

(v) if the judgment debtor, being a defendant in the proceedings giving rise to such judgment, had an office or place of business in the United Kingdom and such proceedings were in respect of a transaction effected through or at such office or place;

(b) in the case of a judgment given in an action of which the subject matter was immovable property or in an action *in rem* of which the subject matter was movable property, if the property in question was, at the time of the proceedings giving rise to such judgment, situate in the United Kingdom;

(c) in the case of a judgment given in an action other than any of the actions mentioned in paragraph (a) or paragraph (b), if the jurisdiction of the court giving such judgment is recognized by the law of Bermuda.

(3) Notwithstanding subsection (2), the courts of the United Kingdom shall not be deemed to have had jurisdiction -

(a) if the subject of the proceedings was immovable property situated outside the United Kingdom; or

(b) except in the cases mentioned in subparagraphs (i), (ii) and (iii) of paragraph (a) and in paragraph (c) of subsection (2), if the bringing of the proceedings

giving rise to a registered judgment was contrary to an agreement under which the dispute in question was to be settled otherwise than by proceedings in the courts of the United Kingdom; or

(*c*) if the judgment debtor, being a defendant in the proceedings giving rise to a registered judgment, was a person who under the rules of public international law was entitled to immunity from the jurisdiction of the courts of the United Kingdom and did not submit to the jurisdiction thereof.

Powers of Supreme Court where appeal pending or judgment not enforceable by execution

5.(1) If on an application to set aside a registration, the applicant satisfies the Supreme Court either than an appeal against the judgment is pending, or that he is entitled and intends to appeal, against such judgment, the Supreme Court may, if it thinks fit, and upon such terms as it may think just, set aside such registration until after the expiration of such period as appears to the Court to be reasonably sufficient to enable the applicant to take the necessary steps to have such appeal disposed of by the competent tribunal.

(2) Where a registration is set aside under subsection (1), or solely for the reason that the judgment was not, at the date of the application for registration thereof, enforceable by execution, the setting aside of such registration shall not operate to prevent a further application to register such judgment when the appeal has been determined or when such judgment becomes enforceable by execution in the United Kingdom, as the case may be.

(3) Where a registration is set aside solely for the reason that the judgment, notwithstanding that it had at the date of the application for registration been partly satisfied, was registered for the whole sum payable thereunder, the Supreme Court shall, on the application of the judgment creditor, order judgment to be registered for the balance remaining payable at that date.

Exclusion of other proceedings in Bermuda

6. No proceedings for the recovery of a sum payable under a judgment to which this Act applies, other than proceedings provided for in this Act, shall be entertained by any court in Bermuda.

General effect of certain judgments

7.(1) Subject to this section, a judgment to which this Act applies or would have applied if a sum of money had been payable thereunder, whether it can be registered or not, and whether, if it can be registered, it is registered or not, shall be recognized in any court in Bermuda as conclusive between the parties thereto in all proceedings founded on the same cause of action and may be relied on by way of defence or counterclaim in any such proceedings.

(2) This section shall not apply in the case of any judgment -

(*a*) where the judgment has been registered and the registration thereof has been set aside on some ground other than -

(i) that a sum of money was not payable under the judgment; or

(ii) that the judgment had been wholly or partly satisfied; or

(iii) that at the date of the application the judgment could not be enforced by execution in the United Kingdom; or

(b) where the judgment has not been registered, and it is shown (whether it could have been registered or not) that if it had been registered the registration thereof would have been set aside on an application for that purpose on some ground other than one of the grounds set out in paragraph (a).

(3) Nothing in this section shall be taken to prevent any court in Bermuda recognizing any judgment as conclusive of any matter of law or fact decided therein if that judgment would have been so recognized before 15 December 1958.

Issue of certificates of judgments

8. Where a judgment under which a sum of money is payable, not being a sum payable in respect of taxes or other charges of a like nature or in respect of a fine or other penalty, has been entered in the Supreme Court against any person and the judgment creditor is desirous of enforcing such judgment in the United Kingdom, the Supreme Court shall, on an application made by the judgment creditor and on payment of such fee as may be prescribed, issue to the judgment creditor a certified copy of the judgment together with a certificate containing such particulars with respect to the action, including the causes of action, and the rate of interest, if any, payable on the sum payable under the judgment, as may be prescribed.

Provided that where execution of a judgment is stayed for any period pending an appeal or for any other reason, an application shall not be made under this section with respect to the judgment until the expiration of that period.

Extension to other countries

9.(1) Where the Governor is satisfied that reciprocal provisions have been made by the Legislature of any part of Her Majesty's dominions outside the United Kingdom for the enforcement within that part of Her Majesty's dominions of judgments obtained in the Supreme Court, the Governor may by Order declare that the application of this Act shall extend to judgments obtained in such courts in that part of Her Majesty's dominions as he may describe in the like manner as it extends to judgments obtained in a superior court in the United Kingdom, and in such case this Act shall apply accordingly.

(2) References in this section to Her Majesty's dominions outside the United Kingdom shall be construed as including references to any territories which are under Her Majesty's protection and any territories in respect of which trusteeship under the United Nations has been accepted by Her Majesty.

Rules; jurisdiction of judge

10.(1) Rules for the carrying into operation of this Act shall be made by the Supreme Court and shall provide -

(a) for the giving of security for costs by persons applying for registration;

(b) for prescribing the matters to be proved on an application for registration and for regulating the mode of proving such matters;

(c) for the serving on the judgment debtor of notice of registration;

(d) for the determination of the period within which an application to have registration set aside may be made and for the extension of such period;

(e) for prescribing the method by which any question arising under this Act regarding the enforceability of such judgment by execution in the United Kingdom, or the interest payable under such judgment, is to be determined;

(f) for prescribing the fees to be paid;

(g) for prescribing any matter which under this Act is required to be prescribed.

(2) Subject to any rule made under subsection (1), any of the powers conferred by this Act on the Supreme Court may be exercised by a judge.

(3) Section 6 of the Statutory Instruments Act 1977 [*title 1 item 3*] shall not apply to rules made under subsection (1).

Repeal

11. [*omitted*]

THE STAMP DUTIES ACT 1976

ARRANGEMENT OF SECTIONS

Part VI - Bills Of Exchange And Promissory Notes

28. Cheques supplied by licensed banks need not bear stamp.
29. Effect of non-compliance in case of certain bills of exchange.
30. Foreign bills and notes.
31. Bills in sets.
32. Unstamped bill of note.
33. Offence: unstamped bill or note.

Part VII - Conveyances

34. Calculation of stamp duty chargeable on conveyance on sale.
35. How consideration on periodical payments to be charged.
36. Provisions where property conveyed in consideration of debt.
37. Special considerations affecting amount of stamp duty chargeable on conveyance on sale.
38. Certain contracts to be chargeable with conveyance duty.
39. Voluntary conveyance inter vivos.

Part VIII - Settlements, Mutual Funds And Unit Trusts Schemes

40. Duty on settlement of money etc.
41. Calculation of duty where several instruments of settlement.
42. Additions to settlements to be made by stamped instrument.
43. Notification of issue of new shares.
44. Notification of issue of new units.
45. Enforcement of sections 42, 43 and 44.
46. Stamp duty on unit trusts.

Part IX - Affidavit Of Value Of Deceased Estate

47. Supreme Court not to grant probate or letter of administration in absence of affidavit as to value of estate.
48. Deductions.
49. Provision for return of duty overpaid.
50. Provision for payment of further duty.
51. Small estates.
52. Liability of estate representative.
53. Power of Registrar to require explanation and proof in support of valuation, and to reassess value.

Part X - Insurance

54. Duty to issue receipts.
55. Exempt policies may cease to be exempt.

Part XI - Miscellaneous Instruments

Part XII - Offences And Supplementary

Part XIII - Miscellaneous

PART I - Interpretation

Interpretation.

1. In this Act, unless the context otherwise requires -

"accident or health policy" means a policy of insurance against the risk of the happening of personal accident, whether fatal or not, disease or sickness, or any class of personal accident, disease or sickness;

"Bermuda property", in relation to an instrument, means property answering the description in subsections (2)(b), (3) and (4) of section 47, but subject -

(a) to the substitution, for the references there to the death of the deceased, of references to the date of execution of the instrument; and

(b) to the deletion of the words "belonging to the deceased" in sub-paragraph (ii) of the said subsection (2)(b);

"bill of exchange" shall have the meaning assigned to it in the Bills of Exchange Act 1934;

"binder" means a cover note or other instrument -

(a) issued by or on behalf of an insurer to an insured person or some other person;

(b) confirming that a contract of insurance has been made between the insurer and the insured person; and

(c) intended to be followed and superseded, and in fact followed and superseded, by a policy of insurance;

"charter party" means any instrument for the charter or hiring of any vessel or aircraft or of some principal part thereof, and any memorandum, letter or other writing (other than a bill of lading) between the master or owner of any vessel or aircraft and any other person for or relating to the freight or conveyance of any money, goods or effects on board any vessel or aircraft;

"cheque" means a bill of exchange drawn on a bank or banker in Bermuda and payable on demand;

"conveyance on sale" includes every instrument, and every decree or order of any court, whereby any real or personal property or any estate or interest in any such property upon the sale thereof is transferred to or vested in a purchaser, or any other person on his behalf or by his direction;

"debenture" includes a debenture, debenture stock and unsecured loan stock;

"deceased person" means person dying after the commencement of this Act;

"duly stamped" as applied to an instrument means that the instrument bears a stamp of not less than the proper amount and that such stamp has been affixed or used in accordance with the law for the time being in force in Bermuda;

"duty" means stamp duty;

"endorsement", in relation to a policy of insurance, means an instrument -

(a) made by an insurer and attached, or intended to be attached, to the policy; and

(b) calculated to modify the effect of the policy in some way;

"equitable mortgage" means an agreement or memorandum, under hand only, relating to the deposit of any title deeds or instruments constituting or being evidence of the title to any property whatever, or creating a charge on such property;

"estate representative" means the executor, original or by representation, or administrator for the time being of a deceased person;

"executed" and "execution" used with reference to instruments not under seal mean signed and signature respectively;

"exempt policy" means -

(a) a policy of insurance written in Bermuda where the risk insured against is situated outside Bermuda including -

(i) real property outside Bermuda;

(ii) personal property ordinarily situated outside Bermuda including vessels or aircraft registered in Bermuda if so situated;

(iii) the life or health of a person ordinarily resident outside Bermuda;

(b) a policy of reinsurance;

"exempted undertaking" means an exempt undertaking for the purposes of section 9 of the Miscellaneous Taxes Act 1976;

"foreign currency security" means a security, not being a share, denominated in a currency other than Bermuda area currency or on which capital moneys, dividends or interest are payable in a currency other than Bermuda area currency, or as respects which the holder has an option to require payment of any capital moneys, dividends or interest in a currency other than Bermuda area currency, and includes the documents commonly known as Eurobonds and analogous securities;

"Head" means head of stamp duty specified in the Schedule;

"instrument" includes every written document;

"insurance" includes "assurance";

"insurance premium receipt" means a receipt for premiums payable under a policy of insurance and where an annuity is taxed as a policy of insurance includes a receipt for premiums payable under an agreement for the grant of an annuity;

"lease" includes a sub-lease;

"legacy" means -

(a) every gift by will or testamentary instrument out of the estate of the testator or of property of which he had power to dispose;

(b) the residue or any share of the residue of estate under a partial or total intestacy;

(c) every gift having the effect of a *donatio mortis* causa;

"life policy" means a policy of insurance upon any life or lives or upon any event or contingency relating to or depending upon any life or lives except a policy of insurance against accident;

"marketable security" means a security of such a description as to be capable of being sold in the stock market in Bermuda and such other markets as may be recognized by the Bermuda Monetary Authority for the purposes of this definition by notice published in the Gazette;

"material" includes every sort of material upon which words or figures can be inscribed;

"Minister" means the Minister of Finance;

"mortgage" means a security by way of mortgage for the payment of any definite and certain sum of money advanced or lent at the time, or previously due, or forborne to be paid, being payable, or for the repayment of money to be thereafter lent, advanced or paid, or which may become due upon an account current, together with any sum already advanced or due, or without, as the case may be; and includes -

(a) any conveyance of any property in trust to be sold or otherwise converted into money intended only as a security, and redeemable before the sale or other disposal thereof, either by express stipulation or otherwise;

(b) any instrument in writing for defeating or making redeemable, or explaining or qualifying any conveyance of property, apparently absolute, but intended only as a security;

(c) any agreement (other than an agreement chargeable with duty as an equitable mortgage), contract or bond accompanied with a deposit of title deeds or with other instruments evidencing a right to property, for making a mortgage or any other security or conveyance as aforesaid of any property comprised in the titled deeds or other instruments or for pledging or charging the same as a security; and

(d) any deed operating as a mortgage of any stock or marketable security;

"mutual fund" shall have the meaning assigned to it in Part XIIA of the Companies Act 1981;

"new share", in relation to a mutual fund, means a share whose issue causes the number of shares in issue immediately after the issue of the share to exceed the largest number of shares that had ever at any one time been in issue before the share was issued; and "new unit", in relation to a unit trust scheme, shall have a corresponding meaning:

Provided that for the purposes of this definition -

(a) the issue of a new share or new unit to a person shall be deemed to include the registration of his entitlement to the shares or unit in a register of shares or unit-holders respectively; and

(b) where shares in a mutual fund or units in a unit trust scheme are subdivided or consolidated into shares or units of an amount different from that fixed by the memorandum of association of the fund or by the trust instrument respectively, the subdivision or consolidation shall be disregarded;

"partnership instrument" includes every agreement relating to the formation, continuance, reorganization or dissolution of any partnership, and every agreement relating to the alteration of any of the terms of any partnership;

"policy of insurance" includes every instrument, except a binder or an endorsement, whereby any contract of insurance is evidenced;

"power of attorney" means any instrument, except a warrant to act as an attorney in any judicial proceedings, empowering a specified person to act in the stead of the person executing it;

"premium", in relation to an insurance premium receipt, includes any consideration for an annuity;

"prescribed" means prescribed by regulations;

"promissory note" shall have the meaning assigned to it in the Bills of Exchange Act 1934;

"receipt" means any instrument, note, memorandum or writing whereby any money, or any bill of exchange or promissory note for money, is acknowledged or expressed to have been received or deposited or paid, or whereby any debt or demand or any part of a debt or demand is acknowledged to have been settled, satisfied or discharged, or which signifies or imports any such acknowledgement, and whether the same is or is not signed with the name of any person;

"Registrar" means the Registrar of the Supreme Court;

"regulations" means regulations under section 77;

"security" (except in sections 32 and 62 or Head 31 or otherwise where reference is intended merely to a document securing an obligation) means -

(a) any document, instrument or writing commonly known as a security;

(b) any document constituting evidence of title to or interest in the capital, assets, property, profits, earnings or royalties of any person or company;

(c) any document constituting evidence of an option, subscription or other interest in or to a security;

(d) any bond, debenture, share, stock, note, unit, unit certificate, participation certificate, certificate of share or interest, pre-organization certificate or subscription;

(e) any agreement providing that money received will be repaid or treated as a subscription to shares, stock, units or interest at the option of the recipient or of any person or company;

(f) any certificate of share or interest in a trust, estate or association;

(g) any profit-sharing agreement or certificate;

(h) any income or annuity contract not issued by a company whose ordinary business consists wholly or mainly of the carrying on of assurance or insurance business;

"settlement" means any non-testamentary disposition in writing whether made voluntarily or upon a good and valuable consideration other than a *bona fide pecuniary* consideration whereby any definite and certain property is settled or agreed to be settled in any manner for any purpose whatsoever;

"share" means any share or debenture in the capital stock or funded debt of any corporation, company or society wherever incorporated and includes stock;

"stamp" means any adhesive or impressed stamp for the time being available for the payment of stamp duty in Bermuda;

"stamped", with reference to material and instruments, applies as well to material and instruments impressed with stamps by means of dies as to material and instruments having adhesive stamps affixed thereto;

"stamp duty" means any duty or tax payable under this Act by affixing or impressing a stamp on the instrument liable to such duty or tax;

"testator" includes the donor of a *donatio mortis causa;*

"unit trust scheme" means any arrangements made for the purpose, or having the effect, of providing, for persons having funds available for investment, facilities for the participation by them, as beneficiaries under a trust, in profits or income arising from the acquisition, holding, management or disposal of any property whatsoever;

"trust instrument" means, in relation to a unit trust scheme, the trust deed or other instrument (whether under seal or not) creating or recording the trusts by virtue of which persons are to participate in the scheme;

"unit" means, in relation to a unit trust scheme, a right or interest (whether described as a unit, as a sub-unit, or otherwise) of a beneficiary under the trust instrument.

PART II - Liability To Stamp Duty

Instruments chargeable to stamp duty.

2. Subject to the provisions of this Act and to the exemptions contained in this Act or other statutory provision, the following instruments shall be chargeable with stamp duty in the amount specified in the Schedule as the proper stamp duty therefor -

(a) every instrument specified in the Schedule as an instrument chargeable with stamp duty which, not having been previously executed by any person, is executed in Bermuda after the commencement of this Act;

(b) every bill of exchange or promissory note drawn or made out of Bermuda after the commencement of this Act and accepted or paid, presented for acceptance or payment, or endorsed, transferred or otherwise negotiated in Bermuda;

(c) every instrument (other than a bill of exchange or promissory note) specified in the Schedule as an instrument chargeable with stamp duty which is executed out of Bermuda after the commencement of this Act, and is brought into Bermuda after such commencement and which requires stamping by virtue of the provisions of section 3.

Instruments executed outside Bermuda.

3.(1) Where an instrument is executed outside Bermuda which would be chargeable with stamp duty under paragraph (a) of section 2 if it were executed in Bermuda, it shall not be valid for any purpose in Bermuda, and in particular it shall not be registered in any register kept pursuant to any statutory provision in Bermuda, unless it is duly stamped under this Act (except that subsection (1) of section 5 shall not apply):

Provided that the provisions of a settlement executed outside Bermuda conferring on any person a power to appoint a trustee of the settlement and any powers supplementary thereto including the power to convey the settled property to such a trustee, shall be valid for the purpose of appointing any such trustee and exercising such supplementary powers notwithstanding that the settlement has not been stamped in accordance with the provisions of this subsection.

(2) For the purposes of this section a person who uses a copy of an instrument in lieu of the original of such instrument shall be deemed to use the original thereof.

Exemptions.

4. No stamp duty shall be payable by the Crown or any agency thereof or chargeable in respect of -

(a) any grant or lease of land where the Crown or any agency thereof is a party;

(b) any instrument for the sale, transfer or other disposition, either absolutely or by way of mortgage or otherwise, of any vessel (including a vessel under construction) or the rights of any person under an agreement for the construction of a vessel;

(c) any instrument for the sale, transfer, lease or other disposition, either absolutely or by way of mortgage or otherwise, of land situate out of Bermuda or any share, estate or interest in land situate out of Bermuda;

(d) any instrument (not being a policy of insurance) which relates exclusively to things to be done out of Bermuda;

(e) any instrument for the transfer on sale of any stock or marketable security issued by or on behalf of any Government or State, including the Government of Bermuda, or of any share or marketable security issued by or on behalf of any corporation, company or body of persons incorporated, formed or established out of Bermuda, except shares registered in a register kept in Bermuda in conformity with any statutory provision;

(f) conveyances or transfers on sale of any personal property situated out of Bermuda by instrument in writing made between parties none of whom is domiciled, resident or incorporated in Bermuda or regularly engaged in any gainful occupation, trade or business in Bermuda;

(g) a bill of exchange drawn on any bank or banker outside Bermuda.

PART III - Provisions Applicable To Instruments Generally

Time and liability to stamping.

5.(1) Subject to the provisions of sections 3 and 10 and Part VI the points of time before which and the periods of time within which the respective instruments must be stamped shall be those specified in the Schedule, and where it is provided in the Schedule that an instrument is to be stamped within a certain period of time after execution, that period of time shall, unless otherwise stated in the Schedule, be reckoned as commencing on the day after the execution of the instrument in question by the person who last executes it.

(2) Where in the Schedule it is specified that an instrument is to be stamped before execution, such instrument must be stamped before execution by any party thereto.

(3) If any instrument which is chargeable with stamp duty is not duly stamped, the person or persons respectively specified in the Schedule as liable for stamping shall be liable, or jointly or severally liable, as the case may be civilly to the Crown.

(4) In addition to the person or persons liable under subsection (3) for stamping an instrument chargeable with stamp duty any person who relies on or presents for registration an instrument drawn, made or executed out of Bermuda which is chargeable with stamp duty shall be liable for stamping such instrument.

(5) Where under this Act more than one person is liable for stamping an instrument chargeable with stamp duty under section 2, the liability shall be joint and several.

Method of stamping.

6.(1) Subject to the provisions of this Act instruments chargeable with stamp duty shall be stamped -

(a) by means of an adhesive stamp in accordance with section 7;

(b) by means of a stamp impressed by a franking machine licensed under section 8;

(c) where the instrument is stamped under subsection (2), by means of mechanically printed figures denoting the amount of stamp duty combined with a stamp impressed upon such figures; or

(d) in such other manner as may be prescribed.

(2) The public officer authorized by the Accountant General shall, on the presentation to him at his office of any instrument for the purposes of being stamped, and subject to section 9, affix thereto a stamp denoting the amount of duty paid.

Adhesive stamps.

7.(1) Stamp duty in an amount not exceeding one dollar may be paid by any adhesive stamp for the time being available for the payment of postage in Bermuda and in amounts greater than one dollar may be paid by any adhesive stamp for the time being available exclusively for payment of revenue in Bermuda or in a combination of such postage stamps (in an amount not exceeding one dollar) and such revenue stamps.

(2) An instrument is not to be deemed duly stamped with an adhesive stamp unless the person required by law to cancel the adhesive stamp cancels the same by writing on or across the stamp his name or initials, or the name or initials of his firm, together with the true date of his so writing, or otherwise effectively cancels the stamp and renders the same incapable of being used for any other instrument, or for any postal purpose, or unless it is otherwise proved that the stamp appearing on the instrument was affixed thereto at the proper time.

(3) Where two or more adhesive stamps are used to denote the stamp duty upon an instrument, each or every stamp is to be cancelled in the manner aforesaid.

(4) Where an instrument, the stamp duty on which is to be paid by an adhesive stamp, is to be stamped within a certain period after any event, the person affixing the adhesive stamp shall cancel it forthwith before he parts with the instrument.

(5) Subject to section and Part VI an instrument, the stamp duty on which is denoted by an adhesive stamp, shall not be deemed to have been duly stamped unless such stamp has been cancelled as required by this section.

(6) Any person who being required by law to cancel an adhesive stamp neglects or refuses duly and effectually to do so in the manner prescribed by subsection (2) shall be guilty of an offence.

Licensing of stamping machines.

8.(1) The Accountant General may license any person to use a machine approved of by him for the purposes of impressing stamps on documents chargeable with stamp duty.

(2) Any such licence may be granted subject to such terms and conditions as the Accountant General may think fit and the Accountant General may revoke any such licence and vary any terms and conditions thereof at any time without giving any reason therefor.

(3) The Accountant General may require any person to whom he grants a licence under this section to give such security as he thinks fit for the payment to him of the stamp duty chargeable on the instruments stamped by any such machine and may from time to time as he sees fit require further security to be given by that person and may, either in the alternative to requiring the giving of security or in addition thereto, require such person to deposit with him from time to time such sums of money as he thinks fit to the credit of that person.

Non-admissibility of unstamped instruments.

9.(1) Subject to subsection (3) and section 10 no instrument chargeable with stamp duty shall be received in evidence in any proceedings whatsoever, except -

(a) in criminal proceedings; and

(b) in civil proceedings on behalf of the Government to recover stamp duty,unless such instrument is duly stamped, whether the point of time before which or the period of time within which such an instrument should be stamped has or has not arrived or expired as the case may be.

(2) No instrument chargeable with stamp duty shall be acted upon, filed or registered by any public officer or by any company unless such instrument is duly stamped, whether the point of time before which or the period of time within which such instrument should be stamped has or has not arrived or expired as the case may be.

(3) Upon the production to any court (other than a criminal court), arbitrator, referee, or public officer, of any instrument which is chargeable with stamp duty and which is not duly stamped, it shall be the duty of such court, arbitrator, referee or public officer to take notice of the omission or insufficiency of the stamp on such instrument and thereupon to take action in accordance with the following rules -

(a) if the point of time before which or the period of time within which the instrument should have been stamped has arrived or expired, as the case may be, and the instrument is one in respect of which a person is specified in the Schedule as being liable for the stamping thereof, the instrument shall be impounded and, unless the instrument has been produced to the Accountant General, shall be forwarded to the Accountant General;

(b) whether or not the instrument is so impounded, before the exclusion or rejection of the instrument the person tendering such instrument shall, if he desires, be given a reasonable opportunity to stamp the instrument and, if such instrument may not be stamped save with the special permission of the Accountant General under section 10, to apply to the Accountant General for such permission.

(4) If a public officer is empowered or required by law to act upon, file, record or register, a duplicate or copy of any instrument, and if the original of such instrument would require to be duly stamped if acted upon, filed, recorded or registered by such public officer, it shall be lawful for such public officer to call for the production of the original instrument or for evidence to his satisfaction that it was duly stamped, and no public officer shall act upon, file, record or register any such duplicate or copy without production of the original instrument duly stamped or of evidence as aforesaid.

(5) If any person whose office it is to enrol, register, or enter in or upon any rolls, books or records any instruments chargeable with duty enrols, registers, or enters any such instrument not being duly stamped or if such person fails to comply with subsection (3) he shall be guilty of an offence.

Stamping by special permission.

10.(1) Where an instrument is chargeable with stamp duty and should have been stamped before a certain event or before the expiration of a certain period but has not been so stamped, it shall be lawful for the Accountant General to give his special permission for the stamping of such instrument if he is satisfied -

(a) that the omission or neglect to stamp duty did not arise from any intention to evade payment of stamp duty or otherwise to defraud; and

(b) that either -

(i) such omission or neglect arose solely from urgent necessity or unavoidable accident and the instrument has been brought to be stamped without delay; or

(ii) that the circumstances of the case are otherwise such as to justify special permission being given.

(2) If the Accountant General grants special permission under subsection (1) for the stamping of any instrument, such instrument may be stamped on payment of the following penalties in addition to the stamp duty -

(a) if the instrument is stamped within three months of the point of time before which, or the expiration of the period of time within which, it should have been stamped, the penalty shall be double the amount of the deficient duty or $10, whichever is the greater amount;

(b) if after three months, four times the amount of the deficient duty or $25, whichever penalty is the greater:

Provided that -

(i) it shall be lawful for the Accountant General to remit the whole or any part of the penalty provided by this subsection;

(ii) the maximum penalty under this subsection shall be $500.

(3) Where an instrument has been duly stamped by special permission under this section, such instrument shall, subject to subsection (4), be deemed to have been duly stamped for the purposes of section 9.

(4) No instrument in respect of which a penalty is payable under this section shall be deemed to be duly stamped unless it bears an endorsement by the Accountant General indicating -

(a) that the penalty has been paid in whole or in part and the amount thereof; or

(b) that the whole of the penalty has been remitted.

Instruments by or in favour of the Crown.

11.(1) Where any instrument is executed by or on behalf of the Government or by any public officer in his official capacity and for an official purpose in a case where but for this section the Government or public officer would be liable to pay the stamp duty chargeable in respect of such instrument, the Government and the public officer shall be exempt from paying such stamp duty.

(2) In a case where the Government or the public officer acting in his official capacity is the only person liable for stamp duty on the instrument, the Accountant General may, notwithstanding subsection (1), stamp such instrument with the stamp denoting that it is not chargeable with any duty.

Appropriated stamps.

12.(1) A stamp which by any word or words on the face of it is appropriated to any particular description of instrument is not to be used, or, if used, is not to be available, for an instrument of any other description.

(2) An instrument falling under the particular description to which any stamp is so appropriated as aforesaid is not to be deemed duly stamped, unless it is stamped with the stamp so appropriated.

Denoting stamps.

13. Where the stamp duty with which an instrument is chargeable depends in any manner upon the duty paid upon another instrument, the payment of the last-mentioned duty shall, upon application to the Accountant General and production of both the instruments, be denoted upon the first-mentioned instrument in such manner as the Accountant General thinks fit.

Duplicates and counterparts.

14. The duplicate or counterpart of an instrument chargeable with stamp duty (except the counterpart of an instrument chargeable as a lease, such counterpart not being executed by or on behalf of any lessor or grantor) is not to be deemed duly stamped unless it is stamped as an original instrument, or unless it appears by some stamp impressed thereon, or by some endorsement made by the Accountant General thereon, or by some other sufficient evidence, that the full and proper duty has been paid upon the original instrument of which it is the duplicate or counterpart.

Value of property.

15.(1) Whenever any stamp duty is payable in respect of a conveyance or transfer of property, the Accountant General may ascertain the value of such property in such manner as he thinks fit.

(2) Where an instrument is chargeable with *ad valorem* duty in respect of -

(a) any money in any currency other than Bermuda area currency as defined for the purposes of the Exchange Control Act 1972;

(b) any stock or marketable security,

the duty shall be calculated on the value, on the day of the date of the instrument, of the money in Bermuda area currency according to the current middle market rate of exchange, or of the stock or security according to the average price thereof.

(3) Where an instrument contains a statement of the current rate of exchange, or average price, as the case may require, and is stamped in accordance with that statement, it is, so far as regards the subject matter of that statement, to be deemed to be truly stamped, unless or until it is shown that the statement is untrue, and that the instrument is in fact insufficiently stamped.

(4) For the purposes of this section the current middle market rate of exchange is the mid point between the buying and selling rates of Bermuda banks for foreign currencies rounded to three decimal places where there are such rates.

How instruments are to be written and stamped.

16.(1) Every instrument written upon stamped material is to be written in such manner, and every instrument partly or wholly written before being stamped is to be so stamped, that the stamp may appear on the face of the instrument, and cannot be used for or applied to any other instrument written upon the same piece of material.

(2) If more than one instrument has been written upon the same piece of material, every one of the instruments is to be separately and distinctly stamped with the duty with which it is chargeable.

Instruments to be separately charged with duty in certain cases.

17. Except where express provision to the contrary is made by this Act -

(a) an instrument containing or relating to several distinct matters is to be separately ad distinctly charged, as if it were a separate instrument, with duty in respect of each of the matters;

(b) an instrument made for any consideration in respect whereof it is chargeable with *ad valorem* duty, and also for any further or other valuable consideration is to be separately and distinctly charged, as if it were a separate instrument, with duty in respect of each of the considerations.

Instrument chargeable under more than one Head.

18. An instrument which is chargeable under more than one Head shall be charged under the Head which imposes the highest duty.

Facts and circumstances affecting duty to be set forth.

19.(1) All facts and circumstances affecting the liability of any instrument to duty, or the amount of the duty with which an instrument is chargeable, are to be fully and truly set forth in the instrument.

(2) Any person who with intent to evade the payment of duty -

(a) executes any instrument in which all the facts and circumstances are not truly and fully set forth as required by subsection (1); or

(b) being employed or concerned in or about the preparation of any instrument neglects or omits fully and truly to set forth therein all the said facts and circumstances, shall be guilty of an offence.

Splitting.

20.(1) Where any minimum amount is prescribed below which stamp duty shall not be payable, no person shall execute more instruments than would ordinarily be necessary for the transaction in question, in order to evade stamp duty by such splitting.

(2) Where a scale is prescribed under which the rate of stamp duty is increased after passing certain limits, no person shall execute more instruments than would ordinarily be necessary for the transaction in question, in order to evade stamp duty by such splitting.

(3) In any question whatsoever arising under this section the onus of proof shall lie upon the person who asserts that there has been no splitting in order to evade stamp duty.

(4) Any person who contravenes the provisions of this section is guilty of an offence.

Periodic stamping of instruments.

21.(1) Where it appears to the Accountant General that an instrument specified in the Schedule will become chargeable to further stamp from time to time after its execution, he may authorize the person liable to pay such further duty to pay it at such periodical intervals as he considers appropriate and not immediately upon the occurrence of the event by reason of which it becomes payable.

(2) The Accountant General in granting such authorization as specified in subsection (1) may impose any conditions or restrictions in relation thereto (including the provision of security by the person so authorized) as he considers appropriate for the securing of the payment of any such stamp duty, and the Accountant General may revoke any such authorization at any time and upon the revocation of any such authorization all stamp duties which but for such authorization would otherwise have been payable shall thereupon become immediately payable.

PART IV - Adjudication With Respect To Liability To Stamp Duty

Adjudication by Accountant General with respect to liability of instrument to stamp duty.

22.(1) The Accountant General may be required by any person, upon payment of such fee therefor as may be prescribed under the Government Fees Act 1965, to express his opinion upon any of the following questions with reference to any executed instrument or any instrument intended to be executed, that is to say -

(a) whether the instrument is chargeable with any stamp duty;

(b) with what amount of stamp duty the instrument is chargeable.

(2) The Accountant General may require the production of the instrument, and also to be furnished with such evidence as he may deem necessary in order to satisfy himself of all the facts and circumstances affecting the liability of the instrument to stamp duty, or the amount of the stamp duty chargeable thereon.

(3) If the Accountant General is satisfied that the instrument is not chargeable with any stamp duty he shall inscribe on the instrument a written note to that effect and shall sign the note accordingly.

(4) If the Accountant General is satisfied that the instrument is chargeable with stamp duty he shall inscribe on the instrument a written note of the amount of duty which in his opinion is chargeable thereon and shall sign the note accordingly.

(5) Every instrument inscribed in the manner prescribed by subsection (3), or on which the amount of duty inscribed in the manner prescribed by subsection (4) has been paid, shall be admissible in evidence and shall be available for all purposes notwithstanding any objections relating to the duty payable thereon.

(6) The following provisions shall have effect with respect to the foregoing provisions of this section -

(a) an instrument upon which the stamp duty has been assessed by the Accountant General shall not, if it is unstamped or insufficiently stamped, be stamped otherwise than in accordance with the assessment;

(b) nothing in this section shall authorize the late stamping of any instrument.

Appeal to Supreme Court against assessment of Accountant General.

23.(1) Any person who is dissatisfied with any assessment made by the Accountant General in pursuance of the provisions of the last foregoing section with respect to the amount of stamp duty chargeable upon an instrument may, within fourteen days after receiving from the Accountant General the instrument duly inscribed in accordance with subsection (4) of that section and on payment of the stamp duty in conformity therewith, appeal to the Supreme Court against the assessment; and for that purpose may by notice served upon the Accountant General require the Accountant General to state and sign a case, setting forth the question upon which his opinion was required, and the assessment made by him.

(2) The Accountant General shall, within fourteen days of the service of such notice upon him, state and sign a case and shall deliver a copy of the case to the person by whom the case is required and a further copy of the case to the Registrar; and the case may within seven days thereafter be set down by such person for hearing by the Supreme Court.

(3) Upon the hearing of the case the Supreme Court shall determine the question submitted, and, if the instrument in question is, in the opinion of the Supreme Court, chargeable with any stamp duty, then the Supreme Court shall assess the amount of the stamp duty with which it is chargeable.

(4) If the Supreme Court determines that the assessment made by the Accountant General was erroneous, then any excess of stamp duty which may have been paid in conformity with the erroneous assessment, together with any fine or penalty which may have been paid in consequence thereof, shall be ordered by the Supreme Court to be repaid to the appellant.

(5) The provisions of the Crown Causes Act 1951 which relate to costs in Crown actions shall have effect in relation to an appeal under this section as though such appeal were a Crown action within the meaning of that Act.

PART V - Allowances

Procedure for obtaining allowance for spoiled stamps.

24. Subject to regulations and to the production of such evidence by affidavit or otherwise as the Accountant General may require, allowance shall be made by the Accountant General for stamps spoiled in the cases hereinafter mentioned -

(a) the stamp on any material inadvertently and undesignedly spoiled, obliterated or by any means rendered unfit for the purpose intended, before the material bears the signature of any person or any instrument written thereon is executed by any party;

(b) any adhesive stamp which has been inadvertently and undesignedly spoiled or rendered unfit for use and has not in the opinion of the Accountant General been affixed to any material;

(c) any adhesive stamp representing a fee capable of being collected by means of such stamp which has been affixed to material;

(d) the stamp on any bill of exchange signed by or on behalf of the drawer which has not been accepted or made use of in any manner whatever or delivered out of his hands for any purpose other than by way of tender for acceptance;

(e) the stamp on any promissory note signed by or on behalf of the maker which has not been made use of in any manner whatever or delivered out of his hands;

(f) the stamp on any bill of exchange or promissory note which from any omission or error has been spoiled or rendered useless, although the same, being a bill of exchange, may have been accepted or endorsed or, being a promissory note, may have been delivered to the payee, provided that another completed and duly stamped bill of exchange or promissory note is produced identical in every particular, except in the correction of the error or omission, with the spoiled bill or note;

(g) the stamp used for any instrument executed by any party thereto -

(i) but afterwards found to be absolutely void from the beginning; or

(ii) but afterwards found unfit, by reason of any error or mistake therein, for the purpose originally intended;

(iii) which has not been made use of or for any purpose whatever and which, by reason of the inability or refusal of some necessary party to sign the same or to complete the transaction according to the instrument, is incomplete and insufficient for the purpose for which it was intended;

(iv) which by reason of the refusal of any person to act under the same, or for want of enrolment or registration within the time required by law, fails of its intended purpose or becomes void;

(v) which is inadvertently and undesignedly spoiled, and in lieu whereof another instrument made between the same parties and for the same purpose is executed and duly stamped, or which becomes useless in consequence of the transaction intended to be thereby effected being effected by some other instrument duly stamped:

Provided that -

(a) the application for relief is made within six months after the stamp has been spoiled or become useless or, in the case of an executed instrument after the date of the instrument or, if it is not dated, within six months after the execution thereof by the person by whom it was first or alone executed, or within such further time as the regulations may prescribe in the case of any instrument sent abroad for execution, or when from unavoidable circumstances any instrument for which another has been substituted cannot be produced within the said period;

(b) in the case of an executed instrument, no legal proceeding has been commenced in which the instrument could or would have been given or offered in evidence, and that the instrument is given up to be cancelled.

Allowance for misused stamps.

25. When any person has inadvertently used for an instrument liable to duty a stamp of greater value than was necessary, or has inadvertently used a stamp for an instrument not liable to any duty, the Accountant General may, on application made within two years after the date of the instrument or, if it is not dated, within six months after the execution thereof by the person by whom it was first or alone executed, and upon the instrument, if liable to duty, being stamped with the proper duty, cancel and allow as spoiled the stamp so misused.

Allowance, how to be made.

26. In any case in which allowance is made for spoiled or misused stamps the Accountant General may give in lieu thereof money to the value of the spoiled or misused stamps or other stamps of the same denomination and value or, if required and he thinks proper, stamps of any other denomination to the same amount in value.

Stamps not wanted may be repurchased.

27. When any person is possessed of a stamp which has not been spoiled or rendered unfit or useless for the purpose intended, but for which he has not immediate use, the Accountant General shall repay to him the value of the stamp in money, upon his delivering up the stamp to be cancelled and proving to the satisfaction of the Accountant General that it was lawfully purchased by him from the Government within the period of two years next preceding the application and with a bona fide intention to use it.

PART VI - Bills Of Exchange And Promissory Notes

Cheques supplied by licensed banks need not bear stamp.

28.(1) The Accountant General may authorize any bank licensed under the Banks Act 1969 to compound for the payment of duty on unstamped cheques on the following conditions -

(a) that the said cheques be drawn and issued on forms to be supplied by the said bank;

(b) that the said bank levy upon or charge to the person to whom such cheques are issued the stamp duty mentioned in the Schedule;

(c) that the said bank do pay on or before the 7th day of January and on or before the 7th day of July in each year to the Accountant General the amount due and collected thereon, up to the previous 31st day of December or the previous 30th day of June as the case may be, as duties on such unstamped cheques.

(2) Cheques drawn and issued on forms supplied or adopted by such bank in accordance with this section shall be deemed to be duly stamped notwithstanding any provision of this Act or of the regulations relating to affixing and cancelling of stamps or the method of denoting the payment of stamp duty.

Effect of non-compliance in case of certain bills of exchange.

29. Notwithstanding any statutory provision to the contrary, a bill of exchange which is presented for acceptance, or accepted, or payable, outside Bermuda or a cheque whether presented for acceptance, or accepted, or payable, outside or inside Bermuda shall not be valid by reason only that it is not stamped in accordance with the provisions of this Act, and any such bill of exchange or cheque which is unstamped or not properly stamped may be received in evidence on payment of the proper duty and penalties as provided by subsection (2) of section 10.

Foreign bills and notes.

30.(1) Where a bill of exchange or promissory note drawn or made outside Bermuda comes into the hands of a person in Bermuda before it is stamped, he shall, before he presents for payment, or endorses, transfers or in any manner negotiates or pays the bill or note, affix thereto a proper adhesive stamp or proper adhesive stamps of sufficient amount, and cancel every stamp so affixed thereto:

Provided as follows -

(a) if at the time when any such bill or note comes into the hands of any *bona fide holder there is* affixed thereto an adhesive stamp effectually cancelled, the stamp shall, so far as relates to the holder, be deemed to be duly cancelled, although it may not appear to have been affixed or cancelled by the proper person; and

(b) if at the time when any such bill or note comes into the hands of any *bona fide holder* there is affixed thereto an adhesive stamp not duly cancelled, it shall be competent for the holder to cancel the stamp as if he were the person by whom it was affixed, and upon his so doing the bill or note shall be deemed duly stamped and as valid and available as if the stamp had been cancelled by the person by whom it was affixed.

(2) Neither of the foregoing provisos is to relieve any person from any fine or penalty incurred by him for not cancelling an adhesive stamp.

Bills in sets.

31.(1) When a bill of exchange is drawn in a set according to the custom of merchants and one of the set is duly stamped, the other or orders of the set shall, unless issued or in some manner negotiated apart from the stamped bill, be exempt from duty; and upon proof of the loss or destruction of a duly stamped bill forming one of a set, any other bill of the set which has not been issued or in any manner negotiated apart from the lost or destroyed bill may, although unstamped, be admitted in evidence to prove the contents of the lost or destroyed bill.

(2) No bills of exchange in sets shall be stamped in which the words "First" and "Second" or "First", "Second" and "Third" are left blank, nor in which the words "Second of the same tenor and date being unpaid" or the like are wholly or partly left blank.

Unstamped bill or note.

32.(1) The person who takes or receives from any other person any bill of exchange or promissory note chargeable with duty and not being duly stamped either in payment or as a security, or by purchase or otherwise, shall not be entitled to recover thereon or to rely upon the same for any purpose whatever.

(2) Notwithstanding anything to the contrary in this Act if any bill of exchange payable on demand or at sight or on presentation is presented for payment unstamped, the person to whom it is presented may affix thereto adhesive stamps to the value of the amount of duty chargeable on that instrument under Head 10 and cancel the same as if he had been the drawer of the bill, and may thereupon pay the sum in the bill mentioned and charge the duty in account against the person by whom the bill was drawn or deduct the duty from the said sum, and the bill is, so far as respects the duty, to be deemed valid and enforceable.

(3) The foregoing subsection is not to relieve any person from any fine or penalty incurred by him in relation to such bill.

Offence: unstamped bill or note.

33. Any person who draws, makes, issues, endorses or transfers or signs otherwise than as a witness, or presents for acceptance or payment or accepts, pays or receives payment of or in any manner negotiates any bill of exchange, or promissory note without the same being duly stamped shall be guilty of an offence.

PART VII - Conveyances

Calculation of stamp duty chargeable on conveyance on sale.

34.(1) Where the consideration for a conveyance on sale consists, wholly or in part, of any shares or marketable security, *ad valorem* duty upon such conveyance shall, in respect of such shares or security, be charged upon the current value thereof.

(2) Where the consideration consists, wholly or in part, of any security not being a marketable security, *ad valorem* duty upon such conveyance shall, in respect of such security, be charged upon the amount due at the date of the conveyance for principal and interest upon the security.

How consideration on periodical payments to be charged.

35.(1) Where the consideration, or any part of the consideration, for a conveyance on sale consists of money payable periodically for a definite period not exceeding twenty years, so that the total amount to be paid can be previously ascertained, the conveyance is to be charged in respect of that consideration with *ad valorem* duty on such total amount.

(2) Where the consideration, or any part of the consideration, for a conveyance on sale consists of money payable periodically for a definite period exceeding twenty years or in perpetuity, or for any indefinite period not terminable with life, the conveyance is to be charged in respect of that consideration with *ad valorem* duty on the total amount which will or may, according to the terms of sale, be payable during the period of twenty years next after the day of the date of the instrument.

(3) Where the consideration, or any part of the consideration, for a conveyance on sale consists of money payable periodically during any life or lives, the conveyance is to be charged in respect of that consideration with *ad valorem* duty on the amount which will or may, according to the terms of sale, be payable during the period of twelve years next after the day of the date of the instrument.

(4) No conveyance on sale chargeable with *ad valorem* duty in respect of any periodical payments, and containing also provision for securing the payments, is to be charged with any duty in respect of such provision, and no separate instrument made in that case for securing the payments is to be charged with any higher duty than $5.00.

Provisions where property conveyed in consideration of debt.

36. Where any property is conveyed to any person in consideration, wholly or in part, of any debt due to him, or subject either certainly or contingently to the payment or transfer of any money or shares, whether being or constituting a charge or incumbrance on the property or not, the debt, money or shares is to be deemed the whole or part, as the case may be, of the consideration in respect whereof the conveyance is chargeable with *ad valorem* duty:

Provided however that where an equity of redemption is so conveyed then the stamp duty applicable thereto shall be based on the consideration referable to such equity of redemption without regard to any mortgage which may be subsisting on such property.

Special considerations affecting amount of stamp duty chargeable on conveyance on sale.

37.(1) Where the property contracted to be sold for one consideration for the whole is conveyed to the purchaser in separate parcels by different instruments, the consideration is to be apportioned as the parties think fit, so that a distinct consideration for each separate parcel is set forth in the conveyance relating thereto, which shall be charged with *ad valorem* duty in respect of such distinct consideration.

(2) Where property contracted to be purchased for one consideration for the whole by two or more persons jointly, or by any person for himself and others, or wholly for others, is conveyed in parcels by different instruments to the persons by or from whom the same was purchased for distinct parts of the consideration, the conveyance of each separate parcel is to be charged with *ad valorem* duty in respect of the distinct part of the consideration therein specified.

(3) Where there are several instruments of conveyance for completing the purchaser's title to the property sold, the principal instrument of conveyance only is to be charged with *ad valorem* duty, and the other instruments are to be charged with such other duty as they are respectively liable to, but the last-mentioned duty shall not exceed the *ad valorem* duty payable in respect of the principal instrument.

(4) Where a person having contracted for the purchase of any property but not having obtained a conveyance thereof, contracts to sell the property to any other person, to whom the property is conveyed immediately, then the conveyance is to be charged in respect of the consideration paid by the sub-purchaser.

(5) Where a person having contracted for the purchase of any property but not having obtained a conveyance thereof contracts to sell the whole, or any part thereof, to any person, and the property is in consequence conveyed by the original seller to different persons in parcels, the conveyance of each parcel is to be charged with *ad valorem* duty in respect only of the consideration paid by the sub-purchaser, without regard to the amount or value of the original consideration.

(6) Where a sub-purchaser takes an actual conveyance of the interest of the person immediately selling to him, which is chargeable with *ad valorem* duty in respect of the consideration paid by him, and is duly stamped accordingly, then any conveyance to be afterwards made to him of the same property by the original seller shall be chargeable only with such other duty as it may be liable to, but not exceeding the *ad valorem* duty.

Certain contracts to be chargeable with conveyance duty.

38.(1) Any contract or agreement for the sale of any equitable estate or interest in any property whatsoever, or for the sale of any estate in any personal property shall be charged with the same *ad valorem* duty, to be paid by the purchaser, as if it were an actual conveyance on sale of the estate, interest or property contracted or agreed to be sold:

Provided that nothing in this subsection shall have the effect of charging *ad valorem* duty upon an instrument chargeable to duty under Head 4.

(2) Where the purchaser has paid the said *ad valorem* duty, and, before having obtained a conveyance or transfer of the property, enters into a contract or agreement for the sale of the property, then such contract or agreement shall, if the consideration for that sale is in excess of that for the original sale, be charged with the *ad valorem* in respect of such excess consideration, and in any other case with the fixed duty of $5.00.

(3) Where duty has been duly paid *ad valorem* in conformity with the foregoing provisions of this section, the conveyance or transfer to the purchaser or sub-purchaser, or any other person on his behalf or by his direction, shall not be chargeable with any duty; and the Accountant General, upon application, shall either denote the payment of the *ad valorem* duty upon the conveyance or transfer, or shall transfer the *ad valorem* duty thereto upon production of the contract or agreement duly stamped.

(4) Where any such contract or agreement is stamped with the fixed duty of $5.00 as aforesaid such contract or agreement shall be regarded as duly stamped for the mere purpose of proceedings to enforce specific performance or to recover damages for the breach thereof.

(5) Where any such contract or agreement is stamped with the said fixed duty, and a conveyance or transfer made in conformity with the contract or agreement is presented to the Accountant General for stamping with the *ad valorem* duty chargeable thereon within the period of six months after the first execution of the contract or agreement, or within such longer period as the Accountant General may think reasonable in the circumstances of the case, the conveyance or transfer shall be stamped accordingly, and the same, and the said contract or agreement, shall be deemed to be duly stamped.

(6) The *ad valorem* duty paid upon any such contract or agreement shall be returned by the Accountant General in case the contract or agreement is afterwards rescinded or annulled, or for any other reason is not substantially performed or carried into effect, so as to operate as, or be followed by, a conveyance or transfer.

Voluntary conveyance inter vivos.

39.(1) The Accountant General may be required to express his opinion under section 22 on any conveyance or transfer operating as a voluntary disposition *inter vivos*, and no such conveyance or transfer shall be deemed to be duly stamped unless the Accountant General has expressed his opinion thereon in accordance with that section.

(2) Any conveyance or transfer (not being a disposition made in favour of a purchaser or incumbrancer or other person in good faith and for valuable consideration) shall, for the purposes of this section, be deemed to be a conveyance or transfer operating as a voluntary disposition *inter vivos*, and the consideration for any conveyance or transfer shall not for this purpose be deemed to be valuable consideration where the Accountant General is of opinion that by reason of the inadequacy of the sum paid as consideration or other circumstances the conveyance or transfer confers a substantial benefit on the person to whom the property is conveyed or transferred.

(3) A conveyance or transfer made for nominal consideration for the purpose of securing the repayment of an advance or loan or made for effectuating the appointment of a new trustee or the retirement of a trustee, whether the trust is expressed or implied, or under which no beneficial interest passes in the property conveyed or transferred, or made to a beneficiary by a trustee or other person in a fiduciary capacity under any trust, whether expressed or implied, shall not be charged with duty as a voluntary conveyance *inter vivos.*

PART VIII - Settlements, Mutual Funds And Unit Trust Schemes

Duty on settlement of money etc.

40. Where any money which may become due or payable upon any life insurance policy, or upon any security, is settled or agreed to be settled, the instrument whereby the settlement is made or agreed to be made shall be charged with *ad valorem* duty as a settlement in respect of that money:

Provided that where in the case of a policy no provision is made for keeping up the policy, the *ad valorem* duty shall be charged only on the value of the policy at the date of the instrument.

Calculation of duty where several instruments of settlement.

41. Where several instruments are executed for effecting the settlement of the same property, and the *ad valorem* duty chargeable in respect of the settlement of the property exceeds $5.00, one only of the instruments shall be charged with the *ad valorem* duty and the instruments not charged with *ad valorem* duty shall be charged with a duty of $5.00.

Additions to settlements to be made by stamped instrument.

42. Every addition of property to a settlement *inter vivos,* being an addition made on or after the date of the commencement of the Stamp Duties Amendment Act 1985, shall be evidenced by an instrument of addition chargeable with duty under Head 40.

Notification of issue of new shares.

43. The secretary of a mutual fund shall, within sixty days of the issue of a new share in the fund, supply to the Accountant General by notice in writing such particulars of the issue as the latter may require for the purpose of calculating stamp duty.

Notification of issue of new units.

44. The trustees of the trust instrument of a unit trust scheme ("the trustees") shall, within sixty days of the issue of a new unit under the scheme, supply to the Accountant General by notice in writing such particulars of the issue as he may require for the purpose of calculating stamp duty.

Enforcement of sections 42, 43 and 44.

45.(1) If section 42 is contravened, each of the trustees of the settlement shall, subject to subsection (4), be guilty of an offence.

(2) If section 43 is contravened, the secretary of the fund shall, subject to subsection (4), be guilty of an offence.

(3) If section 44 is contravened, each of the trustees shall, subject to subsection (4), be guilty of an offence.

(4) It shall be a defence -

(a) for a person charged with an offence under subsection (2) to prove that he took all reasonable steps to avoid; and

(b) for a person charged with an offence under subsection (1) or (3) to prove that he took all reasonable steps to avoid or prevent, the commission of the offence.

Stamp duty on unit trusts.

46. The trust instrument of a unit trust scheme shall be chargeable with duty under Head 21.

PART IX - Affidavit Of Value Of Deceased Estate

Supreme Court not to grant probate or letter of administration in absence of affidavit as to value of estate.

47.(1) The Supreme Court shall not grant probate of the will or letters of administration of the estate of a deceased person nor shall it direct the resealing of a foreign grant (within the meaning of section 18 of the Administration of Estates Act 1974) without first requiring and receiving from the person applying for the probate, letters of administration or resealing or from some other competent person an affidavit that the estate of the deceased for or in respect of which the probate or letters of administration is or are to be granted or in respect of which a foreign grant is to be resealed, exclusive of what the deceased had been possessed of or entitled to as trustee for any other person and not beneficially, is of the value of a certain sum to be therein specified to the best of the deponent's knowledge, information and belief, in order that the proper stamp duty may be paid on such affidavit.

(2) For the purposes of this section -

(a) the estate of a deceased person shall include -

(i) all the property of the deceased at the time of his death and all property of which the deceased was at the time of his death competent to dispose;

(ii) property in which the deceased had an interest ceasing at his death, to the extent to which a benefit arises for someone else by reason of the cesser:

Provided that the purposes of this provision -

(aa) where the deceased's interest in the property was that of a joint tenant, a benefit shall be deemed to arise as aforesaid upon his death, and the value of that benefit shall be deemed to be the value of the interests of all the joint tenants divided by their number; and

(bb) there shall be disregarded any interest that the deceased had in the property as the holder of an office or as the recipient of the benefits of a charity or as a corporation sole;

(iii) money payable to the deceased's estate under any policy of insurance:

Provided that in the case of a deceased person who is not domiciled in Bermuda such money shall only be deemed to form part of his estate if such money is payable in Bermuda or in Bermuda area currency;

(iv) property taken as a *donatio mortis causa* made by the deceased;

(b) the term "property means -

(i) real and personal property of any kind situated or being in Bermuda, and the proceeds of the sale thereof and any investment for the time being representing the same;

(ii) the value of any vessel or aircraft or any share of a vessel or aircraft belonging to the deceased which is registered in Bermuda, notwithstanding such vessel or aircraft, at the time of the death of the deceased, may have been at sea or elsewhere out of Bermuda.

(3) The term "property" in subsection (2) shall not include -

(a) any moneys in a bank licensed under the Banks Act 1969 or in a deposit company licensed under the Deposit Companies Act 1974, being moneys denominated in a currency other than Bermuda area currency; or

(b) any security held in an exempted undertaking as defined in section 1 of the Exempted Undertakings Tax Protection Act 1966; or

(c) any security evidencing participation in a mutual fund business or unit trust scheme in either case carried on by a company formed in Bermuda, provided the security is denominated in a currency other than Bermuda area currency; or

(d) any security to the extent that it represents foreign currency securities (including any shares in any company formed outside Bermuda or in any exempt undertaking) or land that is situate outside Bermuda, being securities or land that are wholly owned by a company formed in Bermuda, provided the latter company is a company as to which the Registrar is satisfied -

(i) that at the time of the deceased's death the company was wholly owned beneficially by individuals not exceeding five in number; and

(ii) that throughout the company's last complete year of business immediately preceding the deceased's death both -

(aa) not less than seventy-five per cent of the assets of the company was in the form of securities, or consisted of land that is situate outside Bermuda, (or partly the one and partly the other); and

(bb) not less than eighty-five per cent of the net income of the company was derived from securities or land such as are described in division (aa) above, (or partly the one and partly the other).

(4) For the purposes of subsection (2) shares, stock or marketable securities which qualify for exemption from duty on transfer under paragraph (e) of section 4 shall be deemed not to be property situated or being in Bermuda.

(5) For the purposes of this section a person shall be deemed competent to dispose of property if he has such an estate or interest therein or such general power, whether exerciseable by instrument *inter vivos* or by will, or both, as would (or would if he were of full age and capacity), enable him to dispose of the property for his own benefit.

(6) For the purposes of this section the value of the property of the deceased at the time of his death shall be deemed to be its value at that time.

(7) In this Part the value of the estate of a deceased person means the value as calculated in accordance with this section as read with section 48.

(8) An affidavit lodged pursuant to subsection (1) may not be inspected by any person except in pursuance of an order made by the Chief Justice upon application by summons for the purpose.

Deductions.

48.(1) In ascertaining the value of the estate for the purposes of section 47 the following deductions shall be made from the value of the estate -

(a) reasonable funeral expenses;

(b) the value of any legacy or other benefit to a surviving spouse;

(c) bequests to charities registered under the Charities Act 1978 or to any body of persons for purposes which are, in the opinion of the Minister, charitable;

(d) all debts and incumbrances incurred or created by the deceased *bona fide* for full consideration in money or money's worth wholly for the deceased's own use and benefit;

Provided that no debt shall be deducted in respect whereof there is a right to reimbursement from any other estate or person or more than once for the same debt or incumbrance charged on different portions of the estate;

(e) the reasonable expenses of valuing any property for the purposes of this Part.

(2) Notwithstanding anything to the contrary in subsection (1), in the case of a deceased person who at the time of his death was not domiciled in Bermuda no deduction shall be made under that subsection for debts due from him to persons resident outside Bermuda unless contracted to be paid in Bermuda or charged on property situated within Bermuda, or unless and to the extent to which it is shown to the satisfaction of the Registrar that the personal property of the deceased person situated in the country in which the person to whom such debts are due resides is insufficient for their payment.

Provision for return of duty overpaid.

49. If at any time after the grant of probate or letters of administration, and during the administration of the estate, the value of the estate as set out in the affidavit furnished in accordance with section 47 is found to exceed the true value of the estate of the deceased, or if at any time within three years after the grant, or such further period as the Accountant General may allow, it appears that no amount or an insufficient amount was deducted on account of debts and funeral expenses, it shall be lawful for the Accountant General, upon proof of the facts to his satisfaction, to return the amount of stamp duty which has been overpaid.

Provision for payment of further duty.

50. If at any time it is discovered that the estate of the deceased was of greater value than the value set out in the affidavit furnished in accordance with section 47 or that any deduction for debts or funeral expenses was made erroneously, the estate representative shall, within six months after the discovery, deliver a further affidavit setting out the true value of the estate to the Registrar, duly stamped for the amount which, with the duty (if any) previously paid on the affidavit in respect of such estate, shall be sufficient to cover the duty chargeable according to the true value thereof, and shall at the same time pay to the Registrar interest upon such amount at the rate of ten *per centum per annum* from the date of such further affidavit, or from such previous date as the Registrar may in the circumstances think proper.

Small estates.

51. Section 47 shall not operate so as to require an affidavit made for the purposes of that section to be furnished prior to the issue of a certificate under section 21 of the Administration of Estates Act 1974, but where such a certificate has been issued without the furnishing of such an affidavit and it is subsequently discovered that the value of the estate exceeds $10,000, section 50 shall apply as though the reference in that section to the value of the estate as set out in the affidavit exceeding the true value of the estate were construed as a reference to the value of the estate exceeding $10,000 and the reference in such section to the estate representative were construed as a reference to the person to whom the certificate under the said section 21 is issued.

Liability of estate representative.

52.(1) The estate representative of every deceased person shall have the power to pay the stamp duty imposed by section 47 as read with Head 2 out of any money for the time being in his hands or to raise the amount of such duty and any interest and expenses properly paid or incurred in respect thereof by the sale or mortgage of the assets of the estate.

(2) The estate representative shall be liable to pay the stamp duty imposed by section 47 as read with Head 2 but his liability shall not exceed the assets which he has received as representative or might but for his own neglect or default have received.

Power of Registrar to require explanation and proof in support of valuation, and to reassess value.

53.(1) The Registrar may, at any time and from time to time within three years from the furnishing of an affidavit under section 47 or section 50 require the estate representative of the deceased person or other person required by this Part to lodge such affidavit or furnish information and explanations and to produce such documentary or other evidence respecting the contents or the particulars verified by the affidavit as the case may seem to him to require.

(2) The Registrar shall, if he is dissatisfied with a declaration of value in an affidavit furnished for the purposes of section 47 or section 50 refer the matter to the Supreme Court.

(3) On a reference to it under subsection (2) the Supreme Court shall ascertain the value of the estate and the stamp duty payable in respect thereof in such manner and by such means as it may think fit, and may, if it thinks fit, as respects any property accept the valuation of any person appointed by the Court for the purposes of this section or so approved for the purpose of making the valuation.

(4) If the stamp duty so assessed exceeds the duty previously paid it shall be lawful for the Supreme Court, and having regard to the merits of the case and the conduct of the estate representative, to direct that the whole or any part of the expenses incident to the making of such assessment shall be paid by the estate representative and any such payment required to be made by the estate representative shall be deemed to be a debt owing to the Consolidated Fund.

(5) The power to make rules of the Supreme Court provided by section 62 of the Supreme Court 1905, shall include power to make rules for regulating, subject to and for the purposes of giving effect to the provisions of this section, the practice and procedure on all matters relating to a reference to it under the provisions of this section.

(6) For the purposes of the Court of Appeal Act 1964 an assessment by the Supreme Court under this section shall be deemed to be a judgment by it in a civil cause or matter.

PART X - Insurance

Duty to issue receipts.

54. Any person who on his own behalf or on behalf of any other person receives or takes credit for any premium payable under a policy of insurance and who does not as soon as practicable after receiving or taking credit for such premium give a receipt in writing therefor, shall where such receipt is chargeable to tax, be guilty of an offence.

Exempt policies may cease to be exempt.

55. Where an exempt policy (not being a policy of reinsurance) has been issued and the risk insured against ceases to be situated outside Bermuda by reason of the risk insured against becoming situated in Bermuda then in respect of any premium paid or anything done under the policy after the occurrence of that event that policy shall no longer be deemed to be an exempt policy for the purposes of this Act.

Compounding of duty on insurance receipts.

56.(1) The Accountant General may authorize any person carrying on insurance business in Bermuda to compound for the payment of duty on policies of insurance or insurance premium receipts on the following conditions -

(a) the policies and receipts bear an endorsement in such manner as the Accountant General may approve to indicate that stamp duty has been paid;

(b) the person so authorized submits within twenty days after the 31st March, the 30th June, the 30th September and the 1st January in each year accounts relating to the period of three months preceding each such date showing the amounts received as premiums during that period, being premiums chargeable to stamp duty;

(c) every account shall be made in such form and shall contain all such particulars as the Accountant General may require;

(d) the duty shall be paid upon the delivery of the account.

(2) The agreement shall be in such form and contain such terms and conditions as the Accountant General may think proper.

(3) In the case of wilful neglect to deliver such an account as is hereby required or to pay the duty in conformity with this section the person shall be liable to a penalty of $10 *per centum* upon the amount of the duty payable for every month, or part of a month, during which the neglect continues.

Records of insurance companies to be open to inspection.

57. Every person carrying on insurance business in Bermuda whether on his own account or on behalf of another person and the managers and any officer or servant of such person shall at all reasonable times permit any person authorized by the Accountant General to inspect all books, records, papers, documents or proceedings in their custody relating to such business the inspection whereof may tend to secure any duty, or to prove or lead to the discovery of any fraud or omission in relation to any duty, and to take such notes and extracts as he may deem necessary, and in case of refusal shall be guilty of an offence:

Provided that nothing in this section shall authorize the Accountant General or person so authorized to inspect the books, records, papers, documents or proceedings of an exempt undertaking issuing only exempt policies.

PART XI - Miscellaneous Instruments

Calculation of stamp duty on securities for future advances of money.

58.(1) A security for the payment or repayment of money to be lent, advanced, or paid, or which may become due upon an account current either with or without money previously due, shall be charged, where the total amount secured or to be ultimately recoverable is in any way limited, with the same duty as a security for the amount so limited.

(2) Where such total amount is unlimited, the security shall be available for such an amount only as the *ad valorem* duty stamped thereon extends to cover, but where any advance or loan is made in excess of the amount covered by that duty the security shall for the purpose of stamp duty be deemed to be a new and separate instrument, bearing date on the date on which the advance or loan was made:

Provided that no money to be advanced for the insurance of any property comprised in the security against damage by fire or for keeping up any policy of life insurance comprised in the security, or for effecting in lieu thereof any new policy, or for the renewal of any grant or lease of any property comprised in the security upon the dropping of any life whereon the property is held, shall be reckoned as forming part of the amount in respect whereof the security is chargeable with *ad valorem* duty.

Special provisions as to leases.

59. Where the consideration or any part of the consideration for which a lease or an agreement for a lease is granted or made consists of a covenant or other undertaking by, or a condition requiring, the lessee to erect a building or otherwise to expend money on the subject-matter of the lease, the amount or value of the consideration shall be deemed to be a premium in respect of which the lease or agreement for the lease is chargeable with *ad valorem* duty in accordance with Head 25(a) or (c).

Certain mortgages of stock to be chargeable as agreements.

60.(1) Every instrument under hand only (not being a promissory note or bill of exchange) given upon the occasion of the deposit of any share warrant or stock certificate to bearer, or foreign or commonwealth share certificate, or any security for money transferable by delivery, by way of security for any loan or guarantee shall be deemed to be an agreement and shall be charged with duty accordingly.

(2) Every instrument under hand only (not being a promissory note or bill of exchange) making redeemable or qualifying a duly stamped transfer, intended as a security, of any marketable security, shall be deemed to be an agreement, and shall be charged with duty accordingly.

(3) A release or discharge of any such instrument shall not be chargeable with any *ad valorem* duty.

Ad valorem duty on exchange or partition of real property.

61. Where on the exchange of any real property for any other real property, or upon the partition or division of any real property, and consideration exceeding in amount or value five hundred dollars is paid or given, or agreed to be paid or given, for equality, the principal or only instrument whereby the exchange or partition or division is effected is to be charged with the same *ad valorem* duty as a conveyance on sale for the same consideration, and where in any such case there are several instruments for completing the title of the parties or any of them, the principal instrument is to be ascertained, and the other instruments are to be charged with duty in the manner hereinbefore provided in the case of several instruments of conveyance.

Calculation of stamp duty on particular securities.

62. A transfer of a duly stamped security, and a security by way of a further charge for money added to money previously secured by a duly stamped instrument, shall not be charged with any duty by reason of its containing any further or additional security for the money transferred or previously secured, or the interest or dividends thereof, or any new covenant, proviso, power, stipulation, or agreement in relation thereto, or any further assurance of the property comprised in the transferred or previous security.

Special provision for companies without shares or capital stock.

63.(1) Notwithstanding anything in any private Act to the contrary, where a company is formed under such an Act without shares or capital stock, stamp duty shall be charged upon the memorandum of association of the company as though references in the Schedule to the share capital of the company were construed as references to the statutory reserves thereof.

(2) In the event of the statutory reserves of such a company as is mentioned in subsection (1) being increased the company shall, within one calendar month thereof file with the Registrar of Companies written notification thereof.

(3) The notification filed under subsection (2) shall, for the purposes of the Schedule be regarded as a memorandum of increased capital and stamp duty shall be charged upon such notification, notwithstanding anything in any private Act to the contrary, at the rate prescribed in the Schedule for such a memorandum.

(4) t is an offence for any company to fail to file a written notification in accordance with subsection (2).

Delivery in escrow.

64. For the removal of doubt it is declared that an instrument delivered in escrow shall not be chargeable to stamp duty until the condition subject to which it has been delivered has been performed; and references in the Schedule to the time of execution of such an instrument shall be construed as references to the time of performance of such condition.

Appraisement.

65. Any person by whom an appraisement or valuation chargeable with stamp duty is made who -

(a) within fourteen days after the making thereof neglects or omits to write out the same in words and figures showing the full amount thereof on duly stamped paper; or

(b) in any other manner discloses the amount of the appraisement or valuation, shall be guilty of an offence.

Annuities.

66.(1) Subject to subsection (2), where upon the sale of any annuity or other right not before in existence such annuity or other right is not created by actual grant or conveyance, but is only secured by bond, warrant of attorney, covenant, contract, or otherwise, the bond or other instrument, or some one of such instruments if there is more than one, is to be charged with the same duty as an actual grant or conveyance, and is for the purposes of this Act to be deemed an instrument of conveyance on sale.

(2) Where an annuity is sold by a person carrying on insurance business, the annuity shall be taxed as an insurance policy, and not as a conveyance, and receipts given for the premiums shall, for the purposes of this Act, be deemed to be insurance premium receipts.

PART XII - Offences And Supplementary

Failure to stamp.

67. If any instrument which is liable to stamp duty is not duly stamped, every person specified in the Schedule as being liable for stamping shall be guilty of an offence and shall be liable on summary conviction therefor to a fine not exceeding $200 or to four times the amount of the unpaid stamp duty, whichever is the greater.

General penalty.

68. Where this Act creates any offence and no penalty is specified therefor the person committing such offence shall be liable on summary conviction therefor to a fine not exceeding $500 and, in addition, if the offence was committed with the intention of avoiding the payment of any stamp duty a fine not exceeding four times the amount of the duty avoided or sought to be avoided.

Penalty for unauthorized dealing in stamps.

69.(1) Any person, not duly appointed to sell and distribute stamps, who deals in any way in stamps, shall be guilty of an offence and shall be liable on summary conviction therefor to a fine not exceeding $200:

Provided that nothing in this section shall prevent the sale or exchange of stamps for philatelic purposes.

(2) In this section "stamps" mean adhesive stamps available exclusively for payment of revenue in Bermuda.

Fraud in relation to duty.

70. Any person who practises or is concerned in any fraudulent act, contrivance or device, with intent to defraud the Government of any stamp duty, shall be guilty of an offence and liable on summary conviction therefor to a fine not exceeding $1,000.

Institution and conduct of prosecutions.

71.(1) No prosecution in respect of any offence punishable under this Act shall be instituted without the sanction of the Accountant General.

(2) The imposition of a fine upon the conviction of any person for a contravention of any provision of this Act shall not relieve such person of the obligation of paying any unpaid duty, including any penalty for late payment under section 10.

(3) Notwithstanding the provisions of section 452 of the Criminal Code a summary offence constituted by the provisions of this Act may be instituted within a period of three months of the date when facts sufficient in the opinion of the Accountant General to justify such a prosecution first come to his notice and, in any prosecution commenced after the expiration of the period specified in the said section 452, a certificate purporting to be under the hand of the Accountant General and specifying the date upon which such facts first came to his notice shall be evidence that such facts first came to his notice upon such date.

Offences by corporations.

72. Where an offence under this Act which has been committed by a body corporate is proved to have been committed with the consent or connivance of, or to be attributable to any default on the part of, a director, manager, secretary or other similar officer of the body corporate, or any person who is purporting to act in any such capacity, he as well as the body corporate shall be guilty of that offence and be liable to be proceeded against accordingly.

PART XIII - Miscellaneous

Books, etc. in the custody of public officers may be inspected without fee.

73. Every public officer having in his custody any registers, books, records, papers, documents or proceedings the inspection where may tend to secure any duty, or to prove or lead to the discovery of any fraud or omission in relation to any duty, shall at all reasonable times permit any person authorized in writing by the Accountant General to inspect for such purposes the registers, books, records, papers, documents or proceedings and to take such notes and extracts as he may deem necessary.

Composition or consolidation of duties.

74. The Minister of Finance may by order published in the Gazette provide for the composition or consolidation of duties in the case of issues by any company or other body corporate of debentures, bonds or other marketable securities.

Conditions and agreements as to stamp duty void.

75. Every condition of sale framed with the view of precluding objection or requisition upon the ground of absence or insufficiency of stamp upon any instrument executed after the 22nd September 1917, and every contract, arrangement, or undertaking for assuming liability on account of absence or insufficiency of stamp upon any such instrument or indemnifying against such liability, absence or insufficiency, shall be void.

Ad valorem duty to be rounded up to nearest whole cent.

76. Where the amount of stamp duty payable upon any instrument is to be calculated by reference to a percentage rate and the result of such calculation is that (but for the provisions of this section) a fraction of a cent of duty would be payable, the amount of duty as so calculated shall be rounded up to the nearest whole cent.

Regulations.

77.(1) The Minister may by regulation -

(a) prescribe any matter or thing which by this Act is required or permitted to be prescribed by regulation;

(b) amend any of the provisions of the Schedule:

Provided that no such amendment shall have the effect of increasing any stamp duty specified in the Schedule or of imposing any new or additional duty not specified therein;

(c) require persons concerned in the management of mutual funds and unit trust schemes to keep such records as the Minister considers necessary or expedient to be kept for the purpose of ensuring that stamp duties that are due are paid;

(d) prescribe the form of affidavit under section 47;

(e) make provision for the better carrying out of the objects and purposes of this Act.

(2) The negative resolution procedure shall apply to regulations made under this section.

(3) Regulations made pursuant to paragraph (c) of subsection (1) may create offences and provide that a person committing any such offence shall be liable on summary conviction to a fine not exceeding $200.

Repeals, savings etc.

78. [Omitted.]

Commencement.

79. [Omitted.]

SCHEDULE

(Section 2)

Nature of Instrument	(a) Stamp Duty (b) Time for Stamping (c) Person Liable
1. AFFIDAVIT, STATUTORY DECLARATION OR DECLARATION IN WRITING ON OATH OR AFFIRMATION MADE BEFORE A PERSON AUTHORIZED BY LAW TO ADMINISTER AN OATH. Exemptions *(a)* Affidavit or declaration made for the immediate purpose of being filed, read, or used in any court, or before any judge or officer of any court. *(b)* Affidavit or declaration required to be made pursuant to any statutory provision relating to marriages. *(c)* Affidavit or declaration made before the Collector of Customs or any officer of the Customs Department under the Revenue Act 1898 or other provision of law. *(d)* Declaration for the purposes of the British Nationality Acts 1948 and 1981 of the United Kingdom.	*(a)* $1. *(b)* 30 days after making *(c)* The person making
2. AFFIDAVIT OF VALUE OF DECEASED ESTATE made for the purposes of this Act	*(a)* **(i)** On the first $100,000 of the value of the estate 2 *per centum;* **(ii)** thereafter, 5 *per centum* of the value of the estate. *(b)* 90 days after the grant of probate or administration or, in the case of a

foreign grant, the resealing thereof at the direction of the Supreme Court, or within such further period as the Registrar or a judge may, on application, allow.

(c) Estate representative or other person acting in the administration of the estate.

Exemptions

The first $10,000 of the value of the estate.
AND *see* PART IX.

3. AGREEMENT, OR ANY MEMORANDUM OF AGREEMENT made under hand only and not otherwise charged with duty, whether the same be the only evidence of a contract, or obligatory upon the parties from its being a written instrument.

(a) $1.

(b) 30 days after execution.

(c) All parties to the agreement.

Exemptions

(a) Agreement or memorandum the subject matter whereof is of the value of less than $50.

(b) Agreement or memorandum for the hire of any labourer, artificer, mechanic or domestic servant.

(c) Contract of service between the Government and a Government employee.

(d) Instrument of apprenticeship.

(e) Subject to Head 5, an agreement or memorandum relating to the sale of any goods, wares or merchandise.

(f) A receipt.

(g) Agreement or memorandum of agreement evidencing a transaction in respect of which a trading fee is charged by a contracts exchange. For the purposes of this exemption -

"contracts exchange" means a contracts exchange that is chargeable to contracts exchange tax under Part VIC of the Miscellaneous Taxes Act 1976;

"trading fee" has the meaning given to it in that Part; and

"transaction" means a transaction carried out on a contracts exchange, being the actual purchase or sale of a contract.

AND *see* section 38.

4. AGREEMENT, OR ANY MEMORANDUM OF AGREEMENT for the sale of land, being an executory agreement not having the effect of a conveyance.	*(a)*	**(i)** The original, $10 **(ii)** each executed counterpart, $1.
	(b)	30 days after execution.
	(c)	All parties to the agreement.
5. AGREEMENT OF INSTALMENT PURCHASE OR HIRE PURCHASE.	*(a)*	$2.
	(b)	30 days after execution.
	(c)	All persons executing.

AGREEMENT OR CONTRACT accompanied by a deposit: *See* Mortgage etc.

AGREEMENT for lease: *See* Lease.

AGREEMENT for sale: *See* Conveyance on Sale and Head 4.

ANNUITY
Conveyance in consideration of, and instrument creating by way of sale: *See* Conveyance on Sale, Policy of Insurance.
Instrument creating by way of security: *See* Mortgage etc.
Premiums for: *See* Insurance Premium Receipt.
AND *See* section 66.

6. APPOINTMENT OF NEW TRUSTEE OF A TRUST OR SETTLEMENT
(including the case where the instrument effecting the appointment is the instrument by which the trust or settlement itself was created ("the original") not falling within Head 16 -

(i) where the original instrument has been duly stamped under this Act, or where duty has ever previously been paid under and in accordance with paragraph (ii) or (iii) of this Head in respect of the appointment of a new trustee of the trust or settlement.

(a) $10.

(b) 30 days after execution

(c) The new trustee*.

(ii) where -

(a) the original instrument was not liable to stamping under this Act; but

(b) the instrument effecting the appointment, whether it is or is not the original instrument, ("the new instrument") is so liable; and

(c) the original instrument was executed two years or more before the date on which the appointment takes effect.

(a) $250.

(b) 30 days after execution

(c) The new trustee*.

(iii) where - *(a)* the original instrument was not liable to stamping under this Act; and *(b)* the new instrument is so liable; but *(c)* the original instrument was executed less than two years before the date on which the appointment takes effect.	*(a)* $250 plus - (i) In respect of Bermuda property in the trust or settlement - *(aa)* on the first $100,000 of the amount or value, 2 per centum of the amount or value; and *(bb)* thereafter, 5 per centum of the amount or value; and (ii) 1/10 *per centum* of the amount or value of other property in the trust or settlement, or $4,000, whichever is less.
	(b) 30 days after execution.
	(c) The new trustee*.

*Where more than one new trustee is being appointed at the same time, the stamp duty payable shall be the same as if one trustee only were being appointed.

AND *see* Head 16.

7. APPOINTMENT on execution of a power of any property by any instrument not being a will or other testamentary disposition.	*(a)* $5.
	(b) 30 days after execution.
	(c) All persons executing.
8. APPRAISEMENT or VALUATION of any property, or of any interest therein, or of the annual value thereof	*(a)* (i) Where the appraisement or valuation does not exceed $10,000 - *per centum*

of the appraisement or valuation;

(ii) in all other cases, $25.

(b) *See* section 65.

(c) The appraiser.

Exemptions

(a) Appraisement or valuation made for the information of one party only, and not being obligatory between the parties either by agreement or by operation of law.

(b) Appraisement or valuation made under any statutory provision or in pursuance of an order of court.

(c) Appraisement or valuation of the assets of a company incorporated in Bermuda with power to redeem or purchase for cancellation its issued shares at the option of, or on the request of, a shareholder, where the purpose of such appraisement or valuation is to determine the market or asset value of the shares.

AND *see* section 65.

ASSIGNMENT

By way of security, or of any security: *see* Mortgage etc. Upon a sale or otherwise: *See* Conveyance.

ATTESTED COPY: *See* Copy.

ATTORNEY, LETTER OR POWER OF: *See* Power of Attorney.

9. AWARD on an arbitration. *(a)* ¼ *per centum* of the

				amount or value awarded but not exceeding a maximum of $25.
		(b)		30 days after the award.
		(c)		The parties to the submission.
	Exemptions			
	(a) Where the amount or value awarded does not exceed $1,000.			
	(b) Awards made by the official arbitrators under the Acquisition of Land Act 1970.			
10.	BILL OF EXCHANGE	*(a)*		2 cents.
	(i) CHEQUE drawn within Bermuda AND *see* section 28	*(b)*	(i)	Where the cheque is drawn on a form issued by banker to customer, before issue of the cheque form to customer;
			(ii)	in any other case, before issue.
		(c)	(i)	The banker issuing the cheque form where the cheque is drawn on a form, where the form issued by banker to customer;
			(ii)	in any other case the drawer.
	(ii) BILL OF EXCHANGE of any other kind whatsoever (except a bank note), if drawn or expressed to be payable, or actually paid, or endorsed, or in any manner negotiated, within Bermuda.	(a)		10 cents.
		(b)		If drawn in Bermuda, before execution. If drawn out of Bermuda, in accordance with section 30.
		(c)		*See* Part VI.

Exemptions

(a) Draft or order drawn by any banker in Bermuda upon any other banker in Bermuda, not payable to bearer or to order, and used solely for the purpose of settling or clearing any account between such bankers.

(b) Cheque or other bill of exchange drawn by the Accountant General or other public officer or person for money payable for any public purpose.

(c) Cheque drawn on any account kept by any court.

(d) Standing order to a banker to make periodical payments.

(e) Travellers cheques.

AND *see* section 4(g) and Part VI.

BILL OF SALE

Absolute: *See* Conveyance.

By way of Security: *See* Mortgage etc.

11. BOND

(i)	Given in pursuance of the Revenue Act 1898 or any other statutory provision.	*(a)*	$2.
		(b)	30 days after execution.
		(c)	All persons executing.
(ii)	On obtaining letters of administration.	*(a)*	$5.
		(b)	30 days after execution.

(c) All persons executing.

(iii) For securing the payment or repayment of money or the transfer or retransfer of stock. *See* Mortgage etc. Marketable Security.

(iv) Of any other kind not specifically Charged with any duty.
(a) $5.
(b) 30 days after execution.
(c) All persons executing.

Exemption

Guarantee, surety and personal performance bond on Government building contracts.

12. CHARTER PARTY
(a) (i) For less than six months, $1;
(ii) for six months or more or for an indefinite period, $10.
(b) 30 days after execution.
(c) All persons executing.

CHEQUE: *See* Bill of Exchange.

CONTRACT: *See* Agreement.

13. (deleted by No. 5 of 1979).

14. CONVEYANCE or TRANSFER on sale of land (not being a conveyance or transfer expressly provided for in Head 15) the duty to be calculated on the amount or value of the consideration on the day of the date of
(a) (i) on the first $100,000 of that amount or value, 1/2 per centum

the instrument.
and

on that amount or value;

AND *see* Part VII and section 4.

(ii) where that amount or value is $500,000 or less

but exceeds $100,000, 2

per centum of that portion of that amount or value which exceeds $100,000; and

(iii) where that amount or value is $1,000,000 or less but exceeds $500,000, 2 per centum of that portion of that amount or value which exceeds $500,000; and

(iv) where that amount or value exceeds $1,000,000, 3 per centum of that portion of that amount or value which exceeds $1,000,000;

(b) 30 days after execution.

(c) All persons executing.

15. CONVEYANCE or TRANSFER on sale other than a conveyance or, transfer to which Head 14 or 16 applies (the duty to be calculated on the amount or value of the consideration on the day of the date of the instrument).

(a) (i) In respect of Bermuda property

(aa) on the first $100,000 of that amount

or value, ½

per centum of that

amount or value;

and

(bb) where that amount or value is $500,000 or less but exceeds $100,000, 1 per centum of that portion of that amount or value which exceeds $100,000; and

(cc) where that amount or value is $1,000,000 or

less but exceeds $500,000, 2 per centum of that portion of that amount or value which exceeds $500,000; and

(dd) where that amount or value exceeds $1,000,000, 3 per centum of that portion of that amount or value which exceeds $1,000,000;

(ii) In respect of property that is not Bermuda property, 1/2 per centum of that amount or value."

(b) 30 days after execution.

(c) All persons executing.

Exemptions

Any conveyance or transfer of, or any contract or agreement for the conveyance or transfer of, any estate or interest in -

(a) Goods, wares or merchandise in the ordinary course of trade.

(b) A trade mark and the proportion of goodwill created thereby.

(c) Shares of a company incorporated in Bermuda with power to redeem or purchase for cancellation its issued shares at the option of, or on the request of, a shareholder, where the conveyance or transfer, or the contract of agreement for the conveyance or transfer, of the shares is effected at the instance of a shareholder who is not resident in Bermuda for the purposes of the

Exchange Control Regulations 1973.

(d) Shares in an exempted company (not being a company within the benefit of paragraph (c)), where at the time of the conveyance or transfer, or the contract or agreement for the conveyance or transfer, ("the transaction"), -

(i) the shares are quoted on a stock exchange that is an appointed stock exchange within the meaning assigned to that expression in subsection (1) of section 25 of the Companies Act 1981; and

(ii) none of the parties to the transaction is resident in Bermuda for the purposes of the Exchange Control Regulations 1973.

(e) Real or personal property between two bodies corporate -

(i) each of which has a share capital; and

(ii) as to which the Accountant General has certified in writing either -

(aa) that one body corporate owns 90% or more of the issued share capital of the other body corporate; or

(bb) that a third person or body of persons owns 90% or more of the issued share capital of each body corporate.

AND *see* Part VII and section 4.

16. CONVEYANCE made for the purpose of effectuating the appointment of a new trustee, if such conveyance is made by some instrument other than the instrument by which the new trustee is appointed.	(a)	$5.
	(b)	30 days after execution.
	(c)	All persons executing

AND *see* Part VII.

17. CONVEYANCE or TRANSFER to effect or having effect of a voluntary disposition *inter vivos.*	(a)	(i) In respect of Bermuda property (aa) on the first $100,000 of the value of the property conveyed, ½ per centum of the value; and (bb) where the value is $500,000 or less but exceeds $100,000, 1 per centum of that portion of the value which exceeds $100,000; and (cc) where the value is $1,000,000 or less but exceeds $500,000, 2 per centum of that portion of the value which exceeds $500,000; and (dd) where the value exceeds $1,000,000, 3 per centum of that portion of the value which exceeds $1,000,000; (ii) In respect of property that is not

Bermuda property, ½ per centum of the value.

(b) 30 days after execution.

(c) All persons executing.

Exemptions

(a) Conveyance of real or personal property to a charity registered as such under the Charities Act 1978 or to anybody of persons whose purposes are, in the opinion of the Minister, charitable.

(b) Conveyance of real or personal property between two bodies corporate -

(i) each of which has a share capital; and

(ii) as to which the Accountant General has certified in writing either -

(aa) that one body corporate owns 90% or more of the issued capital of the other body corporate; or

(bb) that a third person or body of persons owns 90% or more of the issued share capital of each body corporate.

(c) Conveyance chargeable to duty as a settlement under Head 40.

(d) Conveyance of shares in an exempted company where the conveyance is one made between persons none of whom is resident in Bermuda for the purposes

of the Exchange Control Regulations 1973.

AND *see* section 39.

CONVEYANCE or TRANSFER of any kind not herein specifically described.	*(a)*	$5
	(b)	30 days after execution.
	(c)	All persons executing.

Exemption

Conveyance of a legacy by the estate representative to the beneficiary.

AND *see* Part VII.

19. COVENANT Any separate deed of covenant(not being an instrument chargeable	*(a)*	$5
with *ad valorem* duty as a conveyance or mortgage) made on the sale or mortgage of any	*(b)*	30 days after execution
property, and incidental thereto.	*(c)*	All persons executing.

DEBENTURE: *See* Mortgage.

20. DECLARATION or revocation of any use or trust under seal of or concerning any	*(a)*	$25.
property by any writing, not being a will, or an instrument chargeable with duty as a	*(b)*	30 days after execution.
settlement.	*(c)*	All persons executing

Exemption

Declaration or revocation of a trust in respect of a director's qualifying share in an exempted company.

21. DEED of any kind whatsoever, not described in this Schedule.	*(a)*	$5.
	(b)	30 days after execution.
	(c)	All persons executing.

DEPOSIT of title deeds: *See* Mortgage etc.

22. DUPLICATE OR COUNTER PART of any instrument chargeable with any duty.	*(a)* Where the duty on the original instrument does not exceed $1, the same duty as on the original.
AND *see* section 14.	In all other cases $1.
	(b) 30 days after execution, or such longer period as may be allowed within which the original must be stamped.
EQUITABLE MORTGAGE: See Mortgage etc.	
23. EXCHANGE (excluding shares and marketable securities).	*(a)* $10 and *ad valorem* duty as on conveyance on sale on any sum paid or agreed to be paid for equality
AND *see* section 61.	
	(b) 30 days after execution.
	(c) All persons executing.
GIFT: *See* Head 17.	
24. INSURANCE PREMIUM RECEIPT.	*(a)* 1 *per centum* of the amount for which the receipt is given rounded up to the nearest cent.
	(b) Before execution.
	(c) The insurer.

Exemptions

Receipts for premiums paid on -

(a) Life policy.

(b) Exempt policy.

(c) Accident or health policy.

(d) Annuity sold by a person carrying on insurance business.

NOTE: Duty is not payable under this Head in respect of any premium which has been taken into account in calculating duty for the purposes of Head 35.

AND *see* Part X and section 66.

25. LEASE AND AGREEMENT FOR LEASE, as beneath -

(a) If granted in consideration of a premium or fine.	*(a)* *Ad valorem* duty as on conveyance on sale on the amount or value of the premium or fine. *(b)* 30 days after execution. *(c)* All persons executing.
(b) If granted in consideration of a rent -	
(i) where the term is not defined or is uncertain.	*(a)* (i) $1.
(ii) where the term specified in the lease does not exceed one year.	(ii) $1.
(iii) where the term specified in the lease exceeds one year but does not exceed three years.	(iii) $5.
(iv) where the term specified in the lease exceeds three years.	(iv) $10. *(b)* 30 days after execution. *(c)* All persons executing.
(c) If the consideration includes both premium or fine and rent.	*(a)* The total ascertained in (a) and (b) of this item *(b)* 30 days after execution.

		(c) All persons executing.
(d)	Surrender or agreement for surrender of - (i) Lease. (ii) Agreement for lease.	(a) $2. (b) 30 days after execution. (c) All persons executing.
(e)	Lease executed in pursuance of a duty stamped agreement for a lease.	(a) $2. (b) 30 days after execution. (c) All persons executing.
(f)	Renewal of lease or agreement for lease or extension of lease or agreement for lease.	As for lease and agreement for lease.
(g)	Transfer or agreement for transfer of lease or agreement for lease.	(a) *Ad valorem* duty as on conveyance on sale on the amount or value of the consideration. (b) 30 days after execution. (c) All persons executing.

AND *see* section 59.

26. LETTER OF ALLOTMENT or any other document having the effect of a letter of allotment of shares in any company or proposed company incorporated in Bermuda or in respect of any loan raised or proposed to be raised by any such company or proposed company, and letter of renunciation.	(a) 10 cents. (b) Before execution. (c) All persons executing.

LETTER OF ATTORNEY: *See* Power of Attorney.

27. MARKETABLE SECURITIES AND SHARES -

(i) Transfer, assignment, disposition or assignation of a marketable security or share -	(a) $2.	
	(b) Before execution.	
	(c) The transferor and transferee.	
(a) upon a sale or the voluntary disposition thereof: *See* Conveyance.		
(b) upon a mortgage thereof - under hand only: See Agreement and section 58 - by deed: *See* Mortgage etc.		
(c) in any case other than sale, voluntary disposition or mortgage.		
(ii) Share warrant to bearer, issued in Bermuda.	(a) ½ *per centum* of the nominal value of the share.	
	(b) Before issue.	
	(c) The body issuing.	
(iii) Share certificate where the share is issued for the first time at a premium in excess of the par value thereof by a company incorporated in Bermuda other than a mutual fund.	(a)	(i) ½ *per centum* of the amount of the premium in the case of a local company;
		(ii) ¼ *per centum* of the amount of the premium in the case of an exempted company.
		Provided that, once duty under this provision, Head 28 and Head 29 amounting in the aggregate to $25,000 has been paid in the case of an exempted company which -

(aa) has, as an object specified in its memorandum of association, the object of carrying on insurance business as defined in the Insurance Act 1978; and

(bb) is registered as an insurer under that Act within six months of the date of the company's incorporation; and

(cc) at all times thereafter remains so registered,

no further duty shall be payable; but so that any duty paid before 6th December, 1985 under this provision or either of those Heads (as then in force) shall count as a credit towards the above amount of $25,000.

(b) Before issue.

(c) The body issuing.

(iv) Notice under section 43 or section 44

(a) 1/10th *per centum* of the price of new shares or new units issued:

Provided that, once duty amounting in the aggregate to $25,000 has been paid in the case of a mutual fund or a unit trust scheme, there shall, as respects that respective fund or scheme, be substituted for the above rate or 1/10th *per centum the lower rate of 1/20th* per centum; but so that any duty paid before 1st January, 1986 -

(i) in respect of a mutual fund, under Head 27(iv), Head 28 or Head 29 (as then in force); or

(ii) in respect of a unit trust scheme, under Head 40 (as then in force), shall count as a credit towards the above amount of $25,000 as respects that fund or scheme.

(b) On delivery of the notice.

(c) In relation to a new share, the mutual fund; in relation to a new unit, the trustees.

(v) Marketable security issued in Bermuda or made or issued by or on behalf of a corporate or unincorporate body incorporated or formed in Bermuda other than a share (not being a debenture).

(a) 1/5th *per centum* of the money secured.

(b) Before issue.

(c) The body issuing.

Exemption

Securities created, constituted or issued under a trust deed or other instrument dutiable under Head 41.

MARRIAGE SETTLEMENT: *See* Settlement.

MEMORANDUM OF ASSOCIATION filed in the office of the Registrar of Companies for the incorporation of a company.

(a) (i) ½ *per centum* of the authorized share capital in the case of a local company;

(ii) ¼ *per centum* of the authorized share capital in the case of an exempted company:

Provided that, once duty amounting in the aggregate to $25,000 has been paid in the case of an exempted company which -

(aa) has as an object specified in its memorandum of association, the object of carrying on insurance business as defined in the Insurance Act 1978; and

(bb) is registered as an insurer under that Act within six months of the date of the company's incorporation; and

(cc) at all times thereafter remains so registered,

no further duty shall be payable; but so that any duty paid before 6th December, 1985 under this Head (as then in force) shall count as a credit towards the above amount of $25,000;

(iii) ½ *per centum* of the reserve fund in the case of a local mutual company;

(iv) ¼ *per centum* of the reserve fund in the case of a mutual company which is not a local mutual company.

(b) Before filing.

(c) The company.

Exemption

The memorandum of association of a mutual fund.

AND *see* Section 10 of the Exempted Partnerships Act 1958.

29. MEMORANDUM OF INCREASED (a) CAPITAL filed under section 45(3) of the Companies Act 1981.

(i) ½ *per centum* of the increased capital in the case of a local company;

(ii) ¼ *per centum* of the increased capital in the case of an exempted company:

Provided that, once duty under this provision, Head 27(iii) and Head 28 amounting in the aggregate to $25,000 has been paid in the case of an exempted company which -

(aa) has, as an object specified in its memorandum of association, the object of carrying on insurance business as defined in the Insurance Act 1978; and

(bb) is registered as an insurer under that Act within six months of the date of the company's incorporation; and

(cc) at all times thereafter

remains so registered, no further duty shall be payable; but so that any duty paid before 6th December, 1985 under this provision or Head 27(iii) or Head 28 (as then in force) shall count as a credit towards the above amount of $25,000.

(b) Before filing.

(c) The company.

Exemption

(a) Memorandum of increased capital of any commingled pension trust funds company (within the meaning of section 1 of the Pension Trust Funds Act 1966).

(b) Memorandum of increased capital of a mutual fund.

AND *see* section 10 of the Exempted Partnerships Act 1958.

30. (deleted by No. 36 of 1984).

31. MORTGAGE, BOND DEBENTURE (except a marketable security otherwise specially charged with duty) and a WARRANT OF ATTORNEY to confess and enter up judgment -

(i) Being the only or principal or primary security.

(a) ¼ *per centum* of the principal sum secured.

(b) 30 days after execution.

(c) All persons executing.

(ii)	Being a collateral or auxillary or additional or substituted security (other than a mortgage executed in pursuance of a duly stamped agreement for a mortgage), or being a mortgage executed by way of further assurance, provided in every case that the principal security, where required to be stamped, was duly stamped.	(a)	1/10th *per centum* of the principal sum secured.
		(b)	30 days after execution.
		(c)	All persons executing.
(iii)	Being an equitable mortgage.	(a)	1/20th *per centum* of the principal sum secured.
		(b)	30 days after execution.
		(c)	All persons executing.
(iv)	Transfer or assignment of any mortgage, bond, debenture or covenant (except a marketable security), or of any money or stock secured by any such instrument, or by any warrant of attorney to enter up judgment, or by any judgment.	(a)	1/10th *per centum* of the principal sum secured.
		(b)	30 days after execution.
		(c)	All persons executing.
(v)	Reconveyance, release, discharge, surrender, resurrender, or renunciation of any mortgage, bond, debenture or covenant or of any money by any warrant of attorney to enter up judgment.	(a)	1/20th *per centum* of the principal sum secured.
		(b)	30 days after execution.
		(c)	All persons executing.
(vi)	Certificate of satisfaction.	(a)	1/100th *per centum* of the principal sum secured.
		(b)	30 days after execution.

	(c)	All persons executing.
(vii) Mortgage executed in pursuance duly stamped under this Head.	(a)	$1.
	(b)	30 days after execution.
	(c)	All persons executing.
(viii) Where further money is added to the money already secured.	(a)	The same duty as a principal security for such further money.
	(b)	30 days after execution.
	(c)	All persons executing.

Exemption

(a) Securities, other than debentures, created, constituted or issued under a trust deed or other instrument dutiable under Head 41.

(b) Any charge -

(i) taken by either -

(aa) an individual resident outside Bermuda or a company, partnership or other body formed outside Bermuda; or

(bb) an exempted company; or

(cc) a bank licensed under the Banks Act 1969,

to secure financial accommodation:

Provided that such accommodation was not granted for

the purpose of, or in connection with, the acquisition by any person of land, or an interest in land, situate in Bermuda; and

(ii) registered under section 55 of the Companies Act 1981,

not being a charge taken on the assets of a local company as defined in the latter Act.

AND *see* sections 58 and 60.

MUTUAL FUNDS: *See* Part VIII and Head 27.

32. NOTARIAL ACT of any kind (except a protest on a bill of exchange or promissory note).

(a) $1.

(b) Before execution.

(c) The notary.

Exemption

The certificate or other act of a notary given or performed outside Bermuda.

33. PARTITION OR DIVISION - Instruments effecting.
on sale on any sum paid or agreed

(a) $10 together with *ad valorem* duty as on a conveyance to be paid for equality.

(b) 30 days after execution.

(c) All persons executing.

AND *see* section 61.

34. PARTNERSHIP instrument.

(a) $10.

(b) 30 days after execution.

(c) All persons executing.

Exemption

Articles of partnership stampable under section 10 of the Exempted Partnerships Act 1958 at the rate fixed under Head 28.

35. POLICY OF INSURANCE or RE-INSURANCE.

(1)	LIFE POLICY not being an exempt policy and ANNUITY sold by a person carrying premiums are collected	(a)	(i)	where the amount insured does not exceed $4,000 and on insurance business. weekly, $1;
			(ii)	in all other cases, $5.
		(b)		90 days after execution.
		(c)		The insurer.
(2)	EXEMPT POLICY.	(a)		Nil.
(3)	ACCIDENT OR HEALTH POLICY.	(a)	(i)	where the policy is non-renewable, is written for a term less than ten days and insures more than four persons, $5;
			(ii)	where the policy is non-renewable, is written for a term less than ten days and insures one person only, 1% of the amount for which the receipt is given rounded up to the nearest cent;
			(iii)	in all other cases, $1 for each person insured.
		(b)		90 days after execution.
		(c)		The insurer.

(4) POLICIES of any kind not being specifically described.

(a) 1 *per centum* of the first premium rounded u up to the nearest cent.

(b) 90 days after execution.

(c) The insurer.

Exemption

(a) Letter of cover or engagement to issue a policy of insurance:

Provided that unless such letter of cover or engagement bears the stamp prescribed in paragraphs (1) to (4) above for such policy nothing shall be claimable thereunder, nor shall it be available for any purpose except to compel the delivery of the policy therein mentioned.

(b) A policy of marine or air cargo insurance on a cargo in transit to Bermuda.

AND *see* Part X.

36. POWER OF ATTORNEY for any purpose whatever or revocation thereof.

(a) $2.50.

(b) 30 days after execution.

(c) The person executing.

Exemption

Power of attorney for appointing a proxy to vote at a specified meeting or revocation thereof.

37. PROMISSORY NOTE of any kind whatsoever (except a bank note), if drawn or expressed to be payable, or actually paid or endorsed, or in any manner negotiated, within

(a) 1/50th *per centum* of the amount promised.

(b) If made within Bermuda, 7 days after execution.

Bermuda.	If made out of Bermuda, in accordance with section 30.
	(c) *See* Part VI.
Exemption	
A promissory note -	
(a) issued by or in favour of an exempt undertaking or its nominees.	
(b) issued by or in favour of the trustees of a trust or settlement which is not resident in Bermuda for the purposes of the Exchange Control Regulations 1973.	
38. PROTEST of any bill of exchange or promissory note.	(a) $1.
	(b) 30 days after execution.
	(c) The notary, or person giving certificate attesting the dishonour.
PROXY: *See* Power of Attorney.	
39. RELEASE OR RENUNCIATION of any property or of any right or interest in any property -	
(i) Upon sale.	*See* conveyance on sale.
(ii) By way of security.	*See* mortgage.
(iii) By way of gift.	*See* Head 17.
(iv) In any other case not otherwise specifically charged with duty.	(a) $5.
	(b) 30 days after execution.
	(c) Every person executing.
40. SETTLEMENT	

(1) INSTRUMENT OF SETTLEMENT OR AGREEMENT FOR SETTLEMENT.

(a) $250 plus -

(i) In respect of Bermuda property (but so that in the valuation of that property there shall be deducted the value of any benefit conferred on a settlor's spouse and the cost of valuing any Bermuda property) -

(aa) on the first $10,000 of the amount or value, nil; and

(bb) on the next $90,000 of the amount or value, 2 per centum of the amount or value; and

(cc) thereafter, 5 per centum of the amount or value;

(For the purposes of this provision -

(1) an interest that a person has under a settlement by reason of being named as a discretionary object in that settlement (or any part of it) is not a benefit conferred on that person under that settlement; and

(2) the word "settlor", in relation to a settlement, includes any person by whom the settlement was made directly or indirectly, and in particular (but without prejudice to the

generality of the preceding words) includes any person who has provided funds directly or indirectly for the purpose of or in connection with the settlement, or has made with any other person a reciprocal arrangement for that other person to make the settlement; and

(ii) 1/10 *per centum* of the amount or value of other property.

(b) 30 days after execution.

(c) All persons executing.

(2) INSTRUMENT OF ADDITION to the corpus of any settlement. total amount of Bermuda property (whether in respect addition or $2,050 in the centum of the Bermuda property

(a) (i) (aa) up to the point at which the duty paid on under this Head of an instrument of otherwise) equals aggregate, 2 per amount or value of added; and

(bb) thereafter, 5 per centum of the amount or value of Bermuda property added; and

(ii) 1/10 *per centum* of the amount or value of other property added.

(b) 30 days after execution.

(c) All persons executing.

Exemptions

(a) Instrument settling real or personal property -

(i) on a charitable organization registered under the Charities Act 1978; or

(ii) in favour of charitable purposes which, in the Minister's opinion, by reason of -

(aa) their connection with Bermuda (being a connection mentioned in the instrument); and

(bb) their benefit to Bermuda warrant the instrument's exemption from duty.

(b) Any instrument within paragraph (1) or (2) -

(i) as respects only duty payable under this Head in relation to property (other than Bermuda property) settled in or added to a settlement on or after 22nd July, 1985;

(ii) as soon as duty amounting in the aggregate to $4,000 has been so paid in relation to that settlement.

(c) Instrument of appointment relating to any property in favour of persons especially named or described as the objects of a power of appointment, where duty has been paid in respect of the same property upon the settlement creating the power or the grant of representation of any will or testamentary instrument creating the power.

(3) SETTLEMENT executed in pursuance (a) $2.

of a duly stamped agreement for a settlement.

(b) 30 days after execution.

(c) All persons executing.

AND *see* Part VIII and, for Imported Settlements, see Head 6.

SHARES: *See* marketable securities.

UNIT TRUSTS: *See* Part VIII and Head 27.

VALUATION: *See* Appraisement.

41. TRUST DEED or other instrument creating, constituting or providing for the issue of a foreign currency security.

(a) $1,000.

(b) 30 days after execution.

(c) All persons executing.

THE STAMP DUTIES (INTERNATIONAL BUSINESSES RELIEF) ACT 1990

(as amended)

ARRANGEMENT OF SECTIONS

Short title.

1. This Act may be cited as the Stamp Duties (International Businesses Relief) Act 1990.

Construction and interpretation.

2.(1) This Act shall be read and construed as one of the Stamp Duties Act 1976 ("the Act").

(2) Without prejudice to subsection (1), any expression that is used in this Act that is also used in the Act has in this Act the meaning that it has in the Act, but subject to subsection (3).

(3) In this Act -

"disposition" means disposition of any kind, whether by way of sale, lease, loan, gift or otherwise;

"exempted company" and "permit company" has respectively the meanings that they have in subsection (1) of section 2 of the Companies Act 1981;

"exempted partnership" has the meaning assigned to it by the Exempted Partnerships Act 1958;

"international business" means any exempted company, permit company, exempted unit trust scheme (as defined in section 1 of the Exempted Undertakings Tax Protection Act 1966) overseas partnership or exempted partnership;

"overseas partnership" has the meaning assigned to it by section 2(1) of the Overseas Partnership Act 1995.

Stamp duty on certain instruments abolished.

3. Notwithstanding anything to the contrary in the Act but subject to section 4, an instrument is exempt from duty if it is an instrument executed on or after 1st April 1990 by an international business (being an international business properly a party to the instrument), or by a person in respect of an interest which he has in, or in property of, an international business, whether or not the instrument has also been executed by some other person.

Exception for instruments disposing of Bermuda property.

4. Section 3 does not have effect in relation to any instrument effecting a disposition, or constituting an agreement for the disposition, of Bermuda property.

THE USA-BERMUDA TAX CONVENTION ACT 1986 (as amended)

ARRANGEMENT OF SECTIONS

Short title.

1. This Act may be cited as the USA-Bermuda Tax Convention Act 1986.

Interpretation.

2.(1) In this Act, unless the context otherwise requires -

"the Agreement" means the arrangements between Bermuda and the United States established by the Convention and the Notes;

"Article" means Article of the Convention;

"business" includes profession or trade;

"the Convention" means the Convention entered into on 11th July, 1986 at Washington D.C. in the United States of America by the U.K. Government (on behalf of the Government of Bermuda) and the U.S. Government relating to the taxation of insurance enterprises and mutual assistance in tax matters, the text of which Convention is set forth in the First Schedule and in relation to which the Protocol of 1988 sets forth certain reservations of the United States;

"document" includes any book, paper, statement, account, writing or record, and any device by means of which material is recorded or stored;

"information" includes documents;

"judge" means Judge of the Supreme Court;

"the Minister" has the meaning given by subsection (2);

"the Notes" means the notes exchanged on 11th July, 1986 between the U.K. Government and the U.S. Government concerning the Convention, the text of which notes, apart from formal matters, is set forth in the Second Schedule;

"premises" includes any place whatsoever and any means of transport;

"the Protocol of 1988" means the Protocol of Exchange of Instruments of Ratification executed at Washington aforesaid on 2nd December, 1988 and set forth in the Third Schedule;

"regulation" means regulation made under section 13;

"request" means an application made pursuant to Article 5 and the Notes, for assistance;

"the U.K. Government" means the Government of the United Kingdom;

"the United States" has the meaning assigned by Article 1;

the "U.S. Government" means the Government of the United States.

(2) In this Act, a reference to the Minister, in relation to any function to be performed by the Minister under this Act, is a reference to the Minister of Finance or such person, being an officer or servant, or an agency, of the Government of Bermuda, as the Minister of Finance may designate to perform the function (with or without a duty to refer back to the Minister of Finance) in his stead as his delegate.

(3) A reference in this Act to the performance of a function includes reference to the performance of a duty or the exercise of a power or right.

Legal effect of this Act.

3.(1) This Act has effect for the purpose of enforcing the giving of assistance by persons in Bermuda in connection with the performance of the obligations assumed by Bermuda under the Agreement.

(2) The Minister, in performing his functions under this Act, is not restricted by any law or any rule of law relating to confidentiality except as expressly provided in the Agreement.

Procedure in respect of a request.

4.(1) A request must be in writing.

(2) A request must be signed by a senior official designated by the U.S. Government.

(3) A request shall contain particulars indicating -

(a) that by the request the U.S. Government seeks information identified in the request; and

(b) that the information is in Bermuda and that a person in Bermuda has or may have the information in his possession, custody or control; and

(c) that the information relates to the carrying out of the laws of the United States mentioned in Article 5; and

(d) that the information relates to the affairs of a person in respect of whom the request has been made under the Agreement ("the taxpayer"); and

(e) where the request has been made pursuant to the first sentence of Article 5, that the taxpayer has, or is believed to have, done some act, or made some omission, justifying the making of that request in respect of him; and

(f) whether or not the taxpayer is a resident of Bermuda or of the United States; and

(g) that the request relates to an examination of the taxpayer in relation to a taxable period of the taxpayer, being a period specified in the request, but so

that, where a request, in seeking information relating to a taxable period so specified, also seeks information relating to a time outside that period, the request must establish the connection between that period and that time.

(4) Subject to subsections (1), (2) and (3), a request shall be in such form as regulations may prescribe.

Power to require production of information.

5.(1) Subject to this section, where the Minister has received a request in respect of which the requirements of section 4 are fulfilled, he shall by notice in writing under this section served upon the person referred to in paragraph (b) of subsection (3) of that section direct him to deliver to the Minister the information referred to in that paragraph.

(2) For the purposes of subsections (3) and (4) of this section, a subsection (2) matter is a matter -

(a) with respect to which information is sought in a request; and

(b) which relates to a person who is not a resident either of Bermuda or of the United States, whether or not the requirements of section 4 are fulfilled in relation to the request.

(3) Where the Minister receives a request which seeks information with respect to a subsection (2) matter, he shall not issue a notice under this section to any person unless the Minister is satisfied that the information is necessary for the proper administration and enforcement of the fiscal laws of the United States.

(4) Where the Minister receives a request which seeks information with respect to a matter which either -

(a) is a subsection (2) matter; or

(b) does not constitute a United States criminal or tax fraud investigation, he shall not issue a notice under this section to any person unless the Minister receives certification from a senior official designated by the Secretary of the Treasury of the United States that the information sought by the request is relevant to and necessary for the determination of the tax liability of a United States taxpayer, or the criminal tax liability of a person under the laws of the United States.

(5) A notice under this section must -

(a) contain the pertinent details of the request to which the notice relates; and

(b) specify the time within which the information sought by the request is to be delivered to the Minister.

(6) The time to be specified in such a notice is 28 days commencing on the day on which the notice was served, or such greater or lesser number of days as the Minister may in any particular case think fit.

(7) Subject to subsections (8) and (9), a person who is directed by such a notice to deliver information to the Minister shall deliver it to the Minister in accordance with the notice if the information is in Bermuda and that person has it in his possession, custody or control.

(8) A person complies with a duty under this section to deliver information to the Minister if he makes the information available to him.

(9) After a notice has been served, the Minister may in any case enlarge the time specified in the notice, either before or after that time has expired, if in his opinion the circumstances warrant.

(10) A direction given in a notice under this section to a person is an absolute defence to any claim brought against him in respect of any act of his that was done, or any omission of his that was made, in good faith in obedience to the direction.

Power to enter premises to obtain information.

6.(1) An officer of the Ministry of Finance may make an application to a judge under and in accordance with the provisions of this section for the issue of a warrant authorizing entry upon premises.

(2) An officer of that Ministry who makes such an application must produce a minute signed by the Minister of Finance himself authorizing the officer to make the application in that particular case.

(3) If on information given on oath by such an officer a judge is satisfied that there is reasonable ground for suspecting that an offence against this Act has been, or is being, or is about to be, committed on any premises, being an offence by reason of which the delivery to the Minister of information sought by a request is endangered, then the judge may issue a warrant in writing authorizing an officer of the Ministry to enter the premises, if necessary by force, at any time within 14 days commencing on the day of the issue of the warrant, and search them.

(4) In issuing a warrant under this section, the judge may impose such restrictions upon the execution of the warrant as he may deem proper in the circumstances.

(5) An officer entering premises by virtue of a warrant under this section may take such other persons and equipment with him as he thinks necessary; and, on leaving premises entered by virtue of a warrant under this section, shall, if they are unoccupied or the occupier is temporarily absent, leave them as effectively secured against trespassers as he found them.

(6) On entering premises by virtue of a warrant under this section, the officer may seize and remove any things whatsoever found there which he has reasonable cause to believe may contain information relevant to a request, and shall deliver any things so seized and removed to the Minister.

(7) Where entry to premises has been made by virtue of a warrant under this section and the officer making the entry has seized any things under the authority of the warrant, he shall prepare a list of them and, if so requested by a person showing himself either -

(a) to be the occupier of the premises; or

(b) to have had possession or custody of those things immediately before the seizure, provide that person with a copy of that list.

(8) Where things are seized under the authority of a warrant and it is shown that access to those things is required for the continued conduct of the business or affairs of any person, the Minister shall afford to that person reasonable access to those things.

Provision supplementary to ss. 5 and 6.

7. Where the Minister obtains material by virtue of section 5 or 6, he shall -

(a) in any event, for 20 days commencing on the day on which he obtains the material, unless he returns it pursuant to paragraph (c), not disclose or reveal to any person the contents or import of the material, and, in particular, if the material in his opinion contains information sought by a request, not, as respects that material, comply with the request;

(b) after the expiry of those 20 days, if the material in his opinion contains information sought by a request, be entitled to make copies of it and keep them and also make them available to others in furtherance of the request;

(c) whether or not the material contains information sought by a request, return the material as soon as practicable to the person from whom he obtained it.

Service of documents.

8.(1) A document to be served under this Act by one person ("the server") on another person ("the subject") is to be treated as properly served on the subject if dealt with as provided for in this section.

(2) The document may be delivered or sent by post to the subject, or addressed to him by name and left at his proper address.

(3) For the purposes of subsection (2), a document sent by post to, or left at, the address last known to the server as a person's address shall be treated as sent by post to, or left at, his proper address.

(4) References in this section to the serving of a document on a person include the giving of the document to him.

Offences.

9.(1) A person who -

(a) contravenes subsection (7) of section 5; or

(b) wilfully obstructs an officer executing a warrant under section 6 or a person lawfully accompanying him pursuant to subsection (5) of that section, is guilty of an offence.

(2) If any person, in or in connection with delivering information pursuant to subsection (7) of section 5, wilfully tampers with it or alters it so that the information is false when received by the Minister, he is guilty of an offence.

(3) If any person without a reasonable excuse destroys or damages any information which he knows that the Minister by a notice under section 5 has directed should be delivered to the Minister, he is guilty of an offence.

(4) A person guilty of an offence may be proceeded against summarily, and is liable on conviction to imprisonment for a term not exceeding six months or to a fine not exceeding $5,000, or to both such imprisonment and such a fine.

Depositions, etc.

10.(1) Where a request so stipulates, the Minister shall obtain the information sought by the request in the form of -

(a) depositions of witnesses; or

(b) original documents or copies of original documents, being depositions so made, and documents or copies so certified or authenticated, as the laws and administrative practices of Bermuda permit.

(2) Regulations shall be made, conferring such functions on such persons as the regulations may specify, so that full effect can be given to subsection (1).

Advisory Committee.

11.(1) The Minister of Finance shall establish and maintain a committee, to be known as "the Tax Convention Advisory Committee", for the purpose of advising him on matters of policy connected with the performance of his functions under this Act.

(2) The Tax Convention Advisory Committee ("the Committee") shall consist of such persons (not fewer than five in number), to be appointed by the Minister of Finance, as he thinks fit, but so that no fewer than three of the Committee's members shall be persons appearing to him to be knowledgeable about the matters dealt with in the Convention.

(3) The Minister of Finance shall appoint a person to be the Committee's chairman.

(4) Subject to Article 6 dealing with confidentiality, the Minister of Finance may refer to the Committee any matter mentioned in subsection (1), and shall take into account any advice that the Committee may tender on that matter.

Judicial review.

12. For the avoidance of doubt, it is hereby declared that nothing in this Act excludes or restricts the right of any person aggrieved by the performance by the Minister of Finance or any other person of any function under this Act to challenge the performance of that function, in so far as it affects him, either by seeking review of it by the Supreme Court and the grant, if thought fit by that Court, of an order under section 10 of the Administration of Justice (Prerogative Writs) Act 1978 or by taking any other action which is lawfully available.

Regulations.

13.(1) The Minister of Finance may make regulations -

(a) prescribing anything that is required or permitted by this Act to be prescribed by regulation, or that is in the opinion of the Minister necessary or convenient to be prescribed for carrying out this Act or giving effect to it; and

(b) creating offences and prescribing penalties (including, if thought fit, imprisonment) for such offences but not exceeding the penalties fixed by section 9.

(2) Regulations are subject to the affirmative resolution procedure.

Crown bound.

14. This Act binds the Crown.

Commencement.

15. This Act commences on such day as the Premier may by notice published in the Gazette appoint.

First Schedule

THE CONVENTION

Convention Between The Government Of The United Kingdom Of Great Britain And Northern Ireland (On Behalf Of The Government Of Bermuda) And The Government Of The United States Of America Relating To The Taxation Of Insurance Enterprises And Mutual Assistance In Tax Matters

The Government of the United Kingdom of Great Britain and Northern Ireland (on behalf of the Government of Bermuda) and the Government of the United States of America, desiring to conclude a convention with respect to the taxation of insurance enterprises and mutual assistance in tax matters, have agreed as follows:

Article 1

General Definitions

1.In this Convention, unless the context otherwise requires:

(a) **(i)** the term "United States" means the United States of America, but does not include Puerto Rico, the Virgin Islands, Guam, or any other United States possession or territory; and

(ii) the term "Bermuda" means the islands in the Atlantic Ocean known as Bermuda;

(b) the term "person" includes an individual, an estate, a trust, a company, a partnership, and any other body of persons;

(c) the term "company" means any body corporate or any entity which is treated as a body corporate for tax purposes;

(d) the term "enterprise of insurance" means an enterprise of which the predominant business activity during the taxable year is the issuing of insurance or annuity contracts or acting as the reinsurer of risks underwritten by insurance companies, together with the investing or reinvesting of assets held in respect of insurance reserves, capital, and surplus incident to the carrying on of the insurance business;

(e) the terms "enterprise of a Covered Jurisdiction" and "enterprise of the other Covered Jurisdiction" mean respectively an enterprise carried on by a resident of a Covered Jurisdiction and an enterprise carried on by a resident of the other Covered Jurisdiction;

(f) the term "competent authority" means:

(i) in the case of the United States, the Secretary of the Treasury or his delegate; and

(ii) in the case of Bermuda, the Minister of Finance or his delegate;

(g) the term "insurance obligation" means any obligation which, in accordance with normal industry practice, an insurer undertakes under the terms of a contract of insurance, to make payments or incur expenses in connection with the insurance protection offered under the contract, including any such obligation to pay claims to or for the benefit of the insured resulting from damages connected with the covered risk, to pay interest on such claims, and to pay the costs of defending an insured against such damages, but in no event including any obligation to pay premiums or other costs of reinsuring the covered risk; and

(h) the term "Covered Jurisdiction" means the United States or Bermuda, as the context requires.

2. As regards the application of the Convention by a Covered Jurisdiction, any term not defined therein shall, unless the context otherwise requires or the competent authorities agree to a common meaning, have the meaning which it has under the laws of that Jurisdiction. For purposes of the United States, the preceding sentence shall refer to laws concerning taxes. The competent authorities may agree to a common meaning of a term for purposes of this Convention.

Article 2

Residence

For purposes of this Convention, the term "resident" of a Covered Jurisdiction means:

(a) in the case of the United States:

(i) any person, other than a company, resident in the United States for the purpose of United States tax; but in the case of a partnership, estate or trust, only to the extent that the income derived by such partnership, estate or trust is subject to United States tax as the income of a resident, either in its hands or in the hands of its partners or beneficiaries; and

(ii) a company created under the laws of the United States or a political subdivision thereof; and

(b) in the case of Bermuda:

(i) an individual who has the status of a legal resident of Bermuda; and

(ii) a company, partnership, trust, or association created under the laws of Bermuda.

Article 3

Permanent Establishment

1. For the purposes of Article 4, except as otherwise specified in this Article, the term "permanent establishment" means a regular place of business through which the business of an enterprise of insurance is wholly or partly carried on.

2. The term "permanent establishment" shall include especially a place of management, a branch, an office and premises used as a sales outlet.

3. The term "permanent establishment" shall also include the furnishing of services, including consultancy, management, technical and supervisory services, within a Covered Jurisdiction by an enterprise of insurance through employees or other persons but only if:

(a) activities of that nature continue within the Jurisdiction for a period or periods aggregating more than 90 days in a twelve-month period, provided that a permanent establishment shall not exist in any taxable year in which such services are rendered in that Jurisdiction for a period or periods aggregating less than 30 days in the taxable year; or

(b) the services are performed within the Jurisdiction for an associated enterprise.

For purposes of this paragraph, two enterprises shall be "associated" if either participates directly or indirectly in the management, control, or capital of the other, or if the same persons participate directly or indirectly in the management, control, or capital of both.

4. Notwithstanding the preceding provisions of this Article, the term "permanent establishment" shall be deemed not to include any one or more of the following:

(a) the maintenance of a regular place of business solely for the purpose of purchasing goods or merchandise, or of collecting information, for the enterprise of insurance; or

(b) the maintenance of a regular place of business solely for the purpose of advertising, for the supply of information, for scientific research or for similar activities which have a preparatory or auxiliary, character, for the enterprise.

5. Notwithstanding the provisions of paragraph 1, 2 and 3, a person (other than an agent of independent status to whom paragraph 6 applies) acting in a Covered Jurisdiction on behalf of an enterprise of insurance of the other Covered Jurisdiction shall be deemed to be a permanent establishment of that enterprise in the first-mentioned Jurisdiction an authority to conclude contracts on behalf of the enterprise, unless his activities are limited to those mentioned in paragraph 4 which, if exercised through a regular place of business, would not make that regular place of business a permanent establishment under the provisions of that paragraph.

6. An enterprise of insurance shall not be deemed to have a permanent establishment in a Covered Jurisdiction merely because it carries on business in that Jurisdiction through a broker, general commission agent, or any other agent of an independent status, provided that such persons are acting in the ordinary course of their business. However, when the activities of such person are devoted substantially on behalf of that enterprise, he shall not be considered an agent of independent status within the meaning of this paragraph if the transactions between the agent and the enterprise were not made under arm's length conditions.

7. The fact that a company which is a resident of a Covered Jurisdiction controls or is controlled by a company which is a resident of the other Covered Jurisdiction, or which carries on business in that other Jurisdiction (whether through a permanent establishment or otherwise), shall not of itself constitute either company a permanent establishment of the other.

Article 4

Taxation of Insurance Enterprises

1. The business profits of an enterprise of insurance of a Covered Jurisdiction derived from carrying on the business of insurance (including insubstantial amounts of income incidental to such business) shall not be taxable in the other Covered Jurisdiction unless the enterprise carries on or has carried on business in the other Jurisdiction through a permanent establishment situated therein. If the enterprise carries on or has carried on business as aforesaid, the business profits of the enterprise may be taxed in the other Jurisdiction but only so much of them as is attributable to that permanent establishment. Nothing in this Convention shall prevent the United States from taxing its residents (as determined under Article 2(a)) and its citizens as if this Convention had not entered into force.

2. Where an enterprise of insurance of one of the Covered Jurisdictions carries on or has carried on business through a permanent establishment in the other Jurisdiction, there shall in each Covered Jurisdiction be attributed to the permanent establishment business profits which would reasonably be expected to have been derived by it, if it were a distinct and independent enterprise engaged in the same or similar activities under the same or similar conditions. In determining the business profits of a permanent establishment in a Covered Jurisdiction through which an enterprise of insurance of the other Jurisdiction carries on or has carried on business, there shall be allowed as deductions, for purpose of tax imposed by the first-mentioned Jurisdiction other than excise taxes on premiums paid to foreign insurers, expenses which are incurred for the purposes of the permanent establishment, including a reasonable allocation of executive and general administrative expenses, research and development expense, interest, and other expenses incurred for the enterprise of insurance as a whole (or the part thereof which includes the permanent establishment), whether incurred in the Jurisdiction in which the permanent establishment is situated or elsewhere. For the purposes of this paragraph, the business profits to be attributed to a permanent establishment shall be determined by the same method year by year unless there is good and sufficient reason to the contrary. Nothing in this Article shall affect taxation by a Covered Jurisdiction of dividends, interest, royalties, gains or compensation for services beneficially owned by a resident of the other Covered

Jurisdiction if such items of income are not attributable to a permanent establishment of the beneficial owner of such income in the first-mentioned Jurisdiction.

3. A person which is a resident of a Covered Jurisdiction and which derives income from sources within the other Covered Jurisdiction shall not be entitled, in the other Covered Jurisdiction, to relief from taxation under this Article if:

(a) per cent or less of the beneficial ownership of such person is owned, directly or indirectly, by any combination of one or more individual residents of a Covered Jurisdiction or citizens of the United States; or

(b) the income of such person is used in substantial part, directly or indirectly, to make distributions (where such distributions are made with respect to beneficial ownership interests and are substantially disproportionate to such interests) to, or to meet liabilities (including liabilities for interest, royalties or other expenses, but not including liabilities, whether or not for interest or other expenses, which constitute insurance obligations) to, persons who are neither residents of either of the Covered Jurisdictions nor citizens of the United States.

If one of the Covered Jurisdictions proposes to deny benefits to a resident of the other Covered Jurisdictions by reason of this paragraph, the competent authorities of the Covered Jurisdictions shall, upon request of the competent authority of the other Covered Jurisdiction, consult each other.

4. The provisions of paragraph 3 shall not apply if the person deriving the income is a company which is a resident of a Covered Jurisdiction in whose principal class of shares there is substantial and regular trading on a recognized stock exchange. For purposes of the preceding sentence, the term "recognized stock exchange" means:

(a) the NASDAQ System owned by the National Association of Securities Dealers, Inc. and any other stock exchange registered with the Securities and Exchange Commission as a national securities exchange for purposes of the Securities Exchange Act of 1934; and

(b) any other stock exchange agreed upon by the competent authorities of the Covered Jurisdictions.

5. Nothing in this Convention shall limit any provisions of the law of either Covered Jurisdiction which permit the distribution, apportionment, or allocation of income, deductions, credits, or allowances between persons, whether or not residents of a Covered Jurisdiction, owned or controlled directly or indirectly by the same interests when necessary in order to prevent evasion of taxes or clearly to reflect the income of any of such persons.

6. The existing taxes to which this Article shall apply in the United States are the Federal income taxes imposed by the Internal Revenue Code (but excluding the accumulated earnings tax and the personal holding company tax), and the excise taxes imposed on insurance premiums paid to foreign insurers. This Article shall, however, apply to the excise taxes imposed on insurance premiums paid to foreign insurers only to the extent that the risks covered by such premiums are not reinsured with a person not entitled to the benefits of this or any other convention which applies to these taxes. This Article shall also apply to any identical or substantially similar taxes which are imposed by the United States after the date of signature of the Convention in addition to, or in place of, the existing taxes, and shall also apply to any tax imposed by Bermuda after the date of signature of the Convention which is identical or substantially similar to the existing United States taxes to which this Article applies, to the same extent as it applies to those existing taxes. The competent authorities of the Covered Jurisdictions shall notify each other of any significant changes which have been made in their respective taxation laws and of any official published material concerning the application of the Convention, including explanations, regulations, rulings, or judicial decisions.

7. The taxation on a permanent establishment which an enterprise of insurance of a Covered Jurisdiction has in the other Covered Jurisdiction shall not be less favorably levied in that other Jurisdiction than the taxation levied on enterprises of insurance of that other Jurisdiction carrying on the same activities. This provision shall not be construed as obliging a Covered Jurisdiction to grant to residents of the other Covered Jurisdiction any personal allowances, reliefs, and reductions for taxation purposes on account of civil status or family responsibilities which it grants to its own residents. The provisions of this paragraph shall not be construed to prevent the United States from imposing an additional tax on the income of a permanent establishment maintained by a resident of Bermuda in the United States. Except where the provisions of paragraph 5 apply, interest, royalties, and other disbursements paid by a resident of a Covered Jurisdiction to an enterprise of insurance of the other Covered Jurisdiction shall, for purposes of determining the taxable profits of such resident, be deductible under the same conditions as if they had been paid to an enterprise of insurance of the first-mentioned Jurisdiction. For purposes of this paragraph, the term "taxation" means taxes which are the subject of this Convention.

Article 5

Mutual Assistance in Tax Matters

The competent authorities of the Covered Jurisdictions shall provide assistance as appropriate in carrying out the laws of the respective Covered Jurisdictions relating to the prevention of tax fraud and the evasion of taxes. In addition, the competent authorities shall, through consultations, develop appropriate conditions, methods, and techniques for providing, and shall thereafter provide, assistance as appropriate in carrying out the fiscal laws of the respective Covered Jurisdictions other than those relating to tax fraud and the evasion of taxes.

Article 6

Confidentiality

Any matters subject to assistance under Article 5 shall be treated as confidential in the same manner as such matters or items would be under the domestic laws of the Covered Jurisdiction requesting the assistance and, in any event, shall be disclosed only:

(a) in the case of the United States, to persons or authorities (including courts and administrative bodies) involved in the assessment, collection, or administration of, the enforcement or prosecution in respect of, or the determination of appeals in relation to, taxes, and

(b) in the case of Bermuda, to the competent authority of Bermuda.

Such persons or authorities shall use such matters or items only for purposes of the assessment, collection, or administration of, the enforcement or prosecution in respect of, or the determination of appeals in relation to, taxes. Such matters or items may be disclosed in public court proceedings or public decisions, but shall not be disclosed to any country other than one of the Covered Jurisdictions for any purpose.

Article 7

Entry into Force and Termination

1. This Convention shall be subject to ratification in accordance with the applicable procedures of each party and instruments of ratification shall be exchanged as soon as possible.

2. The Convention shall enter into force upon the exchange of instruments of ratification and its provisions shall have effect:

(a) in respect of excise taxes on insurance premiums paid to foreign insurers, for premiums paid or credited on or after January 1, 1986;

(b) in respect of income taxes imposed on the business profits derived by an enterprise of insurance, for such profits derived in taxable years beginning on or after the first day of the calendar year in which this Convention enters into force;

(c) in respect of mutual assistance covered by the first sentence of Article 5, for taxable years not barred by the statute of limitations of the Covered Jurisdiction requesting such assistance; provided, however, that neither Covered Jurisdiction shall be required by Article 5 to provide such assistance with respect to taxable years beginning prior to January 1, 1977; and

(d) in respect of mutual assistance covered by the second sentence (and not also described in the first sentence) of Article 5, for taxable years not barred by the statute of limitations of the Covered Jurisdiction requesting such assistance; provided, however, that neither Covered Jurisdiction shall be required by Article 5 to provide such assistance with respect to:

(i) taxable years beginning prior to January 1, 1977; or

(ii) taxable years beginning prior to the entry into force of the Convention if the provisions of such assistance would cause or result in the breach of an obligation to maintain confidentiality of information under the laws of such Jurisdiction in effect on the date of signature of the Convention.

2. The Convention shall continue in force indefinitely, but either party may give notice of termination to the other party on or after June 30 of the year following the calendar year in which this Convention enters into force and in such event the Convention shall terminate on the first day of the seventh full calendar month following that in which the notice is given.

Second Schedule

The Text Of The Notes

(1) The United States Government noted that in order to implement the relief from excise taxes pursuant to paragraph 1 of Article 4 of the Convention it would be necessary to establish procedures which would, *inter alia*, ensure that companies claiming the benefits of that paragraph are entitled to such benefits and, in the case of refunds, that the amount and recipient of such refunds are properly determined. Representatives of Bermuda assured the representatives of the United States Government of Bermuda's willingness to establish such procedures as may be mutually agreed to ensure that relief from the excise tax is obtained by appropriate persons.

(2) The United States Government noted that paragraph 3 of Article 4 of the Convention limits the availability of the exemption granted to insurance enterprises by either Covered Jurisdiction under the Convention to persons resident in the other Covered Jurisdiction which (i) are more than 50 per cent owned, directly or indirectly, by individual residents of the Covered Jurisdiction or US citizens; and (ii) do not use their income in substantial part, directly or indirectly, to make certain payments to persons who are neither residents of a Covered Jurisdiction nor US citizens. The United States Government indicated that, for purposes of the ownership test in that provision, it would not treat any individual as owning "indirectly" through an intermediary entity any beneficial interest in an entity resident in one of the Covered Jurisdictions if the evidence of and rights to the ownership of any interest in such intermediary entity are in bearer form. For purposes of the second test, the term "liabilities" refers to payments which reduce gross premium payments or are deductible against gross income, and includes interest, royalties, and premiums paid in connection with reinsuring risks. Also, if the sum of (i) the ratio which reinsurance premium payments bears to gross premiums less return premiums and (ii) the ratio which payments of other liabilities bears to (a) gross premiums less return premiums and less reinsurance premium payments plus (b) gross income from all other activities, is no more than 50 per cent, such payments will not generally be considered "substantial", provided that in appropriate circumstances a lower aggregate percentage will be considered "substantial".

(3) The United States Government expressed its concern that the obligations of a Covered Jurisdiction not be construed to establish an obligation to provide assistance with respect to matters other than those relating to the domestic laws of a Covered Jurisdiction respecting taxes. The representatives of the United States and Bermuda agreed that the intended scope of Article 5 of the Convention is limited to assistance relating to the domestic laws of the Covered Jurisdictions concerning taxes.

(4) Representatives of Bermuda expressed concerns as to the policies of the United States Government regarding assistance that might relate to persons not resident in one of the two Covered Jurisdictions and matters that do not constitute a criminal investigation. The representatives of the United States Government discussed with the representatives of Bermuda the United States' policies relating to information exchange. The representatives of the United States and Bermuda agreed that, where the United States requests assistance with respect to a matter which (i) relates to a person not resident in one of the two Covered Jurisdictions or (ii) does not constitute a United States criminal or tax fraud investigation, a senior official designated by the Secretary of the Treasury shall certify such request as being relevant to and necessary for the determination of the tax liability of a person under the laws of the United States. The representatives of the United States and Bermuda further agreed that, in connection with any assistance relating to persons not resident in one of the two Covered Jurisdictions, it shall be established to the satisfaction of the competent authority of the requested Jurisdiction that such assistance is necessary for the proper administration and enforcement of the fiscal laws of the requesting Jurisdiction. Where such necessity has been duly established, the competent authorities shall consult as to the appropriate form of such assistance.

(5) The representatives of the United States and Bermuda agreed that, subject to the limitations described in an agreement to procedures referred to in paragraph (4) above, it is intended that the mutual assistance to be provided under Article 5 of the Convention come into effect under the limitations of Article 7 as follows:

(i) Subject to paragraph (iv), Bermuda's obligation under the Convention to provide assistance with respect to civil and criminal tax matters relating to taxable years of a taxpayer beginning after the entry into force of the Convention will not be limited by an confidentiality restrictions of Bermudian law, other than those relating to solicitor-client privilege.

(ii) With respect to matters relating to taxable years of a taxpayer beginning before the entry into force of the Convention (but beginning on or after January 1, 1977 and not barred by the statute of limitations), paragraph 2(d)(ii) of Article 7 limits Bermuda's obligation to provide assistance with respect to civil tax matters (other than civil fraud) if the provision of such assistance would entail breach of an obligation to maintain confidentiality of information under the laws of Bermuda in effect on the date of signature of the Convention. Under this standard, confidential information would only include information protected by Bermudian statutory and common law. It is understood that under Bermudian common law confidential information would include information protected by the common law solicitor-client privilege and banker-client privilege. It was agreed that if a taxpayer claims that other categories of information are protected under Bermudian common law, and if the United States so requests, the Government of Bermuda will have such a claim determined in the courts of Bermuda.

(iii) Bermuda's obligation under subparagraph 2(c) of Article 7 to provide assistance with respect to criminal tax matters (and tax matters involving civil fraud) relating to taxable years of a taxpayer beginning before the entry into force of the Convention (but on or after January 1, 1977 and not barred by the statute of limitations) would only be limited by the confidentiality obligations of the solicitor-client privilege.

(iv) Bermuda's obligation under the Convention to provide assistance with respect to civil tax matters (other than civil fraud) relating to a taxpayer's taxable years beginning after the entry into force of the Convention will not require it to cause any person to breach a legal obligation to maintain confidentiality of documents or information, properly asserted by such person under the laws of Bermuda as in effect on the date of signature of the Convention, where such documents or information were created in or derived from periods prior to the date of entry into force of the Convention. However, the limitation on Bermuda's obligation described in the preceding sentence will not apply to documents or information created in or derived from a date preceding the entry into force of the Convention that are relevant to a request relating to taxable years after the entry into force of the Convention and are of a kind that have a continuing operational effect. For example, if assistance is requested with respect to a taxpayer's bank transactions occurring after the entry into force of the Convention and the signature card for the account in question was executed prior to the entry into force of the Convention, Bermuda's obligation to provide assistance with respect to such a signature card would not be affected by confidentiality restrictions. Similarly, if a taxpayer's depreciation deduction for a year after entry into force of the Convention is under examination, Bermuda's obligation to provide assistance with respect to information about the purchase price of the property in question, if such property was acquired before the entry into force of the Convention, would not be affected by any confidentiality restrictions of Bermudian law.

(6) The representatives of the United States Government expressed concerns regarding whether assistance would be provided in a form which would permit its use in judicial or administrative proceedings. The representatives of the United States and Bermuda agreed that under Article 5 of the Convention, it was intended that, if specifically requested by a competent authority of a Covered Jurisdiction, the competent authority of the other covered Jurisdiction shall provide information in the form of depositions of witnesses and authenticated copies of original documents (including books, papers, statements, records, accounts and writings) to the same extent such depositions and documents can be obtained under the laws and administrative practices of that other Jurisdiction.

(7) Representatives of Bermuda also expressed concerns as to the scope for use of unilateral compulsory measures by one Covered Jurisdiction to obtain documents, records, or other materials located in the territory of the other covered Jurisdiction, and within the scope of assistance under the Convention, after entry into force of the Convention. In this context the representatives of the United States Government confirmed that, with respect to documents, records, or other materials in the custody of a resident of a Covered Jurisdiction and located in the territory of that Jurisdiction, it shall be the policy of the United States, where practicable, to request assistance pursuant to the provisions of the Convention before using unilateral measures.

(8) The representatives of the United States Government inquired whether shares of a company organized under the laws of Bermuda could be issued in bearer form. The representatives of Bermuda informed the United States representatives that the laws of Bermuda did not permit the issuance of company shares to an unnamed person.

(9) The United States representatives sought clarification that matters that were the subject of assistance under the Convention but that are made public in accordance with Article 6 of the

Convention would not be further subject to Article 6. The representatives of the United States and Bermuda agreed that matters that are the subject of assistance under the Convention but that are made public in accordance with the Convention would not be further subject to Article 6.

(10) The representatives of the Government of the United States observed that, under the legal system applicable in Bermuda, the Convention is not self-executing and that legislation would be required in order to implement the provisions of the Convention. The representatives of Bermuda understood that instruments of ratification would not be exchanged until such legislation as may be required to implement the provisions of the Convention has been enacted. It was further understood that the Convention would be ratified and other necessary steps, such as the adoption of implementing legislation necessary to meet the obligations of the Convention, would be taken so as to permit the exchange of instruments of ratification at the earliest possible date.

(11) The representatives of Bermuda inquired whether, following the entry into force of the Convention, the Secretary of the Treasury of the United States would be prepared to certify that assistance under the Convention, and subject to the understanding of this Note, would be satisfactory for purposes of section 927(e)(3) of the Internal Revenue Code of 1954, as amended ("the Code"), relating to countries qualifying as a jurisdiction in which a Foreign Sales Corporation (FSC) may be organized. The representatives of Bermuda also inquired whether the assistance provided for in the Convention, subject to the understandings of this Note, would be satisfactory for purposes of eligibility for convention tax benefits under section 274(h)(6) of the Code.

The representatives of the United States stated that upon entry into force of the Convention, and subject to the understandings contained in this Note, the Secretary of the Treasury, or his delegate, will be prepared to certify Bermuda for purposes of section 927(e)(3) of the Code such that a company organized under the laws of Bermuda may qualify as a FSC. Such certification would be published in the Federal Register and may be terminated effective six months after the date of publication of a notice of termination in the Federal Register. The United States Government also stated that, upon entry into force of the Convention, the Secretary of the Treasury, or his delegate, will be prepared to execute on behalf of the United States Government an executive agreement satisfying the requirements of section 274(h)(6) of the Code, which would incorporate by cross-reference the provisions of Articles 5 and 6 of the Convention and this Note, and would allow persons incurring expenses for attending business conventions in Bermuda to claim deductions for such expenses as though Bermuda were included as part of the "North American area".

(12) The representatives of Bermuda emphasized the necessity of including in the Convention additional provisions intended to prevent changes in US income tax treaty policy from adversely affecting the economic position of Bermuda's insurance and tourism industries relative to those of US treaty partners in similar circumstances under current US tax treaty policy. The United States representatives were not able to accept such provisions. However, the United States Government recognizes that insurance and tourism currently play a vital role in the Bermudian economy. If, in the future, the income tax treaty policies of the United States change in a manner which would have a material, adverse effect on such Bermudian business activities, compared with existing circumstances, the United States Government would be prepared to reopen the discussions in order to take account of such change in policies.

Third Schedule

The Protocol Of Exchange Of Instruments Of Ratification

The undersigned, John Swan, Premier of Bermuda, and George P. Shultz, Secretary of State of the United States of America, being duly authorised for the purpose by their respective Governments, have met for the purpose of exchanging instruments of ratification of the Convention between the Government of the United Kingdom of Great Britain and Northern Ireland (on behalf of the Government of Bermuda) and the Government of the United States of America relating to the Taxation of Insurance Enterprises and Mutual Assistance in Tax Matters, with a related Exchange of Notes, signed at Washington on July 11, 1986. The United States ratification is subject to the following reservations:

(1) Effective January 1, 1990, said Convention shall not operate to prevent the imposition by the United States of any excise taxes on insurance premiums paid to foreign insurers, whether or not such premiums constitute income of an enterprise of insurance of a Covered Jurisdiction; and

(2) Said Convention shall in no event operate to prevent the imposition by the United States of any excise taxes on insurance premiums paid to foreign insurers except with respect to insurance premiums that either:

(a) constitute income of an enterprise of insurance of a Covered Jurisdiction carried on by a company in a taxable year in which the company is a controlled foreign corporation within the meaning of section 957(a) or (b) of title 26 of the United States Code as in effect for such taxable year; or

(b) constitute income of an enterprise of insurance of a Covered Jurisdiction carried on by a company in a taxable year in which:

(i) the company is subject to the rules of section 953(c) of the Internal Revenue Code of 1986, and

(ii) the company is a controlled foreign corporation within the meaning of section 957(a) of the Internal Revenue Code of 1986 as modified by section 953(c)(1) of said Code, and

the premiums constitute related person insurance income within the meaning of section 953(c) of the Internal Revenue Code of 1986.

The respective instruments of ratification having been compared and found to be in due form, the exchange took place this day.

IN WITNESS WHEREOF, the respective Plenipotentiaries have signed the present Protocol of Exchange of Instruments of Ratification.

Capital Preservation Through Global Investing

By Adam Starchild

Investing globally is one of the most successful ways to accomplish capital preservation and growth. In books such as *The Complete Guide to Tax Havens* and *The Conservative Wealthbuilder: Capital Preservation Through Global Investing*, Adam Starchild reveals how you can create an ultimate global portfolio of investments to hedge against inflation, taxes, confiscations, market, fluctuations, currency devaluations, economic and political turmoil...

Starchild reveals the little-known investment secrets that he has been giving to his clients for the past few decades. His recommendations are not high-flying investment tips, but rather solid, conservative recommendations that over time will help build a healthy nest-egg for you.

You will learn how to build a secret stash of cash that:

You can access at any time

Is tax-free and seizure proof

Pays competitive dividends and interest

And has no government reporting requirements (even for Americans)

In fact, if you had put $ 10,000 each year into this investment or the last twenty years you would have $590,697 today!

You will also discover:

How to accumulate income tax-free

Why offshore mutual funds should form a vital part of your global portfolio

How to invest in gold, silver and platinum and the investor potential of these precious metals

Why Switzerland should play an essential part in any global nest-egg strategy

How and where to best form an offshore trust in order to provide tax and creditor protection for your investments

How to invest tax-free in the United States

Everything you need to get yourself started on a global path to a secure fortune is in *The Conservative Wealthbuilder*. Starchild's techniques have been used by many of the world's wealthiest people for decades, including presidents, kings, Arab sheiks... And now for the first time they are available to you. They have been tested and proven over time. You will not find a safer, surer path to financial security than that mapped out for you in this unique work!

Just published (ISBN 0894990500), *The Conservative Wealthbuilder* is available through major bookstores and online booksellers. Also recently published (ISBN 1893713105) *The Complete Guide to Tax Havens* provides a wealth of information on forming offshore corporations and trusts.

The following sections are excerpts from *The Conservative Wealthbuilder* and other books by Adam Starchild:

Investing for the Offshore Entity

Investing for the offshore entity is just as important as creating the corporation or trust in the first place. Failure to invest the corpus and reinvest the income is one of the surest ways to squander the benefits that come from creation of an offshore corporation or trust. Astute choices in investment can lead to the realization of personal financial goals and, potentially, financial freedom. A problem often arises when one considers where to invest his money because there are so many options. Selecting the wrong ones can, at best, hinder the achievement of financial goals, and, at the worst, result in financial ruin. It is important to bear in mind that the investing is as important as the creation and structuring of the offshore entity.

Asset Allocation — The Key To Successful Investing

One of the newest forms of investments in America is called asset allocation. Basically what it means is that one investment is "allocated" to a number of different types of investments by a professional investment allocator. The reason for this allocation is that no one type of investment is the best in all investment climates, and no one type of investment is usually appropriate for all of one person's investment money.

By using an asset allocation program, a person can invest a large amount of his principal in one place, gaining ease of tracking the investment, while attaining the advantage of having a number of different investments to serve his different investment objectives.

The asset allocator performs the service for the investor of allocating varying amounts of a total investment into different areas of investing, such as income stocks, growth stocks, small capitalization stocks, etc., and a variety of fixed income securities.

For modest to medium-sized investments, one method of attaining even more diversification of investments, and expertise in the actual details of the investments, is to allocate the investment among various top-rated mutual funds. As is well known, mutual funds can perform a number of important tasks for the investor. Diversification among a large number of stocks is possible for even a relatively small sum of money. Expertise is available on any type of investment at a relatively low price. Last, there is great liquidity with ease of purchasing and selling.

The actual allocation into different mutual funds will depend upon three principal criteria:

(1) What is the risk to reward profile of the individual investor,

(2) What is the need of the investor for predictable current income as opposed to the desire for capital gains, and

(3) What is the state of the economic and investment cycles at the particular moment in time.

The first and most important criteria are clearly the needs of the investor. These outweigh any thoughts of where any market may be going or where an allocator believes that the most money can be made. The first need which needs to be addressed is the risk which the investor is prepared to accept. All investment involves some degree of risk, but that risk can rage from the minor risk of how inflation can impact an investment in the next 90 days, to the risk of a high flying initial public offering in a company which may have no earnings and no prospect for earnings in the foreseeable future.

The amount of risk which is appropriate for an individual investor depends upon both the investors actual economic situation and his psychological attitudes towards risk of loss. Human temperament plays a very large role in determining risk tolerance. For example, if a person remembers a period of his or her past where they did not have enough money to make ends meet, they may be very adverse to taking any risk at all. Their attitude may be, "We worked hard for that money, and we don't want to lose it."

Others may have almost the opposite approach. They may never have known deprivation, and may have earned a good income all their life. Their attitude may be that they can live very well on their current earnings, and so any savings can be used to speculate. If the speculation turns out to be successful, that will be great and they can raise their standard of living even further. But if the speculation doesn't work out, that's OK too because they will simply continue living as they have.

Thus a good investment allocator will first determine what the needs of his clients are with respect to risk. One method is to determine first how much money is needed to maintain the current standard of living of the investor, and if he or she is not yet retired, how much of the investment will be needed when they do retire. Whatever amount is needed for these purposes is then designated as income producing principal and is invested accordingly into low-risk, high-yielding investments.

The balance can then be invested according to the investor's wishes into areas which can offer the promise of large capital gains in the future. This is the risk portion of the principal, and care must be taken so that the allocator and the investor agree on what amount of risk is to be taken.

The third and equally important task of allocating is to attempt to maximize the return to the investor from the changes in the economic cycle. When business has been in a slump and starts to turn up with both interest rates and inflation low, the largest profits are typically made in the stock market. But as the economy continues to expand, interest rates will rise and so will inflation. These factors make the prognosis for the economy less rosy, and the stock market may start to gyrate, and then fall. Perhaps gently at first and then more rapidly. So the stock market is definitely not the place to be.

At the same time that the stock market is suffering from inflation, the price of hard assets such as gold, oil, and real estate could well be rising rapidly. It is in these areas that fortunes are made during inflationary periods in the economy.

And then as the economy finally begins to cool down due to the effect of high interest rates, interest rates will begin to fall nd the big money may be made by investing in long-term non-callable bonds.

Thus a good allocator must keep in mind the needs of the individual investor and the current status of the economy. And of course he must have an intimate familiarity with specific investments which are available to investors. Whether they be stocks, bonds, or fixed income securities, the allocator must know which are appropriate for the investor and which will likely do well in the present stage of the economy.

As with options in the preceeding chapter, the expertise of Max G. Ansbacher is once again quite useful. His credentials in the stock market are equally impressive. The second book he wrote is titled *How to Profit from the Coming Bull Market* and it was published in the summer of 1981 near the bottom of the long bear market which had actually begun in 1973.

This book explained how and why a strong bull market was about to start on Wall Street. At the time it was published the book was largely ignored by a public which had grown cynical about a stock market which seemed to do nothing but go sideways or down, year after year.

But just one year after Mr. Ansbacher's book was published, the market suddenly took off like a rocket in August 1982, igniting one of its greatest bull markets ever and establishing Mr. Ansbacher's reputation as an insightful student of the stock market.

We recently asked Mr. Ansbacher what his philosophy was concerning asset allocation. He replied, "Asset allocation is probably the most important single aspect of any investment program. And yet what is so strange about it is that it is often not even considered by investors. Some people will have most of their money in the stock market most of the time, unaware of the large risks which the market sometimes contains. Others believe in bonds, and continue to invest most or all of their money there, apparently unaware that in the 1970's and early 1980's the bond market was the biggest money loser of any investment. I would say that asset allocation is not just important, it is the key to successful investing."

Mr. Ansbacher went follows a deliberatly planned, carefully crafted strategy when handling an asset allocation account for a client. "The first thing I do is to talk to the client in whatever depth is necessary to determine the proper risk profile for the client. This depends upon his current financial situation and what he foresees for his future situation as well as his psychological feelings towards money and the potential loss of money. The second thing I do is to make an outline of the client's need for current income. This naturally has a great deal of influence on how we can invest the funds."

"Only after this has been done, do I then discuss with the client where I think the financial markets are heading and where the best returns are likely to be made in the future. The first step in actually making the investments are to decide upon the proportion of money going into each class of investments. The second part is to select the actual investments. For a number of reasons, I select from among the thousands of mutual funds which are available in the U.S. They range all the way from bond to preferred stocks, to common stocks of all types. There is usually a time and a place for almost all of them, but we try to pick the best one for that particular client at that particular time in the client's life, and in the life of the markets."

Mr. Ansbacher explained that his minimum investment is $100,000, and that he works with some of the biggest mutual fund organizations in the U.S., including Fidelity, Dreyfus and other mutual fund management firms. He does not bill his clients for a fee or commission for the work he does, because his compensation is paid to him by the mutual funds.

We have always believed that to be a good asset allocator is one of the most difficult tasks in the investment world, because it requires so many different considerations. To see just what kind of factors Mr. Ansbacher considers we asked him how he would go about planning an asset allocation program we asked him about a potential (though fictitious) client: a 50-year-old German married man who earns the equivalent of $200,000 a year and has a well-funded pension plan with his company. He is in good health and plans to retire at about the age of 65. We asked Mr. Ansbacher to assume that this man comes to him with $300,000 to invest. Here is how Mr. Ansbacher went about making his asset allocation process.

Mr. Ansbacher's recommendation? "The first question I have is about the amount of $300,000. Since he has a pension plan with his company, it is obviously not pension money. It is also a rather large amount for a person earning $200,000 to want to invest in the U.S. Is it inherited money? Does his wife earn money? Is this his life savings? Did he make a successful investment? The reason I ask this question is that it is very important to know if the money is replaceable. If it is inherited, will there be more to follow, or is this all? First I would want to know whether there will be more money coming in or not."

"Second, I would want to know more about his potential future obligations. Do he or his wife having living parents or other relatives who may need financial support in the future? How much support, if any, does he expect that his children will need in the future? Does he have disability insurance or a company plan in case he becomes disabled before he retires? Is there some specific financial goal that he has, such as acquiring a vacation home, yacht or other item which will require a substantial amount of ready cash. All these factors related to the amount of risk which I would want to take."

"The next set of considerations center around his financial situation now. Since he lives in Germany, this means that he pays a high tax on income such as dividends and interest, but pays no capital gains tax. Right away that sways me into investments which are likely to have high capital gains. I would want to know whether the $200,000 he earns covers all of his current expenses, or whether his current standard of living is so high that he needs extra income each year."

"Once we have the answers to these questions, we can begin to solve the problem of how best to allocate this investment. If there are no likely financial needs coming up in the future, and if at the time of the investment I decide that the stock market is not over priced or likely to decline for other reasons, I would place most of the money into various stock funds. I am particularly fond of funds which use value investing, which means that they pick stocks based upon how large an amount of earnings one gets for each dollar invested. This is another way of saying that they seek out stocks with high quality and low price/earnings ratios."

"The reason I like value investing is that many studies have shown that low price/earnings stocks outperform other stocks in normal markets. And in down markets heir inherent value keeps them from falling as far as others. The second group of stocks I would pick would be senior growth stocks. This means stocks which grow year after year because they are gaining market share, or because they are in a solid growth industry. Examples of this are some pharmaceutical companies which are constantly creating new and better drugs, or highly efficient national retail chains which are constantly gaining market share over local competitors."

"One advantage which growth stocks have for this particular client is that they usually don't pay a very large dividend, which fits right in which his local tax structure. Depending upon the wishes of the client, we would consider some gold stocks as a hedge against inflation. And we might add some mutual funds which specialize in large capitalization companies, because these are the tried and proven winners among all the competition in the economy, and often outperform other stocks when the economy softens."

"I would also place a portion of the assets into a short or medium term bond fund for three reasons:

(1) This could be a source of money in case an emergency arose which required a withdrawal from the fund,

(2) It is a reserve in case some outstanding bargains come up for investment, and

(3) It is a hedge against a downturn in the stock market."

Of course the actual percentage allocations would be discussed with the client. The actual funds selected would depend upon their performance records at the time of the investment. And in general, much of the allocation would depend upon the state of the economy at the time of the investment."

Good advice. From a man well-qualified to give it.

Investing in Options

Another vehicle to consider investing your money is in options. Specifically, trading options on stocks or on a stock index (such as the Standard & Poor's 500 Index). This is route is particularly appealing to foreigners, since the gain or loss from trading in options is a capital gain, and any profits made by a foreigner from trading in such options are free from any tax imposed by the United States.

But, as many investors already know, options are notoriously speculative and most people who try trading in them wind up losing money. Therefore, in order to take advantage of this tax benefit, it is first imperative to find a method of trading options which has a good probability of actually making money.

Almost any method of trading options which has the chance of making an above average return also carries a commensurate high degree of risk. But some practitioners of the arcane art of options trading do manage to do better than others over the years. One such person who has done very well for his clients is Max G. Ansbacher, Chairman of Ansbacher Investment Management, Inc., located in the prestigious Rockefeller Center complex in New York City.

Mr. Ansbacher has a long and distinguished involvement with options. In fact, he is the author of the first book published on the modern form of options, titled *The New Options Market, Revised and Enlarged Edition,* first published in 1975. Today, he manages accounts for investors in both the U.S. and overseas.

What sets Mr. Ansbacher apart from many others is that he has an excellent record of bringing in above average profits for his clients. Since most people who buy options seem to lose money, we asked Mr. Ansbacher what the key was to his success. He replied, "Yes, I agree that most people who buy options do seem to lose money. But what many people don't realize is that the money which the options buyers lose, doesn't disappear from the face of the earth. Rather it becomes the profits of the options *sellers*. And therefore, I concentrate in *selling* options."

What Mr. Ansbacher was saying is that options trading is actually a zero sum game when one looks at the total overall economic effect. This means that buying and selling options has no overall impact on the economy. It neither creates any money or lose any (except transaction costs). If the sellers make money, the buyers lose money. And if the buyers make money, then the sellers must lose money.

Since the options *buyers* tend to be the ones who lose money, it therefore must be true that the options *sellers* are the ones who make money over the long run. "The options buyers tend to be less sophisticated than the sellers," Mr. Ansbacher explained. "They don't always carefully assess the chances that their stocks will really go up enough to make money when they buy a call. Similarly, if people think a stock or a stock market is going to go down, they often over estimate how much it is going to go down. They will buy a put which is going to lose money unless the stock makes a really unusually large move within a relatively short period of time. These are the options I sell."

Of course there is not an investment program yet invented which makes money on every single trade, and option selling is no exception. Mr. Ansbacher said, "Certainly there are times when we have losses, but we believe that the probability lies with the sellers. And so we usually find that every loss is matched by many more winners."

If you do become involved in selling options, the best advise is: proceed with caution! Never forget that the risk factor is high. How does a veteran like Mr. Ansbacher control this risk? He said that the first defense was to control the number of options which he sells. "I usually sell only about one fifth the number of options which margin rules permit me to do. The second line of defense is that I use stop loss orders, which in most instances will automatically get me out of the options before the losses rise to a point which I consider unacceptable."

He continued, "The most interesting line of defense and the most important from the point of view of making money, is that I sell out-of-the-money options. This means that I sell options which have a strike price which is a distance away from the current price of the underlying security." We should point out that a strike price is the level at which an option becomes effective.

What Mr. Ansbacher means is that if a stock is 100, for example, he will not sell the 100 strike price call, because it is tool likely that the stock will go above 100 and he might lose money. Instead, he might sell the call with a strike price of 120. The stock would have to be above 120 at the option's expiration for the seller of the option to sustain a loss. Obviously it is less likely that a stock will go up 20 points than it will merely go up a few points. So, by selling out-of-the-money options, Mr. Ansbacher is able to shift the probabilities in his favor.

Another major decision which an options trader has to make is whether to be trading calls, which go up in price when a stock goes up, or puts which go up in price when the stock goes down. Mr. Ansbacher said that he makes this decision based upon a number of factors, including his long experience in the field. "One of the factors I rely upon, is my own Ansbacher Index. This Index tells me whether the puts or the calls are higher priced. Since I am selling these options, I will generally choose to sell the ones which are higher priced. I believe the Index also gives an indication of which way the stock market is likely to go in the intermediate future." Thus, Mr. Ansbacher can sell options on the stock market which will be profitable for his clients if the market moves as The Ansbacher Index indicates it is likely to do.

The minimum account which Mr. Ansbacher accepts is US$100,000, and he accepts accounts from people residing anywhere in the world. Depending upon the type of account, the investor will receive monthly or quarterly statements giving the exact value of the account.

For more information contact:

Ansbacher Investment Management, Inc.
Attn: New Clients Information
45 Rockefeller Plaza, 20th Floor
New York NY 10111
telephone: (212) 332-3280
fax: (212) 332-3283; Attn: New Clients Information

Swiss Financial Experts

JML Swiss Investment Counselors

Swiss investment managers are experienced in working with investors from around the world. Most are fluent in English and have substantial experience in managing various types of investments. They are comfortable managing an investor's entire portfolio if he wishes; however, for investors who prefer to make their own financial decisions, Swiss advisers are happy to offer their expertise to the degree it is required. They can help you manage your investments, or manage them for you - whichever arrangement makes you feel more comfortable. For the entrepreneur who devotes much of his energy to building his venture, the efficiency and competence of Swiss investment managers can be a major attraction.

A fine example of a Swiss money management company is JML Swiss Investment Counselors. Founded by Jurg M. Lattman, who has been providing expert financial advice to investment professionals, bankers, economists, and private investors around the world since 1973, JML experts monitor global economic indicators and trends and provide their clients with some of the best financial advice available anywhere. They make it a simple matter to invest in Swiss annuities as well as take advantage of other global investment options.

One of the leaders in Swiss financial management is JML Swiss Investment Counsellors, a firm which offers a unique style of financial management. Clients can customize and control their own portfolios and still receive comprehensive management advice from some of the world's best experts on financial matters.

Recognizing that investors have differing goals, time frames, and tolerance for risk, JML's managers work with their individual clients to help them target their unique objectives. This naturally requires continued surveillance and analysis of worldwide economic trends, political events, financial markets, currencies, and other factors which could make some investments particularly attractive and others most unfavora•
ble. Few individuals have the time or

- expertise to undertake this kind of evaluation themselves.
- In any event, JML clumps the various opportunities that are available to investors into five separate categories for consideration by its Personal Portfolio Management Program clients:
- Cash Equivalents. Principal and interest are guaranteed for finite terms are provided.
- Blue Chips. The investment portfolio consists of high-quality securities purchased for long-term capital appreciation potential.
- Trading. The portfolio consists of securities which are bought and sold for short-term capital appreciation.
- Trends. Often referred to a cyclical portfolios, securities are selected on the basis of economic forecasts by industry, sector, or country. The investor normally needs to wait about six years to realize significant annual returns.
- Visions. The most speculative of the five categories, investments are selected from opportunities in emerging markets and new technologies. It may take ten or more years to realize larger annual yields.

For more information on JML write:

JML Jurg M. Lattmann AG
Swiss Investment Counsellors
Germaniastrasse 55, Dept. 212
CH-8033 Zurich, Switzerland
telephone: +41 1 368 8233
fax: +41 1 368 8299; marking the fax "Attn: Dept. 212"

Weber Hartmann Vrijhof & Partners

While there are many excellent Swiss investment financial managers, another one of particular note is the management firm of Weber Hartmann Vrijhof & Partners. Offering management services for the portfolios of both individuals and companies, the firm excels at providing personal attention to its clients. Weber Hartmann Vrijhof & Partners was established in 1992 by Hans Weber, Robert Vrijhof, and Adrian Hartmann. The three men have substantial experience in finance and investment. Weber managed Foreign Commerce Bank (FOCOBANK) in Switzerland for nearly 30 years as its president and CEO, Vrijhof was a former vice-president and head of FOCOBANK'S portfolio management group, and Hartmann was head of FOCOBANK'S North American subsidiary in Vancouver. Weber Hartmann Vrijhof & Partners offers specialized investment services designed to meet the individual needs of their clients.

The minimum opening portfolio to be managed by this firm is $250,000 or equivalent. The management team here normally recommends that a portion of the portfolio be invested in hard currencies other than the U.S. dollar including the Swiss franc, French franc, German mark, and Dutch guilder. Respected for their conservative approach to portfolio management, the partners assist clients with opening a custodial account at one of the major private Swiss banks, so that all client securities are held by the bank, not the investment manager.

A large percentage of their clients are based in the United States. One of their main goals has always been to get a certain portion of their clients' wealth out of the U.S. dollar and into European hard currencies such as Swiss francs, Deutschmarks, and Dutch guilders, and then build a portfolio with a mix of bonds and shares.

If you wish to learn more about the services the firm offers, contact them at:

Weber Hartmann Vrijhof & Partners, Ltd.
Attn: New Clients Department
Zurichstrasses 110B
CH-8134 Adilswil
Switzerland
Tel: +41 1 709-11-15
Fax: +41 1 709-11-13, please mark fax "Attn: New Clients Department"

Even though many investors recognize that Switzerland is a center of finance and investment, they do not realize the vast scope of the investment options offered by Swiss financial institutions and companies. Switzerland is a prime spot for investment for numerous reasons, most importantly for the strength of its currency, security of its financial system, and steady returns on investment.

Dunn & Hargitt: Offshore Managed Commodities Accounts

An offshore managed commodities account is typical of the type of investment that is available to an offshore corporation or trust, but is not available to Americans.

The Dunn & Hargitt International Group, founded in 1961, has specialized in doing research for developing Portfolio Management Programs that have the potential of providing investors with a high return on their capital by investing in a diversified portfolio trading in the commodity, currency, precious metals, and financial futures markets in the United States and throughout the world.

The Dunn & Hargitt group offers investors the possibility of participating in several of the different pools that are managed by them by investing through the investment programs that are offered by their affiliate, Winchester Life in Gibraltar, but which are actually managed by The Dunn & Hargitt International Group.

At the time of publication they are offering three possible investment alternatives, including The Winchester Life Umbrella Account (which allows 100% of a client's money to be invested in a diversified futures portfolio), The Winchester Life 100% Guaranteed Investment Account (in which Lloyds Bank acts as custodian trustee and US Government Zero Coupon Treasury Bonds are set aside to guarantee the client's capital), and The Winchester Life 150%

Guaranteed Investment Account (which is a similar program, but guaranteeing that the client will receive at least 150% of the value deposited with a maturity date at least ten years in the future).

The average net return for the 150% Guaranteed Investment Account over the last six years would have been 22% a year. The average net return on the 100% Guaranteed Investment Account over the last six years would have been 27% a year. The average annual net return for The Winchester Life Umbrella Account over the last twelve years would have been 35% a year.

The minimum accounts accepted are $20,000 for The Winchester Life Umbrella Account, $20,000 for The Winchester Life 100% Guaranteed Account, and $50,000 for The Winchester Life 150% Guaranteed Account.

Although commodities are a speculative form of investment, investors everywhere are diversifying part of their portfolios to take part in the considerable potential profit opportunities that are available in the commodity, currency, precious metals and financial futures markets. The programs devised by the Dunn & Hargitt International Group will make profits if significant trends develop in either direction; i.e. up or down. This does not mean that short term results are always profitable, however the Dunn & Hargitt proven trading systems can provide above average returns over the longer term. Their objective is to make a profit for their clients of between 20% and 40% per annum and their computer trading systems are geared to this level of performance.

For more information, contact:

The Dunn & Hargitt International Group
Department S-697
P.O. Box 3186
Road Town, Tortola
British Virgin Islands

The structure of the Dunn & Hargitt Group has been established so that no taxes are withheld from the client's investment on the international commodity, currency, precious metals and financial futures markets. Because of this they can only manage money for investors who are neither citizens nor residents of the United States, United Kingdom, or Belgium, and they will not mail their brochures to those countries.

The Dunn & Hargitt International Group offers complete confidentiality to all of its clients, and will not reveal any information on a client or on its accounts to any third parties.

Sources of Help in Forming Offshore Entities

Skye Fiduciary Services Limited

Skye Fiduciary Services Limited, based in the Isle of Man, are specialist consultants, designers and trustees and managers of offshore and international fiduciary structures.

They were established in 1991 by Charles Cain to provide specialist consultancy and management services in respect of offshore fiduciary structures, specializing in clients from or connected to the USA. The beginnings of Skye Fiduciary Services Limited go back over twenty

years. In 1972, their Executive Chairman, Charles Cain, after some years working in international banking in East Africa and the United Kingdom, returned to his native country as the managing director of a merchant bank. Three years later he resigned to start his own business, which became, by 1989, the largest corporate and trust management business in the Isle of Man. In 1989, however, as a consequence of an illness, he sold out to a large financial services group.

In 1991, fully recovered, he established Skye Fiduciary Services Limited.

From its executive office in the Isle of Man, Skye Fiduciary Services Limited provides a design and management service relating to offshore companies and trusts.

Unlike many firms that simply provide offshore corporations, one of Sky's major functions is to provide trade management services. These include:

- arranging and supervising appropriate banking and trade finance
- facilities and services.
- trade documentation
- exchange control planning
- double tax treaty planning.
- administration of trading entities
- arranging bank Letters of Credit and other financial instruments
- arranging leasing, invoice discounting and credit factoring
- arranging tax efficient vehicles for transferring royalties and other
- income flows derived from intellectual property rights.
- offshore joint venture vehicles and holding structures for US persons
- international trading structures.

For more information contact:

Skye Fiduciary Services Limited
Attn: New Clients Information
2 Water Street
Ramsey, Isle of Man 1M8 1JP
Great Britain
Telephone: +44 1624 816117
Fax: +44 1624 816645; attn: New Clients Information

ICS Trust (Asia) Limited

The other firm I can personally give my highest recommendation to is ICS Trust (Asia) Limited, based in Hong Kong.

The handover of the former British Crown Colony of Hong Kong to China is complete, and it is now called the Hong Kong Special Administrative Region, generally abbreviated to Hong Kong S.A.R., even on official documents.

As more than one local businessman has put it, "now that the politicians and journalists are gone (from covering the handover), we can get down to *business*." This attitude is typical of Hong Kong, still a true capitalist center. In fact, many of the wealthy who left to obtain second citizenships in Canada, Australia, and elsewhere, have now returned home to continue building their fortunes.

Offshore re-invoicing can be a very useful tool for exporters as well as importers, since it allows for the accumulation of tax-free profits in an offshore environment.

Through re-invoicing, an offshore corporation is established as an international intermediary between importers and their suppliers or between exporters and their customers. The offshore corporation can thus either 1) buy products, on behalf of the importer, at the negotiated price level and then sell, or re-invoice, these same products to the importer at a higher price, thereby accumulating profits offshore where there is no tax liability and significantly reducing profits in the country of destination where there is tax liability, or 2) buy products at discount prices from the exporter, thereby creating a very small profit in the exporting country with tax liability and sell, or re-invoice, these same products at market value prices to overseas buyers, thereby accumulating profits offshore where there is no tax liability.

In order to be profitable, offshore re-invoicing operations need to be situated in an environment where import-export transactions are either tax-free or low tax (in relation to the onshore portion of the operation).

Once the offshore company has been established, the management corporation needs to acquire the services of a post office box, a telex, a telephone, and a facsimile for its use. When all this is in place, the management company can begin re-invoicing. An offshore service provider can arrange these services.

The merchandise can be sent directly to the exporter's client or to the importer. The only functions performed in the offshore haven are the preparation and dispatch of the new invoice and the management of the funds in the way instructed by the client and complying with local regulations.

The major advantage of Hong Kong is simply that it is a real business center, not just a tax haven. One of the consequences of that is the ability to add value to services that are provided in only skeleton form in other tax havens. The reinvoicing business is a prime example. Most tax haven jurisdictions host a number of trading companies that do nothing more than reinvoicing. But one Hong Kong firm has now developed this traditional service into a "real" business mode, with an ability to arrange local trade financing. This is a healthy step away from traditional tax havenry into a true offshore **business** center.

ICS Trust Company Limited is part of the ICS International group of companies headquartered in Hong Kong. This highly successful entrepreneurial group was started by Elizabeth L. Thomson. Elizabeth describes herself as "a lawyer by profession" (2 law degrees, a member of 4 Law Societies internationally), "an entrepreneur by choice"! She has helped innumerable people start new enterprises in many parts of the globe and is well known in Hong Kong for her work with women entrepreneurs.

With a staff of 40 at ICS, every aspect of your business is covered — from deciding to incorporate, to obtaining financing from the bank, to managing your paper work including Letters of Credit, to investing your hard earned profits! ICS is truly a "one stop shop" for entrepreneurs.

Their clients range from multinational companies for whom they run Direct Import Programs worth millions of dollars to individuals who seek tax sheltering and estate planning on an international scale. As an entrepreneurial group, they attract many entrepreneurs as clients — business people who have grown their business to a level of maturity and profits that requires expansion into Asia for many diverse reasons.

Instead of just a paper thin traditional tax haven reinvoicing company, with ICS you can develop a real business in Hong Kong. With their extensive banking contacts, ICS professionals will "shop" for the best letter of credit facilities that Hong Kong's competitive banking scene can offer, likely better facilities than you can find at home. Depending upon the client, ICS can often arrange letter of credit banking facilities for clients with either a low or zero margin deposit, usually required by the opening bank. By freeing up your collateral and capital, they provide you with more purchasing power to increase sales and gain higher profits.

Most of these reinvoicing transactions are usually effected such that they are tax free in Hong Kong. There is no withholding tax on dividends so it is often possible to engage in international trade through a HK company and obtain dividends from that company tax free.

ICS will also work with international banks and factors in Hong Kong and overseas to arrange financing, secured primarily on the strength of purchase orders from your clients. Working with banks, factories, shipping companies and freight forwarders, ICS will structure a transaction to increase the likelihood of obtaining flexible, low cost facilities.

The goods do not need to go through HK for us to use a HK vehicle to pass title. Most of their clients ship from a third country direct to their own country.

Although the traditional Hong Kong focus is on firms who trade in goods, it is also possible to use these structures in cases where services are to be provided from overseas. For example, a firm could contract out a study to a company in Hong Kong. This Hong Kong company could then sub-contract out the work to a third party firm and the profit kept in Hong Kong, tax free.

If you import goods from Asia for sale to large chains, ICS can help you expand your credit facilities and increase your domestic sales by establishing and running a Direct Import Program for you. Combined with their international trade finance capabilities, the Direct Import Program is a powerful tool for generating more profits.

The primary goal of the Direct Import Program is to maximize your profits by making your customers perceive that they are buying "direct." This is achieved by:

- setting up a subsidiary company in Hong Kong
- getting your buyers to open their L/C or orders to this subsidiary
- liaising with suppliers to ensure goods are to specification.

The Direct Import Program works because of two powerful reasons:

- The trend in the retail industry is for buyers to "buy direct" from the Orient. Having a subsidiary in Hong Kong which receives orders or L/Cs greatly enhances this perception.
- Large retail chains often can obtain freight and insurance at significant savings because of their economies of scale. Selling FOB Asia can often result in a lower selling price for the importer but with the same profit.

ICS will set up and manage the subsidiary company for you, and prepare financing proposals for presentation to local banks. When everything is complete, goods are shipped directly from the Asian factory to the customer. The fact that you are now seen as an Asian supplier (and not the middleman) is often an important factor that clinches the deal. The added prestige of a Hong Kong office makes the customer think he or she is buying "direct" and therefore receiving the lowest price.

To get started, you should contact ICS with as much detail as possible about your business and its trading activities.

For further information, contact:

Mr. Kishore K. Sakhrani
Director
ICS Trust (Asia) Limited
Suite 605-6
Nine Queens's Road, Central
Hong Kong
Telephone: +852-2854-4544
Fax: +852-2543-5555

Britannia Corporate Management Limited

A consulting business specializing in the formation of offshore corporations and trusts is Britannia Corporate Management Limited, located in the Cayman Islands. Its president, Gary F. Oakley, is a Canadian with 17 years of Cayman Islands residency. Britannia is licensed to manage investment holding and trading companies, real estate holding companies, patent holding companies, and insurance holding companies. It is licensed to incorporate and manage corporations registered in the Cayman Islands. As such, the firm can service as the registered office of a corporation, provide its secretary, officers and directors, or undertake any day-to-day functions that may be required. More information can be obtained by writing the following:

Britannia Corporate Management Limited
Attn: New Clients Information
P. O. Box 1968
Whitewall Estates, Grand Cayman
Cayman Islands

Britannia can be reached by fax at +1 345 949 0716, marking your fax to "New Clients Information."

You will be well-advised and well-serviced in the hands of any of these fine companies.

About the Author

Over the past 25 years, Adam Starchild has been the author of over two dozen books, and hundreds of magazine articles, primarily on business and finance. His articles have appeared in a wide range of publications around the world -- including *Business Credit, Euromoney, Finance, The Financial Planner, International Living, Offshore Financial Review, Reason, Tax Planning International, The Bull & Bear, Trust & Estates*, and many more.

Now semi-retired, he was the president of an international consulting group specializing in banking, finance and the development of new businesses, and director of a trust company.

Although this formidable testimony to expertise in his field, plus his current preoccupation with other books-in-progress, would not seem to leave time for a well-rounded existence, Starchild has won two Presidential Sports Awards and written several cookbooks, and is currently involved in a number of personal charitable projects.

His personal website is at http://www.adamstarchild.com

www.ingramcontent.com/pod-product-compliance
Ingram Content Group UK Ltd.
Pitfield, Milton Keynes, MK11 3LW, UK
UKHW051455290926
15471UKWH00008B/1221

9 781893 713345

INDEX TO GENERA AND SPECIES OF AMOEBAE

The principal references to amoebae included in the key are indicated by bold-face type.